special events pg 24

Historical re-enactments, gardening festivals, country & craft fairs, concerts, fireworks, car and steam rallies.

accommodation pg 31

Historic properties which offer accommodation - from basic comfort to ultimate luxury.

civil wedding venues pg 32

Places where the ceremony itself can take place and may also provide facilities for receptions.

corporate hospitality pg 35

Properties able to accommodate corporate functions, wedding receptions and events.

plant sales pg 39

Properties and gardens offering collections of rare and unusual plants not generally available.

websites pg 42

Access property and related heritage websites quickly and easily by using the direct links found at

www.hudsonsguide.co.uk

open all year pg 43

Properties and/or their grounds included in this list are open for all or most of the year.

education pg 48

Properties providing facilities for schools/educational groups.

Access to Grant Aided Properties - page 541

English Heritage, as well as managing and opening properties in its care, gives grants towards the cost of repairing outstanding buildings in private, National Trust and other ownerships, subject to appropriate public access being given.

FROM THE EDITOR

*In his foreword to this edition
Sir Simon Jenkins, who in the past few years
during research for his book "England's
Thousand Best Houses", must have visited
more historic houses than anyone, refers to
them as "the finest dispersed gallery of
architecture, art and landscape in Europe".*

*The buildings featured in Hudson's, their
associated contents, gardens and landscape
settings, represent much of what is truly British. Their contribution to the nation is
both cultural and economic. Their role in generating tourism, both international and
domestic, is enormous, but we should heed Simon Jenkins' plea. Where possible we
should ensure that these buildings have life and do not become soulless museums.*

*There are many ways to enjoy the houses in this book: many have Civil wedding
licences; others have facilities for hosting wedding receptions and corporate events;
and a few offer accommodation – so it's possible to get married, party and sleep in
historic and picturesque surroundings! Throughout the year there are many events
and other activities at properties open to the public. Some of these, arranged
before our publication date, feature in our Special Events Index. More recent and
extensive information can be found on our website (www.hudsonsguide.co.uk). This
most popular and extensively used portal website leads you in an easy and
structured way to the best heritage sites in Britain.*

Norman Hudson OBE

Pentire Head , Cornwall   ©National Trust Photographic Library/Joe Cornish

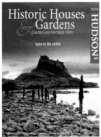

Hudson's Historic Houses & Gardens

Publisher and Editor-in-Chief	Norman Hudson
Editorial	Lucy Denton / Fiona Rolt
Production Co-ordinator	Adrian Baggett
Administration	Jennie Carwithen
Page Make-up	Rika Baggett
Graphic Design/Page Layout	KC Graphics
Maps	Taurus Graphics
Scanning & Pre-press	Spot-On Design & Print
Sales	Fiona Rolt
Printed by	Körner Rotationsdruck
UK & European Distribution	Portfolio - tel: 020 8997 9000
USA Distribution	The Globe Pequot Press - tel: 001 203 458 4505

Published by:
Norman Hudson & Company
High Wardington House,
Upper Wardington, Banbury,
Oxfordshire OX17 1SP, UK
Tel: 01295 750750
Fax: 01295 750800
enquiries@hudsonsguide.co.uk
www.hudsonsguide.co.uk
ISBN: 1 904387 02 0

Co-published in the USA by:
The Globe Pequot Press
246 Goose Lane, Guilford,
Connecticut 06437, USA

**Library of Congress
Cataloging-in-Publication
data is available.**

ISBN: 0-7627-3577-5

UK Cover: © Lindisfarne Castle, National Trust Photo Library/Joe Cornish

US Cover: Audley End House © English Heritage Photo Library

Frontispiece: Holnicote Estate, Somerset
© National Trust Photographic Library/Joe Cornish

This book is a guide to the finest dispersed gallery of architecture, art and landscape in Europe. When I set out a decade ago to discover England's best old buildings I little imagined how limited this search was becoming.

The United Kingdom is woefully careless of its cities, towns, even villages. Few of the buildings in this book are urban. The concept of an entire protected townscape, as in France or Italy, is almost unknown. Even conservation areas are vulnerable. Meanwhile the 2004 Planning Act treats farmland and countryside outside the National Parks as available for development. One day the "thousand best" buildings may be the sole relics of pre-20th century Britain, in a landscape of eternal suburbia.

In this climate the concept of an historic building intact with its surroundings is specially precious. Houses have always needed "cross-subsidy", usually from estate income. As farm revenue declines and tax relief is squeezed, the sale of land and contents to keep roofs on houses is increasing. And houses face other challenges. The competition from other leisure attractions puts them under relentless pressure to keep the past abreast of the present.

I believe houses and those who guard them need to be as flexible over uses as they must be vigilant over fabric. The survival of great houses and their estates cannot be aided by their "dis-integration". On the other hand far too many have become art historical museums, empty, unlived-in, ruins in spirit if not also in fact. I longed to see occupants running about these places, sleeping in bedrooms, cooking in kitchens, eating in dining rooms, even a cost in convenience, access and wear and tear. A house without inhabitants is like a school without children.

There is money aplenty in Britain. It should be harnessed by the country house movement. The spirit of the Victorians should return to restore, rebuild and occupy many ruined shells. Their custodians must employ stories to bring them back to life. A building that has abandoned its prime purpose, habitation, and lost the tellers of stories will soon lose its appeal to visitors. And if it does that it will lose its reason for surviving. So sally forth, *Hudson's* in hand, to keep these places breathing.

Simon Jenkins
author, "England's Thousand Best Houses"

Cottesbrooke Hall & Gardens, Northamptonshire

The HHA Friends scheme
provides amazing value for the interested house and gardens visitor

Athelhampton, Dorset

Southside House, London

The HHA is a group of highly individualistic and diverse properties most of which are still lived-in family houses. They range from the great palaces to small manor houses.

Many HHA member properties are open to the public and offer free admission to Friends of the HHA.

Eyam Hall, Derbyshire

Forde Abbey & Gardens, Dorset

Castle Howard, Yorkshire

Duart Castle, West Highlands & Islands

Minterne Gardens, Dorset

HISTORIC HOUSES ASSOCIATION

Become a Friend of the HHA and visit nearly 300 privately owned houses and gardens for FREE.

HISTORIC HOUSES ASSOCIATION

**join on line
www.hha.org.uk**

Other benefits:

* Receive the quarterly magazine of the HHA which gives news and features about the Association, its members and our heritage

* Take advantage of organised tours in the UK and overseas

* Join the specially arranged visits to houses, some of which are not usually open to the public

KINGSTON BAGPUIZE HOUSE, OXFORDSHIRE

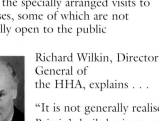

Richard Wilkin, Director General of the HHA, explains . . .

LEVENS HALL GARDENS, CUMBRIA

"It is not generally realised that two-thirds of Britain's built heritage remains in private ownership. There are more privately-owned houses, castles and gardens open to the public than are opened by the National Trust, English Heritage and their equivalents in Scotland and Wales put together.

Successive Governments have recognised the private owner as the most economic and effective guardian of this heritage. But the cost of maintaining these properties is colossal, and the task is daunting. The owners work enormously hard and take a pride in preserving and presenting this element of Britain's heritage.

The HHA helps them do this by:

* *representing their interests in Government*
* *providing an advisory service for houses – taxation, conservation, security, regulations, etc.*
* *running charities assisting disabled visitors, conserving works of art and helping promote educational facilities*

There is a fascinating diversity of properties to visit free with a Friends of the HHA card – from the great treasure houses such as Blenheim and Castle Howard through to small manor houses. What makes these places so special is their individuality and the fact that they are generally still lived in – often by the same family that has owned them through centuries of British history. As well as the stunning gardens which surround the houses, there are over 60 additional wonderful gardens to visit.

The subscription rate remains outstanding value for money. Individual Friend: £33. Double Friends living at the same address: £52 (each additional Friend living at same address, £16 – only available to holders of a Double Membership). If you wish to become a Friend of the HHA, and I very much hope you will, then you can join, using your credit/debit card by calling 01462 896688 or simply fill in the form below."

HOLKHAM HALL, NORFOLK

Membership: Single £33, Double £52, £16 additional Friend at same address. Members of NADFAS, CLA and NACF are offered special rates of £30 Individual and £49 Double (at same address).

'Years spent as an archaeologist working on ruins cannot equal the pleasure of living in the real thing.'

When did you last stay in a pineapple?

The Landmark Trust is a charity that rescues and restores worthwhile historic buildings and gives them a new life by offering them for holidays.

By sleeping, eating and living in a building you can study it at leisure, be there early and late and in all lights and weather. You will come to know it and its habits and understand why and how its builders made it as they did.

Beamsley Hospital, North Yorkshire, a circular stone Almshouse built in the 16th century.

Sleeps 5 people.

The Pineapple is just one of the buildings featured in the Landmark Trust Handbook, your first step to staying at some of the country's finest buildings.

Browsing through its 212 pages, you will find details of 178 buildings from the humblest of cottages to the most ornamental of banqueting houses, each one is remarkable in some way for its architecture, history or setting.
The Handbook is far more than a holiday guide with a description of each building, local maps showing places of interest and detailed plans of the accommodation.

The 20th Edition of the Landmark Trust Handbook currently costs £9.50 when sent to a UK address, which is refundable on your first booking. Payment can be made online **www.landmarktrust.org.uk** or by telephoning our Booking Office on **01628 825925** using MasterCard, Visa, Switch, Delta, sterling cheque.

Stogursey Castle, Somerset, a thatched gatehouse on the site of a ruined 13th century castle.

Sleeps 4 people.

The Landmark Trust
Shottesbrooke, Maidenhead, Berkshire, SL6 3SW

Scobbiscombe Beach – View of the cliffs and sea, Northern Ireland

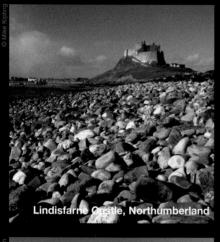

Lindisfarne Castle, Northumberland

Fowey – Cliffs and blue sea, Cornwall

THE NATIONAL TRUST

National Trust & SeaBritain 2005

SeaBritain 2005 is to be a year-long celebration of our illustrious maritime history and close relationship with the sea. At its heart is the bicentenary of the Battle of Trafalgar on 21 October.

The National Trust, with more than 600 miles of diverse coastline around England, Wales and Northern Ireland and numerous magnificent properties with strong seafaring links, has a wealth of knowledge to impart and treasures to share.

continued >

There are iconic places on the coast, such as The Giant's Causeway in Northern Ireland, a World Heritage Site and renowned for its polygonal columns of layered basalt. This remarkable natural feature resulting from a volcanic eruption 60 million years ago has attracted visitors for centuries. Beautiful sand dunes in places like the Gower Peninsula in Wales and the spectacular White Cliffs of Dover, are all in the care of the Trust.

Off the Northumberland coast lie the Farne Islands, one of Europe's most important seabird sanctuaries and home to more than 20 different species including Puffins, Eider Ducks and four species of Tern. A few miles to the North is Lindisfarne (Holy Island) with the Castle made habitable by Lutyens for Edward Hudson, founder of *Country Life* magazine (see front cover

and feature article on p438). Just to the South, dominating a lonely stretch of Northumberland's beautiful coastline, lies Dunstanburgh Castle which can only be reached on foot along paths following the rocky shore.

At the most Southerly point of mainland Britain is The Lizard, the turning point of one of the busiest shipping lanes in the world. The coastline on either side is dramatic and exciting, offering cliff walks, rare wildflowers and interesting geological features. The area is also historically important: it was here that Marconi's wireless experiments took place in 1901 and these are celebrated at the restored Lizard Wireless Station at Bass Point.

Legendary names in maritime history such as Sir Francis Drake also have connections with the Trust. Drake's home was Buckland near

Plymouth, a former Cistercian Monastery from where he planned his attack on the Spanish Armada. This 700 year old building incorporating the remnants of the 13th century Abbey Church and with its marvellous 16th century Great Hall, sits in a secluded valley above the River Tavy. The house not only contains memorabilia from Drake's time of occupation but also of Sir Richard Grenville, his seafaring rival. Here you can see also an Elizabethan garden and a recently unveiled handcrafted plasterwork ceiling in the Drake Chamber.

The Carews, a famous Tudor seafaring family, made Antony in Cornwall their home for almost 600 years. This wonderful property, containing collections of paintings,

continued >

Cliffs and pinnacles in the sea. Corfe Castle Estate, Dorset

furniture and textiles and overlooking grounds landscaped by Humphry Repton, has a façade of silvery grey Pentewan stone.

Medieval Compton Castle in Devon, with a dramatic built form dating from the 14th and 16th centuries, has been the family seat of the Gilberts through generations; Sir Humphrey Gilbert (1539-1583) was half-brother to Sir Walter Raleigh as well as the coloniser of Newfoundland. In this fortified manor house there is a splendid reconstructed medieval Great Hall. It is possible to retrace the footsteps of Admiral Lord Nelson at The Kymin (a landmark dedicated to the glories of the British Navy). This is a most interesting hill picked out on the skyline with two early 19th century buildings, one of which is an unusual circular banqueting house. Nelson, Sir William and Lady Emma Hamilton visited in 1802 and ascended the steep path to the top where a naval temple was built two years before in tribute to the Admirals who fought against the French and more personally to the great Sea Lord and his victory at the Nile.

Even inland there are naval connections. At Melford Hall in Suffolk there were four admirals in the family all called Admiral Sir Hyde Parker. Paintings of naval engagements by Dominique Serres line the walls of his house. It was in 1578 that Queen Elizabeth I was

continued >

St Michael's Mount, Cornwall
© National Trust Photographic Library / David Noton

© National Trust Photographic Library / Joe Cornish

Burton Bradstock, Dorset

© National Trust Photographic Library / David Noton

Golden Cap, Dorset

© National Trust Photographic Library / Joe Cornish

Cornwall

© National Trust Photographic Library / Leo Mason

Cornwall

received here and possibly saw the panelled Banqueting Hall which is a glorious survivor. The Hyde Parker family were in residence from 1786 and the decorative legacy of their occupation is in evidence with furniture, porcelain and important books in a Regency library.

Vast panoramic paintings adorn the Dining Room at Berrington Hall in Herefordshire as a tribute to Admiral Rodney, a hero of the American War of Independence and father-in-law of Anne, daughter of the Hall's owner, Thomas Harley the 3rd Earl of Oxford.

Seascapes are another legacy of National Trust houses, with J M W Turner's works being one of the great features of Petworth House in Sussex, while in a glorious setting on the Menai Strait lies Plas Newydd where Rex Whistler's largest ever mural featuring Neptune dominates the Dining Room.

Tyntesfield in North Somerset, recently acquired by the Trust, indirectly owes its very existence to the sea. The Gibbs family who built it made their fortune transporting guano (bird droppings used for fertiliser) around the world, amassing in the process many of the chattels now on display in the house.

At Souter Lighthouse, boldly painted in red and white on the Tyne and Wear coast, the visitor can see the Engine Room, Light Tower and Keeper's living quarters. This landmark opened in 1871, was the first to use alternating electric current. In the Compass Room visitors can learn about storms at sea, communications from ship-to-shore, pirates and smugglers, lighthouse life, lighting the seas and shipwrecks. Another maritime land-mark is South Foreland Lighthouse standing on the White Cliffs of Dover: this was the site of Faraday's work in pioneering the use of electricity in lighthouses and was the first to display an electrically powered signal.

During SeaBritain 2005 there will be a variety of special events taking place in locations throughout England, Wales and Northern Ireland. These will show how the coast has shaped our lives as a place of industry, inspiration and leisure.

Runswick Bay, Yorkshire

![The National Trust logo]

THE NATIONAL TRUST

To find out more about National Trust properties near you visit www.nationaltrust.org.uk or call 0870 458 4000

Runswick Bay, Yorkshire

White Park Bay, Northern Ireland

ENGLISH HERITAGE 2005

Superb historic sites and action-packed events

From magnificent former royal palaces to mighty
coastal castles and awe-inspiring monuments,
English Heritage's historic properties can be
found in cities, along coastline and in
countryside up and
down the land.

ENGLISH HERITAGE

Many of English Heritage's properties play host to an extensive programme of events staged to inspire, inform and entertain visitors of all ages, with period musicians, storytellers, historic interpreters and guides found on sites countrywide, which enrich and enhance any visit.

The highlight of the events calendar is **Festival of History**, held for the third year in August. Celebrating the rich variety of England's social and military history, Festival of History offers something for all the family to enjoy. Spectacular **arena shows** promise thrilling military displays, while visitors can wander through colourful living history encampments and enjoy authentic period entertainment.

Other highlights for 2005 include the maritime events taking place at some of English Heritage's coastal sites in support of **Sea Britain 2005** – an initiative of the National Maritime Museum at Greenwich, in celebration of Britain's relationship with sea.

ENGLISH HERITAGE

We will also be holding events to commemorate the 60th anniversary of V-E Day.

For those who enjoy watching historic action, a series of **battle re-enactments** are played out at sites around the country, including that most famous of battles, the Battle of Hastings, 1066, at Battle Abbey, which was built by William the Conqueror.

Bringing back the days of chivalry, romance and royal sporting entertainment, **Grand Medieval Jousts** are held regularly countrywide and throughout August at Carisbrooke Castle on the Isle of Wight. **Falconry displays**, with highly-trained birds of prey flying free, provide breathtaking demonstrations of this ancient art – once the sport of kings.

For history-lovers who enjoy walking, there's a superb series of guided **Battlefield Hikes** to the places where some of the most significant battles were fought, and there is also an extensive programme of talks on offer.

Historic properties provide a stunning backdrop to all kinds of outdoor productions, with **theatre** ranging from Shakespeare to 18th-century murder mysteries, and **musical evenings** spanning classical, jazz, rock and pop. Seasonal **garden and craft shows** allow visitors to purchase top quality products in magnificent historic surroundings.

All English Heritage events are suitable for families but **Children's Festivals**, fun days, crafts workshops, puppet shows, teddy bear picnics, storytelling and period entertainment are also held for younger visitors. Seasonal celebrations include traditional St George's Day festivals, Easter egg trails and activities for all ages at Hallowe'en and Christmas.

There is also a lively programme of one-day and overnight heritage trips to historic sites – **Tours Through Time** – run in conjunction with Brookland Travel (tel: 08451 212 863).

English Heritage members can enjoy free entry to sites with up to six children, plus free or discounted entry to special events. For more information on properties, events or membership, please call English Heritage customer services on 0870 333 1181 quoting HUDS, or visit **www.english-heritage.org.uk**

ENGLISH HERITAGE

The Churches Conservation Trust cares for over 330 churches in England of exceptional historic, architectural, or archaeological importance which are no longer needed for regular parish use.

The Trust encourages public appreciation and enjoyment of these churches. Our website, **www.visitchurches.org.uk** provides everything you need to know to visit a church, including background, directions, opening arrangements and images. The Lumley Chapel, Cheam, Surrey, pictured here, is just one of our outstanding churches. All have something special to offer and can be visited *free* throughout the year.

Overleaf you will find a selection of some of the exceptional churches in our care. For further information visit our website. Alternatively, send off for our free guides using the tear off slip.

Caring for historic churches throughout England for all to enjoy

THE CHURCHES
CONSERVATION TRUST

www.visitchurches.org.uk

NORFOLK

Barton Bendish, St Mary

The westernmost of two remaining churches in this tiny village, St Mary's is set in open country, flanked by trees and, with its thatched roof, has considerable charm. This 14th century church has a complicated history: the tower fell during a storm in 1710 and the present cupola was erected in 1789, while the fine west door, with some unusual features, is from the demolished third church in the village – Pevsner called it 'one of the half dozen best… Norman doorways in England'. Inside are a strange collection of old pews, a 14th century wall painting, a Carolean altar table dated 1633, a number of interesting memorials reflecting changing fashions in style down the years, and an atmosphere of wonderful still, white simplicity.

6m E of Downham Market off A122
TF 710 055
Keyholder nearby

DORSET

Portland, St George, Reforne

Impressively large and solitary on the bleak top of the Isle of Portland, itself a dramatic and strange part of England, St George's was described by Pevsner as 'the most impressive 18th century church in Dorset'. The large cruciform building was constructed of local Portland stone in 1754–66, to the design of Thomas Gilbert, a local mason. Its grand conception, probably based on St Paul's Cathedral, may reflect Wren's connections with Portland and its quarries. The interior is singularly complete of its date with twin pulpits and lecterns, box pews and galleries surviving intact, and an elegant font signed by William Gilbert, the architect's brother. In the vast treeless churchyard are some 400 tombstones, many of naval interest, with fascinating inscriptions.

Easton, Isle of Portland
SY 686 720
Open Easter-Sep 2–5.
At other times keyholder nearby

BERKSHIRE

East Shefford, St Thomas

This simple little church enjoys a delightful pastoral setting in meadows beside the River Lambourn. Its origins are pre-Norman, the chancel was added in the 13th century, windows altered in the 15th, the south chapel added in the 16th and the brick porch in the 18th, but its pleasing rustic exterior gives no hint of the treasures inside. There are striking very early wall paintings above the chancel arch and post-Reformation painted texts on other walls, a Norman tub font, an early mediaeval tomb, and some old glass. Two splendid tombs, one of c.1450 in alabaster and another of 1524 in marble, commemorate members of the Fettiplace family who lived at the Manor House from the 13th to the 16th century.

2m NE of M4 Junction 14/5m NE of Hungerford
off A338 at Great Shefford
SU 391 747
Open daily

DEVON

Satterleigh, St Peter

This charming little church is set by a farmyard in the hills above the Mole valley, away from any village. It is mainly 15th century, with an aisleless nave, a wooden bell-cote and a south porch leading to a remarkable mediaeval door in its original wooden frame. Although the church was much restored in 1852, when the chancel was rebuilt, the feeling inside is of an arrangement for 17th or 18th century worship, with its pulpit, sounding board and reading desk, a solid tympanum and several homely runs of hat pegs. There is a Royal Arms of 1726 above the door, and the bells are almost unique in still being fitted with half-wheels, which went out of fashion 300 years ago.

4m SW of South Molton off B3226
SS 667 225
Open daily

SUFFOLK

South Elmham, All Saints

All Saints was probably the oldest of the ten parishes forming the ancient Saxon township of South Elmham and the church stands at the end of a lane behind the 17th century moated Church Farm. Built of local flint-rubble, it has a charming round tower, early Norman in origin but much restored in the 19th century. The lean in the south aisle wall adds to the charm of the bright interior. The massive early-13th-century font, a few mediaeval benches and some attractive old stained glass are also noteworthy, and the 11th century tower arch is filled with an elaborately carved 17th century door and panelling. The Suffolk Wildlife Trust cares for the churchyard which abounds with wild flowers in the early summer.

5m S of Bungay
TM 330 828
Open daily

ESSEX

Halstead, Holy Trinity

Built in 1843–44, by celebrated Victorian architect Sir George Gilbert Scott, to serve Halstead's community west of the River Colne, Holy Trinity is one of the first examples of a Gothic Revival church in the Early English style. Its tall tower and fine brick-built broach spire form a prominent and handsome feature of this north Essex market town. The lofty and dignified proportions of the interior again demonstrate the beauty of Early English architecture in gault brick. Graceful arcades divide the lofty clerestoried nave from the aisles. Furnishings by Scott include the plain functional benches in the nave and aisles, and the font. There is some fine 20th century woodcarving, and colourful stained glass of the 19th and 20th centuries.

½m SW of town centre, near A131
TL 808 305
Keyholder nearby

EAST SUSSEX

Hove, St Andrew

Set back from the seafront, this Regency church was built to serve the expanding resorts of Hove and Brighton. Designed in 1827 by the famous architect Sir Charles Barry, its Italian Renaissance style perfectly matches the symmetry and grandeur of the neighbouring squares and terraces. Extended in the 1880s, the church was further beautified in 1925 when Randoll Blacking added superb baldacchinos for altar and font to fulfil the parish priest's desire that St Andrew's should become 'a little bit of Italy in Waterloo Street'. The domed ceiling of the chancel depicts the Sun, Saturn and stars. A fine series of 19th century monuments forms an excellent introduction to the good and great who worshipped here in the church's heyday.

Waterloo Street, just off the seafront near
Brunswick Square
TQ 299 043
Open Tue–Sat 11am–4pm.
Group tours by arrangement at other times
(01273 326491)

NORTH YORKSHIRE

Fylingdales, St Stephen Old Church

This intriguing period-piece of 1821–22 stands prominently on its hillside above Robin Hood's Bay looking out to sea. Externally it appears severe and windswept; internally it is a rare and unaltered example of a church furnished for the preaching of the Word – a real 'preaching box' which has escaped re-ordering – with galleries to the north and west, box pews below and a superb three-decker pulpit half way along the south side. The sea is a recurring theme throughout and there are memorials to the shipwrecked in church and churchyard, a list of rescues by the lifeboat and a model of *SS Pretoria*. Rare survivals are the 'maiden's garlands', which were carried in the funeral procession of a maiden.

5m SE of Whitby off A171
NZ 942 059
Keyholder nearby

SURREY

Cheam, Lumley Chapel

Situated within the churchyard of 19th century St Dunstan's, Lumley Chapel is the former chancel and only surviving portion of the original late-11th century church demolished in 1864 when the present building was constructed. John, Lord Lumley refurnished the chapel in the 1590s as a burial place for himself and his two wives. Memorials to the Lumley family and other local residents display carving and craftsmanship of the highest order. The most elaborately designed and detailed is the marble monument to Lumley's first wife Jane, through whom he inherited nearby Nonsuch Palace. The chapel also contains a collection of late mediaeval brasses from the former Fromond Chapel. 20th century stained glass in the east window includes the arms of the Lumley family.

Off A2043 Malden Road (next to Cheam
Library)
TQ 243 638
Keyholder nearby

NORTHAMPTONSHIRE

Aldwincle, All Saints

Approached along the curved street of an attractive stone village, the pinnacled and carved 15th century tower of All Saints' dominates the surrounding countryside. The church has been disused, though not neglected, for over a hundred years. Of earlier date than the tower, the rest of the church with its uncluttered interior is equally impressive, and its very emptiness allows a finer appreciation of the beautiful limestone arcades and arches. The Chambre chantry chapel of 1489 is also of exceptional quality. A brass in the chancel commemorates William Aldwynckle who died in 1463, and there is also some 15th century stained glass. John Dryden was born at the former rectory opposite, baptised at All Saints' and lived for many years at Aldwincle.

2m N of Thrapston off A605
TL 011 875
Keyholder nearby

WEST YORKSHIRE

Harewood, All Saints

The 15th-century church of All Saints lies within the park of Harewood House. Much restored by Sir George Gilbert Scott in 1862–63, its rather severe interior houses a spectacular and fascinating collection of alabaster tombs, dating from 1419 to 1510. Six pairs of intricately carved effigies, virtually without rival in England, provide a unique history of mediaeval armour and costume, and the development of the art of alabaster carving for which England was justly famed throughout Europe. The earliest shows Judge William Gascoigne in the robes of Lord Chief Justice. The latest, to Edward Redman and his wife, is probably the finest: the carving of the face may be a true portrait of the man, rare in mediaeval times.

6m N of Leeds, off A61
SE 314 451
Open Wed–Sun, Apr–Oct 10am–5pm.
At other times keyholder nearby

CUMBRIA

Vale of Lune, St Gregory

St Gregory's owes its existence to the construction of the Low Gill to Ingleton branch of the London & North-Western Railway. The church was built in the early 1860s by the Upton family, to provide continued employment for the Scripture Reader to the navvies following completion of the railway. Attached to a cottage it is a plain building of Westmorland stone and slate roofs surmounted by a glazed lantern. By contrast, inside a delightful and colourful series of stained glass windows by Frederick George Simon depict river scenes, trees and plants, as well as birds and animals found locally. These were installed in about 1900 when the church was refurnished. The furnishings in local oak are of remarkably good quality.

1m W of Sedbergh on A684 near M6 Junction 37
SD 634 922
Open daily

Churches in the care of The Churches Conservation Trust

All churches on the map are opened regularly or have keyholders nearby.
For further information visit
www.visitchurches.org.uk

- Churches featured
- Churches in the care of The Churches Conservation Trust

Complete and send to The Churches Conservation Trust, 1 West Smithfield, London, EC1A 9EE

Name.. Title ....

Address.. Postcode ....

Please send me:

Full list of churches in the care of The Churches Conservation Trust ☐

County Guides, please specify county(ies) ....

Why not visit our website? www.visitchurches.org.uk

HHH6

THE CHURCHES
CONSERVATION TRUST

Cadw is the executive agency of the Welsh Assembly Government exercising the National Assembly for Wales's statutory responsibilities to protect, conserve and promote an appreciation of the built heritage of Wales.

Cadw gives grant-aid for the repair or restoration of outstanding historic buildings. Usually it is a condition of the grant that the owner or occupier should allow some degree of public access to the property. Conditions of grant remain in force for ten years.

Details of properties grant aided by Cadw and to which the public currently enjoy a right of access can be found on Cadw's website: **www.cadw.wales.gov.uk/placestovisit**

This contains a wide range of information, including details of buildings and monuments in its care. If you experience any difficulty in exercising the right of access indicated, please write to Cadw at the address below or contact us via telephone or e-mail.

Cadw encourages you to visit these properties, as well as buildings and monuments in its care.

✛ **Cadw**

Llywodraeth Cynulliad Cymru
Welsh Assembly Government

Plas Carew, Cefn Coed, Nantgarw, Cardiff CF15 7QQ Telephone: 029 2050 0200 E-mail: cadw@wales.gsi.gov.uk

Compton Verney House.
©Compton Verney / John Kippin

Portrait of a Boy aged Two,
(1608) Marcus Gheeraerts the Younger
Prudence Cuming Associates © Compton Verney

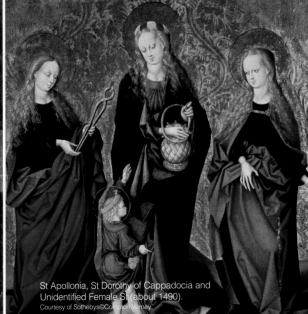

St Apollonia, St Dorothy of Cappadocia and
Unidentified Female St (about 1490).
Courtesy of Sothebys©Compton Verney

The Gallery.
© Compton Verney / Richard Bryant

Compton Verney

After a long period of dereliction, Compton Verney in Warwickshire has been rescued, restored and transformed into a major art venue with diverse collections from sources worldwide.

The influential Verney family began purchasing lands in the area of Compton Murdak in the early 15th century and soon after, the area became known as Compton Verney. The first dwelling on this land had a great hall and octagonal turrets, though by the early 18th century this house had been reconstructed as a baroque courtyard house, possibly to the designs of Vanbrugh.

The eminent Scottish architect, Robert Adam, transformed it into a neo-classical mansion in the 1760s by adding two wings to the main body of the house, a library, an octagonal study and a lofty Corinthian portico. Three sides of the courtyard house were demolished, giving Compton Verney its

A Farmer and his Prize Heifer (about 1844) maker unknown (British).
© Compton Verney / Hugh Kelly

The Dentist (about 1770).
Attributed to John Collier.
© Compton Verney / Hugh Kelly

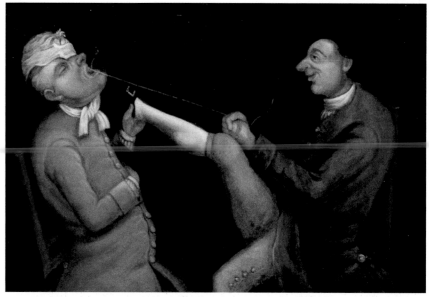

© Compton Verney / Richard Bryant

present 'U' shape. This exceptional house looks out over an impressive naturalistic landscape, designed by the celebrated 'Capability' Brown, who was also the architect of the chapel, completed in 1780.

In 1921, the last of the Verneys left and the house was sold. It was subsequently owned by a soap manufacturer and racehorse owner and then was used as a set for occasional film shoots.

In 1993, what had become a dilapidated building, was bought by the Peter Moores Foundation which established the Compton Verney House Trust to transform the mansion into a gallery of international standard through a programme of renovation and new-build. The British philanthropist, Sir Peter Moores, established the Foundation in 1964 in order to distribute funding to the arts.

Now, in the new galleries and in a learning centre adjoining the house, designed by architects Stanton Williams, one can examine and appreciate art in an outstanding location. The permanent collections comprise works from celebrated periods and places, from Italian paintings from Naples to bronzes and pottery from China to German medieval art. From Tang equestrian figures dating from 700-800BC to the Marx-Lambert collection of popular art, so many unique works spanning so many different ages can be seen here.

Of interest is the compilation of British 'Folk' Art, the largest collection of such works in the country; including weather vanes, trade signs and a collection of naïve paintings, created in the 18th and 19th centuries by artists with no formal training. These are remarkably distinctive with an appealing simplicity. The subject matter of these charming pictures illuminates much about the social history of Britain; some works were created by travelling sign painters.

Here, in this exceptional art gallery, among its 800 works of art, there are also British portraits with sitters such as Henry VIII and lesser known figures, such as the Elizabethan courtier, Thomas Knyvet.

Compton Verney now houses a historic permanent collection of art, much of which has never been on public view before, as well as running a programme of temporary exhibitions and specially commissioned contemporary art. The gallery offers a wide range of learning opportunities including formal education sessions for schools, practical art workshops, family activities, adult art workshops and outreach projects within the local community.

Compton Verney House and Gallery.
©Compton Verney

Interior of the Gallery.
Brett Prestige © Compton Verney

A View of Posillipo (about 1700–01) Gaspare Vanvitelli.
Prudence Cuming Associates © Compton Verney

Fairground Carousel Pig.
© Compton Verney / Hugh Kelly

Whirligig: Pony & Trap.
© Compton Verney / Hugh Kelly

A Female Saint, (1515-20)
Tilman Riemenschneider.
Courtesy of Sothebys © Compton Verney

Harriet, Lady Fawkener (about 1760) Jean-Etienne Liotard.
© Compton Verney / Christopher Foster

Tang Equestrian Figures
(about 700 - 800BC).
www.kenadlard.co.uk©Compton Verney

The Incredulity of St Thomas
(1620) Bernardo Strozzi.
© Compton Verney / Jack Ross

28-29

Eastnor Castle, Herefordshire
Knight's Treasure Hunt.

28-29

Highclere Castle & Gardens, Hampshire
International Horse Trials.

SEPTEMBER

1-11

Blenheim Palace, Oxfordshire
"Churchills' Destiny" exhibition to celebrate the anniversaries of the end of World War II and the death of Sir Winston Churchill. Based on Sir Winston Churchill and his hero John Churchill, who won the Battle of Blenheim, 1704. Admission included in ticket.

1-30

Compton Verney, Warwickshire
Luc Tuymans: New Work. James Coleman.

1-30

Fairfax House, Yorkshire
'Restoration' – York Civic Trust celebrates the 21st anniversary of its rescue of Fairfax House with this special exhibition.

3-4

RHS Garden Wisley, Surrey
Clematis Festival (Plant Centre event, free of charge, no entry into Garden needed).

3-4

RHS Garden Wisley, Surrey
Craft Demonstration Weekend.

3-25

RHS Garden Wisley, Surrey
Sculpture Exhibition, Surrey Sculpture Society.

8-11

Blenheim Palace, Oxfordshire
FEI Blenheim Petplan European Eventing Championships.

10-11

Beaulieu, Hampshire
International Autojumble.

10-11

Parham House & Gardens, Sussex
"Autumn Flowers at Parham House", a celebration of flower arranging, Parham style.

13

RHS Garden Wisley, Surrey
Veggie Tasting Day.

14

RHS Garden Wisley, Surrey
Bulb Bonanza (Plant Centre event, free of charge, no entry into Garden needed).

15

Easton Walled Gardens, Lincolnshire
RHS Autumn Bulb Workshop in association with Walkers Bulbs, 11am-4pm – tips for ordering and planting Autumn bulbs.

16-18

Goodwood House, Sussex
Motorsport Revival (advance tickets only).

17-18

Groombridge Place Gardens, Kent
War of the Roses Skirmish.

24-25

Kentwell Hall & Gardens, Suffolk
Re-Creations of Tudor Daily Life: Tudor Michaelmas, 11am-5pm.

 **O C T O B E R**

1-2

Eastnor Castle, Herefordshire
Festival of Fine Food & Drink.

1-31

Compton Verney, Warwickshire
Luc Tuymans: New Work. James Coleman.

1-31

Fairfax House, Yorkshire
'Restoration' – York Civic Trust celebrates the 21st anniversary of its rescue of Fairfax House with this special exhibition.

6-9

Highclere Castle & Gardens, Hampshire
"Spirit of the Horse".

9

RHS Garden Harlow Carr, Yorkshire
Mushroom Day – educational and fun. Forays, displays, advice, identification, competitions and quizzes, suitable for everyone. No booking required, normal garden entrance fee applies, 10am-4pm.

16

Harewood House, Yorkshire
Autumn Glory.

16

Kentwell Hall & Gardens, Suffolk
Timber Day, 12 noon-5pm.

16

RHS Garden Wisley, Surrey
Fritillaria Society AGM and Show, 11am-4pm.

21

RHS Garden Wisley, Surrey
Apple Day and Festival.

21-23

Arley Hall & Gardens, Cheshire
Arley Hall Antiques and Fine Art Fair.

22-23

RHS Garden Harlow Carr, Yorkshire
Apple Event, 10am-4pm.

22-23

RHS Garden Wisley, Surrey
Apple Tasting Weekend (Plant Centre event, free of charge, no entry into Garden needed).

22-23

Stowe House, Buckinghamshire
Christmas Fayre.

22-30

Blenheim Palace, Oxfordshire
"Haunting Tales for Hallowe'en" with costumed entertainment.

29

Beaulieu, Hampshire
Fireworks Spectacular.

29

RHS Garden Wisley, Surrey
Cyclamen Autumn Show, 11am-4pm.

29-30

Burton Agnes Hall, Yorkshire
Michaelmas Fair.

29-30

Groombridge Place Gardens, Kent
Halloween in the Spooky Forest.

29-30

Kentwell Hall & Gardens, Suffolk
Re-Creations of WWII Daily Life: House Requisitioned, 11am-5pm.

31

Burton Constable Hall, Yorkshire
Hallowe'en Ghost Tours.

N O V E M B E R

1-30

Fairfax House, Yorkshire
'Restoration' – York Civic Trust celebrates the 21st anniversary of its rescue of Fairfax House with this special exhibition.

5

Groombridge Place Gardens, Kent
Fireworks Spectacular set to music.

5

RHS Garden Harlow Carr, Yorkshire
Pumpkin Day, 10am-4pm.

5-13

RHS Garden Wisley, Surrey
Woodturning and Crafts (Plant Centre event, free of charge, no entry into Garden needed).

12-30

Blenheim Palace, Oxfordshire
Christmas at Blenheim Palace – experience the finery and traditions of Christmas at the Palace.

D E C E M B E R

1

Kelmarsh Hall, Northamptonshire
Christmas Fair, 6-8.30pm. Fabulous gifts, choirs, music, mulled wine and mince pies. Admission £4.

1-11

Blenheim Palace, Oxfordshire
Christmas at Blenheim Palace – experience the finery and traditions of Christmas at the Palace.

1-31

Fairfax House, Yorkshire
'Restoration' – York Civic Trust celebrates the 21st anniversary of its rescue of Fairfax House with this special exhibition. Also, 'Keeping of Christmas' – 18th century celebrations and table displays based on family papers and invoices of the period.

2

Kelmarsh Hall, Northamptonshire
Christmas Fair, 11am-5pm. Fabulous gifts, choirs, music, mulled wine and mince pies. Admission £4.

10-11

RHS Garden Wisley, Surrey
Christmas Weekend (Plant Centre event, free of charge, no entry into Garden needed).

17-18

RHS Garden Wisley, Surrey
Christmas Weekend (Plant Centre event, free of charge, no entry into Garden needed).

This information is intended only as a guide, please check with individual properties before travelling.

More information on Special Events can be obtained by visiting individual property websites, see www.hudsonsguide.co.uk for quick access.

Places Offering **Accommodation**

The historic properties listed below are not hotels. Their inclusion indicates that accommodation can be arranged, often for groups only. The type and standard of rooms offered vary widely – from the luxurious to the utilitarian.
Full details can be obtained from each individual property.

Somerley

ENGLAND

SCOTLAND

Florence Court.

WALES

NORTHERN IRELAND

Weston Park

Tower of London.

Syon Park.

🪴 Plant Sales

Properties where plants are offered for sale

Scampston Walled Garden.

White Cliffs of Dover, Kent. ©National Trust Photographic Library

England

london

London, England's vibrant capital city, contains not just the 'must-see' attractions such as Buckingham Palace and the Tower of London, but also many smaller and no less interesting properties. Go east to Spitalfields and visit 18 Folgate Street, a time capsule of 18th century London. Open to the general public for the first time in 2005 will be Clarence House, formerly the home of HM Queen Elizabeth the Queen Mother and now the official residence of her grandson – His Royal Highness the Prince of Wales.

The huge open spaces of the London parks are the envy of capital cities around the world. From Regent's Park in the north to Battersea Park south of the river, via Hyde Park and St James's, it is possible to walk for some miles hardly touching a pavement. As well as relaxing in the Royal Parks, find time to visit The Chelsea Physic Garden: founded in 1673, it is the second oldest botanic garden in Britain. The riverside gardens of the Royal Hospital in Chelsea provide the venue for the world-famous Chelsea Flower Show held in the last week of May. As for entertainment – whether you are looking for theatres, museums or international sporting events, classical music or world class rock concerts, London has them all. This cosmopolitan capital has something to attract everyone, whatever their taste or interest. The city is constantly evolving, and London's newer attractions, such as the London Eye, are proving every bit as popular as some of her more established landmarks.

The Houses of Parliament. © Mike Kipling.

The British Airways London Eye.

The Banqueting House, London.

© English Heritage Photo Library/Nigel Corrie

The Waterloo Gallery, Apsley House, London

national maritime museum

royal observatory l longitude zero l greenwich

The Octagon Room.

Portrait of Captain James Cook (1728-1779), by
William Hodges (1744 - 1797).

Meridian Line and Observatory.

Greenwich c.1752 by Canaletto.

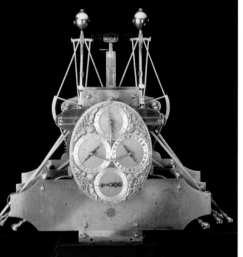
Harrison's H1 marine timekeeper.

Portrait of Henrietta Maria.

A North Sea Breeze on the Dutch Coast c1855 by E W Cook.

national maritime museum
greenwich london

Britain's maritime connections have shaped the nation and established Britain's place in the world.

SeaBritain 2005 is a celebration of this achievement. Ships that left these shores to explore or trade around the globe returned with exotic commodities and people that changed Britain forever. Industrialists built their wealth in world markets; and colonies were established on distant continents. Our kitchens, gardens and restaurants are dependent on the products of the global garden. Here, in Greenwich, is told the story of Britain and the sea.

SeaBritain 2005 is a major event, with the Trafalgar Festival at its core, focusing on the Trafalgar Weekend of 21-23 October. This marks the 200th anniversary of the Battle of Trafalgar and the death of Admiral Lord Nelson. But at the National Maritime Museum, the story of Britain and the sea goes even further and deeper.

Sir Christopher Wren designed these impressive buildings on the instructions of Charles II. They were intended to be viewed on approach from the Thames, adopting the existing Queen's House as the focal point. Designed by Inigo Jones for Anne of Denmark and completed in the reign of Charles I, the Queen's House was used by Henrietta Maria as a private garden house for her most privileged circle. It pre-dates the Banqueting House in Whitehall, thereby introducing the classical proportions of Palladian architecture to England. Its rooms are hung with a splendid collection of portraits, seascapes and historical paintings by eminent artists. The Great Hall, the Tulip Staircase, Orangery and Loggia all show the elegance of the Stuart period.

The Royal Observatory, also built by Sir Christopher Wren (to house the Astronomer Royal) stands at the highest point in the Park. The first Astronomer Royal, Flamsteed, established Greenwich's reputation, though it was only under the fifth incumbent, Nevil Maskelyne, that the Nautical Almanac made the Observatory's greatest contribution by providing the solution to the problem of longitude.

It is here that the visitor can stand astride the Meridian Line, Longitude Zero, adopted by international agreement in 1884 as the defining point for longitude measurement and time for the whole world. At one o'clock daily, the 1833 red time-ball drops to signal Greenwich time.

Flamsteed House contains the 17th century Astronomer's apartments, Wren's elegant Octagon Room and a gallery of Harrison's impressive marine timekeepers, which featured in the popular 'Longitude' film and book. The 'Time for the Navy' room shows how clocks were checked and regulated before long voyages and a modern astronomy section is a foretaste of an impressive new Space Science Centre due to open in 2007.

▸ For further details about the National Maritime Museum, see page 69.

Portrait of Lord Nelson by Abbot.

©English Heritage Photo Library/Nigel Corrie.

Map 3

APSLEY HOUSE

www.english-heritage.org.uk/visits

Apsley House (also known as No. 1 London) is the former residence of the first Duke of Wellington.

The Duke made Apsley House his London home after a dazzling military career culminating in his victory over Napoleon at Waterloo in 1815. Wellington enlarged the house (originally designed and built by Robert Adam between 1771 - 78) adding the magnificent Waterloo Gallery by Benjamin Dean Wyatt which holds many of the masterpieces from the Duke's extensive painting collection. It has been the London home of the Dukes of Wellington ever since.

The seventh Duke gave the house and contents to the Nation in 1947, with apartments retained for the family. With its collections of outstanding paintings, porcelain, silver, sculpture, furniture, medals and memorabilia largely intact and the family still in residence, Apsley House is the last great aristocratic town house in London.

Owner:
English Heritage

▶ **CONTACT**

The Administrator
Apsley House
Hyde Park Corner
London W1J 7NT

Tel: 020 7499 5676
Fax: 020 7493 6576

Administrator:
020 7495 8525

▶ **LOCATION**
OS Ref. TQ284 799

N. side of
Hyde Park Corner

Underground:
Hyde Park Corner exit 1
Piccadilly Line.

▶ **OPENING TIMES**

24 March - 31 October
Tue - Sun & BHs
10am - 5pm.

1 November - 31 March
Tue - Sun
10am - 4pm.
Closed 24 - 26 Dec & 1 Jan.

▶ **ADMISSION**

Adult £4.95
Conc. £3.70
Children £2.50
Child (under 5yrs) ... Free

15% discount on groups of 11 or more. Free for English Heritage members and for Overseas Visitor Pass holders.

©English Heritage Photo Library/Nigel Corrie.

ℹ No photography in house.

📷 Partial.

♿ Partial.

🚶 By arrangement.

🎧 Free. English, French, Spanish & German.

🅿 In Park Lane.

🐕 Guide dogs only

✳

🛡 Tel for details.

THE BANQUETING HOUSE

www.banqueting-house.org.uk

The magnificent Banqueting House is all that survives of the great Palace of Whitehall which was destroyed by fire in 1698. It was completed in 1622, commissioned by King James I, and designed by Inigo Jones, the noted classical architect. In 1635 the main hall was further enhanced with the installation of 9 magnificent ceiling paintings by Sir Peter Paul Rubens, which survive to this day. The Banqueting House was also the site of the only royal execution in England's history, with the beheading of Charles I in 1649.

The Banqueting House is open to visitors, as well as playing host to many of society's most glittering occasions.

Map 3

Owner:
Historic Royal Palaces

▶ **CONTACT**

The Banqueting House
Whitehall
London SW1A 2ER

General Enquiries:
0870 751 5178
Functions:
0870 751 5185 / 5186

▶ **LOCATION**

OS Ref. TQ302 801

Underground:
Westminster,
Embankment and
Charing Cross.

Rail: Charing Cross.

▶ **OPENING TIMES**

All Year
Mon - Sat
10am - 5pm
Last admission 4.30pm.

Closed
24 December - 1 January,
Good Friday and other
public holidays.

NB. Liable to close at
short notice for
Government
functions.

▶ **ADMISSION**

Enquiry line for
admission prices:
0870 751 5178

 Concerts.
No photography inside.

Banquets.

Undercroft suitable.

Video and audio guide.

None.

Welcome.

CONFERENCE/FUNCTION		
ROOM	SIZE	MAX CAPACITY
Main Hall	110' x 55'	400
Undercroft	64' x 55'	350

Andrew Holt / The Royal Collection © 2004 HM Queen Elizabeth II

Map 3

Owner:
Official Residence of
Her Majesty The Queen

▶ **CONTACT**

Ticket Sales &
Information Office
Buckingham Palace
London SW1A 1AA

Tel: 020 7766 7300
Groups (15+):
020 7766 7321
Fax: 020 7930 9625

e-mail:
buckinghampalace@
royalcollection.org.uk

▶ **LOCATION**

OS Ref. TQ291 796

Underground:
Green Park, Victoria,
St James's Park.

Rail: Victoria.

Sightseeing tours

A number of tour
companies include a
visit to Buckingham
Palace in their
sightseeing tours. Ask
your concierge or hotel
porter for details.

BUCKINGHAM PALACE
THE STATE ROOMS
THE QUEEN'S GALLERY
THE ROYAL MEWS

www.royal.gov.uk

Buckingham Palace is the official London residence of Her Majesty The Queen and serves as both home and office. Its 19 State Rooms, which open for eight weeks a year, form the heart of the working palace. They are used extensively by The Queen and members of the Royal Family to receive and entertain their guests on State, ceremonial and official occasions. The State Rooms are lavishly furnished with some of the finest treasures from the Royal Collection – paintings by Rembrandt, Rubens, Van Dyck; sculpture by Canova; exquisite examples of Sèvres porcelain, and some of the most magnificent English and French furniture in the world. The garden walk offers superb views of the Garden Front of the Palace and the 19th-century lake.

Adjacent to Buckingham Palace are the Royal Mews and The Queen's Gallery. The Royal Mews is one of the finest working stables in existence and houses both the horse-drawn carriages and motor cars used for coronations, State visits, royal weddings and the State Opening of Parliament.

The Queen's Gallery, situated adjacent to Buckingham Palace, hosts a programme of changing exhibitions of magnificent works of art from the Royal Collection. Exhibitions in 2005 include *Enchanting the Eye: Dutch Paintings of the Golden Age* (11 February - 30 October), followed by *Canaletto in Venice* (11 November - 26 February 2006).

Both exhibitions will be shown alongside *Treasures from the Royal Collection*, which will include paintings by Duccio, Clouet, Rubens, Van Dyck, Claude and Lely, works by Fabergé, as well as furniture, sculpture and ceramics, jewellery, silver and gold.

Johannes Vermeer, *A Lady at the Virginals with a Gentleman*, c.1662-5/ The Royal Collection © 2005 HMQueen Elizabeth II.

THE QUEEN'S GALLERY

State Postilion Jackets David Cripps/The Royal Collection © 2005 HM Queen Elizabeth II

▶ **OPENING TIMES**

As Buckingham Palace is a working royal palace, opening arrangements may change at short notice.
Please check before planning a visit.

The State Rooms
August - September
Daily: 9.30am - 6.30pm (last admission 4.15pm).

Tickets available during August & September from the Ticket Office in Green Park.

The Queen's Gallery
All year except
10 Jan - 10 Feb, 25 Mar & 25/26 Dec and between exhibitions.
10am - 5.30pm (last admission 4.30pm).
Entry by timed ticket.

The Royal Mews
5 March - 31 October daily except Fridays:
11am - 4pm.
Closed 25 Mar, 28 May, 4 & 11 Jun and during State Visits.
Extended opening hours during August & September.

To pre-book your tickets telephone the Ticket Sales & Information Office or visit the website.

Private Evening Tours are available to Groups (15+) contact 020 7766 7322.

▶ **ADMISSION**

**The State Rooms,
The Queen's Gallery,
The Royal Mews**
For admission prices please call the Ticket Sales & Information Office.
Group (15+) discounts available, ask for details.

No photography inside.

Wheelchair users are required to pre-book.

The Royal Mews.

The State Rooms and some exhibitions.

None.

Guide dogs only.

© English Heritage Photo Library

CHISWICK HOUSE ⊞

www.english-heritage.org.uk/visits

Chiswick House is internationally renowned as one of the first and finest English Palladian villas. Lord Burlington, who built the villa from 1725 - 1729, was inspired by the architecture and gardens of ancient Rome and this house is his masterpiece. His aim was to create a fit setting to show his friends his fine collection of art and his library. The opulent interior features gilded decoration, velvet walls and painted ceilings. The important 18th century gardens surrounding Chiswick House have, at every turn, something to surprise and delight the visitor from the magnificent cedar trees to the beautiful Italianate gardens with their cascade, statues, temples, urns and obelisks.

Venue Hire and Hospitality

English Heritage offers exclusive use of Chiswick House in the evenings and Saturday afternoons for dinners, receptions and weddings.

Map 3

Owner:
English Heritage

▶ **CONTACT**
Visits:
House Manager
Chiswick House
Burlington Lane
London   W4 2RP

Tel: 020 8995 0508

Venue Hire and Hospitality:
Hospitality Manager
Tel: 020 7973 3292

▶ **LOCATION**
OS Ref: TQ210 775

Burlington Lane
London W4.

Rail: ¼ mile NE of
Chiswick Station.

Tube: Turnham Green,
¾ mile

Bus: 190, E3.

▶ **OPENING TIMES***

Summer
24 March - 31 October
Wed - Sun & BHs,
10am - 5pm.
Closes at 2pm on Sats.

Winter
1 Nov - 31 March 2006
Pre-booked group
tours only.

▶ **ADMISSION***

Adult £4.00
Child (5-15yrs)....... £2.00
Conc £3.00
Groups
(11+) .... 15% discount

© English Heritage Photo Library

🛍 ℹ WCs. Filming, plays, photographic shoots.

☕ Café in grounds not managed by English Heritage.

🍴 Private & corporate hospitality.

♿ Please call in advance. WC.

🧍 Personal guided tours must be booked in advance. Colour guide book £2.50.

🎧 Free audio tours in English, French & German.

📷 Free if booked in advance. Tel: 020 7973 3485.

🐕 Guide dogs in grounds.

🔔 Civil Wedding Licence.

🅿

🛡 Tel for details.

English Heritage Photo Library/Jonathan Bailey

Map 3

ELTHAM PALACE ⊞

www.english-heritage.org.uk/visits

Owner:
English Heritage

▶ **CONTACT**

Eltham Palace
Court Yard
Eltham
London SE9 5QE

Visits:
Property Secretary
Tel: 020 8294 2548

Venue Hire and Hospitality:
Hospitality Manager
Tel: 020 8294 2577

▶ **LOCATION**

OS Ref. TQ425 740

M25/J3, then A20 towards Eltham. The Palace is signposted from A20 and from Eltham High Street. A2 from Central London.

Rail: 20 mins from Victoria or London Bridge Stations to Eltham or Mottingham, then 15 min walk.

The epitome of 1930s chic, Eltham Palace dramatically demonstrates the glamour and allure of the period.

Bathe in the light flooding from a spectacular glazed dome in the Entrance Hall as it highlights beautiful blackbeam veneer and figurative marquetry. It is a *tour de force* only rivalled by the adjacent Dining Room – where an Art Deco aluminium-leafed ceiling is a perfect complement to the bird's-eye maple walls. Step into Virginia Courtauld's magnificent gold-leaf and onyx bathroom and throughout the house discover lacquered, 'ocean liner' style veneered walls and built-in furniture.

A Chinese sliding screen is all that separates chic '30s Art Deco from the medieval Great Hall. You will find concealed electric lighting, centralised vacuum cleaning and a loud-speaker system that allowed music to waft around the house. Authentic interiors have been recreated by the finest contemporary craftsmen. Their appearance was painstakingly researched from archive photographs, documents and interviews with friends and relatives of the Courtaulds.

Outside you will find a delightful mixture of formal and informal gardens including a rose garden, pergola and loggia, all nestled around the extensive remains of the medieval palace.

English Heritage Photo Library/Jonathan Bailey

CONFERENCE/FUNCTION	
ROOM	MAX CAPACITY
Great Hall	300 standing 200 dining
Entrance Hall	100 seated
Drawing Room	120 standing 80 theatre-style
Dining Room	80 standing 10 dining

i WCs. Filming, plays and photographic shoots.

□

🍷 Exclusive private and corporate hospitality.

♿ WC.

🚶 Guided tours on request.

🎧 Free. English, German & French.

P Coaches must book.

✖

▮

🎭 Tel for details.

▶ **OPENING TIMES***

24 March - 31 October
Sun - Wed
10am - 5pm.

1 November - 21 December
Sun - Wed
10am - 4pm.

1 February - 31 March
Sun - Wed
10am - 4pm.

Closed 22 Dec - 31 Jan.

Groups visits must be booked two weeks in advance.

Venue Hire and Hospitality
English Heritage offers exclusive use of the Palace on Thu, Fri or Sat for daytime conferences, meetings and weddings and in the evenings for dinners, concerts and receptions.

▶ **ADMISSION***

House and Grounds

Adult	£7.30
Child	£3.70
Conc.	£5.50
Family (2+3)	£18.30

Grounds only

Adult	£4.60
Child	£2.30
Conc.	£3.50

Crown Copyright: Historic Royal Palaces

Crown Copyright: Historic Royal Palaces

Map 3

Managed by:
Historic Royal Palaces

▶ **CONTACT**

Kensington Palace
London W8 4PX

Recorded Information:
0870 751 5170

Venue Hire and Corporate Hospitality:
0870 751 5184

All Other Enquiries:
0870 751 5176

▶ **LOCATION**

OS Ref. TQ258 801

In Kensington Gardens.

Underground:
Queensway on Central Line, High Street Kensington on Circle & District Line.

KENSINGTON PALACE STATE APARTMENTS

www.kensington-palace.org.uk

Kensington Palace has seen such momentous events as the death of George II and the birth of the future Queen Victoria. Visitors today enjoy the tranquillity and calm away from the hustle and bustle of this popular part of London.

The palace is home to the magnificent Royal Ceremonial Dress Collection, a display of court and ceremonial outfits dating from the 18th century. Multi-language sound guides lead visitors through the excitement of court presentation. The collection includes dresses worn on state occasions by Her Majesty The Queen as well as 14 of Diana, Princess of Wales's evening dresses.

During 2005 the special exhibition – *Memories of Royal Occasions, The Queen's Working Wardrobe*

1945-1972, is included in the admission price and brings together outfits worn by Elizabeth II as first Princess and then Queen. Highlights include the black velvet evening dress by Norman Hartnell worn to a 1956 Royal Film Performance where she met stars including Marilyn Monroe and Brigitte Bardot.

The multi-lingual sound guides also take visitors around the magnificent State Apartments, including the lavishly decorated Cupola Room where Queen Victoria was baptised, and the beautifully restored King's Gallery.

Most recently the rooms making up the private apartment of Princess Margaret have been opened for special exhibitions and displays.

▶ **OPENING TIMES**

March - October
Daily, 10am - 6pm
(last admission 5pm)

Nov - Feb
Daily, 10am - 5pm
(last admission 4pm)

Closed 24 - 26 Dec.

▶ **ADMISSION**

Telephone Information Line for admission prices:
0870 751 5170

Advance Ticket Sales:
0870 751 5180

Group bookings
0870 751 7070
Quote Hudson's.

Crown Copyright, HRP

No photography indoors.

The Orangery (located nearby) serves light refreshments.

Partial.

Nearby. Cars and coaches.

Welcome, please book.
0870 751 5192.

 In grounds, on leads. Guide dogs only in Palace.

FUNCTIONS

ROOM	MAX CAPACITY
Orangery	250 receptions 150 dinners
Victoria Garden Rooms	100 receptions 50 dinners

©English Heritage Photo Library/Paul Highnam

Map 3

KENWOOD HOUSE ⌗

www.english-heritage.org.uk/visits

Kenwood, one of the treasures of London, is an idyllic country retreat close to the popular villages of Hampstead and Highgate.

The house was remodelled in the 1760s by Robert Adam, the fashionable neo-classical architect. The breathtaking library or 'Great Room' is one of his finest achievements.

Kenwood is famous for the internationally important collection of paintings bequeathed to the nation by Edward Guinness, 1st Earl of Iveagh. Some of the world's finest artists are represented by works such as a Rembrandt *Self Portrait*, Vermeer's *The Guitar Player; Mary, Countess*

Howe by Gainsborough and paintings by Turner, Reynolds and many others.

As if the house and its contents were not riches enough, Kenwood stands in 112 acres of landscaped grounds on the edge of Hampstead Heath, commanding a fine prospect towards central London. The meadow walks and ornamental lake of the park, designed by Humphry Repton, contrast with the wilder Heath below. The open air concerts held in the summer at Kenwood have become part of London life, combining the charms of music with the serenity of the lakeside setting.

Owner:
English Heritage

▶ CONTACT

Kenwood House
Hampstead Lane
London   NW3 7JR

Visits:
The House Manager
Tel: 020 8348 1286

▶ LOCATION

OS Ref. TQ271 874

M1/J2. Signed off A1, on leaving A1 turn right at junction with Bishop's Ave, turn left into Hampstead Lane. Visitor car park on left.

Bus: London Transport 210.

Rail: Hampstead Heath.

Underground:
Archway or Golders Green Northern Line then bus 210.

English Heritage Photo Library

English Heritage Photo Library

▶ OPENING TIMES

24 March - 31 October, Daily: 10am - 5pm*.

1 November - 31 March Daily: 10am - 4pm*.

Closed 24 - 26 December & 1 January.

*House open at 10.30am on Wednesdays & Fridays.

Venue Hire and Hospitality
Events are available for up to 100 guests in the Service Wing. Please ring company of Cooks on 020 8341 5384.

▶ ADMISSION

House & Grounds: Free. Donations welcome.

ℹ️ WCs. Concerts, exhibitions, filming. No photography in house.

🍽 Exclusive private and corporate hospitality.

♿ Ground floor access. WC.

☕ Available in the Brew House.

🚶 Available on request (in English). Please call for details.

🎧 English, French, Italian & German.

🅿 West Lodge car park on Hampstead Lane. Parking for the disabled.

🎒 Free when booked in advance on 020 7973 3485.

❄️

🎭 Tel for details.

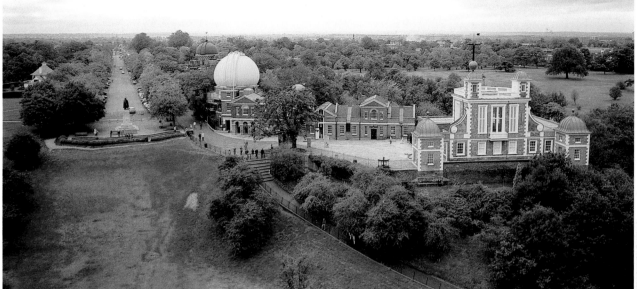

© National Maritime Museum

Owner: National
Maritime Museum

▶ **CONTACT**

Groups: Robin Scates
Events: Eleanor Goody
Park Row, Greenwich
London SE10 9NF

Tel: 020 8858 4422
Fax: 020 8312 6632

Visit Bookings:
Tel: 020 8312 6608
Fax: 020 8312 6522
e-mail:
bookings@nmm.ac.uk
Functions:
Tel: 020 8312 6644/6693
Fax: 020 8312 6572

▶ **LOCATION**
OS Ref. TQ388 773

Within Greenwich Park
on the S bank of the
Thames at Greenwich.
Travel by river cruise or
Docklands Light Railway
(Cutty Sark station).
M25 (S) via A2. From
M25 (N) M11, A12 and
Blackwall Tunnel.

ROYAL OBSERVATORY, NATIONAL MARITIME MUSEUM & QUEEN'S HOUSE
www.nmm.ac.uk

Playing a leading role in the 2005 SeaBritain festival and Trafalgar celebrations these Greenwich attractions are beautifully situated within the historic royal park at Greenwich. Throughout the year there will be events and exhibitions to celebrate Britain's maritime past, present and future.

Illustrated above is Flamsteed House (Wren 1675) built to accommodate the first Astronomer Royal. The Meridian Building defines Longitude 0° as the base point for calculation of the World's time zones. Visitors enjoy a panoramic view over London from the famous Dome of Greenwich to the Dome of St Paul's Cathedral. Displays include the Harrison marine timekeepers and also cover historical and modern astronomy.

The modern National Maritime Museum galleries

chart Britain's history of seafaring and empire. Nelson's uniform coat is on display. Contemporary themes are tackled and there are thought-provoking displays on empire, slavery, immigration and the ocean environment.

The annual exhibition (7 July to 13 November 2005) compares the stories of Nelson and Napoleon and is sumptuously illustrated with artefacts with direct personal associations. Admission charge.

The Queen's House (Inigo Jones 1635) is significant as the first classical house in England. Called a House of Delights by Henrietta Maria, the Great Hall, Orangery and 'Tulip' stairs provide an elegant setting for the art and photographic exhibitions on display for the SeaBritain festival.

▶ **OPENING TIMES**

Daily, 10am - 5pm (later opening in summer). Last admission 30 mins prior. Varies at New Year and Marathon Day (17 Apr).

Closed 24 - 26 December.

Gallery talks and drama (see notices on arrival).

Special Exhibitions National Trust/ Magnum photography from 23 March

Nelson & Napoléon 7 July – 13 November

▶ **ADMISSION**

Free admission except for special exhibition: Nelson & Napoléon
Adult £9.00
Child £4.00
Conc £6.00

ROOM	SIZE	MAX CAPACITY
Queen's House	40' x 40'	Dining 120 Standing 200 Conference 120
Observatory, Octagon Rm	25' x 25'	Dining 60 Standing 150
NMM Upper Court	140' x 70'	Dining 500 Standing 1000
NMM Lecture Theatre		Conference 120

CONFERENCE/FUNCTION

Battle of Trafalgar 21 October 1805 (JMW Turner)   © National Maritime Museum London, Greenwich Hospital Collection

No photography.

Partial. WC.

Licensed.

Limited for coaches.

Guide dogs only.

Sampson Lloyd

ST PAUL'S CATHEDRAL

www.stpauls.co.uk

Map 3

Owner: Dean & Chapter of St Paul's Cathedral

▶ CONTACT

Mark McVay
The Chapter House
St Paul's Churchyard
London   EC4M 8AD

Tel: 020 7246 8348
020 7246 8346

Fax: 020 7248 3104

e-mail: chapterhouse@ stpaulscathedral.org.uk

▶ LOCATION
OS Ref. TQ321 812

Central London.

Underground:
St Paul's,
Mansion House,
Blackfriars, Bank.

Rail: Blackfriars,
City Thameslink.

Air: London Airports.

A Cathedral dedicated to St Paul has stood at the heart of the City of London for 1400 years, a constant reminder of the spiritual life in this busy commercial centre.

The present St Paul's, the fourth to occupy the site, was built between 1675 - 1710. Sir Christopher Wren's masterpiece rose from the ashes of the previous Cathedral, which had been destroyed in the Great Fire of London.

Over the centuries, the Cathedral has been the setting for royal weddings, state funerals and thanksgivings. Admiral Nelson and the Duke of Wellington are buried here, Queen Victoria celebrated her gold and diamond jubilees and Charles, Prince of Wales married Lady Diana Spencer. Most recently, St Paul's hosted the thanksgiving service for the 100th birthday of HM Queen Elizabeth the Queen Mother. On 4 June 2002 the Cathedral hosted the National Service of Thanksgiving for the Golden Jubilee of HM The Queen.

Hundreds of memorials pay tribute to famous statesmen, soldiers, artists, doctors and writers and mark the valuable contributions to national life made by many ordinary men and women.

The soaring dome, one of the largest in the world, offers panoramic views across London from the exterior galleries. Inside, a whisper in the Whispering Gallery can be heard on the opposite side.

2005 will see the completion of a major programme of cleaning and repair on the interior, allowing visitors to experience the Cathedral as we imagine Sir Christopher Wren originally conceived it. Nearly 300 years of dirt has been removed returning the Portland stonework to its natural creaminess, revealing the delicacy of carvings and brilliance of the Byzantine-style mosaics. This is part of a £40m programme of work for the building's approaching tercentenary.

Far more than a beautiful landmark, St Paul's Cathedral is a living symbol of the city and nation it serves.

▶ OPENING TIMES

Mon - Sat, 8.30am - 4.30pm, last admission 4pm.

Guided tours: daily, 11.30am, 1.30pm and 2pm.

Tours of the Triforium: Mon & Thur, 11.30am & 2.30pm.

All tours are subject to an additional charge.

Cathedral Shop & Café:
9am - 5.30pm,
Sun, 10.30am - 5pm.

Restaurant:
11am - 5.30pm.

Service Times
Mon - Sat
7.30am Mattins (Sat 8.30am)
8am Holy Communion (said)
12.30pm Holy Communion (said)
5pm Choral Evensong

Sun: 8am Holy Communion (said)
10.15am Choral Mattins & sermon
11.30am Choral Eucharist & sermon
3.15pm Choral Evensong & sermon
6pm Evening service

The Cathedral may be closed to tourists on certain days of the year. It is advisable to phone or check our website for up-to-date information.

▶ ADMISSION

Adult £8.00
Child £3.50
OAP/Student £7.00
Groups (10+)
Adult £7.50
Child £3.00
OAP/Student £6.50

Sampson Lloyd

constructionphotography.com

ROOM	MAX CAPACITY
Conference Suite	100 (standing)

No photography, video or mobile phones.   Partial.   Licensed.

None for cars, limited for coaches.   Guide dogs only.

© Spencer House / Mark Fiennes

Map 3

SPENCER HOUSE

www.spencerhouse.co.uk

▶ **CONTACT**

Jane Rick
Director
Spencer House
27 St James's Place
London   SW1A 1NR

Tel: 020 7514 1958
Fax: 020 7409 2952

Info Line: 020 7499 8620

▶ **LOCATION**

OS Ref. TQ293 803

Central London:
off St James's Street,
overlooking
Green Park.

Underground:
Green Park.

All images are
copyright of Spencer
House Ltd and may not
be used without the
permission of
Spencer House Ltd.

Spencer House, built 1756 - 66 for the 1st Earl Spencer, an ancestor of Diana, Princess of Wales (1961-97), is London's finest surviving 18th century town house. The magnificent private palace has regained the full splendour of its late 18th century appearance, after a painstaking ten-year restoration programme.

Designed by John Vardy and James 'Athenian' Stuart, the nine state rooms are amongst the first neo-classical interiors in Europe. Vardy's Palm Room, with its spectacular screen of gilded palm trees and arched fronds, is a unique Palladian setpiece, while the elegant mural decorations of Stuart's Painted Room reflect the 18th century passion for classical Greece and Rome. Stuart's superb gilded furniture has been returned to its original location in the Painted Room by courtesy of the V&A and English Heritage. Visitors can also see a fine collection of 18th century paintings and furniture, specially assembled for the house, including five major Benjamin West paintings, graciously lent by Her Majesty The Queen.

The state rooms are open to the public for viewing on Sundays. They are also available on a limited number of occasions each year for private and corporate entertaining during the rest of the week.

© Spencer House / Mark Fiennes

▶ **OPENING TIMES**

All Year
(except January & August)
Suns, 10.30am - 5.45pm.

Last tour 4.45pm.

Tours begin approximately every 20 mins and last 1hr 10 mins. Maximum number on each tour is 20.

Mon mornings for pre-booked groups only.

Open for corporate hospitality except during January & August.

▶ **ADMISSION**

Adult £9.00
Conc.* £7.00

* Students, Friends of V&A, Tate Gallery and Royal Academy (all with cards), children under 16 (no under 10s admitted), Senior Citizens (with identification). Group size: min 15 - 60.

Prices include guided tour.

SPECIAL EVENTS

FEB 15, 22 & MAR 1
6.30pm.
Lecture Series - "Carpets, Carrara and Chandeliers" Craftsmen in Conversation at Spencer House.
For further information telephone 020 7499 8620 or see www.spencerhouse.co.uk

SPECIFIC SUNDAYS
The authentically restored garden of this 18th century London palace will be open to the public on specific Sundays during Spring and Summer.

For updated information telephone 020 7499 8620 or see our website.

CONFERENCE/FUNCTION

ROOM	MAX CAPACITY
Receptions	400
Lunches & Dinners	130
Board Meetings	40
Theatre Style Meetings	100

ℹ️ No photography inside House or Garden. 🍽️ ♿ House only ramps and lifts. WC.

🚶 Obligatory. Comprehensive colour guidebook £3.50. 🅿️ None. 🚫 🔔

Map 3

Owner: The Duke of Northumberland

▶ **CONTACT**

Estate Office
Syon House
Syon Park
Brentford
TW8 8JF

Tel: 020 8560 0882
Fax: 020 8568 0936

e-mail: info@
syonpark.co.uk

▶ **LOCATION**
OS Ref. TQ173 767

Between Brentford and Twickenham, off the A4, A310 in SW London.

Rail: Kew Bridge or Gunnersbury Underground then Bus 237 or 267.

Air: Heathrow 8m.

SYON PARK 🏛

www.syonpark.co.uk

Described by John Betjeman as 'the Grand Architectural Walk', Syon House and its 200 acre park is the London home of the Duke of Northumberland, whose family, the Percys, have lived here for 400 years.

Originally the site of a late medieval monastery, excavated by Channel 4's *Time Team*, Syon Park has a fascinating history. The present house has Tudor origins but contains some of Robert Adam's finest interiors, which were commissioned by the 1st Duke in the 1760s. The private apartments and State bedrooms are available to view. The house is regularly used for feature films and productions.

Within the 'Capability' Brown landscaped park

are 40 acres of gardens which contain the spectacular Great Conservatory designed by Charles Fowler in the 1820s. The House and Great Conservatory are available for corporate and private hire.

Syon House is an excellent venue for small meetings, lunches and dinners in the Duke's private dining room (max 22). The State Apartments make a sumptuous setting for dinners, concerts, receptions, launches and wedding ceremonies (max 120). Marquees can be erected on the lawn adjacent to the house for balls and corporate events. The Great Conservatory is available for summer parties, launches and wedding receptions (max 150).

WEDDING/FUNCTION

ROOM	SIZE	MAX CAPACITY
Great Hall	50' x 30'	120
Great Conservatory	60' x 40'	150
Marquee		1000

▶ **OPENING TIMES**

House
23 March - 30 October
Wed, Thur, Sun & BHs
11am - 5pm
(open Good Fri &
Easter Sat).

Other times by appointment for groups.

Gardens
Daily (except 25 & 26 Dec)
10.30am - 5.30pm or dusk if earlier.

▶ **ADMISSION**

House and Gardens
Adult £7.50
Child/Conc. £6.50
Family (2+2) £17.00

Gardens only
Adult £3.75
Child/Conc. £2.50
Family (2+2) £9.00
Groups (15 - 50 persons)

House & Gardens
(Group bookings)
Adult £7.00
Child/Conc. £6.00

ℹ No photography in house. Indoor adventure playground.

🏠 🌱 Garden centre.

🍽 ♿ Partial.

🍴

🧍 By arrangement. 🎧

🅿 ♿

🐕 Guide dogs only.

🔔 ❄

🛡 Tel for details.

THE TOWER OF LONDON

www.tower-of-london.org.uk

Map 3

Managed by:
Historic Royal Palaces

▶ **CONTACT**

The Tower of London
London   EC3N 4AB

**Recorded
Information Line:**
0870 756 6060

**Venue Hire and
Corporate Hospitality:**
0870 751 5183

All Other Enquiries:
0870 751 5177

▶ **LOCATION**

OS Ref. TQ336 806

Underground:
Tower Hill on
Circle/District Line.

**Docklands Light
Railway:**
Tower Gateway Station.

Rail: Fenchurch Street
Station and
London Bridge Station.

Bus: 15, 25, 42,
78, 100, D1.

Riverboat: From
Charing Cross,
Westminster or
Greenwich to
Tower Pier.

For over 900 years the Tower has served as a royal residence, a fortress, mint, armoury, menagerie, a prison and place of execution.

Start your visit with a Yeoman Warder tour. Better known as Beefeaters, the Yeoman Warders provide an introductory tour detailing the dark and sometimes deadly history of the Tower. Meanwhile, costumed interpreters bring to life the history in daily re-enactments on the south lawn.

The magnificent Crown Jewels remain one of the main attractions. See the Star of Africa, the world's largest cut diamond, mounted in the Sceptre, part of the Coronation Regalia. Also in the collection is the Imperial State Crown, still worn by The Queen

annually at the State Opening of Parliament.

Prisoners and imprisonment is a popular subject and following the recent representation in the Bloody and Beauchamp Towers, displays incorporate the latest audio and visual effects to create a very different experience. Learn more about how prisoners filled their time whilst confined in those very rooms at the Tower and contemplate the reality compared to the myth of Tower imprisonment!

Stand on the execution site, visit the White Tower housing displays of Tudor Arms and Armour and take in the Torture exhibition in the Wakefield Tower.

▶ **OPENING TIMES**

Summer
1 March - 31 October
Daily
Tues - Sat: 9am - 6pm
(last admission 5pm)
Mons & Suns: 10am - 5pm.

Winter
1 November - 28 February
Tues - Sat: 9am - 5pm
Mons & Suns: 10am - 4pm
(last admission 4pm).

Closed 24 - 26 December
and 1 January.

Buildings close 30 minutes
after last admission.

▶ **ADMISSION**

Telephone Information
Line for admission prices:
0870 756 6060

Advance Ticket Sales:
0870 756 7070

Group bookings:
0870 751 7070
Quote Hudson's.

No photography in
Jewel House.

0870 751 5183.

Partial. WC.

Yeoman Warder tours are
free and leave front entrance
every ¹/₂ hr.

None for cars. Coach
parking nearby.

Welcome. To book 0870
751 5191.

Guide dogs only.

www.tower-of-london.org.uk

2 WILLOW ROAD

HAMPSTEAD, LONDON NW3 1TH

Tel: 020 7435 6166 **e-mail:** 2willowroad@nationaltrust.org.uk

Owner: The National Trust **Contact:** The Custodian

The former home of Erno Goldfinger, designed and built by him in 1939. A three-storey brick and concrete rectangle, it is one of Britain's most important examples of modernist architecture and is filled with furniture also designed by Goldfinger. The interesting art collection includes works by Henry Moore and Max Ernst.

Location: OS Ref. TQ270 858. Hampstead, London.

Open: 6 - 27 Mar, 6 - 27 Nov: Sat, 12 noon - 5pm. 1 Apr - 30 Oct: Thurs - Sat, 12 noon - 5pm. Open Good Fri. Last admission 4.30pm. Tours: 12 noon, 1 & 2 pm. Unrestricted access for unguided visits 3 - 5pm.

Admission: Adult £4.60, Child £2.30, Family £11.50. Joint ticket with Fenton House £6.40. Private groups are welcome throughout the year outside public afternoon opening times. Groups must be 5+, booking essential.

♿Small ground floor area accessible, filmed tour of whole house available.

18 FOLGATE STREET

Spitalfields, East London E1 6BX

Tel: 020 7247 4013 **Fax:** 020 7377 5548 **www.**dennissevershouse.co.uk

Owner: Spitalfields Historic Buildings Trust **Contact:** Mick Pedroli

A time capsule furnished and decorated to tell the story of the Jervis family, Huguenot silk weavers from 1724 - 1919.

Location: OS Ref. TQ335 820. ¹/₂ m NE of Liverpool St. Station. E of Bishopsgate (A10), just N of Spitalfields Market.

Open: "Silent Night" every Mon evening. Booking required. 1st & 3rd Sun each month: 2 - 5pm. Mons following these Suns 12 noon - 2pm.

Admission: "Silent Night" Mons £12, Suns £8. Monday afternoons £5.

♿Partial. 🎟Obligatory by private bookings. ✸ 📺 Tel for details.

ALBERT MEMORIAL ♯

Princes Gate, Kensington Gore SW7

Tel: 020 7495 0916 (Booking Agency)

Contact: Richard Skinner on 020 7495 5504

An elaborate memorial by George Gilbert Scott to commemorate the Prince Consort.

Location: OS Ref. TQ266 798. Victoria Station 1¹/₂ m, South Kensington Tube ¹/₂ m.

Open: All visits by booked guided tours; Sunday afternoons only. Tours last 45 mins and are weather dependent so please ring for confirmation. Times and prices subject to change from April 2005.

Admission: Adult £4.

APSLEY HOUSE ♯

See page 62 for full page entry.

THE BANQUETING HOUSE

See page 63 for full page entry.

BLEWCOAT SCHOOL 🌿

23 Caxton Street, Westminster, London SW1H 0PY

Tel: 020 7222 2877

Owner: The National Trust **Contact:** Janet Bowden

Built in 1709 at the expense of William Green, a local brewer, to provide an education for poor children. Used as a school until 1926, it is now the NT London Gift Shop and Information Centre.

Location: OS Ref. TQ295 794. Near the junction with Buckingham Gate.

Open: All year: Mon - Fri, 10am - 5.30pm. Easter - Christmas: Thurs, 10am - 7pm. Also Sat 19 Nov - 24 Dec: 10am - 4pm. Closed BHs.

BOSTON MANOR HOUSE

Boston Manor Road, Brentford TW8 9JX

Tel: 020 8560 5441

Owner: Hounslow Cultural & Community Services **Contact:** Jerome Farrell

A fine Jacobean house built in 1623.

Location: OS Ref. TQ168 784. 10 mins walk S of Boston Manor Station (Piccadilly Line) and 250yds N of Boston Manor Road junction with A4 - Great West Road, Brentford.

Open: Apr - end Oct: Sat, Sun & BHs, 2.30 - 5pm. Due to structural works during 2004/05 please check times prior to your visit. Park open daily.

Admission: Free.

BRUCE CASTLE MUSEUM

Haringey Libraries, Archives & Museum Service,

Lordship Lane, London N17 8NU

Tel: 020 8808 8772 **Fax:** 020 8808 4118 **e-mail:** museum.services@haringey.gov.uk

Owner: London Borough of Haringey

A Tudor building. Sir Rowland Hill (inventor of the Penny Post) ran a progressive school at Bruce Castle from 1827.

Location: OS Ref. TQ335 906. Corner of Bruce Grove (A10) and Lordship Lane, 600yds NW of Bruce Grove Station.

Open: All year: Wed - Sun & Summer BHs (except Good Fri), 1 - 5pm. Organised groups by appointment.

Admission: Free.

BUCKINGHAM PALACE

See page 64 for full page entry.

BURGH HOUSE

New End Square, Hampstead, London NW3 1LT

Tel: 020 7431 0144 **Buttery:** 020 7431 2516 **Fax:** 020 7435 8817

e-mail: burghhouse@talk21.com **www.**burghhouse.org.uk

Owner: London Borough of Camden **Contact:** Ms Helen Wilton

A Grade I listed building of 1703 in the heart of old Hampstead with original panelled rooms, "barley sugar" staircase banisters and a music room. Home of the Hampstead Museum, permanent and changing exhibitions. Prize-winning terraced garden. Regular programme of concerts, art exhibitions, and meetings. Receptions, seminars and conferences. Rooms for hire. Special facilities for schools visits. Wedding receptions.

Location: OS Ref. TQ266 859. New End Square, E of Hampstead underground station.

Open: All year: Wed - Sun, 12 noon - 5pm. Sats by appointment only. BH Mons, 2 - 5pm. Closed Christmas fortnight, Good Fri & Easter Mon. Groups by arrangement. Buttery: Wed - Sun, 11am - 5.30pm. BHs, 1 - 5.00pm.

Admission: Free.

📷 📶 ♿Ground floor & grounds. WC. 🍴Licensed buttery. 🍴 🎟By arrangement. 🅿None. 🔲By arrangement. 🦮 Guide dogs only. 🔺 ✸

CAPEL MANOR GARDENS

BULLSMOOR LANE, ENFIELD EN1 4RQ

www.capel.ac.uk

Tel: 020 8366 4442 **Fax:** 01992 717544

Owner: Capel Manor Charitable Organisation **Contact:** Miss Julie Ryan

These extensive, richly planted gardens are delightful throughout the year offering inspiration, information and relaxation. The gardens include various themes - historical, modern, walled, rock, water, sensory and disabled and an Italianate Maze, Japanese Garden and 'Gardening Which?' demonstration and model gardens. Capel Manor is a College of Horticulture and runs a training scheme for professional gardeners originally devised in conjunction with the Historic Houses Association.

Location: OS Ref. TQ344 997. Minutes from M25/J25. Tourist Board signs posted.

Open: Daily in summer: 10am - 5.30pm. Last ticket 4.30pm. Check for winter times.

Admission: Adult £5, Child £2, Conc. £4, Family £12. Charges alter for special show weekends and winter months.

📷 ♿Grounds. WC. 🍴 🅿 🐕In grounds, on leads. ✸ 📺 Tel for details.

CARLYLE'S HOUSE 🌿

24 Cheyne Row, Chelsea, London SW3 5HL

Tel: 020 7352 7087 **Fax:** 020 7352 5108 **e-mail:** carlyleshouse@nationaltrust.org.uk

Owner: The National Trust **Contact:** The Custodian

Atmospheric home of the writer Thomas Carlyle and his wife Jane from 1834-1881. There is a small walled garden and the surrounding streets are rich in literary and artistic associations.

Location: OS Ref. TQ272 777. Off the King's Road and Oakley Street, or off Cheyne Walk between Albert Bridge and Battersea Bridge on Chelsea Embankment.

Open: 23 Mar - 30 Oct: Wed - Fri (incl. Good Fri), 2 - 5pm; Sat, Sun & BH Mons, 11am - 5pm. Last admission 4.30pm.

Admission: Adult £4, Child £2. Tel for groups visits and guided tours.

🎟By arrangement for groups. 📺 Tel for details.

CHAPTER HOUSE ⌗
East Cloisters, Westminster Abbey, London SW1P 3PE
Tel: 020 7654 4834   **www**.westminster-abbey.org
Owner: English Heritage   **Managed by:** Dean & Chapter of Westminster
The Chapter House, built by the Royal masons c1250 and faithfully restored in the 19th century, contains some of the finest medieval sculpture to be seen and spectacular wall paintings. The building is octagonal, with a central column, and still has its original floor of glazed tiles, which have been newly conserved. Its uses have varied and in the 14th century it was used as a meeting place for the Benedictine monks of the Abbey and as well as for Members of Parliament.
Location: OS Ref. TQ301 795.
Open: Daily, 10am - 4pm. Liable to be closed at short notice on State & Holy occasions. Closed Good Fri, 24 - 26 Dec & 1 Jan.
Admission: Integral part of tour of Westminster Abbey.

CHELSEA PHYSIC GARDEN
66 ROYAL HOSPITAL ROAD, LONDON SW3 4HS
www.chelseaphysicgarden.co.uk
Tel: 020 7352 5646   **Fax:** 020 7376 3910
e-mail: enquiries@chelseaphysicgarden.co.uk
Owner: Chelsea Physic Garden Company
The second oldest botanic garden in Britain, founded in 1673. For many years these 4 acres of peace and quiet, with many rare and unusual plants, were known only to a few. Specialists in medicinal plants, tender species and the history of plant introductions.
Location: OS Ref. TQ277 778. Off Embankment, between Chelsea & Albert Bridges. Entrance - Swan Walk. Underground: Sloane Square/South Kensington.
Open: 3 Apr - 30 Oct: Weds, 12 noon - 5pm & Suns, 2 - 6pm. Special winter openings: 6 & 13 Feb: 11am - 3pm.
Admission: Adult £5, Child £3, OAP £5, Conc. £3. Carers for disabled: Free.
Partial. WCs. By arrangement. Guide dogs only. Tel for details.

CHISWICK HOUSE ⌗   *See page 65 for full page entry.*

CHURCH FARMHOUSE MUSEUM
Greyhound Hill, London NW4 4JR
Tel: 020 8203 0130   **e-mail:** gerrard.roots@barnet.gov.uk
www.churchfarmhousemuseum.co.uk
Owner: London Borough of Barnet   **Contact:** Gerrard Roots
The building is a Grade II* 1660s farmhouse with Victorian additions, in a small public garden. There are three 19th century furnished rooms - dining room (decorated for a Victorian Christmas each December), kitchen and laundry room. Four temporary exhibitions - social history and the decorative arts - are held annually.
Location: OS Ref. TQ228 896. Greyhound Hill is a turning off the A41 (Watford Way) in Hendon. 1/2 m from M1/J2.
Open: All year. Mon - Thurs, 10am - 1pm & 2 - 5pm; Sat, 10am - 1pm & 2 - 5.30pm; Sun, 2 - 5.30pm. Closed: Christmas Day, Boxing Day and New Year's Day.
Admission: Free. Groups restricted to no more than 30 people.
Photography by permission. Unsuitable. By arrangement. Limited. No coaches. Guide dogs only.

Mark Fiennes/The Royal Collection © 2005, HM Queen Elizabeth II

CLARENCE HOUSE
ST. JAMES'S PALACE, LONDON SW1A 1BA
www.royal.gov.uk
Tel: 020 7766 7303   **Fax:** 020 7930 9625   **e-mail:** information@royalcollection.org.uk
Owner: Official Residence of His Royal Highness, The Prince of Wales
Contact: Ticket Sales & Information Office
Clarence House is the official residence of HRH The Prince of Wales. It was originally built by John Nash in the early 19th century for William IV and was the London home of Her Majesty Queen Elizabeth The Queen Mother. Visitors are given a guided tour of the five rooms on the ground floor.
Location: OS Ref. TQ291 798 Underground: Green Park, St. James's Park. Rail: Victoria.
Open: Please contact the Ticket Sales Information Office on 020 7766 7303.
Admission: Please contact the Ticket Sales Information Office on 020 7766 7303.
No photography inside. Wheelchair users are required to pre-book. Obligatory. Guide dogs only.

COLLEGE OF ARMS
Queen Victoria Street, London EC4V 4BT
Tel: 020 7248 2762   **Fax:** 020 7248 6448   **e-mail:** enquiries@college-of-arms.gov.uk
Owner: Corp. of Kings, Heralds & Pursuivants of Arms
                              Contact: The Officer in Waiting
Mansion built in 1670s to house the English Officers of Arms and their records.
Location: OS Ref. TQ320 810. On N side of Queen Victoria Street, S of St Paul's Cathedral.
Open: Earl Marshal's Court only; open all year (except BHs, State and special occasions) Mon - Fri, 10am - 4pm. Group visits (up to 10) by arrangement only. Record Room: open for tours (groups of up to 20) by special arrangement in advance with the Officer in Waiting.
Admission: Free (groups by negotiation).

EASTBURY MANOR HOUSE ⌗
Eastbury Square, Barking, Essex IG11 9SN
Tel: 020 8724 1002   **Fax:** 020 8724 1003   **e-mail:** eastburyhouse@lbbd.gov.uk
Owner: The National Trust   **Contact:** Sarah Willis
Eastbury Manor is a unique example of a medium sized Elizabethan Manor House with attractive grounds. Leased to the London Borough of Barking and Dagenham and used for a variety of events and arts and heritage activites. In addition Eastbury can be hired for business conferences, Civil wedding ceremonies and education days.
Location: OS TQ457 838. In Eastbury Square off Ripple Road off A13, 10 mins S from Upney Station. Buses 287, 368 or 62.
Open: All Year: Mons & Tues and 1st & 2nd Sat of the month, 10am - 4pm.
Admission: Adult £2.50, Child 65p, Conc. £1.25, Family £5. Groups (15+) by arrangement: £2pp.
In Eastbury Square. In grounds only. Tel for details.

ELTHAM PALACE ⌗   *See page 66 for full page entry.*

Corporate Hospitality see page 35

NT Photographic Library: Nadia MacKenzie

FENTON HOUSE ❧

WINDMILL HILL, HAMPSTEAD, LONDON NW3 6RT

Tel/Fax: 020 7435 3471   **Infoline:** 01494 755563

e-mail: fentonhouse@nationaltrust.org.uk

Owner: The National Trust   **Contact:** The Custodian

A delightful late 17th century merchant's house, set among the winding streets of Old Hampstead. The charming interior contains an outstanding collection of Oriental and European porcelain, needlework and furniture. The Benton Fletcher Collection of beautiful early keyboard instruments is also housed at Fenton and the instruments are sometimes played by music scholars during opening hours. The walled garden has a formal lawn and walks, an orchard and vegetable garden and fine wrought-iron gates. Telephone for details of demonstrations and porcelain tours.

Location: OS Ref. TQ262 860. Visitors' entrance on W side of Hampstead Grove. Hampstead Underground station 300 yds.

Open: 5 - 20 Mar: Sat & Sun, 2 - 5pm. 23 Mar - 30 Oct: Wed - Fri, 2 - 5pm, Sat & Sun, 11am - 5pm. Groups at other times by appointment.

Admission: Adult £4.80, Child £2.40, Family £12. Groups (15+) £4. Joint ticket with 2 Willow Road, £6.40.

ℹ️No picnics in grounds. ♿Ground floor. Braille guide. 🎫Demonstration tours. 🅿️None. ✖ ♿Send SAE for details.

©English Heritage Photo Library/Anne Hyde

Chiswick House.

FORTY HALL

FORTY HILL, ENFIELD, MIDDLESEX EN2 9HA

www.enfield.gov.uk/fortyhall

Tel: 020 8363 8196   **Fax:** 020 8367 9098   **e-mail:** forty.hall@enfield.gov.uk

Contact: London Borough of Enfield   **Contact:** Gavin Williams

This beautiful Grade I listed Jacobean House built in 1629 for Sir Nicholas Rainton, Lord Mayor of London, is a location for festivals, events and guided tours throughout the year. The 273-acre estate includes formal gardens, wildflower meadows and the site of Elsyng Palace, owned by Henry VIII and Elizabeth I.

Location: OS Ref. TQ336 985. 1m from M25/J25, just off A10. Tourist Board sign posted.

Open: All Year: Wed - Sun, 11am - 4pm.

Admission: Free.

🔲 ♿Partial. WCs. 🎫 🎫By arrangement. 🅿️Ample for cars. Limited for coaches. 🔲 🐕In grounds, on leads. ✳

THE FOUNDLING MUSEUM

40 Brunswick Square, London WC1N 1AZ
Tel: 020 7841 3600 **Fax:** 020 7841 3601
Owner: The Foundling Museum
Site of London's first home for abandoned children. Established in 1739. The museum charts the history of the Foundling Hospital and its residents until its closure in 1953.
Location: OS Ref. TQ303 822. Underground: Russell Square.
Open: Tues - Sat, 10am - 6pm; Sun, 12 noon - 6pm.
Admission: Adult £5, Child up to 16yrs Free, Conc. £3. Special rates apply for groups and schools.

FULHAM PALACE & MUSEUM

Bishop's Avenue, Fulham, London SW6 6EA
Tel: 020 7736 5821 **Fax:** 020 7736 3233
Owner: London Borough of Hammersmith & Fulham & Fulham Palace Trust
Former home of the Bishops of London (Tudor with Georgian additions and Victorian Chapel). The gardens, famous in the 17th century, now contain specimen trees and a knot garden of herbs.
Location: OS Ref. TQ240 761.
Open: Closed for restoration works from 31 March 2005. Please tel for further details.
Admission: Gardens: Free.

Peter Aprahamian

FREUD MUSEUM

20 MARESFIELD GARDENS, LONDON NW3 5SX

www.freud.org.uk

Tel: 020 7435 2002 **Fax:** 020 7431 5452 **e-mail:** info@freud.org.uk
Contact: The Director
The Freud Museum was the home of Sigmund Freud after he escaped the Nazi annexation of Austria. The house retains its domestic atmosphere and has the character of turn of the century Vienna. The centrepiece is Freud's study which has been preserved intact, containing his remarkable collection of antiquities: Egyptian, Greek, Roman, Oriental and his large library. The Freuds brought all their furniture and household effects to London; fine Biedermeier and 19th century Austrian painted furniture. The most famous item is Freud's psychoanalytic couch, where his patients reclined. Fine Oriental rugs cover the floor and tables. Videos are shown of the Freud family in Vienna, Paris and London.
Location: OS Ref. TQ265 850. Between Swiss Cottage and Hampstead. Nearest Underground: Finchley Road on the Jubilee and Metropolitan lines.
Open: Wed - Sun (inc) 12 noon - 5pm.
Admission: Adult £5, Child under 12 Free, Conc. £2. Coach groups by appointment.
▣ ♿ Ground floor. 🅿 Limited. 🐕 Guide dogs only. ✺

THE GEFFRYE MUSEUM

KINGSLAND ROAD, LONDON E2 8EA

www.geffrye-museum.org.uk

Tel: 020 7739 9893 **Fax:** 020 7729 5647 **e-mail:** info@geffrye-museum.org.uk
Owner: Independent Charitable Trust
The Geffrye presents the changing style of the English domestic interior from 1600 to the present day through a series of period rooms. The displays lead the visitor on a walk through time, from the 17th century with oak furniture and panelling, past the refined splendour of the Georgian period and the high style of the Victorians, to 20th century modernity. The museum's displays are complemented by a walled herb garden and a series of period gardens.
Location: OS Ref. TQ335 833. 1m N of Liverpool St. Buses: 242, 149, 243, 67 & 394. Underground: Liverpool St. or Old St.
Open: Museum: Tue - Sat, 10am - 5pm. Sun & BH Mon, 12 noon - 5pm. Closed Mon (except BHs) Good Fri, Christmas Eve, Christmas Day, Boxing Day & New Year's Day. Gardens: Apr - Oct.
Admission: Free.
▣ ⊤ ♿ ▣ ⊓ ▣ ▣ ✺ ⊟ Tel for details

GUNNERSBURY PARK & MUSEUM

Gunnersbury Park, London W3 8LQ
Tel: 020 8992 1612 **Fax:** 020 8752 0686 **e-mail:** gp-museum@cip.org.uk
Owner: Hounslow and Ealing Councils   **Contact:** Lynn Acum
Built in 1802 and refurbished by Sydney Smirke for the Rothschild family.
Location: OS Ref. TQ190 792. Acton Town Underground station. 1/4 m N of the junction of A4, M4 North Circular.
Open: Apr - Oct: daily: 1 - 5pm. Nov - Mar: daily: 1 - 4pm. Victorian kitchens summer weekends only. Closed Christmas Day & Boxing Day. Park: open dawn - dusk.
Admission: Free. Donations welcome.

LOCAL FOOD

Greenwich Whitebait

Whitebait are tiny fish, normally floured and fried whole and served in a mound on a plain white plate with slices of thin buttered brown bread and a wedge of lemon. In the 17th century the best whitebait in the world were caught at Greenwhich in July and August, and special whitebait dinners were given in local inns. Londoners would come out from the city to spend whole days walking along the riverbank, watching the ships and eating whitebait.

🎭 Special Events Index see page 24

HAM HOUSE ✤

HAM, RICHMOND, SURREY TW10 7RS

www.nationaltrust.org.uk/hamhouse

Tel: 020 8940 1950   **Fax:** 020 8332 6903   **e-mail:** hamhouse@nationaltrust.org.uk

Owner: The National Trust   **Contact:** The Property Manager

Ham House, set on the banks of the Thames near Richmond, is perhaps the most remarkable Stuart house in the country. Formerly the home of the influential Duke and Duchess of Lauderdale, Ham was a centre for Court intrigue throughout the 17th century. In its time, the house was at the forefront of fashion and retains much of its interior decoration from that period. The sumptuous textiles, furniture and paintings collected by the couple are shown in 26 rooms. The gardens are a remarkable survival of English formal gardening and are being gradually restored to their former glory. Statues of *Venus Marina* and *Mercury* have recently returned to the garden. The 18th century dairy, decorated with cast iron cows' legs supporting marble work surfaces

and hand-painted Wedgwood tiles, is now on view as is the 17th century still house, used for distilling alcohol and perfumes.

Location: OS Ref. TQ172 732. 1$^1/_2$ m from Richmond and 2m from Kingston. On the S bank of the River Thames, W of A307 at Petersham.

Open: House: 19 Mar - 30 Oct: Sat - Wed, 1 - 5pm. Gardens: All year, Sat - Wed, 11am - 6pm. Closed 25/26 Dec & 1 Jan. Special Christmas shop. Christmas lunches Dec. Some evening opening for Christmas for Gardens/shop/café.

Admission: House & Garden: Adult £7.50, Child £3.75, Family £18.75. Garden only: Adult £3.50, Child £1.75, Family £8.75. Booked groups (15+): Adult £6.

▢ ▢ ▢ ▢ Partial. WC. ▢ ▢ ▢ ▢ ▢ Guide dogs. ▢ ▢ Tel for details.

HANDEL HOUSE MUSEUM

25 BROOK STREET, LONDON W1K 4HB

www.handelhouse.org

Tel: 020 7495 1685   **Fax:** 020 7495 1759   **e-mail:** mail@handelhouse.org

Owner: The Handel House Trust Ltd   **Contact:** Letty Porter

Handel House Museum is located at 25 Brook Street, where the great baroque composer, George Frideric Handel lived for 36 years, and where he wrote such timeless masterpieces as *Zadok the Priest, Messiah* and *Music for the Royal Fireworks*. The elegantly refurbished interiors create the perfect setting for 18th century furniture and fine art, evoking the spirit of Georgian London. This landmark address is also brought to life by an inspiring programme of live music, events and activities for adults and families. The Thursday evening concerts every week are particularly popular, and you are recommended to book well in advance.

Location: OS Ref. TQ286 809. Central London, between New Bond St and Grosvener Square. Bond Street Tube.

Open: Tue - Sat, 10am - 6pm (Thur until 8pm). Suns, 12 noon - 6pm. Closed Mons. Groups by arrangement.

Admission: Adult £5, Child £2, Conc. £4.

ℹ️No inside photography. ▢ ▢ ▢ By arrangement. ▢ ▢ ✳

Tower of London – Jewel House circa 1820.

HOGARTH'S HOUSE
Hogarth Lane, Great West Road, Chiswick, London W4 2QN
Tel: 020 8994 6757

Owner: Hogarth House Foundation   **Contact:** Jerome Farrell
This late 17th century house was the country home of William Hogarth, the famous painter, engraver, satirist and social reformer between 1749 and his death in 1764.
Location: OS Ref. TQ213 778. 100 yds W of Hogarth roundabout on the Great West Road - junction of Burlington Lane. Car park in named spaces in Hogarth Business Centre behind house and Chiswick House grounds.
Open: Tue - Fri, 1 - 5pm (Nov - Mar: 1 - 4pm). Sat, Sun & BH Mons, 1 - 6pm (Nov - Mar: 1 - 5pm). Closed Mon (except BHs), Good Fri, Christmas Day, Boxing Day & Jan.
Admission: Free.

JEWEL TOWER ⌗
Abingdon Street, Westminster, London SW1P 3JY
Tel: 020 7222 2219   **www.**english-heritage.org.uk/visits

Owner: English Heritage   **Contact:** Visitor Operations Team
Built c1365 to house the personal treasure of Edward III. One of two surviving parts of the original Palace of Westminster. Now houses an exhibition on 'Parliament Past and Present'.
Location: OS Ref. TQ302 794. Opposite S end of Houses of Parliament (Victoria Tower).
Open: 2 Jan - 23 Mar: daily, 10am - 4pm. 24 Mar - 31 Oct: daily, 10am - 5pm. 1 Nov - 31 Mar: daily, 10am - 4pm. Closed 24 - 26 Dec & 1 Jan.
Admission: Adult £2.60, Child £1.30, Conc. £2.
⌖ ⊠ ✸ ▣ Tel for details.

DR JOHNSON'S HOUSE
17 Gough Square, London EC4A 3DE
Tel: 020 7353 3745   **e-mail:** curator@drjohnsonshouse.org

Owner: The Trustees
Fine 18th century house, once home to Dr Samuel Johnson, the celebrated literary figure, famous for his English dictionary.
Location: OS Ref. TQ314 813. N of Fleet Street.
Open: Oct - Apr: Mon - Sat, 11am - 5pm. May - Sept: Mon - Sat, 11am - 5.30pm. Closed BHs.
Admission: Adult £4.50, Child £1.50 (under 10yrs Free), Conc. £3.50. Family £10. Groups: £3.50.

KEATS HOUSE
Keats Grove, Hampstead, London NW3 2RR
Tel: 020 7435 2062   **Fax:** 020 7431 9293
e-mail: keatshouse@corpoflondon.gov.uk
www.keatshouse.org.uk   **www.**cityoflondon.gov.uk/keats

Owner: Corporation of London   **Contact:** The Manager
Regency home of the poet John Keats (1795 - 1821).
Location: OS Ref. TQ272 856. Hampstead, NW3. Nearest Underground: Belsize Park & Hampstead.
Open: Apr - end Nov: Tue - Sun & BHs, 12 noon - 5pm. Visits by appointment: Tue - Sun, 10am - 12 noon. Nov - end Mar: Tue - Fri, 1 - 5pm, Sats/Suns & BHs, 12 noon - 5pm.
Admission: Adult £3, Under 16s Free, Conc. £1.50 (may change Apr 2005).
⌖ ⌨ Ground floor & garden. **P** None. ▣ ⊠ Guide dogs only. ✸

KENSINGTON PALACE STATE APARTMENTS
See page 67 for full page entry.

KENWOOD HOUSE ⌗
See page 68 for full page entry.

LSO ST LUKE'S
THE UBS AND LSO MUSIC EDUCATION CENTRE
161 Old Street, London EC1V 9NG
Tel: 020 7490 3939   **Minicom:** 020 7490 8299   **Fax:** 020 7566 2881
e-mail: alaw@lso.co.uk
www.lso.co.uk/lsostlukes   **Contact:** Alison Law, Events Manager
Formerly St Luke's Church, a Grade I listed Hawksmoor church built in 1733. LSO St Luke's is the new home for the London Symphony Orchestra's music education and community programme, LSO Discovery. The church was derelict for 40 years, but has been rebuilt and opened in early 2003 with state-of-the-art facilities.
Location: OS Ref. TQ325 824. On corner of Old Street and Helmet Row, 5mins walk from Old Street Station (Northern Line, National Rail).
Open: By appointment only. Contact the Events Manager.
Admission: Free.
⌖ ⓘ By arrangement. **P** No cars, limited for coaches. ▣ ⊠ Guide dogs only.

©HRP 2002

Tower of London – Traitors' Gate.

LEIGHTON HOUSE MUSEUM

12 HOLLAND PARK ROAD, KENSINGTON, LONDON W14 8LZ

www.rbkc.gov.uk/leightonhousemuseum

Tel: 020 7602 3316 **Fax:** 020 7371 2467
e-mail: museums@rbkc.gov.uk

Owner: Royal Borough of Kensington & Chelsea
Contact: Curator

Leighton House was the home of Frederic, Lord Leighton 1830 - 1896, painter and President of the Royal Academy, built between 1864 - 1879. It was a palace of art designed for entertaining and to provide a magnificent working space in the studio, with great north windows and a gilded apse. The Arab Hall is the centrepiece of the house, containing Leighton's collection of Persian tiles, a gilt mosaic frieze and a fountain. Victorian paintings by Leighton, Millais and Burne-Jones are on display.

Location: OS Ref. TQ247 793. Nearest underground: High Street Kensington (exit staircase turn left, take first right for Melbury Road after Commonwealth Institute. Leighton House is located in Holland Park Road, the first left. Bus: 9, 10, 27, 28, 33, 49, 328 (to Commonwealth Institute).

Open: Daily, except Tues, 11am - 5.30pm. Also open Spring/Summer BHs. Guided tours on Wed & Thur, 2.30pm. Closed 25/26 Dec.

Admission: Adult £3, Conc £1. Family £6. Guided tours free on Weds & Thurs. Joint group guided tour with Linley Sambourne House £10pp.

🚫 ℹ️No photography. 🅃 ♿Unsuitable.
𝑓Wed & Thurs at 2.30pm. 🅾 🅿None. ✖ ❄
📺 Tel for details.

THE LAW SOCIETY'S HALL

113 Chancery Lane, London WC2A 1PL

Tel: 020 7320 9555 **Fax:** 020 7320 5955 **e-mail:** m&e@lawsociety.org.uk
www.uniquevenue.lawsociety.org.uk

Owner: The Law Society   **Contact:** Heidi Carlsen

This historic London venue, designed by Vulliamy in the Neo-Classical style, opened in 1832. 18 stunning air-conditioned function suites are available to accommodate meetings, conferences, or banquets. The Common Room, with its green marble pilasters and mahogany panelling, lends itself perfectly to wedding receptions.

Location: OS Ref. TQ311 812. Underground: Blackfriars, Temple, Chancery Lane. Rail: Blackfriars, Charing Cross, Waterloo.

Open: All year: daily, 9am - 11pm for pre-booked functions only.

Admission: Please contact for details.

ℹ️Not open to general public except for functions. 🅃 ♿ ☕Licensed. 🍴Licensed.
🅿Limited. None for coaches. 🐕Guide dogs only. 🅰

LINDSEY HOUSE 🌿

100 Cheyne Walk, London SW10 0DQ

Tel: 020 7447 6605 **Fax:** 01494 463310

Owner: The National Trust   **Contact:** Area Manager

Part of Lindsey House was built in 1674 on the site of Sir Thomas More's garden, overlooking the River Thames. It has one of the finest 17th century exteriors in London. Ground floor entrance hall, main staircase and gardens only open to the public.

Location: OS Ref. TQ268 775. On Cheyne Walk, W of Battersea Bridge near junction with Milman's Street on Chelsea Embankment.

Open: 11 May, 15 Jun, 14 Sept & 12 Oct: 2 - 4pm.

Admission: Free.

©HRP 2002

Tower of London guide in 16th/17th century costume.

LINLEY SAMBOURNE HOUSE

18 STAFFORD TERRACE, LONDON W8 7BH

www.rbkc.gov.uk/linleysambournehouse

Info: 020 7602 3316 (ext 305 Mon - Fri) **or** 07976 060160 (Sats & Suns)
Fax: 020 7371 2467 **e-mail:** museums@rbkc.gov.uk
Owner: The Royal Borough of Kensington & Chelsea   **Contact:** Curatorial staff
Linley Sambourne House is the former home of the Punch cartoonist Edward Linley Sambourne and his family. Almost unchanged over the course of the last century, the house provides a unique insight into the life of an artistic middle-class family. The majority of the original decoration and furnishings remain in situ exactly as left by the Sambournes. All visits are by guided tour with special dramatic tours available and an introductory video. Larger groups can visit jointly with Leighton House Museum just 10 minutes walk away.

Location: OS Ref. TQ252 794. Parallel to Kensington High St, between Phillimore Gardens & Argyll Rd. Bus: 9, 10, 27, 28, 31, 49, 52, 70 & C1. Underground: Kensington High St. Parking on Sun in nearby streets.
Open: 5 Mar - 11 Dec: Sats & Suns; tours leaving at 10am, 11.15am, 1pm, 2.15pm and 3.30pm. Pre-booking is advised. At other times for booked groups (10+), by appointment. Larger groups (12+) will be divided for tours of the House. Access for Group tours: Mon - Fri.
Admission: Adult £6, Child (under 18yrs) £1, Conc £4. Groups (12+): Min £60.00. Joint group (10+) guided tour with Leighton House Museum £10pp.
⬛ ℹ️No photography. Obligatory. ⓟNone. ⬛ Guide dogs only. ✳️

English Heritage Photo Library

MARBLE HILL HOUSE ⌗

RICHMOND ROAD, TWICKENHAM TW1 2NL

www.english-heritage.org.uk/visits

Tel: 020 8892 5115
Owner: English Heritage   **Contact:** Visitor Operations Team
This beautiful villa beside the Thames was built in 1724 - 29 for Henrietta Howard, mistress of George II. Here she entertained many of the poets and wits of the Augustan age including Alexander Pope and later Horace Walpole. The perfect proportions of the villa were inspired by the work of the 16th century Italian architect, Palladio. Today this beautifully presented house contains an important collection of paintings and furniture, including some pieces commissioned for the villa when it was built. Summer concerts.
Location: OS Ref. TQ174 736. A305, 600yds E of Orleans House.
Open: 24 Mar - 31 Oct: Sat, 10am - 2pm, Sun & BHs, 10am - 5pm. 1 Nov - 31 Mar: Pre-booked group tours only.
Admission: Adult £4, Child £2, Conc. £3.
⬛ Ⓣ ♿Ground floor. WC. ⬛Summer only. ⬛ ⓟ ⬛ Tel for details.

MORDEN HALL PARK 🍃

Morden Hall Road, Morden SM4 5JD

Tel: 020 8545 6850   **Fax:** 020 8687 0094
e-mail: mordenhallpark@nationaltrust.org.uk
Owner: The National Trust   **Contact:** The Property Manager
Former deer park has an extensive network of waterways, ancient hay meadows and wetlands. Workshops now house local craftworkers.
Location: OS Ref. TQ261 684. Off A24 and A297 S of Wimbledon, N of Sutton.
Open: All year: daily. NT shop & tea shop: 10am - 5pm (closed: 25/26 Dec & 1 Jan). Car park closes 6pm.
Admission: Free.

WILLIAM MORRIS GALLERY

Lloyd Park, Forest Road, Walthamstow, London E17 4PP

Tel: 020 8527 3782   **Fax:** 020 8527 7070
Owner: London Borough of Waltham Forest   **Contact:** The Keeper
Location: OS Ref. SQ372 899. 15 mins walk from Walthamstow tube (Victoria line). 5 - 10 mins from M11/A406.
Open: Tue - Sat and first Sun each month, 10am - 1pm and 2 - 5pm.
Admission: Free for all visitors but a charge is made for guided tours which must be booked in advance.

🌱 **Plant Sales Index** see page 39

London - England

MYDDELTON HOUSE GARDENS
Bulls Cross, Enfield, Middlesex EN2 9HG
Tel: 01992 702200   **Owner:** Lee Valley Regional Park Authority
Created by the famous plantsman E A Bowles.
Location: OS Ref. TQ342 992. ¼ m W of A10 via Turkey St. ¾ m S M25/J25.
Open: Apr - Sept: Mon - Fri, 10am - 4.30pm, Suns & BH Mons, 12 noon - 4pm. Oct - Mar: Mon - Fri, 10am - 3pm.
Admission: Adult £2.30, Conc. £1.70. Prices may change from April 2005.

THE OCTAGON, ORLEANS HOUSE GALLERY
Riverside, Twickenham, Middlesex TW1 3DJ
Tel: 020 8831 6000   **Fax:** 020 8744 0501   **e-mail:** galleryinfo@richmond.gov.uk
Owner: London Borough of Richmond-upon-Thames   **Contact:** The Curator
Outstanding example of baroque architecture by James Gibbs c1720. Art gallery.
Location: OS Ref. TQ168 734. On N side of Riverside, 700yds E of Twickenham town centre, 400yds S of Richmond Road. Vehicle access via Orleans Rd only.
Open: Tue - Sat, 1 - 5.30pm, Sun & BHs, 2 - 5.30pm (Oct - Mar closes 4.30pm). Closed Mons. Garden: open daily, 9am - sunset.
Admission: Free.

© National Trust Photographic Library

OSTERLEY PARK ✣
JERSEY ROAD, ISLEWORTH, MIDDLESEX TW7 4RB

Tel: 020 8232 5050   **Fax:** 020 8232 5080   **Infoline:** 01494 755566
e-mail: osterley@nationaltrust.org.uk   **www**.nationaltrust.org.uk/osterley/
Owner: The National Trust   **Contact:** Visitor Services Manager
Osterley's four turrets look out across one of the last great landscaped parks in suburban London, its trees and lakes an unexpected haven of green. Originally built in 1575, the mansion was transformed in the 18th century into an elegant villa by architect Robert Adam. The classical interior, designed for entertaining on a grand scale, still impresses with its specially made tapestries, furniture and plasterwork. The magnificent 16th century stables survive largely intact.

Location: OS Ref. TQ146 780. Access via Thornbury Road on N side of A4.
Open: House: 5 - 20 Mar: Sat & Sun; 23 Mar - 30 Oct: Wed - Sun, 1 - 4.30pm. Park & Pleasure Grounds: All year: daily, 9am - 7.30pm. Open BH Mons & Good Fri. Park & Pleasure Grounds close dusk if earlier than 7.30pm. Park closes early before major events. Car park closed: 25 & 26 Dec.
Admission: Adult £4.90, Child £2.40, Family £12.20, Groups (15+) £4. Park & Pleasure Grounds: Free. Car Park: £3.50.

▢ ⊤ ⬓ Tel for details. ⬛ ▯ ▥ ⬚ On leads in park. ▲ ✱ ⬓ Tel for details.

PALACE OF WESTMINSTER
London SW1A 0AA
Tel: 020 7219 3000   **First Call:** 0870 906 3773   **Info:** 020 7219 4272
Fax: 020 7219 5839   **Contact:** Information Office
The first Palace of Westminster was erected on this site by Edward the Confessor in 1042 and the building was a royal residence until a devastating fire in 1512. After this, the palace became the two-chamber Parliament for government - the House of Lords and the elected House of Commons. Following a further fire in 1834, the palace was rebuilt by Sir Charles Barry and decorated by A W Pugin.
Location: OS Ref. TQ303 795. Central London, W bank of River Thames. 1km S of Trafalgar Square. Underground: Westminster.
Open: Aug - Oct (exact dates TBA, please ring for details). At other times by appointment. Ring Infoline.
Admission: Adult £7, Child/Conc. £5. 3 Big Ben: Free. (2003 prices.)

PITZHANGER MANOR-HOUSE
Walpole Park, Mattock Lane, Ealing W5 5EQ
Tel: 020 8567 1227 **Fax:** 020 8567 0595
e-mail: pmgallery&house@ealing.gov.uk **www**.ealing.gov.uk/pmgallery&house
Owner: London Borough of Ealing **Contact:** Gill Bohee

Pitzhanger Manor House is a restored Georgian villa, once owned and designed by the architect Sir John Soane (1753 - 1837). Rooms in the house continue to be restored using Soane's highly individual ideas in design and decoration. Exhibitions of contemporary art are programmed year-round and sited in both the adjacent Gallery and the House.

Location: OS Ref. TQ176 805. Ealing, London.

Open: All year: Tue - Fri, 1 - 5pm. Sat, 11am - 5pm. Summer Sunday Openings, please ring for details. Closed Christmas, Easter, New Year and BHs.

Admission: Free.

By arrangement. Limited. In grounds, on leads.

RED HOUSE
Red House Lane, Bexleyheath DA6 8JF
Tel: 01494 755588 (Booking line: Mon - Fri, 9.30am - 4pm)
Owner: The National Trust

Commissioned by William Morris in 1859 and designed by Philip Webb, Red House is of enormous international significance in the history of domestic architecture and garden design. The garden was designed to "clothe" the house with a series of sub-divided areas that still clearly exist today. Inside, the house retains many of the original features and fixed items of furniture designed by Morris and Webb, as well as wall paintings and stained glass by Burne-Jones.

Location: OS Ref. TQ48 1750. Off A221 Bexleyheath. Visitors will be advised on how to reach the property when booking. Nearest rail station Bexleyheath, 15 mins' walk.

Open: Mar - Sep: Wed - Sun, 11am - 5pm; Oct - Dec: Wed - Sun, 11am - 4.15pm. Closed Christmas Day, Boxing Day, 1 Jan - 14 Feb. Open Easter Sun, Good Fri, BH Mons. Admission by pre-booked guided tour only.

Admission: Adult £6, Child £3, Family £15.

No WC. Ground floor only. Limited.
No Parking on site. Parking at Danson Park (15 min walk). 90p parking charge at weekends and BHs. Disabled drivers can pre-book (limited parking).

©HRP 2002

Kensington Palace – The Orangery.

ROYAL OBSERVATORY NATIONAL MARITIME MUSEUM & QUEEN'S HOUSE

See page 69 for full page entry.

ST GEORGE'S CATHEDRAL, SOUTHWARK
Westminster Bridge Road, London SE1 7HY
Tel: 020 7928 5256 **Fax:** 020 7202 2189
e-mail: info@southwark-rc-cathedral.org.uk **Contact:** Canon James Cronin

Neo-Gothic rebuilt Pugin Cathedral bombed during the last war and rebuilt by Romily Craze in 1958.

Location: OS Ref. TQ315 794. Near Imperial War Museum. 1/2 m SE of Waterloo Stn.

Open: 8am - 6pm, every day, except BHs.

Admission: Free.

ST JOHN'S GATE
MUSEUM OF THE ORDER OF ST JOHN
ST JOHN'S GATE, LONDON EC1M 4DA
www.sja.org.uk/museum

Tel: 020 7324 4070 **Fax:** 020 7336 0587 **e-mail:** museum@nhq.sja.org.uk
Owner: The Order of St John **Contact:** Pamela Willis

Early 16 century Gatehouse (1504 - 2004), Priory Church and Norman Crypt. The remarkable history of the Knights Hospitaller, dedicated to caring for the sick and dating back to the 11th century, is revealed in collections including furniture, paintings, armour, stained glass and other items. Notable associations with Shakespeare, Hogarth, Edward Cave, Dr Johnson, Dickens, David Garrick and many others. In Victorian times, St John Ambulance was founded here and a modern interactive gallery tells its story.

Location: OS Ref. TQ317 821. St. John's Lane, Clerkenwell. Nearest Underground: Farringdon.

Open: Mon - Fri: 10am - 5pm. Sat: 10am - 4pm. Closed BHs & Sat of BH weekend. Tours: Tue, Fri & Sat at 11am & 2.30pm. Reference Library: Open by appointment.

Admission: Museum Free. Tours of the building: £5, OAP £3.50 (donation).

Ground floor. WC. Guide dogs only.

Reg. Charity No. 1077265

ST PAUL'S CATHEDRAL

See page 70 for full page entry.

SIR JOHN SOANE'S MUSEUM
13 Lincoln's Inn Fields, London WC2A 3BP
Tel: 020 7405 2107 **Fax:** 020 7831 3957 **www**.soane.org
Owner: Trustees of Sir John Soane's Museum **Contact:** Julie Brock

The celebrated architect Sir John Soane built this in 1812 as his own house. It now contains his collection of antiquities, sculpture and paintings.

Location: OS Ref. TQ308 816. E of Kingsway, S of High Holborn.

Open: Tue - Sat, 10am - 5pm. 6 - 9pm, first Tue of the month. Closed BHs & 24 Dec.

Admission: Free. Groups must book.

SOUTHWARK CATHEDRAL

London Bridge, London SE1 9DA

Tel: 020 7367 6700 **Fax:** 020 7367 6730 **Visitors' Officer:** 020 7367 6734
e-mail: cathedral@dswark.org.uk **www**.southwark.anglican.org/cathedral
Owner: Church of England **Contact:** Visitors' Officer
London's oldest gothic building and a place of worship for over 1,000 years, Southwark Cathedral has connections with Chaucer, Shakespeare, Dickens and John Harvard. Included in the new riverside Millennium buildings are: the Cathedral Shop, Refectory, and Archaeological Chamber.
Location: OS Ref. TQ327 803. South side of London Bridge, near Shakespeare's Globe and Tate Modern.
Open: Daily: 8.30am - 6pm. Weekday services: 8am, 12.30pm and 5.30pm. Sat services, 9am and 4pm. Sun services: 9am, 11am, 3pm & 6.30pm. Cathedral Shop: daily, 10am - 6pm, Sun, 11am - 5pm.
Admission: Recommended donation of £4 per person. Booked groups (min 10): Adult £4, Child £2, Conc. £3.50. Trade discounts available.
ⓘIndoor photography & video recording with permit. 🖾 🆃 🖿 Partial. WCs. 🖿
🖾 Licensed. 🖾 By arrangement. 🖾 🅿None. 🖿 🖾 Guide dogs only. 🖾
🖾 Tel for details.

SPENCER HOUSE

See page 71 for full page entry.

STRAWBERRY HILL

ST MARY'S, STRAWBERRY HILL, WALDEGRAVE ROAD, TWICKENHAM TW1 4SX

Tel: 020 8240 4224 /Appointments: 020 8240 4044
Contact: The Conference Office
Horace Walpole converted a modest house at Strawberry Hill into his own version of a gothic fantasy. It is widely regarded as the first substantial building of the Gothic Revival and as such is internationally known and admired. A century later Lady Frances Waldegrave added a magnificent wing to Walpole's original structure. Lady Waldegrave's suite of rooms can be hired for weddings, corporate functions and conferences. Please telephone for details.
Location: OS Ref. TQ158 722. Off A310 between Twickenham & Teddington.
Open: 1 May - 25 Sept: Suns, 2 - 3.30pm. Tours commence between 2pm & 3.30pm, please tel: 020 8240 4224 for confirmation, or to make an appointment 020 8240 4044.
Admission: Adult £5.50, OAP £4.75. Group bookings: £4.75.
ⓘConferences. 🖾 🖿 🖾 🖾

SOUTHSIDE HOUSE 🏠

3 WOODHAYES ROAD, WIMBLEDON, LONDON SW19 4RJ

www.southsidehouse.com

Tel: 020 8946 7643 **e-mail:** info@southsidehouse.com
Owner: The Pennington-Mellor-Munthe Charity Trust **Contact:** The Administrator
Described by connoisseurs as an unforgettable experience, Southside House provides an enchantingly eccentric backdrop to the lives and loves of generations of the Pennington Mellor Munthe families. Maintained in traditional style, without major refurbishment, and crowded with the family possessions of centuries, Southside offers a wealth of fascinating family stories.

Behind the long façade are the old rooms, still with much of the original furniture and a superb collection of art and historical objects. John Pennington's great granddaughter, Hilda, married Axel Munthe, the charismatic Swedish doctor and philanthropist. The preservation of the house was left to their youngest son who led a life of extraordinary adventure during the Second World War. Malcolm Munthe's surviving children continue to care for the property.

The gardens are as fascinating as the house, with a series of sculptural "rooms" linked by water and intriguing pathways.

Location: OS Ref. TQ234 706. On S side of Wimbledon Common (B281), opposite Crooked Billet Inn.
Open: Easter Saturday - 3 Oct: Weds, Sats, Suns & BH Mons. Guided tours on the hour 2, 3 & 4pm. Other times throughout the year by arrangement with the Administrator.
Admission: Adult £5, Child £2.50 (must be accompanied by an adult), OAP £4, Family £10.
🖿 Unsuitable. 🖾 Obligatory. 🅿 Limited. 🖿 🖾

LOCAL FOOD

Latkes

Wonderful Jewish potato cakes made with grated potato, flavoured with chopped onions, sold in the East End and from Jewish delicatessens.

SUTTON HOUSE ✤

2 & 4 HOMERTON HIGH STREET, HACKNEY, LONDON E9 6JQ

Tel: 020 8986 2264   **e-mail:** suttonhouse@nationaltrust.org.uk

Owner: The National Trust   **Contact:** The Property Manager

A rare example of a Tudor red-brick house, built in 1535 by Sir Rafe Sadleir, Principal Secretary of State for Henry VIII, with 18th century alterations and later additions. Restoration revealed many 16th century details, even in rooms of later periods. Notable features include original linenfold panelling and 17th century wall paintings.

Location: OS Ref. TQ352 851. At the corner of Isabella Road and Homerton High St.

Open: Historic rooms: 21 Jan - 18 Dec: Fri & Sat, 1 - 5pm, Sun, 11.30am - 5pm. Café, Shop & Art Gallery: 19 Jan - 18 Dec: Wed - Sun, 11.30am - 5pm. Open BH Mons 11.30am - 5pm. Closed Good Fri.

Admission: Adult £2.50, Child 50p, Family £5.50. Group visits by prior arrangement.

🗔 ♿ Ground floor only. WC. ☕ 🎨 🅿 None. ■ ▲ ❋ ☗ Tel for details.

WELLINGTON ARCH ⌗

HYDE PARK CORNER, LONDON W1J 7JZ

www.english-heritage.org.uk/visits

Tel: 020 7930 2726   **Venue Hire and Hospitality:** 020 973 3292

Owner: English Heritage   **Contact:** Visitor Operations Team

Newly restored and opened to the public for the first time in April 2001, Wellington Arch has had a chequered history. Originally designed in 1825 by Decimus Burton as a grand entrance to Buckingham Palace and gateway to Green Park, its lavish ornamentation was never finished. An equestrian statue of the Duke of Wellington, hoisted upon the Arch in 1846, was judged to be far too large, and caused public outcry. Plans to remove it were halted when the Duke himself announced that he would take such an action as a personal insult. The statue remained the scorn of London and beyond until 1882 when growing traffic congestion around Hyde Park Corner led to Wellington Arch being dismantled and moved to its current position. The equestrian statue was removed and the arch remained bare until 1912 when the magnificent 'Quadriga' that you see today took its place.

Location: OS Ref. TQ285 798. Hyde Park Corner Tube Station.

Open: 2 Jan - 23 Mar: Wed - Sun, 10am - 4pm. 24 Mar - 31 Oct: Wed - Sun & BHs, 10am - 5pm. 1 Nov - 31 Mar: Wed - Sun, 10am - 4pm. Closed 24 - 26 Dec & 1 Jan.

Admission: Adult £3, Child £1.50, Conc. £2.30. Groups (11+) 15% discount.

🗔 ⊤ ♿ 🎨 Mondays for groups only. ❋ ☗ Tel for details.

SYON PARK 🏛   *See page 72 for full page entry.*

THE TOWER BRIDGE EXHIBITION

Tower Bridge, London SE1 2UP

Tel: 020 7940 3985   **Fax:** 020 7357 7935

Owner: Corporation of London   **Contact:** Emma Parlow

One of London's most unusual and exciting exhibitions is situated inside Tower Bridge. Enjoy spectacular views from the high level walkways.

Location: OS Ref. TQ337 804. Adjacent to Tower of London, nearest Underground: Tower Hill.

Open: 1 Apr - 30 Sep: 10am - 5.30pm (last ticket). 1 Oct - 31 Mar: 9.30am - 5pm (last ticket). Closed 25 Dec.

Admission: Adult £5.50, Child £3, Conc. £4.25. (Prices subject to change from April 2005.)

THE TOWER OF LONDON   *See page 73 for full page entry.*

EMERY WALKER'S HOUSE

7 Hammersmith Terrace, London W6 9TS

Tel: 020 8741 4104 or 07779 145372   **e-mail:** info@emerywalker.org.uk
www.emerywalker.org.uk

Owner: The Emery Walker Trust   **Contact:** Monica Grose-Hodge - Assistant Curator

Emery Walker, friend and advisor to William Morris, lived in this riverside house for 30 years and it preserves the only authentic Arts and Crafts urban interior in Britain, with furniture, wallpapers, textiles and ceramics by Morris & Co, Philip Webb, William de Morgan, etc. Small, pretty garden. It has never been open to the public before and may not be again as its future is uncertain.

Location: OS Ref. TQ221 782. Between Chiswick Mall and South Black Lion Lane in Hammersmith, parallel with King Street (Buses 27, 190, 267, 391, H91). Underground: Stamford Brook or Ravenscourt Park (District Line, both 7 mins walk) or Hammersmith (Piccadilly Line, 15 mins walk). Very limited metered on-street parking.

Open: Apr - Jul: Thur & Fri, 10am - 4pm. Strictly by pre-booked, timed ticket with guide – max group size of eight.

Admission: Adult £6, Conc. £3.50. No children under 12yrs.

ℹ No photography inside house. No WC. Refreshments available locally. ♿ Limited access to ground floor, no access to garden. 🎨 Obligatory. 🛏

THE 'WERNHER COLLECTION' AT RANGER'S HOUSE ⌗

Chesterfield Walk, Blackheath, London SE10 8QX

Tel: 020 8853 0035   **www.**english-heritage.org.uk/visits

Owner: English Heritage   **Contact:** House Manager

This attractive red-brick villa built c1700 on the edge of Greenwich Park houses the 'Wernher Collection': the life-time collection of self-made millionaire, Julius Wernher. A superb display of fine and decorative arts with objects dating from 3BC to the 19th-century, and including a stunning array of Renaissance jewellery as well as paintings, sculpture, furniture, tapestries, enamels and ivories.

Location: OS Ref. TQ388 768. N of Shooters Hill Road.

Open: 24 Mar - 30 Sept: Wed - Sun & BHs, 10am - 5pm. 1 Oct - 31 Mar: pre-booked guided tours. Closed 22 Dec - 28 Feb.

Admission: Adult £5.30, Child £2.70, Conc. £4.

ℹ WC. 🗔 ♿ Limited, lift available. 🅿 ■ 🐕 Guide dogs only. ☗ Tel for details.

WESTMINSTER CATHEDRAL

Victoria, London SW1P 1QW

Tel: 020 7798 9055   **Fax:** 020 7798 9090   **www.**westminstercathedral.org.uk

Owner: Diocese of Westminster   **Contact:** Revd Mgr Mark Langham

The Roman Catholic Cathedral of the Archbishop of Westminster. Spectacular building in the Byzantine style, designed by J F Bentley, opened in 1903, famous for its mosaics, marble and music. Westminster Cathedral celebrated the Centenary of its foundation in 1995.

Location: OS Ref. TQ293 791. Off Victoria Street, between Victoria Station and Westminster Abbey.

Open: All year: 7am - 7pm. Please telephone for times at Easter & Christmas.

Admission: Free. Lift charge: Adult £3. Child £1.50. Family (2+4) £7.

🗔 ♿ Ground floor. ☕ 🎨 Prior booking required. 🅿 None. ■ Worksheets & tours. 🐕 Guide dogs only. ❋

south east

Eight counties make up the South East region. Most are easily accessible in a day trip from London, and all offer a wealth of architectural interest as well as opportunities for rest and relaxation. Kent is not only 'the garden of England', with acres of fruit orchards and hop gardens, but also houses the site of the centre of the Anglican faith at Canterbury Cathedral, founded by St Augustine, the first Archbishop of Canterbury, in 597AD. Following the murder of St Thomas à Becket in 1170, the Cathedral became a place of pilgrimage, which it remains today. In each of the south eastern counties you will find world-famous properties such as Windsor Castle (Berkshire), Blenheim Palace (Oxfordshire), and Leeds Castle (Kent) which must not be missed – but try to find time to visit the lesser known treasures as well. Stowe Landscape Gardens (Buckinghamshire), Broughton Castle (Oxfordshire) and Great Dixter House & Gardens (Sussex) are among those that give a deeper insight into Britain's heritage and history both architectural and horticultural.

Sussex. © National Trust Photographic Library

Hampton Court Palace.

Cliveden, Buckinghamshire.

Reculver Towers and Roman Fort.

Hampton Court Palace – Vine Harvest.

berkshire
buckinghamshire
hampshire
kent
oxfordshire
surrey
sussex
isle of wight

waddesdon manor

16th century château style | decorative art | elegance

waddesdon manor

Waddesdon Manor was built at the end of the 19th century (1874-89) by Baron Ferdinand de Rothschild in the style of a French 16th century château. Baron Ferdinand was an inspired collector and the house was designed to accommodate his fine collection of French 18th century furniture, Sèvres porcelain, English portraits and other exceptional examples of the decorative arts. When Ferdinand died in 1898 he left Waddesdon to his sister, Miss Alice. Upon her death the house passed to James de Rothschild, a cousin from the French side of the family. In 1957, in order to ensure its future in perpetuity, Waddesdon was bequeathed to the National Trust by James de Rothschild, although his widow, Dolly, continued to manage the house until her death in 1988. The Rothschild family maintains an active interest in the running of Waddesdon through a family charitable trust under the chairmanship of Lord Rothschild.

Waddesdon has rich musical associations through Baron Ferdinand and its collections. This year these are explored through displays and interpretation throughout the House. Waddesdon is also celebrating the publication of a new catalogue, 'Drawings for Architecture, Design and Ornament' with an exhibition in the Drawings Room.

One of the finest Victorian gardens in Britain can be found here with the parterre, seasonal displays, colourful shrubs and statuary. The grounds are a peaceful and pleasant place to walk. Following the rediscovery of 'the Baron's Walk' which opened up an area giving wonderful views of the House and surrounding landscape, 'Miss Alice's Drive' has been restored. Originally created to make it easier for carriage horses to be brought up to the House, it forms a delightful stroll through the woodland, linking the Manor and the Stables, with views across the Vale to Bicester.

At the heart of the grounds is the Aviary, housing over 100 birds of around 36 different species, it is also known for breeding endangered species. The gardens around the Aviary have been recently recreated following Baron Ferdinand's scheme and the Aviary has been transformed, painted and guilded in homage to German Rococo pavilions that inspired its design.

There are two licensed restaurants at Waddesdon both serving the highest quality, fresh food. The Manor Restaurant serves breakfasts and snacks, then lunch and afternoon teas, whereas the Stables Restaurant offers a cold buffet, plâts du jour, snacks and sandwiches throughout the day. The Summerhouse and Coffee Bar are handy places too for a quick snack or drink, open weather permitting.

The Shops at Waddesdon should also be visited. The Gift Shop has not only postcards, greeting cards and stationery items but exclusive ceramics and beautifully designed textiles. The Wine Shop and Wine Warehouse sell one of the most comprehensive ranges of Rothschild wine in the world. With wines starting from under £5.00 up to several hundred the range caters for all pockets and occasions.

Waddesdon provides a unique setting for corporate and private entertaining. The Dairy, situated on the Estate beside a lake, is only open for private events. Together with The Stables, The Manor Restaurant and The Wine Cellars it is an ideal venue for meetings, conferences, wine tastings, anniversary and Christmas parties, lunches and dinners.

With so much to enjoy Waddesdon makes a great day out!

▸ For further details about Waddesdon Manor see page 97.

South East - England

Windsor Castle. Peter Packer/The Royal Collection © 2005 HM Queen Elizabeth II

WINDSOR CASTLE
ST GEORGE'S CHAPEL &
FROGMORE HOUSE
www.royal.gov.uk

Map 3

Owner:
Official Residence of
Her Majesty The Queen

▶ **CONTACT**
Ticket Sales &
Information Office
Buckingham Palace
London SW1A 1AA

Tel: 020 7766 7304
Groups (15+):
020 7766 7321
Fax: 020 7930 9625

e-mail: windsor@
royalcollection.org.uk

▶ **LOCATION**
OS Ref. SU969 770

M4/J6, M3/J3.
20m from central
London.

Rail: Regular service
from London Waterloo
and London
Paddington.

Coach: Victoria Coach
Station - regular service.

Sightseeing tours:
Tour companies
operate a daily service
with collection from
many London hotels.
Ask your hotel
concierge or porter
for information.

Whichever way you approach the town of Windsor, the view is dominated by the dramatic outline of Windsor Castle, the largest inhabited castle in the world and the oldest royal residence to have remained in continuous use by the monarchs of Britain. Today, along with Buckingham Palace and the Palace of Holyroodhouse in Edinburgh, it is one of the official residences of Her Majesty The Queen.

Windsor's rich history spans more than 900 years but, as a working royal palace, the Castle plays a large part in the official work of The Queen and members of the Royal Family today. The magnificent State Rooms are furnished with some of the finest works of art from the Royal Collection, including paintings by Rembrandt and drawings by Leonardo da Vinci. Visitors should not miss the Castle Precinct Tours (which depart at regular intervals from the Admission Centre), Queen Mary's Dolls' House, a masterpiece in minature, and the last and largest suit of armour made for Henry VIII.

Within the precincts is St George's Chapel, one of the most beautiful ecclesiastical buildings in England, Ten monarchs are buried here, including Henry VIII with his favourite wife, Jane Seymour.

Frogmore House has been a favourite royal retreat for over 300 years. It is open to visitors on a limited number of days during the year. Guided pre-booked group visits are available throughout August and September. Please contact the Ticket Sales & Information Office for details.

St George's Chapel, Windsor Castle.
Dennis Gilbert /The Royal Collection © 2005 HM Queen Elizabeth II

Frogmore House.
© 2005 HM Queen Elizabeth II

The Crimson Drawing Room.
Mark Fiennes / The Royal Collection © 2005 HM Queen Elizabeth II

▶ **OPENING TIMES**
March - October:
Daily except 25 Mar & 28 - 30 Apr: 9.45am - 5.15pm
(27 Mar, 1 - 5.15pm; 24 Apr, 9.45am - 12.30pm).
Last admission 4pm.

November - February:
Daily except 10 - 21 Jan & 25/26 Dec, 9.45am - 4.15pm.
Last admission 3pm.

Opening arrangements may change at short notice. 24-hr info line 01753 831118.

Private Evening Tours of the Castle for groups contact 020 7766 7322.

St George's Chapel is closed to visitors on Sundays as services are held throughout the day. Worshippers are welcome.

The State Rooms are closed during Royal and State visits.

Frogmore House & Mausoleum
17 - 19 May and 27 - 29 Aug. For prices (Frogmore House & Mausoleum only) contact 020 7766 7305.

Private tours of the house for pre-booked groups (15+) 2 Aug - 29 Sept. Contact 020 7766 7321.

▶ **ADMISSION**
For admission prices please call our Ticket Sales Information on 020 7766 7304.
Groups (15+)
Discounts available.

All information correct at time of going to print.

▣ **SPECIAL EVENTS**
With the exception of Sundays, the Changing of the Guard takes place at 11am daily from April to the end of June and on alternate days at other times of the year.

ⓘ No photography.   📷 ♿ 🎧 Audio Tours Windsor Castle.   🅿 None.   ▣ 🐕 Guide dogs only.   ❄

©National Trust Photographic Library

BASILDON PARK ❧

LOWER BASILDON, READING, BERKSHIRE RG8 9NR

www.nationaltrust.org.uk/basildonpark

Tel: 0118 984 3040   **Infoline:** 01494 755558   **Fax:** 0118 976 7370
e-mail: basildonpark@nationaltrust.org.uk
Owner: The National Trust   **Contact:** The Property Manager

An elegant, classical house designed in the 18th century by Carr of York and set in rolling parkland in the Thames Valley. The house has rich interiors with fine plasterwork, pictures and furniture, and includes an unusual Octagon Room and a decorative Shell Room. Basildon Park has connections with the East through its builder and was the home of a wealthy industrialist in the 19th century. It was rescued from dereliction in the mid 20th century. Small flower garden, pleasure grounds, 400 acres of parkland with woodland walks.

Location: OS Ref. SU611 782. 2¹/₂ m NW of Pangbourne on the west side of the A329, 7m from M4/J12.
Open: House: 23 Mar - 30 Oct: daily except Mon & Tue (open BH Mons), 1 - 5.30pm. Park, Garden & Woodland Walk: as house 11am - 5.30pm. Property closes at 4pm from 19 - 21 Aug. Shop as house plus 2 Nov - 18 Dec: 12 noon - 4pm.
Admission: House, Park & Garden: Adult £5, Child £2.50, Family £12.50. Park & Garden only: Adult £2.40, Child £1.20. Family £6. Groups (15+) by appointment: £3.70.

⬛ 🅿 ♿ 🍴 🎟 By appointment 🅿 In grounds. 🐕 On leads, in grounds only. 🏠
🛏 Tel for details.

DONNINGTON CASTLE ⌗

Newbury, Berkshire
Tel: 01424 775705   **www**.english-heritage.org.uk/visits
Owner: English Heritage   **Contact:** Battle Abbey

Built in the late 14th century, the twin towered gatehouse of this heroic castle survives amidst some impressive earthworks.
Location: OS Ref. SU463 691. 1 mile N of Newbury off B4494.
Open: All year: Any reasonable time (exterior viewing only).
Admission: Free.
♿ Steep slopes within grounds. 🅿 🐕 On leads. ✳

©Savill Garden

DORNEY COURT 🏠

WINDSOR, BERKSHIRE SL4 6QP

www.dorneycourt.co.uk

Tel: 01628 604638   **e-mail:** palmer@dorneycourt.co.uk
Owner/Contact: Mrs Peregrine Palmer

Just a few miles from the heart of bustling Windsor lies "one of the finest Tudor Manor Houses in England", *Country Life*. Grade I listed with the added accolade of being of outstanding architectural and historical importance, the visitor can get a rare insight into the lifestyle of the squirearchy through 550 years, with the Palmer family, who still live there today, owning the house for 450 of these years. The house boasts a magnificent Great Hall, family portraits, oak and lacquer furniture, needlework and panelled rooms. A private tour on a 'non-open day' takes around 1¹/₂ hours, but when open to the public this is reduced to around 40 mins. The adjacent 13th century Church of St James, with Norman font and Tudor tower can also be visited, as well as the adjoining Plant Centre in our walled garden where light lunches and full English cream teas are served in a tranquil setting throughout the day.
Location: OS Ref. SU926 791. 5 mins off M4/J7, 10mins from Windsor, 2m W of Eton.
Open: May: BH Suns & Mons; Aug: daily except Sats, 1.30 - 4pm (last admission).
Admission: Adult: £6, Child (10yrs +) £4. Groups (10+): By arrangement all year.
ℹ Film & photographic shoots. No stiletto heels. 🌸 Garden centre. 🍴
♿ Garden centre. 🍽 🎟 🅿 🛏 🐕 Guide dogs only. ✳

Savill Garden, Berkshire.

ETON COLLEGE

Windsor, Berkshire SL4 6DW

Tel: 01753 671177 **Fax:** 01753 671029 **e-mail:** r.hunkin@etoncollege.org.uk

Owner: Eton College **Contact:** Rebecca Hunkin

Eton College, founded in 1440 by Henry VI, is one of the oldest and best known schools in the country. The original and subsequent historic buildings of the Foundation are a part of the heritage of the British Isles and visitors are invited to experience and share the beauty of the ancient precinct which includes the magnificent College Chapel, a masterpiece of the perpendicular style.

Location: OS Ref. SU967 779. Off M4/J5. Access from Windsor by footbridge only. Vehicle access from Slough 2m N.

Open: Mar - early Oct: Times vary, best to check with the Visits Office.

Admission: Ordinary admissions and daily guided tours during the season at 2.15pm and 3.15pm. Groups by appointment only. Rates vary according to type of tour.

⬛ 🔲 ♿Ground floor. WC. 🎦 🅿 Limited. 🦮Guide dogs only.

TAPLOW COURT 🏠

BERRY HILL, TAPLOW, Nr MAIDENHEAD, BERKS SL6 0ER

www.sgi-uk.org

Tel: 01628 591209 **Fax:** 01628 773055

Owner: SGI-UK **Contact:** Michael Yeadon

Set high above the Thames, affording spectacular views. Remodelled mid-19th century by William Burn. Earlier neo-Norman Hall. 18th century home of Earls of Orkney and more recently of Lord and Lady Desborough who entertained 'The Souls' here. Tranquil gardens & grounds. Anglo-Saxon burial mound. Permanent and temporary exhibitions.

Location: OS Ref. SU907 822. M4/J7 off Bath Road towards Maidenhead. 6m off M40/J2.

Open: House & Grounds: 29 May - 31 Jul & 11 Sept: Sun & BH Mons, 2 - 5.30pm. Groups at other times by appointment.

Admission: No charge. Free parking.

⬛ ♿ 🛒 🎦 ♨ 🅿 🦮Guide dogs only. 🛏Tel for details.

SAVILL GARDEN

WINDSOR GREAT PARK, BERKSHIRE SL4 2HT

www.savillgarden.co.uk

Tel: 01753 847518 **Fax:** 01753 847536 **e-mail:** savillgarden@thecrownestate.co.uk

Owner: Crown Estate Commissioners **Contact:** Jan Bartholomew

World-renowned 35 acre woodland garden, providing a wealth of beauty and interest in all seasons. Spring is heralded by hosts of daffodils, masses of rhododendrons, azaleas, camellias, magnolias and much more. Roses, herbaceous borders and countless alpines are the great features of summer, and the leaf colours and fruits of autumn rival the other seasons with a great display.

Location: OS Ref. SU977 706. Wick Lane, Englefield Green. Clearly signposted from Ascot, Bagshot, Egham and Windsor. Nearest station: Egham.

Open: Mar - Oct: 10am - 6pm. Nov - Feb: 10am - 4pm.

Admission: Apr - May: Adult £5.50, Child (6-16yrs) £2.50, Conc. £5. Jun - Oct: Adult £4.70, Child (6-16yrs) £1.50, Conc. £4.20. Nov - Mar: Adult £3.50, Child (6-16yrs) £1.25, Conc. £3. Child under 6 Free.

ℹ️Film & photographic shoots. ⬛ 🌱Plant centre. ♿Grounds. WC. 🍴Licensed. 🎦For groups, by appointment. 🦮Guide dogs only. ❋

WELFORD PARK

Newbury, Berkshire RG20 8HU

Tel: 01488 608203/608691

Owner/Contact: Mr J Puxley

A Queen Anne house, with attractive gardens and grounds. Riverside walks.

Location: OS Ref. SU409 731. On Lambourn Valley Road. 6m NW of Newbury.

Open: 16 - 21 & 30 May; 4 - 17 & 20 - 30 Jun (closed 26 & 28 Jun); 29 Aug: 11am - 5pm. Home made cream teas available for groups (10+), must book 7 days in advance.

Admission: Booked House Tour: Adult £5, OAP & Child over 8yrs £3.50. Grounds: Free except when occasionally open in aid of charities.

♿Grounds. 🦮On leads, in grounds.

WINDSOR CASTLE, ST GEORGE'S CHAPEL & FROGMORE HOUSE

See page 92 for full page entry.

🔔 **Civil Wedding Venues** see page 32

Windsor Castle – The King's Bedchamber.
© The Royal Collection © 2004, Her Majesty Queen Elizabeth II

STOWE HOUSE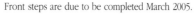

www.stowe.co.uk

Map 5

Owner:
Stowe House
Preservation Trust

▶ **CONTACT**

The Commercial Office
Stowe School
Buckingham
MK18 5EH

Tel: 01280 818282/280
(Mon-Fri) or
01280 818166
(Info Line, House only)
or 01280 822850
Gardens

Fax: 01280 818186
House only

e-mail:
sses@stowe.co.uk
House only

▶ **LOCATION**

OS Ref. SP666 366

From London, M1 to
Milton Keynes, 1½ hrs
or Banbury 1¼ hrs,
3m NW of Buckingham.

Bus: Buckingham 3m.

Rail: Milton Keynes 15m.

Air: Heathrow 50m.

CONFERENCE/FUNCTION

ROOM	MAX CAPACITY
Roxburgh Hall	460
Music Room	120
Marble Hall	150
State Dining Rm	160
Garter Room	180
Memorial Theatre	120

Stowe owes its pre-eminence to the vision and wealth of two owners. From 1715 to 1749 Viscount Cobham, one of Marlborough's Generals, continuously improved his estate, calling in the leading designers of the day to lay out the gardens, and commissioning several leading architects – Vanbrugh, Gibbs, Kent and Leoni – to decorate them with garden temples. From 1750 to 1779 Earl Temple, his nephew and successor continued to expand and embellish both Gardens and House. The House is now a major public school. The magnificently restored North Front is well worth a visit. The Central Pavilion and South Front steps are due to be completed March 2005.

Around the mansion is one of Britain's most magnificent landscape gardens now in the ownership of the National Trust. Covering 325 acres and containing no fewer than 6 lakes and 32 garden temples, it is of the greatest historic importance. During the 1730s William Kent laid out in the Elysian Fields at Stowe, one of the first 'natural' landscapes and initiated the style known as 'the English Garden'. 'Capability' Brown worked there for 10 years, not as a consultant but as head gardener, and in 1744 was married in the little church hidden between the trees.

ℹ Indoor swimming pool, sports hall, tennis court, squash courts, astroturf, parkland, cricket pitches and golf course. No photography in house.

🗓 International conferences, private functions, weddings, and prestige exhibitions. Catering on request.

♿ Visitors may alight at entrance. Allocated parking areas. WC in garden area. 'Batricars' available.

☕🍴 Morning coffee, lunch and afternoon tea available by pre-arrangement only, for up to 100.

🚶 For parties of 15 - 60 at additional cost. Tour time: house and garden 2½ - 4½ hrs, house only 1½ hrs.

🅿 Ample.

🚫

🐕 In grounds on leads.

🔔 Civil Wedding Licence.

♿ Available. ❄

▶ **OPENING TIMES**

House

19/20 Feb; 12/13 Mar:
Sat & Sun for guided tours only at 2pm.

25 Mar - 17 Apr plus
Easter Monday:
Wed - Sun, 12 noon - 5pm with guided tour at 2pm. Last admission 4pm.

30 May - 3 June:
Wed - Sun (plus BH Mon) for guided tours only at 2pm.

3 Jul - 25 Aug:
Wed - Sun (plus BH Mon), 12 noon - 5pm with guided tour at 2pm. Last admission 4pm.

31 Aug - 16 Oct:
Wed - Sun for guided tours only at 2pm.

19/20 Nov; 17/18 Dec:
Sat & Sun for guided tours only at 2pm.

Group visits by arrangement throughout the year.

NB: Times may vary. Please telephone to check 01280 818166 (Info Line) or 01280 818282 /280 (Mon - Fri).

▶ **ADMISSION**

Adult £2.00
Child (under 16yrs)... £1.00
Guided Tours
Adult £3.00
Child (8 - 16yrs) £1.50

(Admission prices correct at time of publication.)

🎭 **SPECIAL EVENTS**

Feb 12 - 13: Homes & Garden Exhibition

Jul 30 - Aug 7: Stowe Opera

Aug 14: Battleproms Concert

Aug 18 - 21: Stowe Music Festival

Oct 22/23: Christmas Fayre

©National Trust, Waddesdon Manor

Map 5

WADDESDON MANOR 🌿

www.waddesdon.org.uk

Waddesdon Manor was built (1874-89), in the style of a 16th century French château, for Baron Ferdinand de Rothschild to entertain his guests and display his vast collection of art treasures. It houses one of the finest collections of French 18th century decorative arts in the world. The furniture, Savonnerie carpets, and Sèvres porcelain rank in importance with the Metropolitan Museum in New York and the Louvre in Paris. There is also a collection of portraits by Gainsborough and Reynolds and works by Dutch and Flemish Masters of the 17th century.

Waddesdon has one of the finest Victorian gardens in Britain, renowned for its colourful parterre, seasonal displays, shady walks and views, fountains and statuary. At its heart lies the rococo-style aviary which houses a splendid collection of exotic birds and is known for breeding endangered species. Thousands of bottles of vintage Rothschild wines are found in the wine cellars.

There is a gift shop, a wine shop with a full selection of Rothschild wines, and two licensed restaurants. A full programme of events is organised throughout the year including special interest days, wine tastings and family events.

▶ CONTACT
Waddesdon
Nr Aylesbury
Buckinghamshire
HP18 0JH

Tel (24-hour recorded info):
01296 653211

Booking & Info (Mon - Fri 10am - 4pm):
01296 653226

Fax: 01296 653212

▶ LOCATION
OS Ref. SP740 169

Between Aylesbury & Bicester, off A41.

Rail: Aylesbury 6m.

©National Trust, Waddesdon Manor

▶ OPENING TIMES
Grounds (incl. Gardens, Aviary, Manor Restaurant, Gift and Wine Shops)
Jan: 8/9, 15/16, 22/23 & 29/30
Feb: 5/6, 12/13, 19/20, 26/27
Mar: 5/6, 12/13, 19/20

and (also Stables Restaurant) from
23 Mar - 23 December
Wed - Sun & BH Mons &
19/20 Dec: 10am - 5pm

House - Main Season (incl Wine Cellars)
23 Mar - 30 Oct
Wed - Sun & BH Mons
11am - 4pm
Last recommended admission 2.30pm.

Bachelors' Wing
23 Mar - 30 Oct: Wed - Fri
11am - 4pm
Space is limited so entry cannot be guaranteed.

House (East Wing) Pre-Christmas
16 Nov - 23 Dec
Wed - Sun & 19/20 Dec
12 noon - 4pm
(from 11am Sats & Suns

▶ ADMISSION
Main Season
House & Grounds
Adult £11.00
Pre-Christmas £8.00
Child (5-16 yrs) £8.00
Pre-Christmas £2.00
Groups (15+)
Adult £8.80
Pre-Christmas £7.20
Child £6.40
Pre-Christmas £1.60
Grounds only
Adult £4.00
Child (5-16 yrs) £2.00
Pre-Christmas ..... Free
Groups (15+)
Adult £3.20
Child £1.60
Pre-Christmas ..... Free

Bachelors' Wing ... £3.00

CLIVEDEN ☘
TAPLOW, MAIDENHEAD SL6 0JA

Tel: 01628 605069 **Infoline:** 01494 755562 **Fax:** 01628 669461
e-mail: cliveden@nationaltrust.org.uk

Owner: The National Trust   **Contact:** Property Manager

152 hectares of gardens and woodland. A water garden, 'secret' garden, herbaceous borders, topiary, a great formal parterre, and informal vistas provide endless variety. The garden statuary is one of the most important collections in the care of The National Trust and includes many Roman antiquities collected by 1st Viscount Astor. The Octagon Temple (Chapel) with its rich mosaic interior is open on certain days, as is part of the house (see below).

Location: OS Ref. SU915 851. 3m N of Maidenhead, M4/J7 onto A4 or M40/J4 onto A404 to Marlow and follow signs. From London by train take Thames Train service from Paddington to Burnham (taxi rank and office adjacent to station).

Open: Estate & Garden: 16 Mar - 30 Oct, daily, 11am - 6pm; 31 Oct - 22 Dec, daily, 11am - 4pm. House (part)& Octagon Temple: 3 Apr - 30 Oct: Thurs & Sun, 3 - 5.30pm. Admission to house by timed ticket, obtainable from information kiosk only. Woodlands: 1 Apr - 30 Oct, daily, 11am - 5.30pm; 31 Oct - 22 Dec & 3 Jan - 31 Mar, daily, 11am - 4pm. Restaurant: 16 Mar - 30 Oct, daily, 11am - 5pm; 6 Nov - 18 Dec, Sat & Sun, 11am - 3pm. Shop: 16 Mar - 30 Oct, daily, 12 noon - 5.30pm; 31 Oct - 22 Dec, daily, 12 noon - 4pm. Some areas of formal garden may be roped off when ground conditions are bad.

Admission: Grounds: Adult £7 Child £3.50, Family £17.50, Groups (must book) £6. House: £1 extra, Child 50p extra. Note: Mooring charge on Cliveden Reach.
Partial. WC. Licensed. Specified woodlands only. Tel for details.

COWPER & NEWTON MUSEUM
Home of Olney's Heritage, Orchard Side, Market Place, Olney MK46 4AJ
Tel: 01234 711516 **e-mail:** cnm@mkheritage.co.uk
www.cowperandnewtonmuseum.org
Owner: Board of Trustees   **Contact:** Mrs J McKillop

Once the home of 18th century poet and letter writer William Cowper and now containing furniture, paintings and belongings of both Cowper and his ex-slave trader friend, Rev John Newton (author of "Amazing Grace"). Attractions include re-creations of a Victorian country kitchen and wash-house, two peaceful gardens and Cowper's restored summerhouse. Costume gallery, important collections of dinosaur bones and bobbin lace, and local history displays.

Location: OS Ref. SP890 512. On A509, 6m N of Newport Pagnell, M1/J14.
Open: 1 Mar - 23 Dec: Tue - Sat & BH Mons, 10am - 1pm & 2 - 5pm. Closed on Good Fri. Open on Sundays in June, July & August, 2 - 5pm.
Admission: Adult £3, Conc. £2, Child & Students (with card) £1.50, Family £7.50.
No photography. Gardens. By arrangement. Guide dogs only.

FORD END WATERMILL
Station Road, Ivinghoe, Buckinghamshire
Tel: 01582 600391   **Contact:** David Lindsey

The Watermill, a listed building, was recorded in 1616 but is probably much older.
Location: OS Ref. SP941 166. 600 metres from Ivinghoe Church along B488 (Station Road) to Leighton Buzzard.
Open: Easter Mon & 2 May - 25 Sept: 2nd & 4th Suns and BHs, 2.30 - 5.30pm. Milling Easter Mon & BHs and 2nd Sun in May, 3 - 5pm.
Admission: Adult £1.20, Child 40p. School Groups: Child 75p, Adults Free.

Lady Mary Wortley Montagu – West Wycombe Park.

NT Photographic Library: Matthew Antrobus

HUGHENDEN MANOR 🌱
HIGH WYCOMBE HP14 4LA

Tel: 01494 755573/ 755565 - Infoline   **Fax:** 01494 474284
e-mail: hughenden@nationaltrust.org.uk
Owner: The National Trust   **Contact:** The Property Manager
2004 Disraeli Bicentenary Year. Home of Prime Minister Benjamin Disraeli from 1847 - 1881, Hughenden has a red brick, 'gothic' exterior. The interior is a comfortable Victorian home and still holds many of Disraeli's pictures, books and furniture, as well as other fascinating mementoes of the life of the great statesman and writer. The surrounding park and woodland have lovely walks, and the formal garden has been recreated in the spirit of Mary Anne Disraeli's colourful designs.
Location: OS165 Ref. SU866 955. 1¹/₂ m N of High Wycombe on the W side of the A4128.

Open: House: 5 - 27 Mar: Sat & Sun, 1 - 5pm; 30 Mar - 30 Oct: Wed - Sun & BH Mon, 1 - 5pm (last admission 4.30pm). Open Good Fri. On BHs and busy days entry is by timed ticket. Gardens open same days as house, 12 noon - 5pm. Shop and Restaurant: open as House 12 noon - 5pm also 31 Oct - 18 Dec: daily, 11am - 4pm. Park & Woodland: All year.
Admission: House & Garden: Adult £5, Child £2.50, Family £12.50. Groups: Adult £4.20, Child £2.10. Group visits outside normal hours £10. Garden only: Adult £1.80, Child 90p. Park & Woodland Free. Small groups only, no groups at weekends or BHs.
🖼 ♿Ground floor only. WC. 🍴 🎫 For booked groups. 🎧
🐕In grounds, on leads. Guide dogs in house & formal gardens. ❄ 🏷 Tel for details.

THE KING'S HEAD 🌱
King's Head Passage, Market Square, Aylesbury, Buckinghamshire HP20 2RW
Tel: 01296 381501   **Fax:** 01296 381502 **e-mail:** kingshead@nationaltrust.org.uk
Owner: The National Trust   **Contact:** The Custodian
This enchanting inn dates back to 1455 and remains a unique place to enjoy real ale or even a glass of Rothschild wine. It has many noteworthy architectural features including a medieval stained glass window, extensive timber framing and an ancient cobbled courtyard. Once a base for Oliver Cromwell it now houses a bookshop, coffee shop and visitor centre.
Location: OS Ref. SP818 138. At NW corner of Aylesbury Market Square.
Open: All year: Mon - Sat, 10am - 3pm and normal pub hours. Guided tours on Wed, Fri & Sat at 2pm.
Admission: Adult £2.10 (incl tour). NT members Free.
🎫 ♿Partial. WC. 🍷 Licensed. 🎫 Obligatory. 🅿 None. ■ 🐕 Guide dogs only. ❄

LONG CRENDON COURTHOUSE 🌱
High St, Long Crendon, Buckinghamshire
Tel: 01494 528051 (Regional Office)   **e-mail:** stowegarden@nationaltrust.org.uk
www.nationaltrust.org.uk
Owner: The National Trust   **Contact:** Nick Phillips
A fantastic opportunity to see very clearly a 15th century building. The exposed timber beams and early oak floorboards are a rare sight.
Location: OS Ref. SP698 091. 3miles N of Thame.
Open: 23 Mar - 28 Sept: Weds: 2 - 6pm. Sats, Suns & BH Mons, 11am - 6pm.
Admission: Adult £1, Child 50p.

JOHN MILTON'S COTTAGE
21 Deanway, Chalfont St. Giles, Buckinghamshire HP8 4JH
Tel: 01494 872313   **e-mail:** info@miltonscottage.org   **www.**miltonscottage.org
Owner: Milton Cottage Trust   **Contact:** Mr E A Dawson
Grade I listed 16th century cottage where John Milton lived and completed 'Paradise Lost' and started 'Paradise Regained'. Four ground floor museum rooms contain important first editions of John Milton's 17th century poetry and prose works. Amongst many unique items on display is the portrait of John Milton by Sir Godfrey Kneller. Well stocked, attractive cottage garden, listed by English Heritage.
Location: OS Ref. SU987 933. ¹/₂ m W of A413. 3m N of M40/J2. S side of street.
Open: 1 Mar - 31 Oct: Tue - Sun, 10am - 1pm & 2 - 6pm. Closed Mons (open BH Mons). Coach parking by prior arrangement only.
Admission: Adult £3, under 15s £1, Groups (20+) £2.
🖼 ♿Ground floor. 🎫 Talk followed by free tour. 🅿 🐕

NETHER WINCHENDON HOUSE 🏠
Aylesbury, Buckinghamshire HP18 0DY
Tel/Fax: 01844 290199   **www.**netherwinchendonhouse.co.uk
Owner/Contact: Mr Robert Spencer Bernard
Medieval and Tudor manor house. Great Hall. Dining Room with fine 16th century frieze, ceiling and linenfold panelling. Fine furniture and family portraits. Former home of Sir Francis Bernard, the last British Governor of Massachussetts Bay. Continuous family occupation since mid-16th century. House altered in late 18th century in the Strawberry Hill Gothick style. Interesting garden and specimen trees.
Location: OS Ref. SP734 121. 2m N of A418 equidistant between Thame & Aylesbury.
Open: 2 - 30 May & 29 Aug: 2.30 - 5.30pm (only conducted tours at ¹/₄ to each hour). Groups at any time by prior written agreement (minimum charge £50, no concessions)
Admission: Adult £5, OAP £4 (no concession at weekends or BHs), Child (under 12yrs) £2. HHA members free (not on special groups).
♿ 🍷 By arrangement. 🎫Obligatory. ❄

❄ **Open All Year Index** *see page 43*

Map 3

Owner:
Earl of Carnarvon

▶ CONTACT

The Castle Office
Highclere Castle
Newbury
Berkshire RG20 9RN

Tel: 01635 253210
Fax: 01635 255315
e-mail: theoffice@
highclerecastle.co.uk

▶ LOCATION

OS Ref. SU445 587

M4/J13 - A34 south,
M3/J8 - A303 - A34
north.

Air: Heathrow M4
45 mins.

Rail: Paddington -
Newbury 45 mins.

Taxi: 4¹/₂ m
07778 156392.

HIGHCLERE CASTLE & GARDENS 🏛

www.highclerecastle.co.uk

Designed by Charles Barry in the 1830s at the same time as he was building the Houses of Parliament, this soaring pinnacled mansion provided a perfect setting for the 3rd Earl of Carnarvon, one of the great hosts of Queen Victoria's reign. The extravagant interiors range from church Gothic through Moorish flamboyance and rococo revival to the solid masculinity in the long Library. Old Master paintings mix with portraits by Van Dyck and 18th century painters. Napoleon's desk and chair rescued from St. Helena sits with other 18th and 19th century furniture.

The 5th Earl of Carnarvon together with Howard Carter, discovered the Tomb of Tutankhamun and the Castle houses a unique exhibition of some of his discoveries. The 7th Earl of Carnarvon was the Queen's Racing Manager and in 1993, to celebrate his 50th year as a leading owner and breeder, the Racing Exhibition was opened offering a fascinating insight into a racing history which dates back four generations. The 8th Earl and his wife take a very personal interest in the Castle and they are often to be seen round and about their home, grounds and gardens.

GARDENS

The magnificent parkland with its massive cedars was designed by 'Capability' Brown. The walled gardens also date from an earlier house at Highclere but the dark yew walks are entirely Victorian in character. The glass Orangery and Fernery add an exotic flavour. The Secret Garden has a romance of its own with a beautiful curving lawn surrounded by densely planted herbaceous gardens. A place for poets and romantics.

🗄 ℹ Conferences, exhibitions, filming, fairs, and concerts (cap. 8000). No photography in the house.

🍽 Receptions, dinners, corporate hospitality.

♿ Visitors may alight at the entrance. WC.

☕ Tearooms, licensed. Lunches for 20+ can be booked.

🅿 Ample.

🎦 Egyptian Exhibition: £4+VAT per child. 1 adult free per every 10 children – includes playgroups, Brownie packs, Guides etc. Nature walks, beautiful old follies, Secret Garden.

🐕 In grounds, on leads.

🔔 Civil Wedding Licence.

🎭 Please visit website.

▶ OPENING TIMES

1 June - 31 August
Mon - Fri, 11am - 4pm
(Gates open 10am).
Last admission 3pm.

▶ ADMISSION

Adult £7.50
Child (4-15yrs)....... £4.00
Conc. £6.00
Wheelchair Pusher... FOC
Family (2+2/1+3). £18.00

Grounds & Gardens only
Adult £4.50
Child (4-15yrs)....... £2.00

Groups (20+)
Adult £5.50
Child (4-15yrs)....... £3.50
Conc. £5.00

Private guided tours at other times may be arranged subject to availability at a minimum cost for up to 40 persons of £800 plus VAT, each additional person £20 plus VAT.

School Groups (to visit Egyptian Exhibition only)
Child ... £4.00 (plus VAT)
1 adult Free for every 10 children. By prior arrangement.

CONFERENCE/FUNCTION

ROOM	SIZE	MAX CAPACITY
Library	43' x 21'	140
Saloon	42' x 29'	120
Dining Rm	37' x 18'	70
Library, Saloon, Drawing Rm, Music Rm, Smoking Rm		500

SOMERLEY

www.somerley.com

Map 3

Owner:
The Earl of Normanton

▶ CONTACT

Danielle Rogers
Somerley
Ringwood
Hampshire BH24 3PL

Tel: 01425 480819
Fax: 01425 478613
e-mail:
events@somerley.com

▶ LOCATION

OS Ref. SU134 080

Off the A31 to
Bournemouth 2m.
London 1³/₄ hrs via
M3, M27, A31.
2m NW of Ringwood.

Air: Bournemouth
International
Airport 5m.

Rail: Bournemouth
Station 12m.

Taxi: A car can be
arranged from the
House if applicable.

CONFERENCE/FUNCTION

ROOM	SIZE	MAX CAPACITY
Picture Gall.	80' x 30'	200
Drawing Rm	38' x 30'	50
Dining Rm	39' x 19'	50
East Library	26' x 21'	30
Old Somerley	40' x 20'	70
Old Game Larder	20' x 20'	30

Sitting on the edge of the New Forest in the heart of Hampshire, Somerley, home of the 6th Earl of Normanton and his three children, is situated in 7,000 acres of meadows, woods and rolling parkland. Designed by Samuel Wyatt in the mid 1700s, the house became the property of the Normanton family in 1825 and has remained in the same family through the years.

Although never open to the public, Somerley is available for corporate events and wedding receptions and its location, along with its seclusion and privacy, provide the perfect environment for conferences and meetings, product launches, lunches and dinners, activity and team building days. With two further facilities available (The Old Game Larder and Old Somerley), the estate's uses are only restricted by an organiser's imagination.

Somerley House only ever hosts one event at a time so exclusivity in an outstanding setting is always guaranteed. From groups as small as eight to perhaps a large dinner for 150, the style of attention and personal service go hand in hand with the splendour of the house and the estate itself.

▶ OPENING TIMES

Privately booked
functions only.

▶ ADMISSION

Privately booked
functions only.

ℹ️ No individual visits, ideal for all corporate events, weddings, activity days and filmwork.

🍷🍴 Dining Room and picture gallery available for private parties.

🅿️ Unlimited.

🛏️ 8 double rooms (7 en-suite).

JANE AUSTEN'S HOUSE

CHAWTON, ALTON, HAMPSHIRE GU34 1SD

www.janeaustenmuseum.org.uk

Tel/Fax: 01420 83262 **e-mail:** enquiries@jahmusm.org.uk

Owner: Jane Austen Memorial Trust **Contact:** The Curator

17th century house where Jane Austen wrote or revised her six great novels. Contains many items associated with her and her family, documents and letters, first editions of the novels, pictures, portraits and furniture. Pleasant garden, suitable for picnics, bakehouse with brick oven and wash tub, houses Jane's donkey carriage.

Location: OS Ref. SU708 376. Just S of A31, 1m SW of Alton, signposted Chawton.

Open: 1 Mar - 30 Nov: daily, 11am - 4.30pm; Dec, Jan & Feb: weekends only. Also open 27 Dec - 2 Jan. Closed 25 - 26 Dec.

Admission: Fee charged.

Bookshop. Ground floor & grounds. WC. Opposite house. Opposite house. Guide dogs only.

BASING HOUSE

Redbridge Lane, Basing, Basingstoke RG24 7HB

Tel: 01256 467294

Owner: Hampshire County Council **Contact:** Alan Turton

Ruins, covering 10 acres, of huge Tudor palace. Recent recreation of Tudor formal garden.

Location: OS Ref. SU665 526. 2m E from Basingstoke town centre. Signposted car parks are about 5 or 10 mins walk from entrance.

Open: 25 Mar - 2 Oct: Wed - Sun & BHs, 2 - 6pm.

Admission: Adult £2, Conc. £1.

BEAULIEU

See pages 104/105 for double page entry.

BISHOP'S WALTHAM PALACE

Bishop's Waltham, Hampshire SO32 1DH

Tel: 01489 892460 **www**.english-heritage.org.uk/visits

Owner: English Heritage **Contact:** Visitor Operations Team

This medieval seat of the Bishops of Winchester once stood in an enormous park. There are still wooded grounds and the remains of the Great Hall and the three storey tower can still be seen. Dower House furnished as a 19th century farmhouse.

Location: OS Ref. SU552 173. In Bishop's Waltham, 5 miles NE from M27/J8.

Open: Grounds: 1 May - 30 Sept: Mon - Fri, 10am - 5pm. Farmhouse: 1 May - 30 Sept: Sun & BH Mons, 10am - 5pm.

Admission: Farmhouse: Adult £2.60, Child £1.30, Conc. £2. Gardens: Free.

WCs. Exhibition. Grounds. Grounds only, on leads. Tel for details.

BOHUNT MANOR GARDENS

Liphook, Hampshire GU30 7DL

Tel/Fax: 01428 727936

Owner: World Wildlife Fund **Contact:** Steve Williams

Woodland gardens with lakeside walk, collection of ornamental waterfowl, herbaceous borders and unusual trees and shrubs.

Location: OS Ref. SU839 310. W side of B2070 at S end of village.

Open: All year: daily, 10am - 5pm.

Admission: Voluntary contributions.

AVINGTON PARK

WINCHESTER, HAMPSHIRE SO21 1DB

www.avingtonpark.co.uk

Tel: 01962 779260 **e-mail:** enquiries@avingtonpark.co.uk

Owner/Contact: Mrs S L Bullen

Avington Park, where Charles II and George IV both stayed at various times, dates back to the 11th century. The house was enlarged in 1670 by the addition of two wings and a classical Portico surmounted by three statues. The State rooms are magnificently painted and lead onto the unique pair of conservatories flanking the South Lawn. The Georgian church, St. Mary's, is in the grounds.

Avington Park is a privately owned stately home and is a most prestigious venue in peaceful surroundings. It is perfect for any event from seminars, conferences and exhibitions to wedding ceremonies and receptions, dinner dances and private parties.

The Conservatories and the Orangery make a delightful location for summer functions, whilst log fires offer a welcome during the winter. Excellent caterers provide for all types of occasion, ranging from breakfasts and light lunches to sumptuous dinners. All bookings at Avington are individually tailor-made and only exclusive use is offered. Several rooms available for Civil wedding ceremonies.

Location: OS Ref. SU534 324. 4m NE of Winchester ½ m S of B3047 in Itchen Abbas.

Open: May - Sept: Suns & BH Mons plus Mons in Aug, 2.30 - 5.30pm. Last tour 5pm. Other times by arrangement, coach parties welcome by appointment all year.

Admission: Adult £4, Child £2.

Conferences. Partial. WC. Obligatory. In grounds, on leads. Guide dogs only in house. Tel for details.

BREAMORE HOUSE & MUSEUM 🏛

BREAMORE, FORDINGBRIDGE, HAMPSHIRE SP6 2DF

www.breamorehouse.com

Tel: 01725 512233 **Fax:** 01725 512858 **e-mail:** breamore@ukonline.co.uk

Owner/Contact: Sir Edward Hulse Bt

Elizabethan manor with fine collections of pictures and furniture. Countryside Museum takes visitors back to the time when a village was self-sufficient.

Location: OS Ref. SU152 191. W Off the A338, between Salisbury and Ringwood.

Open: Easter weekend; Apr: Tue & Sun; May, Jun, Jul & Sept: Tue, Wed, Thur, Sat, Sun & all hols. Aug: daily except Mons. House: 2 - 5.30pm. Countryside Museum: 1 - 5.30pm. Last admission 4.15pm.

Admission: Combined ticket for house and museum: Adult £6, Child £4, OAP £5, Family £15.

🔲 ♿ Ground floor & grounds. WC. ☑ 🐕 €

© Lord Romsey

BROADLANDS

ROMSEY, HAMPSHIRE SO51 9ZD

www.broadlands.net

Tel: 01794 505010 **Event Enquiry Line:** 01794 505020 **Fax:** 01794 518605 **e-mail:** admin@broadlands.net

Owner: Lord & Lady Romsey **Contact:** Estate Manager

Broadlands, the home of Viscount Palmerston and The Earl Mountbatten of Burma, is open to the public by guided tour only. The Mountbatten Exhibition depicts the life and times of Lord Mountbatten. Limited tours, which include items normally available by appointment, are offered on certain days.

Location: OS Ref. SU355 204. On A3090 at Romsey.

Open/Admission: Details of opening times and admission charges can be obtained from the website, or by telephone.

🔳 ♿ Ground floor. WC. 🔳 Obligatory. 🐕 Guide dogs only.

CALSHOT CASTLE ♯

Calshot, Fawley, Hampshire SO45 1BR

Tel: 023 8089 2023 **www**.english-heritage.org.uk/visits

Owner: English Heritage **Contact:** Hampshire County Council

Henry VIII built this coastal fort in an excellent position, commanding the sea passage to Southampton. The fort houses an exhibition and recreated pre-World War I barrack room.

Location: OS Ref. SU488 025. On spit 2 miles SE of Fawley off B3053.

Open: 25 Mar - 31 Oct: daily, 10am - 4pm.

Admission: Adult £2.50, Child £1.50, Conc. £1.80, Family £6.

ℹ️ WCs. 🔲 🅿 🐕

ELING TIDE MILL

The Toll Bridge, Eling, Totton, Southampton, Hampshire SO40 9HF

Tel: 023 8086 9575 **e-mail:** info@elingtidemill.org.uk

Owner: Eling Tide Mill Trust Ltd & New Forest District Council

Contact: Mr David Blackwell-Eaton

Location: OS Ref. SU365 126. 4m W of Southampton. ¹/₂ m S of the A35.

Open: All year: Wed - Sun and BH Mons, 10am - 4pm. Closed 25/26 Dec. (Prices valid until April 2005.)

Admission: Adult £2, Child £1, OAP £1.50, Family £5.50. Discounts for groups.

EXBURY GARDENS & STEAM RAILWAY 🏛

EXBURY, SOUTHAMPTON, HAMPSHIRE SO45 1AZ

www.exbury.co.uk

Tel: 023 8089 1203 **Fax:** 023 8089 9940

Owner: Edmund de Rothschild Esq **Contact:** Estate Office

HHA/Christie's Garden of the Year 2001. A spectacular 200-acre woodland garden showcasing the world famous Rothschild collection of rhododendrons, azaleas and camellias. Daffodil meadow, Rock Garden, new Exotic Garden and herbaceous borders ensure year-round interest. The Steam Railway enchants visitors of all ages, passing through a Summer Garden, and featuring a bridge, tunnel, viaduct and causeway. A beautiful venue for Wedding receptions (except May) and corporate events. Exbury celebrates its 50th anniversary of opening in 2005.

Location: OS Ref. SU425 005. 11m SE of Totton (A35) via A326 & B3054 & minor road. In New Forest.

Open: 26 Feb - 6 Nov: daily, 10am - 5.30pm. Call for winter opening arrangements.

Admission: High Season (21 March - 5 June*): Adult £7, Child (3-15yrs) £1.50, OAP/Group £6.50 (OAPs £6, Tues - Thurs), Family (2+3) £17, Railway £3, Rover Ticket not available. Low Season: Adult £5, Child (3-15yrs) £1, OAP/Group £4.50, Family (2+3) £12, Railway £2.50, Rover Ticket £3.50. Child under 3yrs Free. Buggies: £3.50. *High Season visitors receive a free Low Season Voucher to see Autumn colours.

🔲 ♿ 📷 ☑ 🍴 Licensed. 🅵 By arrangement. 🔳 🅿 🐕 In grounds, on leads. ☑ Tel for details.

FORT BROCKHURST ♯

Gunner's Way, Gosport, Hampshire PO12 4DS

Tel: 023 9258 1059 **www**.english-heritage.org.uk/visits

Owner: English Heritage **Contact:** Visitor Operations Team

This 19th century fort was built to protect Portsmouth. Today its parade ground, moated keep and sergeants' mess are available to hire as an exciting setting for functions and events of all types. The fort is also open to visitors, when tours will explain the exciting history of the site and the legend behind the ghostly activity in cell no. 3.

Location: OS196, Ref. SU596 020. Off A32, in Gunner's Way, Elson on N side of Gosport.

Open: Please telephone for details.

Admission: Adult £2.60, Child £1.30, Conc. £2.

ℹ️ WCs. ♿ Grounds and ground floor only. 🐕 Dogs on leads (restricted areas).

FURZEY GARDENS
Minstead, Lyndhurst, Hampshire SO43 7GL

Tel: 023 8081 2464 **Fax:** 023 8081 2297

Owner: Furzey Gardens Charitable Trust   **Contact:** Maureen Cole

Location: OS Ref. SU273 114. Minstead village ¹/₂ m N of M27/A31 junction off A337 to Lyndhurst.

Open: Please contact property for details.

GREAT HALL & QUEEN ELEANOR'S GARDEN
Winchester Castle, Winchester, Hampshire SO23 8PJ

Tel: 01962 846476   **Fax:** for bookings 01962 841326

www.hants.gov.uk/discover/places/great-hall.html

Owner: Hampshire County Council   **Contact:** Custodian

The only surviving part of Henry III's medieval castle at Winchester, this 13th century hall was the centre of court and government life. The Round Table closely associated with the legend of King Arthur has hung here for over 700 years. Queen Eleanor's garden is a faithful representation of the medieval garden visited by Kings and Queens of England.

Location: OS Ref. SU477 295. Central Winchester. SE of Westgate archway.

Open: All year: daily, 10am - 5pm. Closed 25/26 Dec. Guided tours and children's quizzes available. Groups are advised to book. Suggested group donation £10. Occasionally closed for Civic events - please see website for details.

Admission: Free. Donations are appreciated towards the upkeep of the Great Hall. By arrangement. ❋

HIGHCLERE CASTLE 📷
& GARDENS
See page 106 for full page entry.

Education Index see page 48

GUILDHALL GALLERY
THE BROADWAY, WINCHESTER SO23 9LJ
www.winchester.gov.uk

Tel: 01962 848289 (gallery) 01962 848269 (office) **Fax:** 01962 848299

e-mail: museums@winchester.gov.uk

Owner: Winchester City Council   **Contact:** Mr C Wardman Bradbury

A constantly changing programme of contemporary exhibitions including painting, sculpture, craft, photography and ceramics.

Location: OS Ref. SU485 293. Winchester - city centre. Situated above the Tourist Office in Winchester's 19th century Guildhall.

Open: Apr - Oct: Mon - Sat, 10am - 5pm; Sun, 12 noon - 5pm. Nov - Mar: Tue - Sat, 10am - 4pm; Sun, 12 noon - 4pm.

Admission: Free.

♿ ❋

NT Photographic Library / Stephen Robson

HINTON AMPNER GARDEN ❧
BRAMDEAN, ALRESFORD, HAMPSHIRE SO24 0LA
www.nationaltrust.org.uk

Tel: 01962 771305   **Fax:** 01962 793101

e-mail: hintonampner@nationaltrust.org.uk

Owner: The National Trust   **Contact:** The Property Manager

"I have learned during the past years what above all I want from a garden: this is tranquillity". so said Ralph Dutton, 8th and last Lord Sherborne, of his garden at Hinton Ampner. He created one of the great gardens of the 20th century, a masterpiece of design based upon the bones of a Victorian garden, in which he united a formal layout with varied and informal planting in pastel shades. It is a garden of all year round interest with scented plants and magnificent vistas over the park and surrounding countryside.

The garden forms the link between the woodland and parkland planting, which he began in 1930, and the house, which he remodelled into a small neo-Georgian manor house in 1936. He made further alterations when the house was reconstructed after a fire in 1960. Today it contains his very fine collection of English furniture, Italian paintings and hard-stones. Both his collection and every aspect of the decoration at Hinton Ampner reflects Ralph Dutton's sure eye and fine aesthetic judgement.

He placed the whole within the rolling Hampshire landscape that he loved and understood so well.

Location: OS Ref. SU597 275. M3/J9 follow signs to Petersfield. On A272, 1m W of Bramdean village, 8m E of Winchester.

Open: House: 29 Mar - 28 Sept: Tues & Weds, also Sats & Suns in Aug, 1.30 - 5pm. Garden: 20 Mar & 26 Mar - 28 Sept, daily except Thur & Fri, 12 noon - 5pm.

Admission: House & Garden: Adult £6, Child (5-16yrs) £3, Child (under 5yrs) Free. Garden only: Adult £5, Child (5-16yrs) £2.50, Child (under 5yrs) Free.

♿ ☕ 🅿 Limited for coaches. 🐕 Guide dogs only.

© Andy Williams

HOUGHTON LODGE 🏠

STOCKBRIDGE, HAMPSHIRE, SO20 6LQ

www.houghtonlodge.co.uk

Tel: 01264 810502 **Fax:** 01264 810063 **e-mail:** info@houghtonlodge.co.uk

Owner/Contact: Captain M W Busk

A haven of peace above the tranquil beauty of the River Test. 5 acres of Grade II* Gardens with fine trees surround 18th Century "Cottage Ornée". Chalk Cob walls surround traditional Kitchen Garden with espaliers and herbs, heated greenhouses, hydroponicum and tropical orchid collection. Formal topiary 'Peacock' Garden. Wild flowers. Artists' materials available. Popular TV/Film location.

Location: OS Ref. SU344 332. 1½ m S of Stockbridge (A30) on minor road to Houghton village.

Open: Garden: 1 Mar - 30 Sept: Sat, Sun & BHs, 10am - 5pm also Mon, Tue, Thur & Fri, 2 - 5pm. House: by appointment.

Admission: Adult £5, Child Free. Groups (35+) (booked): Adult £4.50.

⊤ ☛ ♿ 🎦 By arrangement. **P** 🐕 In grounds, on leads. ▲

KING JOHN'S HOUSE & HERITAGE CENTRE

CHURCH STREET, ROMSEY, HAMPSHIRE SO51 8BT

www.kingjohnshouse.org.uk

Tel/Fax: 01794 512200 **e-mail:** annerhc@aol.com

Owner: King John's House & Tudor Cottage Trust Ltd **Contact:** Anne James

Three historic buildings on one site: Medieval King John's House, containing 14th century graffiti and rare bone floor, Tudor Cottage complete with traditional tea room and Victorian Heritage Centre with recreated shop and parlour. Beautiful period gardens, special events/exhibitions and children's activities. Gift shop and Tourist Information Centre. Receptions and private/corporate functions.

Location: OS Ref. SU353 212. M27/J3. Opposite Romsey Abbey, next to Post Office.

Open: Apr - Sept: Mon - Sat, 10am - 4pm. Oct - Mar: Heritage Centre only. Limited opening on Sundays. Evenings also for pre-booked groups.

Admission: Adult £2.50, Child 50p, Conc. £2. Heritage Centre only: Adult £1.50, Child 50p, Conc. £1. Discounted group booking by appointment.

📷 ⊤ ♿ Partial. ☛ 🎦 By arrangement. **P** Off Latimer St with direct access through King John's Garden. ■ 🐕 Guide dogs only. ❋ ♿ Tel for details.

HURST CASTLE ⌗

Keyhaven, Lymington, Hampshire PO41 0PB

Tel: 01590 642344 www.english-heritage.org.uk/visits

Owner: English Heritage **Contact:** (Managed by) Hurst Castle Services

This was one of the most sophisticated fortresses built by Henry VIII, and later strengthened in the 19th and 20th centuries, to command the narrow entrance to the Solent. There is an exhibition in the Castle, and two huge 38-ton guns form the fort's armaments.

Location: OS196 Ref. SZ319 898. On Pebble Spit S of Keyhaven. Best approach by ferry from Keyhaven. 4 miles SW of Lymington.

Open: 25 Mar - 31 Oct: daily, 10.30am - 5.30pm. Café: open Apr - May weekends & Jun - Sept: daily. Times subject to change in 2005.

Admission: Adult £3, Child £1.80, Conc. £2.70. Prices subject to change April 2005.

ℹ WCs. ♿ Unsuitable. ☛ 🐕 Dogs on leads (restricted areas).

MEDIEVAL MERCHANTS HOUSE ⌗

58 French Street, Southampton, Hampshire SO1 0AT

Tel: 023 8022 1503 www.english-heritage.org.uk

Owner: English Heritage **Contact:** Visitor Operations Team

The life of the prosperous merchant in the Middle Ages is vividly evoked in this recreated, faithfully restored 13th century townhouse.

Location: OS Ref. SU419 112. 58 French Street. ¼ mile S of Bargate off Castle Way. 150yds SE of Tudor House.

Open: 24 Mar - 30 Sept: Sat, Sun & BHs, 10am - 5pm.

Admission: Adult £3.30, Child £1.70, Conc. £2.50.

📷 ♿ 🏠 🐕

Somerley .

NT Photographic Library

MOTTISFONT ABBEY & GARDEN

MOTTISFONT, Nr ROMSEY, HAMPSHIRE SO51 0LP

www.nationaltrust.org.uk/places/mottisfontabbey/

Tel: 01794 340757 **Fax:** 01794 341492 **Recorded Message:** 01794 341220
e-mail: mottisfontabbey@nationaltrust.org.uk

Owner: The National Trust **Contact:** The Property Manager

The Abbey and Garden form the central point of an 809 ha estate including most of the village of Mottisfont, farmland and woods. A tributary of the River Test flows through the garden forming a superb and tranquil setting for a 12th century Augustinian priory which, after the Dissolution, became a house. It contains the spring or "font" from which the place name is derived. The magnificent trees, walled gardens and the National Collection of Old-fashioned Roses combine to provide interest throughout the seasons. The Abbey contains a drawing room decorated by Rex Whistler and the cellarium of the old Priory. In 1996 the Trust acquired Derek Hill's 20th century picture collection.

Location: OS185 Ref. SU327 270. Signposted off A3057 Romsey to Stockbridge road, 4½ m N of Romsey. Also signposted off B3084 Romsey to Broughton. Station: Dunbridge (U) ¾ m.

Open: Garden only: 5 - 20 Mar: Sat & Sun, 11am - 4pm. House & Garden: 21 Mar - 3 Jun: daily except Thur & Fri, 11am - 5pm (Garden 6pm); 4 - 26 Jun: daily, 11am - 5pm (Garden 8.30pm); 27 Jun - 31 Aug: daily except Fri, 11am - 5pm (Garden 6pm); 1 Sept - 30 Oct: daily except Thur & Fri, 11am - 5pm (Garden 6pm). Shop: same as Garden but closed 5 Feb - 20 Mar. Kitchen Café: as House (last orders 5pm). Open Good Fri, 11am - 6pm. Last adm. 1 hr before closing.

Admission: Adult £7, Child (5-18yrs) £3.50, Family £17.50. Group (15+) discount available; for every five paying visitors, sixth visitor goes free.

▢ ♿ Partial. ☕ ⟨⟩Licensed. **P** ♿Guide dogs only. ▣ ☎Tel for details.

NETLEY ABBEY ⌗

Netley, Southampton, Hampshire

Tel: 01424 775705 **www.**english-heritage.org.uk/visits

Owner: English Heritage **Contact:** Battle Abbey

A peaceful and beautiful setting for the extensive ruins of this 13th century Cistercian abbey converted in Tudor times for use as a house.

Location: OS Ref. SU453 089. In Netley, 4 miles SE of Southampton, facing Southhampton Water.

Open: Any reasonable time.

Admission: Free.

♿ **P** ♿Dogs on leads. ▣

NORTHINGTON GRANGE ⌗

New Alresford, Hampshire

Tel: 01424 775705 **www.**english-heritage.org.uk/visits

Owner: English Heritage **Contact:** Battle Abbey

Northington Grange and its landscaped park as you see it today, formed the core of the house as designed by William Wilkins in 1809. It is one of the earliest Greek Revival houses in Europe.

Location: OS 185, SU562 362. 4 miles N of New Alresford off B3046 along farm track - 450 metres.

Open: 24 Mar - 31 Oct: daily 10am - 6pm (closes 5pm in Oct, & 3pm in Jun & July for Opera evenings). 1 Nov - 31 Mar : daily 10am - 4pm. Closed 24-26 Dec and 1 Jan.

Admission: Free.

♿ Wheelchair access (with assistance). **P** ♿Dogs on leads. ▣

PORTCHESTER CASTLE ⌗

Portsmouth, Hampshire PO16 9QW

Tel/Fax: 023 9237 8291 **www.**english-heritage.org.uk/visits

Owner: English Heritage **Contact:** Visitor Operations Team

The rallying point of Henry V's expedition to Agincourt and the ruined palace of King Richard II. This grand castle has a history going back nearly 2,000 years including the most complete Roman walls in Europe. New interactive exhibition telling the story of the castle and interactive audio tour.

Location: OS196, Ref. SU625 046. On S side of Portchester off A27, M27/J11.

Open: 24 Mar - 30 Sept: daily, 10am - 6pm. 1 Oct - 31 Mar: daily, 10am - 4pm. Closed 24 - 26 Dec & 1 Jan.

Admission: Adult £3.70, Child £1.90, Conc. £2.80. 15% discount for groups (11+).

ℹWCs. Exhibition. ▢ ♿Partial. ▢ **P** ♿In grounds, on leads. ▣ ☎Tel for details.

PORTSMOUTH CATHEDRAL

Portsmouth, Hampshire PO1 2HH

Tel: 023 9282 3300 **Fax:** 023 9229 5480 **Contact:** Rosemary Fairfax

Maritime Cathedral founded in 12th century and finally completed in 1991. A member of the ship's crew of Henry VIII's flagship Mary Rose is buried in Navy Aisle.

Location: OS Ref. SZ633 994. 1½ m from end of M275. Follow signs to Historic Ship and Old Portsmouth.

Open: 7.45am - 6pm all year. Sun service: 8am, 9.30am, 11am, 6pm. Weekday: 6pm (Choral on Tues and Fris in term time).

Admission: Donation appreciated.

SANDHAM MEMORIAL CHAPEL ✿

Burghclere, Nr Newbury, Hampshire RG20 9JT

Tel/Fax: 01635 278394 **e-mail:** sandham@nationaltrust.org.uk
www.nationaltrust.org.uk/Sandham

Owner: The National Trust **Contact:** The Custodian

This red brick chapel was built in the 1920s for the artist Stanley Spencer to fill with paintings inspired by his experiences of the First World War. Influenced by Giotto's Arena Chapel in Padua, Spencer took five years to complete what is arguably his finest achievement. The chapel is set amidst lawns and orchards with views across Watership Down. Pictures best viewed on a bright day.

Location: OS Ref. SU463 608. 4m S of Newbury, ½m E of A34, W end of Burghclere.

Open: 5 - 20 Mar & 5 - 27 Nov: Sat & Sun, 11am - 4pm. 23 Mar - 30 Oct: Wed - Sun, 11am - 5pm. Open BH Mons. Dec - Feb 2006: by appointment only.

Admission: Adult £3, Child £1.50. Groups by prior arrangement, no reduction.

♿Portable ramp for entrance. ⟨f⟩By arrangement. ▣ ♿In grounds, on leads. ▣

SOMERLEY

See page 107 for full page entry.

STRATFIELD SAYE HOUSE ⌂

Stratfield Saye, Basingstoke RG7 2BZ

Tel: 01256 882882 **Fax:** 01256 881466 **www.**stratfield-saye.co.uk

Owner: The Duke of Wellington **Contact:** The Administrator

Family home of the Dukes of Wellington since 1817.

Location: OS Ref. SU700 615. Equidistant from Reading (M4/J11) & Basingstoke (M3/J6) 1½ m W of the A33.

Open: 25 - 28 Mar (Easter weekend) & 11 Jul - 7 Aug: daily, 11.30am (Sats & Suns, 10.30am) - 3.30pm (last admission).

Admission: Adult £7.50, Child £4, OAP/Student £6.50. Groups (max 40, must book): Adult £9, OAP £8.

▢ ♿ WC. ☕ ⟨f⟩Obligatory. **P** ♿Guide dogs only.

TITCHFIELD ABBEY ⌗

Titchfield, Southampton, Hampshire

Tel: 01329 842133 **www.**english-heritage.org.uk/visits

Owner: English Heritage **Contact:** The Titchfield Abbey Association

Remains of a 13th century abbey overshadowed by the grand Tudor gatehouse. Reputedly some of Shakespeare's plays were performed here for the first time. Under local management of Titchfield Abbey Society.

Location: OS Ref. SU544 067. ½ mile N of Titchfield off A27.

Open: 25 Mar - 30 Sept: daily, 10am - 6pm (5pm in Oct). 1 Nov - 31 Mar (closed 25 Dec): daily, 10am - 4pm. Times subject to change in 2005.

Admission: Free.

♿ **P** ♿Dogs on leads. ▣

NT Photographic Library: Andrea Jones

THE VYNE ❧

SHERBORNE ST JOHN, BASINGSTOKE RG24 9HL

www.nationaltrust.org.uk

Tel: 01256 883858 **Infoline:** 01256 881337 **Fax:** 01256 881720

e-mail: thevyne@nationaltrust.org.uk

Owner: The National Trust   **Contact:** The Property Manager

Built in the early 16th century for Lord Sandys, Henry VIII's Lord Chamberlain, the house acquired a classical portico in the mid-17th century (the first of its kind in England) and contains a fascinating Tudor chapel with Renaissance glass, a Palladian staircase and a wealth of old panelling and fine furniture. The attractive grounds feature herbaceous borders and a wild garden, with lawns, lakes and woodland walks. Weddings & Functions: Stone Gallery licensed for Civil Weddings. Receptions and private/corporate functions in Walled Garden or Brewhouse restaurant.

Location: OS Ref. SU639 576. 4m N of Basingstoke between Bramley & Sherborne St John.

Open: House: 26 Mar - 30 Oct: Sat & Sun, 11am - 5pm; 23 Mar - 26 Oct: Mon - Wed, 1 - 5pm. Grounds/Shop/Restaurant: 5 Feb - 20 Mar: Sat & Sun; 23 Mar - 30 Oct: Sat - Wed; 4 Feb - 26 Mar 2006: Sat & Sun, 11am - 5pm. Open BH Mons & Good Fri. Shop & Restaurant also 3 Nov - 23 Dec, Thur - Sun, 11am - 3pm. Group visits: 23 Mar - 26 Oct: Mon - Wed, by appointment only.

Admission: House & Grounds: Adult £7, Child £3.50, Family £17.50, Groups £5.50. Grounds only: Adult £4, Child £2.

ⓘ No photography in house. ⬜ ⬜ ⬜ ⬜ ⬜ ⬜ ⬜ P ⬜ ⬜ ⬜ Tel for details.

LOCAL FOOD

Watercress

Hampshire's association with watercress goes back to the early 19th century when it was a staple of the working classes and was most often used for breakfast in a sandwich. If people were too poor and could not afford bread they would just eat the watercress. Known as 'poor man's bread' it was, and is, grown commercially in the clear chalk streams of Hampshire, and was then taken by train to Covent Garden for sale. Grown today by the same traditional growing methods as in the past - in washed gravel beds bathed in fresh flowing spring water - watercress is one of the world's most pure and 'ancient' vegetables with a heritage stretching back well over twenty centuries. Its peppery leaf is excellent served with orange segments as a salad and dressed with olive oil and orange juice. It's delicious with an omelette or scrambled eggs, or as an accompaniment for game bird dishes, or simply made into a smooth, vibrant green soup which can be served hot or cold. (see page 114).

GILBERT WHITE'S HOUSE & THE OATES MUSEUM

THE WAKES, HIGH STREET, SELBORNE, ALTON GU34 3JH

Tel: 01420 511275

Owner: Oates Memorial Trust   **Contact:** Mrs Carey Hides

Charming refurbished 18th century house, home of Rev Gilbert White, author of *The Natural History of Selborne*. Lovely garden with many plants of the Georgian era. Tea parlour with fare based on 18th century recipes and excellent gift shop. Exhibition on Captain Oates of Antarctic fame.

Location: OS Ref. SU741 336. On W side of B3006, in village of Selborne 4m NW of the A3.

Open: 1 Jan - 24 Dec: 11am - 5pm. Groups by prior arrangement.

Admission: Adult £5, Child £3, OAP £4.50.

ⓘ No photography in house. ⬜ ⬜ ⬜ Partial. ⬜ ⬜ By arrangement. P ⬜ Guide dogs only. ⬜ ⬜ Tel for details.

WINCHESTER CATHEDRAL

Winchester, Hants SO23 9LS

Tel: 01962 857200 **Fax:** 01962 857201 **www.**winchester-cathedral.org.uk

The Cathedral was founded in 1079.

Location: OS Ref. SU483 293. Winchester city centre.

Open: 8.30am - 6pm. East end closes 5pm. Access may be restricted during services. Weekday services:7.40am, 8am, 5.30pm. Sun services: 8am, 10am, 11.15am, 3.30pm.

Admission: Recommended donations. Adult £3.50, Conc. £2.50. Photo permits £2, Video permits £3. Library & Triforium Gallery: £1, Tower & Roof tours: £3 (age restrictions 12 - 70). Groups (10+) must book, tel: 01962 857225. Special tours available.

©National Trust Photographic Library

WINCHESTER CITY MILL ✤

BRIDGE STREET, WINCHESTER

www.nationaltrust.org.uk/winchestercitymill

Tel/Fax: 01962 870057 **e-mail:** anne.aldridge@nationaltrust.org.uk

Owner: The National Trust **Contact:** Anne Aldridge

Spanning the River Itchen and rebuilt in 1744 on an earlier medieval site, this corn mill has a chequered history. The machinery is completely restored making this building an unusual survivor of a working town mill. It has a delightful island garden and impressive mill races roaring through the building.

Location: OS Ref. SU485 293. M3/J9 & 10. St Swithun's Bridge nr King Alfred's statue. 15 min walk from station.

Open: 5 - 27 Mar: Sat & Sun; 28 Mar - 10 Apr & 4 Jul - 23 Dec: Mon - Sun; 13 Apr - 3 Jul: Wed - Sun; 11am - 5pm. Last entry 4.30pm.

Admission: Adult £3, Child £1.50, Family £7.50. NT members Free.

⬜ 🅰Partial. 🅸By arrangement. 🅿Nearby public car park. ◼ 🅧

©English Heritage Photo Library/Jonathan Bailey

Hurst Castle.

WOLVESEY CASTLE ⌗

College Street, Wolvesey, Winchester, Hampshire SO23 8NB

Tel: 01962 854766 **www.**english-heritage.org.uk/visits

Owner: English Heritage **Contact:** Visitor Operations Team

The fortified palace of Wolvesey was the chief residence of the Bishops of Winchester and one of the greatest of all medieval buildings in England. Its extensive ruins still reflect the importance and immense wealth of the Bishops of Winchester, occupants of the richest seat in medieval England. Wolvesey was frequently visited by medieval and Tudor monarchs and was the scene of the wedding feast of Philip of Spain and Mary Tudor in 1554.

Location: OS Ref. SU484 291. ¾ mile SE of Winchester Cathedral, next to the Bishop's Palace; access from College Street.

Open: 25 Mar - 30 Sept: daily, 10am - 5pm. Times subject to change.

Admission: Free.

⬜ 🅰Grounds. 🅧In grounds, on leads.

LOCAL FOOD

Watercress Soup

A traditional Hampshire recipe.

Two good bunches of watercress rinsed, thoroughly, destalked and roughly chopped
2 medium potatoes, peeled and sliced
White ends of 4 slim leeks, sliced
50g butter
1.5l light chicken stock, vegetable bouillon or water
2 cloves garlic, peeled and finely sliced
150ml double or single cream, or yoghurt
Grated nutmeg to serve (optional)
Salt and freshly ground black pepper

Melt the butter in a large pan, add the potatoes, leeks, garlic and watercress, season with salt and stir to coat with the butter.
Cover and sweat over a very low heat for 15 minutes, stirring occasionally. Add the stock or water, bring to the boil, reduce the heat and simmer, covered, for 15 minutes or until the potatoes are soft.
Allow to cool and liquidise well, then stir in the cream or yoghurt and reheat gently. Single cream and yoghurt may curdle if the temperature gets too hot. Add a few good grinds of black pepper, then check and if necessary adjust the seasoning. Serve plain, or with some drizzled cream, some grated nutmeg and a sprig of watercress to garnish.

Somerley.

Map 4

Owner:
Mr & Mrs D Kendrick

BOUGHTON MONCHELSEA PLACE

www.boughtonmonchelseaplace.co.uk

Boughton Monchelsea Place is a battlemented manor house dating from the 16th century, set in its own country estate just outside Maidstone, within easy reach of London and the channel ports. This Grade I listed building has always been privately owned and is still lived in as a family home.

From the lawns surrounding the property there are spectacular views over unspoilt Kent countryside, with the historic deer park in the foreground. These views are shared by the 20 acre event site set back a little way from the house. A wicket gate leads from the grounds to the medieval church of St Peter, with its rose garden and ancient lych gate. At the rear of the house are to be found a pretty courtyard and walled gardens, together with an extensive range of Tudor barns and outbuildings.

Inside the house, rooms vary in character from Tudor through to Georgian Gothic; worthy of note are the fine Jacobean staircase and sundry examples of heraldic stained glass. Furnishings and paintings are mainly Victorian, with a few earlier pieces; the atmosphere is friendly and welcoming throughout.

The premises are licensed for Civil marriage ceremonies, although wedding receptions in the house may only be held on weekday afternoons. In addition we welcome conferences, group visits, location work and all types of corporate, private and public functions, but please note times of availability. Use outside these hours is sometimes possible, subject to negotiation. All clients are guaranteed exclusive use of this prestigious venue.

▶ CONTACT
Mrs M Kendrick
Boughton
Monchelsea Place
Boughton Monchelsea
Nr Maidstone
Kent ME17 4BU

Tel: 01622 743120
Fax: 01622 741168

e-mail: mk@
boughtonmonchelsea
place.co.uk

▶ LOCATION
OS Ref. TQ772 499

On B2163, 5 1/2 m from M20/J8 or 4 1/2 m from Maidstone via A229.

▶ OPENING TIMES
All year by prior arrangement only.

House & Garden
Not open to individual visitors.

Group visits/ house tours:
(10-50),
Mon - Thur, 9am - 4pm.

Private functions:
Mon - Fri, 9am - 9pm.

Outdoor Event Site
365 days a year:
8am - 11.30pm.

▶ ADMISSION
Gardens &
Guided House Tour
Adult £5.00

Venue Hire
Prices on application.

Day Delegate Rate
From £40.

▶ SPECIAL EVENTS
Mar 27/28
Classic Car & Transport Show.

Jul 12 - 17
Open Air Shakespeare 'Twelfth Night'.

i Film location.

By arrangement.

By arrangement.

By arrangement.

CONFERENCE/FUNCTION		
ROOM	SIZE	MAX CAPACITY
Entrance Hall	25' x 19'	50 Theatre
Dining Room	31' x 19'	50 Dining
Drawing Room	28' x 19'	40 Reception
Courtyard Room	37' x 13'	60 Theatre

NTPL / Rupert Truman

Map 4

Owner:
The National Trust

▶ **CONTACT**

The Property Manager
Chartwell
Westerham
Kent   TN16 1PS

Tel: 01732 866368
01732 868381

Fax: 01732 868193

e-mail: chartwell@
nationaltrust.org.uk

▶ **LOCATION**
OS Ref. TQ455 515

2m S of Westerham,
forking left off B2026.

Bus: 246 from Bromley
South and 401 from
Sevenoaks (Suns &
BHs only).
Please check times.

CHARTWELL

www.nationaltrust.org.uk/chartwell

The family home of Sir Winston Churchill from 1924 until the end of his life. He said of Chartwell, simply *'I love the place - a day away from Chartwell is a day wasted'*. With magnificent views over the Weald of Kent it is not difficult to see why.

The rooms are left as they were in Sir Winston & Lady Churchill's lifetime with daily papers, fresh flowers grown from the garden and his famous cigars. Photographs and books evoke his career, interests and happy family life. Museum and exhibition rooms contain displays and sound recordings and superb collections of memorabilia from Sir Winston's political career, including uniforms and a 'siren-suit'.

The garden studio contains Sir Winston's easel and paintbox, as well as many of his paintings. Terraced and water gardens descend to the lake, the gardens also include a golden rose walk, planted by Sir Winston and Lady Churchill's children on the occasion of their golden wedding anniversary, and the Marlborough Pavilion decorated with frescoes depicting the battle of Blenheim. Visitors can see the garden walls that Churchill built with his own hands, as well as the pond stocked with the golden orfe he loved to feed.

The Mulberry Room at the restaurant can be booked for meetings, conferences, lunches and dinners. Please telephone for details.

▶ **OPENING TIMES**

19 March - 3 July and
1 Sept - 30 October
Wed - Sun & BHs
11am - 5pm.

5 July - 31 August
Tue - Sun & BHs
11am - 5pm.

Last admission 4.15pm.

▶ **ADMISSION**

House, Garden & Studio
Adult £8.00
Child £4.00
Family £20.00

Garden & Studio only
Adult £4.00
Child £2.00
Family £10.00

NTPL / Andreas von Einsiedel

NTPL / Ian Shaw

Conference facilities.   Partial. WC. Please telephone before visit.   Licensed.
By arrangement.   P In grounds, on leads.   Tel for details.

Map 4

CHIDDINGSTONE CASTLE

EDENBRIDGE

www.chiddingstone-castle.org.uk

Owner:
Denys Eyre Bower
Bequest Reg.
Charity Trust

▶ **CONTACT**

Mrs R Vernon
Chiddingstone Castle
Edenbridge
Kent TN8 7AD

Tel: 01892 870347

▶ **LOCATION**
OS Ref. TQ497 452

B2027, turn to
Chiddingstone at Bough
Beech, 1m further on
to crossroads, then
straight to castle.

10m from Tonbridge,
Tunbridge Wells and
Sevenoaks. 4m
Edenbridge. Accessible
from A21 and M25/J5.

London 35m.

Bus: Enquiries:
Tunbridge Wells TIC
01892 515675.

Rail: Tonbridge,
Tunbridge Wells,
Edenbridge then taxi.
Penshurst then 2m walk.

Air: Gatwick 15m.

Henry Streatfeild, Squire of Chiddingstone, intoxicated by the current passion for medieval chivalry, embarked on the transformation of his ancient home into a fantasy castle in 1803, the first major commission of young William Atkinson, which a contemporary guidebook predicted would be the 'fairest house' in Kent. After five hectic years work ceased, leaving a random mixture of old and new. The Establishment was not impressed: today, we find the place enchanting. In 1955 the now decrepit castle was bought by the distinguished collector Denys Bower – greater than Beckford or Burrell. They had wealth and expert agents –

he had neither. He died in 1977, leaving everything to the Nation, for the enjoyment of posterity, to be run as a living home, not a museum. The place is now administered by a registered private Charitable Trust. The restoration of the fabric being completed, the Trust is now improving the display of the collections, as contemplated by Denys Bower: Royal Stuart portraits and mementoes, Japanese lacquer (the finest private collection in the West), Egyptian and oriental antiquities. The 35-acre landscaped park (listed garden of Kent) has been restored – a haven for wildlife, providing idyllic walks.

▶ **OPENING TIMES**

Summer

Easter Hol, All BHs.

June - September

Thur: 2 - 5.30pm

Sun & BHs:
11.30am - 5.30pm
Last admission 5pm.

Winter

Open only for specially
booked groups (20-80).
First Sun in Dec: Christmas
Fair, 10.30am - 4pm –
please enquire.

Great Hall

▶ **ADMISSION**

Adult	£5.00
Child*	£3.00
OAP	£5.00
Student	£5.00

Groups** (Booked 20-80)
Adult	£4.00
Child*	£3.00
OAP	£4.00
Student	£4.00

* Child under 16yrs
accompanied by paying adult.
Under 5 yrs Free.

** Usual hours, other times by
appointment. School groups
only by appointment.

CONFERENCE/FUNCTION		
ROOM	SIZE	MAX CAPACITY
Assembly Rm	14' x 35'	50
Seminar Rms	15' x 15'	
Stable Block	36' x 29'	

ℹ️ Conferences, receptions, concerts. No photography in house; no smoking, prams/buggies, large bags or mobile phones.

🛍️

🍸 Available for special events. Wedding receptions.

♿ Partial (grounds unsuitable). WC.

☕ Licensed.

🅿️ Ample for cars. Limited for coaches, please book.

📚 Teachers' pack. Educational programme.

🐕 In grounds, on leads.

🔔 ❄️

🛡️ **SPECIAL EVENTS**
Chiddingstone may be
closed without notice for
Special Events.

CHIDDINGSTONE CASTLE...

Stable Lecture Room

The Assembly Room

The Seminar Room

SMALL CONFERENCES AND FUNCTIONS:

We have some facilities for small conferences and functions. They can provide a delightful alternative to traditional hotel accommodation, and are ideal for training or get-away-from-it-all meetings. They must be seen prior to booking. More details on request.

CIVIL MARRIAGES:

The Great Hall is licensed by Kent County Council, and is specially attractive to those who desire the dignity of a church ceremony without the religious aspect. We offer all features of wedding celebrations, including reception of guests and refreshments.

EDUCATION:

We welcome visits from schools who wish to use the collections in connection with classroom work. No anxiety for the teachers (admitted free). The children are safe here, can picnic and play in the grounds. Dr Nicholas Reeves F.S.A, Honorary Curator, is responsible for educational developments. Please enquire.

© Photographs Ron Vernon.

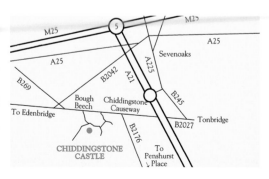

Map 4

COBHAM HALL 🏛

www.cobhamhall.com

Cobham Hall is now a leading Girls Boarding & Day School, and has been visited by several English monarchs from Elizabeth I to Edward VIII. Charles Dickens used regularly to walk through the grounds from his house in Higham to the Leather Bottle Public House in Cobham Village.

Cobham Hall is one of the largest, finest and most important houses in Kent, it is an outstanding beautiful red brick mansion in Elizabethan, Jacobean, Carolean and 18th century styles, it yields much interest to the students of art, architecture & history. The Elizabethan Wings were begun in 1584, whilst the central section, which contains the Gilt Hall, was wonderfully decorated by John Webb.

Further rooms were decorated by James Wyatt in the 18th century.

In 1883 the Hon Ivo Bligh, later the 8th Earl of Darnley, led the victorious English cricket team against Australia bringing the Ashes home to Cobham.

GARDENS

The Park was landscaped for the 4th Earl by Humphry Repton, and is now gradually being restored. The Gothic Dairy, Aviary and the Pump House are all being restored. The gardens are beautiful at all times of the year but especially delightful in the spring when the spring flowers are out in full bloom.

Owner:
Cobham Hall
School

▶ **CONTACT**

Mr N Powell
Bursar
Cobham Hall, Cobham
Kent DA12 3BL

Tel: 01474 823371
Fax: 01474 825904
e-mail:
taylorb@cobhamhall.
com

▶ **LOCATION**
OS Ref. TQ683 689

Situated adjacent to the A2/M2. ¹/₂ m S of A2 4m W of Strood. 8m E of M25/J2 between Gravesend & Rochester.

London 25m
Rochester 5m
Canterbury 30m

Rail: Meopham 3m
Gravesend 5m
Taxis at both stations.

Air: Gatwick 45 mins.
Heathrow 60 mins,

ℹ️ Conferences, business or social functions, 150 acres of parkland for sports, corporate events, open air concerts, sports centre, indoor swimming pool, art studios, music wing, tennis courts, helicopter landing area. Filming and photography. No smoking.

🍽 In-house catering team for private, corporate hospitality and wedding receptions. (cap. 100).

♿ House tour involves 2 staircases, ground floor access for w/chairs.

☕ Cream teas 2 - 5pm on open days. Other meals by arrangement.

🚶 Obligatory guided tours; tour time 1¹/₂ hrs. Garden tours arranged outside standard opening times.

🅿 Ample. Pre-booked coach groups are welcome any time.

▦ Guide provided, Adult £4.50, Child / OAP £3.50.

🐕 In grounds, on leads.

🛏 18 single and 18 double with bathroom. 22 single and 22 double without bathroom. Dormitory. Groups only.

🔔

▶ **OPENING TIMES**

March:
20, 23, 25, 27, 28, 30.

April:
3, 6, 10.

July:
6, 10, 13, 17, 20, 24, 27, 31.

August:
3, 7, 10, 14, 17, 21, 24, 28, 31.

House:
2 - 5pm. Last tour at 4pm.

Dates could change, please telephone to confirm.

▶ **ADMISSION**

Adult £4.50
Child (4-14yrs.) £3.50
OAP £3.50

Gardens & Parkland
Self-guided tour £1.50

Historical/Conservation tour of Grounds
(by arrangement)

Per person £3.50

▶ **SPECIAL EVENTS**

MAR 25, 27 & 29
Easter Opening
(+ House open 2 - 5pm).

APR 3
National Garden Scheme Day
(+ House open 2 - 5pm).

JUL 17
National Garden Scheme Day.
(+ House open 2 - 5pm).

CONFERENCE/FUNCTION

ROOM	SIZE	MAX CAPACITY
Gilt Hall	41' x 34'	180
Wyatt Dining Rm	49' x 23'	135
Clifton Dining Rm	24' x 23'	75
Activities Centre	119' x 106'	300

English Heritage Photo Library / Jonathan Bailey

THE HOME OF CHARLES DARWIN

www.english-heritage.org.uk/visits

Map 4

Owner:
English Heritage

▶ CONTACT

Visitor Operations Team
Down House
Luxted Road
Downe
Kent   BR6 7JT

Tel: 01689 859119
Fax: 01689 862755

▶ LOCATION

OS Ref, TQ431 611

In Luxted Road, Downe, off A21 near Biggin Hill.

Rail: From London Victoria or Charing Cross.

Bus: Orpington (& Bus R8) or Bromley South (& Bus 146). Buses R8 & 146 do not run on Sunday.

A visit to Down House is a fascinating journey of discovery for all the family. This was the family home of Charles Darwin for over 40 years and now you can explore it to the full.

See the actual armchair in which Darwin wrote *'On the Origin of Species'*, which shocked and then revolutionised the way we think about the origins of mankind. His study is much the same as it was in his lifetime and is filled with belongings that give you an intimate glimpse into both his studies and everyday life.

At Down House you will discover both sides of Darwin - the great thinker and the family man.

Explore the family rooms where the furnishings have been painstakingly restored. An audio tour narrated by Sir David Attenborough will bring the house to life and increase your understanding of Darwin's revolutionary theory. Upstairs you will find state-of-the-art interpretation of the scientific significance of the house – especially designed to inspire a younger audience.

Outside, take the Sandwalk which he paced daily in search of inspiration, then stroll in lovely gardens. Complete your day by sampling the delicious selection of home-made cakes in the tea room.

▶ OPENING TIMES*

Wed - Sun & BHs on the following dates:

2 February - 23 March 10am - 4pm.

24 March - 30 September 10am - 6pm.

October: 10am - 5pm.

November - 19 December 10am - 4pm.

Closed:
19 Dec 2005 - 31 Jan 2006

* Times subject to change.

▶ ADMISSION

Adult £6.60
Child £3.30
Conc. £5.00
Family (2+3) £16.50

Groups (11+)
.... 15% discount

Tour leader and coach driver have free entry. 1 extra place for every 20 additional people.

WCs.

Free. English, French, German, Japanese & for visually impaired.

Limited for coaches.

Guide dogs only.

Closed January.

Tel for details.

English Heritage Photo Library / Jonathan Bailey

English Heritage Photo Library

Map 4

DOVER CASTLE ▢

AND THE SECRET WARTIME TUNNELS

www.english-heritage.org.uk/visits

Journey deep into the White Cliffs of Dover and discover the top secret World War II tunnels. Through sight, sound and smells, relive the wartime drama of the underground hospital as a wounded Battle of Britain pilot is taken to the operating theatre in a bid to save his life. Discover how life would have been during the planning days of the Dunkirk evacuation and Operation Dynamo as you are led around the network of tunnels and casements housing the communications centre.

Above ground you can explore the magnificent medieval keep and inner bailey of King Henry II. Visit the evocative Princess of Wales' Royal Regiment Museum. There is also the Roman Lighthouse and Anglo-Saxon church to see or take an audio tour of the intriguing 13th-century underground fortifications and medieval battlements. Enjoy magnificent views of the White Cliffs from Admiralty lookout.

See the exciting 'Life Under Siege' exhibition, and discover, through a dramatic light and sound presentation, how it must have felt to be a garrison soldier defending Dover Castle against the French King in 1216. In the Keep, see a reconstruction of the castle in preparation for a visit from Henry VIII and visit the hands-on exhibition explaining the travelling Tudor court. The land train will help you around this huge site.

Throughout the summer there are many fun events taking place, bringing the castle alive through colourful enactments and living history.

Owner:
English Heritage

▶ **CONTACT**

Visitor Operations Team
Dover Castle
Dover
Kent CT16 1HU

Tel: 01304 211067
Info Line: 01304 201628

Venue Hire and Hospitality:
Hospitality Manager
Tel: 01304 211067

▶ **LOCATION**

OS Ref. TR326 416

Easy access from A2 and M20. Well signed from Dover centre and east side of Dover.
2 hrs from central London.

Rail: London Charing Cross or Victoria
1¹/₂ hrs.

Bus: Freephone
0870 6082608.

CONFERENCE/FUNCTION

ROOM	MAX CAPACITY
The Castle Keep	standing 120 dining 90
Keep Yard Café	theatre-style 150
Secret Wartime Tunnels	standing 120 dining 80 theatre-style 80
Marquee on Palace Green	standing 400 dining 265

ℹ WCs. 📷 Two.

🍷 Exclusive private and corporate hire. Tel: 01034 211067.

♿ Lift for access to tunnels. Courtyard and grounds, some very steep slopes.

🍴 3 restaurants, hot and cold food and drinks.

🚶 Tour of tunnels approx. every 20 mins, more at peak times when a 30 min. wait can occur.

Ⓟ Ample. Groups welcome, discounts available. Free entry for drivers. One extra place for each additional group of 20.

▥ Free visits available for schools. Education centre. Pre-booking essential.

❄

🛡 Tel for details.

English Heritage Photo Library

▶ **OPENING TIMES***

Summer

24 March - 30 June & September:
Daily, 10am - 6pm.

July & August:
Daily, 9.30am - 6.30pm.

October:
Daily, 10am - 5pm.

Winter

1 November - 31 January
Thur - Mon, 10am - 4pm.
(Closed 24 - 26 Dec & 1 Jan.)

1 February - 31 March
Daily, 10am - 4pm.

NB. Keep closes at 5pm on days when events are booked.

Venue Hire and Hospitality

English Heritage offers exclusive use of the Castle Keep or Tunnels in the evenings for receptions, dinners, product launches and themed banquets.

▶ **ADMISSION**

Adult £8.95
Child £4.50
Conc. £6.70
Family (2+3) £22.40

Groups: 15% discount for groups (11+).

Map 4

Owner:
Groombridge Asset
Management

▸ **CONTACT**

The Estate Office
Groombridge Place
Groombridge
Tunbridge Wells
Kent TN3 9QG

Tel: 01892 863999
01892 861444

Fax: 01892 863996

e-mail: office@
groombridge.co.uk

▸ **LOCATION**

OS Ref. TQ534 375

Groombridge Place
Gardens are located on
the B2110 just off the
A264. 4m SW of
Tunbridge Wells and
9m E of East Grinstead.

Rail: London Charing
Cross to Tunbridge
Wells 55mins.
(Taxis).

Air: Gatwick.

GROOMBRIDGE PLACE GARDENS 🏛

www.groombridge.co.uk

There's magic and mystery, history and intrigue, romance and peace at this beautiful venue – which provides such an unusual combination of a traditional heritage garden with the excitement, challenge and contemporary landscaping of the ancient woodland – appealing to young and old alike.

First laid out in 1674 on a gentle, south-facing slope, the formal walled gardens are set against the romantic backdrop of a medieval moat, surrounding a classical Restoration manor house (not open to the public) and were designed as outside rooms. These award-winning gardens include magnificent herbaceous borders, the enchanting White Rose Garden with over 20 varieties of white roses, a Secret Garden with deep shade and cooling waters in a tiny hidden corner, Paradise Walk and Oriental Garden, the Knot Garden and Nut Walk and the Drunken Garden with its crazy topiary. The gardens feature wonderful seasonal colour throughout spring, summer and autumn.

In complete contrast on a high hillside above the walled gardens and estate vineyard is the Enchanted Forest, where quirky and mysterious gardens have been developed in the ancient woodland by innovative designer, Ivan Hicks, to challenge the imagination. Children love the Dark Walk, Tree Fern Valley, Village of the Groms, the Serpent's Lair and the Mystic Pool, the Romany Camp, Double Spiral and the Giant Swings Walk. There are also Birds of Prey flying displays three times a day, a canal boat cruise to and from the Forest – plus a full programme of special events.

▸ **OPENING TIMES**

Summer
Gardens
21 March - 5 November
Daily, 9.30am - 6pm (or
dusk if earlier).

The house is not open
to visitors.

▸ **ADMISSION**

Adult £8.50
Child* (3-12yrs)........ £7.00
Senior £7.20
Family (2+2) £29.50
Groups (20+)
Adult £7.00
Child/School...........£5.25
Senior ....£6.00/£5.25
Student £6.00
School Youth £5.25

*Child under 3yrs Free.

ℹ Film location.

🛍

❄

♿ Partial. WCs.

☕ 🍴 Licensed.

🏃 By arrangement.

🅿 Limited for coaches.

▪

🐕 Guide dogs only.

🔔

▾ **SPECIAL EVENTS**
APR 24
A Celebration of
St George's Day
JUN 11 - 19
Midsummer Garden
Celebration
AUG 7
Wings, Wheels and Steam.
NOV 5
Fireworks Spectacular set
to music

123

HEVER CASTLE & GARDENS 🏛

www.hevercastle.co.uk

Map 4

Owner:
Hever Castle Ltd

▶ CONTACT

Anne Watt
Hever Castle
Hever, Edenbridge
Kent TN8 7NG

Infoline: 01732 865224
Fax: 01732 866796
e-mail:
mail@HeverCastle.co.uk

▶ LOCATION

OS Ref. TQ476 450

Exit M25/J5 & J6
M23/J10,
1¹⁄₂ m S of B2027 at
Bough Beech,
3m SE of Edenbridge.

Rail: Hever Station
1m (no taxis),
Edenbridge Town
3m (taxis).

Hever Castle dates back to 1270, when the gatehouse, outer walls and the inner moat were first built. 200 years later the Bullen (or Boleyn) family added the comfortable Tudor manor house constructed within the walls. This was the childhood home of Anne Boleyn, Henry VIII's second wife and mother of Elizabeth I. There are many items relating to the Tudors, including two books of hours (prayer books) signed and inscribed by Anne Boleyn. The Castle was later given to Henry VIII's fourth wife, Anne of Cleves.

In 1903, the estate was bought by the American millionaire William Waldorf Astor, who became a British subject and the first Lord Astor of Hever. He invested an immense amount of time, money and imagination in restoring the castle and grounds. Master craftsmen were employed and the castle was filled with a magnificent collection of furniture, tapestries and other works of art.

'From Castles to Country Houses' the Miniature Model Houses exhibition, a collection of 1/12 scale model houses, room views and gardens, depicts life in English Country Houses.

GARDENS

Between 1904-8 over 30 acres of formal gardens were laid out and planted, these have now matured into one of the most beautiful gardens in England. The unique Italian garden is a four acre walled garden containing a superb collection of statuary and sculpture. The award-winning gardens include the Rose garden and Tudor garden, a traditional yew maze and a 110 metre herbaceous border. A water maze has been added to the other water features in the gardens. The Sunday Walk Garden has a stream meandering through a mature woodland with borders filled with specimen plants.

Summer
1 March - 30 November
Daily:
Grounds: 11am - 6pm.
Castle: 12 noon - 6pm.
Last admission 5pm.

Winter
March & November
Grounds: 11am - 4pm.

Castle: 12 noon - 4pm.

▶ ADMISSION

Castle & Gardens
Adult £9.20
Child (5-14 yrs) £5.00
OAP £7.70
Family (2+2).......... £23.40

Groups (15+)
Adult £7.80
Child (5-14 yrs) £4.80
OAP £7.30
Student (15-19yrs).... £6.80

Gardens only
Adult £7.30
Child (5-14 yrs) £4.80
OAP £6.30
Family (2+2).......... £19.40

Groups (15+)
Adult £6.40
Child (5-14 yrs) £4.60
OAP £6.10
Student (15-19yrs) £6.00

Pre-booked private guided tours are available before opening, during season.

CONFERENCE/FUNCTION

ROOM	SIZE	MAX CAPACITY
Dining Hall	35' x 20'	70
Breakfast Rm	22' x 15'	12
Sitting Rm	24' x 20'	20
Pavilion	96' x 40'	250
Moat Restaurant	25 'x 60'	75

ℹ ⚇ Suitable for filming, conferences, corporate hospitality, weddings, product launches. Outdoor heated pool, tennis court and billiard room. No photography in house.

▢ Gift, garden & book.

🍽 250 seat restaurant available for functions wedding receptions, etc.

♿ Access to gardens, ground floor only (no ramps into castle), restaurants, gift shop, book shop and water maze. Wheelchairs available. WC.

🍴 Two licensed restaurants. Supper provided during open air theatre season. Pre-booked lunches and teas for groups.

🧍 Pre-booked tours in mornings. 1 Mar - 30 Nov. Tour time 1 hr. Tours in French, German, Dutch, Italian and Spanish (min 20). Garden tours in English only (min 15).

🅿 Free admission and refreshment voucher for driver and courier. Please book, group rates for 15+.

▦ Welcome (min 15). Private guided tours available (min 25). 1:6 ratio (up to 8 year olds: 1:10 9yrs+. Free preparatory visits for teachers during opening hours. Please book.

🐕 In grounds, on leads.

❄ Tudor Village.

🎭 Call infoline: 01732 865224.

©NTPL/Andrew Butler.

Map 4

Owner:
The National Trust

▶ **CONTACT**

The Property Manager
Ightham Mote
Ivy Hatch
Sevenoaks
Kent TN15 0NT

Tel: 01732 810378
Info: 01732 811145
Fax: 01732 811029

e-mail: ighthammote@
nationaltrust.org.uk

▶ **LOCATION**
OS Ref. TQ584 535

6m E of Sevenoaks off
A25. 2¹/₂ m S of
Ightham off A227.

IGHTHAM MOTE 🌳

www.nationaltrust.org.uk/ighthammote

Beautiful moated manor house covering 650 years of history from medieval times to the 1960s. Discover the stories and characters associated with the house from the first owners in 1320 to Charles Henry Robinson, the American businessman who bequeathed Ightham Mote to the National Trust in 1985.

The visitor route includes the newly refurbished Great Hall and Jacobean staircase, along with the Old Chapel, Crypt, Tudor Chapel with painted ceiling, Drawing Room with Jacobean fireplace, frieze and 18th century hand-painted Chinese wallpaper, and Victorian Billiards Room.

A major conservation programme has recently been completed which has facilitated the opening of the South-West Quarter, including for the first time the apartments of Mr Robinson. It is now possible to enjoy the most extensive visitor route available to date. A special exhibition 'Conservation in Action' explains the project and gives insights into the techniques and skills used.

Extensive gardens with lakes and woodland walk. Surrounding 550 acre estate also provides many country walks including way-marked routes.

Free introductory talks, garden and tower tours. Varied events programme including open-air concerts, children's events, and lecture lunches through the season. 'IM20' – A celebration of 20 years' ownership and care by the National Trust. Group & Educational Tours available. For details please telephone: 01732 810378.

Charles Henry Robinson's Bedroom. © Stuart Page Architect

▶ **OPENING TIMES**

18 March - 30 October:
Daily except Tues & Sats.

Gardens, Shop & Restaurant: 10am - 5.30pm (last admission 5pm).

House: 10.30am - 5.30pm (last admission 5pm).

Restaurant & Shop evening and winter opening times, please call property.

▶ **ADMISSION**

Adult	£7.00
Child	£3.50
Family	£17.50

Groups (booked)
Adult	£6.00
Child	£3.00

🛍️
♿ Ground floor. WC.
🍴
🐕 On leads, Estate only.
🛡️ Tel for details.

Knole ©National Trust Photographic Library.

KNOLE 🐝

www.nationaltrust.org.uk

Map 4

Owner:
The National Trust

▶ CONTACT

Property Manager
Knole
Sevenoaks
Kent TN15 0RP

Tel: 01732 462100

Info: 01732 450608

Fax: 01732 465528

e-mail: knole@
nationaltrust.org.uk

Knole's fascinating historic links with Kings, Queens & the nobility, as well as its well-known literary links with Vita Sackville-West and her intimate friend, Virginia Woolf, make this one of the most intriguing houses in England. Thirteen superb state-rooms are laid out much the same as they were in the 17th century, to impress visitors by the wealth and standing of those living there. The house includes rare furniture, paintings by Gainsborough, Van Dyck and Reynolds, as well as many 17th century tapestries, some of which came from the royal palaces of Hampton Court and Whitehall.

Learn about the history of the billiard cue and what gentlemen used to strengthen their sword arm! From the lives of the servants to the reckless behaviour of

the aristocracy, every room in Knole holds its own secrets and nearly 500 years of history.

The house inspired not only Vita Sackville-West, who was born at Knole, to write her best-selling novel *The Edwardians* but was also the setting for Virginia Woolf's famous novel *Orlando*.

Knole is set at the heart of the only remaining medieval deer park in Kent where Sika and Fallow deer still roam freely amongst ancient oak, beech and chestnut trees, as they have since the days of Henry VIII. It is the ideal spot to enjoy a picnic or just to sit back and relax and watch the world go by.

Pre-booked groups can take advantage of exclusive guided tours of the house while it is closed to the general public. Please telephone for further information.

▶ LOCATION

OS Ref. TQ532 543

M25/J5.
25m SE of London.
Just off A225 at S end of
High Street, Sevenoaks.

Rail: ½ hr from
London Charing Cross
to Sevenoaks.

Bus: Arriva 402
Tunbridge Wells -
Bromley North.

Knole, The Great Stairs. ©National Trust Photographic Library.

Knole, The King's Bedroom. ©NTPL

🛍 Full range of NT goods and souvenirs of Knole.

♿ Wheelchair access to Green Court, Stone Court and Great Hall. WC.

🍽 Serving morning coffee, lunch and teas. Also ice-creams and snacks in courtyard.

🚶 Guided tours for pre-booked groups. By arrangement.

🅿 Ample.

📚 Welcome. Contact Education Officer.

🐕 Guide dogs only.

❄ Park open all year to pedestrians.   Tel for details.

▶ OPENING TIMES

House
19 March - 30 October:
Wed - Sun & BH Mons,
12 noon - 4pm.
Last admission 3.30pm.

Exclusive guided tours for pre-booked groups while house is closed to public, Wed, Fri & Sat, 11am. Please telephone for further information.

Garden
This year the garden will be open every Wednesday from 19 Mar - 30 Oct, 11am - 4pm. Last entry 3pm.

Shop & Tearoom
As House: 10.30am - 5pm.

Christmas Shop
November - December:
Wed - Sun, 11am - 4pm.

▶ ADMISSION

House
Adult £6.40
Child £3.20
Family £16.00
Groups (booked 15+)
Adult £5.50
Child £2.75

Parking £2.50

Garden £2.00

NT members Free.

LEEDS CASTLE & GARDENS

www.leeds-castle.com

Map 4

Owner:
Leeds Castle
Foundation

▶ **CONTACT**

Marketing Department
Leeds Castle
Maidstone
Kent ME17 1PL

Tel: 01622 765400
Fax: 01622 735616

▶ **LOCATION**

OS Ref. TQ835 533

From London to
A20/M20/J8, 40m, 1 hr.
7m E of Maidstone,
¼ m S of A20.

Rail: Combined ticket
available, train
and admission.
London - Bearsted.

Coach: Nat Express/
Greenline coach and
admission from Victoria.

Air: Gatwick 45m.
Heathrow 65m.

Channel Tunnel: 25m.

Channel Ports: 38m.

This "loveliest castle in the world", surrounded by 500 acres of magnificent parkland and gardens and set in the middle of a natural lake, is one of the country's finest historic properties. Leeds is also proud to be one of the Treasure Houses of England.

The site of a Saxon royal manor, a Norman fortress and a royal palace to the Kings and Queens of England, the chequered history of Leeds Castle continues well into the 20th century. The last private owner, the Honourable Olive, Lady Baillie, purchased the Castle in 1926. Her inheritance helped to restore the Castle and, prior to her death, she established the Leeds Castle Foundation, which now preserves the Castle for the nation and hosts important

international conferences.

The Castle has a fine collection of paintings, tapestries and furnishings and is also home to a unique collection of antique dog collars. The Park and Grounds include the colourful and quintessentially English Culpeper Garden, the delightful Wood Garden, and the terraced Lady Baillie Garden with its views over the tranquil Great Water. The Aviary houses over 100 rare and endangered species from around the world and, next to the Vineyard can be discovered the Maze with its secret underground grotto.

A highly popular and successful programme of Special Events is arranged throughout the year, details of which can be found on the website.

▶ **OPENING TIMES**

Summer
1 April - 31 October
Daily, 10am - 5pm (last adm).

Winter
1 November - 31 March
Daily, 10am - 3pm (last adm).

Special private tours for pre-booked groups by appointment.

Castle & Grounds closed 25 Jun & 2 July prior to open air concerts and 5 Nov prior to Grand Firework Spectacular.

Culpeper Garden

▶ **ADMISSION**

Castle, Park & Gardens

15 Mar - 31 Oct
Adult £13.00
Child (4 -15yrs) £9.00
OAP/Student £11.00
Family (2+3) £39.00

Group 15+ prices
from 15 Mar - 31 Oct
Adult £9.50
Child (4 -15yrs) £6.50
OAP/Student £8.50

Call for rates for visitors with disabilities or visit our website.

A guidebook is published in English, French, German, Dutch, Spanish, Italian and Japanese.

CONFERENCE/FUNCTION

ROOM	SIZE	MAX CAPACITY
Fairfax Hall	19.8 x 1m	200
Gate Tower	9.8 x 5.2m	50
Culpeper	7.65 x 7.34m	40
Terrace	8.9 x 15.4m	80

Residential conferences, exhibitions, sporting days, clay shooting, falconry, field archery, golf, croquet and heli-pad. Talks can be arranged for horticultural, viticultural, historical and cultural groups. No radios.

Corporate hospitality, large scale marquee events, wedding receptions, buffets and dinners.

Land train for elderly/disabled, wheelchairs, wheelchair lift, special rates. WC.

Restaurants, a tearoom, group lunch menus. Refreshment kiosks.

Guides in rooms. French, Spanish, Dutch, German, Italian and Russian speaking guides.

Free parking.

Welcome, outside normal opening hours, private tours. Teacher's resource pack and worksheets.

Tel for details. €

Map 4

PENSHURST PLACE & GARDENS

www.penshurstplace.com

Owner:
Viscount De L'Isle

▶ CONTACT

Bonnie Vernon
Penshurst Place
Penshurst
Nr Tonbridge
Kent TN11 8DG

Tel: 01892 870307
Fax: 01892 870866

e-mail: enquiries
@penshurstplace.com

▶ LOCATION

OS Ref. TQ527 438

From London M25/J5
then A21 to
Hildenborough,
B2027 via Leigh;
from Tunbridge Wells
A26, B2176.

Visitors entrance at SE
end of village,
S of the church.

Bus: Maidstone &
District 231, 232, 233
from Tunbridge Wells.

Rail: Charing Cross/
Waterloo - Hildenborough,
Tonbridge or Tunbridge
Wells; then taxi.

Penshurst Place is one of England's greatest family-owned stately homes with a history going back six and a half centuries.

In some ways time has stood still at Penshurst; the great House is still very much a medieval building with improvements and additions made over the centuries but without any substantial rebuilding. Its highlight is undoubtedly the medieval Barons' Hall, built in 1341, with its impressive 60ft-high chestnut-beamed roof.

A marvellous mix of paintings, tapestries and furniture from the 15th, 16th and 17th centuries can be seen throughout the House, including the helm carried in the state funeral procession to St Paul's Cathedral for the Elizabethan courtier and poet, Sir Philip Sidney, in 1587. This is now the family crest.

GARDENS

The Gardens, first laid out in the 14th century, have been developed over successive years by the Sidney family who first came to Penshurst in 1552. A twenty-year restoration and re-planting programme undertaken by the 1st Viscount De L'Isle has ensured that they retain their historic splendour. He is commemorated with a new Arboretum, planted in 1991. The gardens are divided by a mile of yew hedges into "rooms", each planted to give a succession of colour as the seasons change. There is also a Venture Playground, Woodland Trail, Toy Museum and a Gift Shop.

A variety of events in the park and grounds take place throughout the season.

🛍️ ℹ️ Product launches, garden parties, photography, filming, fashion shows, receptions, archery, clay pigeon shooting, falconry, parkland for hire. Conference facilities. Adventure playground & parkland & riverside walks. No photography in house.

🍸 Private banqueting, wedding receptions.

♿ Limited, disabled and elderly may alight at entrance. WC.

🍴 Licensed tearoom (waitress service can be booked by groups of 20+).

🏃 Mornings only by arrangement, lunch/dinner can be arranged. Out of season tours by appointment. Guided tours of the gardens and house.

🅿️ Ample. Double decker buses to park from village.

📚 All year by appointment, discount rates, education room and packs.

🐕 Guide dogs only

🔔

❄️

💍 Tel for details.

CONFERENCE/FUNCTION

ROOM	SIZE	MAX CAPACITY
Sunderland Room	45' x 18'	100
Barons' Hall	64' x 39'	250
Buttery	20' x 23'	50

▶ OPENING TIMES

Summer
6 - 19 March:
Sats & Suns only.
19 March - 30 October
Daily.

House
Daily, 12 noon - 4pm.

Grounds
Daily, 10.30am - 6pm.

Shop
Open all year.

Winter
Open to Groups by
appointment only
(see Guided Tours).

▶ ADMISSION

House & Gardens
Adult £7.00
Child* £5.00
Conc. £6.50
Family (2+2) £20.00
Groups (20+)
Adult £6.50

Garden only
Adult £5.50
Child* £4.50
Conc. £5.00
Family (2+2) £17.00

Garden Season
Ticket £35.00

House Tours (pre-booked)
Adult £7.50
Child £4.50

Garden Tours (pre-booked)
Adult £8.50
Child £5.00

House & Garden ... £11.00

* Aged 5-16yrs; under 5s Free.

SQUERRYES COURT 🏛
MANOR HOUSE & GARDENS

www.squerryes.co.uk

Squerryes Court is a beautiful 17th century manor house which has been the Warde family home since 1731. It is surrounded by 10 acres of attractive and historic gardens which include a lake, restored parterres and an 18th century dovecote. Squerryes is 22 miles from London and easily accessible from the M25. There are lovely views and peaceful surroundings. Visitors from far and wide come to enjoy the atmosphere of a house which is still lived in as a family home.

There is a fine collection of Old Master paintings from the Italian, 17th century Dutch and 18th century English schools, furniture, porcelain and tapestries all acquired or commissioned by the family in the 18th century. General Wolfe of Quebec was a friend of the family and there are items connected with him in the Wolfe Room.

GARDENS

These were laid out in the formal style but were re-landscaped in the mid 18th century. Some of the original features in the 1719 Badeslade print survive. The family have restored the formal garden using this print as a guide. The garden is lovely all year round with bulbs, wild flowers and woodland walks, azaleas, summer flowering herbaceous borders and roses.

Map 4

Owner:
John St A Warde Esq

▶ CONTACT

Mrs P A White
Administrator
Squerryes Court
Westerham
Kent   TN16 1SJ

Tel: 01959 562345
or 01959 563118

Fax: 01959 565949

e-mail: squerryes.court
@squerryes.co.uk

▶ LOCATION
OS Ref. TQ440 535

10 min from M25/J5 or 6 off A25, ½ m W from centre of Westerham

London 1-1½ hrs.

Rail: Oxted Station 4m.
Sevenoaks 6m.

Air: Gatwick,
30 mins.

▶ OPENING TIMES

Summer
27 March - 29 September
Wed, Thu, Sun &
BH Mons.

Grounds:
11.30am - 5pm
House: 1 - 5pm
Last admission 4.30pm.

NB. Pre-booked groups welcome any day except Saturday during season.

Winter
October - 31 March
Closed.

▶ ADMISSION

House & Garden
Adult	£5.50
Child (under 16yrs)...	£3.00
Senior	£5.00
Family (2+2)..........	£13.00
Groups (20+)	
Adult	£4.80
Child (under 14yrs)...	£3.00

Garden only
Adult	£3.60
Child (under 16yrs)...	£2.00
Senior	£3.30
Family (2+2)............	£7.50
Groups (20+, booked)	
Adult	£3.30
Child (under 16yrs)...	£2.00

© Clive Boursnell

CONFERENCE/FUNCTION

ROOM	SIZE	MAX CAPACITY
Hall	32' x 32'	60
Old Library	20' x 25' 6"	40

ℹ Suitable for conferences, product launches, filming, photography, outside events, garden parties. No photography in house. Picnics permitted in grounds.

⌂ Small.

⊤ Wedding receptions (marquee).

♿ Limited access in house and garden. WCs.

☕ Teas and light refreshments on open days. Licenced.

🧍 For pre-booked groups (max 55), small additional charge. Owner will meet groups by prior arrangement. Tour time 1 hr.

🅿 Limited for coaches.

🐕 On leads, in grounds.

BEDGEBURY NATIONAL PINETUM
Goudhurst, Cranbrook, Kent TN17 2SL
Tel: 01580 211781 **Fax:** 01580 212423
Owner: Forestry Commission **Contact:** Mrs Elspeth Hill
Location: OS Ref. TQ714 337 (gate on B2079). 7m E of Tunbridge Wells on A21, turn N on B2079 for 1m.
Open: All year: daily, 10am – 5pm (or dusk if earlier).
Admission: Please telephone for prices.

BOUGHTON MONCHELSEA PLACE
See page 116 for full page entry.

BELMONT 🏠
BELMONT PARK, THROWLEY, FAVERSHAM ME13 0HH
www.belmont-house.org

Tel: 01795 890202 **Fax:** 01795 890042 **e-mail:** belmontadmin@btconnect.com
Owner: Harris (Belmont) Charity **Contact:** Mr J R Farmer
Belmont is a charming late 18th century country mansion by Samuel Wyatt, set in delightful grounds, including a restored 2 acre kitchen garden and a greenhouse. The seat of the Harris family since 1801 it is beautifully furnished and contains interesting items from India and Trinidad as well as the unique clock collection formed by the 5th Lord.
Location: OS Ref. TQ986 564. 4½ m SSW of Faversham, off A251.
Open: 1 Apr - 30 Sept: Sats, Suns & BH Mons, 2 - 5pm. Last admission to house 4.15pm. Gardens: Sat - Thurs, 10am - 6pm. Groups (15+): Mon - Thurs, by appointment.
Admission: House & Garden: Adult £5.25, Child £2.50, Conc. £4.75. Groups (15+): Adult £4.75, Child £2.50. Garden: Adult £2.75, Child £1. Prices subject to change April 2005.
ⓘ No photography in house. 🏠 ♿ Partial. WC. 🔌 🎫 Obligatory. 🅿
🐕 On leads only.

CHART GUNPOWDER MILLS
Chart Mills, Faversham, Kent
Tel: 01795 534542 **e-mail:** faversham@btinternet.com
Owner: Swale Borough Council **Contact:** John Breeze
Oldest gunpowder mill in the world. Supplied gunpowder to Nelson for the Battle of Trafalgar, and Wellington at Waterloo.
Location: OS Ref. TQ615 015. M2/J6. W of town centre, access from Stonebridge Way, off West Street.
Open: Apr - Oct: Sat, Sun & BHs, 2 - 5pm, or by arrangement.
Admission: Free.

CHARTWELL 🌿
See page 117 for full page entry.

CHIDDINGSTONE CASTLE 🏠
See pages 118/119 for double page entry.

COBHAM HALL 🏠
See page 120 for full page entry.

DANSON HOUSE
DANSON PARK, BEXLEYHEATH, KENT DA6 8HL
www.dansonhouse.com

Tel: 020 8303 6699 **Fax:** 020 8304 6641 **e-mail:** info@dansonhouse.com
Owner: Bexley Heritage Trust **Contact:** Martin Purslow, Director
The most significant building at risk in London in 1995, Robert Taylor's villa, with William Chambers' additions, now restored for the nation and open to the public for the first time in 30 years. Restored 1760s interiors include magnificent dining room paintings by Charles Pavillon and rare George England organ.
Location: OS Ref. TQ475 768. Signposted off the A2 and A221 Danson Park, Bexley, 5 minutes London-bound from M25 J/2. Nearest stations: Welling or Bexleyheath (10 min walk), or B15 bus to Danson Park.
Open: Good Friday - 30 Oct: Wed, Thur, Sun & BH Mons, 11am - 5pm (guided tours). Last entry 4.15pm. Pre-booking recommended. Pre-booked group & educational tours at other times all year.
Admission: Adult £5, Child (with adult) Free, OAP. £4.50.
🏠 🍴 ♿ WCs. 🔌 Licenced. 🎫 Obligatory. 🅿 Limited for coaches. ⬛ 🔀 ⬛ ❄

DEAL CASTLE ⊞
VICTORIA ROAD, DEAL, KENT CT14 7BA
www.english-heritage.org.uk/visits

Tel: 01304 372762 **Venue hire and Hospitality:** 01304 211067
Owner: English Heritage **Contact:** Visitor Operations Team
Crouching low and menacing, the huge, rounded bastions of this austere fort, built by Henry VIII, once carried 119 guns. A fascinating castle to explore, with long, dark passages, battlements and a huge basement. The interactive displays and exhibition give a fascinating insight into the castle's history.
Location: OS Ref. TR378 521. SE of Deal town centre.
Open: 24 Mar - 30 Sept: daily, 10am - 6pm.
Admission: Adult £3.70, Child £1.90, Conc. £2.80.
ⓘ WCs. 🏠 🍴 Exclusive private & corporate hospitality. ♿ Restricted. 🔌
🅿 Coach parking on main road. 🐕 Guide dogs only. 🎫 Tel for details.

THE HOME OF ⬚   *See page 121 for full page entry.*
CHARLES DARWIN

DODDINGTON PLACE GARDENS 🏛
Doddington, Nr Sittingbourne, Kent ME9 0BB
Tel: 01795 886385
Owner: Mr & Mrs Richard Oldfield   **Contact:** Mrs Richard Oldfield
10 acres of landscaped gardens in an area of outstanding natural beauty.
Location: OS Ref. TQ944 575. 4m N from A20 at Lenham or 5m SW from A2 at
Ospringe, W of Faversham.
Open: 27 March (Easter Day) - 26 June: Suns only plus 7 & 28 Aug & 11 & 18 Sept:
2 - 5pm; BH Mons 11am - 5pm. Groups at other times by appointment. Coaches by
appointment.
Admission: Adult £3.50, Child 75p. Discount for groups.

DOVER CASTLE ⬚   *See page 122 for full page entry.*
AND THE SECRET
WARTIME TUNNELS

DYMCHURCH MARTELLO TOWER ⬚
Dymchurch, Kent
Tel: 01304 211067   www.english-heritage.org.uk/visits
Owner: English Heritage   **Contact:** Visitor Operations Team
Built as one of 74 such towers to counter the threat of invasion by Napoleon,
Dymchurch is perhaps the best example in the country. Fully restored. You can climb
to the roof which is dominated by an original 24-pounder gun complete with
traversing carriage.
Location: OS189, Ref. TR102 294. In Dymchurch, access from High Street.
Open: Aug BH.
Admission: Adult £2, Child £1, Conc. £1.50.
⛔

EASTBRIDGE HOSPITAL OF ST THOMAS
High Street, Canterbury, Kent CT1 2BD
Tel: 01227 471688   **Fax:** 01227 781641   **e-mail:** eastbridge@freeuk.com
www.eastbridgehospital.co.uk   **Contact:** The Warden
Medieval pilgrims' hospital with 12th century undercroft, refectory and chapel.
Location: OS189, Ref. TR148 579. S side of Canterbury High Street.
Open: All year (except Good Fri, Christmas Day & 29 Dec): Mon - Sat, 10am - 4.45pm.
Includes Greyfriars Franciscan Chapel, House & Garden. Easter Mon - 27 Sept: Mon -
Sat, 2 - 4pm.
Admission: Adult £1, Child 50p, Conc. 75p.

NTPL / Jerry Harpur

NTPL / Jerry Harpur

EMMETTS GARDEN 🌿
IDE HILL, SEVENOAKS, KENT TN14 6AY
www.nationaltrust.org.uk/emmetts

Tel: 01732 750367/868381 (Chartwell office) **Info:** 01732 751509
e-mail: emmetts@nationaltrust.org.uk
Owner: The National Trust   **Contact:** The Property Manager
    (Chartwell & Emmetts Garden, Mapleton Road, Westerham, Kent TN16 1PS)
Influenced by William Robinson, this charming and informal garden was laid out in
the late 19th century, with many exotic and rare trees and shrubs from across the
world. Wonderful views across the Weald of Kent – with the highest treetop in Kent.
There are glorious shows of daffodils, bluebells, azaleas and rhododendrons, then

acers and cornus in autumn, also a rose garden and rock garden.
Location: OS Ref. TQ477 524. 1½ m N of Ide Hill off B2042. M25/J5, then 4m.

Open: 19 Mar - 30 May: Tue - Sun; 1 Jun - 3 Jul: Wed - Sun, 6 Jul - 30 Oct: Wed, Sat
& Sun; 11am - 5pm. Last admission 4.15pm. Open BH Mons.

Admission: Adult £4 (£6 with guide book), Child £1, Family £9, Group £3.50.
◻ ♿ Steep in places. WC. Buggy from car park to garden entrance.
▣ ✖ In grounds, on leads. ▣ Tel for details.

FINCHCOCKS

FINCHCOCKS, GOUDHURST, KENT TN17 1HH

www.finchcocks.co.uk

Tel: 01580 211702   **Fax:** 01580 211007   **e-mail:** katrina@finchcocks.co.uk

Owner: Mr Richard Burnett   **Contact:** Mrs Katrina Burnett

In 1970 Finchcocks was acquired by Richard Burnett, leading exponent of the early piano, and it now contains his magnificent collection of some eighty historical keyboard instruments: chamber organs, harpsichords, virginals, spinets and early pianos. About half of these are restored to full concert condition and are played whenever the house is open to the public. The house, with its high ceilings and oak panelling, provides the perfect setting for music performed on period instruments, and Finchcocks is now a music centre of international repute. Many musical events take place here.

There is a fascinating collection of pictures and prints, mainly on musical themes, and a special exhibition on the theme of the 18th century pleasure gardens, which includes costumes and tableaux.

Finchcocks is a fine Georgian baroque manor noted for its outstanding brickwork, with a dramatic front elevation attributed to Thomas Archer. The present house was built in 1725 for barrister Edward Bathurst. Despite having changed hands many times, it has undergone remarkably little alteration and retains most of its original features. The beautiful grounds, with their extensive views over parkland and hop gardens, include the newly restored walled garden, which provides a dramatic setting for special events.

Location: 1m S of A262, 2m W of Goudhurst. 5m from Cranbrook, 10m from Tunbridge Wells, 45m from London (1½ hrs). Rail: Marden 6m (no taxi), Paddock Wood 8m (taxi), Tunbridge Wells 10m (taxi).

Open: Easter Sun - end Sept: Sun & BH Mons, plus Wed & Thurs in Aug, 2 - 6pm. Groups & indivduals: Mid Mar - end Oct & Dec at other times by arrangement. Closed Nov, Jan - early Mar).

Admission: Adult £8, Child £4, Student £5. Garden only: Adult £2.50, Child 50p. Group (25+): Charge dependent on numbers and programme.

🖼️ 👥 ℹ️ Music events, conferences, seminars, promotions, archery, ballooning, filming, television. Instruments for hire. No videos in house, photography by permission only. 🍽️ Private and corporate entertaining, weddings. 🅿️ Limited. WC. Suitable for visually handicapped. 🍴 Licensed. Picnics permitted in grounds. 🚶 Musical tours/recitals. Tour time: 2½ - 4 hrs. 🅿️ Pre-booked groups (25 - 100) welcome from Apr - Oct. 🎹 Opportunity to play instruments. Can be linked to special projects and National Curriculum syllabus. ✕ ♪ Music a speciality. ♿

GAD'S HILL PLACE

GAD'S HILL SCHOOL, HIGHAM, ROCHESTER, KENT ME3 7PA

www.significantevents.co.uk/gadshillplace

Tel: 01634 318825   **e-mail:** ghp@significantevents.co.uk

Owner: Gad's Hill School   **Contact:** Katherine Hersey-Meade

The home of Charles Dickens, set in 11 acres of Kentish countryside and the inspiration for some of his best loved novels. Ground floor rooms including drawing room, conservatory and study are open for guided public viewing with a self-guided tour of the gardens.

Location: OS Ref. TQ709 708. On the A226 Rochester-Gravesend Road in Higham. Entrance to the car park is in Crutches Lane.

Open: May - Oct: First Sun of the month, 2 - 5pm. Dickens Festival Weekends: 2 - 5pm. Please telephone to check opening times and special events.

Admission: Adult £3.75, Child £1.75, Conc. £3.

🖼️ 🍽️ ♿ Partial. WCs. 🍴 Licenced. 🚶 Obligatory. 🅿️ 🚌 Guide dogs only. ♪ ♿ Tel for details.

GODINTON HOUSE & GARDENS

GODINTON LANE, ASHFORD, KENT TN23 3BP

www.godinton-house-gardens.co.uk

Tel: 01233 620773   **Fax:** 01233 647351   **e-mail:** ghpt@godinton.fsnet.co.uk

Owner: Godinton House Preservation Trust   **Contact:** Mr D Bickle

"An ancient estate in a magnificent park with thrilling formal gardens now splendidly restored – one of Kent's finest" – *The Times*. Jacobean house with fascinating history and marvellous collection of furniture, pictures and porcelain. The great yew hedge encloses contrasting formal, wild, Italian and walled gardens. Caravan Club site on Estate.

Location: OS Ref. TQ981 438. Godinton Lane, off A20 Ashford to Lenham (M20/J9).

Open: House: 25 Mar - 9 Oct: Fri - Sun, 2 - 5.30pm. Gardens: 19 Mar - 9 Oct: Thur - Mon, 2 - 5.30pm. Special tours and opening for booked groups.

Admission: House & Gardens: Adult £6. Gardens only: Adult £3. Children Free.

ℹ️ No photography in house. Groups must book. ✕ ♿ Partial. WC. 🍽️ When house open. 🚶 Obligatory (house only). 🅿️ ■ ✕ ♿ Tel for details.

GOODNESTONE PARK GARDENS

Goodnestone Park, Nr Wingham, Canterbury, Kent CT3 1PL
Tel/Fax: 01304 840107 **e-mail:** enquiries@goodnestoneparkgardens.co.uk
www.goodnestoneparkgardens.co.uk
Owner/Contact: The Lady FitzWalter
The garden is approximately 14 acres, set in 18th century parkland. A new gravel garden was planted in 2003. There are many fine trees, a woodland area and a large walled garden with a collection of old-fashioned roses, clematis and herbaceous plants. Jane Austen was a frequent visitor, her brother Edward having married a daughter of the house.
Location: OS Ref. TR254 544. 8m ESE of Canterbury, 1½ m E of B2046, at S end of village. The B2046 runs from the A2 to Wingham, the gardens are signposted from this road.
Open: 28 Mar - 30 Sept: Weekdays (except Tue & Sat), 11am - 5pm. 27 Mar - 2 Oct: Suns, 12 noon - 5pm.
Admission: Adult £4, Child (under 12yrs) 50p, OAP £3.50, Student £2.50, Family (2+2) £6.50. Groups (20+): Adult £3.50. Guided garden tours: £5.50.

GROOMBRIDGE PLACE GARDENS

See page 123 for full page entry.

GREAT COMP GARDEN

COMP LANE, PLATT, BOROUGH GREEN, KENT TN15 8QS

www.greatcomp.co.uk

Tel: 01732 886154
Owner: R Cameron Esq   **Contact:** Mr W Dyson
One of the finest gardens in the country, comprising ruins, terraces, tranquil woodland walks and sweeping lawns with a breathtaking collection of trees, shrubs, heathers and perennials, many rarely seen elsewhere. The truly unique atmosphere of Great Comp is further complemented by its Festival of Chamber Music held in July/September.
Location: OS Ref. TQ635 567. 2m E of Borough Green, B2016 off A20. First right at Comp crossroads. ½ m on left.
Open: 1 Apr - 31 Oct: daily, 11am - 5.30pm.
Admission: Adult £4, Child £1. Groups (20+) £3.50, Annual ticket: Adult £12, OAP £8.
Teas daily. Guide dogs only. Tel for details.

HALL PLACE & GARDENS

BOURNE ROAD, BEXLEY, KENT DA5 1PQ

www.hallplaceandgardens.com

Tel: 01322 526574 **Fax:** 01322 522921 **e-mail:** martin@hallplaceandgardens.com
Managed by: Bexley Heritage Trust   **Contact:** Mr Martin Purslow
A fine Grade I listed country house built c1537 for Lord Mayor of London, Sir John Champneys. The house stands at the centre of award winning gardens with magnificent topiary, a herb garden, a secret garden, Italianate garden and inspirational herbaceous borders on the banks of the River Cray at Bexley. In its former walled gardens is a plant nursery and sub-tropical plant house where you can see ripening bananas in mid-winter. The house boasts a panelled Tudor Great Hall and minstrels' gallery and many period rooms including a vaulted long gallery and splendid drawing room with a fine 17th century plaster ceiling. There is a shop and numerous exhibitions, including an opportunity to purchase artists' work throughout the year.

Various rooms including the Great Hall are available to hire for weddings and other events. Its close proximity to London makes it an ideal location for photographic, film and television use. Extensive Education & Outreach Service available.
Location: OS Ref. TQ502 743. On the A2 less than 5m from the M25/J2 (London bound).
Open: 1 Apr - 31 Oct: Mon - Sat, 10am - 5pm; Sun & BHs, 11am - 5pm. 1 Nov - 31 Mar: Tue - Sat, 10am - 4.15pm.
Admission: Free. Pre-arranged guided tours (10+): Adult £3.
House, lift & WC. Licensed. By arrangement. Guide dogs only. Tel for details.

David Winston, Period Piano Company

RESTORATION HOUSE 🏛

17 – 19 CROW LANE, ROCHESTER, KENT ME1 1RF

www.restorationhouse.co.uk

Tel: 01634 848520 **Fax:** 01634 880058

Owner: R Tucker & J Wilmot   **Contact:** Robert Tucker

Unique survival of an ancient city mansion deriving its name from the stay of Charles II on the eve of The Restoration. Beautiful interiors with exceptional early paintwork related to decorative scheme 'run up' for Charles' visit. The house also inspired Dickens to situate 'Miss Havisham' here.

'Interiors of rare historical resonance and poetry', *Country Life*. Fine English furniture and pictures (Mytens, Kneller, Dahl, Reynolds and several Gainsboroughs). Charming interlinked walled gardens of ingenious plan in a classic English style. A private gem. 'There is no finer pre-Civil war town house in England than this' – Simon Jenkins, *The Times*.

Location: OS Ref, TQ744 683. Historic centre of Rochester, off High Street, opposite the Vines Park.

Open: 2 Jun - 30 Sept: Thurs & Fris also Sat 4 June, 10am - 5pm.

Admission: Adult £5.50 (includes 24 page illustrated guidebook), Child £2.75, Conc £4.50. Booked group (8+) tours: £6.50pp.

ℹ️ No stiletto heels. No photography in house. ♿ Unsuitable.
📷 1st Thurs in month. 🎟 By arrangement. 🅿 None. 🦮 Guide dogs only.

RICHBOROUGH ROMAN FORT ⌗

Richborough, Sandwich, Kent CT13 9JW

Tel: 01304 612013   www.english-heritage.org.uk/visits

Owner: English Heritage   **Contact:** Visitor Operations Team

This fort and township date back to the Roman landing in AD43. The fortified walls and the massive foundations of a triumphal arch which stood 80 feet high still survive. The inclusive audio tour and the museum give an insight into life in Richborough's heyday as a busy township.

Location: OS Ref. TR324 602. 1½ miles NW of Sandwich off A257.

Open: 24 Mar - 30 Sept: daily, 10am - 6pm.

Admission: Gardens: Adult £3.70, Child £1.90, Conc. £2.80.

ℹ️ Museum. 📷 ♿ Ground floor. 🎧 🅿 🦮 Guide dogs only. 📞 Tel for details.

RIVERHILL HOUSE 🏛

Sevenoaks, Kent TN15 0RR

Tel: 01732 458802/452557 **Fax:** 01732 458802

Owner: The Rogers Family   **Contact:** Mrs Rogers

Small country house built in 1714.

Location: OS Ref. TQ541 522. 2m S of Sevenoaks on E side of A225.

Open: Garden: Easter - 19 June: Suns & BH weekends, 11am - 5pm. House: open only to pre-booked groups of adults (20+) on any day: Apr, May & Jun.

Admission: Adult £3, Child 50p. Pre-booked groups: £4.50.

ROCHESTER CASTLE ⌗

The Lodge, Rochester-upon-Medway, Medway ME1 1SX

Tel: 01634 402276   www.english-heritage.org.uk/visits

Owner: English Heritage   **Contact:** Visitor Operations Team
(Managed by Medway Council)

Built in the 11th century. The keep is over 100 feet high and with walls 12 feet thick.

Location: OS Ref. TQ743 685. By Rochester Bridge. Follow A2 E from M2/J1 & M25/J2.

Open: 1 Apr - 30 Sept: daily, 10am - 6pm. 1 Oct - 31 Mar: daily, 10am - 4pm. Closed 24 - 26 Dec & 1 Jan.

Admission: Adult £4, Child £3, Family £11. Prices subject to change April 2005.

ℹ️ WCs. 📷 🎧 🦮 📞

ROCHESTER CATHEDRAL

Garth House, The Precinct, Rochester, Kent ME1 1SX

Tel: 01634 401301 **Fax:** 01634 401410

e-mail: visitsofficer@rochestercathedraluk.org

Rochester Cathedral has been a place of Christian worship since its foundation in 604AD. The present building is a blend of Norman and gothic architecture with a fine crypt and Romanesque façade. The first real fresco in an English Cathedral for 800 years is now on view to the public.

Location: OS Ref. TQ742 686. Signed from M20/J6 & A2/M2/J3. Best access from M2/J3.

Open: All year: 8.30am - 5pm. Visiting may be restricted during services.

Admission: Suggested donation. Adult £3. Guided groups: £3.50 (£3 until 31 Mar), please book on above number. Separate prices for schools.

ℹ️ Photography permit £1. 📷 ♿ 🎟 🎫 By arrangement. 🅿 🦮 📞

ROMAN PAINTED HOUSE

New Street, Dover, Kent CT17 9AJ

Tel: 01304 203279

Owner: Dover Roman Painted House Trust   **Contact:** Mr B Philp

Discovered in 1970. Built around 200AD as a hotel for official travellers. Impressive wall paintings, central heating systems and the Roman fort wall built through the house.

Location: OS Ref. TR318 414. Dover town centre. E of York St.

Open: Apr - Sept: 10am - 5pm, except Mons.

Admission: Adult £2, Child/OAP 80p.

ST AUGUSTINE'S ABBEY ⌗

Longport, Canterbury, Kent CT1 1TF

Tel: 01227 767345   www.english-heritage.org.uk/visits

Owner: English Heritage   **Contact:** Visitor Operations Team

The Abbey, founded by St. Augustine in 598, is a World Heritage Site. Take the free interactive audio tour which gives a fascinating insight into the Abbey's history and visit the museum displaying artifacts uncovered during archaeological excavations of the site.

Location: OS Ref. TR154 578. In Canterbury ½ mile E of Cathedral Close.

Open: 24 Mar - 30 Sept: daily, 10am - 6pm. 1 Oct - 31 Mar: Wed - Sun, 10am - 4pm. Closed 24 - 26 Dec & 1 Jan. Times subject to change.

Admission: Adult £3.70, Child £1.90, Conc. £2.80. 15% discount for groups (11+).

📷 ♿ Grounds. 🎧 Free. 🅿 Nearby. 🦮 Guide dogs only. 📞 Tel for details.

ST JOHN'S COMMANDERY ⌗

Densole, Swingfield, Kent

Tel: 01304 211067   www.english-heritage.org.uk/visits

Owner: English Heritage   **Contact:** Dover Castle

A medieval chapel built by the Knights Hospitallers. It has a moulded plaster ceiling and a remarkable timber roof and was converted into a farmhouse in the 16th century.

Location: OS Ref. TR232 440. 2 miles NE of Densole on minor road off A260.

Open: Any reasonable time for exterior viewing. Internal viewing by appointment only.

Admission: Free.

🦮 📞

SCOTNEY CASTLE GARDEN & ESTATE ❧

LAMBERHURST, TUNBRIDGE WELLS, KENT TN3 8JN

www.nationaltrust.org.uk/scotneycastle

Tel: 01892 891081 **Fax:** 01892 890110 **e-mail:** scotneycastle@nationaltrust.org.uk
Owner: The National Trust **Contact:** Property Manager
One of England's most romantic gardens designed by Edward Hussey in the picturesque style. Dramatic vistas from the terrace of the new Scotney Castle, built in the 1830s, lead down to the ruins of a 14th century moated castle. Rhododendrons, kalmia, azaleas and wisteria flower in profusion. Roses and clematis scramble over the remains of the Old Castle, which is open for the summer. In autumn the garden's glowing colours merge with the surrounding woodlands where there are many country walks to be explored all year round.
Location: OS Ref. TQ688 353. Signed off A21 1m S of Lamberhurst village.
Open: Garden & Shop: 5 - 13 Mar: Sat & Sun; 18 Mar - 31 Oct: Wed - Sun, 11am - 6pm. Last admission 5pm. Old Castle: 1 May - 25 Sept: 11am - 5.30pm. All year for estate walks.
Admission: Adult £4.80, Child £2.40.
⬜ ⬆ ♿ Grounds (but steep parts). ⬛ 🅿 🐕Outside garden only, on leads. ♿ Tel for details. ✱

SISSINGHURST CASTLE GARDEN ❧

SISSINGHURST, CRANBROOK, KENT TN17 2AB

www.nationaltrust.org.uk/sissinghurst

Tel: 01580 710700 **Infoline:** 01580 710701
e-mail: sissinghurst@nationaltrust.org.uk
Owner: The National Trust **Contact:** The Administration Assistant
One of the world's most celebrated gardens, the creation of Vita Sackville-West and her husband Sir Harold Nicolson. Developed around the surviving parts of an Elizabethan mansion with a central red-brick prospect tower, a series of small, enclosed compartments, intimate in scale and romantic in atmosphere, provide outstanding design and colour throughout the season. The study, where Vita worked, and library are also open to visitors.
Location: OS Ref. TQ807 383. 2m NE of Cranbrook, 1m E of Sissinghurst village (A262).
Open: 19 Mar - 30 Oct: Fri - Tues, including BHs & Good Fri, 11am - 6.30pm; Sat, Sun, BHs & Good Fri, 10am - 6.30pm. Last admission 1 hour before closing or dusk if earlier.
Admission: Adult £7.50, Child £3.50, Family (2+3) £18.50. Group discounts (11-50) on Mons only. NT members Free.
⬜ ⬆ ♿WCs. ⬛ 🍴Licensed. 🅿Ample. Limited for coaches. 🐕Grounds only, on leads. Guide dogs only in Garden.

SMALLHYTHE PLACE ❧

TENTERDEN, KENT TN30 7NG

www.nationaltrust.org.uk/smallhytheplace

Tel: 01580 762334 **Fax:** 01580 761960
e-mail: smallhytheplace@nationaltrust.org.uk
Owner: The National Trust **Contact:** Assistant Property Manager
This early 16th century half-timbered house was home to Shakespearean actress Ellen Terry from 1899 to 1928. The house contains many personal and theatrical mementoes, including her lavish costumes. The grounds include the barn theatre and beautiful cottage garden. Many events take place in the grounds and the theatre.
Location: OS Ref. TQ893 300. 2m S of Tenterden on E side of the Rye road B2082.
Open: 5 - 20 Mar, Sats & Suns. 26 Mar - 29 Oct: daily except Thur & Fri (open Good Fri), 11am - 5pm, last admission 4.30pm.
Admission: Adult £4.25, Child £2, Family £10.
ℹ️No photography in house. ⬆ ♿ Ground floor only. 🅿 Limited. 🐕On leads, in grounds. ♿ Tel for details.

ARDINGTON HOUSE

www.ardingtonhouse.com

Map 3

Owner:
The Baring Family

▶ CONTACT

Nigel Baring
Ardington House
Wantage
Oxfordshire OX12 8QA

Tel: 01235 821566
Fax: 01235 821151
e-mail: info@
ardingtonhouse.com

▶ LOCATION
OS Ref. SU432 883

12m S of Oxford, 12m
N of Newbury,
2¹/₂ m E of Wantage.

Just a few miles south of Oxford stands the hauntingly beautiful Ardington House. Surrounded by well-kept lawns, terraced gardens, peaceful paddocks, parkland and its own romantic island this Baroque house is the private home of the Barings. You will find it in the attractive village of Ardington, close to the Ridgeway on the edge of the Berkshire Downs.

Built by the Strong brothers in 1720 with typical Georgian symmetry, the House is also famous for its Imperial Staircase. Leading from the Hall, the staircase is considered by experts to be one of the finest examples in Britain.

Away from the crowds and the hustle of the workplace Ardington House provides a private and secluded setting. The calm, exclusive use environment allows for weddings, offsite board meetings, conferences and workshops utilising the splendid gardens and grounds. There is a heated outdoor swimming pool, tennis court, croquet lawn and trout river. Close by is the ancient Ridgeway Path, a popular place for walking or mountain biking.

Ardington House is licensed to hold civil wedding ceremonies. Receptions can range from drinks and intimate dining in the house, to a full dinner and dance reception using marquees in the grounds.

Poet Laureate Sir John Betjeman wrote of the homeliness and warmth of Ardington House, and the rooms have seen many special occasions and important visitors in the past with this tradition being continued. The astonishing mixture of history, warmth and style you'll find at Ardington truly does place it in a class of its own.

▶ OPENING TIMES

2 - 6, 9 - 13, 16 - 20 May:
2.30 - 4.30pm.

1 - 5, 8 - 12, 15 - 19 August:
2.30 - 4.30pm.

Guided tours at 2.30pm.

▶ ADMISSION
House & Gardens

Adult £4.50

CONFERENCE/FUNCTION

ROOM	MAX CAPACITY
Imperial Hall	
Theatre Style	80
U shape	30
Cabaret	40
Oak Room	
Theatre Style	40
U shape	20
Cabaret	30
Music Room	
Theatre Style	40
U shape	20
Cabaret	30

ℹ️ Conferences, product launches, films.

🍸 Lunches and teas by arrangement for groups.

🚶 By members of the family.

🅿️ Free.

🐕 Guide dogs only.

🔔

🛎️ Tel for details.

BLENHEIM PALACE 🏛

www.blenheimpalace.com

Map 5

Owner:
The Duke of Marlborough

▶ CONTACT

Operations Director
Blenheim Palace
Woodstock OX20 1PX

Tel: 08700 602080
Fax: 01993 810570
e-mail: administrator@
blenheimpalace.com

▶ LOCATION

OS Ref. SP441 161

From London, M40, A44
(1½ hrs), 8m NW of
Oxford. London 63m
Birmingham 54m.

Air: Heathrow 60m.
Birmingham 50m.

Coach: From London
(Victoria) to Oxford.

Rail: Oxford Station.

Bus: Oxford
(Cornmarket) -
Woodstock.

'As we passed through the entrance archway and the lovely scenery burst upon me', wrote Lady Randolph Churchill on her first visit to Blenheim, *'Randolph said with pardonable pride "This is the finest view in England"'*

This year there are new splendours to admire at Blenheim including the restoration of the 10th Duke's "Secret Garden" close to the Palace, as well as a whole calendar of events and a special exhibition to commemorate the anniversary of the death of Sir Winston Churchill. The Palace, home of the 11th Duke of Marlborough and birthplace of Sir Winston Churchill, was built for John Churchill, 1st Duke of Marlborough, by Sir John Vanbrugh between the years 1705 and 1722 after the land and a sum of £240,000 were given to the Duke by Queen Anne and a grateful nation in recognition of his great victory over the French

and Bavarians. It is now considered a masterpiece of the English Baroque style.

The original gardens were designed by Queen Anne's gardener Henry Wise, with later alterations by Lancelot "Capability" Brown which included the creation of Blenheim's most outstanding feature, the lake. In more recent times the French architect, Achille Duchêne, built the formal gardens to the east and west of the Palace. The combination of house, gardens and park was recognised as uniquely important when Blenheim was listed as a World Heritage Site.

The Pleasure Gardens area includes the Marlborough Maze, the Butterfly House, the Herb and Lavender Garden and the Adventure Play Area, but still keeps the atmosphere of Vanbrugh's original walled kitchen garden.

🛍 Four Shops.

ℹ Filming, product launches, activity days. No photography in house.

🍽 Corporate hospitality, including dinners and receptions and team building events.

♿ Car park for the disabled. Adapted toilets.

☕🍴 1 Restaurant, 2 Cafés. Group enquiries welcome (up to 150). Menus on request.

🚶 In off peak season; guides in rooms in peak season. Private and language tours may be pre-booked.

🅿 Unlimited for cars and coaches.

🏆 Sandford Award holder since 1982. Teacher pre-visits welcome.

🐕 Dogs on leads in Park. Registered assistance dogs only in house and garden.

❄

🎫 Full programme. Tel for details.

▶ OPENING TIMES

Summer - Palace
12 February - 30 October
Daily
31 October - 11 December:
Wed - Sun

10.30am - 4.45pm
Last admission 4.45pm.

Winter - Park only
12 December - Mid
February
Daily, 9am - Dusk.

The Duke of Marlborough reserves the right to close the Palace or Park or to amend admission prices without notice.

▶ ADMISSION

House & Grounds

Peak Period 25 - 28 Mar &
28 May – 11 Sept

Adult £13.00
Child £7.50
Conc £10.50
Family £35.00

Groups (15+)
Adult £9.75
Child £5.10
Conc £8.75

Off Peak Period: 12 Feb -
11 Dec (except above dates)

Adult £11.50
Child £6.00
Conc £9.00
Family £30.00

Groups (15+)
Adult £8.75
Child £4.65
Conc £7.75

Park only
Mid Dec - mid Feb

Adult £2.00
Child £1.00

Park & Gardens

Peak Period 25 - 28 Mar &
28 May – 11 Sept

Adult £8.00
Child £4.00
Conc £6.00
Family £20.00

Groups (15+)
Adult £5.75
Child £2.90
Conc £4.75

Off Peak Period: 12 Feb -
11 Dec (except above dates)

Adult £6.00
Child £2.00
Conc £4.00
Family £14.00

Groups (15+)
Adult £4.50
Child £1.50
Conc £3.50

Private tours by
appointment only,
prices on request.

CONFERENCE/FUNCTION

ROOM	SIZE	MAX CAPACITY
Orangery		200
Great Hall	70' x 40'	150
Saloon	50' x 30'	72
with Great Hall		450
with Great Hall & Library		750
Library	180' x 30'	300

141

BROUGHTON CASTLE

www.broughtoncastle.demon.co.uk

Map 5

Owner:
Lord Saye & Sele

▶ **CONTACT**

Mrs J Moorhouse
Broughton Castle
Broughton
Nr Banbury
Oxfordshire
OX15 5EB

Tel: 01295 722547
Fax: 01295 276070

e-mail:
admin@broughton
castle.demon.co.uk

▶ **LOCATION**

OS Ref. SP418 382

Broughton Castle is
2¹/₂ m SW of Banbury
Cross on the B4035,
Shipston-on-Stour -
Banbury Road.
Easily accessible from
Stratford-on-Avon,
Warwick, Oxford,
Burford and the
Cotswolds. M40/J11.

Rail: From London/
Birmingham to Banbury.

Broughton Castle is essentially a family home lived in by Lord and Lady Saye & Sele and their family.

The original medieval Manor House, of which much remains today, was built in about 1300 by Sir John de Broughton. It stands on an island site surrounded by a 3-acre moat. The Castle was greatly enlarged between 1550 and 1600, at which time it was embellished with magnificent plaster ceilings, splendid panelling and fine fireplaces.

In the 17th century William, 8th Lord Saye & Sele, played a leading role in national affairs. He opposed Charles I's efforts to rule without Parliament and Broughton became a secret meeting place for the King's opponents.

During the Civil War William raised a regiment and he and his four sons all fought at the nearby Battle of Edgehill. After the battle the Castle was besieged and captured.

Arms and armour from the Civil War and other periods are displayed in the Great Hall. Visitors may also see the gatehouse, gardens and park together with the nearby 14th century Church of St Mary, in which there are many family tombs, memorials and hatchments.

GARDENS

The garden area consists of mixed herbaceous and shrub borders containing many old roses. In addition, there is a formal walled garden with beds of roses surrounded by box hedging and lined by more mixed borders.

▶ **OPENING TIMES**

Summer
Easter Sun & Mon
1 May - 15 September
Weds & Suns
2 - 5pm.

Also Thurs in July and
August and all BH Suns
& Mons
2 - 5pm.

Groups welcome on
any day and at any time
throughout the year
by appointment.

▶ **ADMISSION**

Adult £6.00
Child (5-15yrs)....... £2.50
OAP/Student £5.00
Groups (15 -100)
Adult £5.50
Child (5-15yrs)....... £2.50
OAP/Student £5.50

ℹ️ Photography allowed in house.

🦽 Partial.

☕ Teas on Open Days. Groups may book morning coffee, light lunches and afternoon teas.

🚶 Available for booked groups.

🅿️ Limited.

🐕 Guide dogs only in house. On leads in grounds.

❄️ Open all year for groups.

26A EAST ST HELEN STREET
Abingdon, Oxfordshire
Tel: 01865 242918 **e-mail:** info@oxfordpreservation.org.uk
www.oxfordpreservation.org.uk
Owner: Oxford Preservation Trust   **Contact:** Ms Debbie Dance
One of best preserved examples of a 15th century dwelling in the area. Originally a Merchant's Hall House with later alterations, features include a remarkable domestic wall painting, an early oak ceiling, traceried windows and fireplaces. The remains of a 17th century boy's doublet found in the roof during restoration works is on display.
Location: OS Ref. SU497 969. 300 yards SSW of the market place and Town Hall.
Open: By prior appointment.
Admission: Free.

ARDINGTON HOUSE 🏛 *See page 140 for full page entry.*

ASHDOWN HOUSE 🌼
Lambourn, Newbury RG17 8RE
Tel: 01793 762209   **e-mail:** ashdownhouse@nationaltrust.org.uk
www.nationaltrust.org.uk
Owner: The National Trust   **Contact:** Coleshill Estate Office
Location: OS Ref. SU282 820. 3¹/₂ m N of Lambourn, on W side of B4000.
Open: House & Garden: 2 Apr - 29 Oct: Wed & Sat, 2 - 5pm. Admission by guided tour at 2.15, 3.15 & 4.15pm. Woodland: All year: daily except Fri, daylight hours.
Admission: House & garden: £2.30. Woodland: Free.
❄

Accommodation Index see page 31

BLENHEIM PALACE 🏛 *See pages 141 for full page entry.*

BROOK COTTAGE
Well Lane, Alkerton, Nr Banbury OX15 6NL
Tel: 01295 670303/670590   **Fax:** 01295 730362
Owner/Contact: Mrs David Hodges
4 acre hillside garden. Roses, clematis, water gardens, colour co-ordinated borders, trees, shrubs.
Location: OS Ref. SP378 428. 6m NW of Banbury, ¹/₂m off A422 Banbury to Stratford-upon-Avon road.
Open: Easter Mon - end Oct: Mon - Fri, 9am - 6pm. Evenings, weekends and all group visits by appointment.
Admission: Adult £4, OAP £3, Child Free.

BROUGHTON CASTLE 🏛 *See page 142 for full page entry.*

BUSCOT OLD PARSONAGE 🌼
Buscot, Faringdon, Oxfordshire SN7 8DQ
Tel: 01793 762209   **e-mail:** buscot@nationaltrust.org.uk
Owner: The National Trust   **Contact:** Coleshill Estate Office
An early 18th century house of Cotswold stone on the bank of the Thames with a small garden.
Location: OS Ref. SU231 973. 2m from Lechlade, 4m N of Faringdon on A417.
Open: 30 Mar - 26 Oct, Weds, 2 - 6pm by written appointment with tenant.
Admission: Adult £1.40, Child 70p, Family £3.50. Not suitable for groups.
ℹNo WCs. ♿Partial.

NTPL / Thames and Chiltern
Part of the Harold Peto Water Garden

BUSCOT PARK 🌼
BUSCOT, FARINGDON, OXFORDSHIRE SN7 8BU
www.buscot-park.com

Tel: Infoline 0845 345 3387 / Office 01367 240786 **Fax:** 01367 241794
e-mail: estbuscot@aol.com
Owner: The National Trust   **Contact:** The Estate Office
(Administered on their behalf by Lord Faringdon)
The 18th century Palladian house contains the Faringdon Collection of fine paintings (including works by Murillo, Reynolds, Rossetti and the famous Briar Rose series by Burne-Jones) and furniture, with important pieces by Adam, Thomas Hope and others. The House is set in parkland, offering peaceful walks through water gardens and a well-stocked walled garden. A tearoom serves delicious home-made cream teas and cakes, and there is ample free parking.
Location: OS Ref. SU239 973. Between Faringdon and Lechlade on A417.

Open: House & Grounds: 25 Mar - 30 Sep: Wed - Fri, 2 - 6pm (last entry to house 5pm). Also open BH Mons & Good Fri and weekends 26/27 Mar; 9/10, 23/24 & 30 Apr; 1, 14/15 & 28/29 May; 11/12 & 25/26 Jun; 9/10 & 23/24 Jul; 13/14 & 27/28 Aug; 10/11 & 24/25 Sep. Grounds only: 25 Mar - 30 Sep: Mon & Tues, 2 - 6pm. Tearoom: as house & grounds, 2.30 - 5.30pm.
Admission: House & Grounds: Adult £6.50, Child £3.25. Grounds only: Adult £4.50, Child £2.25. Groups must book in writing, or by fax or e-mail. Booking required by disabled visitors wishing to use powered mobility vehicle.
ℹNo photography in house. 🎭Fully equipped theatre. ♿Partial, tel for details.
🍖BBQ lunches for groups by arrangement. ⓟAmple for cars, 2 coach spaces.
🐕May be exercised in overflow car park only.

143

CHASTLETON HOUSE

Chastleton, nr Moreton-in-Marsh, Oxfordshire GL56 0SU

Tel/Fax: 01608 674355 **Infoline:** 01494 755560 **e-mail:** chastleton@nationaltrust.org.uk

Owner: The National Trust   **Contact:** The Custodian

One of England's finest and most complete Jacobean houses, dating from 1607. It is filled with a mixture of rare and everyday objects and the atmosphere of four hundred years of continuous occupation by one family. The gardens have a Jacobean layout and the rules of modern croquet were codified here.

Location: OS Ref. SP248 291. 6m ENE of Stow-on-the-Wold. 1¹/2 miles NW of A436. Approach only from A436 between the A44 (W of Chipping Norton) and Stow.

Open: 23 Mar - 1 Oct: Wed - Sat, 1 - 5pm, last admission 4pm. 5 - 29 Oct: Wed - Sat, 1 - 4pm, last admission 3pm. Admission for all visitors (including NT members) by timed tickets booked in advance. Bookings can be made by telephone (01494 755585) on weekdays between 9.30am - 4pm.

Admission: Adult £6, Child £3. Family £15. Groups by appointment £5.

Partial. Coaches limited to 25 seat minibuses. Guide dogs only.

CHRIST CHURCH CATHEDRAL

The Sacristy, The Cathedral, Oxford OX1 1DP

Tel: 01865 276154   **Contact:** Mr Jim Godfrey

12th century Norman Church, formerly an Augustinian monastery, given Cathedral status in 16th century by Henry VIII. Private tours available.

Location: OS Ref. SP515 059. Just S of city centre, off St Aldates. Entry via Meadow Gate visitors' entrance on S side of college.

Open: Mon - Sat: 9am - 5pm. Suns: 1 - 5pm (last entry 4.30pm) closed Christmas Day. Services: weekdays 7.20am, 6pm. Suns: 8am, 10am, 11.15am & 6pm. Areas of the college (especially the Great Hall & Cathedral) are closed at various times during the year. Please telephone to check before visit.

Admission: Adult £5, Child under 5 Free, Conc. £4, Family £10.

COGGES MANOR FARM MUSEUM

Church Lane, Witney, Oxfordshire OX28 3LA

Tel: 01993 772602 **Fax:** 01993 703056

e-mail: info@cogges.org **WWW**.cogges.org

Administered by: West Oxfordshire District Council **Contact:** Victoria Beaumont

The Manor House dates from the 13th century, rooms are furnished to show life at the end of the 19th century. Daily cooking on the Victorian range. On the first floor, samples of original wallpapers and finds from under the floorboards accompany the story of the history of the house. In one of the rooms, rare 17th century painted panelling survives. Farm buildings, including two 18th century barns, stables and a thatched ox byre, display farm implements. Traditional breeds of farm animals, hand-milking demonstration each day. Seasonal produce from the walled kitchen garden sold in the museum shop.

Location: OS Ref. SP362 097. Off A40 Oxford - Burford Rd. Access by footbridge from centre of Witney, 600 yds. Vehicle access from S side of B4022 near E end of Witney.

Open: Apr - end Oct: Tue - Fri & BH Mons, 10.30am - 5.30pm; Sat & Sun, 12 noon - 5.30pm. Closed Good Fri. Early closing in Oct.

Admission: Please telephone for details.

Ground floor. WCs. In grounds, on leads.

DEDDINGTON CASTLE

Deddington, Oxfordshire

Tel: 01424 775705 **www**.english-heritage.org.uk/visits

Owner: English Heritage   **Contact:** Battle Abbey

Extensive earthworks concealing the remains of a 12th century castle which was ruined as early as the 14th century.

Location: OS Ref. SP471 316. S of B4031 on E side of Deddington, 17 miles N of Oxford on A423. 5 miles S of Banbury.

Open: Any reasonable time.

Admission: Free.

On leads.

DITCHLEY PARK

Enstone, Oxfordshire OX7 4ER

Tel: 01608 677346 **www**.ditchley.co.uk

Owner: Ditchley Foundation   **Contact:** Brigadier Christopher Galloway

The most important house by James Gibbs, with magnificent interiors by William Kent and Henry Flitcroft. For three centuries the home of the Lee family, restored in the 1930s by Ronald and Nancy (Lancaster) Tree, it was frequently used at weekends by Sir Winston Churchill during World War II.

Location: OS Ref. SP391 214. 2m NE from Charlbury. 13 miles NW of Oxford.

Open: Visits only by prior arrangement with the Bursar, weekdays preferred.

Admission: £5 per person (minimum charge £40).

THE GARDEN HOUSE

DENCHWORTH MANOR, WANTAGE, OXFORDSHIRE, OX12 0DX

www.denchworthmanor.com

Tel: 01235 967414 **Fax:** 01235 868452

e-mail: info@denchworthmanor.com

Owner: Lady Beaverbrook   **Contact:** Jane Ford

Built in 1668 as a Woolstore, the property has been transformed into an elegant two-storey house. Upstairs is a wonderful open room with high ceilings and unique criss-crossing beams; downstairs is a comfortable and warm room with open fire. Surrounded by stunning grounds, wide peaceful lawns, a formal herb garden, dovecote and half moat.

Location: OS Ref. SU381 918. 1hr from Heathrow, Denchworth is between the M40 & M4, S of Oxford and equi-distant from Oxford, Newbury and Swindon.

Open: By arrangement for weddings, corporate hospitality and other functions.

Admission: Please contact for details.

GREAT COXWELL BARN

Great Coxwell, Faringdon, Oxfordshire

Tel: 01793 762209 **e-mail:** greatcoxwellbarn@nationaltrust.org.uk

Owner: The National Trust   **Contact:** Coleshill Estate Office

A 13th century monastic barn, stone built with stone tiled roof, which has an interesting timber construction.

Location: OS Ref. SU269 940. 2m SW of Faringdon between A420 and B4019.

Open: All year: daily at reasonable hours.

Admission: £1.

NT Photographic Library / Nick Meers

LOCAL FOOD

Banbury Cakes

These oval cakes date back to Tudor days. The first recorded recipe was published in 1615, in Gervase Markham's 'The English Hous-wife'. They were originally sold from special lidded baskets and wrapped in white cloths to keep them warm. Banbury Cakes have evolved from what was a spicy fruit cake to the mincemeat filled puff pastry case that we know today. The cakes were produced by a baker in Banbury, from where, according to Jane Grigson, their popularity spread with the advent of The Great Western Railways so that they became staple fare at stations along the line.
They were traditionally eaten during Whitsun.

GREYS COURT ❧

ROTHERFIELD GREYS, HENLEY-ON-THAMES, OXFORDSHIRE RG9 4PG

Infoline: 01494 755564 **Tel:** 01491 628529 **e-mail:** greyscourt@nationaltrust.org.uk
Owner: The National Trust   **Contact:** The Custodian

Rebuilt in the 16th century and added to in the 17th, 18th and 19th centuries, the house is set amid the remains of the courtyard walls and towers of a 14th century fortified house. A Tudor donkey wheel, well-house and an ice house are still intact, and the garden contains Archbishop's Maze, inspired by Archbishop Runcie's enthronement speech in 1980.

Location: OS Ref. SU725 834. 3m W of Henley-on-Thames, E of B481.

Open: House: 6 Apr - 30 Sept: Wed - Fri & 1st Sat in month, 2 - 5pm. Garden & Tearoom: 2 - 30 Mar & 5 - 26 Oct: Wed; 2 Apr - 30 Sept: Tues - Sat, 2 - 5.30pm. All open BH Mons but closed Good Fri.

Admission: House & Garden: Adult £5.20, Child £2.60, Family £13. Garden only: £3.70, Child £1.80, Family £9.20. Coach parties must book in advance.

♿ Grounds partial. WCs. 🐕 🐾 In car park only, on leads. 🎫 Contact Custodian.

KINGSTON BAGPUIZE HOUSE ▥

ABINGDON, OXFORDSHIRE OX13 5AX

www.kingstonbagpuizehouse.org.uk

Tel: 01865 820259 **Fax:** 01865 821659 **e-mail:** virginiagrant@btinternet.com
Owner/Contact: Mrs Francis Grant

A family home, this beautiful house originally built in the 1660s was remodelled in the early 1700s in red brick with stone facings. It has a cantilevered staircase and panelled rooms with some good furniture and pictures. Set in mature parkland, the gardens, including shrub border and woodland garden, contain a notable collection of trees, shrubs, perennials and bulbs including snowdrops, planted for year round interest. A raised terrace walk leads to an 18th century panelled gazebo with views of the house and gardens, including a large herbaceous border and parkland. Available for wedding receptions, special events, corporate functions, product launches and filming. Facilities for small conferences.

Location: OS Ref. SU408 981. In Kingston Bagpuize village, off A415 Abingdon to Witney road S of A415/A420 intersection. Abingdon 5m, Oxford 9m.

Open: BH Sun & Mons: Feb: 5/6, 19/20. Mar: 13, 27/28. Apr: 3, 16/17. May: 1/2, 15, 29/30. June: 12 & 26. July: 3, 16/17 & 24. Aug: 6/7, 28/29. Sept: 10/11 & 25. Oct: 9. 2 - 5.30pm.. Last tour of house 4pm. House: guided tours only. Last entry to garden 5pm.

Admission: House & Garden: Adult £4.50, Child (5-15) £2.50, (admission to house not recommended for children under 5yrs), Conc. £4. Gardens: £2.50 (child under 16yrs Free). Groups (20-80) by appointment throughout the year, prices on request.

ℹ No photography in house. 📷 🍴 🚋 ♿ Grounds. WC.
🐕 Home-made cakes. Light meals for groups by appointment.
🅿 🛈 Obligatory 🚌 ❋

MAPLEDURHAM HOUSE & WATERMILL

MAPLEDURHAM, READING RG4 7TR

www.mapledurham.co.uk

Tel: 01189 723350 **Fax:** 01189 724016 **e-mail:** mtrust1997@aol.com

Owner: The Mapledurham Trust   **Contact:** Mrs Lola Andrews

Late 16th century Elizabethan home of the Blount family. Original plaster ceilings, great oak staircase, fine collection of paintings and a private chapel in Strawberry Hill Gothick added in 1797. Interesting literary connections with Alexander Pope, Galsworthy's *Forsyte Saga* and Kenneth Grahame's *Wind in the Willows*. 15th century watermill fully restored producing flour and bran which is sold in the giftshop.

Location: OS Ref. SU670 767. N of River Thames. 4m NW of Reading, 1¹/2 m W of A4074.

Open: Easter - Sept: Sats, Suns & BHs, 2 - 5.30pm. Last admission 5pm. Midweek parties by arrangement only (Tue - Thur). Mapledurham Trust reserves the right to alter or amend opening times or prices without prior notification.

Admission: Please call 01189 723350 for details.

⬜ 🔲 ♿ Grounds. WCs. ⬛ 🅿 🏠 Guide dogs only.
🏠 11 holiday cottages (all year). ♨ Tel for details.

Stonor Park near Henley from the book 'Historic Family Homes & Gardens from the Air'.

MILTON MANOR HOUSE

MILTON, ABINGDON, OXFORDSHIRE OX14 4EN

Tel: 01488 71036

Owner: Anthony Mockler-Barrett Esq   **Contact:** Helen Hall

Dreamily beautiful mellow brick house, traditionally designed by Inigo Jones, with a celebrated Gothick library (pictured on right) and a startling Catholic chapel. One of *England's Thousand Best Houses*. Lived in by the family; pleasant, relaxed and informal atmosphere. Park with fine old trees, stables (pony rides usually available); Treehouse in the garden, Stockade in the woods. Walled garden, woodland walk, two lakes, variety of charming annuals and unusual ornaments. Plenty to see and enjoy for all ages, picnickers welcome.

Location: OS Ref. SU485 924. Just off A34, village and house signposted, 9m S of Oxford, 15m N of Newbury. 3m from Abingdon and Didcot.

Open: 1 - 31 Aug: 12 noon - 5pm. Guided tours of house: 2pm, 3pm, 4pm. Also all BH weekends: Easter - end Aug: open 12 noon - 5pm. For weddings etc. please write to the Administrator.

Admission: House & Gardens: Adult £5, Child £2.50. House: Guided tours only. Garden, Woodland & Grounds only: Adult £3, Child £1.50. Easter Egg Hunt on Easter w/end. Georgian/Stuart weekend on Aug BH weekend. Groups by arrangement throughout the year. For group bookings only please fax or phone 01235 831287.

🔲 ♿ Grounds. ⬛ 🔧 Obligatory. 🅿 Free. 🏠 Guide dogs only. ✳
🏠 1 holiday flat (Easter to September). ♨ Tel for details.

MINSTER LOVELL HALL & DOVECOTE ⌗
Witney, Oxfordshire
Tel: 01424 775705 **www**.english-heritage.org.uk/visits
Owner: English Heritage   **Contact:** Battle Abbey
The ruins of Lord Lovell's 15th century manor house stand in a lovely setting on the banks of the River Windrush.
Location: OS Ref. SP324 114. Adjacent to Minster Lovell Church, ¹/₂ mile NE of village. 3 miles W of Witney off A40.
Open: Any reasonable time.
Admission: Free.
⌖ On leads. ❄

PRIORY COTTAGES
1 Mill Street, Steventon, Abingdon, Oxfordshire OX13 6SP
Tel: 01793 762209
Owner: The National Trust   **Contact:** Coleshill Estate Office
Former monastic buildings, converted into two houses. South Cottage contains the Great Hall of the original priory.
Location: OS Ref. SU466 914. 4m S of Abingdon, on B4017 off A34 at Abingdon West or Milton interchange on corner of The Causeway and Mill Street, entrance in Mill Street.
Open: The Great Hall in South Cottage only: 30 Mar - 28 Sept: Wed, 2 - 6pm, by written appointment with the tenant.
Admission: Adult £1.10, Child 50p, Family £2.70.

Cogges Manor Farm – Threshing machine.

ROUSHAM HOUSE
Nr STEEPLE ASTON, BICESTER, OXFORDSHIRE OX25 4QX
www.rousham.org

Tel: 01869 347110/07860 360407
Owner/Contact: Charles Cottrell-Dormer Esq
Rousham represents the first stage of English landscape design and remains almost as William Kent (1685 - 1748) left it. One of the few gardens of this date to have escaped alteration. Includes Venus' Vale, Townesend's Building, seven-arched Praeneste, the Temple of the Mill and a sham ruin known as the 'Eyecatcher'. The house was built in 1635 by Sir Robert Dormer. Excellent location for fashion, advertising, photography etc.

Location: OS Ref. SP477 242. E of A4260, 12m N of Oxford, S of B4030, 7m W of Bicester.
Open: House: Easter Sun & Mon then May - Sept: Suns & BH Mons 2 - 4.30pm. Garden: All year: daily, 10am - 4.30pm. Pre-booked groups all year at any time.
Admission: House: £3. Garden: Adult £4. No children under 15yrs.

⌖Partial. ⓘObligatory. Ⓟ ⌖ ❄

Education Index see page 48

RYCOTE CHAPEL ⌗
Rycote, Oxfordshire
Tel: 01424 775705 **www**.english-heritage.org.uk/visits
Owner: English Heritage   **Contact:** Battle Abbey
A 15th century chapel with exquisitely carved and painted woodwork. It has many intriguing features, including two roofed pews and a musicians' gallery.
Location: OS165 Ref. SP667 046. 3 miles SW of Thame, off A329. 1¹/₂ miles NE of M40/J7.
Open: 24 Mar - 24 Sept: Fri - Sun & BHs, 2 - 6pm. Times subject to change.
Admission: Adult £2.60, Child £1.30, Conc. £2. 15% discount for groups (11+).
▢ ⌖ Ⓟ ⌖

STONOR 🏠

HENLEY-ON-THAMES, OXFORDSHIRE RG9 6HF

www.stonor.com

Tel: 01491 638587 **Fax:** 01491 639348 **e-mail:** jweaver@stonor.com

Owner: Lord & Lady Camoys   **Contact:** The Administrator - John Weaver

Family home of Lord and Lady Camoys and generations of their family for over 800 years. Stonor, surrounded by deer park, sits in a beautiful wooded valley. The House and Chapel date from the 12th century, with 14th and 18th century additions and changes. Internal features include rare furniture, artworks and family portraits. Mass has been celebrated continuously since medieval times in the Chapel, sited close by a pagan stone circle. St Edmund Campion sought refuge here during the Reformation. An exhibition celebrates his life and work. Enclosed hillside gardens at the rear offer outstanding views of the park. Springtime daffodils are a major attraction.

Location: OS Ref. SU743 893. 1 hr from London, M4/J8/9. A4130 to Henley-on-Thames. On B480 NW of Henley. A4130/B480 to Stonor. Rail: Henley-on-Thames Station 5m.

Open: 27 Mar - 25 Sept: Suns & BH Mons, also Weds 6 July - 28 Sept. House: 2 - 5.30pm. Garden: 1 - 5.30pm. Tearoom: 2 - 5.30pm (from 1pm for lunch if pre-booked). Private groups by arrangement: Apr - Sept, Tues - Thurs.

Admission: House, Garden & Chapel: Adult £6, Child (under 14yrs) Free. Garden & Chapel: Adult £3.50. Schools £2.50 pp, 1 teacher for every 10 children admitted free. Private guided tours (20+): £7pp (one group payment). School groups £4pp, 1 teacher per 10 children admitted free.

🔲 ℹ️ No photography in house. 🚾 ♿ Unsuitable for physically disabled. 🍽️ Licensed. 🎫 For 20-60. 🅿️ 100yds away. 🐕 In grounds on leads. 🛏️ Tel for details.

SWALCLIFFE BARN

Swalcliffe Village, Banbury, Oxfordshire

Tel: 01295 788278   **Contact:** Jeffrey Demmar

15th century half cruck barn, houses agricultural and trade vehicles. Exhibition of 2500 years of Swalcliffe history.

Location: OS Ref. SP378 378. 6m W of Banbury Cross on B4035.

Open: Easter - end Oct: Suns & BHs, 2 - 5pm.

Admission: Free.

WATERPERRY GARDENS

WATERPERRY, Nr WHEATLEY, OXFORDSHIRE OX33 1JZ

www.waterperrygardens.co.uk

Tel: 01844 389254 **Fax:** 01844 339883

e-mail: office@waterperrygardens.fs.net.co.uk

Owner: School of Economic Science   **Contact:** P Maxwell

Here is the chance to enjoy the order of careful cultivation. See one of Britain's finest herbaceous borders which flowers continually from May to October. Rose garden; alpine gardens, formal garden, shrub borders, perennial borders and river walk.

Location: OS Ref. SP630 063. Oxford 9m, London 52m M40/J8, Birmingham M40/J8A 42m. Well signposted locally.

Open: Apr - Oct: 9am - 5.30pm. Nov - Mar: 9am - 5pm.

Admission: Adult £4, Child £2.50 (under 10yrs Free), OAP £3.50. Groups (20+) £3.25. Nov - Mar: all £2.

🔲 🎫 ♿ Partial. 🍽️ 🎫 By arrangement. 🅿️ Limited for coaches. ■ ✖️ ❋

The Colleges of Oxford University

All Souls' College
High Street
Tel: 01865 279379
Founder: Archbishop Henry Chichele 1438
Open: Mon - Fri, 2 - 4pm (4.30pm in summer)

Balliol College
Broad Street
Tel: 01865 277777
Founder: John de Balliol 1263
Open: Daily, 2 - 5pm

Brasenose College
Radcliffe Square
Tel: 01865 277830
Founder: William Smythe, Bishop of Lincoln 1509
Open: Daily, 10 - 11.30am (tour groups only) & 2 - 4pm (5pm in summer)

Christ Church
St. Aldates
Tel: 01865 286573
Founder: Cardinal Wolsey/ Henry VIII 1546
Open: Mon - Sat, 9am - 5.30pm; Sun, 1 - 5.30pm

Corpus Christi College
Merton Street
Tel: 01865 276700
Founder: Bishop Richard Fox 1517
Open: Daily, 1.30 - 4.30pm

Exeter College
Turl Street
Tel: 01865 279600
Founder: Bishop Stapleden of Exeter 1314
Open: Daily, Term time 2 - 5pm.

Green College
Woodstock Road
Tel: 01865 274770
Founder: Dr Cecil Green 1979
Open: By appointment only.

Harris Manchester College
Mansfield Road
Tel: 01865 271011
Founder: Lord Harris of Peckham 1996
Open: Chapel only: Mon - Fri, 8.30am - 5.30pm. Sat, 9am - 12 noon.

Hertford College
Catte Street
Tel: 01865 279400
Founder: TC Baring MP 1740
Open: Daily, 10am - Noon & 2pm - dusk.

Jesus College
Turl Street
Tel: 01865 279700
Founder: Dr Hugh Price (Queen Elizabeth I) 1571
Open: Daily, 2 - 4.30pm

Keble College
Parks Road
Tel: 01865 272727
Founder: Public money 1870
Open: Daily, 2 - 5pm

Kellogg College
Wellington Square
Tel: 01865 274300
Founder: Kellogg Foundation 1990
Open: Mon - Fri, 9am - 5pm

Lady Margaret Hall
Norham Gardens
Tel: 01865 274300
Founder: Dame Elizabeth Wordsworth 1878
Open: Gardens: 10am - 5pm

Linacre College
St Cross Road
Tel: 01865 271650
Founder: Oxford University 1962
Open: By appointment only.

Lincoln College
Turl Street
Tel: 01865 279800
Founder: Bishop Richard Fleming of Lincoln 1427
Open: Mon - Sat, 2 - 5pm; Sun, 11am - 5pm

Magdalen College
High Street
Tel: 01865 276000
Founder: William of Waynefleete 1458
Open: Oct - June: 1pm - 6pm/dusk (whichever is the earlier) and July - 30 Sept: 12 noon - 6pm

Mansfield College
Mansfield Road
Tel: 01865 270999
Founder: Free Churches 1995
Open: Mon - Fri, 9am - 5pm.

Merton College
Merton Street
Tel: 01865 276310
Founder: Walter de Merton 1264
Open: Mon - Fri, 2 -4pm; Sat & Sun, 10am - 4pm

New College
Holywell Street
Tel: 01865 279555
Founder: William of Wykeham, Bishop of Winchester 1379
Open: Daily, 11am - 5pm (summer); 2 - 4pm (winter)

Nuffield College
New Road
Tel: 01865 278500
Founder: William Morris (Lord Nuffield) 1937
Open: Daily, 9am - 5pm.

Oriel College
Oriel Square
Tel: 01865 276555
Founder: Edward II/Adam de Brome 1326
Open: Daily, 1 - 4pm

Pembroke College
St Aldates
Tel: 01865 276444
Founder: James I 1624
Open: By appointment only.

Queen's College
High Street
Tel: 01865 279120
Founder: Robert de Eglesfield 1341
Open: By prior appointment through the Tourist Information Office.

Somerville College
Graduate House, Woodstock Road
Tel: 01865 270600
Founder: Association for the Education of Women 1879
Open: 2 - 5.30pm

St. Anne's College
56 Woodstock Road
Tel: 01865 274800
Founder: Association for the Education of Women 1878
Open: 9am - 5pm

St. Antony's College
62 Woodstock Road
Tel: 01865 284700
Founder: M. Antonin Bess 1948
Open: By appointment only.

St. Catherine's College
Manor Road
Tel: 01865 271700
Founder: Oxford University 1964
Open: 9am - 5pm

St. Cross College
St. Giles
Tel: 01865 278490
Founder: Oxford University 1965
Open: Not open to the public.

St. Edmund Hall
Queens Lane
Tel: 01865 279000
Founder: St. Edmund Riche of Abingdon c.1278
Open: Daily, daylight hours.

St. Hilda's College
Cowley Place
Tel: 01865 276884
Founder: Miss Dorothea Beale 1893
Open: Daily, 2 - 5pm

St. Hugh's College
St. Margarets Road
Tel: 01865 274900
Founder: Dame Elizabeth Wordsworth 1886
Open: 10am - 4pm

St. John's College
St. Giles
Tel: 01865 277300
Founder: Sir Thomas White 1555
Open: 1 - 5pm (or dusk)

St. Peter's College
New Inn Hall Street
Tel: 01865 278900
Founder: Rev. Christopher Charvasse 1928
Open: 10am - dusk

Trinity College
Broad Street
Tel: 01865 279900
Founder: Sir Thomas Pope 1554-5
Open: Mon - Fri 10am - Noon and 2 - 4pm. Sat & Sun in term, 2 - 4pm; Sat & Sun in vacation 10am - Noon and 2 - 4pm.

University College
High Street
Tel: 01865 276602
Founder: Archdeacon William of Durham 1249
Open: Not open to the public.

Wadham College
Parks Road
Tel: 01865 277900
Founder: Nicholas & Dorothy Wadham 1610
Open: Term time: daily, 1 - 4.15pm.
Vacation: daily, 10.30 - 11.45am & 1 - 4.15pm.

Wolfson College
Linton Road
Tel: 01865 274100
Founder: Oxford University 1966
Open: Daylight hours.

Worcester College
Walton Street
Tel: 01865 278300
Founder: Sir Thomas Cookes 1714
Open: Daily, 2 - 5pm.

This information is intended only as a guide. Times are subject to change due to functions, examinations, conferences, holidays, etc. You are advised to check in advance opening times and admission charges which may apply at some colleges, and at certain times of the year. Visitors wishing to gain admittance to the Colleges (meaning the Courts, not to the staircases & students' rooms) are advised to contact the Tourist Information Office. It should be noted that Halls normally close for lunch (12 - 2pm) and many are not open during the afternoon. Chapels may be closed during services. Libraries are not normally open, and Gardens do not usually include the Fellows' garden. Visitors, and especially guided groups, should always call on the Porters Lodge first. Groups should always book in advance. Dogs, except guide dogs are not allowed in any colleges.

For further details contact: Oxford Information Centre, 15 - 16 Broad Street, Oxford OX1 3AS
Tel: +44 (0)1865 726871   Email: tic@oxford.gov.uk   Fax: +44 (0)1865 240261
Image © Adrian Baggett.

South East - England

National Trust Photographic Library - Clandon Park

National Trust Photographic Library, Hatchlands Park

Map 3

Owner:
The National Trust

▶ CONTACT

The Property Manager
Clandon Park &
Hatchlands Park
East Clandon
Guildford
Surrey GU4 7RT

Tel: 01483 222482
Fax: 01483 223176
e-mail: hatchlands@
nationaltrust.org.uk

▶ LOCATION

Clandon
OS Ref. TQ042 512
At West Clandon
on the A247,
3m E of Guildford.

Rail: Clandon BR 1m.

Hatchlands
OS Ref. TQ063 516
E of East Clandon
on the A246 Guildford -
Leatherhead road.

Rail: Clandon BR
2¹/₂ m, Horsley 3m.

CONFERENCE/FUNCTION

ROOM	SIZE	MAX CAPACITY
Marble Hall Clandon Pk	40' x 40'	160 seated 200 standing

CLANDON PARK & HATCHLANDS PARK

www.nationaltrust.org.uk/clandonpark

Clandon Park & Hatchlands Park were built during the 18th century and are set amidst beautiful grounds. They are two of England's most outstanding country houses and are only five minutes' drive apart.

Clandon Park is a grand Palladian mansion, built c1730 by the Venetian architect, Leoni and notable for its magnificent two-storey marble hall. The house is rightly acclaimed for its remarkable collection of 18th century porcelain, textiles and furniture, which includes the Ivo Forde Meissen collection of Italian comedy figures and a series of Mortlake tapestries. The attractive gardens feature a parterre, grotto, Dutch garden and a Maori

© David Mees

house with a fascinating history. Clandon is also home to the Queen's Royal Surrey Regiment Museum. The excellent restaurant is renowned for its Sunday lunches - booking is advisable.

Hatchlands Park was built in 1756 for Admiral Boscawen and is set in a beautiful 430 acre Repton park offering a variety of park and woodland walks. There is also a small garden by Gertrude Jekyll flowering from late May to early July. Hatchlands contains splendid interiors by Robert Adam, decorated in appropriately nautical style. The rooms are hung with the Cobbe Collection of old master paintings and portraits, initially formed in the 18th century. It includes works by Bernini, Guercino, Poussin, Van Dyck, Gainsborough and Zoffany.

Hatchlands also houses the Cobbe Collection of keyboard instruments, the world's largest group of early keyboard instruments owned or played by famous composers such as Purcell, J C Bach, Mozart, Chopin, Liszt, Mahler and Elgar. Notable too are Marie Antoinette's piano and the instrument on which the world's most performed opera, Bizet's Carmen, was composed.

There are frequent concerts on instruments of the collection. For information contact:
The Cobbe Collection Trust, tel. 01483 211474 or visit www.cobbecollection.co.uk.

🏛 ℹ Clandon Park. Tel: 01483 222482. No photography.

🍷 For Clandon weddings and receptions tel: 01483 222502.

♿ Hatchlands suitable. Clandon partially suitable. WCs.

🍽 Hatchlands: 01483 211120.

🍴 Licensed. Clandon: 01483 222502.

🎭 Clandon - by arrangement.

🎧 Hatchlands only.

📖 Children's quizzes available.

🅿 🐕 Guide dogs only.

🔔 Clandon only.   📷 Tel: 1483 222482.

▶ OPENING TIMES

Clandon - House
13 March - 30 October
Tue - Thur, Suns &
BH Mons, Good Fri
& Easter Sat
11am - 5pm.

Garden
As house.

Museum
13 March - 30 October
Tue - Thur & Suns,
BH Mons, Good Fri
& Easter Sat
12 noon - 5pm.

Hatchlands - House
27 March - 30 October
Tue - Thur,
Suns & BH Mon,
Fris in August only.
2 - 5.30pm.

Park Walks
27 March - 30 October:
Daily
11am - 6pm.

▶ ADMISSION

Clandon:
House/Grounds........ £6.00
 Child £3.00
 Family £15.00
Pre-booked Groups
 Adult £5.00

Hatchlands
House/Grounds........ £6.00
 Child £3.00
 Family £15.00
 Park Walks only £3.00
 Child £1.50
Pre-booked Groups
 Adult £5.00

Combined ticket
Clandon/Hatchlands . £9.00
 Child £4.50
 Family £22.50

Map 3

THE COBBE COLLECTION
AT HATCHLANDS

www.cobbecollection.co.uk

Owner:
The National Trust

▶ **CONTACT**

Cobbe Collection Trust
Hatchlands Park
East Clandon
Guildford
Surrey
GU4 7RT

Tel: 01483 211474
Fax: 01483 225922

e-mail: enquiries@
cobbecollection.co.uk

The Cobbe Collections are set in sumptuous rooms designed by Robert Adam. The house, given to the National Trust with few contents, has been let to Mr & Mrs Alec Cobbe since 1987 and is lived in as a family home. The resulting arrangement of pictures, furniture, *objéts d'art* and the celebrated collection of keyboards, spanning 400 years and formerly belonging to some of the greatest names of classical music, has been called 'one of the most beautiful musical museums in the world'. The family art collection, formed initially in the 18th century, includes pictures by Allori, Bernini, Guercino, Poussin, Van Dyck, Gainsborough, Zoffany and many others.

World headlines were occasioned by the identification in 2002, among family portraits, of the most youthful picture of Shakespeare's friend and patron, Henry Wriothesley, 3rd Earl of Southampton, formerly thought to have been of Lady Norton!

The instruments in the collection, all in playing order, are used in lunchtime recitals on Wednesdays, master classes and evening concerts and tours from April to July and in October, giving an opportunity to hear the sounds of instruments played by Purcell, JC Bach, Mozart, Beethoven, Chopin, Liszt and Mahler.

▶ **OPENING TIMES**

Hatchlands - House
27 March - 30 October
Tue - Thur,
Suns & BH Mon,
Fris in August only.
2 - 5.30pm.

Park Walks
27 Mar - 30 Oct: Daily
11am - 6pm.

▶ **ADMISSION**

Hatchlands
House/Grounds £6.00
　　Child £3.00
　　Family £15.00
Park Walks only........ £3.00
　　Child £1.50

Pre-Booked Groups
　　Adult £5.00

Combined ticket
Clandon/Hatchlands . £9.00
　　Child £4.50
　　Family £22.50

▶ **LOCATION**
OS Ref. TQ063 516

E of East Clandon, N of A246 Guildford to Leatherhead road.

© David Mees

🛍
♿ Suitable. WCs.
☕
🍴 Licensed. No booking required, except for groups, tel: 01483 222502
🎧
📱 Children's quizzes .
🅿
🐕 Guide dogs only.
📷 01483 222482.

151

Crown Copyright: Historic Royal Palaces

HAMPTON COURT PALACE

www.hampton-court-palace.org.uk

Map 3

Managed by:
Historic Royal Palaces

▶ **CONTACT**

Hampton Court Palace
Surrey
KT8 9AU

Recorded info:
0870 752 7777
All other enquiries:
0870 751 5175

Venue Hire and Corporate Hospitailty
0870 751 5182

▶ **LOCATION**

OS Ref. TQ155 686

From M25/J15 and A312, or M25/J12 and A308, or M25/J10 and A307.

Rail: From London Waterloo direct to Hampton Court (32 mins).

Henry VIII's magnificent riverside palace also proved to be the favoured home of both George II and William III. Sir Christopher Wren remodelled the south and east fronts in the beautiful baroque style, creating the 'English Versailles'.

Today there are six routes to explore. Multi-lingual sound guides and costumed guided tours help visitors get the most from a visit. Henry VIII's State Apartments include the Great Hall and Chapel Royal, whilst the King's Apartments reveal William III's ceremonial life. The vast Tudor kitchens are alive with the smell of herbs, authentic dishes from the period and the roaring fire.

The gardens are a delight all of their own, and the Garden Exhibition charts the evolution of the Palace's gardens, as well as giving inside information on conservation and plant care. During the summer, tours are available with the gardeners or costumed guides. In springtime Florimania kicks off the season with historic flower arranging in the Queen's Apartments.

For art lovers the lower Orangery in the South Gardens holds Andrea Mantegna's *Triumphs of Caesar*, a sequence of nine paintings, part of the Royal Collection. Painted during the period c1484-1505 they are considered to be one of the most important works of the Italian Renaissance.

Crown Copyright: Historic Royal Palaces

FUNCTION ROOMS

ROOM	SIZE	MAX CAPACITY
Great Hall	88'6" x 35'6"	280/400
Cartoon Gallery	22'6" x 116'	220/350
Gt Watching Chamber	66'6" x 25'	120
Painted Room	33'3" x 21'3"	50/100
King's Guard Chamber	60'3" x 36'4"	120/150
Public Dining Room	31'6" x 55'6"	50/150

▶ **OPENING TIMES**

Summer
March - October
Tue - Sun:
9.30am - 6pm
Mon: 10.15am - 6pm.
(last admission 5.15pm)

Winter
November - February
Tue - Sun:
9.30am - 4.30pm
Mon: 10.15am - 4.30pm
(last admission 3.45pm)

Closed 24 - 26 December.

▶ **ADMISSION**

Telephone Information Line for admission prices:
0870 752 7777.

Advance Ticket Sales:
0870 753 7777.

Group Bookings
0870 7517070,
Quote *Hudson's*.

Information Centre. No photography indoors.

Motorised buggies available at main entrance. WCs.

Ample for cars, coach parking nearby.

Rates on request 0870 7515190.

In grounds, on leads. Guide dogs only in Palace.

For a full list of special events please telephone for details.

Map 3

LOSELEY PARK 🏛

www.loseley-park.com

Owner:
Mr Michael
More-Molyneux

▶ CONTACT

Nicky Rooney
Loseley Park
Guildford
Surrey GU3 1HS

Tel: 01483 405120
Fax: 01483 302036

e-mail: enquiries@
loseley-park.com

▶ LOCATION

OS Ref. SU975 471

30m SW of London,
leave A3 S of Guildford
on to B3000.
Signposted.

Bus: 1¼ m
from House.

Rail: Farncombe 1½ m,
Guildford 2m,
Godalming 3m.

Air: Heathrow 30m,
Gatwick 30m.

CONFERENCE/FUNCTION

ROOM	SIZE	MAX CAPACITY
Tithe Barn	100' x 18'	200
Marquee	sites available	
Great Hall	70' x 40'	100
Drawing Rm	40' x 30'	50
Walled Gdn	Marquee	sites
Chestnut Ldg	18' x 38'	50

Loseley Park, built in 1562 by Sir William More to entertain Queen Elizabeth I, is a fine example of Elizabethan architecture, its mellow stone brought from the ruins of Waverley Abbey now over 850 years old. The house is set amid magnificent parkland grazed by the Loseley Jersey herd. Many visitors comment on the very friendly atmosphere of the house, it is a country house, the family home of descendants of the builder.

Furniture has been acquired by the family and includes an early 16th century Wrangelschrank beautifully inlaid with many different woods, a Queen Anne cabinet, Georgian armchairs and settee, a Hepplewhite four-poster bed and King George IV's coronation chair. The King's bedroom has Oudenarde tapestry and a carpet commemorating James I's visit. Also many fine paintings and portraits of family members. A beautiful and unique chimney piece carved out of a single piece of chalk to a design by Holbein. A Christian Cancer Help Centre meets twice monthly. Loseley House is available for dinners, functions and Civil weddings.

GARDEN

A magnificent Cedar of Lebanon presides over the front lawn. Parkland adjoins the lawn and a small lake adds to the beauty of Front Park. Walled Garden: Based on a Gertrude Jekyll design. Five gardens exist each with their own theme and character, making up the whole. These include the award-winning rose garden containing over 1,000 bushes, a magnificent vine walk, colourful fruit and flower garden and the serene fountain garden. Other features include a vegetable garden and moat walk. HDRA Seed Library plants.

🏠 🌷 ℹ️ Chapel. New lakeside walk. Business launches & promotions. 10 - 12 acre field can be hired in addition to the lawns. Fashion shows, archery, garden parties, shows, rallies, filming, parkland, moat walk & terrace. Lectures can be arranged on the property, its contents, gardens & history. Picnic area, home to Jersey herd since 1916; No unaccompanied children, no photography in house, no videos on estate. All group visits must be booked in advance.

🍽 Special functions, banquets and conference catering. Additional marquees for hire. Wedding receptions.

♿ May alight at entrance to property. Access to all areas except house first floor. WCs.

☕ Courtyard Tea Room.

🍴 Lunchtime restaurant.

🚶 Obligatory. Tour time for house, 40 mins.

🅿️ 150 cars, 6 coaches. Summer overflow car park.

🐕 Guide dogs only. 🔔 ❄️

▶ OPENING TIMES

Summer
Garden, Shop, Tea Room & Lunchtime Restaurant
May - September
Tues - Sun & BH Mons
in May & Aug,
11am - 5pm.

Loseley House
(guided tours)
May - Aug
Tues - Thurs and Suns
BH Mons in May & Aug,
1 - 5pm.

All Year (Private Hire)
Tithe Barn, Chestnut Lodge, House, Walled Garden and Grounds available for private/business functions, Civil weddings and receptions. Off-road 4 x 4 course.

▶ ADMISSION

House & Gardens
Adult £6.00
Child (5-16yrs) £3.00
Conc. £5.00
Child (under 5yrs) ...... Free

Booked Groups (10+)
Adult £5.50
Child (5-16yrs) £2.50
Conc. £4.50

Garden & Grounds only
Adult £3.00
Child (5-16yrs) £1.50
Conc. £2.50

Booked Groups (10+)
Adult £2.75
Child (5-16yrs) £1.25
Conc. £2.25

🎭 SPECIAL EVENTS
Please telephone for details.

153

Map 3

Owner:
Painshill Park Trust

▶ CONTACT

Visitor Management
Painshill Park
Portsmouth Road
Cobham
Surrey
KT11 1JE
Tel: 01932 868113
Fax: 01932 868001

e-mail:
info@painshill.co.uk

PAINSHILL PARK 🏛

www.painshill.co.uk

A unique award-winning restoration of England's 18th century heritage, Painshill Park is one of the most important 18th century parks in Europe. Within its 160 acres, its Hamilton Landscapes are a work of art that influenced the future of England's countryside and culture. Between 1738 and 1773 the Hon Charles Hamilton transformed barren heathland into a sequence of subtle and surprising vistas. Around the 14 acre serpentine lake, he assembled a series of carefully designed views known as the Hamilton Landscapes. The visitor moves from scene to scene; past the vineyard to an evergreen amphitheatre and on to the Gothic Temple, from the magical crystal grotto to a ruined Mausoleum, from a wild wood to the colourful flower beds that surround the site of the

Temple of Bacchus. Following years of dereliction the Landscapes have been restored to their original pre-eminence, winning the Europa Nostra Medal for exemplary restoration. Available for corporate and private hire, location filming, wedding receptions, etc.

Full Education Programme available – Lifelong Learning for ages 5 - 95. All Key Stages. Adult Higher Education and Informal Learning. Discover American Roots at Painshill Park. In July 2005 the first stage of The Painshill Park Heritage Plant Project will open with a major exhibition recreating the 18th century exchange of plants between Europe and America. Over 250 years on, retrace the journey of these seeds from American wilds to English landscapes.

▶ OPENING TIMES

March - October:
Tue - Sun & BH Mons,
10.30am - 6pm
(last admission 4.30pm).

November - February:
Wed - Sun & BH Mons
(closed Christmas Day),
11am - 4pm/dusk if earlier
(last admission 3pm).

▶ ADMISSION

Adult £7.00
Child (5-16yrs)...........£3.50
Under 5yrs ....Free
Conc £6.00
Family (2+2) £20.00

Multiple Season £75.00
Single Season £35.00
2 Adults Season £45.00

Pre-booked
groups (10+) £5.80

▶ LOCATION
OS Ref. TQ099 605

M25/J10 to London. W of Cobham on A245. Entrance 200 yds E of A245/A307 roundabout.

ℹ Marquee site.

🍽

♿

🍷 Licensed.

🎨 By arrangement.

🅿

♿

🐕 Guide dogs only and 'Special Dogs on a Lead Days'.

❄

BOX HILL

The Old Fort, Box Hill Road, Box Hill, Tadworth KT20 7LB
Tel: 01306 885502 **Fax:** 01306 875030 **e-mail:** boxhill@nationaltrust.org.uk
www.nationaltrust.org.uk/northdowns
Owner: The National Trust   **Contact:** Head Warden
An outstanding area of woodland and chalk downland, long famous as a destination
for day-trippers from London.
Location: OS Ref. TQ171 519. 1m N of Dorking, 1^1/$_2$m S of Leatherhead on A24.
Open: Shop, Information Centre and Servery: All year, daily (except 25/26 Dec & 1 Jan),
11 - 5pm or dusk.
Admission: Countryside: Free. Car/coach park £2, NT members Free.

❋

CAREW MANOR DOVECOTE

Church Road, Beddington, Surrey SM6 7NH
Tel: 020 8770 4781 **Fax:** 020 8770 4777 **e-mail:** sutton.museum@ukonline.co.uk
www.sutton.gov.uk
Owner: London Borough of Sutton   **Contact:** Ms V Murphy
An early 18th century octagonal brick dovecote with around 1200 nesting boxes and
the original potence (circular ladder). Opened for tours with the adjacent late
medieval Grade I listed Great Hall of Carew Manor.
Location: OS Ref. TQ295 652. Just off A232 at entrance to Beddington Park.
Open: Tours: Suns only, 24 Apr, 15 May, 3 Jul & 25 Sept: 2 & 3.30pm.
Admission: £3.50.

CLANDON PARK & HATCHLANDS PARK

See page 150 for full page entry.

Hampton Court Palace – Tudor Christmas.

©HRP 2002

❋ Open All Year Index see page 43

NT Photographic Library

NTPL / John Bethall

CLAREMONT LANDSCAPE GARDEN

PORTSMOUTH ROAD, ESHER, SURREY KT10 9JG
www.nationaltrust.org.uk/claremont

Tel: 01372 467806 **Fax:** 01372 464394 **e-mail:** claremont@nationaltrust.org.uk
Owner: The National Trust   **Contact:** The Property Manager
One of the earliest surviving English landscape gardens, restored to its former glory.
Begun by Sir John Vanbrugh and Charles Bridgeman before 1720, the garden was
extended and naturalised by William Kent. 'Capability' Brown also made
improvements. Features include a lake, island with pavilion, grotto, turf
amphitheatre, viewpoints and avenues.
Location: OS Ref. TQ128 632. On S edge of Esher, on E side of A307 (no access

from Esher bypass).
Open: Jan - end Mar, Nov - end Dec: daily except Mons: 10am - 5pm or sunset if
earlier. Apr - end Oct: daily: Mon - Fri, 10am - 6pm, Sats, Suns & BHs, 10am - 7pm. NB:
Garden closes for major events in July, please check in advance. Closed 25 Dec.
Admission: Adult £5, Child £2.50. Family (2+2) £12.50. Groups (15+), Adult £4.20,
Child £2.10. Discount if using public transport. Coach groups must book; no coach
groups on Suns.
☐ ♿ Limited. WC. ▣ 🐕 No dogs (Apr - Oct). ▣ Tel for details.

THE COBBE COLLECTION AT HATCHLANDS

See page 151 for full page entry.

DAPDUNE WHARF

River Wey Navigations, Wharf Road, Guildford GU1 4RR
Tel: 01483 561389 **Fax:** 01483 531667 **e-mail:** riverwey@nationaltrust.org.uk
www.nationaltrust.org.uk/riverwey
Owner: The National Trust   **Contact:** Wharf Warden
Dapdune Wharf is the centrepiece of one of The National Trust's most unusual properties, the River Wey Navigations.
Open: 19 Mar - 30 Oct: Thur - Mon, 11am - 5pm. River trips as for Wharf.
Admission: Adult £3.50, Child £2, Family £10. NT members Free. Boat Trip: Adult £2.50, Child £1.50.Groups (booked, min 15): Adult £3.
🎫 ♿ 💻 By arrangement. ■ **P** Limited. 🐕 In grounds, on leads.

FARNHAM CASTLE

Farnham, Surrey GU9 0AG
Tel: 01252 721194 **Fax:** 01252 711283 **e-mail:** info@farnhamcastle.com
Owner: The Church Commissioners   **Contact:** Farnham Castle
Bishop's Palace built in Norman times by Henry of Blois. Tudor and Jacobean additions.
Location: OS Ref. SU839 474. 1/2 m N of Farnham town centre on A287.
Open: All year: Weds, 2 - 4pm except Christmas & New Year.
Admission: Adult £2.50, Child/Conc £1.50.

FARNHAM CASTLE KEEP

Castle Hill, Farnham, Surrey GU6 0AG
Tel: 01252 713393 **www.**english-heritage.org.uk/visits
Owner: English Heritage   **Contact:** Visitor Operations Team
Used as a fortified manor by the medieval Bishops of Winchester, this motte and bailey castle has been in continuous occupation since the 12th century. You can visit the large shell-keep enclosing a mound in which are massive foundations of a Norman tower.
Location: OS Ref. SU839 474. 1/2 mile N of Farnham town centre on A287.
Open: 24 Mar - 30 Sept: Sats, Suns, & BHs: 10am - 5pm.
Admission: Adult £2.60, Child £1.30, Conc. £2.
🎫 ♿ Ground floor & grounds. 🎫 Free. **P** 🐕 In grounds, on leads.

GODDARDS

Abinger Common, Dorking, Surrey RH5 6TH
Tel: 01628 825920 or 01628 825925 (bookings) **www.**landmarktrust.org.uk
Owner: The Lutyens Trust, leased to The Landmark Trust **Contact:** The Landmark Trust
Built by Sir Edwin Lutyens in 1898 - 1900 and enlarged by him in 1910. Garden by Gertrude Jekyll. Given to the Lutyens Trust in 1991 and now managed and maintained by the Landmark Trust, which let buildings for self-catering holidays. The whole house, apart from the library, is available for up to 12 people. Full details of Goddards and 178 other historic buildings available for holidays are featured in The Landmark Handbook (price £9.50 refundable against booking), from The Landmark Trust, Shottesbrooke, Maidenhead, Berkshire SL6 3SW.
Location: OS Ref. TQ120 450. 4¹/₂ m SW of Dorking on the village green in Abinger Common. Signposted Abinger Common, Friday Street and Leith Hill from A25.
Open: Strictly by appointment. Must be booked in advance, including parking, which is very limited. Visits booked for Weds afternoons from the Wed after Easter until the last Wed of Oct, between 2.30 - 5pm. Only those with pre-booked tickets will be admitted.
Admission: £3. Tickets available from Mrs Baker on 01306 730871, Mon - Fri, 9am & 6pm. Visitors will have access to part of the garden and house only.
🐕

GREAT FOSTERS

Stroude Road, Egham, Surrey TW20 9UR
Tel: 01784 433822 **Fax:** 01784 472455 **e-mail:** enquiries@greatfosters.co.uk
www.greatfosters.co.uk
Owner: The Sutcliffe family   **Contact:** Karen Kennedy
Grade II* listed garden. Laid out in 1918 by W H Romaine-Walker in partnership with G H Jenkins, incorporating earlier features. The site covers 50 acres and is associated with a late 17th century country house, converted to an hotel in 1927. The main formal garden is surrounded on three sides by a moat thought to be of medieval origin and is modelled on the pattern of a Persian carpet. Garden also includes a sunken rose garden and avenue of lime trees.
Location: OS Ref. TQ015 694. M25 J/13, follow signs to Egham town centre. Under motorway bridge, left at roundabout. Left at the mini roundabout into Vicarage Rd. Right at next roundabout. Over M25. Left into Stroude Rd. 500 yds on left.
Open: All year.
Admission: Free.
♿ Partial. WC. **P** 🐕 Guide dogs only. ✳

GUILDFORD HOUSE GALLERY

155 High Street, Guildford, Surrey Gu1 3AJ
Tel/Fax: 01483 444742 (Guildford Borough Council)
www.guildfordhouse.co.uk
Owner/Contact: Guildford Borough Council
A beautifully restored 17th century town house with a number of original features including a finely carved staircase, panelled rooms and decorative plaster ceilings. A varied temporary exhibition programme including paintings, photography and craft work. Exhibition and events leaflet available. Lecture and workshop programme. Details on application.
Location: OS Ref. SU996 494. Central Guildford on High Street.
Open: Tue - Sat, 10am - 4.45pm.
Admission: Free.
🎫 💻 🍴 Public car park nearby. **P** 🐕 Guide dogs only. ✳ 💷 Tel for details.

HAMPTON COURT PALACE

See page 152 for full page entry.

HATCHLANDS PARK & CLANDON PARK

See page 150 for full page entry.

HONEYWOOD HERITAGE CENTRE

Honeywood Walk, Carshalton, Surrey SM5 3NX
Tel: 020 8770 4297 **Fax:** 020 8770 4297
e-mail: lbshoneywood@ukonline.co.uk **www.**sutton.gov.uk
Owner: London Borough of Sutton   **Contact:** The Curator
A 17th century listed building next to the picturesque Carshalton Ponds, containing displays on many aspects of the history of the London Borough of Sutton plus a changing programme of exhibitions and events on a wide range of subjects. Attractive garden at rear.
Location: OS Ref. TQ279 646. On A232 approximately 4m W of Croydon.
Open: Wed - Fri, 11am - 5pm. Sat, Suns & BH Mons, 10am - 5pm. Free admission to shop & tearooms.
Admission: Adult £1.25, Child 60p, under 5 Free. Groups by arrangement.
🎫 ♿ Ground floor. WC. 💻 🍴 **P** Limited. ■ 🐕 Guide dogs only. ✳ 💷 Tel for details.

KEW GARDENS

Kew, Richmond, Surrey TW9 3AB
Tel: 020 8332 5655 **Fax:** 020 8332 5610   **Contact:** Visitor Information
Kew Gardens, now a World Heritage Site, is a mixture of stunning vistas, magnificent glasshouses and beautiful landscapes beside the River Thames. This once Royal residence represents nearly 250 years of historical gardens and today its 121 hectares are home to over 30,000 types of plants from rainforest to desert.
Location: OS Ref. TQ188 776. A307. Junc. A307 & A205 (1m Chiswick roundabout M4).
Open: 9.30am, daily except 24/25 Dec. Closing time varies according to the season. Please telephone for further information.
Admission: Adult £8.50, Child (under 17yrs) Free, Conc. £6. (2004 prices.)

©HRP 2002

Hampton Court Palace – The Sunken Garden.

LEITH HILL ✠
Coldharbour, Surrey
Tel: 01306 711777 **Fax:** 01306 712153 **www**.nationaltrust.org.uk/northdowns
Owner: The National Trust   **Contact:** Head Warden
The highest point in south-east England, crowned by an 18th century Gothic tower, from which there are magnificent views. The surrounding woodland contains ancient stands of hazel and oak, and there is a colourful display of rhododendrons in May - Jun.
Location: OS Ref. TQ139 432. 1m SW of Coldharbour A29/B2126.
Open: Tower: 18 Mar - 30 Oct: Fri - Sun, and Weds in Aug, 10am - 5pm. 5 Nov - 12 Mar: Sats & Suns, 10am - 3.30pm. Open all BHs (closed 25 Dec). Wood & Estate: All year: daily.
Admission: Tower: £1, Child 50p. Rhododendron Wood: £2 per car. (2 circular nature trails with leaflet.)
ⓘNo vehicular access to summit. ⓹Partial. ⓓWhen Tower open. ⓕGuided walks.
ⓅParking at foot of hill, ¹/₂m walk from Tower. ⓗNot in picnic area or Tower. ✳

LITTLE HOLLAND HOUSE
40 Beeches Avenue, Carshalton, Surrey SM5 3LW
Tel: 020 8770 4781 **Fax:** 020 8770 4777
e-mail: valary.murphy@sutton.gov.uk **www**.sutton.gov.uk
Owner: London Borough of Sutton   **Contact:** Ms V Murphy
The home of Frank Dickinson (1874 - 1961) artist, designer and craftsman, who dreamt of a house that would follow the philosophy and theories of William Morris and John Ruskin. Dickinson designed, built and furnished the house himself from 1902 onwards. The Grade II* listed interior features handmade furniture, metal work, carvings and paintings produced by Dickinson in the Arts and Crafts style.
Location: OS Ref. TQ275 634. On B278 1m S of junction with A232.
Open: First Sun of each month & BH Suns & Mons (excluding Christmas & New Year), 1.30 - 5.30pm.
Admission: Free. Groups by arrangement, £3pp (includes talk and guided tour).
ⓘNo photography in house. ⓹Ground floor. ⓕBy arrangement.
ⓗGuide dogs only. ✳

LOSELEY PARK 🏛   *See page 153 for full page entry.*

PAINSHILL PARK 🏛   *See page 154 for full page entry.*

OAKHURST COTTAGE ✠
HAMBLEDON, GODALMING, SURREY GU8 4HF
Tel: 01483 208477 **e-mail:** oakhurstcottage@nationaltrust.org.uk
Owner: The National Trust   **Contact:** Winkworth Arboretum
A small 16th century timber-framed cottage, painted by both Helen Allingham and Myles Birket Foster, containing furniture and artefacts reflecting two or more centuries of continuing occupation. There is a delightful cottage garden and a small barn containing agricultural implements.
Location: OS Ref. SU965 385. Hambledon, Surrey.
Open: 23 Mar - 30 Oct: Weds, Thurs, Sats, Suns & BH Mons. Strictly by appointment, 2 - 5pm.
Admission: Adult £4, Child £2 (incl guided tour). No reduction for groups.
⓹Unsuitable. ⓕObligatory, by arrangement. ⓅLimited. ⓗ

POLESDEN LACEY ✠
GREAT BOOKHAM, Nr DORKING, SURREY RH5 6BD
www.nationaltrust.org.uk/polesdenlacey

Tel: 01372 452048 **Infoline:** 01372 458203 **Fax:** 01372 452023
e-mail: polesdenlacey@nationaltrust.org.uk
Owner: The National Trust   **Contact:** The Property Manager
Originally an elegant 1820s Regency villa in a magnificent landscape setting. The house was remodelled after 1906 by the Hon Mrs Ronald Greville, a well-known Edwardian hostess. Her collection of fine paintings, furniture, porcelain and silver are still displayed in the reception rooms and galleries. Extensive grounds, walled rose garden, lawns and landscaped walks.
Location: OS Ref. TQ136 522. 5m NW of Dorking, 2m S of Great Bookham, off A246.

Open: House: 16 Mar - 6 Nov: Wed - Sun, 11am - 5pm also BH Mons starting with Easter. Grounds: All year: daily, 11am - 6pm/dusk. Last admission to house ¹/₂ hr before closing.
Admission: Garden, grounds & landscape walks: Adult £5, Child £2.50, Family £12.50. House: Adult £3 extra, Child £1.50 extra, Family £7.50 extra. All year, booked groups £6.50 (house, garden & walks).

⧉ ⊞ ⓹ ⊞Licensed. ⓅLimited for coaches. ⓗIn grounds on leads. ✳
⊞ Tel: 01372 452048 for info.

RHS GARDEN WISLEY

Nr WOKING, SURREY GU23 6QB

www.rhs.org.uk

Tel: 01483 224234 **Fax:** 01483 211750

Owner/Contact: The Royal Horticultural Society

A garden to enjoy all year round with something to see for everyone. Wisley provides the visitor with ideas and inspiration and the benefit of experience from experts. The Wisley Plant Centre with plants for sale, The Wisley Shop with books and gifts and for refreshments the Café, Restaurant and coffee shops.

Location: OS Ref. TQ066 583. On A3 N of Guildford nr. M25 J/10. Brown Signs.

Open: All year: daily (except Christmas Day), Mon - Fri, 10am - 6pm (4.30pm Nov - Feb). Sat & Sun, 9am - 6pm (4.30pm Nov - Feb). Last entry 1 hr before closing.

Admission: RHS Members: Free. Adult £7, Child (6-16yrs) £2, Child (under 6) Free. Groups (10+): Adult £5.50, Child £1.60.

◻ ⊛ ⬧ Wheelchairs available tel: 01483 211113 & special map. WC. ☞ ⬚ Licensed. ⬧ By arrangement. ◻ P ▣ ⬧ Guide dogs only. ⊛ ⬚

RAMSTER GARDENS

Ramster, Chiddingfold, Surrey GU8 4SN

Tel: 01428 654167 **Fax:** 01428 658345

Owner/Contact: Mrs M Gunn

20 acres of woodland and shrub garden.

Location: OS Ref. SU950 333. 1½ m S of Chiddingfold on A283.

Open: 9 Apr - 26 Jun: daily, also 29/30 Oct, 5/6 Nov: 10am - 5pm.

Admission: Adult £4, Child Free.

RUNNYMEDE ✿

Egham, Surrey

Tel: 01784 432891 **Fax:** 01784 479007 **e-mail:** runnymede@nationaltrust.org.uk www.nationaltrust.org.uk

Owner: The National Trust   **Contact:** The Head Warden

Runnymede is an attractive area of riverside meadows, grassland and broadleaf woodland, rich in diversity of flora and fauna, and part-designated a Site of Special Scientific Interest. It was on this site, in 1215, that King John sealed Magna Carta.

Location: OS Ref. TQ007 720. 2m W of Runnymede Bridge, on S side of A308, M25/J13.

Open: All year. Riverside Car park (grass): Apr - 30 Sept: daily, 9am - 7pm. Tearoom Car park (hard standing): daily, all year, 8.30am - 5pm (later in Summer).

Admission: Fees payable for parking (NT members Free), fishing & mooring.

◻ ⬧ Partial. ☞ ⬧ P ⊛ ⬚ Tel for details.

WHITEHALL

1 Malden Road, Cheam, Surrey SM3 8QD

Tel/Fax: 020 8643 1236 **e-mail:** curators@whitehallcheam.fsnet.co.uk www.sutton.gov.uk

Owner: London Borough of Sutton   **Contact:** The Curator

A Tudor timber-framed house, c1500 with later additions, in the heart of Cheam village conservation area. Displays on the history of the house and the people who lived here, plus nearby Nonsuch Palace, Cheam School and William Gilpin (Dr Syntax). Changing exhibition programme and special event days throughout the year. Attractive rear garden features medieval well from c1400.

Location: OS Ref. TQ242 638. Approx. 2m S of A3 on A2043 just N of junction with A232.

Open: Wed - Fri, 2 - 5pm; Sat, 10am - 5pm; Sun & BH Mons, 2 - 5pm.

Admission: Adult £1.25, Child (under 16yrs) 60p, Child under 5yrs Free. Groups by arrangement.

◻ ⬧ Ground floor. ☞ ⬧ ◻ ▣ ⬧ Guide dogs only. ⊛ ⬚ Tel for details.

NTPL / D Sellman

WINKWORTH ARBORETUM ✿

HASCOMBE ROAD, GODALMING, SURREY GU8 4AD

www.nationaltrust.org.uk/winkwortharboretum

Tel: 01483 208477 **Fax:** 01483 208252

e-mail: winkwortharboretum@nationaltrust.org.uk

Owner: The National Trust   **Contact:** Head Arborist

Established in the 20th century, the hillside arboretum now contains over 1,000 different shrubs and trees, many of them rare. The most impressive displays are in spring for bluebells and azaleas, and in autumn for colour and wildlife. In the summer it is an ideal place for family visits and a picnic. Following dam restoration work, a new wetland area is being developed. The upper lake has been restored.

Location: OS Ref. SU990 412. Near Hascombe, 2m SE of Godalming on E side of B2130.

Open: All year round: daily during daylight hours. May be closed due to high winds. Boathouse: Apr - Nov.

Admission: Adult £4.50, Child (5-16yrs) £2, Family (2+2) £10 (additional family member £1.75). Discounts for 15 or more.

◻ ⬧ Limited. WC. ☞ ⬧ In grounds, on leads. ⊛

ARUNDEL CASTLE

www.arundelcastle.org

A thousand years of history is waiting to be discovered at Arundel Castle in West Sussex. Dating from the 11th century, the Castle is both ancient fortification and stately home of the Dukes of Norfolk and Earls of Arundel.

Set high on a hill, this magnificent castle commands stunning views across the River Arun and out to sea. Climb the Keep, explore the battlements, wander in the grounds and recently restored Victorian gardens and relax in the Fitzalan Chapel garden.

The Castle suffered extensive damage during the English Civil War and the process of structural restoration began in earnest in the 18th century and continued up until 1900. It was one of the first private residences to have electricity and central heating and has its own fire engine, which is still on view today.

Inside the Castle, 20 rooms are open to the public including the vast Baron's Hall with its fine collection of 16th century furniture, the Armoury with a unique assemblage of armour and weaponry, tapestries hang above the Grand Staircase leading to the renovated Victorian bedrooms and bathrooms, paintings by Van Dyck, Gainsborough, Canaletto and others, together with the personal possessions of Mary, Queen of Scots, including the gold and enamel rosary that she carried to her execution.

There are special events throughout the season, including jousting, medieval re-enactments and falconry.

Map 3

Owner:
Arundel Castle
Trustees Ltd

▶ CONTACT

The Comptroller
Arundel Castle
Arundel
West Sussex
BN18 9AB

Tel: 01903 883136
or 01903 882173

Fax: 01903 884581

e-mail: info@
arundelcastle.org

▶ LOCATION

OS Ref. TQ018 072

Central Arundel, N of A27
Brighton 40 mins,
Worthing 15 mins,
Chichester 15 mins.
From London A3 or
A24, 1¹/₂ hrs.
M25 motorway, 30m.

Bus: Bus stop 100 yds.

Rail: Station ¹/₂ m.

Air: Gatwick 25m.

No photography inside the Castle. Guidebooks in French & German.

Most areas accessible. Visitors may alight at the entrance, before parking in the allocated areas. WCs.

Restaurant seats 140. Special rates for booked groups. Self-service restaurant in Castle serves home-made food. Groups must book in advance for morning coffee, lunch or afternoon tea.

Pre-booked groups only. Tour time 1¹/₂ hrs. Tours available in Japanese.

Ample. Coaches can park free in town coach park.

Items of particular interest include a Norman Motte & Keep, Armoury & Victorian bedrooms. Special rates for schoolchildren (aged 5-15) and teachers.

Tel for details.

▶ OPENING TIMES

Summer
25 March - 31 October
Daily (except Sats)
Grounds, gardens, shop,
Fitzalan Chapel and Keep
Restaurant
11am - 5pm.

Castle Rooms
12 noon - 5pm.
Last admission 4pm.

Winter
1 November - 24 March
Pre-booked groups only.

▶ ADMISSION

Summer
Adult £11.00
Child (5-16yrs) £7.50
Conc. £9.00
Family (2+5 max). £31.00
Groups (20+)
Adult £9.00
Child (5-16yrs) £6.00
Conc. £7.50

Pre-booked Groups
(subject to minimum fee)
Mornings.............. £11.00
Evenings £17.00
Saturdays £17.00

Winter
Pre-booked groups
(subject to minimum fee).
All entries £17.00

NTPL/ Rupert Truman

Map 4

BATEMAN'S ❧

www.nationaltrust.org.uk/batemans

Owner:
The National Trust

▶ **CONTACT**

The Property Manager
Bateman's
Burwash
Etchingham
East Sussex   TN19 7DS

Tel: 01435 882302

Fax: 01435 882811

e-mail: batemans@
nationaltrust.org.uk

▶ **LOCATION**
OS Ref. TQ671 238

¹/₂ m S of Burwash
off A265.

Rail: Etchingham 3m,
then bus (twice daily).

Air: Gatwick 40m.

Built in 1634 and home to Rudyard Kipling for over 30 years, Bateman's lies in the richly wooded landscape of the Sussex Weald. Visit this Sussex sandstone manor house, built by a local ironmaster, where the famous writer lived from 1902 to 1936. See the rooms as they were in Kipling's day, including the study where the view inspired him to write some of his well-loved works including *Puck of Pook's Hill* and *Rewards and Fairies*. Find the mementoes of Kipling's time in India and illustrations from his famous *Jungle Book* tales of *Mowgli, Baloo and Shere Khan*.

Wander through the delightful Rose Garden with its pond and statues, with Mulberry and Herb gardens and discover the wild garden, through which flows the River Dudwell. Through the wild garden, you will find the Mill where you can watch corn being ground on most Saturday and Wednesday afternoons and one of the world's first water-driven turbines installed by Kipling to generate electricity for the house. In the garage, see a 1928 Rolls Royce, one of several owned by Kipling who was a keen early motorist.

Savour the peace and tranquillity of this beautiful property which Kipling described as *'A good and peaceable place'* and of which he said *'we have loved it, ever since our first sight of it…'*.

There is a picnic glade next to the car park, or you can enjoy morning coffee, a delicious lunch or afternoon tea in the licensed tearoom where there is special emphasis on using local produce. The well-stocked gift shop offers the largest collection of Kipling books in the area.

▶ **OPENING TIMES**

19 March - 30 October:
Sat - Wed, Good Fri &
BH Mons
11am - 5.00pm.
Last admission 4.30pm.

▶ **ADMISSION**

House & Garden
Adult £5.90
Child £2.95
Family (2+3) £14.75
Groups..................... £4.90

Ground floor & grounds.
WC. Computerised virtual tour of upper floors.

Licensed.

Tel for details.

NTPL/ Geoffrey Frosh

Map 3

GOODWOOD HOUSE

www.goodwood.co.uk

Seated at the heart of one of the world's finest sporting estates, Goodwood House is the ancestral home of the Dukes of Richmond, direct descendants of King Charles II. Two of the three great wings of Goodwood House were built just after 1800, to house the earlier art treasures. This year the focus is on *The Richmonds at War:* Wellington, Napoleon, and the Duchess of Richmond's Ball. The emphasis is thus on the Regency Period. This exhibition-trail ties in with events at other venues in 2005, celebrating Nelson and *Sea Britain*.

Today, the flinted and turreted Goodwood House continues to encapsulate the innovation and party spirit that have been the signature tune of the Dukes of Richmond for three hundred years. Set in the strongly coloured, gilded, Regency interiors, the art collection comprises fine French furniture and tapestries, Sèvres porcelain, glorious views of London by Canaletto and sporting scenes on the estate by George Stubbs. There are hundreds of other superb paintings. Special pieces are regularly rotated and displayed. Items are also available for viewing by written appointment. Arrangements to see the books can be made by written application to the Curator (there is a charge for these viewings).

Still inhabited by the family, Goodwood exudes the glamour of a ducal seat. It is not only a beautiful house to visit on an Open Day, but is also renowned for its elegant entertaining, enjoying a worldwide reputation for excellence as a location for unforgettable weddings, parties and other events. With horseracing, motorsport, aviation, a hotel and sports centre and two golf courses at hand, there is something for everyone at Glorious Goodwood.

Owner:
The Earl of March

▶ CONTACT

Curator's PA
Goodwood House
Goodwood
Chichester
West Sussex PO18 0PX

Tel: 01243 755048
01243 755042
(Weddings)
Fax: 01243 755005
Recorded info:
01243 755040
e-mail: curator
@goodwood.co.uk
or weddings@
goodwood.co.uk

▶ LOCATION

OS Ref. SU888 088

3¹/₂m NE of Chichester.
A3 from London then
A286 or A285. M27/A27
from Portsmouth or
Brighton.

Rail: Chichester 3¹/₂m
Arundel 9m.

Air: Heathrow 1¹/₂ hrs
Gatwick ³/₄ hr.

CONFERENCE/FUNCTION

ROOM	SIZE	MAX CAPACITY
Ballroom	79' x 23'	200
11 other rooms also available		

▶ OPENING TIMES

Summer
20 March - 3 October:
Most Sun & Mon
afternoons. (Check
recorded information.)

1 - 31 Aug:
Sun - Thur, 1 - 5pm.

Closed 24 April,
15/16 May & 18 Sept.
It will also be closed over
two consecutive weekends
for the Festival of Speed,
probably 3/4 & 10/11 July.

Connoisseurs' Days
13 & 26 April, 18 May,
20 Sept, 20 Oct.
Special tours for groups:
must be booked.

▶ ADMISSION

House
Adult £7.00
Child (12 - 18yrs)...... £3.00
Child (under 12 yrs) ... Free
Senior £6.00
Groups (20 - 200)
Open Day £6.00
Morning................ £8.50
Connoisseur £9.00

Goodwood Photo Collection

Goodwood Photo Collection

▶ SPECIAL EVENTS

July 8 - 10*
Motorsport Festival of Speed.
July 26 - 30
Festival Race Meeting.
Sept 16 - 18*
Motorsport Revival.

*Advance tickets only.
Please visit our website.

Conference facilities. No photography. Highly trained guides. Shell House optional extra on Connoisseurs' Days or by Group Appointment, or written request.

Obligatory. Ample.

In grounds, on leads. Guide dogs only in house.

Civil Wedding Licence.

Map 3

Owner:
R Loder Esq

▶ **CONTACT**

R Loder Esq
Leonardslee Gardens
Lower Beeding
Horsham
West Sussex   RH13 6PP

Tel: 01403 891212
Fax: 01403 891305

e-mail: gardens@
leonardslee.com

▶ **LOCATION**
OS Ref. TQ222 260

M23 to Handcross then
B2110 (signposted
Cowfold) for 4m.
From London:
1 hr 15 mins.

Rail: Horsham
Station 4^1/$_2$ m

Bus: No. 17 from
Horsham and Brighton

LEONARDSLEE
LAKES & GARDENS

www.leonardslee.com

Leonardslee represents one of the largest and most spectacular woodland gardens in England, in a most magnificent setting, only a few miles from the M23. Begun 200 years ago, and enlarged by Sir Edmund Loder since 1889, it is still maintained by the Loder family today. The 240 acre (100 hectare) valley is world famous for its spring display of azaleas and rhododendrons around the seven lakes, giving superb views and reflections.

The famous *rhododendron loderi*, was raised by Sir Edmund Loder in 1901. The original plants can still be seen in the garden. In May, the fragrance of their huge blooms pervades the air throughout the valley. The delightful Rock Garden, is a kaleidoscope of colour in May, then new plantings of *Hydrangeas*, *Cornus* and *Kalmias* give colour in the summer months.

A fine collection of Bonsai, including specimen Bonsai maples and choice group plantings show this living art-form to perfection. At Leonardslee, not only flora but fauna are welcome too! Wallabies (used as mowing machines!) have lived wild in parts of the valley for over 100 years, and deer, (Sika, Fallow and Axis) may be seen in the parklands. Ducks, geese and swans adorn the lakes where large carp glide.

Other attractions include the Loder family collection of Victorian motorcars (1889 - 1900), which provide a fascinating view of the different designs adopted by the first pioneers of the automobile industry, while the 'Behind the Dolls House' exhibition shows a country estate of 100 years ago, all in miniature ^{1}/$_{12}$th scale, and has proved so popular that it has been extended.

▶ **OPENING TIMES**

Summer
1 April - 31 October
Daily 9.30am - 6pm

Winter
1 November - 31 March
Closed to the general public.

Available for functions.

▶ **ADMISSION**

April, June - October
  Adult £6.00

May (Mon - Fri)
  Adult £7.00

May (Sats, Suns & BH Mons)
  Adult £8.00

  Child (anytime) £4.00

Groups
April, June - October
  Adult £5.00

May: (Mon - Fri) £6.00
Sat, Sun & BH Mons:. £7.00

  Child (anytime) £3.50

▶ **SPECIAL EVENTS**

MAY
Early May Bonsai Weekend.

JUN 25/26
West Sussex Country
Craft Fair.

CONFERENCE/FUNCTION	
ROOM	MAX CAPACITY
Clock Tower	100

📷✳ℹ️ Photography - landscape & fashion, film location.

🍴 Restaurant available for private and corporate function in the evenings and out of season.

♿ Unsuitable.

☕🍴 Restaurant & café. Morning coffee, lunch and teas.

🅿 Ample. Refreshments free to coach drivers. Average length of visit 3 - 5 hours.

Geoff Hamilton/The National Trust

Map 3

Owner:
The National Trust

▶ **CONTACT**

The Administration
Office
Petworth House
Petworth
West Sussex   GU28 0AE

Tel: 01798 342207

Info Line: 01798 343929

Fax: 01798 342963

e-mail: petworth@
nationaltrust.org.uk

▶ **LOCATION**
OS Ref. SU976 218

In the centre of
Petworth town
(approach roads
A272/A283/A285)
Car park signposted.

Rail: Pulborough
5¼ m.

PETWORTH HOUSE & PARK

www.nationaltrust.org.uk/petworth

Petworth House is one of the finest houses in the care of the National Trust and is home to an art collection that rivals many London galleries. Assembled by one family over 350 years, it includes works by Turner, Van Dyck, Titian, Claude, Gainsborough, Bosch, Reynolds and William Blake.

The state rooms contain sculpture, furniture and porcelain of the highest quality and are complemented by the old kitchens in the Servants' Quarters. The Carved Room contains some of

Grinling Gibbons' finest limewood carvings.

Petworth House is also the home of Lord and Lady Egremont and extra family rooms are open on weekdays by kind permission of the family (not Bank Holidays).

Petworth Park is a 700 acre park landscaped by 'Capability' Brown and is open to the public all year free of charge. Spring and autumn are particularly breathtaking and the summer sunsets over the lake are spectacular.

NTPL / Rupert Truman

🏬 ℹ️ Events throughout the year. Large musical concerts in the park. Baby feeding and changing facilities, highchairs. Pushchairs admitted in house but no prams, please. No photography in house.

🛍️ Contact Retail & Catering Manager on 01798 344975.

♿ Car park is 800 yards from house; there is a vehicle available to take less able visitors to House.

🍴 Licensed.

🚶 By arrangement with the Administration Office on variety of subjects.

🎧 Audio House Tours.

🅿️ 800 yards from house. Coach parties alight at Church Lodge entrance, coaches then park in NT car park. Coaches must book in advance.

🏫 Welcome. Must book. Teachers' pack available.

🐕 Guide dogs only in house. Dogs in park only.

❄️ 💍 Tel for details.

▶ **OPENING TIMES**

House
19 March - 30 October
Daily except Thurs & Fris
but open Good Fri,
11am - 5pm.

Last admission to House
4.30pm.

Extra rooms shown on
Mons, Tues & Weds,
not BH Mons.

Pleasure Ground
5 - 16 March for spring
bulbs and events,
12 noon - 4pm.

19 March - 30 October
Daily except Thurs & Fris,
11am - 6pm.

Park
All year: Daily, 8am - sunset.

Shop & Restaurant:
5 - 16 March for Mothering
Sunday lunches and events,
12 noon - 4pm.

19 March - 30 October
Daily except Thurs & Fris,
11am - 5pm.

▶ **ADMISSION**

**House & Pleasure
Ground**
Adult £7.50
Child (5-17yrs) £4.00
Child (under 5 yrs) ..... Free
Family (2+3) £19.00

Groups (pre-booked 15+)
Adult £6.50

Park Only .... Free

Pleasure Ground
Adult £2.00
Children £1.00

NT Members Free.

THE ROYAL PAVILION

www.royalpavilion.org.uk

Map 3

Owner:
Brighton & Hove
City Council

▶ **CONTACT**

Visitor Services
The Royal Pavilion
Brighton
East Sussex BN1 1EE

Tel: 01273 290900

Fax: 01273 292871

▶ **LOCATION**

The Royal Pavilion is in
the centre of Brighton
easily reached by road
and rail. From London
M25, M23, A23 -
1 hr 30 mins.

Rail: Victoria to
Brighton station
50 mins.
15 mins walk from
Brighton station.

Air: Gatwick 20 mins.

Universally acclaimed as one of the most exotically beautiful buildings in the British Isles, the Royal Pavilion is the former seaside residence of King George IV.

Originally a simple farmhouse, in 1787 architect Henry Holland created a neo-classical villa on the site. It was later transformed into its current Indian style by John Nash between 1815 and 1822. With interiors decorated in the Chinese style and an astonishingly exotic exterior, this Regency Palace is quite breathtaking.

Magnificent decorations and fantastic furnishings have been re-created in the recent extensive restoration programme. From the opulence of the main state rooms to the charm of the first floor bedroom suites, the Royal Pavilion is filled with astonishing colours and superb craftsmanship.

Witness the magnificence of the Music Room with its domed ceiling of gilded scallop-shaped shells and hand-knotted carpet, and promenade through the Chinese bamboo grove of the Long Gallery.

Lavish menus were created in the Great Kitchen, with its cast iron palm trees and dazzling collection of copperware, and then served in the dramatic setting of the Banqueting Room, lit by a huge crystal chandelier held by a silvered dragon.

Set in restored Regency gardens replanted to John Nash's elegant 1820s design, the Royal Pavilion is an unforgettable experience.

Visitors can discover more about life behind the scenes at the Palace during the last 200 years with a specially commissioned interactive multimedia presentation. Public guided tours take place daily at 11.30am and 2.30pm for a small additional charge.

ⓘ Location filming and photography, including feature films, fashion shoots and corporate videos.

🛍 Gift shop with souvenirs unique to the Royal Pavilion.

🍽 Spectacular rooms available for prestigious corporate and private entertaining and wedding receptions.

♿ Access to ground floor only. Tactile and signed tours can be booked in advance with Visitor Services Tel: 01273 292820/2.

☕ Tearooms with a balcony providing sweeping views across the restored Regency gardens.

🧍 Tours in English, French and German and other languages by prior arrangement. General introduction and specialist tours provided.

🅿 Close to NCP car parks, town centre voucher parking. Coach drop-off point in Church Street, parking in Madeira Drive. Free entry for coach drivers.

▣ Specialist tours relating to all levels of National Curriculum, must be booked in advance with Visitor Services. Special winter student rates. Slide lecture presentations by arrangement.

🔔 Civil Wedding Licence.

❄

▶ **OPENING TIMES**

Summer
April - September
Daily: 9.30am - 5.45pm
Last admission at 5pm.

Winter
October - March
Daily: 10am - 5.15pm
Last admission at 4.30pm.

Closed 24 (from 2.30pm),
25/26 December.

▶ **ADMISSION**

Adult £5.95
Child £3.50
Conc. £4.20
Groups (20+)
Adult £4.95

Prices valid until 31.3.2005

 SPECIAL EVENTS

**AUTUMN, WINTER
& SPRING:**
Children's Events.

Please telephone for details
of other events throughout
the year.

CONFERENCE/FUNCTION

ROOM	MAX CAPACITY
Banqueting Room	200
Great Kitchen	90
Music Rm	180
Queen Adelaide Suite	100
Small Adelaide	40
William IV	80

SAINT HILL MANOR

Map 3

Owner:
Church of Scientology

▶ **CONTACT**

Mrs Liz Ostermann
Saint Hill Manor
Saint Hill Road
East Grinstead
West Sussex RH19 4JY

Tel: 01342 326711
Fax: 01342 317057

e-mail:
info@hubbardfoundation.
co.uk

▶ **LOCATION**
OS Ref. TQ383 359

2m SW of East
Grinstead. At Felbridge,
turn off A22, down
Imberhorne Lane and
over crossroads into
Saint Hill Road,
200yds on right.

Rail: East Grinstead
station.

Air: 15 mins drive from
Gatwick airport.

Built 1792 by Gibbs Crawfurd. One of the finest Sussex sandstone buildings in existence and situated near the breathtaking Ashdown Forest. Subsequent owners included Edgar March Crookshank and the Maharajah of Jaipur. In 1959, Saint Hill Manor's final owner, acclaimed author and humanitarian L Ron Hubbard, acquired the Manor, where he lived for many years with his family. As a result of the work carried out under Mr Hubbard's direction, the Manor has been restored to its original beauty, including the uncovering of fine oak wood panelling, marble fireplaces and plasterwork ceilings. Other outstanding features of this lovely house include an impressive library of Mr Hubbard's works, elegant winter garden, and delightful Monkey Mural painted in 1945 by Winston Churchill's nephew John Spencer Churchill. This 100-foot mural depicts many famous personalities as monkeys, including Winston Churchill. Also open to the public are 59 acres of landscaped gardens, lake and woodlands. Ideal for corporate functions and also available as a film location. Annual events include open-air theatre, arts festivals, classical and jazz concerts.

▶ **OPENING TIMES**

All year
Daily, 2 - 5pm,
on the hour.

Groups welcome
throughout the year.

▶ **ADMISSION**

Free.

🍷
♿ Ground floor.
☕ Teas available.
🚶 Obligatory.
🅿
🐾
❄

🛡 **SPECIAL EVENTS**

Open-air theatre, concerts and festivals in summer – please telephone for details.

©NTPL 2004

SHEFFIELD PARK GARDEN

www.nationaltrust.org.uk/sheffieldpark

Map 4

Owner:
The National Trust

▶ **CONTACT**

Jo Hopkins
Visitor Services &
Marketing Manager
Sheffield Park
East Sussex
TN22 3QX

Tel: 01825 790231
Fax: 01825 791264

e-mail: sheffieldpark@
nationaltrust.org.uk

▶ **LOCATION**

OS Ref. TQ415 240

Midway between East
Grinstead and Lewes,
5m NW of Uckfield on
E side of A275.

A magnificent 120 acre landscaped garden. The centrepiece of this internationally renowned, garden is the four lakes that mirror the unique planting and colour that each season brings. Displays of spring bulbs as the garden awakens, and a stunning exhibition of colour in May, of rhododendrons and the National Collection of Ghent Azaleas. Water lilies dress the lakes during the summer months. Visitors to the garden during the summer months can enjoy a leisurely walk perhaps pausing to sit on a seat to enjoy the tranquil ambience. In the autumn the garden is transformed by trees planted specifically for their autumn colour including *Nyssa sylvatica*, *Amelanchier* and *Acer palmatum*. These and other fine specimen trees, particularly North American varieties, produce displays of gold, orange and crimson. *Gentiana sino-ornata* offers two borders of amazing 'Gentian Blue' colour during the autumn months. The garden is open throughout the year and has something for all, whether a quiet stroll or a family gathering, allowing the children to participate in the many activities offered. Special Events run throughout the year, including Bat Walk, Teddy Bears' Picnic, Open-air Concerts and Garden Tours..

▶ **OPENING TIMES**

1 January - 13 February:
Sat & Sun,
10.30am - 4pm.

15 February - 30 April &
June - September:
Tue - Sun & BH Mons,
10.30am - 6pm.

May & October:
Daily, 10.30am - 6pm.

November - 22 December:
Tue - Sun, 10.30am - 4pm.

Last admission to the
garden 1 hour before
closing or dusk if earlier.

▶ **ADMISSION**

Adult	£5.50
Child	£2.75
Family	£13.75
Groups (15+)	
Adult	£4.70
Child	£2.35

Joint Ticket available with
Bluebell Railway.

NT, RHS individual &
Great British Heritage Pass
members Free.

Partial. WC.

(not NT).

By arrangement.

Guide dogs only.

Tel for details.

©NTPL 2004

NT Photographic Library: David Sellman

Map 3

UPPARK

www.nationaltrust.org.uk/uppark

A fine late 17th century house set high on the South Downs with magnificent sweeping views to the sea. The drama of the 1989 fire and restoration adds to the magic of this romantic house.

The elegant Georgian interior houses a famous Grand Tour collection that includes paintings by Pompeo Batoni, Luca Giordano, and Joseph Vernet, with furniture and ceramics of superb quality. The famous 18th century dolls' house with original contents is one of the star items in the collection, and provides a rare insight into life in a great house 300 years ago.

The restaurant in the Georgian kitchen in the East

Pavilion serves a delicious menu using local produce. The West Pavilion houses the beautiful stables and the atmospheric and romantic Dairy. The complete servants' quarters in the basement are shown as they were in Victorian days when H G Wells' mother was housekeeper. From the basement visitors leave the house via the subterranean passages.

The fine, peaceful, historic garden is now fully restored in the early 19th century 'Picturesque' style, with flowering shrubs and under-plantings of bulbs, perennials and herbaceous plants in a magical woodland and downland setting.

Owner:
The National Trust

▶ CONTACT

The Property Manager
Uppark
South Harting
Petersfield   GU31 5QR

Tel: 01730 825415

Info Line: 01730 825857

Fax: 01730 825873

e-mail: uppark
@nationaltrust.org.uk

▶ LOCATION
OS Ref. 197 SU781 181

5m SE of Petersfield
on B2146, 1½ m S of
South Harting.

Bus: Stagecoach Sussex
Bus 54 (not Sun).

Rail: Petersfield 5½ m.

▶ OPENING TIMES
20 March - 27 October:
Daily except Fris & Sats.

House: 1 - 5pm
(opens 12 noon on Suns
in Aug, 11am on BH Mons;
closes 4pm in Oct).

Last admission 4.15pm
(3.30pm in Oct).

Print room open on 1st
Mon of each month.

Grounds & Garden
11am - 5.30pm
(4.30pm in Oct).

Shop & Restaurant:
11.30am - 5.30pm
(4.30pm in Oct).

▶ ADMISSION
**House, Garden &
Exhibition**

Adult £6.00
Child £3.00
Family £15.00
Groups (15+)
must book................ £5.00

Booked group guided tours:
mornings by arrangement.

Special group catering
arrangements: please
telephone for details.

NT members Free.

NB. To avoid congestion
timed tickets will be used
on BH Suns and Mons,
and on Suns in August.

ℹ️ Pushchairs on weekdays
only. No photography, large
bags or sharp heeled shoes in
the house.

🎄 Tel for Xmas opening.

♿ WC. Wheelchairs
available.

🍴 Licensed.

🅿️ Coaches must pre-book.

🐕 On leads, in Car Park (no
shade) & woodland only.

🏰 Tel for details.

NT Photographic Library: Nadia MacKenzie

CONFERENCE/FUNCTION

ROOM	MAX CAPACITY
Restaurant	50
Lower Servants Hall	50

167

South East - England

NTPL / Andrew Butler

ALFRISTON CLERGY HOUSE ✤

THE TYE, ALFRISTON, POLEGATE, EAST SUSSEX BN26 5TL

Tel: 01323 870001 **Fax:** 01323 871318 **e-mail:** alfriston@nationaltrust.org.uk
Owner: The National Trust **Contact:** The Property Manager
Step back into the Middle Ages with a visit to this 14th century thatched Wealden 'Hall House'. Trace the history of this building which in 1896 was the first to be acquired by the National Trust. Discover what is used to make the floor in the Great Hall and visit the excellent shop with its local crafts. Explore the delightful cottage garden and savour the idyllic setting beside Alfriston's parish church, with stunning views across the meandering River Cuckmere. An intriguing variety of shops, pubs and restaurants in Alfriston village make this a wonderful day out.
Location: OS Ref. TQ521 029. 4m NE of Seaford, just E of B2108.
Open: 5 - 13 Mar: Sats & Suns, 11am - 4pm. 18 Mar - 31 Oct: daily except Tue & Fri, 10am - 5pm. 2 Nov - 18 Dec: daily except Tue & Fri, 11am - 4pm.
Admission: Adult £3.10, Child £1.55, Family (2+3) £7.75. Pre-booked groups £2.65.
ℹ️ No WCs. 📷 🅿️ Parking in village car parks.

ANNE OF CLEVES HOUSE

52 Southover High Street, Lewes, Sussex BN7 1JA

Tel: 01273 474610 **Fax:** 01273 486990 **e-mail:** anne@sussexpast.co.uk
www.sussexpast.co.uk
Owner: Sussex Past **Contact:** Mr Stephen Watts
This 16th century timber-framed Wealden hall-house was given to Anne of Cleves as part of her divorce settlement from Henry VIII in 1541, and contains wide-ranging collections of Sussex interest. Furnished rooms give an impression of life in the 17th and 18th centuries. Artefacts from Lewes Priory, Sussex pottery and Wealden ironwork.
Location: OS198 Ref. TQ410 096. S of Lewes town centre, off A27/A275/A26.
Open: 1 Jan - 28 Feb: Tue - Sat, 10am - 5pm. 1 Mar - 31 Oct: Tue - Sat, 10am - 5pm; Sun, Mon & BHs, 11am - 5pm. 1 Nov - 31 Dec: Tue - Sat, 10am - 5pm. Closed 24 - 27 Dec.
Admission: Adult £3, Child £1.50, Conc. £2.70, Family (2+2) £7.60 or (1+4) £6.10. Groups (15+): Adult £2.70, Child £1.30, Conc. £2.40. Combined ticket with Lewes Castle is also available.
📷 ℹ️ By arrangement. 🅿️ Limited (on road). ■ 🐕 Guide dogs only. ▲ ❋ 👑 Tel for details.

ARUNDEL CASTLE

See page 159 for full page entry.

ARUNDEL CATHEDRAL

Parsons Hill, Arundel, Sussex BN18 9AY

Tel: 01903 882297 **Fax:** 01903 885335
e-mail: aruncath1@aol.com **Contact:** Rev J Scott
French Gothic Cathedral, church of the RC Diocese of Arundel and Brighton built by Henry, 15th Duke of Norfolk and opened 1873.
Location: OS Ref. TQ015 072. Above junction of A27 and A284.
Open: Summer: 10am - 4pm. Winter: 9am - dusk. Mass at 10am each day. Sun Masses: 8am, 9.30am & 11am, Vigil Sat evening: 6.30pm. Shop open in the summer, Mon - Fri, 10am - 4pm and after services and on special occasions and otherwise at request.
Admission: Free.

English Heritage Photo Library / Jonathan Bailey

English Heritage Photo Library / York

1066 BATTLE OF HASTINGS ⌗
ABBEY & BATTLEFIELD

BATTLE, SUSSEX TN33 0AD

www.english-heritage.org.uk/visits

Tel: 01424 773792 **Fax:** 01424 775059
Owner: English Heritage **Contact:** Visitor Operations Team
Visit the site of the 1066 Battle of Hastings. A free interactive audio tour will lead you around the battlefield and to the exact spot where Harold fell. Explore the magnificent abbey ruins and see the fascinating exhibition in the gate house and '1066 Prelude to Battle' exhibition. Children's themed play area.
Location: OS Ref. TQ749 157. Top of Battle High Street. Turn off A2100 to Battle.

Open: 24 Mar - 30 Sept: daily, 10am - 6pm. 1 Oct - 31 Mar: daily 10am - 4pm. Closed 24 - 26 Dec & 1 Jan.
Admission: Adult £5.30, Child £2.70, Conc. £4, Family £13.30. 15% discount for groups (11+). English Heritage members free.

ℹ️ WCs nearby. 📷 ♿ Ground floor & grounds. 🅿️ Charge payable. 📷 Free.
🐕 In grounds, on leads. ❋ 👑 Tel for details.

BATEMAN'S 🦋

See page 160 for full page entry.

BAYHAM OLD ABBEY ⌗

Lamberhurst, Sussex

Tel/Fax: 01892 890381   **www**.english-heritage.org.uk/visits

Owner: English Heritage   **Contact:** Visitor Operations Team

These riverside ruins are of a house of 'White' Canons, founded c1208 and preserved in the 18th century, when its surroundings were landscaped to create its delightful setting. Two rooms in the Georgian Dower House are also open to the public.

Location: OS Ref. TQ651 366. 1¼ miles W of Lamberhurst off B2169.

Open: 24 Mar - 30 Sept: daily, 10am - 5pm. Closed 1 Oct - 31 Mar. Times subject to change April 2005.

Admission: Adult £3.30, Child £1.70, Conc. £2.50.

▢ ♿ Grounds. WC. 🅿 🐕 In grounds, on leads.

BIGNOR ROMAN VILLA

Bignor Lane, Bignor, Nr Pulborough, West Sussex RH20 1PH

Tel/Fax: 01798 869259   **e-mail:** bignorromanvilla@care4free.net

Owner: Mr J R Tupper   **Contact:** Ging Allison – Curator

One of the largest villas to be open to the public in Great Britain, with some of the finest mosaics all *in situ* and all under cover, including Medusa, Venus & Cupid Gladiators and Ganymede. Discovered in 1811 and open to the public since 1814. See the longest mosaic on display in Great Britain at 24 metres. Walk on original floors dating back to circa 350 AD. We have a small café and picnic area available for Villa visitors only.

Location: OS Ref. SU987 146. 6m N of Arundel, 6m S of Pulborough A29. 7m S of Petworth A285.

Open: Mar & Apr: Tue - Sun & BHs, 10am - 5pm; May & Oct: daily, 10am - 5pm. Jun - Sept: daily, 10am - 6pm.

Admission: Adult £4.20, Child £1.80, OAP £3. Groups (10+): Adult £3.35, Child £1.45, OAP £2.40. Guided tours (max 30 per tour) £19.50.

▢ ♿ Partial. 🖱 *ⅈ* By arrangement. 🅿 🍴 🐕

Wilmington Priory.

😊 **Special Events Index** see page 24

BODIAM CASTLE 🦋

BODIAM, Nr ROBERTSBRIDGE, EAST SUSSEX TN32 5UA

www.nationaltrust.org.uk/bodiamcastle

Tel: 01580 830436   **Fax:** 01580 830398   **e-mail:** bodiamcastle@nationaltrust.org.uk

Owner: The National Trust   **Contact:** The Property Manager

Built in 1385 to defend the surrounding countryside and as a comfortable dwelling for a rich nobleman, Bodiam Castle is one of the finest examples of medieval architecture. The virtual completeness of its exterior makes it popular with adults, children and film crews alike. Inside, although a ruin, floors have been replaced in some of the towers and visitors can climb the spiral staircase to enjoy superb views of the Rother Valley and local steam trains from the battlements. Discover more of its intriguing past in the Museum and Audio Visual Presentation, and wander in the peacefully romantic Castle grounds.

Location: OS Ref. TQ782 256. 3m S of Hawkhurst, 2m E of A21 Hurst Green.

Open: 8 Jan - 6 Feb: Sats & Suns, 10am - 4pm. 7 Feb - 30 Oct: daily including Good Fri, Easter Sat & Sun, 10am - 6pm. 5 Nov - 12 Feb 2006: Sats & Suns, 10am - 4pm. Last admission 1 hour before closing.

Admission: Adult £4.40, Child £2.20, Family (2+3) £11. Groups (15+) £3.60. Car parking £2 per car.

ⅈ Small museum. ▢ ♿ Ground floor & grounds. 🍴 🅿

🖱 Teacher and student packs and education base.   ❋ 🎫 Tel for details.

BORDE HILL GARDEN, 🏛
PARK & WOODLAND

HAYWARDS HEATH, WEST SUSSEX RH16 1XP

www.bordehill.co.uk

Tel: 01444 450326 **Fax:** 01444 440427 **e-mail:** info@bordehill.co.uk

Owner: Mr & Mrs A P Stephenson Clarke   **Contact:** Sarah Brook

Glorious heritage and collector's garden, listed Grade II*, set within 200 acres of spectacular parkland and woodland. Breathtaking botanical collection of rare trees, shrubs, rhododendrons, azaleas, roses and herbaceous borders. Intimate 'garden rooms' with stunning views and magical parkland and lakeside walks. Rich autumn colour followed by winter's architectural splendour. Ideal location for filming and photographic shoots.

Location: OS Ref. TQ324 265. 1¹/₂m N of Haywards Heath on Balcombe Road, 3m from A23. 45mins from Victoria Station.

Open: All year: daily, 10am - 6pm (dusk if earlier).

Admission: Adult £6, Child £3.50, OAP £5. RHS members Free Jan - Feb & Nov - Dec.

❄

BOXGROVE PRIORY ⊞

Boxgrove, Chichester, Sussex

Tel: 01424 775705   www.english-heritage.org.uk/visits

Owner: English Heritage   **Contact:** Battle Abbey

Remains of the Guest House, Chapter House and Church of this 12th century priory, which was the cell of a French abbey until Richard II confirmed its independence in 1383.

Location: OS Ref. SU909 076. N of Boxgrove, 4 miles E of Chichester on minor road N of A27.

Open: Any reasonable time.

Admission: Free.

P 🐕 ❄

BRAMBER CASTLE ⊞

Bramber, Sussex

Tel: 01424 775705   www.english-heritage.org.uk/visits

Owner: English Heritage   **Contact:** Battle Abbey

The remains of a Norman castle gatehouse, walls and earthworks in a splendid setting overlooking the Adur valley.

Location: OS Ref. TQ187 107. On W side of Bramber village NE of A283.

Open: Any reasonable time.

Admission: Free.

P Limited. 🐕 On leads. ❄

CAMBER CASTLE ⊞

Camber, Nr Rye, East Sussex

Tel: 01797 223862   www.english-heritage.org.uk/visits

Owner: English Heritage   **Contact:** Rye Harbour Nature Reserve

A fine example of one of many coastal fortresses built by Henry VIII to counter the threat of invasion during the 16th century. Monthly guided walks of Rye Nature Reserve including Camber Castle: telephone for details.

Location: OS189, Ref. TQ922 185. Across fields off A259, 1 mile S of Rye off harbour road.

Open: 1 Jul - 30 Sept: Sat & Sun, 2 - 5pm. Last admission 4.30pm. Times subject to change April 2005.

Admission: Adult £2, Child/Conc. £1. Accompanied children, free. Friends of Rye Harbour Nature Reserve, free. Prices subject to change April 2005.

♿ Unsuitable. 🎧 By arrangement. P None. 🐕 Guide dogs only.

CHARLESTON

CHARLESTON, FIRLE, NR LEWES, EAST SUSSEX BN8 6LL

www.charleston.org.uk

Tel: 01323 811265 **Fax:** 01323 811628 **e-mail:** info@charleston.org.uk

Owner: The Charleston Trust   **Contact:** Visitor Manager

Charleston was discovered in 1916 by Virginia Woolf and became the country home of her sister, Vanessa Bell and her unconventional household, including fellow artist Duncan Grant. Charleston became a focal point for the group of artists, writers and intellectuals known as Bloomsbury. The artists decorated the walls, furniture and ceramics with their own designs inspired by Italian fresco painting and Post-impressionism. Creativity extended to the garden, with its mosaics and statues and the subtle masses of colour used in the planting. Charleston has been described as 'one of the most difficult and imaginative feats of restoration current in Britain.'

Location: OS Ref. TQ490 069. 7m E of Lewes on A27 between Firle & Selmeston. Rail, bus, taxi & airport.

Open: 23 Mar - 30 Oct: Wed - Sun, 2 - 6pm (Last entry 5pm). Jul & Aug: Wed - Sat, 11.30am - 6pm; Sun, 2 - 6pm (Last entry 5pm). Nov & Dec Christmas Shopping: Sat & Sun, 1 - 4pm. Guided visits: Wed - Sat; Unguided on Suns. Open BH Mons. 'A Day in the Life of Charleston' tour on Fris: Apr - Jun, Sept & Oct, special themed tour of the House, including Vanessa Bell's studio and the kitchen.

Admission: Adult £6, Child £4.50, Conc. (Weds & Thurs only) £5, Student £4, Disabled £4.50, Family £16.50. Themed Fridays: £7. Groups (10-48): Adult £5.50, Student £4, School £2.

ℹ Filming and photography by arrangement. 📷 🎫 🍴
♿ Partial. Access leaflet available. WC. 🚼 🎧 Obligatory except Sun & BH Mons.
P 🍴 🐕 Guide dogs only.

CHICHESTER CATHEDRAL
Chichester, Sussex PO19 1PX

Tel: 01243 782595 **Fax:** 01243 812499 **e-mail:** visitors@chichestercathedral.org.uk
www.chichestercathedral.org.uk   **Contact:** Mrs P Utting

In the heart of the city, this fine Cathedral has been a centre of Christian worship and community life for 900 years.

Location: OS Ref. SU860 047. West Street, Chichester.

Open: Summer: 7.15am - 7pm, Winter: 7.15am - 6pm. Choral Evensong daily (except Wed) during term time.

Admission: Donation.

✳

LOCAL FOOD

Sussex Pond Pudding

This wonderful steamed suet pudding has its competitors in both Kent and Hampshire - but this Sussex version is the best. A whole lemon is pricked all over to encourage the juice to flow and placed in the centre of a suet lined pudding dish with buttter and sugar. It is then baked for approximately three hours. When cooked the pudding is inverted into a deep dish. When the crust is cut the lemon sauce flows from the centre of the pudding creating a pond, from where the pudding derives its name.

CLINTON LODGE GARDEN
FLETCHING, EAST SUSSEX TN22 3ST

Tel: 01825 722952 **Fax:** 01825 723967 **e-mail:** collum@fs.life.co.uk
Owner: Sir Hugh and Lady Collum   **Contact:** Lady Collum

Caroline house enlarged by the Earl of Sheffield for his daughter when she married Sir Henry Clinton, one of three generals at Waterloo. The 18th century façade is set in a tree lined lawn, flanked by a newly created canal and overlooking parkland. The 6 acre garden reflects periods of English gardening history and includes a knot garden, mediaeval style herb garden with camomile paths and turf seats, potager, wild flower garden, pre-Raphaelite inspired allée, pleached lime walks; garden of old roses, double blue, white and yellow herbaceous borders; orchard planted with crinums and many yew and beech hedges.

Location: OS Ref. TQ428 238. In centre of village behind tall yew and holly hedge.

Open: 5/6, 17 & 24 Jun, 1 & 8 Jul & 5 Aug. NGS days. Other times by arrangement.

Admission: NGS Days: £4 + £2 for teas. Private groups £6pp (min charge £100).
ⓘ WCs. ♿ Unsuitable. ⊡ 🎦 By arrangement. 🅿 Parking for cars & coaches. 🐕 Guide dogs only. €

Jeremy Whitaker

FIRLE PLACE 🏛
FIRLE, LEWES, EAST SUSSEX BN8 6LP

www.firleplace.co.uk

Tel: 01273 858307 (Enquiries) **Events:** 01273 858567
Fax: 01273 858188 **Restaurant:** 01273 858307 **e-mail:** gage@firleplace.co.uk
Owner: The Rt Hon Viscount Gage

Firle Place is the home of the Gage family and has been for over 500 years. Set at the foot of the Sussex Downs within its own parkland, this unique house originally Tudor, was built of Caen stone, possibly from a monastery dissolved by Sir John Gage, friend of Henry VIII. Remodelled in the 18th century it is similar in appearance to that of a French château. The house contains a magnificent collection of Old Master paintings, fine English and European furniture and an impressive collection of Sèvres porcelain collected mainly by the 3rd Earl Cowper from Panshanger House, Hertfordshire.

Events: The Great Tudor Hall can, on occasion, be used for private dinners, with drinks on the Terrace or in the Billiard Room. A private tour of the house can be

arranged. The paddock area is an ideal site for a marquee. The park can be used for larger events, using the house as a backdrop.

Restaurant: Enjoy the licensed restaurant and tea terrace with views over the garden for luncheon and cream teas.

Location: OS Ref. TQ473 071. 4m S of Lewes on A27 Brighton/Eastbourne Road.

Open: Easter & BH Sun/Mon. Jun - Sept: Wed, Thur, Sun & BHs, 2 - 4.30pm. Dates and times subject to change without prior notice.

Admission: Adult £5.75, Child £3, Conc. £5.25.

ⓘ No photography in house. 📷 ⊡ ♿ Ground floor & restaurant. 🍴 Licensed. ⊡ Tea Terrace. 🎦 Wed & Thur. 🅿 🐕 In grounds on leads. 🛏 Tel for details.`

FISHBOURNE ROMAN PALACE

SALTHILL ROAD, FISHBOURNE, CHICHESTER, SUSSEX PO19 3QR

www.sussexpast.co.uk

Tel: 01243 785859   **Fax:** 01243 539266   **e-mail:** adminfish@sussexpast.co.uk

Owner: Sussex Past   **Contact:** David Rudkin

A Roman site built around AD75. A modern building houses part of the extensive remains including a large number of Britain's finest *in situ* mosaics. The museum displays many objects discovered during excavations and an audio-visual programme tells Fishbourne's remarkable story. Roman gardens have been reconstructed and include a museum of Roman gardening.

Please note that owing to an exciting redevelopment programme to protect the mosaics, certain areas of the Palace may be temporarily inaccessible during 2005. This should not affect the overall enjoyment of your visit.

Location: OS Ref. SU837 057. 1¹/₂ m W of Chichester in Fishbourne village off A27/A259.

Open: 1 Feb - 15 Dec: daily. Feb, Nov - 15 Dec: 10am - 4pm. Mar - Jul & Sept - Oct: 10am - 5pm. Aug: 10am - 6pm. 16 Dec - 31 Jan (excluding Christmas): Sats & Suns, 10am - 4pm.

Admission: Adult £5.40, Child £2.80, Conc. £4.60, Family (2+2): £13.80, Registered disabled £4.10. Groups (20+): Adult £4.50, Child £2.60, Conc. £4.10.

▢ ⊞ ⧖ ⬛ ⚗ By arrangement. **P** ▪ ♿Guide dogs only. ❋ ☑ Tel for details.

GLYNDE PLACE ⌂

GLYNDE, Nr LEWES, EAST SUSSEX BN8 6SX

www.glyndeplace.com

Tel/Fax: 01273 858224   **e-mail:** glyndeplace@glyndeplace.com

Owners: Viscount & Viscountess Hampden   **Contact:** Sue Tester

Glynde Place is a magnificent example of Elizabethan architecture commanding exceptionally fine views of the South Downs. Amongst the collections of 400 years of family living can be seen a fine collection of 17th and 18th century portraits of the Trevors, a room dedicated to Sir Henry Brand, Speaker of the House of Commons 1872 - 1884 and furniture, embroidery and silver. Plus a collection of 18th century Italian masterpieces.

Location: OS Ref. TQ456 093. Sign posted off of A27, 4m SE of Lewes at top of village. Rail: Glynde is on the London/Eastbourne and Brighton/Eastbourne mainline railway.

Open: May - Aug: Weds, Suns & BHs, 2 - 5pm (last admission to House 4.45pm). Private viewings by appointment.

Admission: House & Garden: Adult £5.50, Child (under 16yrs) £2.75. Garden: Adult £2, Child (under 16yrs) £1. Child under 12yrs Free. CPRE 2 for 1. Groups (25+) by appointment.

▢ ⊞ ⟳ ⬛ ⚗ **P**Free. ♿ Guide dogs only. ☑Tel for details.

GOODWOOD HOUSE ⌂   *See page 161 for full page entry.*

Jonathan Buckley

GREAT DIXTER HOUSE & GARDENS ⌂

NORTHIAM, RYE, EAST SUSSEX TN31 6PH

www.greatdixter.co.uk

Tel: 01797 252878   **Fax:** 01797 252879   **e-mail:** office@greatdixter.co.uk

Owner: Christopher Lloyd   **Contact:** Perry Rodriguez

Great Dixter, built c1450 is the birthplace of Christopher Lloyd, gardening author. The house boasts the largest surviving timber-framed hall in the country. The gardens feature a variety of topiary, pools, wild meadow areas and the famous Long Border and Exotic Garden.

Location: OS Ref. TQ817 251. Signposted off the A28 in Northiam.

Open: 25 Mar - 30 Sept: Tue - Sun, 2 - 5pm.

Admission: House & Garden: Adult £6.50, Child £2. Gardens only: Adult £5, Child £1.50. Groups (25+) by appointment.

ℹNo photography in House. ▢ ⊞ ⚗Obligatory. **P** Limited for coaches. ♿ Guide dogs only.

St Mary's Bramber.

David Sellman

HAMMERWOOD PARK
EAST GRINSTEAD, SUSSEX RH19 3QE
www.hammerwoodpark.com

Tel: 01342 850594 **Fax:** 01342 850864 **e-mail:** latrobe@mistral.co.uk
Owner/Contact: David Pinnegar

Built in 1792 as an Apollo's hunting lodge by Benjamin Latrobe, architect of the Capitol and the White House, Washington DC. Owned by Led Zepplin in the 1970s, rescued from dereliction in 1982. Teas in the Organ Room; mural by French artists in the hall; and a derelict dining room still shocks the unwary. Guided tours (said by many to be the most interesting in Sussex) by the family.

Location: OS Ref. TQ442 390. 3¹/₂ m E of East Grinstead on A264 to Tunbridge Wells, 1m W of Holtye.

Open: 1 June - end Sept: Wed, Sat & BH Mon, 2 - 5pm. Guided tour starts 2.05pm. Private groups: Easter - Jun. Coaches strictly by appointment. Small groups any time throughout the year by appointment.

Admission: House & Park: Adult £6, Child £2. Private viewing by arrangement.

ⓘ Conferences. ⓣ 🔲 🔳 Obligatory. ◼ 🔲 In grounds. 🏨 B&B. ✳
📺 Tel for details. €

HIGH BEECHES WOODLAND 🏠 & WATER GARDENS
HIGH BEECHES, HANDCROSS, SUSSEX RH17 6HQ
www.highbeeches.com

Tel: 01444 400589 **Fax:** 01444 401543 **e-mail:** gardens@highbeeches.com
Owner: High Beeches Gardens Conservation Trust (Reg. Charity)
                                                    Contact: Sarah Bray

Explore 25 acres of magically beautiful, peaceful woodland and water gardens. Daffodils, bluebells, azaleas, naturalised gentians, autumn colours. Rippling streams, enchanting vistas. Four acres of natural wildflower meadows. Rare plants. Marked trails. Recommended by Christopher Lloyd. Enjoy lunches and teas in the new tearoom and tea lawn in restored Victorian farm building.

Location: OS Ref. TQ275 308. S side of B2110. 1m NE of Handcross.

Open: 18 Mar - 31 Oct: daily except Weds, 1 - 5pm (last adm. 4.30pm). Coaches/ guided tours anytime, by appointment only.

Admission: Adult £5, Child (under 14yrs) Free. Season ticket (12 months): £15. Concession for groups (30+). Guided tours for groups £8pp.

🔲 ♿ Partial. Tearoom fully accessible. 🍴 Licensed. 🔏 By arrangement. 🅿 🔳
📺 Tel for details. €

HERSTMONCEUX CASTLE GARDENS
HAILSHAM, SUSSEX BN27 1RN
www.herstmonceux-castle.com

Tel: 01323 833816 **Fax:** 01323 834499 **e-mail:** c_dennett@isc.queensu.ac.uk
Owner: Queen's University, Canada   **Contact:** C Dennett

This breathtaking 15th century moated Castle is within 500 acres of parkland and gardens (including Elizabethan Garden) and is ideal for picnics and woodland walks. At Herstmonceux there is something for all the family. For information on our attractions or forthcoming events tel: 01323 834457.

Location: OS Ref. TQ646 104. 2m S of Herstmonceux village (A271) by minor road. 10m WNW of Bexhill.

Open: 16 Apr - 23 Oct (but closed Sat 30 July): daily, 10am - 6pm (last adm. 5pm). Closes 5pm from Oct.

Admission: Grounds & Gardens: Adults £4.50, Child under 15yrs & Students £3 (child under 5 Free), Conc. £3.50, Family £12. Group rates/bookings available.

ⓘ Visitor Centre. 📷 ♿ Limited for Castle Tour. 🔲 🔏 🅿 🔳 On leads. ◼
📺 Tel for details.

HIGHDOWN GARDENS
Littlehampton Road, Goring-by-Sea, Worthing, Sussex BN12 6PE
Tel: 01903 501054
Owner: Worthing Borough Council   **Contact:** C Beardsley Esq
Unique gardens in disused chalk pit, begun in 1909.
Location: OS Ref. TQ098 040. 3m WNW of Worthing on N side of A259, just W of the Goring roundabout.
Open: 1 Apr - 30 Sept: Mon - Fri, 10am - 6pm. W/ends & BHs, 10am - 6pm. 1 Oct - 30 Nov: Mon - Fri, 10am - 4.30pm. 1 Dec - 31 Jan: 10am - 4pm. 1 Feb - 31 Mar: Mon - Fri, 10am - 4.30pm.
Admission: Free.

LAMB HOUSE 🔳
West Street, Rye, Sussex TN31 7ES
Tel: 01797 229542 **Fax:** 01797 223492
Owner: The National Trust   **Contact:** Winchelsea Office
A delightful brick-fronted house dating from the early 18th century and typical of the attractive town of Rye. This was the home of writer Henry James from 1898 to 1916, and later of author E F Benson. There is a charming walled garden.
Location: OS Ref. TQ920 202. In West Street, facing W end of church.
Open: 26 Mar - 29 Oct: Weds & Sats only, 2 - 6pm.
Admission: Adult £2.90, Child £1.40, Family (2+3) £7.25. Group: £2.50.

LEONARDSLEE LAKES & GARDENS
See page 162 for full page entry.

LEWES CASTLE &
BARBICAN HOUSE MUSEUM

169 HIGH STREET, LEWES, SUSSEX BN7 1YE

www.sussexpast.co.uk

Tel: 01273 486290 **Fax:** 01273 486990 **e-mail:** castle@sussexpast.co.uk

Owner: Sussex Past   **Contact:** Dr Sally White

Lewes's imposing Norman castle offers magnificent views across the town and surrounding downland. Barbican House, towered over by the Barbican Gate, is home to an interesting museum of local history and archaeology. A superb scale model of Victorian Lewes provides the centrepiece of a 25 minute audio-visual presentation telling the story of the county town of Sussex.

Location: OS198 Ref. TQ412 101. Lewes town centre off A27/A26/A275.

Open: Daily (except Mons in Jan & 24 - 27 Dec). Tue - Sat: 10am - 5.30pm; Sun, Mon & BHs, 11am - 5.30pm. Castle closes at dusk in winter.

Admission: Adult £4.40, Child £2.20, Conc. £3.90 Family (2+2) £11.40 or (1+4) £9. Groups (15+): Adult £3.90, Child £1.80, Conc. £3.30. Combined ticket with Anne of Cleves House available.

⬜ ♿ Unsuitable. 👤 By arrangement. 🔳 🐕 Guide dogs only. ❄ ♨ Tel for details.

MARLIPINS MUSEUM

High Street, Shoreham-by-Sea, Sussex BN43 5DA

Tel: 01273 462994 or 01323 441279   **e-mail:** marlipins@sussexpast.co.uk

www.sussexpast.co.uk

Owner: Sussex Past   **Contact:** Helen Poole

Shoreham's local and especially maritime history is explored at Marlipins, an important historic building of Norman origin.

Location: OS198 Ref. TQ214 051. Shoreham town centre on A259, W of Brighton.

Open: 3 May - 1 Oct: Tue - Sat & BH Mons, 10.30am - 4.30pm.

Admission: Adult £2, Child £1, Conc. £1.50. Groups (15+): Adult £1.75, Child 80p, Conc. £1.25.

Nymans Garden.

MERRIMENTS GARDENS

HAWKHURST ROAD, HURST GREEN, EAST SUSSEX TN19 7RA

www.merriments.co.uk

Tel: 01580 860666 **Fax:** 01580 860324 **e-mail:** info@merriments.co.uk

Owner: Family owned   **Contact:** Mrs Alana Sharp

Set in 4 acres of gently sloping Weald farmland, a naturalistic garden which never fails to delight. The garden is planted according to the prevailing conditions and many areas are planted only using plants suited for naturalising and colonising their environment. This natural approach to gardening harks back to the days of William Robinson and is growing in popularity, especially in Northern Europe. Most of the garden however is crammed with deep curved borders, colour themed and planted in the great tradition of English gardening. These borders use a rich mix of trees, shrubs, perennials, grasses and many unusual annuals which ensure an arresting display of colour, freshness and vitality in the garden right through to its closing in autumn.

Location: OS198, Ref. TQ737 281. Signposted off A21 London - Hastings road, at Hurst Green.

Open: Apr - Sept: Mon - Sat, 10am - 5pm, Suns, 10.30am - 5pm.

Admission: Adult £4, Child £2. Groups (15+) by arrangement £3.50pp.

⬜ ♿ 🔳 Licensed. 🍴 👤 By arrangement. 🅿 🐕 In grounds, on leads.

©National Trust Photographic Library/Stephen Robson

MICHELHAM PRIORY

UPPER DICKER, HAILSHAM, SUSSEX BN27 3QS

www.sussexpast.co.uk

Tel: 01323 844224   **Fax:** 01323 844030   **e-mail:** adminmich@sussexpast.co.uk

Owner: Sussex Past   **Contact:** Chris Tuckett

Set on a medieval moated island surrounded by superb gardens, the Priory was founded in 1229. The remains after the Dissolution were incorporated into a Tudor farm and country house that now contains a fascinating array of exhibits. Grounds include a 14th century gatehouse, working watermill, physic and cloister gardens and Elizabethan great barn.

Location: OS Ref. TQ557 093. 8m NW of Eastbourne off A22/A27. 2m W of Hailsham.

Open: 1 Mar - 30 Oct: Tue - Sun & BH Mons & daily in Aug. Mar & Oct: 10.30am - 4.30pm. Apr - Jul & Sept: 10.30am - 5pm. Aug: 10.30am - 5.30pm.

Admission: Adult £5.40, Child £2.80, Conc. £4.60, Family (2+2) £13.80, Registered disabled & carer £2.70 each. Groups (15+): Adult/Conc. £4.35, Child £2.50.

Licensed. By arrangement. Ample for cars & coaches Guide dogs only. Tel for details.

NYMANS GARDEN

Handcross, Haywards Heath, Sussex RH17 6EB

Tel: 01444 400321/405250   **Fax:** 01444 400253   **www**.nationaltrust.org.uk/nymans
e-mail: nymans@nationaltrust.org.uk

Owner: The National Trust   **Contact:** The Property Manager

One of the great gardens of the Sussex Weald, with rare and beautiful plants, shrubs and trees from all over the world. Wall garden, rose garden, pinetum, laurel walk and romantic ruins.

Location: OS Ref. TQ265 294. On B2114 at Handcross.

Open: 18 Feb - 31 Oct: daily except Mon & Tue (open BHs), 11am - 6pm (sunset if earlier). House: 24 Mar - 31 Oct: as garden, last entry at 4.30pm. Garden: 6 Nov - 20 Feb: Sats & Suns, 11am - 4pm.

Admission: Adult £6.50, Child £3.25, Family £16.25. Pre-booked Groups (15+) £5.50. Winter weekends: Adult £3.25, Child £1.60, Family £8. Booked groups: £2.75. RHS members Free.

Grounds. WC. Licensed. Wed & Sat only. Tel for details.

PALLANT HOUSE GALLERY

9 North Pallant, Chichester, West Sussex PO19 1TJ

Tel: 01243 774557   **Fax:** 01243 536038

Owner: Pallant House Gallery Trust   **Contact:** Reception

The Gallery of Modern Art in the south. A Queen Anne townhouse and a contemporary extension showcasing the best of 20th century British Art.

Location: OS Ref. SU861 047. City centre, SE of the Cross.

Open: Re-opens summer 2005. Please telephone for details.

Admission: Please telephone for details.

MONK'S HOUSE

Rodmell, Lewes BN7 3HF

Tel: 01372 453401 (Regional Office)

Owner: The National Trust   **Contact:** Regional Office

A small weather-boarded house, the home of Leonard and Virginia Woolf until Leonard's death in 1969.

Location: OS Ref. TQ421 064. 4 m E of Lewes, off former A275 in Rodmell village, near church.

Open: 2 Apr - 29 Oct: Weds & Sats, 2 - 5.30pm. Last admission 5pm. Groups by arrangement with tenant.

Admission: Adult £2.90, Child £1.45, Family £7.25.

MOORLANDS

Friar's Gate, Crowborough, East Sussex TN6 1XF

Tel: 01892 652474

Owner: Dr & Mrs Steven Smith   **Contact:** Dr Steven Smith

This marvellously atmospheric garden is again open to the public after building alterations. The garden is on three levels. From a herbaceous border and Spring dell planted with pieris, camellias, rhododendrons and hellebores, go across a yew hedge lawn down to the river level with bridges across it to an area which, in late Summer, shows the bamboos and ornamental grasses at their best. Streams and ponds are planted with primulas, irises and other water loving plants. Many unusual trees, planted 20 years ago, have now reached maturity, particularly the Autumn colouring acers. It is a garden for every season.

Location: OS Ref. TQ498 329. 2m NW of Crowborough. From B2188 at Friar's Gate, take left fork signposted 'Crowborough Narrow Road', entrance 100yds on left. From Crowborough crossroads take St John's Road to Friar's Gate.

Open: 1 Apr - 1 Oct: Weds, 11am - 5pm. Also for National Garden Scheme: 26 Jun, 2 - 6pm.

Admission: Adult £3, Child Free.

On NGS Day. On leads.

Glynde Place from the book 'Historic Family Homes & Gardens from the Air'.

175

PARHAM HOUSE & GARDENS 🏛

PARHAM PARK, STORRINGTON, Nr PULBOROUGH, WEST SUSSEX RH20 4HS

www.parhaminsussex.co.uk

Tel: 01903 742021   **Info Line:** 01903 744888   **Fax:** 01903 746557
e-mail: enquiries@parhaminsussex.co.uk

Owner: Parham Park Trust   **Contact:** Patricia Kennedy

Friendly staff give a warm welcome to this stunning Elizabethan house with award-winning gardens, set in the heart of a medieval deer park below the South Downs. The light, panelled rooms, from Great Hall to magnificent Long Gallery, house an important collection of contemporary paintings, furniture, needlework and working clocks, all complemented by informal arrangements of flowers, freshly cut twice a week from the four acre walled garden. Light lunches and cream teas are served in the 15th century Big Kitchen (licensed), and souvenirs and gifts can be purchased from the shop, with plants on sale from the garden shop.

"Garden Weekend" annual event: 9/10 July. "Autumn Flowers at Parham House", a celebration of flower arranging, Parham style: 10/11 September. We regret that HHA passes are not valid for Special Event weekends.

Location: OS Ref. TQ060 143. Midway between Pulborough & Storrington on A283.

Open: Easter Sun - end Sept: Wed, Thur, Sun & BH Mon afternoons (also Tue & Fri afternoons in Aug); 9 Jul & 10 Sept. Guided groups by arrangement at other times. Picnic area, Big Kitchen & Gardens: 12 noon - 6pm. House: 2 - 6pm. Last entry 5pm.

Admission: House & Gardens: Adult £6.50, Child (5-15yrs) £2.50, OAP £5.50, Family (2+2) £15.50. Unguided booked groups (20+) £5. Gardens only: Adult £5, Child £1, OAP £4.50, Family (2+2) £10.

ℹ No photography in house. 🖼 🎫 ♿ Partial. 🍽 Licensed. 👪 🅿 ⬛
🐕 In grounds, on leads. 🎗 Special charges may apply.

PASHLEY MANOR GARDENS 🏛

TICEHURST, WADHURST, EAST SUSSEX TN5 7HE

www.pashleymanorgardens.com

Tel: 01580 200888   **Fax:** 01580 200102   **e-mail:** info@pashleymanorgardens.com

Owner: Mr & Mrs James A Sellick   **Contact:** Claire Baker

HHA/Christie's Garden of the Year 1999. The gardens offer a sumptuous blend of romantic landscaping, imaginative plantings and fine old trees, fountains, springs and large ponds. This is a quintessential English garden of a very individual character with exceptional views to the surrounding valleyed fields. Many eras of English history are reflected here, typifying the tradition of the English Country House and its garden.

Pashley prides itself on its delicious food. Home-made soups, ploughman's lunches with pickles and patés, fresh salad from the garden (whenever possible), home-made scones and delicious cakes, filter coffee, specialist teas, fine wines -

served on the terrace or in the Garden Room café. The gift shop caters for every taste… from postcards and local honey to traditional hand-painted ceramics and tapestry cushions. A wide selection of plants and shrubs, many of which grow at Pashley, are available for purchase.

Location: OS Ref. TQ 707 291. On B2099 between A21 and Ticehurst village.

Open: 5 Apr - 29 Sept: Tues, Weds, Thurs, Sats & all BH Mons, 11am - 5pm. Oct: Mon - Fri, 10am - 4pm Garden only (restaurant & shop closed).

Admission: £6. Groups (20+): £5.50. Coaches must book. Please telephone for details.

🖼 🎫 🍴 ♿ Partial. 🍽 Licensed. 👪 By arrangement. 🅿 🐕 Guide dogs only.
🎗 Tel for details.

PETWORTH COTTAGE MUSEUM

346 High Street, Petworth, West Sussex GU28 0AU

Tel: 01798 342100

Owner: Petworth Cottage Trust   **Contact:** Curator

Step into a Leconfield Estate Cottage furnished as if it were 1910. Lighting is by gas, heating by coal-fired range. The scullery has a stone sink and a copper for the weekly wash.

Open: Apr - Oct: Wed - Sun & BH Mons, 2 - 4.30pm.

Admission: Adult £2.50, Child (under 14yrs 50p. Group visits by arrangement.

PETWORTH HOUSE & PARK *See page 163 for full page entry.*

PEVENSEY CASTLE

Pevensey, Sussex BN24 5LE

Tel/Fax: 01323 762604   **www.**english-heritage.org.uk/visits

Owner: English Heritage   **Contact:** Visitor Operations Team

Originally a 4th century Roman Fort, Pevensey was the place where William the Conqueror landed in 1066 and established his first stronghold. The Norman castle includes the remains of an unusual keep within the massive walls. Free audio tour tells the story of the Castle's 2,000 year history.

Location: OS Ref. TQ645 048. In Pevensey off A259.

Open: 24 Mar - 30 Sept: daily, 10am - 6pm. 1 Oct - 31 Mar: Sat & Sun only, 10am - 4pm. Closed 24 - 26 Dec & 1 Jan.

Admission: Adult £3.70, Child £1.90, Conc. £2.80. 15% discount for groups of 11+. WC. Grounds. Free. In grounds, on leads. Tel for details.

PRESTON MANOR

PRESTON DROVE, BRIGHTON, EAST SUSSEX BN1 6SD

www.prestonmanor.virtualmuseum.info

Tel: 01273 292770   **Fax:** 01273 292771

Owner: Brighton & Hove City Council

A delightful Manor House which powerfully evokes the atmosphere of an Edwardian gentry home both 'upstairs' and 'downstairs'. Explore more than twenty rooms over four floors – from the servants' quarters, kitchens and butler's pantry in the basement to the attic bedrooms and nursery on the top floor. Plus charming walled gardens, pets' cemetery and 13th century parish church.

Location: OS Ref. TQ303 064. 2m N of Brighton on the A23 London road.

Open: Please call 01273 292770 for details of 2005 opening arrangements.

Admission: Adult £3.80, Child £2.20, Conc. £3.15. Groups (20+) £3.25. Prices valid until 31 Mar 2005.

No photography. Gift kiosk. Unsuitable. By arrangement. For coaches. Spring, Summer & Autumn half-term. Easter, Summer & Christmas. Children's activities all year round. Tel for details.

Plant Sales Index see page 39

THE PRIEST HOUSE

NORTH LANE, WEST HOATHLY, SUSSEX RH19 4PP

www.sussexpast.co.uk

Tel: 01342 810479   **e-mail:** priest@sussexpast.co.uk

Owner: Sussex Past   **Contact:** Antony Smith

Standing in the beautiful surroundings of a traditional cottage garden on the edge of Ashdown Forest, The Priest House is an early 15th century timber-framed hall-house. In Elizabethan times it was modernised into a substantial yeoman's dwelling. Its furnished rooms now contain 17th and 18th century furniture, kitchen equipment, needlework and household items. A formal herb garden contains over 150 different herbs.

Location: OS187 Ref. TQ362 325. In triangle formed by Crawley, East Grinstead and Haywards Heath, 4m off A22, 6m off M23.

Open: 1 Mar - 30 Oct: Tue - Sat & BHs plus Mons during Aug: 10.30am - 5.30pm; Sun, 12 noon - 5.30pm.

Admission: Adult £2.70, Child £1.35, Conc. £2.40. Groups (15+): Adult/Conc. £2.40, Child £1.25.

Partial. By arrangement. Limited (on street). In grounds, on leads.

THE ROYAL PAVILION *See page 164 for full page entry.*

LOCAL FOOD

Cider

Cider is certainly one of the great national drinks of Britain but it was most likely introduced by the Normans sometime after the Conquest in 1066. The best Sussex ciders have a less acid and less harsh flavour than some West Country ciders, because they are made from dessert apples. They are fermented dry and are almost wine-like in character.

ST MARY'S HOUSE & GARDENS 🏛

BRAMBER, WEST SUSSEX BN44 3WE
www.stmarysbramber.co.uk

Tel/Fax: 01903 816205 **e-mail:** info@stmarysbramber.co.uk

Owner: Mr Peter Thorogood

This enchanting, medieval timber-framed house is situated in the downland village of Bramber. The fine panelled interiors include the unique Elizabethan 'Painted Room' with its intriguing *trompe l'oeil* murals, give an air of tranquillity and timelessness. Once the home of the real Algernon and Gwendolen brilliantly portrayed in Oscar Wilde's comedy, *The Importance of Being Earnest,* St Mary's was said to be the setting for the Sherlock Holmes story, *The Musgrave Ritual,* and has served as a location for a number of television series including the world-famous *Dr Who.* The formal gardens with amusing animal topiary include an exceptional example of the 'Living Fossil' tree, Gingko biloba, and a mysterious ivy-clad 'Monk's Walk'. In the 'Secret Garden' can still be seen the Victorian fruit-wall, potting shed, circular orchard,

and woodland walk. St Mary's is a house of fascination and mystery. Many thousands of visitors have admired its picturesque charm and enjoyed its atmosphere of friendliness and welcome, qualities which make it a visit to remember.

Location: OS Ref. TQ189 105. Bramber village off A283. From London 56m via M23/A23 or A24. Bus from Shoreham to Steyning, alight St Mary's, Bramber.

Open: May - 30 Sept: Suns, Thurs & BH Mons, 2 - 6pm. Last entry 5pm. Groups at other times by arrangement.

Admission: House & Gardens: Adult £6, Child £2.50, Conc. £5. Groups (25+) £5.50.

ℹ️ No photography in house. 🔲 📶 ♿ Unsuitable. 🍴
𝒇 Obligatory for groups (max 60). Visit time 2½ hrs. 🅿 30 cars, 2 coaches.
🔲 ✖ ⬆ 🎭 Tel for details.

SAINT HILL MANOR   *See page 165 for full page entry.*

SHEFFIELD PARK GARDEN 🌿   *See page 166 for full page entry.*

SACKVILLE COLLEGE

HIGH STREET, EAST GRINSTEAD, WEST SUSSEX RH19 3BX
www.sackville-college.co.uk

Tel: 01342 326561

Owner: Board of Trustees   **Contact:** College Co-ordinator

Built in 1609 for Richard Sackville, Earl of Dorset, as an almshouse and overnight accommodation for the Sackville family. Feel the Jacobean period come alive in the enchanting quadrangle, the chapel, banqueting hall with fine hammerbeam roof and minstrel's gallery, the old common room and warden's study where "Good King Wenceslas" was composed. Chapel weddings by arrangement.

Location: A22 to East Grinstead, College in High Street (town centre).

Open: 15 Jun - 15 Sep: Wed - Sun, 2 - 5pm. Groups all year by arrangement.

Admission: Adult £3, Child £1. Groups: (10 - 60) no discount.

ℹ️ Large public car park adjacent to entrance. 🔲 📶 📶 🍴 ♿ Partial.
𝒇 Obligatory. 🅿 Limited. 🔲 ✖ Guide dogs only. ❄ By arrangement.
🎭 Tel for details.

Borde Hill Garden.

STANDEN ✤

EAST GRINSTEAD, WEST SUSSEX RH19 4NE
www.nationaltrust.org.uk/standen

Tel: 01342 323029   **Fax:** 01342 316424   **e-mail:** standen@nationaltrust.org.uk

Owner: The National Trust   **Contact:** The Property Manager

Dating from the 1890s and containing original Morris & Co furnishings and decorations, Standen survives today as a remarkable testimony to the ideals of the Arts and Crafts Movement. The property was built as a family home by the influential architect Philip Webb and retains a warm, welcoming atmosphere. Details of Webb's designs can be found everywhere from the fireplaces to the original electric light fittings.

Location: OS Ref. TQ389 356. 2m S of East Grinstead, signposted from B2110.

Open: House, Garden, Shop & Restaurant: 18 Mar - 30 Oct: Wed - Sun & BHs. 11am - 5pm (last admission to house 4.30pm). Garden, Shop & Restaurant: 5 Nov - 18 Dec: Sat & Sun, 11am - 3pm.

Admission: House & Garden: £6.50, Family £16. Garden only: £3.90. Joint ticket with same day entry to Nymans Garden £10, available Wed - Fri. Groups: £5.50, Wed - Fri only, only if booked in advance.

▢ ⚗ ⊤ ⬧ Partial. WC. ⍾ Licensed. 🅿 ▣
🐕 In woods on leads, not in garden. ☏ Tel for details.

STANSTED PARK 🏛

STANSTED PARK, ROWLANDS CASTLE, HAMPSHIRE   PO9 6DX

www.stanstedpark.co.uk

Tel: 023 9241 2265   **Fax:** 023 9241 3773   **e-mail:** enquiry@stanstedpark.co.uk

Owner: Stansted Park Foundation   **Contact:** House Administrator

'One of the South's most beautiful stately homes' set amongst 1750 acres of glorious park and woodland, Stansted House gives an insight into the social history of an English country house in its heyday. The State Rooms, containing Bessborough family furniture, portraits and a colourful collection of bird paintings, contrast with the Servants Quarters' equally interesting domestic artefacts. Visit the ancient Chapel which inspired Keats, the Bessborough Arboretum and the Stansted Maze.

Annual events include the Garden Show, Antiques Fairs, Outdoor Concerts and a Craft Fair. Please contact the House for more information.

Location: OS Ref. SU761 103. Follow brown heritage signs from A3 Rowlands Castle or A27 Havant. Rail: Mainline station, Havant. Taxis: Rowlands Castle no taxis 30 minute walk.

Open: House & Chapel: Easter Sun - 26 Sept: Suns & Mons, 1 - 5pm (last entry 4pm). Also Jul & Aug: Sun - Wed. House closed during events. Grounds: All year, restricted access on Sats and during events.

Admission: House, Grounds, Chapel: Adult £5.50, Child (5-15yrs) £3.50, Conc. £4.50, Family (2+3) £14.50. Groups/educational visits by arrangement.

⚗ ⊤ Private & corporate hire. ⬧ Partial. ▣ 🄵 By arrangement. 🅿 ▣
🐕 Guide dogs only. ⬖ ❄ Grounds. ☏ Tel for details.

South East - England

UPPARK ✿
See page 167 for full page entry.

WAKEHURST PLACE ✿
Ardingly, Haywards Heath, Sussex RH17 6TN

Tel: 01444 894066 **Fax:** 01444 894069 **e-mail:** wakehurst@kew.org. **www.**kew.org
Owner: The National Trust (managed by Royal Botanic Gdns) **Contact:** The Administrator
A superb collection of exotic trees, shrubs and other plants, many displayed in a geographic manner. Extensive water gardens, a winter garden, a rock walk and walled gardens. The Loder Valley Nature Reserve can be visited by prior arrangement.
Location: OS Ref. TQ339 314. 1¹/₂ m N of Ardingly, on B2028.
Open: Daily (not 25 Dec & 1 Jan). Feb & Oct: 10am - 5pm. Mar: 10am - 6pm. Apr - end Sept: 10am - 7pm. Nov - end Jan 2004: 10am - 4pm. Mansion, seed bank and restaurant closed 1hr before gardens.
Admission: Adult £7, Child (under 17yrs) Free, Conc. £5.
◻ ♿Ground floor & part of grounds. 🍴 ♿ Tel for details.

WEALD & DOWNLAND OPEN AIR MUSEUM
Singleton, Chichester, Sussex PO18 0EU

Tel: 01243 811348 **www.**wealddown.co.uk
Over 45 original historic buildings. Interiors and gardens through the ages.
Location: OS Ref. SU876 127. 6m N of Chichester on A286. S of Singleton.
Open: 1 Mar - 31 Oct: daily, 10.30am - 6pm. Nov - Feb: Wed, Sat & Sun, 10.30am - 4pm. 26 Dec - 1 Jan: daily, 10.30am - 4pm.
Admission: Adult £7.50, Child/Student £4, OAP £6.50. Family (2+3) £20. Group rates on request.
◻ ♿ ♿ ♿ 🍴 🔨 🅿 🚻 🛏 🔔 ❄ ♿ Tel for details.

© Skyscan

WEST DEAN GARDENS 🏛
WEST DEAN, CHICHESTER, WEST SUSSEX PO18 0QZ

www.westdean.org.uk

Tel: 01243 818210 **Fax:** 01243 811342 **e-mail:** gardens@westdean.org.uk
Owner: The Edward James Foundation **Contact:** Jim Buckland, Gardens Manager
Visiting the Gardens you are immersed in a classic 19th century designed landscape with its 2¹/₂ acre walled kitchen garden, 13 original glasshouses dating from the 1890s, 35 acres of ornamental grounds, 240 acre landscaped park and the 49 acre St Roche's arboretum, all linked by a scenic 2¹/₄ mile parkland walk. Features of the grounds are a lavishly planted 300ft long Edwardian pergola terminated by a flint and stone gazebo and sunken garden. The Visitor Centre (free entry) houses a licensed restaurant and an imaginative garden shop.
Location: OS Ref. SU863 128. SE side of A286 Midhurst Road, 6m N of Chichester.
Open: 1 Mar - 31 October: daily. Mar, Apr & Oct: 11am - 5pm. May - Sept: 10.30am - 5pm.
Admission: Adult £5.50, Child £2, Over 60s £5. Groups (20+): Adult £5, Child £2.
ℹ No photography in house. ◻ 🍴 🚻 ♿ ♿ 🍴Licensed. 🅿 Limited for coaches. 🔨 By arrangement. 🚻 🐕 Guide dogs only. ♿ Tel for details.

WILMINGTON PRIORY
Wilmington, Nr Eastbourne, East Sussex BN26 5SW

Tel: 01628 825920 or 825925 (bookings) **www.**landmarktrust.org.uk
Owner: Leased to the Landmark Trust by Sussex Archaeological Society
                                                          Contact: The Landmark Trust
Founded by the Benedictines in the 11th century, the surviving, much altered buildings date largely from the 14th century. Managed and maintained by the Landmark Trust, which lets buildings for self-catering holidays. Full details of Wilmington Priory and 178 other historic buildings available for holidays are featured in The Landmark Handbook (price £9.50 refundable against booking), from The Landmark Trust, Shottesbrooke, Maidenhead, Berkshire, SL6 3SW.
Location: OS Ref. TQ543 042. 600yds S of A27. 6m NW of Eastbourne.
Open: Grounds, Ruins, Porch & Crypt: on 30 days between Apr - Oct. Whole property including interiors on 8 of these days. Contact the Landmark Trust for details. Available for self-catering holidays for up to 6 people throughout the year.
Admission: Free entry on open days.
🚻

Pashley Manor from the book 'Historic Family Homes & Gardens from the Air'.

Raymond Woodham

English Heritage Photo Library

OSBORNE HOUSE ⌗

Map 3

Owner:
English Heritage

▶ **CONTACT**

The House
Administrator
Osborne House
Royal Apartments
East Cowes
Isle of Wight
PO32 6JY

Tel: 01983 200022
Fax: 01983 297281

**Venue Hire and
Hospitality:**
Tel: 01983 200022

▶ **LOCATION**
OS Ref. SZ516 948

1 mile SE of East Cowes.

Ferry: Isle of Wight
ferry terminals.

East Cowes 1¹/₂ miles
Tel: 02380 334010.

Fishbourne 4 miles
Tel: 0870 582 7744.

CONFERENCE/FUNCTION

ROOM	MAX CAPACITY
Durbar Hall	standing 80 seated 50
Upper Terrace	standing 250
Walled Gardens	standing 100
Marquee	Large scale events possible

Osborne House was the peaceful, rural retreat of Queen Victoria, Prince Albert and their family; they spent some of their happiest times here.

Many of the apartments have a very intimate association with the Queen who died here in 1901 and have been preserved almost unaltered ever since. The nursery bedroom remains just as it was in the 1870s when Queen Victoria's first grandchildren came to stay. Children were a constant feature of life at Osborne (Victoria and Albert had nine). Don't miss the Swiss Cottage, a charming chalet in the grounds built for the Royal children to play and entertain their parents in.

Enjoy the beautiful gardens with their stunning views over the Solent and the fruit and flower Victorian Walled Garden. The Durbar Wing has been refurbished. With interactive screens it displays the exquisite Indian gifts given by the Indian people to Queen Victoria.

English Heritage Photo Library

ℹ️ WCs. Suitable for filming, concerts, drama. No photography in the House. Children's play area. WC.

🛍️

🍽️ Private and corporate hire.

♿ Wheelchairs available, access to house via ramp, ground floor access only. WC.

☕🍴 Teas, coffees and light snacks. Waitress service in Swiss Cottage tearoom and new digby trout restaurant overlooking the terrace.

🅿️ Ample.

▪️ Visits free, please book. Education room available.

❄️

▶ **OPENING TIMES***

House
24 March - 30 September
Daily: 10am - 6pm.
Last admission 4pm.

May close earlier on concert days, please telephone for details.

1 - 31 October
Sun - Thur:
10am - 4pm.

1 November - 31 March
Sun - Thur: 10am - 4pm.
Guided tours only. Last tour 2.30pm.
Pre-booking essential on 01983 200022.

Closed 24 - 26 December & 1 January.

* Times subject to change.

▶ **ADMISSION***

House & Grounds
Adult £8.95
Child (5-15yrs) £4.50
Child under 5yrs ..... Free
Conc. £6.70
Family (2+3) £22.40

Grounds only
Adult £5.30
Child (5-15yrs) £2.70
Child under 5yrs ..... Free
Conc. £4.00
Family (2+3) £13.30

Groups (11+) 15% discount. Tour leader and driver have free entry.
1 extra free place for every additional 20 paying.

APPULDURCOMBE HOUSE

Wroxall, Shanklin, Isle of Wight

Tel: 01983 852484   www.english-heritage.org.uk/visits

Owner: English Heritage   **Contact:** Mr & Mrs Owen

The bleached shell of a fine 18th century Baroque style house standing in grounds landscaped by 'Capability' Brown. An exhibition displays prints and photographs depicting the history of the house. Falconry Centre.

Location: OS Ref. SZ543 800. 1/2 mile W of Wroxall off B3327.

Open: 19 Feb - 31 Oct: daily, 10am - 3pm (5pm Easter weekend & May - Sept). Last entry 1hr before closing.

Admission: House: Adult £2.50, Child £1.50, Conc. £2.25, Family £7. Falconry Centre: Adult £4.75, Child £2.75, Conc. £4.25, Family £12.50. Combined Ticket: Adult £5.75, Child £3.25, Conc. £5.25, Family £15.

□ ⊔ P Limited. ⊠ In grounds, on leads. ✱ ⊎ Tel. for details.

BEMBRIDGE WINDMILL

Correspondence to: NT Office, Strawberry Lane, Mottistone, **Isle of Wight PO30 4EA**

Tel: 01983 873945   www.nationaltrust.org.uk

Owner: The National Trust   **Contact:** The Custodian

Dating from around 1700, this is the only windmill to survive on the Island. Much of its original wooden machinery is still intact and there are spectacular views from the top.

Location: OS Ref. SZ639 874. 1/2 m S of Bembridge off B3395.

Open: 21 Mar - 30 Jun & 1 Sept - 30 Oct: daily except Sat; 1 Jul - 31 Aug: daily, 10am - 5pm. Open Easter Sat.

Admission: Adult £2, Child £1, Family £6. All school groups are conducted by a NT guide; special charge applies.

□ ⊡ ⓘBy arrangement. P 100 yds. ⊠ ⊠Guide dogs only.

BRIGHSTONE SHOP & MUSEUM

North St, Brighstone, Isle of Wight PO30 4AX

Tel: 01983 740689

Owner: The National Trust   **Contact:** The Manager

The traditional cottages contain a National Trust shop and Village Museum (run by Brighstone Museum Trust) depicting village life in the late 19th century.

Location: OS Ref. SZ428 828. North Street, Brighstone, just off B3399.

Open: 4 Jan - 24 Mar: Mon - Sat, 10am - 1pm. 25 Mar - 28 May: Mon - Sat, 10am - 4pm. 29 May - 30 Oct: daily, 10am - 5pm (Suns from 12 noon). 31 Oct - 24 Dec: Mon - Sat, 10am - 4pm. 28 - 31 Dec: Wed - Sat, 10am - 4pm.

Admission: Free.

⟁Partial. ✱

Accommodation Index see page 31

Yarmouth Castle.

CARISBROOKE CASTLE

NEWPORT, ISLE OF WIGHT PO30 1XY

www.english-heritage.org.uk/visits

Tel: 01983 522107   **Fax:** 01983 528632

Owner: English Heritage   **Contact:** Visitor Operations Team

The island's Royal fortress and prison of King Charles I before his execution in London in 1648. See the famous Carisbrooke donkeys treading the wheel in the Well House or meet them in the donkey centre. Don't miss the castle story in the gatehouse, the museum in the great hall and the interactive coach house museum. Guided tours available in summer.

Location: OS196 Ref. SZ486 877. Off the B3401, 1 1/4 miles SW of Newport.

Open: 24 Mar - 30 Sept: daily, 10am - 6pm. 1 Oct - 31 Mar: daily, 10am - 4pm. Closed 24 - 26 Dec & 1 Jan.

Admission: Adult £5.30, Child £2.70, Conc. £4, Family (2+3) £13.30. 15% discount for groups (11+).

ⓘWCs. □ ⟁ ⊡ P ⊠In grounds, on leads. ✱ ⊎ Tel. for details.

MORTON MANOR

Brading, Isle of Wight PO36 0EP

Tel/Fax: 01983 406168   **e-mail:** mortonmanor-iow@amserver.com

Owner/Contact: Mr J A J Trzebski

Refurbished in the Georgian period. Magnificent gardens and vineyard.

Location: OS Ref. SZ603 863 (approx.). 1/4 m W of A3055 in Brading.

Open: Easter - end Oct: daily except Sats, 10am - 5.30pm. Last admission 4.30pm.

Admission: Adult £4.75, Child £2.25, Conc. £4.25, Group £3.75.

MOTTISTONE MANOR GARDEN

Mottistone, Isle of Wight PO30 4ED

Tel: 01983 741302   www.nationaltrust.org.uk

Owner: The National Trust   **Contact:** The Gardener

A haven of peace and tranquillity with colourful herbaceous borders and a backdrop of the sea making a perfect setting for the historic Manor House. An annual open air Jazz Concert is held in the grounds in July.

Location: OS Ref. SZ406 838. 2m W of Brighstone on B3399.

Open: 20 Mar - 30 Oct: Sun - Thur, 11am - 5.30pm. House: Aug BH Mon only: 2 - 5.30pm. Guided tours for NT members on that day 10am - 12 noon.

Admission: Adult £3, Child £1.50, Family £7.50.

□ ⟁Limited access for wheelchair users. ⊡ P ⊠ ⊠In grounds, on leads.

NEEDLES OLD BATTERY

West High Down, Totland, Isle of Wight PO39 0JH

Tel: 01983 754772   www.nationaltrust.org.uk

Owner: The National Trust   **Contact:** The Property Manager

High above the sea, the Old Battery was built in the 1860s against the threat of French invasion. Exhibition of History of Battery. Stunning views.

Location: OS Ref. SZ300 848. Needles Headland W of Freshwater Bay & Alum Bay (B3322).

Open: 20 Mar - 30 Jun, 1 Sept - 30 Oct: daily except Fri (open Good Fri); Jul & Aug: daily, 10.30am - 5pm. Closes in bad weather; please telephone on day of visit to check.

Admission: Adult £3.60, Child £1.80. Special charge for guided tours.

⟁Partial. ⊡ ⓘBy appointment. ⊠ ⊠In grounds, on leads.

NUNWELL HOUSE & GARDENS
Coach Lane, Brading, Isle of Wight PO36 0JQ

Tel: 01983 407240

Owner: Col & Mrs J A Aylmer   **Contact:** Mrs J A Aylmer

Nunwell has been a family home for five centuries and reflects much architectural and Island history. King Charles I spent his last night of freedom here. Jacobean and Georgian wings. Finely furnished rooms. Lovely setting with Channel views and five acres of tranquil gardens including walled garden. Family military collections.

Location: OS Ref. SZ595 874. 1m NW of Brading. 3m S of Ryde signed off A3055.

Open: 29/30 May & 4 Jul - 7 Sept: Mon - Wed, 1 - 5pm. House tours: 1.30, 2.30 & 3.30pm. Groups welcome by arrangement throughout the year.

Admission: Adult £4, Pair of Adults £7.50 (inc guide book), Child (under 10yrs) £1, OAP/Student £3.50. Garden only: Adult £2.50.

▣ ⓘObligatory. 🅿 🐕 Guide dogs only. ✳

OLD TOWN HALL 🌿
Newtown, Isle of Wight

Tel: 01983 531785   **www.**nationaltrust.org.uk

Owner: The National Trust   **Contact:** The Custodian

A charming small 18th century building that was once the focal point of the 'rotten borough' of Newtown.

Location: OS Ref. SZ424 905. Between Newport and Yarmouth, 1m N of A3054.

Open: 20 Mar - 29 Jun, 4 Sept - 26 Oct: Mon, Wed & Sun; 3 Jul - 31 Aug: Sun - Thur, 2 - 5pm. Open Good Fri & Easter Sat.

Admission: Adult £1.80, Child 90p, Family £4.50.

🅿 Limited. 🐕 Guide dogs only.

OSBORNE HOUSE ⛉
See page 181 for full page entry.

See page 181 for full page entry.

YARMOUTH CASTLE ⛉
Quay Street, Yarmouth, Isle of Wight PO41 0PB

Tel: 01983 760678   **www.**english-heritage.org.uk/visits

Owner: English Heritage   **Contact:** Visitor Operations Team

This last addition to Henry VIII's coastal defences was completed in 1547 and is, unusually for its kind, square with a fine example of an angle bastion. It was garrisoned well into the 19th century. It houses exhibitions of paintings of the Isle of Wight and photographs of old Yarmouth.

Location: OS Ref. SZ354 898. In Yarmouth adjacent to car ferry terminal.

Open: 1 Apr - 30 Sept: Sun - Thurs, 11am - 4pm.

Admission: Adult £2.60, Child £1.30, Conc. £2.

▣ ♿Ground floor. 🅿 None. 🐕 In grounds, on leads.

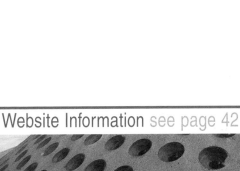

©National Trust Photographic Library/Martin Trelawny

The Needles Old Battery.

south west

As you travel west from London, so the landscape changes. Neat lanes and small fields become less common and are replaced by a wilder countryside. The houses are built of stone rather than brick, villages are few and far between, and the pace of life slows. The moorlands of Devon and Cornwall are among the most dramatic in Britain, contrasting with the unspoilt beaches. There is a warm welcome for the visitor from local residents and wonderful local produce to be sampled. Cliff top walks are well signed and present a perfect opportunity to take exercise in the invigorating sea air away from the crowds. Do not miss Athelhampton House & Gardens (Dorset) or Powderham Castle (Devon). For keen gardeners, The Lost Gardens of Heligan (Cornwall) contain over 200 acres of superb working Victorian gardens and pleasure grounds. The climate on the Scilly Isles means exotic and sub-tropical plants can be grown. If time permits, day trips to the islands can be made by helicopter, boat or plane from Newquay or Penzance.

Cornwall.

Old Sarum, Wiltshire

Lizard Oenins la, Cornwall

Cornwall

channel islands
cornwall
devon
dorset
gloucestershire
somerset
wiltshire

godolphin house

15th century | granite | continuing restoration

godolphin house

s o u t h   w e s t

"It looks like one of Inigo Jones's fairy castles for a masque at the Stuart court in which he married the battlements of medieval chivalry with the newfangled Classism of summer climes." Sir Roy Strong

Approaching through open country, Godolphin's presence is sensed rather than seen. The remains of little ancient avenues and plantations come up close, adding to the sense of mystery and surprise, hiding the house in trees. It is a great house on an intimate scale, grand but endearing. You won't find the rolling, landscaped park or the sweeping carriage drive leading up to a Georgian mansion here. Godolphin, the house, its gardens and grounds pre-date all that. They come from an altogether stranger and more obscure period.

The sensations are strong and clear however, of beauty and of age, because what you see is real; there is no attempt to deceive your eye or your feelings by fakery, or to iron-out the venerable signs of passing time.

The surfaces at Goldolphin are rich, cobbling of quartz and daisy-studded grass, weathered granite walls, reflections on leaded panes, well-modelled plasterwork, rich effects in pictures and textiles. These time-honoured qualities make that telling link between us and the Godolphin Justice of the Peace who violently robbed the King of Portugal's ship, wrecked in 1526 or the Elizabethan knight who reported the first sighting of the Armada in 1588

"…Nine sayle of great shippes between Sylly and Ushant – bearing in northeast…and their sayles all crossed over with a red cross…".

They remind us of the civilised plans commenced by Francis and Dorothy and of the poet brother Sidney Godolphin, to be cut short by the Civil War, or the quiet success of one of 16 children rising to the top of Queen Anne's government. Behind it all are the thousands who generated the wealth below ground or in the Godolphin tin works.

The Godolphins, who were courtiers from the early 16th century, brought metropolitan architecture to this distant place, where it married with our West Cornish granite idiom producing this extraordinary building. Then, by the mid-18th century, they dwindled away and the old house became derelict, reduced to a farmhouse and forgotten. Artists found it in the 20th century, which saw a recovery in its fortunes. Public money has enabled Godolphin's private owners to commence a slow and gentle but none-the-less major programme of specialist repair. Three quarters of the house has been saved and now they are raising the money to complete it, and to revive the great medieval gardens – work to be seen in progress.

▶ For further details about Godolphin House see page 194.

SAUSMAREZ MANOR

www.sausmarezmanor.co.uk

The home of the Seigneurs de Sausmarez since c1220 with a façade built at the bequest of the first Governor of New York.

An entrancing and entertaining half day encompassing something to interest everyone. The family have been explorers, inventors, diplomats, prelates, generals, admirals, privateers, politicians and governors etc, most of whom left their mark on the house, garden or the furniture.

The sub-tropical woodland garden is crammed with such exotics as banana trees, tree ferns, ginger, 300 plus camellias, lilies, myriads of bamboos, as well as the more commonplace hydrangeas, hostas etc.

The sculpture in the art park with its 200 or so pieces by artists from a dozen countries is the most comprehensive in Britain. The dolls' house collection displays pieces from 1830 onwards and is the third largest dedicated collection in Britain. The pitch and put is a cruelly testing 500m 9 hole par 3. The Copper, Tin and Silversmith demonstrates his ancient skills in the large barn. The two lakes are a haven for ornamental wildfowl and some of the sculpture.

Sausmarez Manor is available for corporate hospitality functions and Civil weddings. It also offers guided tours, welcomes schools (has education programmes), and has a tearoom, café and gift shop.

Sea Guernsey is celebrating the *History of the Heroes of the Sea*, and much of the Activities, Pageants, and Dramas are taking place here.

Map 2

Owner:
The Seigneur de Sausmarez

▶ CONTACT

Peter de Sausmarez
Sausmarez Manor
Guernsey
Channel Islands
GY4 6SG

Tel: 01481
235571/235655
Fax: 01481 235572

e-mail:
sausmarezmanor@
cwgsy.net

▶ LOCATION

2m S of St Peter Port,
clearly signposted.

▶ OPENING TIMES

Easter - End Oct
Daily: 10am - 5pm

Guided tours of House
Mon - Thurs:
10.30 & 11.30am.
Additional 2pm tour
during high season.

▶ ADMISSION

There is no overall charge
for admission.

Doll's House £3.50
Sub Tropical Garden . £4.00
Sculpture Trail £4.00
Pitch & Putt.............. £4.50
Putting...................... £1.00
House Tour £6.50

Discounts for Children,
Students, OAPs &
Organised Groups.

Partial.

Guided tours of House.

Holiday flat on the
ground floor.

€

National Trust/ Jon Hicks

COTEHELE

www.nationaltrust.org.uk

Map 1

Owner:
The National Trust

▶ **CONTACT**

Lewis Eynon
Property Manager
Cotehele
St Dominick
Saltash, Cornwall
PL12 6TA

Tel: 01579 351346
Fax: 01579 351222

e-mail:
cotehele@nationaltrust.
org.uk

▶ **LOCATION**

OS Ref. SX422 685
1m SW of Calstock by
foot. 8m S of Tavistock,
4m E of Callington,
15m from Plymouth
via the Tamar bridge
at Saltash

Trains: Limited service
from Plymouth to
Calstock (1¼ m uphill)

Boats: Limited (tidal)
service from Plymouth
to Calstock Quay
(Plymouth Boat
Cruises)
Tel: 01752 822797

River ferry: Privately
run from Calstock to
Cotehele Quay.
Tel: 01579 351346

Buses: Western
National (seasonal
variations)
Tel: 01752 222666

Cotehele, owned by the Edgcumbe family for nearly 600 years, is a fascinating and enchanting estate set on the steep wooded slopes of the River Tamar. Exploring Cotehele's many and various charms provides a full day out for the family and leaves everyone longing to return.

The steep valley garden contains exotic and tender plants which thrive in the mild climate. Remnants of an earlier age include a mediaeval stewpond and domed dovecote, a 15th-century chapel and 18th-century tower with fine views over the surrounding countryside. A series of more formal gardens, terraces, an orchard and a daffodil meadow surround Cotehele House.

One of the least altered medieval houses in the country, Cotehele is built in local granite, slate and sandstone. Inside the ancient rooms, unlit by electricity, is a fine collection of textiles, tapestries, armour and early dark oak furniture.

National Trust /Tymn Lintell

The chapel contains the oldest working domestic clock in England, still in its original position.

A walk through the garden and along the river leads to the quay, a busy river port in Victorian times. The National Maritime Museum worked with the National Trust to set up a museum here which explains the vital role that the Tamar played in the local economy. As a living reminder, the restored Tamar sailing barge *Shamrock* (owned jointly by the Trust and the National Maritime Museum) is moored here.

A further walk through woodland along the Morden stream leads to the old estate corn mill which has been restored to working order.

This large estate with many footpaths offers a variety of woodland and countryside walks, opening up new views and hidden places. The Danescombe Valley, with its history of mining and milling, is of particular interest.

ℹ️ No photography in house. *NPI National Heritage Award winners 1996 & 1999.*

🛍️ National Trust shop. 🌸

🍷 Available for up to 90 people.

♿ 2 wheelchairs at Reception. Hall & kitchen accessible. Ramps at house, restaurant and shop. Most of garden is very steep with loose gravel. Riverside walks are flatter (from Cotehele Quay) & Edgcumbe Arms is accessible. WCs near house and at Quay. Parking near house & mill by arrangement.

☕🍴 Barn restaurant daily (except Fri), 19 Mar - 31 Oct, plus limited opening from 12 Feb. Tel for details of pre-Christmas opening. At the Quay, Edgcumbe Arms offers light meals daily, 19 Mar - 31 Oct. Both licensed.

🅿️ Near house and garden and at Cotehele Quay. No parking at mill.

🚶 Groups (15+) must book with Property Office and receive a coach route (limited to two per day). No groups Suns & BH weekends. Visitors to house limited to 80 at any one time. Please arrive early and be prepared to queue. Avoid dull days. Allow a full day to see estate.

🐕 Under control welcome only on woodland walks.

❄️

▶ **OPENING TIMES**

House & Restaurant
19 Mar - 31 Oct: Daily
except Fris (but open
Good Fri), 11am - 5pm
(Oct: 11am - 4.30pm).
Last admission 30 mins
before closing time.

Mill
19 Mar - 31 Oct: Daily
except Fris (but open
Good Fri plus Fris in July
& August) 1 - 5.30pm
(closes 4.30pm during Oct,
6pm July & Aug).

Garden
All year: Daily,
10.30am - dusk.

▶ **ADMISSION**

House, Garden & Mill
Adult £7.40
Family £18.50
1-Adult Family £11.10
Pre-booked Groups .. £6.40

Garden & Mill only
Adult £4.40
Family £11.00
1-Adult Family £6.60

*Groups must book in
advance with the
Property Office.
No groups Suns or BHs.

NT members free.
You may join here.

NTPL/ R Truman

Map 1

Owner:

The National Trust

▶ **CONTACT**

Property Manager
Lanhydrock
Bodmin
Cornwall   PL30 5AD

Tel: 01208 265950
Fax: 01208 265959

e-mail: lanhydrock@
nationaltrust.org.uk

▶ **LOCATION**

OS Ref. SX085 636

2¹/₂ m SE of Bodmin,
follow signposts from
either A30,
A38 or B3268.

LANHYDROCK 🌿

www.nationaltrust.org.uk

Lanhydrock is the grandest and most welcoming house in Cornwall, set in a glorious landscape of gardens, parkland and woods overlooking the valley of the River Fowey.

The house dates back to the 17th century but much of it had to be rebuilt after a disastrous fire in 1881 destroyed all but the entrance porch and the north wing, which includes the magnificent Long Gallery with its extraordinary plaster ceiling depicting scenes from the Old Testament. A total of 50 rooms are on show today and together they reflect the entire spectrum of life in a rich and splendid Victorian household, from the many servants' bedrooms and the fascinating complex of kitchens, sculleries and larders to the nursery suite where the Agar-Robartes children lived, learned and played, and the grandeur of the dining room with its table laid and ready.

Surrounding the house on all sides are gardens ranging from formal Victorian parterres to the wooded higher garden where magnificent displays of magnolias, rhododendrons and camellias climb the hillside to merge with the oak and beech woods all around. A famous avenue of ancient beech and sycamore trees, the original entrance drive to the house, runs from the pinnacled 17th-century gatehouse down towards the medieval bridge across the Fowey at Respryn.

NTPL/ Andreas von Einsiedel

NT/Jon Hicks

🚫 No photography in house.

🍵 By arrangement.

♿ Suitable. Braille guide. WC.

☕

🍴 Licensed restaurant

🐕 In park, on leads. Guide dogs only in house.

🅿 Limited for coaches.

❄ Please telephone for details.

▶ **OPENING TIMES**

House:
19 Mar - 30 Oct:
Daily except Mons
(but open BH Mons)
11am - 5.30pm.
Oct: 11am - 5pm.

Last admission ¹/₂ hr
before closing.

Garden:
All year: Daily.
10am - 6pm.
Charge levied from
12 Feb - 30 Oct.

Refreshments available
12 Feb - 30 Oct: Daily.
Nov - Jan: limited opening
(tel for details).

Plant Sales:
12 Feb - 18 Mar: Daily
11am - 4pm
19 Mar - 30 Sept: Daily
11am - 5.30pm.
Oct: Daily
11am - 5pm.

Shop:
Jan - 11 Feb: Sat & Sun,
11am - 4pm.
12 Feb - 18 Mar, 31 Oct -
24 Dec & 27 - 31 Dec:
Daily, 11am - 4pm.
19 Mar - 30 Sept: Daily
11am - 5.30pm.
Oct: Daily
11am - 5pm.

▶ **ADMISSION**

**House, Garden &
Grounds**
   Adult £7.90
   Family £19.75
   1-Adult Family £11.85
   Groups.................. £6.90

**Garden &
Grounds only** £4.40

National Trust/ Peter Cade

ANTONY HOUSE & GARDEN ❧
& ANTONY WOODLAND GARDEN

TORPOINT, CORNWALL PL11 2QA

www.nationaltrust.org.uk

Antony House & Garden Tel: 01752 812191

Antony Woodland Garden Tel: 01752 812364

e-mail: antony@nationaltrust.org.uk

Antony House & Garden Owner: The National Trust

Antony Woodland Garden Owner: Carew Pole Garden Trust

Superb 18th-century house on the Lynher estuary, grounds landscaped by Repton. Formal garden with sculptures & National Collection of day lilies; woodland garden with magnolias, rhododendrons & National Collection of Camellia japonica.

Location: OS Ref. SX418 564. 5m W of Plymouth via Torpoint car ferry, 2m NW of Torpoint.

Open: House & Garden: 28 Mar - 27 Oct: Tue - Thur & BH Mons. Also Suns in June, July & Aug: 1.30pm - 5.30pm. Last adm. 4.45pm. Restaurant open from 12.30pm. Woodland Garden (not NT) 1 Mar - 30 Oct: daily except Mon & Fri (open BH Mons), 11am - 5.30pm.

Admission: House & Garden: £5, Family £12.50, 1-Adult Family £7.50. Groups £4.30pp. NT Garden only: £2.60. Woodland Garden: Adult £4 (Free to NT members on days when the house is open). Joint Gardens-only tickets: Adult £4.20. Groups £3.50.

🅾 ♿ Braille guide. 🍴 🅿 ✖

BOSVIGO

Bosvigo Lane, Truro, Cornwall TR1 3NH

Tel/Fax: 01872 275774 **e-mail:** bosvigo.plants@virgin.net **www**.bosvigo.com

Owner: Michael & Wendy Perry **Contact:** Michael Perry

A series of small, densely planted 'rooms', each with its own colour theme, surround the Georgian house (not open). The Woodland Walk is crammed full of small spring treasures, whilst the herbaceous garden 'rooms' give non-stop colour from June to the end of September. Small specialist nursery attached.

Location: OS Ref. SW815 452. ³/₄ m W of Truro city centre. Turn off A390 down Dobbs Lane just W of Sainsbury foodstore.

Open: Mar - end Sept: Thur & Fri, 11am - 6pm.

Admission: Adult £3.50, Child (5-15yrs) £1. No group concessions.

♿ ♿ Partial. 🅿 Limited. ✖

BURNCOOSE NURSERIES & GARDEN

Gwennap, Redruth, Cornwall TR16 6BJ

Tel: 01209 860316 **Fax:** 01209 860011 **e-mail:** burncoose@eclipse.co.uk **www**.burncoose.co.uk

Owner/Contact: C H Williams

The Nurseries are set in the 30 acre woodland gardens of Burncoose.

Location: OS Ref. SW742 395. 2m SE of Redruth on main A393 Redruth to Falmouth road between the villages of Lanner and Ponsanooth.

Open: Mon - Sat: 9am - 5pm, Suns, 11am - 5pm. Gardens and Tearooms open all year (except Christmas Day).

Admission: Nurseries: Free. Gardens: Adult/Conc. £2. Child Free. Group conducted tours: £2.50 by arrangement.

🅾 ♿ ♿ Grounds. WCs. 📷 🏧 By arrangement. 🅿 ✖ In grounds, on leads. ✱

BOCONNOC

ESTATE OFFICE, BOCONNOC, LOSTWITHIEL, CORNWALL PL22 0RG

www.boconnocenterprises.co.uk

Tel: 01208 872507 **Fax:** 01208 873836 **e-mail:** adgfortescue@btinternet.com

Owner/Contact: Anthony Fortescue Esq

Bought with the famous Pitt Diamond in 1717, Boconnoc remains one of Cornwall's best kept secrets. Home to three Prime Ministers, its unique combination of history, architecture, picturesque landscape and one of the great Cornish gardens created ideal film locations for *Poldark* and *The Three Musketeers*. King Charles I and the architect Sir John Soane played an influential part in Boconnoc's history. Groups visit the Boconnoc House restoration project, the gardens, church, Golden Jubilee lake walk and the Georgian Bath House. Ideal for private and corporate events, conferences, activities; weddings and receptions and holiday houses for long or short breaks.

Location: OS Ref. 148 605. A38 Plymouth, Liskeard or from Bodmin to Dobwalls, then A390 to Middle Taphouse.

Open: House & Garden: 17 Apr - 29 May: Suns, also Tues & Weds in May: 2 - 5.30pm. Groups (15-255) by appointment all year.

Admission: House: £3, Garden £3. Child under 12yrs Free.

🅾 🍴 ♿ Partial. 📷 🏧 By arrangement. 🅿 ■ ✖ In grounds, on leads.
🛏 8 doubles, 1 single, 3 ensuite. 🔔 Applied for. ✱ 📅 2/3 Apr: Cornwall Garden Society Spring Flower Show. 15 - 17 Jul: Liskeard Steam & Vintage Fair.

PENCARROW 🏠
BODMIN, CORNWALL PL30 3AG
www.pencarrow.co.uk

Tel: 01208 841369 **Fax:** 01208 841722 **e-mail:** pencarrow@aol.com

Owner: Molesworth-St Aubyn family   **Contact:** J Reynolds

Still owned and lived in by the family. Georgian house and Grade II* listed gardens. Superb collection of pictures, furniture and porcelain. Marked walks through 50 acres of beautiful formal and woodland gardens, Victorian rockery, Italian garden, over 700 different varieties of rhododendrons, lake and ice house.

Location: OS Ref. SX040 711. Between Bodmin and Wadebridge. 4m NW of Bodmin off A389 & B3266 at Washaway.

Open: 27 Mar - 27 Oct: Sun - Thur, 11am - 4pm (last tour). Gardens: 1 Mar - 31 Oct: daily.

Admission: House & Garden: Adult £7.50, Child £3.50. Family £21. Garden only: Adult £4, Child £1. Groups (by arrangement): House & Garden: groups 20-30 £6.50, 31+ £5.50; Gardens only: groups 20-30 £3.50, 31+ £3. Discounts not normally available on Fri & Sat.

ℹ️ Craft centre, small children's play area, self-pick soft fruit. 🚻 🍵 By arrangement. ♿ ● Licensed. 🍴 🛈 Obligatory. 🅿️ 🔲 🚌 Grounds only. 🔺✱ 🐕 Tel for details.

PINE LODGE GARDENS & NURSERY
Holmbush, St Austell, Cornwall PL25 3RQ

Tel: 01726 73500   **Fax:** 01726 77370   **e-mail:** garden@pine-lodge.co.uk
www.pine-lodge.co.uk

Owner/Contact: Mr & Mrs R H J Clemo

30 acres with over 6,000 plants all labelled. Herbaceous and shrub borders. Many water features, pinetum, arboretum, Japanese garden, wild flower meadow, lake with waterfowl and black swans. Plant hunting expeditions every year to gather seeds for our nursery which contain very unusual plants, many rare. The gardens were given a Highly Commended Award by the Cornwall Tourist Board for 2002. Plenty of seats in the gardens.

Location: OS Ref. SX044 527. Signposted on A390.

Open: 1 Mar - 31 Oct: daily, 10am - 6pm, last ticket 5pm.

Admission: Adult £5, Child £3.

ℹ️ WC. 🚻 ● 🅿️ 🚌

LOCAL FOOD

Stargazy Pie

This somewhat macabre looking dish has its fishy contents staring upwards from a pastry case! Arranged in a circular dish like the spokes of a wheel, sardines, pilchards or small herrings are left with their heads on and stuffed with parsley and onion. The gaps between the fishes are filled with chopped bacon and egg and then the whole dish is covered with a pastry lid with the heads peeking out. A wavy effect is created by shaping the pastry and it is then glazed with egg yolk or milk infused with saffron, and baked. The Cornish village of Mousehole celebrates each 23 December by baking Stargazy Pie to commemorate a local fisherman who saved the village from a hungry Christmas one stormy winter.

© English Heritage Photo Library. © Skyscan Balloon Photography

PENDENNIS CASTLE ⛨
FALMOUTH, CORNWALL TR11 4LP
www.english-heritage.org.uk/pendennis

Tel: 01326 316594   **Fax:** 01326 319911   **e-mail:** customers@english-heritage.org.uk
Venue and Hire Hospitality: 01326 310106

Owner: English Heritage   **Contact:** Visitor Operations Team

Pendennis and its neighbour, St Mawes Castle, face each other across the mouth of the estuary of the River Fal. Built by Henry VIII in 16th century as protection against threat of attack and invasion from France. Extended and adapted over the years to meet the changing threats to national security from the French and Spanish and continued right through to World War II. It withstood five months of siege during the Civil War before becoming the penultimate Royalist Garrison to surrender on the mainland. Pendennis today stands as a landmark, with fine sea views and excellent site facilities including a hands-on discovery centre, exhibitions, a museum, guardhouse, shop and tearoom. Excellent special events venue.

Location: OS Ref. SW824 318. On Pendennis Head.

Open: 24 Mar - 30 Jun: daily, 10am - 5pm (4pm Sats). 1 Jul - 31 Aug: daily, 10am - 6pm (4 pm Sats). 1 - 30 Sept: daily 10am - 5pm (4pm Sats), 1 Oct - 31 Mar: daily, 10am - 4pm. Closed 24 - 26 Dec & 1 Jan. The Keep will close for 1hr at lunch on Sats when events are booked.

Admission: Adult £4.60, Child £2.30, Conc. £3.50, Family £11.50. 15% discount for groups (11+). Prices subject to change April 2005.

🔲 🍵 ♿ Partial. ● 🛈 By arrangement. 🅿️ 🔲 🚌 In grounds only. 🔺✱ 🐕 Tel for details.

PRIDEAUX PLACE

PADSTOW, CORNWALL PL28 8RP

Tel: 01841 532411 **Fax:** 01841 532945 **e-mail:** office@prideauxplace.fsnet.co.uk
Owner/Contact: Peter Prideaux-Brune Esq

Tucked away above the busy port of Padstow, the home of the Prideaux family for over 400 years, is surrounded by gardens and wooded grounds overlooking a deer park and the Camel estuary to the moors beyond. The house still retains its 'E' shape Elizabethan front and contains fine paintings and furniture as well as an exhibition reflecting its emergence as a major international film location. The impressive outbuildings have been restored in recent years and the 16th century plaster ceiling in the great chamber has been uncovered for the first time since 1760.

Location: OS Ref. SW913 756. 5m from A39 Newquay/Wadebridge link road. Signposted by Historic House signs.

Open: House & Grounds: Easter Sun - 31 Mar, 8 May - 6 Oct: Sun - Thur, 1.30 - 4pm (last tour). Grounds & Tearoom: Easter Sun - 6 Oct: Sun - Thur, 12.30 - 5pm. Open all year for pre-booked groups (15+), discounts apply.

Admission: House & Grounds: Adult £6.50, Child £2. Grounds only: Adult £2, Child £1. Groups (15+) discounts apply.

📷 ⊤ By arrangement. 🖟 Ground floor & grounds. 🖢 🐾 Obligatory. 🖼 By arrangement. 🐕 In grounds, on leads. 🅰 ❊

RESTORMEL CASTLE ⌗

Lostwithiel, Cornwall PL22 0BD

Tel: 01208 872687 **e-mail:** customers@english-heritage.org.uk
www.english-heritage.org.uk/restormel

Owner: English Heritage   **Contact:** Visitor Operations Team

Perched on a high mound, surrounded by a deep moat, the huge circular keep of this splendid Norman castle survives in remarkably good condition. It is still possible to make out the ruins of Restormel's Keep Gate, Great Hall and even the kitchens and private rooms.

Location: OS200 Ref. SX104 614. 1¹/2 m N of Lostwithiel off A390.

Open: 24 Mar - Oct: daily, 10am - 5pm (6pm in Jul & Aug; 4pm in Oct). Winter: closed.

Admission: Adult £2.30, Child £1.20, Conc. £1.70. 15% discount for groups (11+).

📷 🅿 Limited for coaches. 🐕 In grounds, on leads. ♿ Tel for details.

ST CATHERINE'S CASTLE ⌗

Fowey, Cornwall

Tel: 0117 9750700

Owner: English Heritage   **Contact:** The South West Regional Office

A small fort built by Henry VIII to defend Fowey harbour, with fine views of the coastline and river estuary.

Location: OS200 Ref. SX118 508. ³/4 m SW of Fowey along footpath off A3082.

Open: Any reasonable time, daylight only.

Admission: Free.

❊

© English Heritage Photo Library

ST MAWES CASTLE ⌗

ST MAWES, CORNWALL TR2 3AA

www.english-heritage.org.uk/stmawes

Tel/Fax: 01326 270526 **Venue Hire and Hospitality:** 01326 310106
e-mail: customers@english-heritage.org.uk/visits

Owner: English Heritage   **Contact:** Visitor Operations Team

The pretty fishing village of St Mawes is home to this castle. On the opposite headland to Pendennis Castle, St Mawes shares the task of watching over the mouth of the River Fal as it has done since Henry VIII built it as a defence against the French. With three huge circular bastions shaped like clover leaves, St Mawes was designed to cover every possible angle of approach. It is the finest example of Tudor military architecture. The castle offers views of St Mawes' little boat-filled harbour, the passenger ferry tracking across the Fal, and the splendid coastline which featured in the *Poldark* TV series. Also the start of some delightful walks along the coastal path.

Location: OS204 Ref. SW842 328. W of St Mawes on A3078.

Open: 24 Mar - 30 June: daily, 10am - 5pm (1pm on Sats). 1 Jul - 31 Aug: daily, 10am - 6pm (1pm on Sats). 1 - 30 Sept: daily, 10am - 5pm daily (1pm on Sats). 1 - 31 Oct: daily, 10am - 4pm. 1 Nov - 31 Mar: Fri - Mon, 10am - 4pm. Closed 24 - 26 Dec & 1 Jan.

Admission: Adult £3.60, Child £1.80, Conc. £2.70. 15% discount for groups (11+).

📷 ⊤ Private & corporate hire. 🖟 Grounds. WC. 🖢 🅿 Limited. 🐕 Guide dogs only. 🅰 ❊ ♿ Tel for details.

Website Information see page 42

www.hudsonsguide.co.uk

ST MICHAEL'S MOUNT

MARAZION, Nr PENZANCE, CORNWALL TR17 0EF

www.stmichaelsmount.co.uk   **www.nationaltrust.org.uk**

Tel: 01736 710507 (710265 tide information)   **Fax:** 01736 719930
e-mail: godolphin@manor-office.co.uk

Owner: The National Trust   **Contact:** The Manor Office

This beautiful island set in Mounts Bay has become an icon for Cornwall, and in turn there are magnificent views when you reach its summit. There the church and castle, whose origins date from the 12th century, have at various times acted as a Benedictine priory, a place of pilgrimage, a fortress, a mansion house and now a magnet for visitors from all over the world. Following the Civil War, the island was acquired by the St Aubyn family who still live in the castle today.

Location: OS Ref. SW515 300. 4m E of Penzance. At Marazion there is access on foot

over causeway at low tide. In the main season, the property is reached at high tide by a short evocative boat trip.

Open: Castle: 21 Mar - 31 Oct: Sun - Fri, 10.30am - 4.45pm (last admission on the island). Nov - Mar: open when tide and weather favourable. Essential to telephone in advance. Garden (not NT): May & Jun: Weekdays only; Jul - Oct: Thur & Fri only, 10.30am - 4.45pm. Church Service: Whitsun - 30 Sept (also Christmas Day, Good Fri & Easter Sun): Sun, 11.15am. All visits subject to weather and tides.

Admission: Adult £5.50, Child (under 17) £2.75, Family £13.75, 1-Adult Family £10.50. Booked groups £5. Gardens (not NT) £3.

⬜ ⓘ 🅿 On mainland (not NT.) 🐕 Not permitted on island. ✱

SAUSMAREZ MANOR 🏠   *See page 190 for full page entry.*

TATE ST IVES

Porthmeor Beach, St Ives, Cornwall TR26 1TG
Tel: 01736 796266   **Fax:** 01736 794480   **e-mail:** tatestivesinfo@tate.org.uk
www.tate.org.uk

Owner: Tate Gallery   **Contact:** Arwen Fitch

Changing displays from the Tate Collection, as well as international modern and contemporary art, focusing on the modern movement that St Ives is famous for. The exhibitions are supported by an extensive range of events. Tate St Ives does close for re-hanging the new exhibitions, however the shop and café (with spectacular views over St Ives) remain open.

Tate St Ives also manages the Barbara Hepworth Museum and Sculpture Garden.

Location: OS Ref. SW515 407. Situated by Porthmeor Beach.
Open: Mar - Oct: daily, 10am - 5.30pm. Nov - Feb: Tue - Sun, 10am - 4.30pm.
Admission: Adult £5.50, Conc. £2.50, Under 18s and Over 60s Free.

⬜ ♿ 🍴 Licensed. ⓘ Daily. 🅿 Nearby. ■ 🐕 Guide dogs only. ✱ 📺 Tel for details.

© English Heritage Photo Library

TINTAGEL CASTLE ⊞

TINTAGEL, CORNWALL PL34 0HE

www.english-heritage.org.uk/tintagel

Tel/Fax: 01840 770328   **e-mail:** customers@english-heritage.org.uk/visits
Owner: English Heritage   **Contact:** Visitor Operations Team

The spectacular setting for the legendary castle of King Arthur on the wild and windswept Cornish coast. Clinging precariously to the edge of the cliff face are the extensive ruins of a medieval royal castle, built by Richard, Earl of Cornwall, younger brother of Henry III. Also used as a Cornish stronghold by subsequent Earls of Cornwall. Despite extensive excavations since the 1930s, Tintagel Castle remains one of the most spectacular and romantic spots in the entire British Isles. Destined to remain a place of mystery and romance, Tintagel will always jealously guard its marvellous secrets.

Location: OS200 Ref. SX048 891. On Tintagel Head, ¹/₂ m along uneven track from Tintagel.
Open: 24 Mar - 31 Oct: daily, 10am - 6pm (5pm in Oct). 1 Nov - 31 Mar: daily, 10am - 4pm. Closed 24 - 26 Dec & 1 Jan.
Admission: Adult £3.90, Child £2, Conc. £2.90. 15% discount for groups (11+).

ⓘ No vehicles. ⬜ 🐕 ✱ 📺 Tel for details.

🎭 **Special Events Index** see page 24

TINTAGEL OLD POST OFFICE ❧
Tintagel, Cornwall PL34 0DB

Tel: 01840 770024 or 01208 74281

Owner: The National Trust   **Contact:** The Custodian

One of the most characterful buildings in Cornwall, and a house of great antiquity, this small 14th-century yeoman farmhouse is full of charm and interest.

Location: OS Ref. SX056 884. In the centre of Tintagel.

Open: 23 Mar - 30 Oct: daily, 11am - 5.30pm (closes 4pm Oct). Last admission 15 mins before closing.

Admission: Adult £2.50, Child £1.20, Family £6.20, 1-Adult Family £3.60. Booked groups £2.10.

LOCAL FOOD

Cornish Pasty

The most famous culinary export from the West Country must be the Cornish Pasty. This was the packed lunch for the working man or schoolchild. Wrapped in a cloth and placed in a lunch tin to preserve the heat, the pasty contained whatever ingredients were available to the family, sweet or savoury. The crimped edge of the short pastry case was originally used to hold the pasty and was not meant to be eaten itself. The habit was to mark a corner of each pasty with the initials of its owner so that each member of the family could have their own favourite filling or so that the owner could be identified if the pasty was put down in the playground or workplace.

TREBAH GARDEN

MAWNAN SMITH, Nr FALMOUTH, CORNWALL TR11 5JZ

www.trebah-garden.co.uk

Tel: 01326 250448   **Fax:** 01326 250781   **e-mail:** mail@trebah-garden.co.uk

Owner: Trebah Garden Trust   **Contact:** V. Woodcroft

Steeply wooded 25 acre sub-tropical ravine garden falls 200 feet from 18th century house to private beach on Helford River. Stream cascading over waterfalls through ponds full of Koi Carp and exotic water plants winds through 2 acres of blue and white hydrangeas and spills out over beach. Huge Australian tree ferns and palms mingle with shrubs of ever-changing colours and scent beneath over-arching canopy of 100 year old rhododendrons and magnolias. The striking Visitor Centre houses a garden shop, plant sales and stylish catering.

Location: OS Ref. SW768 275. 4m SW of Falmouth, 1m SW of Mawnan Smith. Follow brown and white tourism signs from Treliever Cross roundabout at A39/A394 junction through Mawnan Smith to Trebah.

Open: All year: daily, 10.30am - 5pm (last admission).

Admission: 1 Mar - 31 Oct: Adult £5.50, Child (5-15yrs)/Disabled £3, Child under 5yrs Free, OAP £5. 1 Nov - 28 Feb: Adult £2.60, Child (5-15yrs)/Disabled £1.40, Child under 5yrs Free, OAP £2.40. RHS members free. NT members: free entry 1 Nov - end Feb.

🏠 ♿ 🅰 Partial. ⬛ 🍴 🅵 By arrangement. 🅿 💻 🐕 On leads. ❋

TRELISSICK GARDEN ❧

FEOCK, TRURO, CORNWALL TR3 6QL

www.nationaltrust.org.uk

Tel: 01872 862090   **Fax:** 01872 865808   **e-mail:** trelissick@nationaltrust.org.uk

Owner: The National Trust   **Contact:** The Property Manager

A garden and estate of rare tranquil beauty with glorious maritime views over the Carrick Roads to Falmouth. The tender and exotic shrubs make this an attractive garden in all seasons. Extensive park and woodland walks beside the river. Art and Craft Gallery. Make your visit a really special day: travel to Trelissick by foot ferry from Truro, Falmouth and St Mawes by Fal River Links Partnerships Ferries, from April to September. Copeland Spode China on display in Trelissick House at 2pm on Thursdays, April to June, September and October, booking advisable 01872 862248.

Location: OS Ref. SW837 396. 4m S of Truro on B3289 above King Harry Ferry.

Open: Garden, Shop, Restaurant, Gallery and Plant Sales: 2 Jan - 11 Feb: Thur - Sun, 11am - 4pm. 12 Feb - 30 October: daily, 10.30am - 5.30pm. 1 Nov - 23 Dec: daily, 11am - 4pm. 27 Dec - 1 Jan: daily, 12 noon - 4pm. Woodland Walks: All year: daily.

Admission: Adult £5, Family £12.50, 1-Adult Family £7.50. Pre-arranged groups £4.30pp. Car Park £3 (refunded on admission). Garden & Copeland Spode China: £7.80 (NT members £3.50).

🏠 ♿ 🅣 By arrangement. 🅰 🍴 🅵 By arrangement. 🅿 Limited for coaches. 🐕 In park on leads; only guide dogs in garden. ❋ 📺 Tel for details.

National Trust/ Giles Oldworthy

TRENGWAINTON GARDEN 🌿

PENZANCE, CORNWALL TR20 8RZ

www.nationaltrust.org.uk

Tel: 01736 363148   **Fax:** 01736 367762

Owner: The National Trust   **Contact:** The Property Manager

Intimate and closely linked to the picturesque stream running through its valley, the garden leads up to a terrace and summer houses with splendid views across Mount's Bay to the Lizard. The walled gardens contain many rare and unusual species which are difficult to grow in the open anywhere else in the country.

Location: OS Ref. SW445 315. 2m NW of Penzance, $^1/_2$ m W of Heamoor on Penzance - Morvah road (B3312), $^1/_2$ m off St. Just road (A3071).

Open: 13 Feb - 30 Oct: Sun - Thur & Good Fri, 10am - 5.30pm (Feb, Mar & Oct: 10am - 5pm). Also open pre-Christmas - telephone for details.

Admission: Adult £4.50, Child £2.20, Family £11.20, 1-Adult Family £6.70. Booked groups: £3.80.

⊡ ♿ ♿Partial. ☕Tea-house. 🐕On leads.

TREWITHEN 🏛

GRAMPOUND ROAD, TRURO, CORNWALL TR2 4DD

www.trewithengardens.co.uk

Tel: 01726 883647   **Fax:** 01726 882301
e-mail: gardens@trewithen-estate.demon.co.uk

Owner: A M J Galsworthy   **Contact:** The Estate Office

Trewithen means 'house of the trees' and the name truly describes this fine early Georgian House in its splendid setting of wood and parkland. Country Life described the house as *'one of the outstanding West Country houses of the 18th century'*. The gardens at Trewithen are outstanding and of international fame. 2004 is the 100th year since George Johnstone inherited and started developing the gardens which now contain a wide and rare collection of flowering shrubs. Some of the magnolias and rhododendron species in the garden are known throughout the world. They are one of two attractions in this country awarded three stars by Michelin. Viewing platforms and a *Camera Obscura* will be an additional interest to visitors.

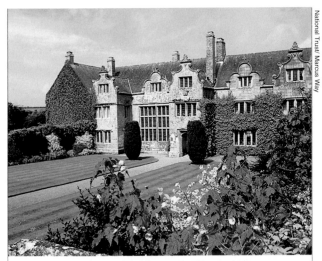

National Trust/ Marcus Way

TRERICE 🌿

KESTLE MILL, Nr NEWQUAY, CORNWALL TR8 4PG

www.nationaltrust.org.uk

Tel: 01637 875404   **Fax:** 01637 879300   **e-mail:** trerice@nationaltrust.org.uk

Owner: The National Trust   **Contact:** The Property Manager

Trerice is an architectural gem and something of a rarity – a small Elizabethan manor house hidden away in a web of narrow lanes and still somehow caught in the spirit of its age. An old Arundell house, it contains much fine furniture, ceramics, glasses and a wonderful clock collection. A small barn museum traces the development of the lawn mower.

Location: OS Ref. SW841 585. 3m SE of Newquay via the A392 & A3058 (right at Kestle Mill).

Open: 20 Mar - 30 Oct: Daily except Tues & Sat: (open Tues 26 Jul - 30 Aug). 11am - 5.30pm (5pm in Oct).

Admission: £5.50, Child £2.75, Family £13.75, 1-Adult Family £8.25. Pre-arranged groups £4.70.

⊡ ♿ ♿Braille & taped guides. WC. ☕Licensed. 🐕Guide dogs only. 🏠

Location: OS Ref. SW914 476. S of A390 between Grampound and Probus villages. 7m WSW of St Austell.

Open: Gardens: 1 Mar - 30 Sept: Mon - Sat, 10am - 4.30pm. Suns in Mar, Apr & May only. House: Apr - Jul & Aug: BH Mons, Mons & Tues, 2 - 4pm.

Admission: Adult (Mar - Jun) £4.75/ (Jul - Sept) £4.25, Child Free. Pre booked groups (20+): Adult (Mar - Jun) £4.25/ (Jul - Sept) £4, Child Free. Combined gardens & house £6.

ℹ️No photography in house. ♿ ♿Partial. WC. ☕ 🎫By arrangement. 🅿️Limited for coaches. 🐕In grounds, on leads.

BICTON PARK BOTANICAL GARDENS

www.bictongardens.co.uk

Map 2

Owner:
Mr & Mrs S E Lister

▶ **CONTACT**

Mr Simon Lister
Bicton Park
Botanical Gardens
East Budleigh
Budleigh Salterton
Devon EX9 7BJ

Tel: 01395 568465

Fax: 01395 568374

e-mail: info@
bictongardens.co.uk

Spanning three centuries of horticultural history, Bicton Park Botanical Gardens are set in the picturesque Otter Valley, near the coastal town of Budleigh Salterton and 10 miles south of Exeter.

The 63-acre park's oldest ornamental area is the Italian Garden, created in the axial style of Versailles landscaper Andre le Notre, c1735. By that time formal designs were becoming unfashionable in England, which may explain why the garden was located out of view of the manor house. Today, the full grandeur of the Italian Garden can be seen from the spacious restaurant in the classically styled Orangery, built at the beginning of the 19th century.

Bicton's high-domed Palm House, one of the world's most beautiful garden buildings, was the first of many developments between 1820 and 1850. Others included an important collection of conifers in the Pinetum, now the subject of a rare species conservation project, and St Mary's Church, where Queen Victoria worshipped.

A large museum reflects changes in agriculture and rural life generally over the past 200 years. The Grade I listed gardens, which are open all year, also feature a narrow-gauge railway which meanders through the garden on its 1½ mile track. Gift shop, garden centre, children's inside and outdoor play areas.

▶ **OPENING TIMES**

Summer
10am - 6pm.

Winter
10am - 5pm.
Closed Christmas Day & Boxing Day.

▶ **ADMISSION**

Adult £5.95
Child £4.95
Conc £4.95
Family (2+2) £19.95

Groups (16-200)
Adult £3.95
Child £2.95
Conc. £3.95

Children under 3yrs Free

▶ **LOCATION**

OS Ref. SY074 856

2m N of Budleigh Salterton on B3178.

Follow the brown signs to Bicton Park from M5/J30 at Exeter.

Rail: Exmouth 5mins, Exeter St Davids 12m.

Air: Exeter Airport 5m.

ⓘ Children's inside & outdoor play areas.

🛍 Garden Centre.

♿

🍴 Licensed.

🧍 By arrangement.

🅿

🐕 In grounds, on leads.

🔔

❄

201

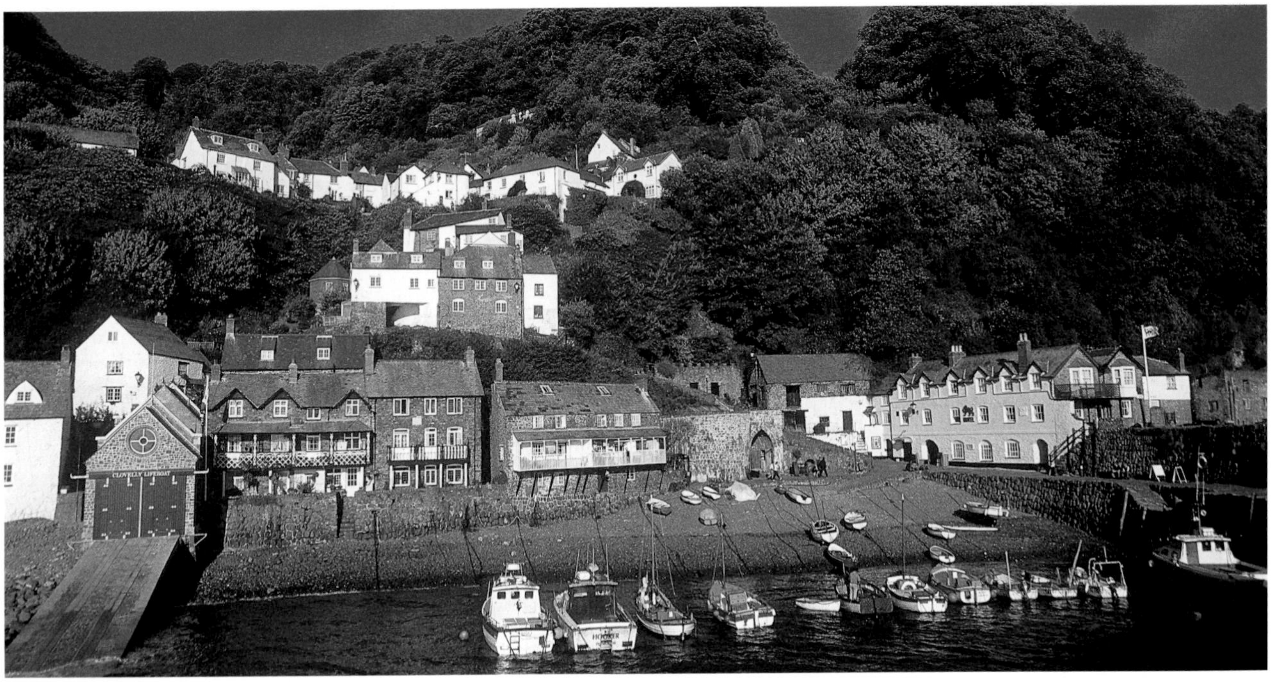

CLOVELLY

www.clovelly co.uk

The ancient seaside village of Clovelly is mentioned in the Domesday Book (c1100 AD), and it is very probable that a settlement existed on the site well before that, in Saxon times. The privately owned village has been sympathetically restored to how it would have appeared in the 19th century and is now a visitor destination in its own right. Access is restricted to pedestrians only, via the Clovelly Visitor Centre. (Land Rover taxi service for those unable to walk). Donkeys are used to transport goods into the village and down the steep lanes to the harbour. There are two museums in the village and an audio visual show in the Visitor Centre detailing the history of the village, as well as local craft workshops and two inns. Extensive coastal and woodland walks.

Map 1

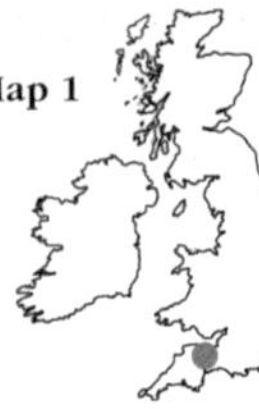

Owner:
Hon John Rous

CONTACT

Visitor Centre
Clovelly
Nr Bideford
N Devon EX39 5TA

Tel: 01237 431781

Fax: 01237 431288

LOCATION

OS Ref. SS248 319

On A39 10 miles W of Bideford, 15 miles E of Bude. Turn off at 'Clovelly Cross Roundabout' and follow signs to car park.

Air: Exeter & Plymouth Airport both 50 miles.

Rail: Barnstaple 19 miles.

Bus: from Bideford.

OPENING TIMES

High season: 9am - 6pm.

Low season: 9am - 4.30pm.

ADMISSION

The entrance fee covers parking and other facilities provided by Clovelly Estate, as well as admission to the audio-visual film, Fisherman's Cottage, and Kingsley Museum.

Adult	£4.00
Child (7 - 16yrs)	£2.75
Child (under 7yrs)	Free
Family (2+2)	£12.00

Group Rates (20+)

Adult	£3.50
Child	£2.50

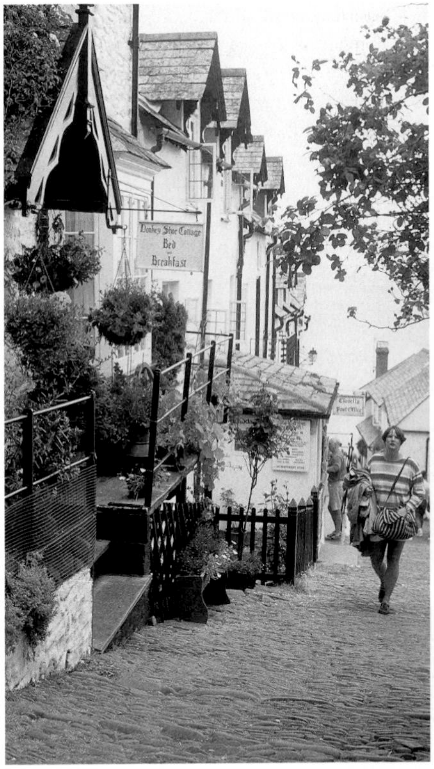

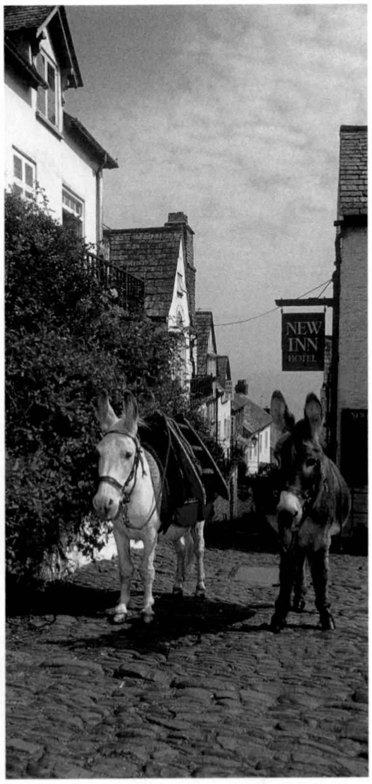

Rubber soled, low heel shoes are recommended. Partial. Around the Visitor Centre. Licensed. Licensed. On leads. 18 double, 1 single, all en suite.

POWDERHAM CASTLE 🏛

www.powderham.co.uk

Map 2

Owner:
The Earl of Devon

▶ **CONTACT**

Mr Tim Faulkner
General Manager
The Estate Office
Powderham Castle
Kenton, Exeter
Devon EX6 8JQ

Tel: 01626 890243
Fax: 01626 890729
e-mail: castle@
powderham.co.uk

**Functions
coordinator:**
Virginia Bowman
01626 890243
ginny@
powderham.co.uk

▶ **LOCATION**

OS Ref. SX965 832

6m SW of Exeter,
4m S M5/J30.
Access from A379 in
Kenton village.

Air: Exeter Airport 9m.

Rail: Starcross
Station 2m.

Bus: Devon General
No: 85, 85A, 85B to
Castle Gate.

Lying in a tranquil deer park with views through the ancient oaks to the Estuary of the River Exe, the castle of Powderham has long been the home of the Earl of Devon. It was built by Sir Philip Courtenay in 1390 but there may have been an earlier house defending the site in Saxon days. The Courtenays owned large parts of the West Country and it was not until the 17th century that Powderham became their principal seat. After some Civil War damage the family carried out some major embellishments and the 18th century saw the addition of the magnificent Grand Staircase and, towards the end of the century, Wyatt's fine Music Room.

The Castle remains a family home and visitors see the State Rooms by entertaining guided tours. The gardens and grounds are largely informal with walks and paths ranging from the springtime Woodland Garden to the old Victorian walled garden that is now home to a national collection of Dianthus, under the care of Whetman's Pinks, who run the Plant Centre at Powderham Country Store. The garden is also home to The Children's Secret Garden, and whilst the terraced Rose Garden has so sadly said goodbye to Timothy (the world's oldest tortoise who died in 2004), a youngster of some 65 years currently resides amongst the animals here. He is also a Timothy but is known as Timmy Two! A free tractor and trailer ride links the grounds and visits Powderham's fine shopping centre, The Country Store, which is open free all year, and helps to make a great all year round destination. Here you will find a Food Hall, Plant Centre, Restaurant, Gift Shop and the House of Marbles. There is also a delightful steam railway in the grounds, and Jousting Knights entertain most days in the summer.

Powderham has a huge events programme with everything from classic vehicles to firework displays and pop concerts. Voted Venue of the Year in 2004, some 150,000 visitors attend shows over the year (see the website for up to date details).

In addition the Castle is a popular venue for weddings, filming, private functions and corporate events, all of which help the Estate to be a diversified success in the modern world whilst retaining the charm of its past.

Summer
20 March - 30 October
Daily*: 10am - 5.30pm
Last admission 4.30pm.

*Except Sat: closed to
public, but available
for private hire.

Powderham Country Store:
Daily, 9am - 5.30pm,
(Suns, 10am - 4.30pm).

Winter
Available for hire for
conferences, receptions and
functions and private tours.

▶ **ADMISSION**

Adult £7.20
Child £4.10
Group rates by arrangement.
(2004 prices.)

🛍 ✂ ℹ Filming, car
launches including 4WD,
vehicle rallies, open air
concerts, etc. Grand piano in
Music Room, 3800 acre estate,
cricket pitch, horse trials
course. Deer park.

🍽 Conferences, dinners,
corporate entertainment.

♿ Limited facilities. Some
ramps. WC.

🍴 Fully licensed restaurant
and coach room access.

🚶 Fully inclusive. Tour time: 1hr.

🅿 Unlimited free parking.
Commission and complimentary
drinks for drivers. Advance
warning of group bookings
preferred but not essential.

🎒 Welcome. Fascinating tour
and useful insight into the life
of one of England's Great
Houses over the centuries.

🐕 In part of grounds, on
leads.

⚜ Civil Wedding Licence.

❄

🛡 See website or tel for
details.

CONFERENCE/FUNCTION

ROOM	SIZE	MAX CAPACITY
Music Room	56' x 25'	170
Dining Room	42' x 22'	100
Ante Room	28' x 18'	25
Library 1	32' x 18'	85
Library 2	31"x18'	85

NTPL / David Garner

A LA RONDE 🌿

SUMMER LANE, EXMOUTH, DEVON EX8 5BD

www.nationaltrust.org.uk

Tel: 01395 265514   **e-mail:** alaronde@nationaltrust.org.uk

Owner: The National Trust   **Contact:** John Rolfe – Custodian

A unique 16-sided house built on the instructions of two spinster cousins, Jane and Mary Parminter, on their return from a grand tour of Europe. Completed c1796, the house contains many 18th century contents and collections brought back by the Parminters. The fascinating interior decoration includes a feather frieze and shell-encrusted gallery which, due to its fragility, can only be viewed on closed circuit television.

Location: OS Ref. SY004 834. 2m N of Exmouth on A376.

Open: 21 Mar - 31 Oct: daily except Fri & Sat, 11am - 5.30pm. Last admission ½ hr before closing.

Admission: Adult £4.50, Child £2.20. No reduction for groups.

National Trust / Andreas Von Einsiedel

ARLINGTON COURT 🌿

Nr BARNSTAPLE, NORTH DEVON EX31 4LP

www.nationaltrust.org.uk

Tel: 01271 850296   **Fax:** 01271 851108   **e-mail:** arlingtoncourt@nationaltrust.org.uk

Owner: The National Trust   **Contact:** Ana Chylak - Property Manager

Nestling in the thickly wooded valley of the River Yeo, stands the 3000 acre Arlington estate. It comprises a delightful and intimate Victorian house full of treasures including collections of model ships, pewter, shells, extensive informal gardens, a formal terraced Victorian garden, a partially restored walled garden and historic parkland with breathtaking woodland and lakeside walks. The working stable yard houses the National Trust's museum of horse-drawn vehicles and offers carriage rides around the gardens.

Location: OS180 Ref. SS611 405. 7m NE of Barnstaple on A39.

Open: 20 Mar - 30 Oct: daily except Sat (open BH weekend Sats), 10.30am - 5pm. House & Carriage Collection open at 11am. Last admission 4.30pm. Garden, shop, tearoom & bat education room: 1 Jul - 31 Aug: Daily including Sats, 10.30am - 4.30pm. 1 Nov - Mar 2006: grounds open during daylight hours.

Admission: House, Garden & Carriage Collection: Adult £6.50, Child £3.20, Family £16.20, 1-Adult family £9.70. Group £5.50. Garden & Carriage Collection only: Adult £4.20, Child £2.10. Sats during July & Aug: Adult £2.60, Child £1.30.

Ground floor & grounds. WC. Licensed. Teachers' pack. In grounds, on leads.

ANDERTON HOUSE

Goodleigh, Devon EX32 7NR

Tel: 01628 825925   **www.**landmarktrust.org.uk

Owner: The Landmark Trust

Anderton House is a Grade II* listed building of an exceptional modern design by Peter Aldington of Aldington and Craig. It was commissioned in 1969 as a family home and is highly evocative of its time, retaining the contemporary features and materials. Anderton House is cared for by The Landmark Trust, a building preservation charity who let it for holidays. Full details of Anderton House and 178 other historic and architecturally important buildings are featured in the Landmark Trust Handbook (price £9.50 refundable against a booking).

Location: OS Ref. SS603 343. In village.

Open: Available for holidays for up to 5 people throughout the year. Open Days on 3/4 Sept: 10am - 4pm.

Admission: Free on Open Days.

BAYARD'S COVE FORT ⌗

Dartmouth, Devon

Tel: 0117 9750700

Owner: English Heritage   **Contact:** South West Regional Office

Set among the picturesque gabled houses of Dartmouth, on the waterfront at the end of the quay, this is a small artillery fort built 1509 - 10 to defend the harbour entrance.

Location: OS Ref. SX879 510. In Dartmouth, on riverfront 200 yds, S of South ferry.

Open: Any reasonable time, daylight hours.

Admission: Free.

BERRY POMEROY CASTLE ⌗

Totnes, Devon TQ9 6NJ

Tel: 01803 866618   **e-mail:** customers@english-heritage.org.uk

www.english-heritage.org.uk/berrypomeroy

Owner: The Duke of Somerset   **Contact:** Visitor Operations Team

A romantic late medieval castle, dramatically sited half-way up a wooded hillside, looking out over a deep ravine and stream. It is unusual in combining the remains of a large castle with a flamboyant courtier's mansion. Reputed to be one of the most haunted castles in the country.

Location: OS202 Ref. SX839 623. 2½ m E of Totnes off A385. Entrance gate ½ m NE of Berry Pomeroy village, then ½ m drive. Narrow approach, unsuitable for coaches.

Open: 24 Mar - Oct: daily, 10am - 5pm (6pm in Jul & Aug; 4pm in Oct).

Admission: Adult £3.30, Child £1.70, Conc £2.50. 15% discount for groups (11+).

Ground floor & grounds. Not EH. No access for coaches. Tel for details.

BICTON PARK BOTANICAL GARDENS

See page 201 for full page entry.

Corporate Hospitality see page 35

BRADLEY MANOR
Newton Abbot, Devon TQ12 6BN
Tel: 01626 354513 **e-mail:** greenway@nationaltrust.org.uk
www.nationaltrust.org.uk
Owner: The National Trust
A delightful small medieval manor house set in woodland and meadows. Still lived in and managed by the donor family.
Location: OS Ref. SX848 709. On Totnes road A381. $^3/_4$ m SW of Newton Abbot.
Open: 5 Apr - 29 Sept: Tue - Thur, 2 - 5 pm. Last admission 4.30pm.
Admission: Adult £3.50, Child £1.75, no reduction for groups.

BRANSCOMBE MANOR MILL, THE OLD BAKERY & FORGE
Branscombe, Seaton, Devon EX12 3DB
Tel: Manor Mill - 01392 881691 Old Bakery - 01297 680333 Forge - 01297 680481
www.nationaltrust.org.uk
Owner: The National Trust   **Contact:** NT Devon Office
Manor Mill, still in working order and recently restored, is a water-powered mill which probably supplied the flour for the bakery, regular working demonstrations. The Old Bakery was, until 1987, the last traditional working bakery in Devon. The old baking equipment has been preserved in the baking room and the rest of the building is now a tearoom. Information display in the outbuildings. The Forge opens regularly and ironwork is on sale - please telephone to check opening times.
Location: OS Ref. SY198 887. In Branscombe $^1/_2$ m S off A3052 by steep, narrow lane.
Open: Manor Mill: 3 Apr - 30 Oct: Suns, 2 - 5pm; also Weds in Jul & Aug. The Old Bakery: 31 Mar - 30 Oct, Wed - Sun, 11am - 5pm.
Admission: Adult £2, Child £1. Manor Mill only.

BUCKFAST ABBEY
Buckfastleigh, Devon TQ11 0EE
Tel: 01364 645500 **Fax:** 01364 643891 **e-mail:** education@buckfast.org.uk
Owner: Buckfast Abbey Trust   **Contact:** The Warden
Location: OS Ref. SX741 674. $^1/_2$ m from A38 Plymouth - Exeter route.
Open: Church & Grounds: All year: 5.30am - 7pm.
Admission: Free.

RHS Garden Rosemoor.

Website Information see page 42
www.hudsonsguide.co.uk

BUCKLAND ABBEY

YELVERTON, DEVON PL20 6EY

www.nationaltrust.org.uk

Tel: 01822 853607 **Fax:** 01822 855448 **e-mail:** bucklandabbey@nationaltrust.org.uk
Owner: The National Trust   **Contact:** Michael Coxson - Property Manager
The spirit of Sir Francis Drake is rekindled at his home with exhibitions of his courageous adventures and achievements throughout the world. One of the Trust's most interesting historical buildings and originally a 13th century monastery, the abbey was transformed into a family residence before Sir Francis bought it in 1581. Fascinating decorated plaster ceiling in Tudor Drake Chamber. Outside there are monastic farm buildings, herb garden, craft workshops and country walks. Introductory video presentation. Beautiful new Elizabethan garden now open. Exciting new gallery displays.

Location: OS201 Ref. SX487 667. 6m S of Tavistock; 11m N of Plymouth off A386. Bus: 55/56 from Yelverton (except Sun).

Open: 12 Feb - 13 Mar: Sat & Sun only, 2 - 5pm. 19 Mar - 30 Oct: daily except Thur, 10.30am - 5.30pm (last adm. 4.45pm). Nov: Sat & Sun only, 2 - 5pm. 3 - 18 Dec: Sats & Suns, 11am - 5pm.

Admission: Abbey & Grounds: Adult £6, Child £3, Family £15, 1-Adult Family £9. Group (15+): Adult £4.60, Child £2.30. Grounds only: Adult £3.20, Child £1.60.

ℹ️ No photography in house. 🏠 🚻 Ground floor & grounds. WC. 🍴 Licensed. 🍴 Licensed. By arrangement. 🅿️ Guide dogs only. ❋

©National Trust Photographic Library

Knightshayes Court.

CADHAY 🏛
OTTERY ST MARY, DEVON EX11 1QT

Tel/Fax: 01404 812999

Owner: Mr R Thistlethwayte   **Contact:** Jo Holloway

Cadhay is approached by an avenue of lime-trees, and stands in an extensive garden, with herbaceous borders and yew hedges, with excellent views over the original medieval fish ponds. The main part of the house was built about 1550 by John Haydon who had married the de Cadhay heiress. He retained the Great Hall of an earlier house, of which the fine timber roof (about 1420 - 1460) can be seen. An Elizabethan Long Gallery was added by John's successor at the end of the 16th century, thereby forming a unique and lovely courtyard with statues of Sovereigns on each side.

Location: OS Ref. SY090 962. 1m NW of Ottery St Mary. From W take A30 and exit at Pattersons Cross, follow signs for Fairmile and then Cadhay. From E, exit at the Iron Bridge and follow signs as above.

Open: Spring BH Sun & Mon; July: Fri; August: Fri and BH Sun & Mon: Sept: Fri, 2 - 6pm. Last tour 5pm.

Admission: Guided tours: Adult £5, Child £2.

♿ Ground floor & grounds. ⊤ Gardens available. 🖊 Obligatory.
🦮 Guide dogs only. 📷 ⬛

David Cripps

NTPL / David Garner

CASTLE DROGO 🌿
DREWSTEIGNTON, EXETER EX6 6PB
www.nationaltrust.org.uk

Tel: 01647 433306   **Fax:** 01647 433186   **e-mail:** castledrogo@nationaltrust.org.uk

Owner: The National Trust   **Contact:** Mark Agnew, Property Manager

Extraordinary granite and oak castle, designed by Sir Edwin Lutyens, which combines the comforts of the 20th century with the grandeur of a Baronial castle. Elegant dining and drawing rooms and fascinating kitchen and scullery. Terraced formal garden with colourful herbaceous borders and rose beds. Panoramic views over Dartmoor and delightful walks in the dramatic Teign Gorge.

Location: OS191 Ref. SX721 900. 5m S of A30 Exeter – Okehampton road.

Open: Castle: 18 Mar - 6 Nov: daily except Tues, 11am - 5pm, 4pm in Oct & Nov (last admission 30 mins before closing). Garden: All year: daily, 10.30am - 5.30pm. Shop & tearoom: 18 Mar - 6 Nov: daily, 10.30am - 5.30pm; Nov & Dec: Fri - Sun, 11am - 4pm.

Admission: House & Garden: Adult £6.50, Child £3.20, Family £16.20, 1-Adult Family £9.70. Group: £5.50. Garden only: Adult £4, Child £2, Group £3.40.

🅿 ⓘ ♿ 2 rooms in castle & grounds. WCs. ⬛ 🖊 By arrangement.
🦮 Guide dogs only in certain areas. ❋

CHAMBERCOMBE MANOR
Ilfracombe, Devon EX34 9RJ

Tel: 01271 802624 **www**.chambercombemanor.co.uk

Owner: Chambercombe Trust   **Contact:** Angela Powell

Guided tours of Norman Manor House which is mentioned in Domesday Book. Hear the legend of Chambercombe and visit Haunted Room. Set in 16 acres of woodland and landscaped gardens. Lady Jane Tea Rooms offering light lunches and cream teas.

Location: OS Ref. SS539 461. East of Ilfracombe between A399 and B3230, follow brown historic house signs. Private car park at end of Chambercombe Lane.

Open: Easter - 30 Oct: Mon & Fri, 10.30am - 5pm; Sun, 2 - 5pm. Last tour 4.30pm.

Admission: Adult £5, Child £3, Conc. £3, Family £14.50. Groups (max 50) conc. apply to Manor.

ⓘ No photography in house. ♿ Partial. ☕ 🚶 Obligatory. 🅿 Limited for coaches. ⬛ 🐕 On leads, in grounds.

CLOVELLY   *See page 202 for full page entry.*

❄ Open All Year Index see page 43

Dartmouth Castle.

COLETON FISHACRE HOUSE & GARDEN ❧
BROWNSTONE ROAD, KINGSWEAR, DARTMOUTH TQ6 0EQ
www.nationaltrust.org.uk

Tel: 01803 752466 **Fax:** 01803 753017 **e-mail:** coletonfishacre@nationaltrust.org.uk

Owner: The National Trust   **Contact:** David Mason, Property Manager

A 9 hectare property set in a stream-fed valley within the spectacular scenery of the South Devon coast. The Lutyensesque style house with art deco-influenced interior was built in the 1920s for Rupert and Lady Dorothy D'Oyly Carte who created the delightful garden, planted with a wide range of rare and exotic plants giving year round interest.

Location: OS202 Ref. SX910 508. 3m E of Kingswear, follow brown tourist signs.

Open: House: 23 Mar - 30 Oct: Weds - Suns & BH Mons, 11am - 4.30pm (last entry at 4pm). Garden & Tearoom: Mar: Sats & Suns only, 11am - 5pm. 23 Mar - 30 Oct: Weds - Suns & BH Mons, 10.30am - 5pm..

Admission: House & Garden: Adult £5.50, Child £2.75. Family £13.75, 1-Adult Family £8.25. Booked groups (15+): Adult £4.70, Child £2.35. Garden only: Adult £4.40, Child £2.10, Booked groups (15+) £3.70.

ⓘ No photography in house. 📷 🚻 ♿ Limited access to grounds. WC. ☕ 🅿 Limited. Coaches must book. 🐕 Assistance dogs only in garden.

LOUGHWOOD MEETING HOUSE

Dalwood, Axminster, Devon EX13 7DU

Tel: 01392 881691 **Fax:** 01392 881954

Owner: The National Trust **Contact:** National Trust Regional Office

Around 1653 the Baptist congregation of the nearby village of Kilmington constructed this simple building dug into the hillside.

Location: OS Ref. SY253993. 4m W of Axminster.

Open: All year, daily.

Admission: Free

ⓘ Pushchairs and baby carriers admitted.
♿ Steep slope from the car park. Ground floor only.
🅿 Very narrow country lanes. No parking for coaches. ❋

LYDFORD CASTLES & SAXON TOWN

Lydford, Okehampton, Devon

Tel: 01822 820320

Owner: English Heritage **Contact:** The National Trust

Standing above the lovely gorge of the River Lyd, this 12th century tower was notorious as a prison. The earthworks of the original Norman fort are to the south. A Saxon town once stood nearby and its layout is still discernible.

Location: OS191 Castle Ref. SX510 848, Fort Ref. SX509 847. In Lydford off A386 8m SW of Okehampton.

Open: Any reasonable time, daylight hours.

Admission: Free.

❋

MARKER'S COTTAGE

Broadclyst, Exeter, Devon EX5 3HR

Tel: 01392 461546

Owner: The National Trust **Contact:** The Custodian

Medieval cob house containing a cross-passage screen decorated with a painting of St Andrew and his attributes.

Location: OS Ref. SX985 973. 1/4 E of B3181 in village of Broadclyst.

Open: 27 Mar - 31 Oct: Sun - Tue, 2 - 5pm.

Admission: Adult £2, Child £1. Joint ticket with Clyston Mill: Adult £3.50, Child £1.75.

MARWOOD HILL

Barnstaple, Devon EX31 4EB

Tel: 01271 342528 **Owner/Contact:** Dr J A Snowdon

20 acre garden with 3 small lakes. Extensive collection of camellias, bog garden. National collection of astilbes.

Location: OS Ref. SS545 375. 4m N of Barnstaple. 1/2 m W of B3230. Signs off A361 Barnstaple - Braunton road.

Open: Dawn to dusk throughout the year.

Admission: Adult £3, Child (under 12yrs) Free.

MORWELLHAM QUAY

Morwellham, Tavistock, Devon PL19 8JL

Tel: 01822 832766 **Fax:** 01822 833808

Owner: The Morwellham & Tamar Valley Trust **Contact:** Anthony Power

Award-winning visitor centre at historic river port.

Location: OS Ref. SX446 697. Off A390 about 15 mins drive from Tavistock, Devon. 5m SW of Tavistock. 3m S of A390 at Gulworthy.

Open: Summer: daily, 10am - 5.30pm, last adm. 3.30pm. Winter: daily, 10am - 4.30pm, last adm. 2.30pm.

Admission: Adult £8.90, Child £6. Family (2+2) £26. Group rate please apply for details. Usual concessions. Prices may be subject to change.

OKEHAMPTON CASTLE

Okehampton, Devon EX20 1JB

Tel: 01837 52844 **e-mail:** customers@english-heritage.org.uk

www.english-heritage.org.uk/okehampton

Owner: English Heritage **Contact:** Visitor Operations Team

The ruins of the largest castle in Devon stand above a river surrounded by splendid woodland. There is still plenty to see, including the Norman motte and the jagged remains of the Keep. There is a picnic area and lovely woodland walks.

Location: OS Ref. SX584 942. 1m SW of Okehampton town centre off A30 bypass.

Open: 24 Mar - Sept: daily, 10am - 5pm (6pm in July & Aug).

Admission: Adult £3, Child £1.50, Conc. £2.30. 15% discount for groups (11+).

📷 ♿ Access difficult for ambulant disabilities. Grounds. WC. 🎧 🅿
🐕 In grounds, on leads. 🎫 Tel. for details.

OLDWAY MANSION

Paignton, Devon

Tel: 01803 201201 **Fax:** 01803 207670

Owner: Torbay Council **Contact:** Facilities Management Officer

Built by sewing machine entrepreneur I M Singer in the 1870s.

Location: OS Ref. SX888 615. Off W side of A3022.

Open: All year: Mon - Sat, 9am - 5pm (except Christmas & New Year). Easter - Oct: Suns, 2 - 5pm. Visitors should note that not all rooms will always be open, access depends on other activities.

Admission: Free.

NTPL / Tony Murdoch

OVERBECK'S MUSEUM & GDN

SHARPITOR, SALCOMBE, SOUTH DEVON TQ8 8LW

www.nationaltrust.org.uk

Tel: 01548 842893 **e-mail:** overbecks@nationaltrust.org.uk

Owner: The National Trust **Contact:** Property Manager

Elegant Edwardian house with diverse collections and luxuriant garden. The scientist Otto Overbeck lived here from 1928 to 1937 and the museum containing his collections of curios and nautical artefacts has an intimate atmosphere. Some of Overbeck's inventions are on show, including the intriguing 'rejuvenator' machine. The house is set in $2^3/_4$ha (7acres) of beautiful exotic gardens with spectacular views over the Salcombe estuary. It enjoys a sheltered microclimate and so is home to many rare plants. There is also a secret room for children with dolls, tin soldiers, other toys and a ghost hunt.

Location: OS Ref. SX728 374. $1^1/_2$ m SW of Salcombe. Signposted from Salcombe (single track lanes).

Open: Museum: 23 Mar - 17 July & 1 - 30 Sept: Sun - Fri & Easter Sat (closed Good Fri), 11am - 5.30pm. 18 Jul - 28 August: daily, 11am - 5.30pm. 2 - 27 Oct: Sun - Thur, 11am - 5pm. Garden: All year: daily, 10am - 6pm.

Admission: House & Garden: Adult £5, Child £2.50, Family £12.50, 1-Adult Family £7.50. Garden only: Adult £4.50, Child £2.25.

ⓘ No photography in house. 📷 🎁 ♿ Partial. 🎫 By arrangement.
🅿 Limited. Charge £3.50 refunded on admission. 🔲 ❌ ❋

POWDERHAM CASTLE 🏰 *See page 203 for full page entry.*

🔔 Civil Wedding Venues see page 32

PUSLINCH

YEALMPTON, PLYMOUTH, DEVON PL8 2NN

Tel: 01752 880555 **Fax:** 01752 880909

Owner/Contact: Sebastian Fenwick

A perfect example of a medium sized early Georgian house in the Queen Anne tradition with fine contemporary interiors. Built in 1720 by the Yonge family.

Location: OS Ref. SX570 509. Yealmpton.

Open: Groups only (min charge £25). All year, except Christmas & Boxing Day, by prior appointment only.

Admission: Adult £5.

ℹ️No photography. 🎫Obligatory. 🅿️ ⚡ ✳️

RHS GARDEN ROSEMOOR

Great Torrington, Devon EX38 8PH

Tel: 01805 624067   **Fax:** 01805 624717

Owner/Contact: The Royal Horticultural Society

A beautiful garden mixing new gardens with Lady Anne's original garden. Something for all interests and tastes whatever the season, from formal gardens to a lake and Arboretum. The Rosemoor Plant Centre stocks a variety of hardy plants, the shop has books and gifts and, for refreshments, there is a café and restaurant. Voted South West Visitor Attraction of the Year 2003.

Location: OS Ref. SS500 183. 1m S of Great Torrington on A3124.

Open: All year except Christmas Day; Apr - Sept: 10am - 6pm. Oct - Mar: 10am - 5pm.

Admission: Adult £5.50, Child (6 - 16yrs) £1.50, Child (under 6yrs) Free. Groups (10+) £4.50. Companion for disabled visitor Free.

Overbeck's – View of the Salcombe Estuary.

SALTRAM 🌼

PLYMPTON, PLYMOUTH, DEVON PL7 1JH

www.nationaltrust.org.uk

Tel: 01752 333500   **Fax:** 01752 336474   **e-mail:** saltram@nationaltrust.org.uk

Owner: The National Trust   **Contact:** Carol Murrin

Saltram stands high above the River Plym in a rolling and wooded landscaped park that now provides precious green space on the outskirts of Plymouth. The house, with its magnificent decoration and original contents, was largely created between the 1740s and 1820s by three generations of the Parker family. It features some of Robert Adam's finest rooms, exquisite plasterwork ceilings, original Chinese wallpapers and an exceptional collection of paintings including many by Sir Joshua Reynolds and Angelica Kauffman. The garden is predominantly 19th-century and contains an orangery and several follies, as well as beautiful shrubberies and imposing specimen trees.

The shop and art gallery offer work for sale from contemporary local artists, and National Trust gifts. A new restaurant opens in July 2005. Corporate business and special functions are very welcome.

Location: OS Ref. SX520 557. From A38, exit 3 miles north of Plymouth City Centre at Marsh Mill's roundabout. Take Plympton exit; continue in right hand lane to third set of traffic lights then turn right onto Cott Hill. At the top of the hill turn right into Merafield Road then right again after 200 yards..

Open: House: 23 Mar - 30 Oct: daily except Fris (open Good Fri), 12 noon - 4.30pm (11.30am - 3.30pm in Oct). Garden: Jan - 22 Dec: daily except Fri (open Good Fri), 11am - 4pm (5pm 23 Mar - 30 Sept). Gallery: Jan - Mar: Sat/Sun; 23 Mar - 22 Dec: daily except Fri (open Good Fri), 11am - 4pm (5pm 23 Mar - 30 Sept). Shop: Jan, 23 Mar - 15 Jul; 10 Oct - 22 Dec: daily except Fri, 11am - 4pm (5pm 23 Mar - 30 Sept); Feb - 22 Mar: Sat/Sun only, 11am - 4pm. 16 July - 30 Sept daily. Tearoom/Restaurant: Jan - Mar: Sat/Sun, 11am - 4pm; 23 Mar - 15 Jul, daily except Fri; 11am - 5pm. 16 July - 30 Sept daily, 11am - 5pm, 1 Oct - 22 Dec: daily except Fri. 11am - 4pm.

Admission: House & Garden: Adult £7, Child £3.50, Family £17.50, 1-Adult Family £10.50. Groups (15+): £5.90. Garden only: Adult £3.50, Child £1.80.

🖼️ ♿ 🍽️ ♿ WC. Braille guide. 👕 🍴 Licensed. 🎫 🖼️ 🅿️
🐕On signed perimeter paths only, on leads. Guide dogs only in house & garden.
✳️ 📺 Tel. for details.

213

©National Trust Photographic Library/Eric Crichton.

HARDY'S COTTAGE ✤

HIGHER BOCKHAMPTON, DORCHESTER, DORSET DT2 8QJ

www.nationaltrust.org.uk

Tel: 01305 262366

Owner/Contact: The National Trust

A small cob and thatch cottage where the novelist and poet Thomas Hardy was born in 1840, and from where he would walk to school every day in Dorchester, six miles away. It was built by his great-grandfather and is little altered. Since the family left the interior has been furnished by the Trust (see also Max Gate). His early novels *Under the Green Wood Tree* and *Far From the Madding Crowd* were written here. Charming cottage garden.

Location: OS Ref. SY728 925. 3m NE of Dorchester, 1/2 m S of A35. 10 mins walk through the woods from car park.

Open: 18 Mar - 31 Oct: daily except Tue & Wed, 11am - 5pm or dusk if earlier.

Admission: £3. No reduction for children or groups.

ℹ️ No WC. 📷 ♿ Partial. 🅿️ No coach parking. 🎦 ✤

HIGHER MELCOMBE

Melcombe Bingham, Dorchester, Dorset DT2 7PB

Tel: 01258 880251

Owner/Contact: Mr M C Woodhouse

Consists of the surviving wing of a 16th century house with its attached domestic chapel. A fine plaster ceiling and linenfold panelling. Conducted tours by owner.

Location: OS Ref. ST749 024. 1km W of Melcombe Bingham.

Open: May - Sept by appointment.

Admission: Adult £2 (takings go to charity).

♿ Unsuitable. 📷 By written appointment only. 🅿️ Limited. 🐕 Guide dogs only.

THE KEEP MILITARY MUSEUM OF DEVON & DORSET

Bridport Rd, Dorchester, Dorset DT1 1RN

Tel: 01305 264066 **Fax:** 01305 250373

e-mail: keep.museum@talk21.com **www**.keepmilitarymuseum.org

Owner: Ministry of Defence (Museums Trustees) **Contact:** The Curator

The courage, humour, tradition and sacrifice of those who served in the Regiments of Devon and Dorset for over 300 years are brought to life using touch screen computers and creative displays in this modern museum situated in a Grade II listed building. View Hardy country from the battlements.

Location: OS Ref. SY687 906. In Dorchester at the top of High West Street.

Open: All year: Apr - Sept: Mon - Sat 9.30am - 5pm (last admission 1hr before closing time). Jul & Aug: Suns also, 10am - 4pm. Oct - Mar: Tue - Sat, 9.30am - 5pm.

Admission: Adult £3, Conc. £2, Family (2+3) £9. Groups (10-50): Adult £2.50, Conc. £1.50.

ℹ️ No flash photography. 📷 🍽️ ♿ 📷 By arrangement. 🅿️ Limited. 🎦
🐕 Guide dogs only. ❄️ 📺 Tel for details.

HIGHCLIFFE CASTLE 🏛️

ROTHESAY DRIVE, HIGHCLIFFE-ON-SEA, CHRISTCHURCH BH23 4LE

www.highcliffecastle.co.uk

Tel: 01425 278807 **Fax:** 01425 280423 **e-mail:** castleman@christchurch.gov.uk

Owner: Christchurch Borough Council **Contact:** The Manager

Built in 1830 in the Romantic and Picturesque style of architecture for Lord Stuart de Rothesay using his unique collection of French medieval stonework and stained glass. Recently repaired externally, it remains mostly unrepaired inside. Five State Rooms house a visitor centre, exhibitions, events and gift shop. Coastal grounds, village trail and nearby St Mark's church. Tea rooms in the Claretian's Wing.

Location: OS Ref. SZ200 930. Off the A337 Lymington Road, between Christchurch

and Highcliffe-on-Sea.

Open: 1 Feb - 23 Dec: daily, 11am - 5pm. Grounds: All year: daily from 7am. Access for coaches. Tearooms closed Christmas Day.

Admission: Adult £2, Child Free. Group (10+) rates available. Guided tours of unrestored areas (may be unsuitable for people with mobility problems - please ring for details): Adult £3.50, Child Free. Grounds: Free.

📷 🍽️ ♿ Partial. WC. 🍽️ 10am - 5pm. 📷 By arrangement. 🅿️ Limited. Parking charge.
🎦 By arrangement. 🐕 In grounds, on leads. 🏨 ❄️ 📺 Tel for details.

Dave Penman

KINGSTON MAURWARD GARDEN

DORCHESTER, DORSET DT2 8PY

www.kmc.ac.uk/gardens

Tel: 01305 215003 **Fax:** 01305 215001 **e-mail:** events@kmc.ac.uk

Contact: Wendy Cunningham

Classical 18th century parkland setting, with majestic lawns sweeping down from the Grade I listed Georgian house to the lake. The Rainbow beds and beautiful herbaceous borders complement the series of 'rooms' within the formal Edwardian garden. National Collections of Penstemons and Salvias. Lakeside walks, animal park, shop, plant centre and refreshments.

Location: OS Ref. SY713 911. 1m E of Dorchester. Roundabout off A35 by-pass.

Open: 5 Jan - 21 Dec: daily, 10am - 5.30pm or dusk if earlier.

Admission: Adult £4, Child £2.50 (under 3yrs Free), Family £12.50. Groups (10+): Adult £3.50. Guided tours (by arrangement) (12+): £5pp.

ℹ️ Conferences. 🅿️ 📷 📶 Wedding receptions. 🅿️ Partial. 🅿️ Licensed. 🅰️ By arrangement. 🅿️ 📶 📶 Guide dogs only. 🅰️ ✳️ 📶 Tel for details.

KINGSTON LACY 🌿

See page 217 for full page entry.

KNOLL GARDENS & NURSERY

Stapehill Road, Hampreston, Wimborne BH21 7ND

Tel: 01202 873931 **Fax:** 01202 870842

Owner: J & J Flude & N R Lucas   **Contact:** Mr John Flude

Nationally acclaimed 6 acre gardens, with 6000+ named plants.

Location: OS Ref. SU059 001. Between Wimborne & Ferndown. Exit A31 Canford Bottom roundabout, B3073 Hampreston. Signposted 1¹/₂ m.

Open: All year: Wed - Sun, 10am - 5pm or dusk if earlier. Closed Christmas & New Year holiday period.

Admission: Adult £4, Child (5-15yrs) £2, OAP £3.50, Student £3. RHS Free. Groups: Adult £3, Child £1.75, Student £2.50. Family (2+2) £9.75.

Sherborne Castle.

Lulworth Castle & Park

Lulworth Castle House

LULWORTH CASTLE & PARK AND LULWORTH CASTLE HOUSE

WAREHAM, DORSET BH20 5QS

www.lulworth.com

Tel: 0845 4501054 **Fax:** 01929 400563 **e-mail:** office@lulworth.com

Owner: The Weld Estate

Surrounded by beautiful parkland this 17th century hunting lodge was destroyed by fire in 1929 and has been restored by English Heritage. Steeped in history the Castle has remained in the same family since 1641. Features include a gallery on the Weld family, reconstructed kitchen, dairy and laundry rooms and a wine cellar. The Chapel is reputed to be one of the finest pieces of architecture in Dorset and houses an exhibition on vestments and recusant silver. **Lulworth Castle House:** Elegantly stands within the Park and has a stunning collection of pictures and furniture. The grounds also include the original kitchen garden to the Castle.

Location: OS Ref. SY853 822. In E Lulworth off B3070, 3m NE of Lulworth Cove.

Open: Castle & Park: All year: Sun - Fri & Easter Sat: 10.30am - 6pm (closes 4pm autumn/winter). Closed 8 - 22 Jan & 24/25 Dec. Lulworth Castle House: 18 May - 20 Jul: Weds, 2 - 5pm. Last admission 4.30pm. Groups by appointment.

Admission: Castle: Adult £7, Child £4, Conc. £6. Groups (10+): Adult £6.30, Child £3.60, Conc. £5.40. Lulworth Castle House: Adult £3, Child Free. Family tickets and joint Castle and Lulworth Castle House admission available. Prices may vary for special events.

📷 📶 🅿️ Partial. WC. 🅿️ Licensed. 🅰️ By arrangement. 📶 🅿️ 📶 In ground, on leads. 📶 5 holiday cottages, tel: 01929 400100. 🅰️ ✳️ 📶 See website or tel for details.

George Wright

MAPPERTON 🏛

BEAMINSTER, DORSET DT8 3NR

www.mapperton.com

Tel: 01308 862645   **Fax:** 01308 863348   **e-mail:** office@mapperton.com

Owner/Contact: The Earl & Countess of Sandwich

Jacobean 1660s manor with Tudor features and Georgian north front. Italianate upper garden with orangery, topiary and formal borders descending to fish ponds and shrub gardens. All Saints Church forms south wing opening to courtyard and stables. Area of outstanding natural beauty with fine views of Dorset hills and woodlands. House and Gardens featured in *Restoration*, *Emma* and *Tom Jones*.

Location: OS Ref. SY503 997. 1m S of B3163, 2m NE of B3066, 2m SE Beaminster, 5m NE Bridport.

Open: House: 30 May & 27 Jun - 5 Aug weekdays & 29 Aug: 2 - 4.30pm, last admission 4pm. Other times by appointment. Garden & All Saints Church: 1 Mar - 31 Oct: daily, 2 - 6pm. Café: Mar - Sept: daily, 12.30 - 5.30pm, for lunch and tea.

Admission: Gardens: £4, House: £2.50. Child (under 18yrs) £2, under 5yrs Free. Groups tours by appointment.

◻ 🏠 ⬚ Partial. 🍷Licensed. 🍴 🎨 By arrangement. ◼ ⓟ Limited for coaches. 🐕 Guide dogs only. ⬛ 💺 Tel for details.

©National Trust Photographic Library

MAX GATE 🌿

ALINGTON AVENUE, DORCHESTER, DORSET DT1 2AA

www.thomas-hardy.connectfree.co.uk

Tel: 01305 262538   **e-mail:** heritage.venues@virgin.net

Owner: The National Trust   **Contact:** The Tenant

Novelist and poet Thomas Hardy designed and lived in this house from 1885 until his death in 1928. Here he wrote *Tess of the d'Urbervilles*, *Jude the Obscure* and *The Mayor of Casterbridge*, as well as much of his poetry. The house contains several pieces of his furniture.

Location: OS Ref. SY704 899. 1m E of Dorchester just N of the A352 to Wareham. From Dorchester follow A352 signs to the roundabout named Max Gate (at Jct. of A35 Dorchester bypass). Turn left and left again into cul-de-sac outside Max Gate.

Open: 20 Mar - 28 Sept: Mons, Weds & Suns, 2 - 5pm. Only hall, dining, drawing rooms & garden open. Private visits, tours & seminars by schools, colleges and literary societies at other times by prior appointment with the tenants, Mr & Mrs Andrew Leah.

Admission: Adult £2.75, Child £1.50.

ⓘNo WC. ⬚ Partial. Braille guide. ⓟ ◼ ⬛

MILTON ABBEY CHURCH

Milton Abbas, Blandford, Dorset DT11 0BZ

Tel: 01258 880215

Owner: Diocese of Salisbury   **Contact:** Chris Fookes

Abbey church dating from 14th century.

Location: OS Ref. ST798 024. 3¹/₂ m N of A354. Between Dorchester/Blandford Road.

Open: Abbey Church: daily 10am - 6pm. Groups by arrangement please.

Admission: By donation except Easter & mid-Jul - end Aug. Adult £2, Child Free.

MINTERNE GARDENS 🏛

Minterne Magna, Nr Dorchester, Dorset DT2 7AU

Owner/Contact: The Lord Digby

Tel: 01300 341370   **Fax:** 01300 341747

If you wish to wander peacefully through 20 wild woodland acres, where magnolias, rhododendrons, eucryphias, hydrangeas, water plants and water lilies provide a new vista at each turn, with small lakes and cascades landscaped in the 18th century, you will be welcome at Minterne, described by Simon Jenkins as 'a corner of paradise'. The home of the Churchill and Digby families for 350 years. The house, which contains magnificent Churchill tapestries and naval and other historical pictures, is open for organised groups only, which may be arranged by prior appointment.

Location: OS Ref. ST660 042. On A352 Dorchester/Sherborne Rd, 2m N of Cerne Abbas.

Open: 1 Mar - 10 Nov: daily, 10am - 7pm.

Admission: Adult £4, accompanied children Free.

⬚Unsuitable. 🐕 In grounds on leads.

English Heritage Photo Library

PORTLAND CASTLE ⌗

CASTLETOWN, PORTLAND, WEYMOUTH, DORSET DT5 1AZ

www.english-heritage.org.uk/portland

Tel: 01305 820539   **Fax:** 01305 860853   **e-mail:** customers@english-heritage.org.uk

Owner: English Heritage   **Contact:** Visitor Operations Staff

Discover one of Henry VIII's finest coastal fortresses. Perfectly preserved in a waterfront location overlooking Portland harbour, it is a marvellous place to visit for all the family whatever the weather. You can try on armour, explore the Tudor kitchen and gun platform, see ghostly sculptured figures from the past, enjoy the superb battlement views or picnic on the lawn in front of the Captain's House. An excellent new audio tour, included in the admission charge, brings the castle's history and characters to life. Visit the 'Contemporary Heritage' Garden.

Location: OS Ref. SY684 743. Overlooking Portland harbour.

Open: 24 Mar - 31 Oct: daily, 10am - 5pm (6pm in Jul & Aug, 4pm in Oct).

Admission: Adult £3.60, Child £1.80, Conc. £2.70. 15% discount for groups (11+).

◻ ⬚Captain's House & ground floor. WCs. 🍷 ◻ ⓟ ◼ ⬛ 💺Tel for details.

ST CATHERINE'S CHAPEL ⌗

Abbotsbury, Dorset

Tel: 0117 9750700 **www**.english-heritage.org.uk/southwest

Owner: English Heritage   **Contact:** The South West Regional Staff

A small stone chapel, set on a hilltop, with an unusual roof and small turret used as a lighthouse.

Location: OS Ref. SY572 848. ½ m S of Abbotsbury by pedestrian track to the hilltop.

Open: Any reasonable time, daylight hours.

Admission: Free.

❋

SANDFORD ORCAS MANOR HOUSE

Sandford Orcas, Sherborne, Dorset DT9 4SB

Tel: 01963 220206

Owner/Contact: Sir Mervyn Medlycott Bt

Tudor manor house with gatehouse, fine panelling, furniture, pictures. Terraced gardens with topiary and herb garden. Personal conducted tour by owner.

Location: OS Ref. ST623 210. 2½ m N of Sherborne, Dorset 4m S of A303 at Sparkford. Entrance next to church.

Open: Easter Mon, 10am - 5pm. May & Jul - Sept: Suns & Mons, 2 - 5pm.

Admission: Adult £3, Child £1.50. Groups (10+): Adult £2.50, Child £1.

🚫Unsuitable. 📷Obligatory. 🐕In grounds, on leads.

Hardy's Cottage.

SHERBORNE CASTLE 🏛

SHERBORNE, DORSET DT9 5NR

www.sherbornecastle.com

Tel: 01935 813182 **Fax:** 01935 816727 **e-mail:** enquiries@sherbornecastle.com

Owner: Mr & Mrs John Wingfield Digby   **Contact:** Castle & Events Manager

Built by Sir Walter Raleigh in 1594, Sherborne Castle has been the home of the Digby family since 1617. Prince William of Orange was entertained here in 1688, and George III visited in 1789. Splendid interiors and collections of art, furniture and porcelain are on view in the Castle. Lancelot 'Capability' Brown created the lake in 1753 and gave Sherborne the very latest in landscape gardening, with magnificent vistas of the surrounding parklands. 40 acres of beautiful lakeside gardens and grounds open for public viewing.

Location: OS Ref. ST649 164. ¾ m SE of Sherborne town centre. Follow brown signs from A30 or A352. ½ m S of the Old Castle.

Open: Castle, Gardens, Shop & Tearoom: 22 Mar - 31 Oct: daily except Mon & Fri (open BH Mons), 11am - 4.30pm last admission. (Castle interior from 2.30pm Sats.) Groups (15+) by arrangement during normal opening hours.

Admission: Castle & Gardens: Adult £7.50, Child (0-15yrs) Free (max 4 accompanied by adult), OAP £7. Groups (15+): Adult/OAP £6.50, Child (0-15yrs) £3. Private views (15+): Adult/OAP £8.50, Child £4.50. Gardens only: Adult/OAP £3.50, Child (0-15yrs) Free (max 4 per adult), no concessions or group rates for gardens only.

🏠 ☕ 🚫Partial. 📹 📷By arrangement. 🐕In grounds, on leads. ♿ 📞Tel for details.

SHERBORNE OLD CASTLE

Castleton, Sherborne, Dorset DT9 3SA

Tel/Fax: 01935 812730 **e-mail:** customers@english-heritage.org.uk
www.english-heritage.org.uk/sherborne

Owner: English Heritage **Contact:** Visitor Operations Staff

The ruins of this early 12th century Castle are a testament to the 16 days it took Cromwell to capture it during the Civil War, after which it was abandoned. A gatehouse, some graceful arcading and decorative windows survive.

Location: OS Ref. ST647 167. ½ m E of Sherborne off B3145. ½ m N of the 1594 Castle.

Open: 24 Mar - 31 Oct: daily, 10am - 5pm (6pm in Jul & Aug, 4pm in Oct). Closed in winter.

Admission: Adult £2.30, Child £1.20, Conc. £1.70. 15% discount for groups of 11+.
Grounds. Limited for cars. No coach parking.

SMEDMORE HOUSE

Smedmore, Kimmeridge, Wareham BH20 5PG

Tel/Fax: 01929 480719

Owner: Dr Philip Mansel **Contact:** Mr B Belsten

The home of the Mansel family for nearly 400 years nestles at the foot of the Purbeck hills looking across Kimmeridge Bay to Portland Bill.

Location: OS Ref. SY924 787. 15m SW of Poole.

Open: 29 May & 4 Sept: 2 - 5pm.

Admission: Adult £3.50, Child under 16 Free.

WHITE MILL

Sturminster Marshall, Nr Wimborne, Dorset BH21 4BX

Tel: 01258 858051 **www.**nationaltrust.org.uk

Owner: The National Trust **Contact:** The Custodian

Rebuilt in 1776 on a site marked as a mill in the Domesday Book, this substantial corn mill was extensively repaired in 1994 and still retains its original elm and applewood machinery (now too fragile to be operative).

Location: OS Ref. ST958 006. On River Stour ½ m NE of Sturminster Marshall from the B3082 Blandford to Wimborne Rd, take road to SW signposted Sturminster Marshall. Mill is 1m on right. Car park nearby.

Open: 26 Mar - 30 Oct: Sats, Suns & BH Mons, 12 noon - 5pm. Admission by guided tour only.

Admission: Adult £3, Child £2. Groups by arrangement.
No WC. Ground floor. Obligatory.
Under close control in grounds and car park.

WOLFETON HOUSE

Nr Dorchester, Dorset DT2 9QN

Tel: 01305 263500 **Fax:** 01305 265090
e-mail: kthimbleby@wolfeton.freeserve.co.uk

Owner: Capt N T L Thimbleby **Contact:** The Steward

A fine mediaeval and Elizabethan manor house lying in the water-meadows near the confluence of the rivers Cerne and Frome. It was much embellished around 1580 and has splendid plaster ceilings, fireplaces and panelling of that date. To be seen are the Great Hall, Stairs and Chamber, Parlour, Dining Room, Chapel and Cyder House. The mediaeval Gatehouse has two unmatched and older towers. There are good pictures and furniture.

Location: OS Ref. SY678 921. 1½ m from Dorchester on the A37 towards Yeovil. Indicated by Historic House signs.

Open: June - end Sept: Mons, Weds & Thurs, 2 - 5pm. Groups by appointment throughout the year.

Admission: £5.

By arrangement. Ground floor. By arrangement. By arrangement.

Cloud's Hill.

BERKELEY CASTLE 🏛

www.berkeley-castle.com

Map 2

Owner:
Mr R J G Berkeley

▶ **CONTACT**

The Custodian
Berkeley Castle
Gloucestershire
GL13 9BQ

Tel: 01453 810332
Fax: 01453 512995
e-mail: info@berkeley-castle.com

▶ **LOCATION**

OS Ref. ST685 990

SE side of Berkeley
village. Midway
between
Bristol & Gloucester,
2m W off the A38.

From motorway
M5/J14 (5m) or
J13 (9m).

Not many can boast of having their private house celebrated by Shakespeare nor of having held it in the possession of their family for nearly 850 years, nor having a King of England murdered within its walls, nor of having welcomed at their table the local vicar and Castle Chaplain, John Trevisa (1342-1402), reputed as one of the earliest translators of the Bible, nor of having a breach battered by Oliver Cromwell, which to this day it is forbidden by law to repair even if it was wished to do so. But such is the story of Berkeley.

This beautiful and historic Castle, begun in 1117, still remains the home of the famous family who gave their name to numerous locations all over the world, notably Berkeley Square in London, Berkeley Hundred in Virginia and Berkeley University in California. Scene of the brutal murder of Edward II in 1327 (visitors can see his cell and

nearby the dungeon) and besieged by Cromwell's troops in 1645, the Castle is steeped in history but twenty-four generations of Berkeleys have gradually transformed a Norman fortress into the lovely home it is today.

The State Apartments contain magnificent collections of furniture, rare paintings by primarily English and Dutch masters, and tapestries. Part of the world-famous Berkeley silver is on display in the Dining Room. Many other rooms are equally interesting including the Great Hall upon which site the Barons of the West Country met in 1215 before going to Runnymede to force King John to put his seal to the Magna Carta.

The Castle is surrounded by lovely terraced Elizabethan Gardens with a lily pond, Elizabeth I's bowling green, and sweeping lawns.

▶ **OPENING TIMES**

25 - 28 Mar (Easter weekend)

11 April - 30 September*
Tues - Sat & BH Mons,
11am - 4pm,
Sun, 2 - 5pm.

October
Sundays only, 2 - 5pm.

The Butterfly House is closed in October.

Last admission 30 mins before closing.

* Except for weekends of 23/24 & 30/31 July: entry via the Joust Mediaeval Festival event only. Opening during April may change due to filming. Please check before your visit.

▶ **ADMISSION**

Global Ticket including Castle, Gardens & Butterfly House

Adult	£7.50
Child (5-16yrs)	£4.50
Child (under 5s)	Free
OAP	£6.00
Family (2+2)	£21.00

Groups (25+ pre-booked)

Adult	£7.00
Child (5-16yrs)	£3.50
OAP	£5.50

Gardens only

Adult	£4.00
Child	£2.00

Butterfly House

Adult	£2.00
Child (5-16yrs)	£1.00
School groups	£0.80
Family (2+2)	£5.00

CONFERENCE/FUNCTION

ROOM	MAX CAPACITY
Great Hall	150
Long Drawing Rm	100

Fashion shows and filming. Butterfly House. No photography inside the Castle.

Wedding receptions and corporate entertainment.

Visitors may alight in the Outer Bailey.

Licensed. Serving lunches and home-made teas.

Free. Max. 120 people. Tour time: One hour. Evening groups by arrangement. Group visits must be booked.

Cars 150yds from Castle, 15 coaches 250yds away. Free.

Welcome. General and social history and architecture.

Map 2

Owner:

Mr David Lowsley-
Williams

▶ **CONTACT**

D Lowsley-Williams
or Caroline
Lowsley-Williams
Chavenage
Tetbury
Gloucestershire
GL8 8XP

Tel: 01666 502329
Fax: 01453 836778
e-mail: info@
chavenage.com

▶ **LOCATION**

OS Ref. ST872 952

Less than 20m
from M4/J16/17 or 18.
1³/₄ m NW of Tetbury
between the B4014 &
A4135. Signed from
Tetbury. Less than 15m
from M5/J13 or 14.
Signed from A46
(Stroud - Bath road)

Rail: Kemble Station 7m.

Taxi: SC Taxis
01666 504195.

Air: Bristol 35m.
Birmingham 70m.
Grass airstrip on farm.

CONFERENCE/FUNCTION

ROOM	SIZE	MAX CAPACITY
Ballroom	70' x 30'	120
Oak Room	25 'x 20'	30

CHAVENAGE 🏛

www.chavenage.com

Chavenage is a wonderful Elizabethan house of mellow grey Cotswold stone and tiles which contains much of interest for the discerning visitor.

The approach aspect of Chavenage is virtually as it was left by Edward Stephens in 1576. Only two families have owned Chavenage; the present owners since 1891 and the Stephens family before them. A Colonel Nathaniel Stephens, MP for Gloucestershire during the Civil War was cursed for supporting Cromwell, giving rise to legends of weird happenings at Chavenage since that time.

Inside Chavenage there are many interesting rooms housing tapestries, fine furniture, pictures and many relics of the Cromwellian period. Of particular note are the Main Hall, where a contemporary screen forms a minstrels' gallery and two tapestry rooms where it is said Cromwell was lodged.

Recently Chavenage has been used as a location for TV and film productions including a Hercule Poirot story *The Mysterious Affair at Styles*, many episodes of the sequel to *Are you Being Served* now called *Grace & Favour*, a *Gotcha* for *The Noel Edmonds' House Party*, episodes of *The House of Elliot* and *Casualty,* in 1997/98 *Berkeley Square* and *Cider with Rosie* and in 2002 the US series *Relic Hunter* III.

Chavenage is especially suitable for those wishing an intimate, personal tour, usually conducted by the owner, or for groups wanting a change from large establishments. Meals for pre-arranged groups have proved hugely popular. It also provides a charming venue for small conferences and functions.

▸ **OPENING TIMES**

Summer

May - September
Easter Sun, Mon
& BHs, 2 - 5pm.

Thurs & Suns
2 - 5pm.

NB. Will open on any day and at other times by prior arrangement for groups.

Winter

October - March
By appointment only
for groups.

▸ **ADMISSION**

Tours are inclusive
in the following prices.

Summer

Adult £5.00
Child (5 - 16 yrs)...... £2.50

CONCESSIONS

By prior arrangement, concessions may be given to groups of 40+ and also to disabled and to exceptional cases.

Winter

Groups only:
Rates by arrangement.

ⓘ Clay pigeon shooting, archery, cross-bows, pistol shooting, ATV driving, small fashion shows, concerts, plays, seminars, filming, product launching, photography. No casual photography in house.

🍽 Corporate entertaining. In-house catering for drinks parties, dinners, wedding receptions. Telephone for details.

♿ Partial. WC.

🍴 Lunches, teas, dinners and picnics by arrangement.

👤 By owner. Large groups given a talk prior to viewing. Couriers/group leaders should arrange tour format prior to visit.

🅿 Up to 100 cars. 2 - 3 coaches (by appointment). Coaches access from A46 (signposted) or from Tetbury via the B4014, enter the back gates for coach parking area.

▪ Chairs can be arranged for lecturing. Tour of working farm, modern dairy and corn facilities can be arranged.

🐕 In grounds on leads. Guide dogs only in house. ❋

Sabina Rüber

SUDELEY CASTLE 🏛

www.sudeleycastle.co.uk

Nestled in the Cotswold Hills, Sudeley Castle is steeped in history. With royal connections spanning the centuries, it has played an important role in the turbulent and changing times of England's past. Once the property of King Ethelred the Unready, the Castle is perhaps best known as home to Queen Katherine Parr, who is buried in St Mary's Church in the gardens. Henry VIII, Anne Boleyn, and Queen Elizabeth I all visited Sudeley and Charles I's nephew, Prince Rupert, established his headquarters here during the Civil War.

Slighted by Cromwell's troops, Sudeley lay neglected and derelict for 200 years before a programme of reconstruction during the 19th century, under the aegis of Sir George Gilbert Scott, restored Sudeley for its new owners, the Dent brothers. This was continued by their nephew John Coucher Dent and his wife, Emma, who threw herself enthusiastically into Sudeley's restoration. The exhibition 'The Lace and Times of Emma Dent'

illuminates both her wide ranging interests and this period of the Castle's history.

Surrounding the Castle are 14 acres of magnificent award-winning gardens. Highlights include the Queen's Garden, famous for its double yew hedges and collection of English roses, the semi-Mediterranean planting in the Secret Garden, the intricate Tudor Knot Garden and the bold planting surrounding the romantic Tithe Barn ruins.

A recent addition is the Pheasantry and Wildfowl Area. This newly landscaped garden attraction is home to a number of rare and endangered pheasants and a variety of wildfowl.

In collaboration with the Meadow Gallery, an exhibition is planned of works by contemporary artists which will respond to the landscape, architecture and gardens of Sudeley. This will include some of the most influential living British and international artists and will be staged in the parkland, gardens and in the dungeons of the castle.

| i | Photography and filming by prior arrangement, Concerts, corporate events and conferences. Product launches and activity days. Sudeley reserves the right to close part or all of the Castle, gardens and grounds and to amend information as necessary. |

🛍 ❄

🍷 Corporate and private events, wedding receptions.

♿ Partial access to the grounds. WC.

🍴 Licensed restaurant.

🚶 Special interest tours can be arranged.

🅿 1,000 cars. Meal vouchers, free access for coach drivers.

✕

13 holiday cottages for 2 - 5 occupants.

🔔 🛡 Tel for details.

CONFERENCE/FUNCTION	
ROOM	MAX CAPACITY
Chandos Hall	80
Banquet Hall & Pavilion	150

BERKELEY CASTLE

See page 225 for full page entry.

BLACKFRIARS PRIORY

Ladybellegate Street, Gloucester

Tel: 0117 9750700   **www.**english-heritage.org.uk/southwest

Owner: English Heritage   **Contact:** The South West Regional Office

A small Dominican priory church converted into a rich merchant's house at the Dissolution. Most of the original 13th century church remains, including a rare scissor-braced roof.

Location: OS Ref. SO830 186. In Ladybellegate St, Gloucester, off Southgate Street and Blackfriars Walk.

Open: Access by guided tour only (Jul & Aug: Sunday pm). Please contact the South West Regional Office.

Admission: Free.

CHEDWORTH ROMAN VILLA

YANWORTH, Nr CHELTENHAM, GLOUCESTERSHIRE GL54 3LJ

www.nationaltrust.org.uk

Tel: 01242 890256   **Fax:** 01242 890909   **e-mail:** chedworth@nationaltrust.org.uk

Owner: The National Trust   **Contact:** The Property Manager

Remains of one of the largest Romano-British villas in the country. Over one mile of walls survives and there are several fine mosaics, two bathhouses, hypocausts, a water-shrine and latrine. Set in a wooded Cotswold combe, the site was excavated in 1864 and still has a Victorian atmosphere. The museum houses objects from the villa and a 15-minute audio-visual presentation gives visitors an insight into the history of this fascinating place. What's new in 2005: Family activity packs.

Location: OS Ref. SP053 135. 3m NW of Fossebridge on Cirencester - Northleach road (A429) via Yanworth or from A436 via Withington. Coaches must approach from Fossebridge.

Open: 1 - 24 Mar: Tues - Sun, 11am - 4pm. 25 Mar - 30 Oct: Tues - Sun, 10am - 5pm; 1 Nov - 13 Nov: Tues - Sun, 10am - 4pm. Open BH Mons. Shop open as Villa. Shop and reception close at above time - visitors already on the property are allowed up to 30min to finish their visit.

Admission: Adult £5, Child £2.50, Family (2+3) £12.50. Booked group tours (max 30 per guide): Schools £16, others £32.

Partial. WC. By arrangement. Adult £1.20, Child 80p. By arrangement. Tel for details.

BOURTON HOUSE GARDEN

BOURTON-ON-THE-HILL GL56 9AE

www.bourtonhouse.com

Tel: 01386 700754   **Fax:** 01386 701081   **e-mail:** cd@bourtonhouse.com

Owner/Contact: Mr & Mrs Richard Paice

Exciting 3 acre garden surrounding a delightful 18th century Cotswold manor house and 16th century tithe barn. Featuring flamboyant borders, imaginative topiary, a unique shade house, a profusion of herbaceous and exotic plants and, not least, a myriad of magically planted pots. The mood is friendly and welcoming, the atmosphere tranquil yet inspiring. The garden... "positively fizzes with ideas". There are a further 7 of parkland where young trees progress apace. 'The Gallery' features contemporary art, craft and design in the tithe barn.

Location: OS Ref. SP180 324. 1³⁄₄ m W of Moreton-in-Marsh on A44.

Open: 25 May - 31 Aug: Wed - Fri; Sept - Oct: Thur & Fri. Also 29/30 May & 28/29 Aug (BH Sun & Mon). 10am - 5pm.

Admission: Adult £5, Child Free.

Partial. By arrangement. Limited for coaches.

CHAVENAGE

See page 226 for full page entry.

DYRHAM PARK

Nr CHIPPENHAM, GLOUCESTERSHIRE SN14 8ER

www.nationaltrust.org.uk

Tel: 01179 372501   **Fax:** 01179 371353   **e-mail:** dyrhampark@nationaltrust.org.uk

Owner: The National Trust   **Contact:** The Property Manager

Dyrham Park was built between 1691 and 1702 for William Blathwayt, William III's Secretary at War and Secretary of State. The rooms have changed little since they were furnished by Blathwayt and their contents are recorded in his housekeeper's inventory. Many fine textiles and paintings, as well as items of blue-and-white Delftware. Restored Victorian domestic rooms open, including kitchen, bells passage, bakehouse, larders, tenants' hall and Delft-tiled dairy.

Location: OS Ref. ST743 757. 8m N of Bath, 12m E of Bristol. Approached from Bath - Stroud road (A46), 2m S of Tormarton interchange with M4/J18.

Open: House: 18 Mar - 30 Oct: Fri - Tue, 12 noon - 4pm, last admission 45 mins before closing. Garden: as house, 11am - 5pm. Park: daily (closed 25 Dec), 11am - 5pm (dusk if earlier). Contact property for winter opening times.

Admission: Adult £8.80, Child £4.35, Family £21.75. Garden & Park only: Adult £3.40, Child £1.70, Family £7.75. Park only (on days when house & garden closed): Adult £2.25, Child £1.10.

Partial. No electric wheelchairs admitted. Licensed. Mons, 11.30am (max 20). House. Only in dog-walking area. Tel for details.

Open All Year Index see page 43

South West - England

FRAMPTON COURT
FRAMPTON-ON-SEVERN, GLOUCESTERSHIRE GL2 7EU
www.framptoncourtestate.uk.com

Tel: 01452 740267 **Fax:** 01452 740698 **e-mail:** clifford.fce@farming.co.uk

Owner: Mr & Mrs Rollo Clifford   **Contact:** Jean Speed

Splendid Georgian family home of the Cliffords, who have lived in Frampton since the Norman Conquest. Built 1732, school of Vanbrugh, set in Grade I listed park and garden with fine views to extensive lake. Superb panelled interiors and period furniture. Also the famous 19th century "Frampton Flora" botanical watercolours. Principal bedrooms available for Bed and Breakfast.

Strawberry Hill Gothic Orangery with a Dutch ornamental canal is available for self catering holidays (tel: 01452 740698).

Location: OS Ref. SO750 078. In Frampton, ¼ m SW of B4071, 3m NW of M5/J13.

Open: By arrangement for groups (10+).

Admission: House & Garden: £5.

ℹ️ No photography in house.
🌿 In Orangery walled garden. Pan Global Plants (tel: 01452 741641), rare plant nursery. ☕ Small. ♿ Garden only. ▣ 📷 Obligatory. 🅿 Coaches limited.
🐕 In grounds, on leads.
🛏 B&B contact Gilian Keightley on 01452 740267. Orangery tel: 01452 740698. ✳

FRAMPTON MANOR
Frampton-on-Severn, Gloucestershire GL2 7EU

Tel: 01452 740268 **Fax:** 01452 740698

Owner: Mr & Mrs Rollo Clifford   **Contact:** Mrs Rollo Clifford

Medieval/Elizabethan timber-framed manor house with walled garden. Reputed 12th century birthplace of 'Fair Rosamund' Clifford, mistress of King Henry II. Wool Barn c1560 and 16th century dovecote.

Location: OS Ref. SO748 080. 3m M5/J13.

Open: House & Garden: open by appointment for groups (10+). Garden: 28 Apr - 23 Jul: Thur & Fri, 2.30 - 5pm.

Admission: House, Garden & Wool Barn: £4.50. Garden only: £3. Wool Barn only £1.

ℹ️ No photography inside. 🌿 ☕ Tearoom for groups. 📷 Obligatory. 🅿
🐕 Tel for details.

GLOUCESTER CATHEDRAL
Chapter Office, College Green, Gloucester GL1 2LR

Tel: 01452 508211 **Fax:** 01452 300469

e-mail: lin@gloucestercathedral.org.uk **www**.gloucestercathedral.org.uk
          Contact: Mrs L Henderson

Daily worship and rich musical tradition continue in this abbey church founded 1300 years ago. It has a Norman nave with massive cylindrical pillars, a magnificent east window with medieval glass and glorious fan-vaulted cloisters. You can also find the tombs of King Edward II and Robert, Duke of Normandy.

Location: OS Ref. SO832 188. Off Westgate Street in central Gloucester.

Open: Daily, 8am until after Evensong. Groups must book via the Chapter Office.

Admission: £3 donation requested.

📷 ☕ ♿ Partial. WC. 🍴 Licensed. 📷 By arrangement. ▣ 🅿 None.
🐕 In grounds, on leads.

HAILES ABBEY ⊞ ✄
Nr Winchcombe, Cheltenham, Gloucestershire GL54 5PB

Tel/Fax: 01242 602398 **e-mail:** customers@english-heritage.org.uk
www.english-heritage.org.uk/hailes

Owner: English Heritage & The National Trust   **Contact:** Visitor Operations Staff

Seventeen cloister arches and extensive excavated remains in lovely surroundings of an abbey founded by Richard, Earl of Cornwall, in 1246. There is a small museum and covered display area.

Location: OS Ref. SP050 300. 2m NE of Winchcombe off B4632. ½ m SE of B4632.

Open: 24 Mar - 31 Oct: daily, 10am - 5pm (6pm in Jul & Aug, 4pm in Oct). Closed in winter.

Admission: Adult £3.30, Child £1.70, Conc. £2.50.

📷 ♿ Partial. WC. 📷 🅿 🐕 In grounds, on leads. 🐕 Tel for details.

NTPL / Nick Meers

HIDCOTE MANOR GARDEN ✄
HIDCOTE BARTRIM Nr CHIPPING CAMPDEN,
GLOUCESTERSHIRE GL55 6LR
www.nationaltrust.org.uk/hidcote

Tel: 01386 438333 **Fax:** 01386 438817 **e-mail:** hidcote@nationaltrust.org.uk

Owner: The National Trust   **Contact:** Visitor Services Manager

One of the most delightful gardens in England, created in the early 20th century by the great horticulturist Major Lawrence Johnston; a series of small gardens within the whole, separated by walls and hedges of different species; famous for rare shrubs, trees, herbaceous borders, 'old' roses and interesting plant species.

Location: OS Ref. SP176 429. 4m NE of Chipping Campden, 1m E of B4632 off B4081. At Mickleton ¼ m E of Kiftsgate Court. Coaches are not permitted through Chipping Campden High Street.

Open: 19 Mar - 30 Oct: Sat - Wed, 10.30am - 6pm (from 3 Oct closes at 5pm), last admission 1hr before closing. Open Good Fri.

Admission: Adult £6.60, Child £3.30, Family (2+3) £16.10.
Groups (15+) Adult £5.90, Child £2.65.

📷 🌿 ♿ Limited. WC. ▣ 🍴 Licensed. 🅿 ▣ 🐕 🐕 Send SAE for details.

©The Landmark Trust

East Banqueting House, Chipping Campden (a Landmark Trust Property, see page 6).

229

OWLPEN MANOR 🏛

Nr ULEY, GLOUCESTERSHIRE GL11 5BZ

www.owlpen.com

Tel: 01453 860261 **Fax:** 01453 860819 **Restaurant:** 01453 860816
e-mail: sales@owlpen.com
Owner: Mr & Mrs Nicholas Mander   **Contact:** Sara Tucker
Romantic Tudor manor house, 1450-1616, with Cotswold Arts & Crafts
associations. Remote wooded valley setting, with 16th and 17th century formal
terraced gardens and magnificent yews. Contains unique painted cloth wall
hangings, family and Arts & Crafts collections. Mill (1726), Court House (1620);
licensed restaurant in medieval Cyder House. Victorian church. *"Owlpen - ah,
what a dream is there!"* - Vita Sackville-West.

Location: OS Ref. ST801 984. 3m E of Dursley, 1m E of Uley, off B4066, by Old
Crown pub.

Open: Apr - Sept: Tue - Sun & BH Mons, 2 - 5pm. Restaurant 12 noon - 5pm.

Admission: Adult £4.80, Child (4-14yrs) £2, Family (2+4) £13.50. Gardens and
Grounds: Adult £2.80, Child £1. Group rates available.

🖼 ⬇Unsuitable. 🍴Licensed. 🅿 🏠Holiday cottages, all seasons, sleep 2 - 9.

PAINSWICK ROCOCO GARDEN 🏛

PAINSWICK, GLOUCESTERSHIRE GL6 6TH

www.rococogarden.co.uk

Tel: 01452 813204 **Fax:** 01452 814888 **e-mail:** paulmoir@rococogarden.co.uk
Owner: Painswick Rococo Garden Trust   **Contact:** P R Moir
Unique 18th century garden restoration situated in a hidden 6 acre Cotswold
combe. Charming contemporary buildings are juxtaposed with winding woodland
walks and formal vistas. Famous for its early spring show of snowdrops. Newly
planted maze.

Location: OS Ref. SO864 106. ¹/₂ m NW of village of Painswick on B4073.

Open: 10 Jan - 31 Oct: daily, 11am - 5pm.

Admission: Adult £4, Child £2, OAP £3.50. Family (2+2) £10.50.
Free introductory talk for pre-booked groups (20+).

🖼 🏠 ♿Partial. WC. 🍴Licensed. 🍴 🅿 🖼 🐕In grounds, on leads. 🖼 ❋
📖 Tel for details.

RODMARTON MANOR 🏛

CIRENCESTER, GLOUCESTERSHIRE GL7 6PF

www.rodmarton-manor.co.uk

Tel: 01285 841253 **Fax:** 01285 841298 **e-mail:** simon.biddulph@farming.co.uk
Owner: Mr & Mrs Simon Biddulph   **Contact:** Simon Biddulph
A Cotswold Arts and Crafts house, one of the last great country houses to be built in
the traditional way and containing beautiful furniture, ironwork, china and
needlework specially made for the house. The large garden complements the house
and contains many areas of great beauty and character including the magnificent
herbaceous borders, topiary, roses, rockery and kitchen garden. Available as a film
location and for small functions.

Location: OS Ref. ST943 977. Off A433 between Cirencester and Tetbury.

Open: House & Garden: 28 Mar, 2 Apr & 2 May - 17 Sept (Weds, Sats & BHs), 2 - 5pm

(Not guided tours). Garden only, for snowdrops,: 13, 17 & 20 Feb: from 1.30pm.
Groups please book. Individuals need not book. Guided tours of the house (last
about 1hr) may be booked for groups (15+) at other times at any time of year
(minimum group charge of £105 applies). Groups (5+) may book to visit the garden
at other times.

Admission: House & Garden: £7, Child (5-15yrs) £3.50. Garden only: £4, Child
(5-15yrs) £1.

ℹ️Colour guidebook & postcards on sale. No photography in house. WCs in garden.
♿Garden & ground floor. 🖼Most open days and groups by appointment.
🖼 By arrangement. 🅿 🖼 🐕Guide dogs only. ❋

ST MARY'S CHURCH ⚏
Kempley, Gloucestershire

Tel: 01179 750700 **www**.english-heritage.org.uk/southwest

Owner: English Heritage   **Contact:** The South West Regional Office

A delightful Norman church with superb wall paintings from the 12th - 14th centuries which were only discovered beneath whitewash in 1871.

Location: OS Ref. SO670 313. On minor road. 1¹/₂ m SE of Much Marcle, A449.

Open: 1 Mar - 31 Oct: daily, 10am - 6pm.

Admission: Free.

⊠

SEZINCOTE ⌂
Moreton-in-Marsh, Gloucestershire GL56 9AW

Tel: 01386 700444

Owner: Mr and Mrs D Peake   **Contact:** Mr E Peake

Exotic oriental water garden by Repton and Daniell. Large semi-circular orangery. House by S P Cockerell in Indian style was the inspiration for Brighton Pavilion.

Location: OS Ref. SP183 324. 2¹/₂ m SW of Moreton-in-Marsh. Turn W along A44 to Broadway and left into gateway just before Bourton-on-the-Hill (opposite the gate to Batsford Park, then 1m drive.

Open: Garden: Thurs, Fris & BH Mons, 2 - 6pm (dusk if earlier) throughout the year except Dec. House: May, Jun, Jul & Sept, Thurs & Fris, 2.30 - 6pm. Groups by written appointment.

Admission: House & Garden: Adult £6 (no children in house). Garden: Adult £4, Child £1.50 (under 5yrs Free).

♿ Unsuitable. ⊠ Guide dogs only. ✳

Westbury Court Garden.

SNOWSHILL MANOR ✤
SNOWSHILL, Nr BROADWAY, GLOUCESTERSHIRE WR12 7JU
www.nationaltrust.org.uk

Tel: 01386 852410 **Fax:** 01386 842822

e-mail: snowshillmanor@nationaltrust.org.uk

Owner: The National Trust   **Contact:** The Property Manager

Snowshill Manor contains Charles Paget Wade's extraordinary collection of craftsmanship and design, including musical instruments, clocks, toys, bicycles, weavers' and spinners' tools and Japanese armour. Due to ongoing conservation work some items may not be available at all times (telephone for details). Run on organic principles, the intimate garden is laid out as a series of outdoor rooms, with terraces and ponds, and wonderful views across the Cotswold countryside.

The Snowshill Costume Collection can be viewed by appointment only at Berrington Hall, please tel: 01568 613720 on Thursdays or Fridays.

Location: OS Ref. SP096 339. 3m SW of Broadway, turning off the A44, by Broadway Green.

Open: House: 25 Mar - 1 May: Thur - Sun, 2 May - 30 Oct: Wed - Sun & BH Mons, 12 noon - 5pm. Garden: as House, 11am - 5.30pm. Restaurant & Shop: as Garden also 5 Nov - 11 Dec: Sat & Sun, 12 noon - 4pm.

Admission: Gardens, Shop & Restaurant: Adult £7, Child £3.50, Family £17.80. Coach & School groups by written appointment only.

⌂ ♿ Partial. ⊞ Licensed. ⊠ ⊡ Tel for details.

MUSEUM OF COSTUME & ASSEMBLY ROOMS

www.museumofcostume.co.uk

Map 2

Owner:
The National Trust

▶ **CONTACT**
For Room Hire:
Mr Tom Deller
Room Hire Manager
Stall Street
Bath BA1 1LZ

Tel: 01225 477734
Fax: 01225 477476

e-mail: tom_deller@
bathnes.gov.uk

Museum Enquiries:
Tel: 01225 477785
Fax: 01225 477743

▶ **LOCATION**
OS Ref. ST750 648

Near centre of Bath,
10m from M4/J18.
Park & Ride or
public car park.

Rail: Great Western
from London Paddington
(regular service)
90 mins approx.

Air: Bristol airport
45 mins.

The Assembly Rooms in Bath are open to the public daily (free of charge) and are also popular for dinners, dances, concerts, conferences and Civil weddings.

Originally known as the Upper Rooms, they were designed by John Wood the Younger and opened in 1771. The magnificent interior consists of a splendid Ball Room, Tea Room and Card Room, connected by two fine octagonal rooms. This plan was perfect for 'assemblies', evening entertainments popular in the 18th century, which included dancing, music, card-playing and tea drinking. They are now owned by The National Trust and managed by Bath & North East Somerset Council, which runs a full conference service.

The building also houses one of the largest and most comprehensive collections of fashionable dress in the world, the Museum of Costume. Its extensive displays cover the history of fashion from the late 16th century to the present day. Hand-held audioguides allow visitors to learn about the fashions on display while the lighting is kept to levels suitable for fragile garments. The 'Dress of the Year' collection traces significant moments in modern fashion history from 1963. For the serious student of fashion, the reference library and study facilities are available by appointment.

The museum shops sell publications and gifts associated with the history of costume and are open daily to all visitors.

▶ **OPENING TIMES**
All Year
January/February &
November/December:
11am - 4pm.
March - October:
11am - 5pm.

Closed 25 & 26 December
Last exit 1hr after closing.

**Special exhibition
for June 2005:**
Jane Austen: Film & Fashion

▶ **ADMISSION**
Assembly Rooms ... Free
Museum of Costume:
Adult £6.25
Child* (summer).... £4.25
Conc. £5.25
Family (2+4) £17.00
Groups (20+)
Adult £5.00
Child* (summer).... £3.60
Child* (winter)....... £3.20

**Joint Saver Ticket with
Roman Baths**
Adult £12.50
Child*.................... £7.30
Conc. £11.00
Family (2+4) £33.50
Groups (20+)
Adult £8.30
Child* (summer).... £5.30
Child* (winter)....... £4.50

* Age 6 - 16yrs.
Child under 6yrs Free.

ROOM	SIZE	MAX CAPACITY
Ballroom	103' x 40'	500/310
Octagon	47' x 47'	120/120
Tea Room	58' x 40'	260/170
Card Room	59' x 18'	80/60

CONFERENCE/FUNCTION

ℹ Conference facilities.
Extensive book & gift shops.
Corporate hospitality. Function facilities.
Suitable. WC.
Hourly. Individual guided tours by arrangement.
🎧 English/Dutch/French/German/Italian/Japanese/Spanish.
P Charlotte Street car park.
Teachers' pack. Guide dogs only.
Civil Weddings/Receptions.

Bath & North East Somerset Council

THE ROMAN BATHS & PUMP ROOM

www.romanbaths.co.uk

Map 2

Owner:
Bath & North East
Somerset Council

▶ **CONTACT**

For Room Hire:
Mr Tom Deller
Stall Street
Bath BA1 1LZ
Tel: 01225 477734
Fax: 01225 477476
e-mail: tom_deller@
bathnes.gov.uk

**For visits to
Roman Baths:**
Tel: 01225 477785
Fax: 01225 477743

▶ **LOCATION**

OS Ref. ST750 648

Centre of Bath,
10m from M4/J18. Park
& Ride recommended.

Rail: Great Western
from London
Paddington, half
hourly service,
1 hr 17 mins duration.

The first stop for any visitor to Bath is the Roman Baths surrounding the hot springs where the city began and which are still its heart. Here you'll see one of the country's finest ancient monuments – the great Roman temple and bathing complex built almost 2000 years ago. Discover the everyday life of the Roman spa and see ancient treasures from the Temple of Sulis Minerva. A host of new interpretive methods bring these spectacular buildings vividly to life and help visitors to understand the extensive remains.

The Grand Pump Room, overlooking the Spring, is the social heart of Bath. The elegant interior of 1795 is something every visitor to Bath should see. You can enjoy a glass of spa water drawn from the fountain, perhaps as an appetiser to a traditional Pump Room tea, morning coffee or lunch. The Pump Room Trio and resident pianists provide live music daily. The Roman Baths shop sells publications and gifts related to the site.

In the evening, the Pump Room is available for banquets, dances and concerts. Nothing could be more magical than a meal on the terrace which overlooks the Great Bath, or a pre-dinner drinks reception by torchlight around the Great Bath itself.

▶ **OPENING TIMES**

January - February:
9.30am - 4.30pm.
March - June: 9am - 5pm.
July - August: 9am - 9pm.
September - October:
9am - 5pm.
November - December:
9.30am - 4.30pm.
Last exit 1 hour after
closing.

Closed 25 & 26 December.

The Pump Room Trio
plays 10am - 12 noon Mon
- Sat and 3 - 5pm Sunday.
During the summer it also
plays from 3 - 5pm, Mon -
Sat. Resident pianists play
at lunch-time.

▶ **ADMISSION**

Roman Baths:

Adult	£9.50
Child (6-16yrs)	£5.30
Conc.	£8.50
Family (2+4)	£25.00
Groups (20+)	
Adult	£6.80
Child* (summer)	£4.00
Child* (winter)	£3.70

**Joint Saver Ticket with
Museum of Costume**

Adult*	£12.50
Child*	£7.30
Conc.	£11.00
Family (2+4)	£33.50
Groups (20+)	
Adult	£8.30
Child* (summer)	£5.30
Child* (winter)	£4.50

* Age 6 - 16yrs.

Child under 6yrs Free.

Bath & North East Somerset Council

[icon] Extensive gift shop.

[icon] Award-winning guide book in English, French and German.

[icon] Comprehensive service for private and corporate entertainment. The Assembly Rooms, Guildhall, Victoria Art Gallery and Pump Room are all available for private hire, contact the Pump Room.

[icon] Free access to terrace. Restricted access to the Museum, special visits for disabled groups by appointment. People with special needs welcome, teaching sessions available.

[icon] Pump Room coffees, lunches and teas, no reservation needed. Music by Pump Room Trio or pianist.

[icon] Hourly. Private tours by appointment.

[icon] English, French, German, Italian, Japanese, Spanish, Dutch.

[icon] City centre car parks available.

[icon] Teaching sessions available. Pre-booking necessary.

[icon] Civil Weddings in two private rooms with photographs around the Great Bath.

[icon]

CONFERENCE/FUNCTION

ROOM	SIZE	MAX CAPACITY
Great Roman Bath		400 summer 200 winter
Pump Rm.	57' x 41'	180
Terrace overlooking Great Bath	83' x 11'	70
Reception Hall	56' x 44'	100
Smoking Rm & Drawing Rm	28' x 16'	40

STONEHENGE ⚏

AMESBURY, WILTSHIRE SP4 7DE

www.english-heritage.org.uk/stonehenge

Tel: 01980 624715 (Information Line)   **Owner:** English Heritage

The mystical and awe-inspiring stone circle at Stonehenge is one of the most famous prehistoric monuments in the world, designated by UNESCO as a World Heritage Site. Stonehenge's orientation on the rising and setting sun has always been one of its most remarkable features. Whether this was simply because the builders came from a sun-worshipping culture, or because – as some scholars have believed – the circle and its banks were part of a huge astronomical calendar, remains a mystery. Visitors to Stonehenge can discover the history and legends which surround this unique stone circle, which began over 5,000 years ago, with a complimentary three part audio tour available in 9 languages (subject to availability).

Location: OS Ref. SU123 422. 2m W of Amesbury on junction of A303 and A344/ A360.

Open: 16 Mar - end May: daily, 9.30am - 6pm. June - Aug: daily, 9am - 7pm. Sept - 15 Oct: daily, 9.30am - 6pm. 16 Oct - 15 Mar: daily, 9.30am - 4pm. Closed 24 - 26 Dec & 1 Jan. Last recommended admission is ½ hr before advertised closing times and the site will be closed promptly 20 mins after the advertised closing times.

Admission: Adult £5.50, Child £2.80, Conc. £4.10. Family (2+3) £13.80. Groups (11+) 10% discount.

ⓘWCs. 🖼 ⬛ 🖥 🎧 ♿ 🅿 ❌ ✳ 🛡 Tel for details.

STONEHENGE HISTORIC LANDSCAPE ✻

3/4 Stonehenge Cottages, Kings Barrows, Amesbury, Wiltshire SP4 7DD

Tel: 01980 664780 (Stonehenge Cottage)

Tel: 01980 623108 (Monument Visitor Centre, EH)

Owner: The National Trust   **Contact:** English Heritage Monument & Visitor Centre

The Trust own 850ha (2100 acres) of downland surrounding the famous monument, including some fine Bronze Age barrow groups and the Cursus, variously interpreted as an ancient racecourse or processional way. The Trust is now managing this historic landscape which forms approximately one third of the Stonehenge World Heritage Site, to conserve archeology, increase access and balance the needs of modern agricultural practice with natural conservation.

Location: OS Ref. SU120 420. 2m W of Amesbury on junction of A303 and A344/ A360.

Open: Tel for details. NT land N of visitor centre: All year, but parts may be closed at the Summer Solstice (21 Jun) for up to 2 days.

Admission: Free. A charge over the peak period (Jun - Oct) may apply.

🖼 ♿Partial. 🐕Not on archaeological walks, under close control at all times. ✳

STOURHEAD ✻

See page 249 for full page entry.

STOURTON HOUSE FLOWER GARDEN

Stourton, Warminster, Wiltshire BA12 6QF

Tel: 01747 840417

Owner/Contact: Mrs E Bullivant

Four acres of peaceful, romantic garden. Daffodils, rhododendrons, roses, hydrangeas and wild flowers.

Location: OS Ref. ST780 340. A303, 2m NW of Mere next to Stourhead car park. Follow blue signs.

Open: Apr - end Nov: Weds, Thurs, Suns, and BH Mons, 11am - 6pm. Plants & dried flowers for sale during the winter on weekdays.

Admission: Adult £3, Child £50p. Subject to increase Apr 2005. Group guided tours by appointment.

WILTON HOUSE 🏛

See page 250 for full page entry.

Stourhead.

NTPL / Nick Meers

Longleat, from the book 'Historic Family Homes & Gardens from the Air'

eastern region

More generally known as East Anglia, this region has magical coastal areas ranging from The Wash in Norfolk down to the Essex marshes. The Norfolk Broads is an area of inland waterways where boats can be hired by the day or the week to explore these fascinating wetlands. East Suffolk was the home of the artist John Constable, and Flatford Bridge Cottage houses a number of his paintings, as well as a display about the artist himself. The half timbered houses, in villages such as Lavenham, are enchanting and contrast with the Norfolk flint found in the north of this region. Cambridge, with its stunning colleges and delightful riverside walks, merits a visit all to itself. Ruben's 'Adoration of the Magi' hangs in King's College Chapel, where it is possible to attend services. Among the major properties that welcome visitors are Sandringham (Norfolk) the country home of HM The Queen, Woburn Abbey (Bedfordshire) and Hatfield House (Hertfordshire). But off the beaten track do find time for The Manor, Hemingford Grey (Cambridgeshire), reputedly one of the oldest continuously inhabited houses in Britain; or visit Copped Hall (Essex), the subject of a remarkable restoration programme by local residents.

Orford Ness, Suffolk © National Trust Photographic Library/Joe Cornish

Holham Hall, Norfolk

Layer Marney Tower, Essex

Audley End House, Essex

bedfordshire

cambridgeshire

essex

hertfordshire

norfolk

suffolk

copped hall

18th century ruin | restoration | transformed

copped hall

e a s t e r n   r e g i o n

Copped Hall, a most spectacular shell of a house, 'undressed' by fire, stands on a remote ridge overlooking landscaped parkland at Epping (Copt is Saxon for hill top). This sublime scene – of ruinous mansion, roofless, its interior walls adorned only with lingering fragments of plaster and stubborn weeds – is a result of a terrible blaze in 1917 which reduced the 18th century main body of the house to a skeletal reminder of its past splendour.

The Hall was built at the other end of the gardens to two earlier structures: a 12th century dwelling subsequently owned by the Abbots of Waltham who remained until the Dissolution of the Monastries; and the Elizabethan mansion of Sir Thomas Heneage, in whose 173 foot long gallery the first performance of Shakespeare's 'A Midsummer Night's Dream' was performed.

Between 1750 and 1758, the existing structure was built by John Sanderson for John Conyers when the 16th century house had become dilapidated and uninhabitable. It was fashioned out of golden brick and designed with starkly dramatic, unadorned classical façades. This contrasts with the visually exciting garden front with its dramatic pediment and curving staircases added by C E Kempe in 1895. Kempe also enlarged the Hall by constructing the north wing and creating a large winter garden and elaborate Italianate terraces.

One morning in May 1917, while the Wythes family were preparing for church, the fire broke out, probably in the southern end of the house in an attic. It was devastating. Much of the furniture was rescued and some of it can now be viewed at the V&A. But it was in 1952, when the estate was sold, that the Hall was stripped of its staircases, remaining timberwork and marble floors. The ancillary buildings, gardens and grounds were maintained until after the war, but again, at the time of the sale, the elaborate garden structures were dismantled and sold, buildings were vandalised and in the 1960s the Winter Garden was dynamited.

In 1995, after a nine year campaign against aggressive development proposals, the site was acquired by the specially formed Copped Hall Trust, whose purpose is to implement a carefully researched programme of restoration for the mansion and grounds. The beautifully austere 1753 classical interior will be restored and the gardens will be mostly restored as they were in 1917. Considerable progress has been made: much garden stonework has been traced to Essex, Herefordshire and Cambridgeshire. Parts of the roof of the Hall have been replaced. The Winter Garden has been excavated and the grounds cleared, shrubs replaced and, for the first time in years, vegetables are being grown in the walled garden. A sleeping beauty is awakening.

▶ For further details about Copped Hall, see page 273.

CASTLE ACRE PRIORY ⌗

Stocks Green, Castle Acre, King's Lynn, Norfolk PE32 2XD

Tel: 01760 755394   **www**.english-heritage.org.uk/visits

Owner: English Heritage   **Contact:** Visitor Operations Team

Explore the romantic ruins of this 12th century Cluniac priory, set in the picturesque village of Castle Acre. The impressive Norman façade, splendid prior's lodgings and chapel, and delightful medieval herb garden should not be missed.

Location: OS Ref. TF814 148. ¼ m W of village of Castle Acre, 5m N of Swaffham.

Open: 24 Mar - 30 Sept: daily, 10am - 6pm. 1 Oct - 31 Mar: Wed - Sun, 10am - 4pm. Closed 24 - 26 Dec & 1 Jan.

Admission: Adult £4.30, Child £2.20, Conc. £3.20. Family £10.80.

🖸 🕭 Ground floor & grounds. 🖸 🅿 🔲 🖾 On leads. ✳ 🖾 Tel for details.

CASTLE RISING CASTLE ⌗

Castle Rising, King's Lynn, Norfolk PE31 6AH

Tel: 01553 631330   **Fax:** 01553 631724

Owner: Greville Howard   **Contact:** The Custodian

Possibly the finest mid-12th century Keep left in England: it was built as a grand and elaborate palace. It was home to Queen Isabella, grandmother of the Black Prince. Still in surprisingly good condition, the Keep is surrounded by massive ramparts up to 120 feet high. Picnic area adjacent tearoom. Free audio tour.

Location: OS Ref. TF666 246. Located 4m NE of King's Lynn off A149.

Open: 1 Apr - 31 Oct: daily, 10am - 6pm, (5pm in Oct). 1 Nov - 31 Mar: Wed - Sun, 10am - 4pm. Closed 24 - 26 Dec & 1 Jan.

Admission: Adult £3.85, Child £2.20, Conc. £3.10. 15% discount for groups (11+). Prices include VAT.

ℹ Picnic area. 🖸 🕭 Grounds. WC. 🖾 🖸 🅿 ✳

DRAGON HALL

115 - 123 King Street, Norwich, Norfolk NR1 1QE

Tel: 01603 663922   **e-mail:** dragon.hall@virgin.net   **www**.dragonhall.org

Owner: Norfolk & Norwich Heritage Trust Ltd   **Contact:** Stephanie Potts

Magnificent medieval merchants' hall described as "one of the most exciting 15th century buildings in England". A wealth of outstanding features include living hall, screens passage, vaulted undercroft, superb timber-framed Great Hall, crown-post roof and intricately carved and painted dragon. Built by Robert Toppes, a wealthy and influential merchant. Dragon Hall is a unique legacy of medieval life, craftsmanship and trade.

Location: OS Ref. TG235 084. SE of Norwich city centre.

Open: Due to renovations in 2005, please telephone to check opening times.

Admission: Adult £2.50, Child £1, Conc. £2.

🖸 🕭 House. 🖟 Obligatory. 🖾 Guide dogs only. ✳

FAIRHAVEN WOODLAND & WATER GARDEN

School Road, South Walsham NR13 6DZ

Tel/Fax: 01603 270449

Owner: The Fairhaven Garden Trust   **Contact:** George Debbage, Manager

180 acre woodland & water garden with private broad in the beautiful Norfolk Broads.

Location: OS Ref. TG368 134. 9m NE of Norwich. Signed on A47 at junction with B1140.

Open: Daily (except 25 Dec), 10am - 5pm, also May - Aug: Wed & Thurs evenings until 9pm.

Admission: Adult £4, Child £1.50 (under 5yrs Free), OAP £3.50. Group reductions.

🌻 Plant Sales Index see page 39

FELBRIGG HALL 🌿

FELBRIGG, NORWICH, NORFOLK NR11 8PR

www.nationaltrust.org.uk

Tel: 01263 837444   **Fax:** 01263 837032   **e-mail:** felbrigg@nationaltrust.org.uk

Owner: The National Trust   **Contact:** The Property Manager

One of the finest 17th century country houses in East Anglia. The hall contains its original 18th century furniture and one of the largest collections of Grand Tour paintings by a single artist. The library is outstanding. The Walled Garden has been restored and features a series of pottager gardens, a working dovecote and the National Collection of Colchicums. The Park, through which there are way-marked walks, is well known for its magnificent and aged trees. There are also walks to the church and lake and through the 500 acres of woods.

Location: OS133 Ref. TG193 394. Nr Felbrigg village, 2m SW of Cromer, entrance off B1436, signposted from A148 and A140.

Open: House: 19 Mar - 30 Oct: daily except Thur & Fri, 1 - 5pm. Gardens: As house, 11am - 5pm. Walled Garden: Also open Thur & Fri, 21 Jul - 2 Sep, 11am - 5pm.

Admission: House & Garden: Adult £6.60, Child £3.10, Family £16.20. Garden only: £2.70. Groups: (except BHs), £5.30. Groups please book with SAE to the Property Manager.

🖸 01263 837040. 🖟 🖾 01263 838237. 🕭 Partial. 🖾 Licensed. 🍴 Licensed. 🖟 By arrangement. 🅿 🖾 In grounds, on leads. 🖾 Tel 01263 837444 for details.

The National Trust

GREAT YARMOUTH ROW HOUSES ⌗
South Quay, Great Yarmouth, Norfolk NR30 2RQ
Tel: 01493 857900
Owner: English Heritage   **Contact:** Visitor Operations Team
Two immaculately presented 17th century Row Houses, a type of building unique to Great Yarmouth. Row 111 House was almost destroyed by bombing in 1942/3 and contains items rescued from the rubble. Old Merchant's House boasts magnificent plaster-work ceilings and displays of local architectural fittings.
Location: OS134, TG525 072. In Great Yarmouth, make for South Quay, by riverside and dock, 1/2 m inland from beach. Follow signs to dock and south quay.
Open: 24 Mar - 31 Oct: Thur - Sun, 12 noon - 5pm.
Admission: Adult £3.30. Child £1.70, Conc. £2.50.

GRIME'S GRAVES ⌗
Lynford, Thetford, Norfolk IP26 5DE
Tel: 01842 810656
Owner: English Heritage   **Contact:** Visitor Operations Team
These remarkable Neolithic flint mines, unique in England, comprise over 300 pits and shafts. The visitor can descend some 30 feet by ladder into one excavated shaft, and look along the radiating galleries, from where the flint used for making axes and knives was extracted.
Location: OS 144, TL818 898. 7m NW of Thetford off A134.
Open: 3 - 31 Mar & 1 - 31 Oct: Thur - Mon, 10am - 5pm. 1 Apr - 30 Sept: daily, 10am - 6pm. Closed: 1 Nov - 28 Feb. Last visit to site 30 mins before close. No entry to the mines for children under 5 yrs.
Admission: Adult £2.60, Child £1.30, Conc. £2, Family £6.50.
⬚ ⬚Exhibition area only. **P** ⬚ Restricted areas. ⬚ ⬚ Tel for details.

HOLKHAM HALL ⌂
See page 281 for full page entry.

HOVETON HALL GARDENS ⌂
Wroxham, Norwich, Norfolk NR12 8RJ
Tel: 01603 782798 **Fax:** 01603 784564 **e-mail:** info@hovetonhallgardens.co.uk
Owner: Mr & Mrs Andrew Buxton   **Contact:** Mrs Buxton
15 acres of rhododendrons, azaleas, woodland and lakeside walks, walled herbaceous and vegetable gardens. Traditional tearooms and plant sales. The Hall (which is not open to the public) was built 1809 - 1812. Designs attributed to Humphry Repton.
Location: OS Ref. TG314 202. 8m N of Norwich. 1 1/2 m NNE of Wroxham on A1151. Follow brown tourist signs.
Open: 27 Mar - 4 Sept: Weds, Fris, Suns & BH Mons, 10.30am - 5pm. Also open Thurs in May & June.
Admission: Adult £4, Child (4-16yrs) £1.50, Senior £4, Wheelchair pusher and user £2pp. Season Ticket: Adult £10.50, Family £22.

LOCAL FOOD

Colchester Oysters

Colchester is renowned for having the some of the best oysters in the world. Only eaten during months with an 'R' in them, oysters are classically eaten raw, but can also be grilled or steamed. They can be teamed up with Samphire, a green vegetable, slightly resembling asparagus, that grows wild on the Norfolk and Suffolk salt marshes.

HOUGHTON HALL ⌂
HOUGHTON, KING'S LYNN, NORFOLK PE31 6UE
www.houghtonhall. com

Tel: 01485 528569 **Fax:** 01485 528167 **e-mail:** enquiries@houghtonhall.com
Owner: The Marquess of Cholmondeley   **Contact:** Susan Cleaver
Houghton Hall is one of the finest examples of Palladian architecture in England. Built in the 18th century by Sir Robert Walpole, Britain's first prime minister. Original designs by James Gibbs & Colen Campbell, interior decoration by William Kent. The House has been restored to its former grandeur, containing many of its original furnishings. The spectacular 5-acre walled garden is divided into areas devoted to fruit and vegetables, elegant herbaceous borders, and a formal rose garden with over 150 varieties – full of colour throughout the summer. The unique Model Soldier

Collection contains over 20,000 models arranged in various battle formations.
Location: OS Ref. TF792 287. 13m E of King's Lynn, 10m W of Fakenham 1 1/2 m N of A148.
Open: Easter Sun - 30 Sept: Weds, Thurs, Suns & BH Mons. House: 1.30 - 5pm (last admission 4.30pm). Gates, Garden, Soldier Museum, Restaurant & Shop: 11am - 5.30pm (last admission 5pm).
Admission: Adult £7, Child (5-16) £3, Family £16. Excluding House: Adult £4.50, Child £2. Group (20+) discounts available, please tel for details.
ⓘ ⬚ ⬚ ⬚ ⬚Licensed. ⬚Licensed. ⬚By arrangement. **P** ⬚ ⬚On leads, in grounds.

kirby hall

gothic & classical | elizabethan | reawakening

© English Heritage Photo Library / John Critchley

© English Heritage Photo Library / Nigel Corrie

© English Heritage Photo Library

© English Heritage Photo Library / John Critchley

kirby hall

east midlands

Kirby Hall is one of England's great Elizabethan houses, run by English Heritage, and is a monument to late 16th century architectural zeal. This stone-built mansion, standing in remarkable solitude in the countryside north of Corby, has richly carved decoration which is exceptional and shows the arrival in England of new ideas in architecture and design.

Begun in 1570 by Sir Humphrey Stafford, it was sold unfinished to Sir Christopher Hatton who completed the house in 1575. The house, with its Great Hall and state rooms, was built for entertaining. Sir Christopher Hatton, once Lord Chancellor to Queen Elizabeth I, lived here and completed the house in the hope of receiving Queen Elizabeth I on one of her annual 'progresses' around the country.

The Hall is constructed on a quadrangle, with its now ruined wings surrounding a courtyard. The porch is one of the most exuberant displays of architectural ornament to be found in England, with its curved top gable and nine tiny columns with Corinthian capitals.

The decoration of the courtyard is one of the most innovative features of Kirby Hall. Around all four sides run pilasters, or columns applied to the wall. They run through both floors of the building and this courtyard is the first example of such details being used to unite the design of a whole façade.

Subsequent generations of Hattons inherited the Hall until Sir Christopher Hatton IV who died in 1706. In the following century the house was occupied less often, the gardens fell into decay and in the 19th century Kirby fell into decline. Sales of the contents were held in 1772 and 1824 and by 1828 the historian John Nichols wrote that Kirby was 'now dismantled and going fast to decay, the furniture, including a fine collection of pictures, statues, &c. having been sold'.

In recent times the house has been the subject of an extensive programme of work to return the Hall to its former glory. A major redecoration and conservation scheme has just been completed using extensive paint and wallpaper research and reinstatement of historic artefacts from the site.

Outside, the elaborate Great Garden with its 'cutwork' parterre is also undergoing restoration and is a fitting setting for this fine house.

▶ For further details about Kirby Hall, see page 396.

Gary Rogers Hamburg

CHATSWORTH

www.chatsworth.org

Map 5

Owner: Trustees of the
Chatsworth Settlement.
Home of the
Devonshire family

▶ CONTACT

Mr John Oliver
Chatsworth
Bakewell
Derbyshire   DE45 1PP

Tel: 01246 582204
01246 565300
Fax: 01246 583536

e-mail: visit@
chatsworth.org

▶ LOCATION

OS Ref. SK260 703

From London
3 hrs M1/J29,
signposted via
Chesterfield.

3m E of Bakewell,
off B6012,
10m W of Chesterfield.

Rail: Chesterfield
Station, 11m.

Bus: Chesterfield -
Baslow, 1¹/₂ m.

The great Treasure House of Chatsworth was first built by Bess of Hardwick in 1552 and has been lived in by the Cavendish family, the Dukes of Devonshire, ever since. The House today owes its appearance to the 1st Duke who remodelled the building at the end of the 17th century, while the 6th Duke added a wing 130 years later. Visitors can see 26 rooms including the run of 5 virtually unaltered 17th century State Rooms and Chapel. There are painted ceilings by Verrio, Thornhill and Laguerre, furniture by William Kent and Boulle, tapestries from Mortlake and Brussels, a library of over 17,000 volumes, sculpture by Cibber and Canova, old master paintings by Rembrandt, Hals, Van Dyck, Tintoretto, Veronese, Landseer and Sargent; the collection of neo-classical sculpture, Oriental and European porcelain and the dazzling silver collection, including an early English silver chandelier. The special 2005 exhibition in the house is a fascinating selection of photographs of eminent 20th century British artists by the photographer Jorge Lewinski, from the remarkable archive of his studio recently purchased for Chatsworth. Chatsworth was voted the nation's favourite stately home in 2003.

GARDEN

The 105 acre garden was created during three great eras in garden and landscape design. The 200 metre Cascade, the Willow Tree fountain and the Canal survive from the 1st Duke's formal garden. 'Capability' Brown landscaped the garden and park in the 1760s. The 6th Duke's gardener, Sir Joseph Paxton, built rockeries and designed a series of glasshouses. He also created the Emperor fountain, one of the tallest gravity-fed fountains in the world. More recent additions include the Rose, Cottage and Kitchen gardens, the Serpentine Hedge, the Maze, and a new Sensory garden.

Farmyard and Adventure Playground. Guide book translations and audio guides in French, German, Italian, Spanish and Japanese.

Wheelchairs in part of the house, and welcome in garden (3 electric, 7 standard available). WCs. Special leaflet.

Rooms available for conferences and private functions. Contact Head of Catering.

Restaurant (max 300); home-made food. Menus on request.

Private tours of house or Greenhouses and Behind the Scenes Days, by arrangement only (extra charges apply). Groups please pre-book.

Cars 100 yds, Coaches 25 yds from house.

Guided tours, packs, trails and school room. Free preliminary visit recommended.

▶ OPENING TIMES

16 March - 21 December.
Daily: 11am - 4.30pm.
The Park is open free
throughout the year.

▶ ADMISSION

House & Garden
Adult £9.50
Child £3.50
OAP/Student £7.50
Family £22.50
Pre-booked groups
Adult £8.00
OAP/Student £6.50
Garden only
Adult £5.75
Child £2.50
OAP/Student £4.25
Family £14.00
**House, Garden
& Scots Suite**
Adult £11.00
Child £4.00
OAP £9.00
Family £25.50
Groups
Adult £9.50
OAP £8.00

**Farmyard &
Adventure Playground**
All £4.25
Groups (5+).......... £3.70
OAP/School £3.00
Child under 3yrs ..... Free

Family ticket for all
attractions £38.00

Rates differ during
Christmas season
(5 Nov - 21 Dec).

▶ SPECIAL EVENTS
Tel for details.

CONFERENCE/FUNCTION	
ROOM	MAX CAPACITY
Hartington Rm.	70
Coffee Rm.	24

Map 5

Owner:
Lord Edward Manners

▶ CONTACT

Janet O'Sullivan
Estate Office
Haddon Hall
Bakewell
Derbyshire
DE45 1LA

Tel: 01629 812855
Fax: 01629 814379

e-mail: info@
haddonhall.co.uk

▶ LOCATION

OS Ref. SK234 663

From London 3 hrs
Sheffield ½ hr
Manchester 1 hr
Haddon is on the
E side of A6 1½ m
S of Bakewell.
M1/J30.

Rail: Chesterfield
Station, 12m.

Bus: Chesterfield
Bakewell.

HADDON HALL 🏛
www.haddonhall.co.uk

Haddon Hall sits on a rocky outcrop above the River Wye close to the market town of Bakewell, looking much as is would have done in Tudor times. There has been a dwelling here since the 11th century but the house we see today dates mainly from the late 14th century with major additions in the following 200 years and some alterations in the early 17th century including the creation of the Long Gallery.

William the Conqueror's illegitimate son Peverel, and his descendants, held Haddon for 100 years before it passed to the Vernon family. In the late 16th century the estate passed through marriage to the Manners family, in whose possession it has remained ever since.

When the Dukedom of Rutland was conferred on the Manners family in 1703 they moved to Belvoir Castle, and Haddon was left deserted for 200 years. This was Haddon's saving grace as the Hall thus escaped the major architectural changes of the 18th and 19th centuries ready for the great restoration at the beginning of the 20th century by the 9th Duke of Rutland. Henry VIII's elder brother Arthur, who was a frequent guest of the Vernons, would be quite familiar with the house as it stands today.

Haddon Hall is a popular location for film and television productions. Recent films include *Jane Eyre* and *Elizabeth*.

GARDENS

Magnificent terraced gardens with over 150 varieties of rose and clematis, many over 70 years old, provide colour and scent throughout the summer.

▶ OPENING TIMES

Summer
24 March - 30 September
Daily: 10.30am - 5pm
Last admission 4pm.

October: Thur - Sun
10.30am - 4.30pm
Last admission 3.30pm.

Winter
November - 23 March
Closed.

▶ ADMISSION

Summer
Adult £7.25
Child (5 -15yrs) £3.75
Conc £6.25
Family (2+3).......... £19.00

Groups (15+)
Adult £6.25
Child (5 -15yrs) £3.25
Conc £5.25

📷 ℹ️ Haddon Hall is ideal as a film location due to its authentic and genuine architecture requiring little alteration. Suitable locations are also available on the Estate.

♿ Unsuitable, steep approach, varying levels of house.

☕ 🍴 Self-service, licensed (max 75). Home-made food.

👤 Special tours £30 extra for groups of 15, 7 days' notice.

🅿 Ample, 450 yds from house. £1 per car.

🎭 Tours of the house bring alive Haddon Hall of old. Costume room also available, very popular!

🐕 Guide dogs only.   🎭 Tel for details.

East Midlands - England

PAVILION GARDENS

www.paviliongardens.co.uk

Map 5

Owner: High Peak
Borough Council

▶ CONTACT

Rachel Hoodith
Pavilion Gardens
St John's Road
Buxton
Derbyshire SK17 6XN

Tel: 01298 23114
Fax: 01298 27622

e-mail:
paviliongardens@
highpeak.gov.uk

▶ LOCATION

OS Ref. SK055 734

Situated on the A6 in
the Peak District,
within easy reach of
Manchester, Sheffield
and the East Midlands.

Rail: Buxton station
$^1/_2$ m.

PAVILION

With Grade II listed buildings dating from 1871
and 23 acres of beautiful Victorian landscaped
gardens in the centre of Buxton on the River Wye,
there are attractions to Suit all tastes and ages.

The Pavilion hosts a range of fairs and events
such as Antique, Book and Toy fairs to Classic Car
Auctions, Tea Dances and Farmers' Markets.

There are facilities for conferences, seminars and
meetings with a capacity to cater for up to
400 people with a full meal menu.

Visitors can also use the Restaurant, Café and
Coffee Lounge or browse in the Food and
Gift Shop, which specialises in locally
produced goods.

GARDENS

Over the last 125 years, various changes have been
made to the Gardens (they hosted the only Open
Tennis Championships in the UK outside
Wimbledon). The Gardens, originally designed by
the eminent landscape gardener Edward Milner,
have recently been restored to their original
Victorian splendour, following a £4.5 million
Heritage Lottery grant.

The bandstand is used on most summer Sundays,
with brass bands playing from 2 - 4pm, when
deckchairs are available on the terrace promenade.

There is also a colourful and relaxing Conservatory,
housing an extensive range of flowers and plants,
and which adjoins the renowned, Frank Matcham
designed, Buxton Opera House.

▶ OPENING TIMES

Every day except
Christmas Day.

Opens: 10am.

▶ ADMISSION

Free entry into building.

Charges vary for different
events and fairs.

ℹ Miniature train in gardens,
crazy golf, adventure play
areas.

🛍 Food & gift shops.

🍽 Wedding receptions,
banquets, functions &
conferences.

♿ Partial.

🍴 Licensed.

🅿 Charge applies

🐕 In gardens on leads.
Guide dogs only in Pavilion.

🔔

❄

🛡 Tel for details.

English Heritage Photo Library/Jonathan Bailey

BOLSOVER CASTLE ⚎

CASTLE STREET, BOLSOVER, DERBYSHIRE S44 6PR

www.english-heritage.org.uk/visits

Tel: 01246 822844

Owner: English Heritage

Contact: Visitor Operations Team

An enchanting and romantic spectacle, situated high on a wooded hilltop dominating the surrounding landscape. Built on the site of a Norman castle, this is largely an early 17th century mansion. Most delightful is the 'Little Castle', with intricate carvings, panelling and wall painting. See the restored interiors of the Little Castle including the only remaining copies of Titian's Caesar Paintings, and the Venus Fountain and statuary. There is also an impressive 17th century indoor Riding House built by the Duke of Newcastle. Enjoy the Visitor and Discovery Centre. Bolsover is now available for Civil weddings, receptions and corporate hospitality. Exciting new interpretation scheme includes Audio/Visual and scale model of

Little Castle. Also contemporary Visitor Centre with information about Bolsover town's development. Picnickers are welcome.

Location: OS120, SK471 707. Signposted from M1/J29, 6m from Mansfield. In Bolsover 6m E of Chesterfield on A632.

Open: 24 Mar - 30 Apr & 1 Sept - 31 Oct: Thur - Mon, 10am - 5pm. 1 May - 31 Aug: daily, 10am - 6pm. 1 Nov - 31 Mar 2006: Thur - Mon, 10am - 4pm. Closes 4pm on Sats. Closed 24 - 26 Dec & 1 Jan.

Admission: Adult £6.60, Child £3.30, Conc. £5, Family £16.50. 15% discount for groups (11+).

⬛ 🚽 ♿Grounds. WC. 🎦Airconditioned café. 🚫 🅾Free with admission. 🅿 ◼
❌ ▲ ❄ 🎗 Tel for details.

NT Photographic Library: Andreas von Einsiedel

NT Photographic Library: Rupert Truman

CALKE ABBEY ❧

TICKNALL, DERBYSHIRE DE73 1LE

www.nationaltrust.org.uk

Tel: 01332 863822   **Fax:** 01332 865272   **e-mail:** calkeabbey@nationaltrust.org.uk

Owner: The National Trust

Contact: The Property Manager

The house that time forgot, this baroque mansion, built 1701 - 3 for Sir John Harpur, is set in a landscaped park. Little restored, Calke is preserved by a programme of conservation as a graphic illustration of the English country house in decline; it contains the family's collection of natural history, a magnificent 18th century state bed and interiors that are virtually unchanged since the 1880s. Walled garden, pleasure grounds and orangery. Early 19th century Church. Historic parkland with Portland sheep and deer. Staunton Harold Church is nearby.

Location: OS128, SK356 239. 10m S of Derby, on A514 at Ticknall between

Swadlincote and Melbourne.

Open: House, Garden & Church: 26 Mar - 30 Oct: Sat - Wed; House: 1 - 5.30pm (ticket office opens 11am); Garden & Church: 11am - 5.30pm. Park: most days until 9pm or dusk. Closed 13 Aug for concert. Shop & Restaurant: 26 Mar - 30 Oct: as house, 10.30am - 5.30pm (shop) & 10.30am - 5pm (restaurant). 5 - 27 Nov & Jan - Mar 2006: Sat & Sun, 11am - 4pm; also 28 Nov - 18 Dec: Sat - Wed, 11am - 4pm.

Admission: All sites: Adult £6.30, Child £3.10, Family £15.70. Garden only: Adult £3.80, Child £1.90, Family £9.50. Discount for pre-booked groups.

⬛ ♿House. Braille guide. Wheelchairs. WCs. 🍴Licensed. 🚫By arrangement.
🐕In park, on leads only. ❄

MELBOURNE HALL & GARDENS 🏛

MELBOURNE, DERBYSHIRE DE73 1EN

www.melbournehall.com

Tel: 01332 862502 **Fax:** 01332 862263

Owner: Lord & Lady Ralph Kerr **Contact:** Mrs Gill Weston

This beautiful house of history, in its picturesque poolside setting, was once the home of Victorian Prime Minister William Lamb. The fine gardens, in the French formal style, contain Robert Bakewell's intricate wrought iron arbour and a fascinating yew tunnel. Upstairs rooms available to view by appointment.

Location: OS Ref. SK389 249. 8m S of Derby. From London, exit M1/J24.

Open: Hall: Aug only (not first 3 Mons) 2 - 5pm. Last admission 4.15pm. Gardens: 1 Apr - 30 Sept: Weds, Sats, Suns, BH Mons, 1.30 - 5.30pm.

Admission: Hall: Adult £3.50, Child £2, OAP £3. Gardens: Adult £3, Child/OAP £2. Hall & Gardens: Adult £5.50, Child £3.50, OAP £4.50.

ℹ Crafts. No photography in house. 🖾 🗼 Partial. 🖵 🎦 Obligatory. 🅿 Limited. No coach parking. 🖾 Guide dogs only.

Patrick Lane

RENISHAW HALL GARDENS 🏛

SHEFFIELD, DERBYSHIRE S31 3WB

www.sitwell.co.uk

Tel: 01246 432310 **Fax:** 01246 430760 **e-mail:** info2@renishaw-hall.co.uk

Owner: Sir Reresby Sitwell Bt DL **Contact:** The Administrator

Home of Sir Reresby and Lady Sitwell. Eight acres of Italian style formal gardens stand in 300 acres of mature parkland, encompassing statues, shaped yew hedges, herbaceous borders, a water garden and lakes. The Sitwell museum, art galleries (display of Fiori de Henriques sculptures and paintings by John Piper) are located in Georgian stables alongside craft workshops and Gallery café, furnished with contemporary art. Beautiful camellias and carpets of daffodils in April.

Location: OS Ref. SK435 786. On A6135 3m from M1/J30, equidistant from Sheffield and Chesterfield.

Open: 24 Mar - 2 Oct: Thurs - Sun & BHs, 10.30am - 4.30pm. Hall is not open to the general public, private groups (25+) only by prior arrangement.

Admission: Garden only: Adult £3.80, Conc. £3. Museum & Galleries: Adult £3.60, Conc. £2.80. Garden, Museum & Galleries: Adult £6.50, Conc. £5. Family (2+3) £21.

🖾 🎦 🥤 🖵 🖾 🎦 By arrangement. 🅿 In grounds, on leads. 🅰 🖾 Bluebell fortnight (28 Apr - 15 May).

PAVILION GARDENS
See page 304 for full page entry

PEVERIL CASTLE ⌗

Market Place, Castleton, Hope Valley S33 8WQ

Tel: 01433 620613 www.english-heritage.org.uk/visits

Owner: English Heritage **Contact:** Visitor Operations Team

There are breathtaking views of the Peak District from this castle, perched high above the pretty village of Castleton. The great square tower of Henry II stands almost to its original height. Formerly known as Peak Castle. Walkway opens up new areas and views from the first floor of the Keep. Peveril Castle is one of the earliest Norman castles to be built in England. Picknickers are welcome.

Location: OS110, SK150 827. S side of Castleton, 15m W of Sheffield on A6187.

Open: 24 Mar - 31 Oct: daily, 10am - 5pm (6pm May - Aug). 1 Nov - 31 Mar: Thur - Mon, 10am - 4pm. Closed 24 - 26 Dec & 1 Jan.

Admission: Adult £3, Child £1.50, Conc. £2.30, Family £7.50. 15% discount for groups (11+).

🖾 🖵 🖾 ❊ 🖾 Tel for details.

SUDBURY HALL ⚘

Ashbourne, Derbyshire DE6 5HT

Tel: 01283 585337 **Fax:** 01283 585139 **e-mail:** sudburyhall@nationaltrust.org.uk

Owner: The National Trust **Contact:** The Property Manager

Late 17th century house with sumptuous interiors. The decoration includes wood carving by Grinling Gibbons, and painted murals and ceilings by Louis Laguerre.

Location: OS Ref. SK160 323. 6m E of Uttoxeter.

Open: 6 Mar - 30 Oct: Wed - Sun & BH Mons & Good Fri. Hall: 1 - 5pm. Grounds: 11am - 6pm. Tearoom: 11.30am - 5pm. Shop: 12.30 - 5pm.

Admission: Adult £5, Child £2, Family (2+3) £11.50. Groups (15+): Adult £4.25, Child £1.50.

🖾 🗼 Limited, braille guide. WC. 🖵 Licensed. 🅿 Car park only. 🅰

SUTTON SCARSDALE HALL ⌗

Chesterfield, Derbyshire

Tel: 01604 735400 (Regional Office) www.english-heritage.org.uk/visits

Owner: English Heritage **Contact:** The East Midlands Regional Office

The dramatic hilltop shell of a great early 18th century baroque mansion.

Location: OS Ref. SK441 690. Between Chesterfield & Bolsover, 1½ m S of Arkwright Town.

Open: Daily in summer: 10am - 6pm (4pm rest of year). Closed 24 - 26 Dec & 1 Jan.

Admission: Free.

🗼 🅿

❊ Open All Year Index see page 43

TISSINGTON HALL 🏠
ASHBOURNE, DERBYSHIRE DE6 1RA
www.tissington-hall.com

Tel: 01335 352200   **Fax:** 01335 352201   **e-mail:** tisshall@dircon.co.uk

Owner/Contact: Sir Richard FitzHerbert Bt

Home of the FitzHerbert family for over 500 years. The Hall stands in a superbly maintained estate village, and contains wonderful panelling and fine old masters. A 10 acre garden and arboretum. Schools very welcome. Award-winning Old Coach House Tearoom, open Apr - Oct: daily; Nov - Mar, Thurs - Sun, 11am - 5pm for coffees, lunch and tea.

Location: OS Ref. SK175 524. 4m N of Ashbourne off A515 towards Buxton.

Open: 28 Mar - 1 Apr, 30 May - 3 Jun: Daily. 19 Jul - 26 Aug: Tue - Fri, & 29/30 Aug.

First tour 1.30pm - last tour 4pm. Groups and societies welcome by appointment throughout the year. Corporate days, weddings and events also available, contact: The Estate Office on 01335 352200. Well-Dressings: 5 - 11 May. Six wells dressed in the village.

Admission: Hall & Gardens: Adult £5.50, Child (10-16yrs) £2.50, Conc. £4.50, Gardens only: Adult £2, Child £1.

No photography in house. Partial. WCs at tearooms. Tearoom adjacent to Hall. Obligatory. Limited. Guide dogs only. Tel for details.

WINGFIELD MANOR ⚏
Garner Lane, South Wingfield, Derbyshire DE5 7NH
Tel: 01773 832060

Owner: Mr S Critchlow (managed by English Heritage)   **Contact:** Visitor Operations Team

Huge, ruined, country mansion built in the mid-15th century. Mary Queen of Scots was imprisoned here in 1569, 1584 and 1585.

Location: OS Ref. SK374 548. S side of B5035, ½ m S of South Wingfield village. Access by 600yd drive (no vehicles). From M1 J28, W on A38, A615 (Matlock road) at Alfreton and turn onto B5035 after 1½ m.

Open: 24 Mar - 30 Oct: Thur - Mon, 10am - 5pm. 1 Nov - 31 Mar: Sat - Sun, 10am - 4pm. Closed 24 - 26 Dec & 1 Jan. The Manor incorporates a working farm. Visitors are requested to respect the privacy of the owners, to keep to visitor routes and refrain from visiting outside official opening times.

Admission: Adult £3.30, Child £1.70, Conc. £2.50.

LOCAL FOOD

Bakewell Pudding

A buttery mixture, flavoured with ground almonds and baked in a light flaky pastry case, is the basis of this traditional Derbyshire recipe. Local legend has it that it was eaten as far back as the 1500s at Haddon Hall but the truth is that it actually appeared some 300 years later. The Bakewell Pudding was first created in 1859 at the coaching inn that is now called the Rutland Arms. The story goes that the cook made a mistake whilst cooking two separate dishes, jam tarts and an almond cake. She poured the ingredients of the second dish into the pastry case of the first. Rather than throw this away, she baked it, the customers liked it, and the rest is history. Sadly this tale is almost certainly apocryphal and today there are three bakeries in the town all laying claim to holding the secret recipe!

Eyam Hall.

East Midlands - England

AUBOURN HALL

Lincoln LN5 9DZ

Tel: 01522 788717 **Fax:** 01522 788199 **e-mail:** cnevile@ukonline.co.uk

Owner/Contact: Christopher Nevile

Late 16th century house with important staircase and panelled rooms. Garden.

Location: OS Ref. SK928 628. 6m SW of Lincoln. 2m SE of A46.

Open: House not open on a regular basis. Garden: Occasional Suns for charity or by arrangement.

Admission: Please contact property for details.

AYSCOUGHFEE HALL MUSEUM & GARDENS

Churchgate, Spalding, Lincolnshire PE11 2RA

Tel: 01775 725468 **Fax:** 01775 762715 **e-mail:** museum@sholland.gov.uk

Owner: South Holland District Council   **Contact:** Museum Manager

A late-medieval wool merchant's house surrounded by five acres of walled gardens.

Location: OS Ref. TF240 230. E bank of the River Welland, 5 mins walk from Spalding town centre.

Open: Reopens to the public from Easter 2005.

BURGHLEY HOUSE 🏛

See page 314 for full page entry

Corporate Hospitality see page 35

BELTON HOUSE ❧

GRANTHAM, LINCOLNSHIRE NG32 2LS

www.nationaltrust.org.uk

Tel: 01476 566116 **Fax:** 01476 579071 **e-mail:** belton@nationaltrust.org.uk

Owner: The National Trust   **Contact:** The Property Manager

Belton, considered by many to be the perfect English Country House, with stunning interiors, fine silver and furniture collections and the remnants of a collection of Old Masters. There are also huge garden scenes by Melchior d'Hondecoeter acquired by the last Earl. The 17th century saloon in the centre of the house is panelled and decorated with intricate limewood carvings of the Grinling Gibbons school. The virtually unaltered north-facing chapel has a baroque plaster ceiling by Edward Gouge. Built in 1685 - 88, Belton offers you a great day out whether you are looking for peace and tranquillity or lots to do. With magnificent formal gardens, Orangery, landscaped park with lakeside walk, woodland adventure playground and

Bellmount Tower. Fine church with family monuments. Winners of "Excellence in Tourism" and Sandford Heritage Education awards 2002.

Location: OS Ref. SK929 395. 3m NE of Grantham on A607. Signed off the A1.

Open: House: 23 Mar - 30 Oct: Wed - Sun (open BH Mons & Good Fri), 12.30 - 5pm. Garden & Park: as house, 11am - 5.30pm (Aug: 10.30am - 5.30pm). Garden only: 5 Nov - 18 Dec: Sat & Sun, 12 noon - 4pm. Park only: on foot from Lion Lodge gates. Shop & Restaurant: 23 Mar - 30 Oct: 11am - 5.15pm. 4 Nov - 18 Dec: Sat & Sun, 12 noon - 4pm.

Admission: Adult £6.80, Child £3.40, Family £16. Discount for groups.

🖾 🕭 Partial. Please telephone for arrangements. 🍴 Licensed. 🅿 📷 🔺

DODDINGTON HALL 🏛

LINCOLN LN6 4RU

www.doddingtonhall.com

Tel: 01522 694308   **Fax:** 01522 682584   **e-mail:** info@doddingtonhall.com

Owner: Mr & Mrs A G Jarvis   **Contact:** The Estate Office

Magnificent Smythson mansion which stands today as it was completed in 1600 with its walled gardens and gatehouse. The Hall is still very much the home of the Jarvis family and has an elegant Georgian interior with a fine collection of porcelain, paintings and textiles, representing 400 years of unbroken family occupation. The five acres of beautiful gardens contain a superb layout of box-edged parterres, sumptuous borders that provide colour in all seasons, and a wild garden with a marvellous succession of spring bulbs and flowering shrubs set amongst mature trees. Private group visits and specialist tours welcomed. Choice of refreshments and meals available in charming restaurant. Please call the Estate Office to discuss your requirements. Sandford Award winning schools project and a nature trail into the nearby countryside. Innovative schools programme. Civil weddings and receptions at Doddington Hall and in The Littlehouse next door.

Location: OS Ref. SK900 710. 5m W of Lincoln on the B1190, signposted off the A46 bypass and A57.

Open: Gardens only: 20 Feb - 28 Sept: Suns & Easter Mon, 2 - 6pm. House & Gardens: 1 May - 28 Sept: Weds, Suns & BH Mons, 2 - 6pm.

Admission: House & Gardens: Adult £5.30, Child £2.65, Family (2 adults & 2 - 4 children of 4 - 14yrs/1 OAP) £14.80. Gardens only: Adult £3.65, Child £1.80. Pre-booked Groups (20+) on open days: Adult £4.80. Special groups (20+) at other times by appointment only £6.80. RHS members free Feb - June.

ⓘ No photography in Hall. No stilettos. 🔲 🍽 🔲 Gardens & ground floor. WC (please call for assistance). 🔲 🍴 ⓕ By prior arrangement. 🅿 🔲 🐕 Guide dogs only. 🔲 🔲 Tel for details.

EASTON WALLED GARDENS

The Garden Office, Easton, Grantham, Lincolnshire NG33 5AP

Tel: 01476 530063   **Fax:** 01476 550116   **e-mail:** info@eastonwalledgardens.co.uk   **www.**eastonwalledgardens.co.uk

Owner: Sir Fred & Lady Cholmeley   **Contact:** Jude Hudson

12 acres of forgotten gardens. Owned by the family since 1500s. Three years ago Lady Cholmeley undertook to revive the gardens. Formal terraces have been cleared, enormous borders reinstated and vistas opened up. A garden for the 21st century emerges. Fantastic snowdrops. Beautiful cut flower garden in summer.

Location: OS Ref. SK938 274. 1m from A1 (between Stamford and Grantham) N of the Colsterworth roundabout. Right onto B6403 and follow signs.

Open: 12 - 20 Feb for snowdrops, 11am - 3pm. 27/28 Mar, 11am - 4pm. Apr - Sept: BH Mons, Weds & Suns, 11am - 4pm.

Admission: Adult £3.50, Child Free.

🔲 🍽 🔲 🔲 Partial. WCs. 🔲 ⓕ By arrangement. 🅿 Ample. 🔲 🐕 Guide dogs only. 🔲

FULBECK MANOR

Fulbeck, Grantham, Lincolnshire NG32 3JN

Tel: 01400 272231   **Fax:** 01400 273545   **e-mail:** fane@fulbeck.co.uk

Owner/Contact: Mr Julian Francis Fane

Built c1580. 400 years of Fane family portraits. Open by written appointment. Guided tours by owner approximately 1¼ hours. Tearooms at Craft Centre, 100 yards, for light lunches and teas.

Location: OS Ref. SK947 505. 11m N of Grantham. 15m S of Lincoln on A607. Brown signs to Craft Centre & Tearooms and Stables.

Open: By written appointment.

Admission: Adult £5. Groups (10+) £4.

ⓘ No photography. 🔲 Unsuitable. WCs. 🔲 🍴 ⓕ Obligatory. 🅿 Ample. Limited for coaches. 🐕 Guide dogs only. 🔲 € .

GAINSBOROUGH OLD HALL ♯

Parnell Street, Gainsborough, Lincolnshire DN21 2NB

Tel: 01427 612669   **www.**english-heritage.org.uk/visits

Owner: English Heritage   **Contact:** Visitor Operations Team

A large medieval house with a magnificent Great Hall and suites of rooms. A collection of historic furniture and a re-created medieval kitchen are on display.

Location: OS121, SK815 895. In centre of Gainsborough, opposite library.

Open: 24 - 26 Mar & 1 Nov - 31 Mar: Mon - Sat, 10am - 5pm. 27 Mar - 31 Oct: Suns, 1 - 4.30pm, Mon - Sat, 10am - 5pm. Closed 24 - 26 & 31 Dec/1 Jan.

Admission: Adult £3.25, Child (5-15yrs) £2.40 (0-5yrs Free), Conc. £2.50, Family £8.80.

ⓘ WC. 🔲 🔲 🔲 🔲

GRIMSTHORPE CASTLE, 🏛   *See page 315 for full page entry*
PARK & GARDENS

GUNBY HALL 🔷

Gunby, Spilsby, Lincolnshire PE23 5SS

Tel: 01909 486411   **Fax:** 01909 486377   **www.**nationaltrust.org.uk

Owner: The National Trust   **Contact:** Regional Office

A red brick house with stone dressings, built in 1700 and extended in 1870s. Within the house, there is good early 18th century wainscoting and a fine oak staircase, also English furniture and portraits by Reynolds. Also of interest is the contemporary stable block, a walled kitchen and flower garden, sweeping lawns and borders and an exhibition of Field Marshal Sir Archibald Montgomery-Massingberd's memorabilia. Gunby was reputedly Tennyson's 'haunt of ancient peace'.

Location: OS122, TF466 672. 2½ m NW of Burgh Le Marsh, 7m W of Skegness. On S side of A158 (access off roundabout).

Open: Ground floor of house & garden: 30 Mar - 28 Sept: Weds, 2 - 6pm. Last admission 5.30pm. Closed BHs. Garden also open Thurs, 2 - 6pm. House & garden also open Tues, Thurs & Fris by written appointment to J D Wrisdale at above address.

Admission: House & Garden: Adult £4.20, Child £2.10, Family £10.50. Garden only: Adult £3, Child £1.50, Family £7.50. No reduction for groups. Access roads unsuitable for coaches which must park in layby at gates ½ m from Hall.

🔲 Grounds. 🐕 In grounds, on leads.

NTPL/ Andrew Butler

78 DERNGATE

82 DERNGATE, NORTHAMPTON NN1 1UH

www.78 derngate.org.uk

Tel: 01604 603407 **Fax:** 01604 603408
e-mail: info@78derngate.org.uk

Owner: 78 Derngate Northampton Trust **Contact:** Sylvia Pinches

Charles Rennie Mackintosh transformed a typical terraced house into a startlingly modern home. It was his last major commission and his only work in England. The house is a testament to a partnership of designer and patron, combining striking interiors with practical solutions to living in a small terrace house.

Location: OS Ref. SP759 603. In the heart of Northampton close to the rear of the Derngate Theatre. Follow Derngate road out of the centre of town

Open: 23 Mar - Nov: Wed - Sun & BH Mons: 10.30am - 5pm. Strictly pre-booked tours only.

Admission: Adult £5.50, Conc. £4. Family (2+2): £13.50.

ⓘNo indoor photography. 🖼 ♿Partial. 🎥Obligatory. 🅿None. ▣
♿Guide dogs only.

CANONS ASHBY 🌿

CANONS ASHBY, DAVENTRY, NORTHAMPTONSHIRE NN11 3SD

www.nationaltrust.org.uk

Tel: 01327 861900 **Fax:** 01327 861909 **e-mail:** canonsashby@nationaltrust.org.uk

Owner: The National Trust **Contact:** The Property Manager

Home of the Dryden family since the 16th century, this Elizabethan manor house was built c1550, added to in the 1590s, and altered in the 1630s and c1710; largely unaltered since. Within the house, Elizabethan wall paintings and outstanding Jacobean plasterwork are of particular interest. A formal garden includes terraces, walls and gate piers of 1710. There is also a medieval priory church and a 70 acre park.

Location: OS Ref. SP577 506. Access from M40/J11, or M1/J16. Signposted from A5 2m S of Weedon crossroads. Then 7m to SW.

Open: 23 Mar - 2 Nov: Sat - Wed. House, Park & Church: 1 - 5.30pm (Oct: 1 - 4.30pm). Gardens: 11am - 5.30pm (Oct: 11am - 4.30pm). Shop & Tearoom: 12 noon - 5pm (Oct: 12 noon - 4.30pm). Gardens, Shop, Tearoom, Park & Church: 5 Nov - 18 Dec: Sats & Suns, 12 noon - 4pm.

Admission: Adult £5.80, Child £2.90, Family £14.50. Garden only: £2. Discount for booked groups, contact Property Manager.

🖼 ♿Some steps. WC. ▣ ♿In Home Paddock, on leads.

ALTHORP *See page 320 for full page entry.*

See page 320 for full page entry.

BOUGHTON HOUSE 🏛 *See page 321 for full page entry.*

See page 321 for full page entry.

Rockingham Castle.

COTON MANOR GARDEN

GUILSBOROUGH, NORTHAMPTONSHIRE NN6 8RQ

www.cotonmanor.co.uk

Tel: 01604 740219 **Fax:** 01604 740838
e-mail: pasleytyler@cotonmanor.fsnet.co.uk

Owner: Ian & Susie Pasley-Tyler **Contact:** Sarah Ball

Traditional English garden laid out on different levels surrounding a 17th century stone manor house. Many herbaceous borders, with extensive range of plants, old yew and holly hedges, rose garden, water garden and fine lawns set in 10 acres. Also wild flower meadow and bluebell wood.

Location: OS Ref. SP675 716. 9m NW of Northampton, between A5199 (formerly A50) and A428.

Open: 25 Mar - 1 Oct: Tue - Sat & BH weekends; also Suns Apr - May: 12 noon - 5.30pm.

Admission: Adult £4.50, Child £2, Conc. £4. Groups: £4.

🖼 🚻 ♿Grounds. WC. 🍴 ▣ 🎥By arrangement. 🅿 ♿

COTTESBROOKE HALL & GARDENS 🏛

COTTESBROOKE, NORTHAMPTONSHIRE NN6 8PF

www.cottesbrookehall.co.uk

Tel: 01604 505808 **Fax:** 01604 505619 **e-mail:** hall@cottesbrooke.co.uk

Owner: Mr & Mrs A R Macdonald-Buchanan   **Contact:** The Administrator

This magnificent Queen Anne house dating from 1702 is set in delightful rural Northamptonshire. Reputed to be the pattern for Jane Austen's *Mansfield Park*, the Hall's beauty is matched by the magnificence of the gardens and views and by the excellence of the picture, furniture and porcelain collections it houses. The Woolavington collection of sporting pictures at Cottesbrooke is possibly one of the finest of its type in Europe and includes paintings by Stubbs, Ben Marshall and many other artists renowned for works of this genre, from the mid 18th century to the present day. Portraits, bronzes, 18th century English and French furniture and fine porcelain are also among the treasures of Cottesbrooke Hall.

In the formal gardens huge 300-year-old cedars set off magnificent double herbaceous borders, pools and lily-ponds. In midsummer, visitors enjoy the splendid array of planters, a sight not to be missed. The Wild Garden is a short walk across the Park and is planted along the course of a stream with its small cascades and arched bridges.

Winner of the *HHA/Christie's Garden of the Year* award in 2000.

Location: OS Ref. SP711 739. 10m N of Northampton near Creaton on A5199 (formerly A50). Signed from J1 on A14.

Open: May - Sept. May & Jun: Wed & Thur, 2 - 5.30pm. Jul - Sept: Thur, 2 - 5.30pm. Open BH Mons (May - Sept), 2 - 5.30pm.

Admission: House & Gardens: Adult £6. Gardens only: Adult £4, Child half price. RHS members Free access to gardens. Private groups welcome by prior arrangement.

ℹ️ No photography in house. Filming & outside events. 🌿 Unusual plants. ⊤ ♿ Gardens. WC. Parking. 🍰 Home-made cakes. 👤 Hall guided tours obligatory. 🅿 🐕

DEENE PARK 🏛   *See page 322 for full page entry.*

EDGCOTE HOUSE

Edgcote, Banbury, Oxfordshire OX17 1AG

Owner/Contact: Christopher Courage

Early Georgian house with good rococo plasterwork.

Location: OS Ref. SP505 480. 6m NE of Banbury off A361.

Open: By written appointment only.

ELEANOR CROSS ⚏

Geddington, Kettering, Northamptonshire

Tel: 01604 735400 (Regional Office) **www.**english-heritage.org.uk/visits

Owner: English Heritage   **Contact:** The East Midlands Regional Office

One of a series of famous crosses, of elegant sculpted design, erected by Edward I to mark the resting places of the body of his wife, Eleanor, when brought for burial from Harby in Nottinghamshire to Westminster Abbey in 1290. Picnickers are welcome.

Location: OS Ref. SP896 830. In Geddington, off A43 between Kettering and Corby.

Open: Any reasonable time.

🐕 ❄️

HADDONSTONE SHOW GARDENS

The Forge House, East Haddon, Northampton NN6 8DB

Tel: 01604 770711 **Fax:** 01604 770027

e-mail: info@haddonstone.co.uk **www.**haddonstone.co.uk

Owner: Haddonstone Ltd   **Contact:** Marketing Director

See Haddonstone's classic garden ornaments in the beautiful setting of the walled manor gardens – including urns, troughs, fountains, statuary, bird baths, sundials and balustrading. The garden is on different levels with shrub roses, conifers, clematis and climbers. The Jubilee garden features a pavilion, temple and Gothic grotto. An Orangery was opened in 2002.

Location: OS Ref. SP667 682. 7m NW of Northampton off A428. Signposted.

Open: Mon - Fri, 9am - 5.30pm. Closed weekends, BHs & Christmas period.

Admission: Free. Groups by appointment only. Not suitable for coach groups.

📷 ♿ 👤 By arrangement. 🅿 Limited. 🐕 Guide dogs only.

HOLDENBY HOUSE GARDENS 🏛 & FALCONRY CENTRE

HOLDENBY, NORTHAMPTONSHIRE NN6 8DJ

www.holdenby.com

Tel: 01604 770074 **Fax:** 01604 770962 **e-mail:** enquiries@holdenby.com

Owner: James Lowther Esq   **Contact:** The Commercial Manager

Just across the fields from Althorp stands Holdenby, a house whose regal history is now complemented by an equally regal collection of birds of prey. Built by Sir Christopher Hatton as the largest house in England in order to entertain Elizabeth I, Holdenby subsequently became the palace and then the prison of Charles I. Now you can see the beautiful gardens, restored with the help of Rosemary Verey and Rupert Golby, and watch magnificent flying displays of birds from our Falconry Centre. Holdenby also welcomes corporate and wedding clients.

Location: OS Ref. SP693 681. M1/J15a. 7m NW of Northampton off A428 & A5199.

Open: Garden & Falconry: Easter - end Sept: Suns, BH Mons, 1 - 5pm. House: 28 March & 30 May only and by appointment. Victorian Easter: 27/28 March. Plant Fair: 29/30 May.

Admission: Garden & Falconry: Adult £4.50 Child (3-15yrs) £3, OAP £4, Family (2+2) £12. Different tariffs apply for special events.

ℹ️ Children's play area. 📷 🌿 ⊤ ♿ Partial. WC. 🍰 Home-made teas. Groups must book. 👤 By arrangement. 🅿 🏅 Sandford Award-winner. 🐕 In grounds, on leads. ⌂ 🛏 Tel for details.

west midlands

The counties of the West Midlands are among some of Britain's best kept secrets. Shakespeare's birthplace of Stratford-upon-Avon justly receives thousands of visitors each year, but travel further west too, into the gloriously unspoilt counties of Herefordshire and Worcestershire. The Wye Valley remains a haven of green fields, cider orchards and a meandering river. Both county towns have beautiful cathedrals which annually host world-famous musical events. Surrounded by the Malvern Hills, the fairytale Eastnor Castle (Herefordshire) has something to interest all visitors, whilst Warwick Castle (Warwickshire) provides exciting living history to entertain all ages within its medieval walls. A new project at the Ryton Organic Gardens (Warwickshire) is their Vegetable Kingdom! The UK's national centre for organic gardening has a new, £2 million fully interactive visitor centre telling the story of Britain's vegetables. A thriving network of canals means you can explore this beautiful part of Britain at a more leisurely pace – boats are readily available for hire – allowing you to get deep into the countryside to places inaccessible by road.

The Avon Canal, Warwickshire. ©Adrian Baggett 2004

Ironbridge Gorge Museums.

Hergest Croft Gardens, Herefordshire. From the book Historic Family Homes and Gardens from the Air.

Hatton, Warwickshire.

herefordshire

shropshire

staffordshire

warwickshire

west midlands

worcestershire

ragley hall

modern sculpture | baroque plasterwork

ragley hall

w e s t m i d l a n d s

Ragley Hall, with its sensational interiors and majestic Great Hall, is a late 17th century marvel designed by Robert Hooke with thrilling later additions and architectural flourishes by Gibbs and Wyatt.

Here in the Warwickshire countryside is enduring family and architectural history: Sir John Conway of Conway Castle purchased Ragley in 1591; and the family found royal favour decades later when King Charles II created his great grandson Earl of Conway. In August 1679, when he was Charles' Secretary of State, Lord Conway invited Robert Hooke, friend of Christopher Wren, scientist and member of the Royal Society, to design the Hall. The result was a grand house befitting Lord Conway's status. Hooke, with his scientific mind and knowledge of French architecture, had designed a symmetrical two-storey central hall with the apartments arranged around it forming an H-plan.

To this formidable structure, much has been added. When Francis, 2nd Lord Conway, inherited Ragley in 1732 it was no more than a 'noble shell'. James Gibbs was summoned to Ragley with instructions to complete the unfinished house and it was during this period that the Great Hall was created – adorned with some of England's finest and most exquisite baroque plasterwork. The stunning combination of Gibbs, responsible for this architectural tour de force, and the Italian Artari brothers, creators of the electrifying plasterwork in the principal rooms, is staggering. Ragley Hall is full of colour and movement with its rolling rococo decorations of swags and flowers; and the brightly painted walls of many of the rooms.

Further rococo decoration was added in the mid-18th century, possibly by Vassali. Later in the 18th century, in 1780, Wyatt embellished the façade of the Hall with an august portico and elegant stairs.

It was here, at Ragley, that the Prince Regent stayed in 1796 and visitors can still see his bedroom at the Hall, complete with the bed made especially for the occasion. Although the Prince of Wales was a close friend of Francis Ingram, 2nd Marquess, his devotion to the Marchioness was one of the many scandals connected with the Prince.

Ragley is home to spectacular collections of 18th century and earlier paintings, china and furniture, built up by generations of the Hertford family. There are also spectacular ceilings decorated with Grisaille panels and insets by Angelica Kauffman.

Not to be missed at Ragley is the breathtaking mural and ceiling decoration 'The Temptation of Christ' by Graham Rust painted between 1969 and 1983. The Hertford family is portrayed gazing down upon spectacular imaginary landscapes alive with exotic birds and animals.

Outside, in the picturesque 'Capability' Brown landscape, Ragley is a working estate with an enchanting rose garden, richly planted borders and mature woodland.

The Jerwood Sculpture Park has recently been opened and includes works by Frink, Armitage, Chadwick and Gormley.

▶ For further details about Ragley Hall, see page 359.

All images © Bryan McDonald

ABBEY DORE COURT GARDEN
Abbey Dore, Herefordshire HR2 0AD
Tel/Fax: 01981 240419
Owner/Contact: Mrs C L Ward
6 acres of new and established garden with a wild river walk leading to a meadow planted with a variety of interesting trees.
Location: OS Ref. SO387 309. 3 m W of A465 midway Hereford - Abergavenny.
Open: Apr - Sept: Sat, Sun, Tue, Thur & BH Mons, 11am - 5.30pm. Other times by appointment.
Admission: Adult £3.50, Child 50p.

BERRINGTON HALL ✕

See page 338 for full page entry.

BROCKHAMPTON ESTATE ✕
Bringsty, Worcestershire WR6 5UH
Tel: 01885 488099/482077   **www.**nationaltrust.org.uk/brockhampton
Owner: The National Trust   **Contact:** The Property Manager
Wood and parkland estate with waymarked walks including Lower Brockhampton, a 14th century moated manor house with timber framed gatehouse.
Location: OS Ref. SO682 546. 2m E of Bromyard on A44.
Open: Lower Brockhampton: 5 - 20 Mar: Sats & Suns, 12 noon - 4pm; 23 Mar - 2 Oct: Wed - Sun, 12 noon - 5pm; 5 - 30 Oct: Wed - Sun, 12 noon - 4pm. Open BH Mons & Good Fri, 12 noon - 5pm. Woodland walks: All year: daily during daylight hours.
Admission: Lower Brockhampton: Adult £3.60, Child £1.80, Family £8.50. Groups (15+) £3. Estate Car Park: £2.
🅿 Partial. ⬛ 🚻 Dogs in woodland walks, on leads. ✳

CROFT CASTLE ✕
Leominster, Herefordshire HR6 9PW
Tel: 01568 780246   **e-mail:** croft@nationaltrust.org.uk   **www.**nationaltrust.org.uk
Owner: The National Trust   **Contact:** The House Manager
Home of the Croft family since Domesday. Walls and corner towers date from 14th and 15th centuries, interior mainly 18th century.
Location: OS Ref. SO455 655. 5m NW of Leominster, 9m SW of Ludlow, approach from B4362.
Open: House: 6 - 28 Mar & 2 - 31 Oct: Sat & Sun; Apr - Sept: Wed - Sun & BH Mons, 1 - 5pm. Garden: 6 - 28 Mar & 2 - 31 Oct: Sat, Sun & BH Mons, 11.30am - 5pm; Apr - Sept: Wed - Fri, 12 noon - 5pm. Park: All year. Tea Room: As House, 11am - 5pm.
Admission: House & Garden: Adult £4.40, Child £2.20, Family £11, Group (15+) £4. Garden only: Adult £3.10, Child £1.50. (2004 prices.)
🚻 🅿 ✳

CWMMAU FARMHOUSE ✕
Brilley, Whitney-on-Wye, Herefordshire HR3 6JP
Tel: 01981 590509
Owner: The National Trust   **Contact:** The Property Manager
A wonderful timber-framed and stone tiled traditional Welsh farmhouse restored from dereliction. There is an informal atmosphere with free guided tours by volunteers and access to all parts of the house.
Location: OS Ref. SO267 514. SW of Kington between A4111 and A438.
Open: 25 - 28 Mar, 28 - 30 May & 27 - 29 Aug: 2 - 5pm. Remainder of year available as holiday cottage.
Admission: Adult £3.20, Child £1.60, Family £7.
ℹ Picnics in garden. 🅿 Ground floor. ⬛ 🍴 🅿 Not suitable for coaches. 🚻 On leads, only in grounds. 🚻 ✳

EASTNOR CASTLE 🏰

See page 339 for full page entry.

GOODRICH CASTLE ⌗
ROSS-ON-WYE, HEREFORDSHIRE HR9 6HY
www.english-heritage.org.uk/visits
Tel: 01600 890538
Owner: English Heritage   **Contact:** Visitor Operations Team
This magnificent red sandstone castle is remarkably complete with a 12th century keep and extensive remains from 13th & 14th centuries. From the battlements there are fine views over the Wye Valley to Symonds Yat. Marvel at the maze of small rooms and the 'murder holes'.
Location: OS162 Ref. SO577 200. 5m S of Ross-on-Wye, off A40.
Open: 24 Mar - 31 Oct: daily, 10am - 5pm (6pm Jun - Aug). 1 Nov - 28 Feb: Thur - Mon, 10am - 4pm. Closed 24 - 26 Dec & 1 Jan.
Admission: Adult £4.30, Child £2.20, Conc. £3.20, Family £10.80. 15% discount for groups (11+).
ℹ WC. ▢ ▢ 🅿 🚻 ✳ 🍽 Tel for details.

Eastnor Castle.

LOCAL FOOD

Beef

The Herefordshire breed of beef, is the backbone of the British beef trade. Easy to recognise by its large white face and chestnut body, over the years this cow has been crossed with Continental breeds to produce leaner meat. There is however now strong support from traditionalists who favour a pure beef herd and who appreciate the flavour that the marbled Herefordshire meat produces.

HELLENS

MUCH MARCLE, LEDBURY, HEREFORDSHIRE HR8 2LY

Tel: 01531 660504   **Fax:** 01531 660501

Owner: Pennington-Mellor-Munthe Charity Trust   **Contact:** The Administrator

Built as a monastery and then a stone fortress in 1292 by Mortimer, Earl of March, with Tudor, Jacobean and Stuart additions and lived in ever since by descendants of the original builder. Visited by the Black Prince, Bloody Mary and the 'family ghost'. Family paintings, relics and heirlooms from the Civil War and possessions of the Audleys, Walwyns and Whartons as well as Anne Boleyn. Also beautiful 17th century woodwork carved by the 'King's Carpenter', John Abel. All those historical stories incorporated into guided tours, revealing the loves and lives of those who lived and died here. Goods and chattels virtually unchanged.

Location: OS Ref. SO661 332. Off A449 at Much Marcle. Ledbury 4m, Ross-on-Wye 4m.

Open: Easter Sun - 3 October: Wed, Thur, Sun & BH Mons. Guided tours only at 2pm, 3pm & 4pm. Other times by arrangement with the Administrator throughout the year.

Admission: Adult £5, Child £2.50, OAP £4, Family ticket £10.

ℹ️No photography inside house. ▣ ♿Partial. 🅣Obligatory. ▣ 🅿️ 🐕In grounds, on leads. 📧Tel for details.

HEREFORD CATHEDRAL

MAPPA MUNDI AND CHAINED LIBRARY EXHIBITION.

Hereford HR1 2NG **www:** herfordcathedral.co.uk

Tel: 01432 374202   **Fax:** 01432 374220   **e-mail:** visits@herefordcathedral.co.uk

Contact: Mrs C Quinto - The Visits Manager

Location: OS Ref. SO510 398. Hereford city centre on A49.

Open: Cathedral: Daily, 9.15am - Evensong. Exhibition: Easter - Oct: Mon - Sat, 10am - 4.15pm, Sun, 11am - 3.15pm; Nov - Easter: Mon - Sat, 11am - 3.15pm.

Admission: Admission only for Mappa Mundi and Chained Library Exhibition: Adult £4.50, OAP/Student/Unemployed £3.50, Child under 5yrs Free. Family (2+3) £10.

🅿️ 🅣 ♿ ▣ 🍴 🅣 ▣ ✳️ 📧Tel for details.

HERGEST COURT

c/o Hergest Estate Office, Kington HR5 3EG

Tel: 01544 230160   **Fax:** 01544 232031   **e-mail:** gardens@hergest.co.uk

Owner/Contact: W L Banks

The ancient home of the Vaughans of Hergest, dating from the 13th century.

Location: OS Ref. SO283 554. 1m W of Kington on unclassified road to Brilley.

Open: Strictly by appointment only through Estate Office.

Admission: Adult £4, Child £1.50. Groups: Adult £3.50, Child £1.

♿Unsuitable. 🅿️Limited. 🐕Guide dogs only. ✳️

HERGEST CROFT GARDENS

KINGTON, HEREFORDSHIRE HR5 3EG

www.hergest.co.uk

Tel: 01544 230160   **Fax:** 01544 232031   **e-mail:** gardens@hergest.co.uk

Owner: W L Banks   **Contact:** Melanie Lloyd

From spring bulbs to autumn colour, this is a garden for all seasons. An old-fashioned kitchen garden has spring and summer borders and roses. Over 59 Champion trees and shrubs grow in one of the finest collections in the British Isles. Holds National Collection of birches, maples and zelkovas. Park Wood is a hidden valley with rhododendrons up to 30 ft tall.

Location: OS Ref. SO281 565. On W side of Kington. ¹/₂ m off A44, left at Rhayader end of bypass. Turn right and gardens are ¹/₄ m on left. Signposted from bypass.

Open: Mar: Sats & Suns. 25 Mar - 30 Oct: daily, 12.30 - 5pm. May & June: daily, 12 noon - 6pm. Season tickets and groups by arrangement throughout the year. Winter by appointment.

Admission: Adult £5, Child (under 16yrs) Free. Pre-booked groups (20+) £4. Pre-booked guided groups (20+) £6pp. Season ticket £17.

ℹ️Gift sales. 🌿Rare plants. ♿Limited. ▣ 🐕In grounds, on leads. ✳️ 📧Tel for details.

🎭 Special Events Index see page 24

IRON BRIDGE ⌗

Ironbridge, Shropshire

Tel: 0121 625 6820 (Regional Office)

Owner: English Heritage   **Contact:** The West Midlands Regional Office

The world's first iron bridge and Britain's best known industrial monument. Cast in Coalbrookdale by local ironmaster, Abraham Darby, it was erected across the River Severn in 1779. Iron Bridge is a World Heritage Site. Visit the recently refurbished Toll House on the Bridge, with interpretation displays.

Location: OS127, SJ672 034. In Ironbridge, adjacent to A4169.

Open: Any reasonable time.

Admission: Free crossing.

LANGLEY CHAPEL ⌗

Acton Burnell, Shrewsbury, Shropshire

Tel: 0121 625 6820 (Regional Office)

Owner: English Heritage   **Contact:** The West Midlands Regional Office

A delightful medieval chapel, standing alone in a field, with a complete set of early 17th century wooden fittings and furniture.

Location: OS126, SJ538 001. 1½ m S of Acton Burnell, on unclassified road 4m E of the A49, 9½ m S of Shrewsbury.

Open: 10am - 5pm. Key at farmhouse. Closed 24- 26 Dec & 1 Jan.

Admission: Free.

LILLESHALL ABBEY ⌗

Oakengates, Shropshire

Tel: 0121 625 6820 (Regional Office)

Owner: English Heritage   **Contact:** The West Midlands Regional Office

Extensive ruins of an abbey of Augustinian canons including remains of the 12th and 13th century church and the cloister buildings. Surrounded by green lawns and ancient yew trees.

Location: OS127, SJ738 142. On unclassified road off the A518, 4m N of Oakengates.

Open: Apr - Sept: 10am - 5pm.

Admission: Free.

LONGNER HALL 🏠

Uffington, Shrewsbury, Shropshire SY4 4TG

Tel: 01743 709215

Owner: Mr R L Burton   **Contact:** Mrs R L Burton

Designed by John Nash in 1803, Longner Hall is a Tudor Gothic style house set in a park landscaped by Humphry Repton. The home of one family for over 700 years. Longner's principal rooms are adorned with plaster fan vaulting and stained glass.

Location: OS Ref. SJ529 110. 4m SE of Shrewsbury on Uffington road, ¼ m off B4380, Atcham.

Open: Apr - Oct: Tues & BH Mons, 2 - 5pm. Tours at 2pm & 3.30pm. Groups at any time by arrangement.

Admission: Adult £5, Child/OAP £3.

ℹ️No photography in house. 🏠 ♿Partial. 📷 By arrangement for groups. 🎦 Obligatory. 🅿️Limited for coaches. 🍴By arrangement. 🐕Guide dogs only. ❋

LUDLOW CASTLE
CASTLE SQUARE, LUDLOW, SHROPSHIRE SY8 1AY
www.ludlowcastle.com

Tel: 01584 873355

Owner: The Earl of Powis & The Trustees of the Powis Estate   **Contact:** Helen J Duce

900 year old castle of the Marches, dates from 1086 and extended over the centuries to a fortified Royal Palace. Seat of government for the Council for Wales and the Marches. Privately owned by the Earls of Powis since 1811. A magnificent ruin set in the heart of medieval Ludlow.

Location: OS Ref. SO509 745. Shrewsbury 28m, Hereford 26m. A49 centre of Ludlow.

Open: Jan: weekends only, 10am - 4pm, Feb - Mar & Oct - Dec: 10am - 4pm. Apr - Jul & Sept: 10am - 5pm. Aug: 10am - 7pm. Last adm. 30mins before closing. Closed 25 Dec.

Admission: Adult £4, Child £2, Conc. £3.50, Family £11. 10% reduction for groups (10+).

📷 ♿Partial. 📷 By arrangement. 🎧 🅿️None. 🍴 🐕 ❋ 📺Tel for details.

MAWLEY HALL
CLEOBURY MORTIMER, DY14 8PN
www.mawley.com

Tel: 020 7495 6702 **Fax:** 020 7409 1810 **e-mail:** administration@mawley.com

Owner: R Galliers-Pratt Esq   **Contact:** Mrs R Sharp

Built in 1730 and attributed to Francis Smith of Warwick, Mawley is set in 18th century landscaped parkland with extensive gardens and walks down to the River Rea. Magnificent plasterwork and a fine collection of English and Continental furniture and porcelain.

Location: OS137, SO688 753. 1m N of Cleobury Mortimer on the A4117 and 7m W of Bewdley.

Open: 18 Apr - 21 Jul: Mons & Thurs, 3 - 5pm and throughout the year by appointment.

Admission: Adult £5, Child/OAP £3.

ℹ️Lunches, dinners & functions in association with Sean Hill of the Michelin starred restaurant, The Merchant House, in Ludlow.

📺 📷 By arrangement. 🅿️ 🍴 🐕In grounds, on leads. ❋

MORETON CORBET CASTLE ⌗

Moreton Corbet, Shrewsbury, Shropshire
Tel: 0121 625 6820 (Regional Office)
Owner: English Heritage   **Contact:** The West Midlands Regional Office
A ruined medieval castle with the substantial remains of a splendid Elizabethan mansion, captured in 1644 from Charles I's supporters by Parliamentary forces.
Location: OS126, SJ561 231. In Moreton Corbet off B5063, 7m NE of Shrewsbury.
Open: Any reasonable time.
Admission: Free.

MORVILLE HALL 🌿

Bridgnorth, Shropshire   WV16 5NB
Tel: 01746 780838
Owner: The National Trust   **Contact:** Dr & Mrs C Douglas
An Elizabethan house of mellow stone, converted in the 18th century and set in attractive gardens.
Location: OS Ref. SO668 940. Morville, on A458 3m W of Bridgnorth.
Open: By written appointment only with the tenants.

OAKLEY HALL   *See page 343 for full page entry.*

PREEN MANOR GARDENS

Church Preen, Church Stretton, Shropshire   SY6 7LQ
Tel: 01694 771207
Owner/Contact: Mrs P Trevor-Jones
Six acre garden on site of Cluniac monastery, with walled, terraced, wild, water, kitchen and chess gardens. 12th century monastic church.
Location: OS Ref. SO544 981. 10m SSE of Shrewsbury. 7m NE of Church Stretton, 6m SW of Much Wenlock.
Open: 1 May: 2 - 5pm; 2 & 23 Jun, 14 & 28 Jul: 2 - 6pm; 2 Oct: 2 - 5pm.
Admission: Adult £3.50, Child 50p.

SHIPTON HALL 🏛

Much Wenlock, Shropshire   TF13 6JZ
Tel: 01746 785225   **Fax:** 01746 785125
Owner: Mr J N R Bishop   **Contact:** Mrs M J Bishop
Built around 1587 by Richard Lutwyche who gave the house to his daughter Elizabeth on her marriage to Thomas Mytton. Shipton remained in the Mytton family for the next 300 years. The house has been described as 'an exquisite specimen of Elizabethan architecture set in a quaint old fashioned garden, the whole forming a picture which as regards both form and colour, satisfies the artistic sense of even the most fastidious'. The Georgian additions by Thomas F Pritchard include some elegant rococo interior decorations. There is some noteworthy Tudor and Jacobean panelling. Family home. In addition to the house visitors are welcome to explore the gardens, the dovecote and the parish church which dates back to Saxon times.
Location: OS Ref. SO563 918. 7m SW of Much Wenlock on B4378. 10m W of Bridgnorth.
Open: Easter - end Sept: Thurs, 2.30 - 5.30pm. Also Suns and Mons of BH, 2.30 - 5.30pm. Groups of 20+ at any time of day or year by prior arrangement.
Admission: Adult £4, Child £2. Discount of 10% for groups (20+).
Unsuitable. By arrangement for groups (20+). Obligatory. Guide dogs only.

SHREWSBURY ABBEY

Shrewsbury, Shropshire   SY2 6BS
Tel: 01743 232723   **Fax:** 01743 240172   **Contact:** Roger Knight
Benedictine Abbey founded in 1083, tomb of Roger de Montgomerie and remains of tomb of St Winefride, 7th century Welsh saint. The Abbey was part of the monastery and has also been a parish church since the 12th century.
Location: OS Ref. SJ499 125. Signposted from Shrewsbury bypass (A5 and A49). 500yds E of town centre, across English Bridge.
Open: All year. Summer: 10am - 4.30pm. Winter: 11am - 3pm.
Admission: Donation. For guided tours, please contact Abbey.

SHREWSBURY CASTLE &
THE SHROPSHIRE REGIMENTAL MUSEUM

Castle Street, Shrewsbury   SY1 2AT
Tel: 01743 358516   **Fax:** 01743 358411   **e-mail:** museums@shrewsbury.gov.uk
www.shrewsburymuseums.com
Owner: Shrewsbury & Atcham Borough Council
Norman Castle with 18th century work by Thomas Telford. Free admission to attractive floral grounds. The main hall houses The Shropshire Regimental Museum and displays on the history of the castle. Open-air theatre, music and events throughout the summer.
Location: OS Ref. SJ495 128. Town centre, adjacent BR and bus stations.
Open: Main building & Museum: Late May BH - end Sept: Tue - Sat, 10am - 5pm; Sun & Mon, 10am - 4pm. Winter: Please call for details. Grounds: Mon - Sat, 10am - 5pm & Suns as above.
Admission: Museum: Adult £2.50, OAP £1.50, Shrewsbury residents, under 18s, Students & members of the regiments Free. Grounds: Free.
ⓘNo photography. 🅿None. Guide dogs only. Tel for details.

SHREWSBURY MUSEUM & ART GALLERY

Barker Street, Shrewsbury, Shropshire   SY1 1QH
Tel: 01743 361196   **Fax:** 01743 358411
e-mail: museums@shrewsbury.gov.uk   **www**.shrewsburymuseums.com
Owner: Shrewsbury and Atcham Borough Council   **Contact:** Mary White
Impressive timber-framed building and attached 17th century brick mansion with archaeology and natural history, geology, social history and special exhibitions, including contemporary art.
Location: OS Ref. SJ490 126. Barker Street.
Open: Late May BH - end Sept: Tue - Sat, 10am - 5pm; Sun & Mon, 10am - 4pm. Rest of year: Tue - Sat, 10am - 4pm. Closed 18 Dec - 3 Jan.
Admission: Free.
ⓘNo photography. Ground floor only. 🅿Adjacent public.
Guide dogs only.

STOKESAY CASTLE ⌗

Nr CRAVEN ARMS, SHROPSHIRE   SY7 9AH

Tel: 01588 672544
Owner: English Heritage   **Contact:** Visitor Operations Team
This perfectly preserved example of a 13th century fortified manor house gives us a glimpse of the life and ambitions of a rich medieval merchant. Lawrence of Ludlow built this country house to impress the landed gentry. Lawrence built a magnificent Great Hall where servants and guests gathered on feast days, but the family's private quarters were in the bright, comfortable solar on the first floor. From the outside the castle forms a picturesque grouping of castle, parish church and timber-framed Jacobean gatehouse set in the rolling Shropshire countryside.
Location: OS148, SO446 787. 7m NW of Ludlow off A49. 1m S of Craven Arms off A49.
Open: 24 Mar - 31 May: Thur - Mon, 10am - 5pm. 1 Jun - 31 Aug: daily, 10am - 6pm. 1 Sept - 31 Oct: Thur - Mon, 10am - 5pm. 1 Nov - 28 Feb: Fri - Sun, 10am - 4pm. Closed 24 - 26 Dec & 1 Jan.
Admission: Adult £4.60, Child £2.30, Conc. £3.50, Family £11.50. 15% discount for groups (11+).
Great Hall & gardens. WC. 🅿 Tel for details.

WENLOCK GUILDHALL

Much Wenlock, Shropshire   TF13 6AE
Tel: 01952 727509
Owner/Contact: Much Wenlock Town Council
16th century half-timbered building has an open-arcade market area.
Location: OS Ref. SJ624 000. In centre of Much Wenlock, next to the church.
Open: 1 Apr - 31 Oct: Mon - Sat, 10.30am - 1pm & 2 - 4pm. Suns: 2 - 4pm.
Admission: Adult 50p, Child Free.

English Heritage Photo Library

DUNWOOD HALL

Longsdon, Nr Leek, Stoke-on-Trent, Staffordshire ST9 9AR

Tel: 01538 372978 **e-mail:** info@dunwoodhall.co.uk

www.dunwoodhall.co.uk

Owner: Dr R V Kemp/C Lovatt   **Contact:** Camilla Lovatt

This fine, unspoiled example of Victorian Gothic Revival architecture was built as the desirable, 1871 country residence of the Mayor of local Potteries' town, Burslem (Josiah Wedgwood's birthplace). It features carved stonework, decorative wrought iron and an impressive three-storey, galleried hall over an extensive Minton encaustic-tile floor.

Location: OS Ref. SJ947 544. On the A53 between Stoke-on-Trent and Leek, 3 miles West of Leek. Regular bus service on A53.

Open: Groups (15 - 50), by arrangement only.

Admission: Please telephone for details.

⬛ⓣ♿Partial. ⬤ 🔲Obligatory. 🅿Limited for cars, arrangements for coaches. 🐕 Guide dogs only. 🛏 3 doubles.

ERASMUS DARWIN HOUSE 🏠

Beacon Street, Lichfield, Staffordshire WA13 7AD

www.erasmusdarwin.org

Tel: 01543 306260 **e-mail:** erasmus.d@virgin.net

Owner: The Erasmus Darwin Foundation   **Contact:** Judith Franklin

Grandfather of Charles Darwin and a founder member of the Lunar Society, Erasmus Darwin (1731-1802) was a leading doctor, scientist, inventor and poet. This elegant Georgian house was his home and contains an exhibition of his life, theories, and inventions. There is also an 18th century herb garden.

Location: OS Ref. SK115 098. Situated at the W end of Lichfield Cathedral Close.

Open: All year. Please telephone for details.

Admission: Adult £2.50, Child/Conc. £2, Family £6. Groups (10-50) £2.

⬛ⓘⓣ♿🔲By arrangement. ⬤ 🅿Disabled only. ⬛ 🐕Guide dogs only. ❄

FORD GREEN HALL

Ford Green Road, Smallthorne, Stoke-on-Trent ST6 1NG

Tel: 01782 233195 **Fax:** 01782 233194

e-mail: ford.green.hall@stoke.gov.uk **www.**stoke.gov.uk/fordgreenhall

Owner: Stoke-on-Trent City Council   **Contact:** Angela Graham

A 17th century house, home to the Ford family for two centuries. The hall has been designated a museum with an outstanding collection of original and reproduction period furniture, ceramics and textiles. There is a Tudor-style garden. The museum has an award-winning education service and regular events. Children's parties available.

Location: OS Ref. SJ887 508. NE of Stoke-on-Trent on B505, signposted from A500.

Open: All year: (closed 25 Dec - 1 Jan), Sun - Thurs, 1 - 5pm.

Admission: Charge applies. Special group packages and packages with other visitor attractions (must book, min 10).

⬛ⓘ♿Partial. WC. ⬤ 🅿 ⬛ 🐕In grounds, on leads. ⬛ ❄ 🔲Tel for details.

IZAAK WALTON'S COTTAGE

Worston Lane, Shallowford, Nr Stafford ST15 0PA

Tel/Fax: 01785 760278

e-mail: ahh@staffordbc.gov.uk **www.**staffordbc.gov.uk.heritage

Owner: Stafford Borough Council   **Contact:** Mark Hartwell

Stafford's rural heritage is embodied in the charming 17th century cottage owned by the celebrated author of *The Compleat Angler*. Izaak Walton's Cottage gives a fascinating insight into the history of angling and the life of a writer whose work remains 'a unique celebration of the English countryside.'

Location: OS Ref. SJ876 293. M6/J14, A5013 towards Eccleshall, signposted on A5013.

Open: May - Aug: Sat & Sun, 1 - 5pm.

Admission: Free. Check for events, charges may apply.

⬛♿Partial. WCs. ⬤ 🅿Limited for cars. 🐕Guide dogs only. ⬛

The Dorothy Clive Garden.

MOSELEY OLD HALL ✠

FORDHOUSES, WOLVERHAMPTON WV10 7HY

Tel: 01902 782808 **e-mail:** moseleyoldhall@nationaltrust.org.uk

Owner: The National Trust   **Contact:** The Property Manager

An Elizabethan timber-framed house encased in brick in 1870; with original interiors. Charles II hid here after the Battle of Worcester. The bed in which he slept is on view as well as the hiding place he used. An exhibition retells the story of the King's dramatic escape from Cromwell's troops, and there are optional, free guided tours. The garden has been reconstructed in 17th century style with formal box parterre, only 17th century plants are grown. The property is a Sandford Education Award Winner.

Location: OS Ref. SJ932 044. 4m N of Wolverhampton between A449 and A460.

Open: 19 Mar - 30 Oct: Sats, Suns, Weds, BH Mons & following Tues. 6 Nov - 18 Dec: Suns. Times: Mar - end Oct: 1 - 5pm (garden, tearoom and shop from 12 noon). BH Mons: 11am - 5pm (whole property). Nov & Dec: 1 - 4pm (shop, garden & tearoom from 12 noon). Sun 6 Mar: pre-season preview: Ground floor of house, garden, tearoom & shop: 1 - 4pm (garden & tearoom from 12 noon). Pre-booked groups at other times.

Admission: Adult £4.80, Child £2.40, Family £12. 6 Mar: Adult £2, Child £1.

🔲 🛗 ♿ Ground floor & grounds. WC. ☕ Tearoom in 18th century barn. 🎟 🅿 🛏 🐕 On leads. 🛏 Tel for details.

SAMUEL JOHNSON BIRTHPLACE MUSEUM

Breadmarket Street, Lichfield, Staffordshire WS13 6LG

Tel: 01543 264972 **Fax:** 01543 258441

Owner: Lichfield City Council   **Contact:** Annette French

The house where his father had a bookshop is now a museum with many of Johnson's personal belongings.

Location: OS Ref. SK115 094. Breadmarket Street, Lichfield.

Open: 1 Apr - 30 Sept: daily: 10.30am - 4.30pm. 1 Oct - 31 Mar: daily, 12 noon- 4.30pm.

Admission: Adult £2.50, Child £1, Conc. £2, Family £6.

SANDON HALL

SANDON, STAFFORDSHIRE ST18 0BZ

www.sandonhall.co.uk

Tel/Fax: 01889 508004 **e-mail:** info@sandonhall.co.uk

Owner: The Earl of Harrowby   **Contact:** Michael Bosson

Ancestral seat of the Earls of Harrowby, conveniently located in the heart of Staffordshire. The imposing neo-Jacobean house was rebuilt by William Burn in 1854. Set amidst 400 acres of glorious parkland, Sandon, for all its grandeur and elegance, is first and foremost a home. The family museum which opened in 1994 has received considerable acclaim, and incorporates several of the State Rooms. The 50 acre landscaped gardens feature magnificent trees and are especially beautiful in May and autumn.

Location: OS Ref. SJ957 287. 5m NE of Stafford on the A51, between Stone and Lichfield, easy access from M6/J14.

Open: 1 May - 23 Dec: for events, functions and for pre-booked visits to the museum and gardens. Evening tours by special arrangement.

Admission: Museum: Adult £4, Child £3, OAP £3.50. Gardens: Adult £1.50, Child £1, OAP £1. NB. Max group size 22 or 45 if combined Museum and Gardens.

🎟 ♿ 🛗 By arrangement. 🎟 Obligatory. 🅿 Limited for coaches. 🐕 In grounds, on leads. 🔲 🛏 Tel for details.

LOCAL FOOD

Staffordshire Oatcakes

A regional delicacy exclusive to North Staffordshire. Similar in appearance to pancakes, Oatcakes are used to wrap both savoury and sweet food and then either grilled or eaten cold. It is said that the Oatcake's origins lie in British Colonial India. Apparently, the Staffordshire soldiers who served in India enjoyed the local flat-bread (roti), and tried to copy it when they came home, using local ingredients of white flour, oatmeal and yeast. Each Oatcake baker has developed their own closely guarded recipe and they can be found in every corner shop, as well as bakeries, in the area.

BADDESLEY CLINTON ❧

www.nationaltrust.org.uk

Enjoy a day at Baddesley Clinton, the medieval moated manor house with hidden secrets! One of the most enchanting properties owned by the National Trust, Baddesley Clinton has seen little change since 1633 when Henry Ferrers 'the Antiquary' died. He was Squire at Baddesley for almost seventy years and remodelled the house over a long period of time, introducing much of the panelling and chimney pieces. Henry was proud of his ancestry and began the tradition at Baddesley of armorial glass, which has continued until the present day. Henry let the house in the 1590s when it became a refuge for Jesuit priests, and hiding places, called 'priest holes', created for their concealment, survive from this era. Pictures painted by Rebecca, wife of Marmion Edward Ferrers, remain to show how the romantic character of Baddesley was enjoyed in the late 19th century when the family also re-created a sumptuously furnished Chapel.

The garden, which surrounds the house, incorporates many features including stewponds: a small lake (the 'Great Pool'); a walled garden with thatched summer house and a lakeside walk with nature trail and wildflower meadow. Make a day of it! Complementary opening times and substantial discounts on joint ticket prices make a combined visit to Baddesley Clinton and Packwood House even more attractive, especially since both properties are only two miles apart.

Map 5

Owner:
The National Trust

▶ CONTACT

The Estate Office
Baddesley Clinton Hall
Rising Lane
Baddesley Clinton
Knowle
Solihull B93 0DQ

Tel: 01564 783294
Fax: 01564 782706

e-mail:
baddesleyclinton@
nationaltrust.org.uk

▶ LOCATION
OS Ref. SP199 715

³/₄m W of A4141
Warwick/Birmingham
road at Chadwick End.

▶ OPENING TIMES

House
2 Mar - 6 Nov:
Wed - Sun, Good Friday
& BH Mons.

Mar, Apr, Oct & Nov:
1.30 - 5pm;

May - end Sept:
1.30 - 5.30pm.

Grounds
2 Mar - 11 Dec:
Wed - Sun, Good Friday
& BH Mons.

Mar, Apr, Oct & 2 - 6 Nov:
12 noon - 5pm;

May - end Sept:
12 noon - 5.30pm;

9 Nov - 11 Dec:
12 noon - 4.30pm.

▶ ADMISSION

Adult £6.60
Child £3.30
Family £16.50
Groups £5.60
Guided tours
(out of hours) £11.20

Grounds only
Adult £3.30
Child £1.65
Combined Ticket with Packwood House
Adult £9.60
Child £4.80
Family £24.00
Groups £8.20

Gardens only
Adult £4.80
Child £2.40

🛍 | 🌿 🍷 ♿ Partial. WC. 🍴 Licensed. 🚶 By arrangement. 🎪 🐕 Guide dogs only. 🎭 Tel for details.

©Coughton Court

Owner:
The National Trust
but the Throckmorton
family lease, part fund
and manage.

▶ **CONTACT**
Sales Office
Coughton Court
Alcester
Warwickshire B49 5JA

Tel: 01789 400777
Fax: 01789 765544

Visitor Information:
01789 762435

e-mail: sales@
throckmortons.co.uk

▶ **LOCATION**
OS Ref. SP080 604

Located on A435,
2m N of Alcester,
8m NW of
Stratford-on-Avon.
18m from Birmingham
City Centre.

Rail: Birmingham
International.

Air: Birmingham
International.

CONFERENCE/FUNCTION

ROOM	SIZE	MAX CAPACITY
Dining Rm	45' x 27'	60
Saloon	60' x 36'	100

The Saloon, which has particularly
good acoustics, is often used for
music recording.

COUGHTON COURT

www.coughtoncourt.co.uk

Coughton Court has been the home of the
Throckmortons since the 15th century and the
family still live here today. The magnificent Tudor
gatehouse was built around 1530 with the north
and south wings completed 10 or 20 years later.
The gables and the first storey of these wings are
of typical mid-16th century half-timbered work.

Of particular interest to visitors is the
Throckmorton family history from Tudor times to
the present generation. On view are family
portraits through the centuries, memorabilia,
furniture, tapestries and porcelain.

A long-standing Roman Catholic theme runs
through the family history which is maintained to
the present day. The house has strong connections
with the Gunpowder plot and also suffered
damage in the Civil War.

GARDENS

The house stands in 25 acres of gardens and
grounds along with two churches and a lake.
The Gardens include a Formal Garden, Elizabethan
Knot Garden, Orchard, Bog Garden and a 1 acre
Walled Garden, now considered to be one of
Britain's finest walled gardens, which features a
spectacular Rose Labyrinth. These beautiful
Gardens have been created and financed by the
Throckmorton family over the past decade. They
are the inspiration and treasured project of
Mrs Clare Throckmorton, translated into reality by
her daughter Christina Williams, garden designer.

ℹ️ Wedding receptions, special occasion
dinners, business meetings, filming, fairs and
corporate activity days. The acoustics of the
Saloon make it ideal for live theatre and
musical concerts. Marquees can be erected in
the grounds. No photography or stiletto heels
in house.

🍴 Private dinners can be provided by
arrangement in the Dining Room, Saloon and
Tudor Rooms. Licensed for Civil Marriage
ceremonies.

♿ Ground floor of house, gardens &
restaurant. WC.

🍽️ Licensed restaurant, 11am - 5.30pm.
Capacity: 100 inside, 60 outside.

🚶 By arrangement. Ask for group organisers
brochure.

🅿️ Unlimited for cars plus 4 coaches.

👩‍🏫 Teacher's pack available.

🐕 Car park only.

🔔 Tel for details.

©Coughton Court

©Coughton Court

▶ **OPENING TIMES**

House
5 March - end March
& October
Sats & Suns only

April - September:
Wed - Sun plus
BH Mons & Tues
(also Tues in July & Aug)
11.30am - 5pm.

Closed Good Friday,
Sats 18 June & 16 July.

House may close early
some Sats due to functions
and events, check prior
to your visit: 01789 762435.

**Gardens, Restaurant,
Shop & Plant Sales:**
Dates as house,
11am - 5.30pm.

Walled Garden
Dates as house,
11.30am - 4.45pm.

Last admissions are $^1/_2$ hr
before closing times.

▶ **ADMISSION**

House & Gardens
Adult £8.60
Child* (5-15yrs)........ £4.30
Family (2+2).......... £24.80
Family (2+3).......... £28.75
Groups (15+)** £7.50

Gardens only
Adult £5.90
Child* (5-15yrs)........ £2.95
Family (2+2).......... £17.00
Family (2+3).......... £19.50
Groups (15+)** £5.15

Parking .... All cars £1.00

*Under 5yrs free.
**Paying visitors.

ARBURY HALL 🏛   *See page 355 for full page entry.*

BADDESLEY CLINTON ❧   *See page 356 for full page entry.*

Corporate Hospitality see page 35

NT Photographic Library

NT Severn SWT / D Sellman

CHARLECOTE PARK ❧

WARWICK CV35 9ER

www.nationaltrust.org.uk

Tel: 01789 470277   **Fax:** 01789 470544   **Events (info & booking):** 07788 658495
e-mail: charlecote.park@nationaltrust.org.uk

Owner: The National Trust   **Contact:** Sal Ransome

Owned by the Lucy family since 1247, Sir Thomas Lucy built the house in 1558. Now, much altered, it is shown as it would have been a century ago, complete with Victorian kitchen, brewhouse and family carriages in the coach house and two bedrooms, a dressing room and the main staircase. A video of Victorian life can be viewed. The formal gardens and informal parkland lie to the north and west of the house. Jacob Sheep were brought to Charlecote in 1756 by Sir Thomas Lucy. It is reputed that William Shakespeare was apprehended for poaching c1583 and Sir Thomas Lucy is said to be the basis of Justice Shallow in Shakespeare's *'Merry Wives of Windsor'*.

Location: OS151, SP263 564. 1m W of Wellesbourne, 5m E of Stratford-upon-Avon.

Open: Please telephone or see our website for opening times, dates, and details of regular events and activities.

Admission: NT members and those joining at Charlecote Park: Free. Adult £6.60, Child (5-16yrs) £3.30, Family £16. Grounds only: Adult £3.30, Child £1.65.

🖷 ⓘ Children's play area. 🚻 ♿ 🖷 🍴 Licensed. 🖬 For booked groups. 🅿 Limited for coaches. 🖬 By arrangement. 🐕 On leads, in car park only.

♿ Tel for details.

© Skyscan

Coughton Court from the book 'Historic Family Homes & Gardens from the Air'.

COMPTON VERNEY
COMPTON VERNEY, WARWICKSHIRE CV35 9HZ
www.comptonverney.org.uk

Tel: 01926 645500 **Fax:** 01926 645501 **e-mail:** info@comptonverney.org.uk
Owner: Compton Verney House Trust **Contact:** Ticketing Desk

Set in a restored 18th century Robert Adam mansion, Compton Verney offers a unique art gallery experience. Surrounded by 120 acres of 'Capability' Brown landscape, the gallery houses a diverse permanent collection, complemented by temporary exhibitions. There is also an extensive programme of events and activities.

Location: OS Ref. SP312 529. 7m E of Stratford-upon-Avon, 10 mins from M40/J12, on B4086 between Wellesbourne and Kineton.

Open: Mar - Oct: Tues - Sun & BH Mons, 11am - 5pm (Thurs closes 8pm). Last entry to Gallery 4.30pm. Nov - Mar: Pre-booked groups only.

Admission: Adult £6, Child (5-16yrs) £2, Conc. £4, Family £14. Groups (10+): Adult £5.40, Conc £4. Tuesdays half price.

ⓘ No photography in the Gallery. ☐ ♿ ☕Licensed. ☕Licensed.
✗ By arrangement. ☐Ample. ■ 🦮 Guide dogs only. ❄ ☂Tel for details.

Arbury Hall.

COUGHTON COURT 📖 🌿   *See page 357 for full page entry.*

FARNBOROUGH HALL 🌿
BANBURY, OXFORDSHIRE OX17 1DU
www.nationaltrust.org.uk

Tel: 01295 690002 (information line)
Owner: The National Trust

A classical mid-18th century stone house, home of the Holbech family for 300 years; notable plasterwork, the entrance hall, staircase and 2 principal rooms are shown; the grounds contain charming late 17th century temples, a $^2/_3$ mile terrace walk and an obelisk.

Location: OS151, SP430 490. 6m N of Banbury, $^1/_2$ m W of A423.

Open: House, Garden & Terrace Walk: 2 Apr - 28 Sept: Weds & Sats, also 1/2 May, 2 - 5.30pm.

Admission: House, Garden & Terrace Walk: Adult £4, Child £2, Family £11. Garden & Terrace Walk only: £2.

♿House & grounds, but steep terrace walk. 🦮 In grounds, on leads.

THE HILLER GARDEN
Dunnington Heath Farm, Alcester, Warwickshire B49 5PD
Tel: 01789 491342 **Fax:** 01789 490439
Owner: A H Hiller & Son Ltd **Contact:** Mr Jeff Soulsby

2 acre garden of unusual herbaceous plants and over 200 rose varieties.
Location: OS Ref. SP066 539. $1^1/_2$ m S of Ragley Hall on B4088 (formerly A435).
Open: All year: daily 10am - 5pm.
Admission: Free.

✻ **Plant Sales Index** see page 39

SPETCHLEY PARK GARDENS

SPETCHLEY PARK, WORCESTER WR5 1RS

www.spetchleygardens.co.uk

Tel: 01453 810303 **Fax:** 01453 511915 **e-mail:** hb@spetchleygardens.co.uk

Owner: Spetchley Gardens Charitable Trust **Contact:** Mr R J Berkeley

This lovely 30 acre private garden contains a large collection of trees, shrubs and plants, many rare or unusual. A garden full of secrets, every corner reveals some new vista, some treasure of the plant world. The exuberant planting and the peaceful walks make this an oasis of beauty, peace and quiet. Deer Park close by.

Location: OS Ref. SO895 540. 2m E of Worcester on A44. Leave M5/J6 or J7.

Open: 25 Mar- 30 Sept: Tue - Fri & BH Mons, 11am - 6pm (last admission at 4pm each open day), Suns, 2 - 6pm (last admission at 4pm each open day). Closed all Sats and all other Mons.

Admission: Adult £5, Child £2. Groups: Adult £4.50, Child £1.90.

THE TUDOR HOUSE

16 Church Street, Upton-on-Severn, Worcestershire WR8 0HT

Tel: 01684 592447/592754

Owner: Mrs Lavender Beard **Contact:** Mrs Wilkinson

Upton past and present, exhibits of local history.

Location: OS Ref. SO852 406. Centre of Upton-on-Severn, 7m SE of Malvern by B4211.

Open: Apr - Oct: daily, 2 - 5pm (4pm on Suns). Winter Suns only, 2 - 4pm. Groups by arrangement.

Admission: Adult £1, Conc. 50p, Family £2.

WICHENFORD DOVECOTE

Wichenford, Worcestershire

Tel: 01743 708100 (Regional Office) **www.**nationaltrust.org.uk

Owner: The National Trust **Contact:** Regional Office

A 17th century half-timbered black and white dovecote.

Location: OS Ref. SO788 598. 5½ m NW of Worcester, N of B4204.

Open: 1 Apr - 31 Oct: daily, 9am - 6pm or sunset if earlier. Closed Good Fri, other times by appointment with Regional Office.

Admission: £1.

English Heritage Photo Library

WITLEY COURT

GREAT WITLEY, WORCESTER WR6 6JT

Tel: 01299 896636

Owner: English Heritage **Contact:** Visitor Operations Team

The spectacular ruins of a once great house. An earlier Jacobean manor house, converted in the 19th century into an Italianate mansion, with porticoes by John Nash. The adjoining church, by James Gibbs, has a remarkable 18th century baroque interior. The gardens, William Nesfield's 'Monster Work' were equally elaborate and contained immense fountains, which survive today. The largest is the Perseus and Andromeda Fountain which has been restored and now fires daily throughout the summer, contact the site for details and timings. The landscaped grounds, parterres, fountains and woodlands have recently been restored to their former glory. The Woodland Walks in the North Park include various species of tree and shrub acquired from all over the world and the new garden in 'The Wilderness' is part of the Contemporary Heritage Garden project.

Location: OS150, SO769 649. 10m NW of Worcester off A443.

Open: 24 Mar - 31 Oct: daily, 10am - 5pm (6pm Jun - Aug). 1 Nov - 28 Feb: Thur - Mon, 10am - 4pm. Closed 24 - 26 Dec & 1 Jan.

Admission: Adult £4.95, Child £2.50, OAP £3.70, Family £12.40. 15% discount for groups (11+).

Visitor welcome point. Grounds. WC. Tel for details.

yorkshire
and the humber

Yorkshire is Britain's largest county, and its countryside has something for everyone: the wild North York Moors, the more gentle Yorkshire Dales, and the flatter landscape of the Humber estuary. The city of York contains constant reminders of its medieval origins, but is as well known for its elegant Jacobean and Georgian architecture. The Jorvik Centre brings back to life the Viking occupation of York, together with sights, sounds and even smells! York Races is always the highlight of the social and sporting year, especially in 2005 when it hosts Royal Ascot whilst that racecourse is being refurbished. Within easy reach of York are grand palaces such as Castle Howard, designed by Sir John Vanbrugh in 1699, and Harewood House, home of HM the Queen's cousin, the Earl of Harewood. But there are also more modest gems to be seen such as Sion Hill Hall, and the gardens at the RHS Harlow Carr are amongst the finest in Britain.

Saltwick Nab, Yorkshire. © National Trust Photographic Library/Joe Cornish

Yorkshire

Runswick Bay, Yorkshire.

© National Trust Photographic Library/Ian Shaw

Skipton Castle, Yorkshire.

Brodsworth Hall, Yorkshire

scampston walled garden

contemporary l innovative l inspirational

scampston walled garden

yorkshire and the humber

Having recently completed the restoration of Scampston Hall – recognised by their winning the *Country Life* 'House of the Year' award – Sir Charles and Lady Legard have turned their attention to the 4½ acre Walled Garden.

The Walled Garden, neglected after the War, was in a state of dereliction and so, in the tradition of gardening excellence at Scampston, Piet Oudolf, the renowned Dutch garden designer, was invited to submit a proposal for its revival. Work began in 1999 and was completed in time for the garden to open to the public in 2004. Meanwhile Piet Oudolf went on the win 'Best in Show' at Chelsea 2000 and was selected to design the Battery Park September 11 Memorial Garden in New York.

His outstanding design for the plot was based on breaking up the space into a series of large 'rooms' enclosed by beech hedges and surrounded by an avenue of lime trees beside the wall on three sides of the garden. The overall scheme is boldly geometric with an enthusiastic use of colour. The main focus of the central area is a perennial flower meadow using a rich palette of reds, yellows and orange. The planting here is Oudolf's signature style and is designed to give a long season of interest. He has a keen appreciation of the shape and texture of plants, and not just in their summer glory; he visualises them in the winter months when their forms are skeletal, coated in hoar frost and spiders' webs, giving a focal point at a time when most gardens are often very bleak.

Here, enclosed by historic walls, there is an appealing modern textural contrast within sections of the garden: in parts there are rigid structural shapes of clipped box and yew, contrasting with soft waves of tall grasses, a closely cropped lawn and a still, reflective pond. Astonishingly, many of the plants selected by Piet Oudolf are propagated on site by the head gardener, Tim Marshall, in order to produce the numbers needed for this huge project (6,000 Molinia grasses were propagated from an original purchase of 50).

From a grassed pyramid 3m high, similar to a 17th century 'prospect mount', it is possible to view the whole garden in its entirety. Every aspect of this garden speaks of quality and not just in the planting. The gravel paths have been constructed from a wheelchair friendly material; the brick paths are of hand made brick meticulously laid and the seats – which have aroused much favourable comment – are a splendid modern design by the young Dutch furniture maker, Piet Hein Eek.

▸ For further details about Scampston, see page 399.

Map 8

BRAMHAM PARK

www.bramhampark.co.uk

Bramham Park is the stunning family home of the Lane Fox family, who are direct descendants of Robert Benson, the founder of Bramham over 300 years ago. The gardens extend to some 66 acres and, with the Pleasure Grounds, extend to over 100 acres.

The focus at Bramham has always been the landscape (the house was merely built as a 'villa' from which to admire it). Inspiration for the design of the Garden at Bramham was French and formal, but the manner in which it was adapted to the national landscape is relaxed and entirely English. It is completely original and few other parks of this period survive; none on

the scale and complexity of Bramham. It is a rare and outstanding example of the formal style of the late 17th century and early 18th century.

Bramham is a garden of walks and vistas, architectural features and reflecting water. A broad vista stretches away at an angle from the house and a number of other allées have focal points – temples and vistas. This creates an experience of anticipation when walking around the grounds.

The house, gardens and surrounding parkland make an ideal venue for events, private dinners, corporate entertaining, product launches and filming.

Owner:
George Lane Fox

▶ **CONTACT**

The Estate Office
Bramham Park
Wetherby
West Yorkshire
LS23 6ND

Tel: 01937 846000
Fax: 01937 846007
e-mail: enquiries@
bramhampark.co.uk

▶ **LOCATION**

OS Ref. SE410 416

A1/M1 1m,
Wetherby 5m,
Leeds 7m,
Harrogate 12m,
York 14m.

Rail: Leeds or York.

Bus: 770; Bus stop
$^1/_2$ m.

Air: Leeds/Bradford
15m.

CONFERENCE/FUNCTION

ROOM	SIZE	MAX CAPACITY
Gallery	80' x 20'	110
Hall	30' x 30'	50
North Room	27' x 48'	100
East Room	20' x 18'	14
Old Kitchen	22' x 23'	50

Map 8

Owner:
English Heritage

▶ **CONTACT**

Visitor Operations Team
Brodsworth Hall
Brodsworth
Nr Doncaster
Yorkshire DN5 7XJ

Tel: 01302 722598

Fax: 01302 337165

e-mail: customers@
english-heritage.org.uk

▶ **LOCATION**
OS Ref. SE507 071

In Brodsworth, 5m NW
of Doncaster off A635.
Use A1(M)/J37.

Rail: Doncaster.

BRODSWORTH HALL ⊞
& GARDENS

www.english-heritage.org.uk/yorkshire

Brodsworth Hall is a rare example of a Victorian country house that has survived largely unaltered. Designed and built in the 1860s it remains an extraordinary time capsule. The now faded grandeur of the reception rooms speaks of an opulent past whilst the cluttered servants' wing, with its great kitchen from the age of Mrs Beeton, recalls a vanished way of life. Careful conservation has preserved the patina of time to produce an interior that is both fascinating and evocative. The Hall is set within beautiful Victorian gardens rich in features which are a delight in any season and are currently being restored to their original design.

New for 2005: Launch of the Victorian gardens - now fully restored to their 1860s heyday.

© English Heritage Photo Library / John Critchley

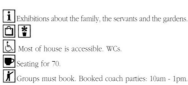

ℹ️ Exhibitions about the family, the servants and the gardens.

♿ Most of house is accessible. WCs.

♿ Seating for 70.

Groups must book. Booked coach parties: 10am - 1pm.

🅿️ 220 cars and 3 coaches. Free.

Education Centre. Free if booked in advance.

Tel for details.

▶ **OPENING TIMES**
Summer

House

19 March - 2 October
Tue - Sun & BH Mons,
1 - 5pm.

3 - 31 October
Sats & Suns,
12 noon - 4pm.

Gardens

19 March - 31 October
Daily,
10am - 6pm.

Winter

**Gardens, Tea Rooms,
Shop & Servants' Wing**

1 November - 31 March
Sats & Suns, 10am - 4pm.

Last admission $1/2$ hr
before closing.

▶ **ADMISSION***
House & Gardens

Adult £6.60
Child (5-15yrs) £3.30
Child (under 5yrs) ...... Free
Conc. £5.00

Groups (11+) 15% discount

Free admission for tour
leaders and coach drivers.

Gardens only

Adult £4.60
Child (5-15yrs) £2.30
Child (under 5yrs) ...... Free
Conc. £3.50

CASTLE HOWARD 🏛

www.castlehoward.co.uk

In a dramatic setting between two lakes with extensive gardens and impressive fountains, this 18th century Palace was designed by Sir John Vanbrugh in 1699. Undoubtedly the finest private residence in Yorkshire, it was built for Charles Howard, 3rd Earl of Carlisle, whose descendants still live here.

With its painted and gilded dome reaching 80ft into the Yorkshire sky, this impressive house has collections of antique furniture, porcelain and sculpture, while its fabulous collection of paintings is dominated by the famous Holbein portraits of Henry VIII and the Duke of Norfolk.

Designed on a heroic scale covering 1,000 acres. The gardens include memorable sights such as the Temple of the Four Winds and the Mausoleum, the New River Bridge and the restored waterworks of the South Lake, Cascade, Waterfall and Prince of Wales Fountain. The walled garden has collections of old and modern roses.

Ray Wood, acknowledged by the Royal Botanic Collection, Kew, as a "rare botanical jewel" has a unique collection of rare trees, shrubs, rhododendrons, magnolias and azaleas.

Map 8

Owner:
The Hon Simon Howard

▶ CONTACT

Visitor Services
Castle Howard
York, North Yorks
YO60 7DA

Tel: 01653 648333
Fax: 01653 648529

e-mail:
house@
castlehoward.co.uk

▶ LOCATION

OS Ref. SE716 701

Approaching from S, A64 to Malton, on entering Malton, take Castle Howard road via Coneysthorpe village. Or from A64 following signs to Castle Howard via the Carrmire Gate 9' wide by 10' high.

York 15m (20 mins), A64. From London: M1/J32, M18 to A1(M) to A64, York/Scarborough Road, 3¹/₂ hrs.

Train: London Kings Cross to York 1hr. 50 mins. York to Malton Station 30 mins.

Bus: Service and tour buses from York Station.

CONFERENCE/FUNCTION

ROOM	SIZE	MAX CAPACITY
Long Gallery	197' x 24'	280
Grecian Hall	40' x 40'	160

▶ OPENING TIMES

Summer
1 March - 6 November
Daily, 10am - 4pm
(last admission).

Winter
Grounds only
November - mid February.

Stable Courtyard (gift shops, farm shop, chocolate shop, plant centre, café) open year round - telephone before setting off is recommended.

Access to Pretty Wood Pyramid is available from 1 July to 31 August. Special tours to newly restored rooms in the house are available by arrangement.
For more information please contact Castle Howard Estate Office on 01653 648444.

▶ ADMISSION

Summer

House & Garden
Adult £9.50
Child (4-16yrs)....... £6.50
Senior £8.50

Garden only
Adult £6.50
Child (4-16yrs)....... £4.50
Senior £6.00

📷✳ℹ Outdoor tours, events, concerts, theatre, exhibitions, historical character guides, adventure playground, plant centre, farm shop, chocolate shop, gift & book shops. Gift fairs, product launches, garden parties, firework displays, banqueting and other events. Suitable for helicopter landing. Used as a film location. No photography in the House unless prior permission is granted.

🍴 Booked private parties and receptions, min. 25.

♿ Transport equipped for wheelchairs. Wheelchair lift in House to main floor. WCs.

☕ Two cafeterias (third open Jul - Sept). Stable Courtyard Café open year round.

👤 Guides posted throughout House. Private tours and lectures by arrangement covering architecture, history, art, collections, House including tours of recently refurbished rooms.

🅿 400 cars, 20 coaches.

🎒 1:10 teacher/pupil ratio required. KS2&3 education pack. Special interest: architecture, art, history, wildlife, horticulture.

❋

Map 8

Owner:
York Civic Trust

▶ **CONTACT**

Mr Peter Brown
Fairfax House
Castlegate
York   YO1 9RN

Tel: 01904 655543
Fax: 01904 652262

e-mail: peterbrown@
fairfaxhouse.co.uk

▶ **LOCATION**
OS Ref. SE605 515

In centre of York
between Castle
Museum and
Jorvik Centre.

London 4 hrs by car,
2 hrs by train.

Rail: York Station,
10 mins walk.

Taxi: Station Taxis
01904 623332.

FAIRFAX HOUSE

www.fairfaxhouse.co.uk

Fairfax House was acquired and fully restored by the York Civic Trust in 1983/84. The house, described as a classic architectural masterpiece of its age and certainly one of the finest townhouses in England, was saved from near collapse after considerable abuse and misuse this century, having been converted into a cinema and dance hall.

The richly decorated interior with its plasterwork, wood and wrought-iron, is now the home for a unique collection of Georgian furniture, clocks,

paintings and porcelain.

The Noel Terry Collection, gift of a former treasurer of the York Civic Trust, has been described by Christie's as one of the finest private collections formed in the 20th century. It enhances and complements the house and helps to create that special 'lived-in' feeling, providing the basis for a series of set-piece period exhibitions which bring the house to life in a very tangible way.

▶ **OPENING TIMES**

Summer

5 February - 31 December

Mon - Thur: 11am - 5pm.
Fridays: Guided tours only at 11am and 2pm.
Saturdays: 11am - 5pm.
Sundays: 1.30 - 5pm.

Last admission 4.30pm.

Winter

Closed
1 January - 4 February & 24 - 26 December.

▶ **ADMISSION**

Adult......................£4.50
Child......... Free with full
                    paying adult.
Conc. £3.75
Groups*
  Adult....................£4.00
  Child....................£1.00
  Conc. £3.25

* Min payment 15 persons.

ℹ️ Suitable for filming. No photography in house. Liveried footmen, musical & dancing performances can be arranged.

🖼️

🍽️ Max. 28 seated. Groups up to 50: buffet can be provided.

♿ Visitors may alight at entrance prior to parking. No WCs except for functions.

🚶 A guided tour can be arranged at a cost of £6. Evening and daytime guided tours, telephone for details. Available in French and German. Tour time: 1½ hrs. Special connoisseur tours available - contact the Director to discuss.

🅿️ 300 cars, 50 yds from house. Coach park is ½ m away, parties are dropped off; drivers please telephone for details showing the nearest coach park and approach to the house.

🛡️ **SPECIAL EVENTS**

MAR 4 - DEC 31
Restoration.

DEC 1 - 31
Keeping of Christmas.

SKIPTON CASTLE

www.skiptoncastle.co.uk

Map 8

▶ CONTACT

Judith Parker
Skipton Castle
Skipton
North Yorkshire
BD23 1AQ

Tel: 01756 792442

Fax: 01756 796100

e-mail: info@
skiptoncastle.co.uk

▶ LOCATION

OS Ref. SD992 520

In the centre of Skipton, at the N end of High Street.

Skipton is 20m W of Harrogate on the A59 and 26m NW of Leeds on A65.

Rail: Regular services from Leeds & Bradford.

Guardian of the gateway to the Yorkshire Dales for over 900 years, this unique fortress is one of the most complete and well-preserved medieval castles in England. Standing on a 40-metre high crag, fully-roofed Skipton Castle was founded around 1090 by Robert de Romille, one of William the Conqueror's Barons, as a fortress in the dangerous northern reaches of the kingdom.

Owned by King Edward I and Edward II, from 1310 it became the stronghold of the Clifford Lords withstanding successive raids by marauding Scots. During the Civil War it was the last Royalist bastion in the North, yielding only after a three-year siege in 1645. 'Slighted' under the orders of Cromwell, the castle was skilfully restored by the redoubtable Lady Anne Clifford and today visitors can climb from the depths of the Dungeon to the top of the Watch Tower, and explore the Banqueting Hall, the Kitchens, the Bedchamber and even the Privy!

Every period has left its mark, from the Norman entrance and the Medieval towers, to the beautiful Tudor courtyard with the great yew tree planted by Lady Anne in 1659. Here visitors can see the coat of arms of John Clifford, the infamous 'Bloody' Clifford of Shakespeare's *Henry VI*, who fought and died in the Wars of the Roses whereupon the castle was possessed by Richard III. Throughout the turbulent centuries of English history, the Clifford Lords fought at Bannockburn, at Agincourt and in the Wars of the Roses. The most famous of them all was George Clifford, 3rd Earl of Cumberland, Champion to Elizabeth I, Admiral against the Spanish Armada and conqueror of Puerto Rico in 1598.

In the castle grounds visitors can see the Tudor wing built as a royal wedding present for Lady Eleanor Brandon, niece of Henry VIII, the beautiful Shell Room decorated in the 1620s with shells and Jamaican coral and the ancient medieval chapel of St John the Evangelist. The Chapel Terrace, with its delightful picnic area, has fine views over the woods and Skipton's lively market town.

▶ OPENING TIMES

All Year
(closed 25 December)

Mon - Sat: 10am - 6pm

Suns: 12 noon - 6pm
(October - February 4pm)

▶ ADMISSION

Adult	£5.20
Child (0-4yrs)	Free
Child (5-17yrs)	£2.70
OAP	£4.60
Student (with ID)	£4.60
Family (2+3)	£14.90

Groups (15+)

Adult	£4.20
Child (0-17yrs)	£2.70

Includes illustrated tour sheet in a choice of nine languages, plus free badge for children.

Groups welcome: Guides available for booked groups at no extra charge.

Unsuitable.

Tearoom. Indoor and outdoor picnic areas.

By arrangement.

Large public coach and car park off nearby High Street. Coach drivers' rest room at Castle.

Welcome. Guides available. Teachers free.

In grounds on leads.

Tel for details.

€

ALDBOROUGH ROMAN SITE ⚏

Main Street, Aldborough, Boroughbridge, North Yorkshire YO51 9EP

Tel: 01423 322768 **e-mail:** customers@english-heritage.org.uk
www.english-heritage.org.uk/yorkshire

Owner: English Heritage   **Contact:** Visitor Operations Team
Site of the principal town of Britain's largest Roman tribe. Discover original Roman mosaics still in situ. A small museum displays finds from the site.

Location: OS Ref. SE405 661. Close to Boroughbridge off A1.

Open: 19 Mar - 30 Sept: Thur - Mon, 10am - 5pm (daily to 6pm in Aug). Closed 1 Oct - 31 Mar.

Admission: Adult £2.60, Child £1.30, Conc. £2. 15% discount for groups (11+).

ℹ️WC. 🔲📷 🐕

ARCHAEOLOGICAL RESOURCE CENTRE

St Saviour's Church, St Saviourgate, York YO1 8NN

Tel: 01904 543403   **Fax:** 01904 627097

e-mail: jorvik@yorkarchaeology.co.uk   **www**.vikingjorvik.com

Owner: York Archaeological Trust   **Contact:** Reservations Team
Housed in the restored medieval church of St Saviour, the ARC offers a glimpse behind the scenes of a leading archaeological unit. Visitors take part in hands-on activities with real finds, investigating a section of a layer from an archaeological dig and even examining Viking-Age artefacts.

Location: OS Ref. SE606 519. Central York, close to the Shambles.

Open: School holidays: Mon - Sat, 11am - 3pm. Term time: Mon - Fri, 10am - 3.30pm. Closed last two weeks of Dec & first week of Jan. For details of opening times on the day of your visit please phone 01904 543403.

Admission: £4.50, Conc. £4. Pre-booked groups (15+) £4 (valid until 31 Mar 2005).

🔲 ⊤ &♿ Partial. 🎧 Obligatory. 🅿 None. 📷 🐕 Guide dogs only.

ASKE HALL 🏛

Richmond, North Yorkshire DL10 5HJ

Tel: 01748 822000   **Fax:** 01748 826611   **e-mail:** mhairi.mercer@aske.co.uk
www.aske.co.uk

Owner: The Marquess of Zetland   **Contact:** Mhairi Mercer
Aske Hall lies in Capability Brown landscaped parkland and has been the family seat of the Dundas family since 1763. This Georgian treasure house boasts exquisite 18th century furniture, paintings and porcelain, including works by Robert Adam, Chippendale, Gainsborough, Raeburn and Meissen.

Location: OS Ref. NZ179 035. 2m SW of A1 at Scotch Corner, 1m from the A66, on the Gilling West road (B6274).

Open: Public Access days as per the website – dates shown. Group tours by appointment only. Mon - Fri, 10am - 3pm.

Admission: House & grounds: Adult £7, Child £5. Groups (10 - 30).

🎧 By arrangement. 🅿 Limited. 🐕 In grounds on leads.

BAGSHAW MUSEUM

Wilton Park, Batley, West Yorkshire WF17 0AS

Tel: 01924 326155   **Fax:** 01924 326164

Owner: Kirklees Cultural Services   **Contact:** Melanie Brook
A Victorian Gothic mansion set in Wilton Park.

Location: OS Ref. SE235 257. From M62/J27 follow A62 to Huddersfield. At Birstall, follow tourist signs.

Open: Mon - Fri, 11am - 5pm. Sat & Sun, 12 noon - 5pm. Pre-booked groups and school parties welcome.

Admission: Free.

BENINGBROUGH HALL & GARDENS 🌿

Beningbrough, North Yorkshire YO30 1DD

Tel: 01904 470666   **Fax:** 01904 470002   **e-mail:** beningbrough@nationaltrust.org.uk

Owner: The National Trust   **Contact:** The Visitor Services Manager
Imposing 18th century house with over 100 portraits from the National Portrait Gallery.

Location: OS Ref. SE516 586. 8m NW of York, 3m W of Shipton, 2m SE of Linton-on-Ouse, follow signposted route.

Open: 12 Mar - 26 Jun: Sat - Wed; 27 Jun - 28 Aug: daily except Thurs; 29 Aug - 30 Oct: Sat - Wed. House: 12 noon - 5pm. Grounds: 11am - 5.30pm.

Admission: House & Garden: Adult £6.30, Child £3.20, Family £14.50. Groups: Adult £5.70, Child £2.60.

🔲⊠♿ Partial. WC. 🍴🅿 Reduced rates for groups (15+), not Suns or BHs. ▣❌▲

🌱 **Plant Sales Index** see page 39

BOLTON ABBEY

SKIPTON, NORTH YORKSHIRE BD23 6EX

www.boltonabbey.com

Tel: 01756 718009   **Fax:** 01756 710535   **e-mail:** tourism@boltonabbey.com

Owner: Trustees of the Chatsworth Settlement   **Contact:** Visitor Manager
Wordsworth, Turner and Landseer were inspired by this romantic and varied landscape. The Estate, centred around Bolton Priory (founded 1154), is the Yorkshire home of the Duke and Duchess of Devonshire and provides 80 miles of footpaths to enjoy some of the most spectacular landscape in England.

Location: OS Ref. SE074 542. On B6160, N from the junction with A59 Skipton - Harrogate road, 23m from Leeds.

Open: All year.

Admission: £5 per car, £3.50 for disabled (occupants free).

🔲⊤&♿ Licensed. 🍴 Licensed. 🎧 By arrangement. 🅿 📷
🐕 In grounds, on leads.   ▣ Devonshire Arms Country House Hotel & Devonshire Fell Hotel nearby. ❋

BOLTON CASTLE 🏛

LEYBURN, NORTH YORKSHIRE DL8 4ET

www.boltoncastle.co.uk

Tel: 01969 623981   **Fax:** 01969 623332   **e-mail:** harry@boltoncastle.co.uk

Owner/Contact: Lord Bolton or Sarah Penty
A fine medieval castle that overlooks beautiful Wensleydale. Bolton Castle celebrated its 600th anniversary in 1999. Set your imagination free as you wander round this fascinating castle, which once held Mary Queen of Scots prisoner for 6 months and succumbed to a bitter Civil War siege. Don't miss the beautiful medieval garden and vineyard.

Location: OS Ref. SE034 918. Approx 6m W of Leyburn. 1m NW of Redmire.

Open: Mar - Nov: daily, 10am - 5pm. Please telephone for winter opening times.

Admission: Adult £5, Child/OAP £3.50, Family £12.

🔲⊤ Wedding receptions. ♿ Partial. ● 🅿 📷 🐕 In grounds, on leads. ▲ ❋

Yorkshire & The Humber - England

BRAMHAM PARK 🏛   *See page 380 for full page entry.*

BROCKFIELD HALL 🏛
Warthill, York YO19 5XJ
Tel: 01904 489362   **e-mail:** clare.brockfield@btinternet.com
Owner/Contact: Mr & Mrs Simon Wood
A fine late Georgian house designed by Peter Atkinson, whose father had been assistant to John Carr of York, for Benjamin Agar Esq. Begun in 1804, its outstanding feature is an oval entrance hall with a fine cantilevered stone staircase curving past an impressive Venetian window. It is the family home of Mr and Mrs Simon Wood. Mrs Wood is the daughter of the late Lord and of Lady Martin Fitzalan Howard. He was the brother of the 17th Duke of Norfolk and son of the late Baroness Beaumont of Carlton Towers, Selby. There are some interesting portraits of her old Roman Catholic family, the Stapletons, and some good English furniture. Permanent exhibition of paintings by Staithes Group Artists (by appointment outside August).
Location: OS Ref. SE664 550. 5m E of York off A166 or A64.
Open: 31 July and Aug: daily except Mons (open Aug BH Mon), 1 - 4pm. Other times by appointment.
Admission: Adult £5, Child £2.
♿ Partial. 🎫Obligatory. 🅿 🚗 Guide dogs only.

BRODSWORTH HALL ⌗   *See page 381 for full page entry.*
& GARDENS

BRONTË PARSONAGE MUSEUM
Church St, Haworth, Keighley, West Yorkshire BD22 8DR
Tel: 01535 642323   **Fax:** 01535 647131   **e-mail:** bronte@bronte.org.uk
www.bronte.info
Owner: The Brontë Society   **Contact:** The Administrator
Georgian parsonage, former home of the Brontë family, now a museum with rooms furnished as in the sisters' day and displays of their personal treasures as seen on BBC1's "In Search of the Brontës".
Location: OS Ref. SE029 373. 8m W of Bradford, 3m S of Keighley.
Open: Apr - Sept: 10am - 5pm, Oct - Mar: 11am - 4.30pm. Daily except 24 - 27 Dec & 2 Jan - 2 Feb.
Admission: Adult £4.90, Child (5-16yrs) £1.60, Conc. £3.60, Family £10.50. Discounts for booked groups.

Civil War Archer at Skipton Castle.

BROUGHTON HALL
SKIPTON, NORTH YORKSHIRE BD23 3AE

www.broughtonhall.co.uk   www.ruralsolutions.co.uk

Tel: 01756 799608   **Fax:** 01756 700357
e-mail: tempest@broughtonhall.co.uk   **e-mail:** info@ruralsolutions.co.uk
Owner: The Tempest Family   **Contact:** The Estate Office
Stephen Tempest built Broughton Hall in 1597 and it was extended in the 18th and 19th centuries into the handsome and graceful form we see today. It is the private home of the Tempest family and is a Grade I listed building, the rooms containing fine Gillow furniture and interesting family portraits. Groups may visit for tours by prior arrangement. A 3,000 acre parkland setting and Italianate gardens which include a stunning conservatory, make Broughton Hall a desirable location for film makers and for corporate and promotional events, the owners being very experienced in successfully meeting the needs of such clients.

Nearby Estate buildings have been skilfully converted into the Broughton Hall Business Park. Here forty companies employ over five hundred people in quality offices in unspoilt historic buildings and peaceful surroundings, thanks to the innovative approach of Rural Solutions, the rural regeneration specialists (01756 799955) who conceived and completed the project.
Location: OS Ref. SD943 507. On A59, 3m W of Skipton midway between the Yorkshire and Lancashire centres. Good air and rail links.
Open: Tours by arrangement.
Admission: £7.

♿ 🚻 🎫 By arrangement. 🅿 ❋

BURTON AGNES HALL 🏛

DRIFFIELD, EAST YORKSHIRE YO25 0ND

www.burton-agnes.com

Tel: 01262 490324 **Fax:** 01262 490513

Owner: Burton Agnes Hall Preservation Trust Ltd **Contact:** Mrs Susan Cunliffe-Lister

A lovely Elizabethan Hall containing treasures collected by the family over four centuries from the original carving and plasterwork to modern and Impressionist paintings. The Hall is surrounded by lawns and topiary yew. The old walled garden contains a maze, potager, jungle garden, campanula collection and colour gardens incorporating giant game boards. Children's corner.

Location: OS Ref. TA103 633. Off A614 between Driffield and Bridlington.

Open: 1 Apr - 31 Oct: daily, 11am - 5pm.

Admission: House & Gardens: Adult £5.50, Child £2.75, OAP £5. Gardens only: Adult £2.75, Child £1.30, OAP £2.50. 10% reduction for groups of 30+.

🖼 ♿ Ground floor & grounds. ⬛ Café. Ice-cream parlour.
🐕 In grounds, on leads. ♿

©National Trust Photographic Library/Andrew Butler

Nunnington Stone Gateway.

Kenneth Berry Studios & Associates

BURTON CONSTABLE HALL 🏛

SKIRLAUGH, EAST YORKSHIRE HU11 4LN

www.burtonconstable.com

Tel: 01964 562400 **Fax:** 01964 563229 **e-mail:** via www.burtonconstable.com

Owner: Burton Constable Foundation **Contact:** Mrs Helen Dewson

One of the most fascinating country houses to survive with its historic collections, Burton Constable is a large Elizabethan mansion set in a 300 acre park with nearly 30 rooms open. The interiors of faded splendour are filled with fine furniture, paintings and sculpture, a library of 5,000 books and a remarkable 18th century 'cabinet of curiosities'. Occupied by the Constable family for over 400 years, the house still maintains the atmosphere of a home. Pleasure grounds with a delightful orangery ornamented with coade stone, a stable block and park landscaped by 'Capability' Brown in the 1770s.

Location: OS Ref. TA193 369. 14m E of Beverley via A165 Bridlington Road, follow Historic House signs. 7m NE of Hull via B1238 to Sproatley then follow Historic House signs.

Open: Hall, Grounds & Tearoom: Easter Sat - 31 Oct: Sat - Thur. Grounds & Tearoom: 12.30 - 5pm. Hall: 1 - 5pm. Last admission 4pm.

Admission: Hall & Grounds: Adult £5.50, Child £2.50, OAP £5, Family £12.50. Grounds only: Adult £1, Child 50p. Groups (20-80): £4.50. Connoisseur Study Visits: prices on request.

ℹ No photography in house. 🖼 ♿ Suitable. WCs. ⬛ 𝑓 By arrangement. 🅿 ⬛
🐕 In grounds on leads. ♿

NEWBURGH PRIORY

COXWOLD, NORTH YORKSHIRE YO61 4AS

Tel: 01347 868435

Owner/Contact: Sir George Wombwell Bt

Originally 1145 with major alterations in 1568 and 1720, it has been the home of the Earls of Fauconberg and of the Wombwell family since 1538. Tomb of Oliver Cromwell (3rd daughter Mary married Viscount Fauconberg) is in the house. Extensive grounds contain a water garden, walled garden, topiary yews and woodland walks.

Location: OS Ref. SE541 764. 4m E of A19, 18m N of York, ¹/₂ m E of Coxwold.

Open: 27 Mar - 29 Jun: Wed & Sun (open Easter Sun & Mon). House: 2.30 - 4.45pm. Garden: 2 - 6pm. Tours every ¹/₂ hour, take approximately 50mins. Booked groups by arrangement.

Admission: House & Grounds: £5.50. Child £1.50. Gardens only: £3, Child Free. Special tours of Private Apartment in addition to the above (Easter Sun & Mon and Weds & Suns 27 Mar - 24 Apr) £6pp.

ⓘNo photography in house. ⬛Partial. ⬛ ⒡Obligatory. ⓟLimited for coaches. ⬛In grounds, on leads. ⬛

NEWBY HALL & GARDENS 🏠 *See page 386 for full page entry.*

NORTON CONYERS 🏠

NR RIPON, NORTH YORKSHIRE HG4 5EQ

Tel/Fax: 01765 640333 **e-mail:** norton.conyers@ripon.org

Owner: Sir James and Lady Graham **Contact:** Lady Graham

Visited by Charlotte Brontë in 1839, Norton Conyers is an original of 'Thornfield Hall' in *Jane Eyre*', and a family legend was an inspiration for the mad Mrs Rochester. House and garden have a friendly, quiet and unspoilt atmosphere. They have been in the Grahams' possession for 381 years. Family pictures, furniture, costumes and ceramics on display. 18th century walled garden near house, with Orangery and herbaceous borders. Small plants sales area specialising in unusual hardy plants. Pick your own fruit in season.

Location: OS Ref. SF319 763. 4m N of Ripon. 3¹/₂m from the A1.

Open: House: 27/28 Mar, 1/2 & 29/30 May, 28/29 Aug; 24 Apr - 21 Aug: Suns; 27 Jun - 2 Jul: daily, 2 - 5pm, last admission 4.40pm. Garden: as House plus Thurs: 12 noon - 4.30pm (10am - 4pm on Thurs), last admission 4.15pm. (When Garden open for charity: 2 - 5pm, last admission 4.40pm.) Groups by appointment.

Admission: House: Adult £5, Child (under 16yrs) Free, OAP £3.50. Garden: Free (donations welcome), but charges are made at charity openings. Groups by arrangement.

ⓘNo interior photography. No high-heeled shoes. ⬛ ⬛ ⬛Partial. WC. ⬛Garden charity openings only. ⒡By arrangement. ⓟ ⬛Guide dogs only in House. In grounds, on leads. ⬛Tel for details.

Wakefield Cathedral.

NOSTELL PRIORY ✷

Doncaster Road, Wakefield, West Yorkshire WF4 1QE

Tel: 01924 863892 **Fax:** 01924 866846 **www.**nationaltrust.org.uk

Owner: The National Trust **Contact:** Visitor Services Manager

Nostell Priory, one of Yorkshire's finest jewels, is an 18th century architectural masterpiece by James Paine.

Location: OS Ref. SE403 175. 6m SE of Wakefield, off A638.

Open: House: 19 Mar - 6 Nov: Wed - Sun, 1 - 5pm; 3 - 11 Dec: daily, 11am - 5pm. Grounds: 5 - 20 Mar: Sats & Suns only, 11am - 5pm; 23 Mar - 6 Nov: Wed - Sun, 11am - 6pm; 3 - 11 Dec: daily, 11am - 4.30pm.

Admission: House & Grounds: Adult £6, Child £3, Family (2+4) £15. Groups (20+) £5.50. Garden only: Adult £3.50, Child £2.50.

ⓘBaby facilities. ⬛ ⬛ ⬛Partial. WC. ⬛ ⒡By arrangement. ⓟ ⬛ ⬛In grounds, on leads. ⬛ ⬛Send SAE for details.

NUNNINGTON HALL ✷

Nunnington, North Yorkshire YO62 5UY

Tel: 01439 748283 **Fax:** 01439 748284

Owner: The National Trust **Contact:** The Property Manager

17th century manor house with magnificent oak-panelled hall, nursery, haunted room, and attics, with their fascinating Carlisle collection of miniature rooms fully furnished to reflect different periods.

Location: OS Ref. SE670 795. In Ryedale, 4¹/₂ m SE of Helmsley, 1¹/₂ m N of B1257.

Open: 12 Mar - 30 Apr: Wed - Sun, 1.30 - 5pm; 1 May - 30 Sept: Wed - Sun (also Tues 31 May - 31 Aug): 1.30 - 5.30pm; 1 - 30 Oct: Wed - Sun, 1.30 - 5pm.

Admission: House & Garden: Adult £5, Child £2.50, Family £12.50. Groups: £4.50. Garden only: Adult £2.50, Child Free.

⬛ ⬛Ground floor and grounds.WC. ⬛ ⬛Guide dogs only. ⬛Tel for details.

ORMESBY HALL

Ladgate Lane, Ormesby, Middlesbrough TS7 9AS

Tel: 01642 324188 **Fax:** 01642 300937 **e-mail:** ormesbyhall@nationaltrust.org.uk

Owner: The National Trust   **Contact:** The House Manager

A mid 18th century house with opulent decoration inside, including fine plasterwork by contemporary craftsmen.

Location: OS Ref. NZ530 167. 3m SE of Middlesbrough.

Open: 25 Mar - 31 Oct: Fri - Mon, 1.30 - 5pm. Shop/Tearoom: as House, 12.30 - 5pm.

Admission: House, grounds & railway: Adult £4.10, Child £2, Family £10.50. Groups £3.50pp. Grounds, railway & exhibition only: Adult £2.90, Child £1.30.

Ground floor & grounds. WC.

PARCEVALL HALL GARDENS

Skyreholme, Skipton, North Yorkshire BD23 6DE

Tel: 01756 720311 **Fax:** 01756 720441 **Contact:** Phillip Nelson (Head Gardener)

Owner: Walsingham College (Yorkshire Properties) Ltd.

Location: OS Ref. SE068 613. E side of Upper Wharfedale, 1½ m NE of Appletreewick. 12m NNW of Ilkley by B6160 and via Burnsall.

Open: 1 Apr - 31 Oct: 10am - 6pm.

Admission: £3.50, Child 50p. RHS Free access May - Aug.

PICKERING CASTLE

Castlegate, Pickering, North Yorkshire YO18 7AX

Tel: 01751 474989 **e-mail:** customers@english-heritage.org.uk

www.english-heritage.org.uk/yorkshire

Owner: English Heritage   **Contact:** Visitor Operations Team

A splendid motte and bailey castle built by William the Conqueror, it was later used as a royal ranch. Discover more of its fascinating history in the chapel exhibition.

Location: OS Ref. SE800 845. In Pickering, 15m SW of Scarborough.

Open: 19 Mar - 30 Sept: daily, 10am - 6pm. 1 - 31 Oct: Thur - Mon, 10am - 4pm. Closed 1 Nov - 31 Mar.

Admission: Adult £3, Child £1.50, Conc. £2.30, Family £7.50. 15% discount for groups (11+).

WCs. Partial. Limited. In grounds, on leads. Tel for details.

PLUMPTON ROCKS

Plumpton, Knaresborough, North Yorkshire HG5 8NA

Tel: 01289 386360 **www.**plumptonrocks.co.uk

Owner: Edward de Plumpton Hunter **Contact:** Robert de Plumpton Hunter

Grade II* listed garden extending to over 30 acres including an idyllic lake, dramatic millstone grit rock formation, romantic woodland walks winding through bluebells and rhododendrons. Declared by English Heritage to be of outstanding interest. Painted by Turner. Described by Queen Mary as 'Heaven on earth'.

Location: OS Ref. SE355 535. Midway between Harrogate and Wetherby on the A661, 1m SE of A661 junction with the Harrogate southern bypass.

Open: Mar - Oct: Sat, Sun & BHs, 11am - 6pm.

Admission: Adult £2, Child/OAP £1.

Unsuitable. By arrangement. Limited for coaches. In grounds, on leads.

RHS GARDEN HARLOW CARR

CRAG LANE, HARROGATE, NORTH YORKSHIRE HG3 1QB

www.rhs.org.uk

Tel: 01423 565418 **Fax:** 01423 530663 **e-mail:** admin-harlowcarr@rhs.org.uk

Owner/Contact: Royal Horticultural Society

Beautiful 58 acre garden with new BBC 'Gardens through Time' to mark the RHS Bicentenary in 2004, flower and vegetable trials, ornamental grasses, woodland and streamside... to name a few. Courses on gardening and horticulture, family events, playground, Gardening Museum, Plant Centre and Gift Shop, Betty's Garden Café, free parking – one of Yorkshire's most relaxing locations.

Location: OS Ref. SE285 543. 1½/2m W from town centre on B6162.

Open: Daily: 9.30am - 6pm (4pm Nov - Feb). Last entry 1 hour before closing.

Admission: Adult £5.50, Child (6-16yrs) £1.50, Child (under 6yrs) Free. Groups (10+): £4.50. Groups must book in advance.

Picnic area. Partial. WC. Licensed. Licensed. By arrangement. Guide dogs only.

© English Heritage Photo Library

RICHMOND CASTLE

TOWER ST, RICHMOND, NORTH YORKSHIRE DL10 4QW

www.english-heritage.org.uk/yorkshire

Tel: 01748 822493 **e-mail:** customers@english-heritage.org.uk

Owner: English Heritage   **Contact:** Visitor Operations Team

Built shortly after 1066 on a rocky promontory high above the River Swale, this is the best preserved castle of such scale and age in Britain. The magnificent Keep, with breathtaking views, is reputed to be the place where the legendary King Arthur sleeps. An exhibition and contemporary garden reflect the castle's military history from the 11th to 20th centuries.

Location: OS Ref. NZ174 006. In Richmond.

Open: 19 Mar - 30 Sept: daily, 10am - 6pm. 1 Oct - 31 Mar: Thur - Mon, 10am - 4pm. Closed 24 - 26 Dec & 1 Jan.

Admission: Adult £3.60, Child £1.80, Conc. £2.70, Family £9. 15% discount for groups (11+).

Interactive exhibition. WCs. Partial. In grounds, on leads. Tel for details.

LOCAL FOOD

Fat Rascals

Whereas Yorkshire Pudding is known the world over, Fat Rascals do not appear to have moved beyond the county boundary! The gloriously named Fat Rascals are a round domed currant tea-cake, with a rich brown crust, made with currants and candied peel, similar to rock buns. They are famously sold in Ilkley and Haworth. It is thought they are based on an old recipe from Turf Cakes. When Yorkshire bakers finished for the day they mixed all the leftovers together and then gave them to farmers up on the moors to bake over a turf fire. When Swiss confectioner Frederick Belmont came to England, he took the Turf Cakes and decorated them with cherry eyes and split almond teeth. He thought they looked like cheeky little rascals and so the Fat Rascal was born.

north west

Four very disparate counties make up the North West Region. Cheshire has two strikingly different faces; the East, more industrial and more rugged where it adjoins the Peak District National Park, and the West, the flatter 'Cheshire Plain', more densely farmed and with easily recognisable red brick buildings; among them Arley Hall whose gardens were recently voted one of the top 50 in Europe. The urban areas of Merseyside and Greater Manchester contain a wealth of industrial architectural history but sadly much of this was lost following bombing in the Second World War. The regeneration of this area has been remarkable. Today Manchester offers a standard of living and lifestyle that is the envy of many other cities in Britain. From the urban to the rural – Cumbria is truly a beautiful county. The Lake District National Park was one of the first National Parks to be created in Britain (in 1951) and covers 880 sq. miles, and is best explored on foot. When exhaustion strikes, the local Mountain Goat bus service provides transport from village to village. No trip to this area would be complete without a visit to Dove Cottage and the Wordsworth Museum (Cumbria), and for children, the Beatrix Potter Gallery (Cumbria) and Hill Top Farm (Cumbria) are a must. A first port of call on the way into the Lake District is Levens Hall (Cumbria), with its world famous Topiary Garden and over to the west, on the coast at Ravenglass is Muncaster Castle (Cumbria), and its fascinating Owl Centre. The Eskdale and Ravenglass Railway (The Ratty) runs from Ravenglass on the coast, up to Boot above Eskdale Green. This miniature railway gives hours of fun for all the family and is a wonderful way to get up the valley before a long downhill walk back to the sea.

Formby Point, Merseyside. © National Trust Photographic Library.

Wordsworth House, Cumbria.

Formby Point, Merseyside.

Carlisle Castle, Cumbria.

Little Moreton Hall, Cheshire

National Trust Photographic Library

cheshire
cumbria
lancashire
merseyside

rufford old hall

decorative ǀ dramatic ǀ haunted

The National Trust Photographic Library

TATTON PARK

www.tattonpark.org.uk

Map 5

Owner:
The National Trust

▶ **CONTACT**

Conferences, exhibitions, weddings etc.
Sheila Hetherington
01625 534406

Party Visits
01625 534428

Tatton Park
Knutsford
Cheshire WA16 6QN

Tel: 01625 534400
info: 01625 534435
Fax: 01625 534403

▶ **LOCATION**
OS Ref. SJ745 815

From M56/J7 follow
signs. From M6/J19,
signed on A56 & A50.

Rail: Knutsford or
Altrincham Station,
then taxi.

Air: Manchester
Airport 6m.

Tatton is one of the most splendid historic estates in Europe. The 1000 acres of parkland are home to herds of red and fallow deer and provide the setting for a Georgian Mansion, over 50 acres of Gardens, Tudor Old Hall and a working Farm. These attractions, plus private functions and a superb events programme attract over 700,000 visits each year.

Archaeologists have found evidence of occupation at Tatton since 8000 BC with the discovery of flints in the park. There is also proof of people living here in the Iron Age, Roman times, Anglo-Saxon and medieval periods.

The neo-classical Mansion by Wyatt is the jewel in Tatton's crown and was built in stages from 1780 - 1813. The Egerton family collection of Gillow furniture, Baccarat glass, porcelain and paintings by Italian and Dutch masters is found in the splendid setting of the magnificent staterooms. In stark contrast, the Victorian kitchens and cellars provide fascinating insight

into life as it would have been 'downstairs'. Guided tours are available for a small extra charge at 12 noon and 12.15pm.

The Gardens extend over 50 acres and feature rare species of plants, shrubs and trees, and in fact are considered to be one of the most important gardens within the National Trust. Features include: a conservatory by Wyatt, Fernery by Paxton, Italian terraced garden and recently restored Japanese garden. The rare collection of plants including rhododendrons, tree ferns, bamboo and pines are the result of 200 years of collecting by the Egerton family.

The Home Farm has traditional breeds of animals including rare sheep and cattle, pigs and horses plus estate workshops. The Tudor Old Hall shows visitors how life would have been at Tatton Park over centuries past for the estate workers. Tours start in the smoky 16th century Great Hall lit by flickering candles and end in the 1950s home of an estate employee.

Summer
19 March - 2 October

Park: Daily, 10am - 7pm.
Gardens: Tue - Sun,
10am - 6pm.

Mansion:
Tue - Sun, 1 - 5pm.
(12 noon & 12.15pm guided tours by timed ticket, limited numbers)

Tudor Old Hall: Guided tours: Sats & Suns, hourly, 12 noon - 4pm.

Farm: Tue - Sun,
12 noon - 5pm.

Restaurant: Tue - Sun,
10am - 6pm.

Gift, Garden & Housekeeper's Store:
Tue - Sun, 10.30am - 5pm.

Winter
3 October - 31 March.

Park: Tue - Sun, 11am - 5pm.

Gardens: Tue - Sun,
11am - 4pm.

Farm: Sat & Sun, 11am - 4pm

Last admissions 1 hour before closing.

(Oct half-term & Dec special opening of Mansion, Farm & Old Hall)

▶ **ADMISSION**

Any two attractions

	Single	Group*
Adult	£4.60	£3.80
Child**	£2.60	£2.10
Family	£12.80	

Mansion, Gardens, Tudor Old Hall, Farm

	Single	Group*
Adult	£3.00	£2.40
Child**	£2.00	£1.60
Family	£8.00	

(50% reduction for NT members to Tudor Old Hall & Farm.)

Parking
Per car £4.00
Coaches...................... Free

*Min. 12 ** Aged 4 - 15yrs.

Tours available outside normal openings phone for details.

CONFERENCE/FUNCTION

Room	Size	Max Capacity
Tenants' Hall	125' x 45'	330 - 400
Foyer	23' x 20'	50 - 100
Tenants' Hall Event Wing - total of 8,000 sq.ft. available		
Lord Egerton's Apartment	20' x 16'	16 - 40
	24' x 18'	19 - 40
Stable Block	31' x 20'	80

Conferences, trade exhibitions, presentations, product launches, concerts and fashion shows. Special family days. Spotlights, stages, dance floor, PA system. The Tenants' Hall seats up to 400 for presentations.

Telephone for details. Dinners, dances, weddings.

Upstairs in Mansion, Tudor Old Hall & areas of farm not accessible. Wheelchairs & electric vehicles available. WCs.

Self-service. Tuck shop.

By arrangement.

200-300 yds away. Meal vouchers for coach drivers.

Award-winning educational programmes, please book. Environmental days, Orienteering, adventure playground.

In grounds, on leads.

Civil Wedding Licence.

Tel for details.

ADLINGTON HALL *See page 410 for full page entry.*

ARLEY HALL & GARDENS
ARLEY, Nr NORTHWICH, CHESHIRE CW9 6NA
www.arleyhallandgardens.com

Tel: 01565 777353 **Fax:** 01565 777465 **e-mail:** enquiries@arleyhallandgardens.com
Owner: Viscount & Viscountess Ashbrook   **Contact:** Estate Secretary

Owned by the same family for over 500 years, Arley is a delightful estate. The gardens, recently described as one of the 50 best in Europe, offer a wide range of plant interest throughout the season. Particular features are the renowned double herbaceous border (c1846), the Quercus Ilex and Pleached Lime Avenues, yew hedges, walled gardens and shrub roses. The Grove (a woodland garden) contains a large collection of rhododendrons, azaleas and other shrubs and exotic trees. The Hall (Grade II*), with family pictures and furniture, is ideal for weddings and other receptions. Chapel by Salvin, Plant Nursery and Restaurant.

Location: OS117, Ref. SJ675 809. 5 miles W Knutsford.
Open: 27 Mar - 2 Oct & Oct weekends. Hall: Tues, Sun & BHs, 12 noon - 4.30pm. Gardens, grounds & Chapel: Tues - Sun & BHs, 11am - 5pm.
Admission: Gardens, grounds & Chapel: Adult £4.70, Child (5-15yrs) £2, OAP £4.20, Family £11.80. Season Ticket £22, Family Season Ticket (2+2) £52. Hall & Gardens: £7.20, Child (5-15yrs) £3, OAP £6.20, Family £18.30. Group discounts available.

[i] Photography in garden only. ☐ ☒ ☒ ☒ Partial. ☒ ☒ ☒ By arrangement. P ☒ ☒ In grounds on leads. ☒ ☒

BEESTON CASTLE
Beeston, Tarporley, Cheshire CW6 9TX
Tel: 01829 260464 **e-mail:** customers@english-heritage.org.uk
www.english-heritage.org.uk/northwest
Owner: English Heritage   **Contact:** Visitor Operations Team

Standing majestically on sheer, rocky crags which fall sharply away from the castle walls, Beeston has stunning views across 8 counties. (Access by steep paths.) "The Castle of the Rock" exhibition outlines the history of the site from pre-historic times through to the Civil War.
Location: OS Ref. SJ537 593. 11m SE of Chester on minor road off A49, or A41. 2m SW of Tarporley.
Open: 24 Mar - 30 Sept: daily, 10am - 6pm. Oct - Mar: daily, 10am - 4pm. Closed 24 - 26 Dec & 1 Jan.
Admission: Adult £3.60, Child £1.80, Conc. £2.70, Family (2+3) £9. 15% discount for groups (11+).

[i] Exhibition. WCs. ☐ ☒ Unsuitable. P ☒ In grounds on leads. ☒ ☒ Tel for details.

CAPESTHORNE HALL *See page 411 for full page entry.*

CHESTER ROMAN AMPHITHEATRE
Vicars Lane, Chester, Cheshire
Tel: 01244 402466 **e-mail:** enquiries@chesteramphitheatre.co.uk
www.chesteramphitheatre.co.uk
Owner: English Heritage, managed by Chester City Council
Contact: Chester City Council

The largest Roman amphitheatre in Britain, partially excavated. Used for entertainment and military training by the 20th Legion, based at the fortress of Deva.
Location: OS Ref. SJ404 660. On Vicars Lane beyond Newgate, Chester.
Open: Any reasonable time.
Admission: Free.

☒ ☒ On leads. ☒

CHOLMONDELEY CASTLE GARDEN 🏛

MALPAS, CHESHIRE SY14 8AH

Tel: 01829 720383 **Fax:** 01829 720877

Owner: The Marchioness of Cholmondeley **Contact:** The Secretary

Extensive ornamental gardens dominated by romantic Gothic Castle built in 1801 of local sandstone. Visitors can enjoy the beautiful Temple Water Garden, Rose Garden and many mixed borders. Lakeside picnic area, children's play areas, rare breeds of farm animals, including llamas, children's corner with rabbits, chickens and free flying aviary birds. Private chapel in the park.

Location: OS Ref. SJ540 515. Off A41 Chester/Whitchurch Rd. & A49 Whitchurch/Tarporley Road. 7m N of Whitchurch.

Open: 25 Mar - 25 Sept: Weds, Thurs, Suns & BHs, 11.30am - 5pm. Also 9 & 23 Oct for Autumn Tints. Groups (25+): other days by prior arrangement at reduced rates. Castle not open to the public

Admission: Adult £4, Child £1.50, no concessions.

🗓 🎡 🍴 ♿ Limited. WCs. 🚭 🐕 In grounds on leads only. ❋

DORFOLD HALL 🏛

ACTON, Nr NANTWICH, CHESHIRE CW5 8LD

Tel: 01270 625245 **Fax:** 01270 628723

Owner/Contact: Richard Roundell

Jacobean country house built in 1616 for Ralph Wilbraham. Family home of Mr & Mrs Richard Roundell. Beautiful plaster ceilings and oak panelling. Attractive woodland gardens and summer herbaceous borders.

Location: OS Ref. SJ634 525. 1m W of Nantwich on the A534 Nantwich - Wrexham road.

Open: Apr - Oct: Tues only and BH Mons, 2 - 5pm.

Admission: Adult £5, Child £3.

🎦 Obligatory. 🅿 Limited. Narrow gates with low arch prevent coaches. 🐕 In grounds on leads.

Patrick Lane

DUNHAM MASSEY 🌺

ALTRINCHAM, CHESHIRE WA14 1SJ

www.nationaltrust.org.uk

Tel: 0161 941 1025 **Fax:** 0161 929 7508

e-mail: dunhammassey@nationaltrust.org.uk

Owner: The National Trust **Contact:** Property Manager

Originally an early Georgian house, Dunham Massey has sumptuous interiors with collections of walnut furniture, paintings and magnificent Huguenot silver. The richly planted garden contains waterside plantings, late flowering azaleas, an Orangery and Elizabethan mount. The surrounding deer park escaped the attentions of 18th century landscape gardeners and contains some notable specimen trees.

Location: OS Ref. SJ735 874. 3m SW of Altrincham off A56. M6/J19. M56/J7. Station Altrincham (BR & Metro) 3m.

Open: House: 19 Mar - 30 Oct: Sat - Wed, 12 noon - 5pm (11am - 5pm Good Fri, BH Sun & Mon). Garden: 19 Mar - 30 Oct: daily, 11am - 5.30pm. Last admission ½ hr before closing. Park open daily, all year.

Admission: House & Garden: Adult £6.50, Child £3.25, Family (2+3 max) £16.25. House or Garden: Adult £4.50, Child £2.25. Park entry: Car £3.80, Coach £10, Motorcycle £1. Groups should telephone for price details.

ℹ️ No photography in house. 🗓 🎡 ♿ Partial. WC. Batricars. 🍴 Licensed. 🎦 Optional. No extra charge. 🅿 🚭 🐕 In grounds, on leads. ❋

GAWSWORTH HALL

MACCLESFIELD, CHESHIRE SK11 9RN

www.gawsworthhall.com

Tel: 01260 223456   **Fax:** 01260 223469   **e-mail:** enquiries@gawsworthhall.com

Owner: Mr and Mrs T Richards   **Contact:** Mr T Richards

Fully lived-in Tudor half-timbered manor house with Tilting Ground. Former home of Mary Fitton, Maid of Honour at the Court of Queen Elizabeth I, and the supposed 'Dark Lady' of Shakespeare's sonnets. Pictures, sculpture and furniture. Open air theatre with covered grandstand - June, July and August, please telephone for details. Situated halfway between Macclesfield and Congleton in an idyllic setting close to the lovely medieval church.

Location: OS Ref. SJ892 697. 3m S of Macclesfield on the A536 Congleton to Macclesfield road.

Open: Easter weekend then 30 Apr - 25 Sept: Sun - Wed and for Special Events & BHs. 19 Jun - 31 Aug: daily, 2 - 5pm.

Admission: Adult £5, Child £2.50. Groups (20+): £4.

🖻 🖼 🅿 🐾 Guide dogs in garden only. 🔺 ♨ Tel for details.

HARE HILL 🌿

Over Alderley, Macclesfield, Cheshire SK10 4QB

Tel: 0161 928 0075 (Regional Office)   01625 584412 (Countryside Office)

www.nationaltrust.org.uk

Owner: The National Trust   **Contact:** The Head Gardener

A woodland garden surrounding a walled garden with pergola, rhododendrons, hollies and hostas. Parkland.

Location: OS Ref. SJ875 765. Between Alderley Edge and Macclesfield (B5087). Turn off N onto Prestbury Road, continue for 3/4 m.

Open: 25 Mar - 8 May & 1 Jun - 30 Oct: Weds, Thurs, Sats & Suns, 10am - 5pm. 9 - 29 May: daily, 10am - 5pm.

Admission: Adult £2.70, Child £1.25. Car park fee £1.50 (refundable on entry to garden). Groups by written appointment c/o Garden Lodge at address above.

🔖 Gravel paths - strong companion advisable. 🐾 On leads in park.

HOLMSTON HALL BARN

Little Budworth, Tarporley, Cheshire CW6 9AY

Tel/Fax: 01829 760366

Owner/Contact: Mr Richard & Dr Yvonne Hopkins

15th century barn. Newly restored.

Location: OS Ref. SJ607 626. Off A49. 2m from Eaton village.

Open: All year by appointment only.

Admission: Free.

✳

LITTLE MORETON HALL 🌿

Congleton, Cheshire CW12 4SDN

Tel: 01260 272018   www.nationaltrust.org.uk

Owner: The National Trust   **Contact:** The Property Manager

Begun in 1450 and completed 160 years later, Little Moreton Hall is regarded as the finest example of a timber-framed moated manor house in the country.

Location: OS Ref. SJ833 589. 4m SW of Congleton on E side of A34.

Open: 20 Mar - 31 Oct: Wed - Sun (open BH Mons & Good Fri), 11.30am - 5pm. 6 Nov - 19 Dec: Sat & Sun, 11.30am - 4pm or dusk.

Admission: Adult £5, Child £2.50, Family £12. Groups: £4.25 (must book).

🖻 🚻 🔖 Braille guide, wheelchair. WCs. 🖼 🍴 🐾 Car park only.

Rode Hall.

LYME PARK 🌿

Disley, Stockport, Cheshire SK12 2NX

Tel: 01663 762023   **Fax:** 01663 765035   www.nationaltrust.org.uk

Owner: The National Trust   **Contact:** The Property Manager

Legh family home for 600 years. Part of the original Elizabethan house survives with 18th and 19th century additions by Giacomo Leoni and Lewis Wyatt. Mortlake tapestries, Grinling Gibbons carvings, unique collection of English clocks.

Location: OS Ref. SJ965 825. Off the A6 at Disley. 6¹/₂ m SE of Stockport.

Open: House: 29 Mar - 30 Oct: Fri - Tue, 1 - 5pm (last adm 4.30pm) (BH Mons & Good Fri, 11am - 5pm). Park: 1 Apr - 31 Oct: daily, 8am - 8.30pm; Nov - Mar: 8am - 6pm. Gardens: 29 Mar - 30 Oct: Fri - Tue, 11am - 5pm.

Admission: House & Garden: £5.80. House only: £4.20. Garden only: £2.70. Park only: car £3.80 (refundable on purchase of adult house & garden ticket), motorbike £2, coach/minibus £6. Booked coach groups Park admission Free. NT members Free.

ⁱNo photography in house. 📷 ⚅Partial. WC. ☻ ⒴Licensed. ⒯By arrangement. ℗ ☻ ✈In park, close control. Guide dogs only in house & garden. ❋

NESS BOTANIC GARDENS

Ness, Neston, Cheshire CH64 4AY

Tel: 01513 530123   **Fax:** 01513 531004

Owner: University of Liverpool   **Contact:** Dr E J Sharples

Location: OS Ref. SJ302 760 (village centre). Off A540. 10m NW of Chester. 1¹/₂ m S of Neston.

Open: 1 Mar - 31 Oct: 9.30am - 5pm. Nov - Feb: 9.30am - 4pm.

Admission: Adult £4.70, Conc £4.30, Child (under 18yrs) Free. 10% discount for groups. Please telephone for details.

NETHER ALDERLEY MILL 🌿

Congleton Rd, Nether Alderley, Macclesfield SK10 4TW

www.nationaltrust.org.uk

Tel: 01625 584412 or 01625 527468 (Quarry Bank Mill Reception)

e-mail: netheralderleymill@national trust.org.uk

Owner: The National Trust   **Contact:** Property Manager

15th century mill beside a tranquil millpond. Heavy framework, low beams and floors connected by wooden ladders, all set beneath an enormous sloping stone roof, help to create this wonderful corn mill.

Location: OS Ref. SJ844 763. 1¹/₂ m S of Alderley Edge, on E side of A34.

Open: 1 Apr - 30 Oct: Wed, Thur, Fri, Sun & BH Mons, 1 - 5pm.

Admission: Adult £2.50, Child £1.20, Family £8. Groups by prior arrangement (max 20).

⒯By arrangement. ℗Limited. Coaches must book. ☻By arrangement. ✈

NORTON PRIORY MUSEUM & GARDENS

TUDOR ROAD, MANOR PARK, RUNCORN WA7 1SX

www.nortonpriory.org

Tel: 01928 569895   **e-mail:** info@nortonpriory.org

Owner/Contact: The Norton Priory Museum Trust

Discover the 800 year old priory range, excavated priory remains, museum gallery, the St Christopher statue – one of the great treasures of medieval Europe – exciting sculpture trail and award winning Walled Garden. Set in 38 acres of tranquil, woodland gardens, Norton Priory also has a coffee shop, retail area and temporary exhibitions gallery.

Location: OS Ref. SJ545 835. 3m from M56/J11. 2m E of Runcorn.

Open: All year: daily, from 12 noon. Telephone for details.

Admission: Adult £4.50, Child/Conc. £3.25, Family £12. Groups £2.95.

📷 ⒯ ⚅Wheelchairs, braille guide, audio tapes & WC. ☻ ⒯By arrangement. ℗ ☻ ✈In grounds, on leads. ❋ ⒰Tel for details.

PEOVER HALL 🏛

OVER PEOVER, KNUTSFORD WA16 9HW

Tel: 01565 632358

Owner: Randle Brooks   **Contact:** I Shepherd

An Elizabethan house dating from 1585. Fine Carolean stables. Mainwaring Chapel, 18th century landscaped park. Large garden with topiary work, also walled and herb gardens.

Location: OS Ref. SJ772 734. 4m S of Knutsford off A50 at Whipping Stocks Inn.

Open: Apr - Oct: House, Stables & Gardens: Mons except BHs, 2 - 5pm. Tours of the House at 2.30 & 3.30pm. Stables & Gardens only: Thurs, 2 - 5pm.

Admission: House, Stables & Gardens: Adult £4.50, Child £3. Stables & Gardens only: Adult £3, Child £2.

☻Mondays only. ⒯Obligatory. ✈

QUARRY BANK MILL & STYAL ESTATE 🌿

Styal, Wilmslow SK9 4LA

Tel: 01625 527468   **Fax:** 01625 539267

e-mail: quarrybankmill.reception@nationaltrust.org.uk   www.nationaltrust.org.uk

Owner: The National Trust   **Contact:** Nikky Braithwaite

Unique Georgian Cotton Mill with working machinery, daily demonstrations and fascinating living history. See the steam engines and mighty watermill in action. Experience the grim conditions in the Apprentice House. Enjoy the beautiful 300 acre Styal Estate.

Location: OS Ref. SJ835 835. 1¹/₂ m N of Wilmslow off B5166. 2¹/₂ m from M56/J5. Styal Shuttle Bus, Airport 2¹/₂ m.

Open: Mill: Apr - Sept: daily, 10.30am - 5.30pm, last adm. 4pm. Oct - Mar: daily except Mons, 10.30am - 5pm, last adm. 3.30pm. Apprentice House & Garden: Tue - Fri, 2 - 4.30pm, Sats/Suns, 11am - 4.30pm.

Admission: Adult £7.30, Child/Conc. £4.50, Family £15 (2+3). Mill only: Adult £5.20, Child/Conc. £3.50. Booked Groups (20+) at child rate.

📷 ⓣ ⚅Partial. ☻ ⒴Licensed. ⒯By arrangement. ℗ ☻ ✈In grounds on leads. ▲ ❋ ⒰Tel for details.

RODE HALL 🏛

CHURCH LANE, SCHOLAR GREEN, CHESHIRE ST7 3QP

www.rodehall.co.uk

Tel: 01270 873237   **Fax:** 01270 882962   **e-mail:** rodehall@scholargreen.fsnet.co.uk

Owner/Contact: Sir Richard Baker Wilbraham Bt

The Wilbraham family have lived at Rode since 1669; the present house was constructed in two stages, the earlier two storey wing and stable block around 1705 and the main building was completed in 1752. Later alterations by Lewis Wyatt and Darcy Braddell were undertaken in 1812 and 1927 respectively. The house stands in a Repton landscape and the extensive gardens include a woodland garden, with a terraced rock garden and grotto, which has many species of rhododendrons, azaleas, hellebores and climbing roses following snowdrops and daffodils in the early spring. The formal rose garden was designed by W Nesfield in 1860 and there is a large walled kitchen garden which is at its best from the middle of June. The icehouse in the park has recently been restored.

Location: OS Ref. SJ819 573. 5m SW of Congleton between the A34 and A50. Kidsgrove railway station 2m NW of Kidsgrove.

Open: 28 Mar - 29 Sept: Weds & BHs and by appointment. Garden only: Tues & Thurs, 2 - 5pm. Snowdrop Walk: 8 - 27 Feb: 12 noon - 4pm.

Admission: House, Garden & Kitchen Garden: Adult £5, OAP £3.50. Garden & Kitchen Garden: Adult £3, OAP £2. Snowdrop Walk: £3.

🛗 ⬛ Home-made teas. 🐕 On leads.

TABLEY HOUSE

KNUTSFORD, CHESHIRE WA16 0HB

www.tableyhouse.co.uk

Tel: 01565 750151   **Fax:** 01565 653230   **e-mail:** inquiries@tableyhouse.co.uk

Owner: The University of Manchester   **Contact:** The Assistant Administrator

The finest Palladian House in the North West, Tabley a Grade I listing, was designed by John Carr of York for the Leicester family. Set in landscaped parkland it contains the first collection of English paintings, including works of art by Turner, Reynolds, Lawrence and Lely. Furniture by Chippendale, Bullock and Gillow and fascinating family memorabilia adorn the rooms. Interesting Tea Room and 17th century Chapel adjoin.

Location: OS Ref. SJ725 777. M6/J19, A556 S on to A5033. 2m W of Knutsford.

Open: Apr - end Oct inclusive: Thurs, Fris, Sats, Suns & BHs, 2 - 5pm.

Admission: Adult £4. Child/Student £1.50. Groups by arrangement.

⬛ 🔲 ⬛ 🅿
🪑 Civil Wedding Licence plus Civil Naming Ceremonies & Re-affirmation of Vows.
📺 Tel for details.

TATTON PARK 🌿   *See page 412 for full page entry.*

See page 412 for full page entry.

WOODHEY CHAPEL

Faddiley, Nr Nantwich, Cheshire CW5 8JH

Tel: 01270 524215

Owner: The Trustees of Woodhey Chapel   **Contact:** Mr Robinson, The Curator

Small private chapel that has been recently restored.

Location: OS Ref. SJ573 528. Proceeding W from Nantwich on A534, turn left 1m W of the Faddiley - Brindley villages onto narrow lane, keep ahead at next turn, at road end obtain key from farmhouse.

Open: Apr - Oct: Sats & BHs, 2 - 5pm, or apply for key at Woodhey Hall.

Admission: Donation box.

Cholmondeley Castle.

© C J Crowder

LEVENS HALL

www.levenshall.co.uk

Map 7

Owner: C H Bagot

▶ **CONTACT**

Peter Milner
Levens Hall
Kendal
Cumbria LA8 0PD

Tel: 01539 560321

Fax: 01539 560669

e-mail: email@
levenshall.fsnet.co.uk

▶ **LOCATION**

OS Ref. SD495 851

5m S of Kendal on the
A6. Exit M6/J36.

Rail: Oxenholme 5m.

Air: Manchester.

Levens Hall is an Elizabethan mansion built around a 13th century pele tower. The much loved home of the Bagot family, visitors comment on the warm and friendly atmosphere. Fine panelling and plasterwork, period furniture, Cordova leather wall coverings, paintings by Rubens, Lely and Cuyp, the earliest English patchwork and Wellingtoniana combine with other beautiful objects to form a fascinating collection.

The world famous Topiary Gardens were laid out by Monsieur Beaumont from 1694 and his design

has remained largely unchanged to this day. Over ninety individual pieces of topiary, some over nine metres high, massive beech hedges and colourful seasonal bedding provide a magnificent visual impact. *"Considered to be in the top ten UK gardens"* – Monty Don.

On Sundays and Bank Holidays 'Bertha', a full size Showman's Engine, is in steam. Delicious home-made lunches and teas are available, together with the award-winning Levens beer 'Morocco Ale', in the Bellingham Buttery.

▶ **OPENING TIMES**

Summer

12 April - 13 October
Sun - Thur
(closed Fris & Sats).

House: 12 noon - 5pm
Last admission 4.30pm.

Gardens, Plant Centre,
Gift Shop & Tearoom:
10am - 5pm.

Winter

Closed.

▶ **ADMISSION**

House & Gardens

Adult	£8.00
Child	£3.80
Family (2+3*)	£22.00

Groups (20+)

Adult	£7.00
Child	£3.50

Gardens

Adult	£5.90
Child	£2.70
Family (2+3*)	£17.00

Groups (20+)

Adult	£5.00
Child	£2.50

*Additional Children at
Group rate.

Evening Tours

House & Garden, for
groups (20+) by prior
arrangement only
(Mon - Thur) £9.00

Gardens guided tour by
the Head Gardener or his
Assistant for groups (20+)
by prior arrangement
only £6.50

Morning Tours

House tours starting
between 10 - 10.30am
for pre-arranged groups
(20+/min charge £160)
..............................£8.00

ⓘ No indoor photography. 🎦 ❋ ♿ Partial. WC. Electric buggy hire. DVD of interior.

☕ Licensed. 🍽 🚶 By arrangement. 🏫 Schools welcome. 🅿 🐕 Guide dogs only.

No admission charge for gift
shop, tearoom and plant
centre.

Map 7

MUNCASTER CASTLE 🏛

GARDENS, OWL CENTRE & MEADOWVOLE MAZE

www.muncaster.co.uk

Owner: Mrs Phyllida Gordon-Duff-Pennington

▶ CONTACT

Peter Frost-Pennington
Muncaster Castle
Ravenglass
Cumbria CA18 1RQ

Tel: 01229 717614
Fax: 01229 717010

e-mail: info@muncaster.co.uk

▶ LOCATION

OS Ref. SD103 965

On the A595 1m S of Ravenglass, 19m S of Whitehaven.

From London 6 hrs, Chester 2¹/₂ hrs, Edinburgh 3¹/₂ hrs, M6/J36, A590, A595 (from S). M6/J40, A66, A595 (from E). Carlisle, A595 (from N).

Rail: Ravenglass (on Barrow-in-Furness-Carlisle Line) 1¹/₂ m.

Air: Manchester 2¹/₂ hrs.

CONFERENCE/FUNCTION

ROOM	MAX CAPACITY
Drawing Rm	120
Dining Rm	50
Family Dining Rm	60
Great Hall	110
Old Laundry	120
Library	40

Top Attraction (up to 100,000 visitors) Cumbria Awards for Excellence 2004.

Muncaster Castle has been owned by the Pennington family since 1208. It has grown from the original pele tower built on Roman foundations to the impressive structure visible today. Outstanding features are the Great Hall and Salvin's Octagonal Library and the Drawing Room with its barrel ceiling.

The haunted castle contains many treasures including beautiful furniture, exquisite needlework panels, tapestries and oriental rugs. The family silver is very fine and is accompanied in the Dining Room by the Ongley Service, the most ornamental set of porcelain ever created by the Derby factory, Florentine 16th century bronzes and an alabaster lady by Giambologna can be seen. The family are actively involved in entertaining their many visitors.

The woodland gardens cover 77 acres and command spectacular views of the Lakeland Fells, with many delightful walks including a 3 hour Wild Walk allowing visitors into areas not previously accessible. From mid-March to June the rhododendrons, azaleas, camellias and magnolias are at their best.

The Owl Centre boasts a fine collection of owls from all over the world. 'Meet the Birds' occurs daily at 2.30pm (Apr - 6 Nov), when a talk is given on the work of the centre. Weather permitting, the birds fly free.

Imagine being a meadow vole - just two and a half inches tall - living in meadowland, where dangers lurk at every turn. It's no picnic. Great for kids of all ages! Muncaster Interactive - a new computer suite in The Old Dairy allows visitors to interact with Muncaster as never before.

Tony Warburton, Director of The World Owl Trust, with Sparky the Barn Owl.

📷 ℹ Church. Suitable for fashion shoots, garden parties, film location, clay pigeon shooting. No photography inside the Castle. Home of the World Owl Trust, run by TV naturalist Tony Warburton.

📶 Wedding receptions. For catering and functions in the Castle Tel: 01229 717614.

♿ By prior arrangement visitors alight near Castle. Wheelchairs for loan. WCs. Special audio tour tapes for the partially sighted/those with learning difficulties. Allocated parking.

☕ 🍴 Creeping Kate's Kitchen (licensed) (max 80) – full menu. Groups can book: 01229 717614 to qualify for discounts.

🚶 🎧 Individual audio tour (40mins) included in price. Private tours with a personal guide (family member possible) can be arranged at additional fee. Lectures by arrangement.

🅿 500 cars 800 yds from House; coaches may park closer.

📖 Guides available. Historical subjects, horticulture, conservation, owl tours.

🐕 In grounds, on leads.

🔔 ❄

▶ OPENING TIMES

Castle
14 February - 6 November
Daily (closed Sat),
12 noon - 5pm.

Gardens & Owl Centre
All year except January:
Daily, 10.30am - 6pm
or dusk if earlier.

'Meet the Birds'
April - 6 November
Daily at 2.30pm.

Watch the wild herons feeding during the 'Heron Happy Hour'.
Daily at 4.30pm.

Winter
Castle closed. Open by appointment for groups.

Darkest Muncaster
A Winter Evening of Magic – see website for details.

▶ ADMISSION

Castle, Gardens, Owl Centre & MeadowVole Maze
Adult £9.00
Child (5-15yrs) £6.00
Under 5yrs .... Free
Family (2+2) £25.00
Groups
Adult £7.50
Child (5-15yrs) £4.50

Gardens, Owl Centre & MeadowVole Maze
Adult £6.00
Child (5-15yrs) £4.00
Under 5yrs .... Free
Family (2+2) £18.00
Groups
Adult £5.50
Child (5-15yrs) £3.00

ABBOT HALL ART GALLERY

See page 418 for full page entry.

ACORN BANK GDN & WATERMILL 🌿

Temple Sowerby, Penrith, Cumbria CA10 1SP

Tel: 01768 361893 **e-mail:** acornbank@nationaltrust.org.uk

www.nationaltrust.org.uk

Owner: The National Trust **Contact:** The Custodian

A one hectare garden protected by fine oaks under which grow a vast display of daffodils. Inside the walls there are orchards with a variety of fruit trees surrounded by mixed borders with shrubs, herbaceous plants and roses. House not open.

Location: Gate: OS Ref. NY612 281. Just N of Temple Sowerby, 6m E of Penrith on A66.

Open: 27 Mar - 31 Oct: daily except Tue, 10am - 5pm. Last admission 4.30pm. Tearoom: 6 - 26 Mar, 11am - 4pm.

Admission: Adult £2.75, Child £1.80, Family £6.80. Pre-arranged groups £2.

🖼 ⛔ Grounds only. WCs. ❋

BEATRIX POTTER GALLERY 🌿

MAIN STREET, HAWKSHEAD, CUMBRIA LA22 0NS

www.nationaltrust.org.uk

Tel: 01539 436355 **Fax:** 01539 436187

e-mail: beatrixpottergallery@nationaltrust.org.uk

Owner: The National Trust **Contact:** Ticket Office / House Steward

An annually changing exhibition of original sketches and watercolours painted by Beatrix Potter for her children's stories. *The Tale of Mrs Tiggy-Winkle* and *The Tale of The Pie & The Patty-Pan* feature for their 100th birthdays. The gallery was once the office of Beatrix Potter's husband, William Heelis. It is ideally matched with a visit to Beatrix Potter's house, Hill Top, two miles away, where she wrote and illustrated many of her children's stories.

Location: OS Ref. SD352 982. 5m SSW of Ambleside. In the Square.

Open: 19 Mar - 30 Oct: Sat - Wed (closed Thur & Fri except Good Fri) 10.30am - 4.30pm. Last admission 4pm. Admission is by timed ticket (incl. NT members).

Admission: Adult £3.50, Child £1.70, Family £8.70. No reduction for groups. Discount for Hill Top ticket holders (not groups). Group booking essential.

ⓘNo photography inside. 🖼 ⛔Assistance dogs only.

BLACKWELL - THE ARTS & CRAFTS HOUSE

See page 419 for full page entry.

BRANTWOOD

Coniston, Cumbria LA21 8AD

Tel: 01539 441396 **Fax:** 01539 441263 **e-mail:** enquiries@brantwood.org.uk

www.brantwood.org.uk

Owner: The Brantwood Trust

Brantwood, the former home of John Ruskin, is the most beautifully situated house in the Lake District. Explore Brantwood's estate and gardens or experience contemporary art in the Severn Studio. Brantwood's bookshop, the Jumping Jenny restaurant and Coach House Craft Gallery combine for a perfect day out.

Location: OS Ref. SD313 959. 2½m from Coniston village on the E side of Coniston Water.

Open: Mid Mar - mid Nov: daily, 11am - 5.30pm. Mid Nov - mid Mar: Wed - Sun, 11am - 4.30pm.

Admission: Adult £5.50, Child £1, Student £4, Family (2+3) £11.50. Garden only: Adult £3.75, Family (2+3) £8. Groups: Adult £4.50, Child £1, Student £3, Garden only: £3.

ⓘNo photography in the house. 🖼❋⛔Partial. ◐Licensed. ⑪Licensed.

Ⓕ By arrangement. ⓟAmple. Limited for coaches. 🖼 ⛔In grounds, on leads. ◮ ❋

BROUGH CASTLE ⚏

Brough, Cumbria

Tel: 01228 591922

Owner: English Heritage **Contact:** Visitor Operations Manager

This ancient site dates back to Roman times. The 12th century keep replaced an earlier stronghold destroyed by the Scots in 1174.

Location: OS Ref. NY791 141. 8m SE of Appleby S of A66. South part of the village.

Open: Any reasonable time.

Admission: Free.

🖼 On leads. ⓟ ❋

BROUGHAM CASTLE ⚏

Penrith, Cumbria CA10 2AA

Tel: 01768 862488

Owner: English Heritage **Contact:** Visitor Operations Team

These impressive ruins on the banks of the River Eamont include an early 13th century keep and later buildings. You can climb to the top of the keep and survey the domain of its eccentric one-time owner Lady Anne Clifford. Exhibition about the Roman fort, medieval castle and Lady Anne Clifford.

Location: OS Ref. NY537 290. 1½ m SE of Penrith, between A66 & B6262.

Open: 24 Mar - 30 Sept: daily, 10am - 6pm. 1 - 31 Oct: Thur - Mon, 10am - 5pm. Times subject to change April 2005.

Admission: Adult £2.60, Child £1.30, Conc. £2. 15% discount for groups (11+).

ⓘWCs. 🖼 ⛔Grounds. ⓟLimited. ◼ 🖼In grounds, on leads. 🖼Tel for details.

CARLISLE CASTLE ⚏

CARLISLE, CUMBRIA CA3 8UR

Tel: 01228 591922

Owner: English Heritage **Contact:** Visitor Operations Team

This impressive medieval castle, where Mary Queen of Scots was once imprisoned, has a long and tortuous history of warfare and family feuds. A portcullis hangs menacingly over the gatehouse passage, there is a maze of passages and chambers, endless staircases to lofty towers and you can walk the high ramparts for stunning views. There is also a medieval manor house in miniature: a suite of medieval rooms furnished as they might have been when used by the castle's former constable. The castle includes the King's Own Royal Border Regimental Museum.

Location: OS Ref. NY397 563. In Carlisle town, at N end of city centre.

Open: 24 Mar - 30 Sept: daily, 9.30am - 6pm. 1 - 31 Oct: daily, 10am - 5pm. 1 Nov - 31 Mar: daily, 10am - 4pm. Closed 24 - 26 Dec & 1 Jan. Times subject to change April 2005.

Admission: Adult £4, Child £2, Conc £3. 15% discount for groups (11+).

🖼 ⛔Partial, wheelchairs available. Ⓕ By arrangement.

ⓟ Disabled parking only. ◼ 🖼 Dogs on leads. ❋ 🖼 Tel for details.

LOCAL FOOD

Cumberland Sauce

A fruity sauce with its main ingredients being redcurrant jelly, oranges and lemons. Usually served with a glazed ham, but suitable for any roast joint of meat.

CARLISLE CATHEDRAL

Carlisle, Cumbria CA3 8TZ

Tel: 01228 548151 **Fax:** 01228 547049   **Contact:** Ms C Baines
Fine sandstone Cathedral, founded in 1122. Medieval stained glass.
Location: OS Ref. NY399 559. Carlisle city centre, 2m from M6/J43.
Open: Mon - Sat: 7.45am - 6.15pm, Suns, 7.45 - 5pm. Closes 4pm between Christmas
Day & New Year. Sun services: 8am, 10.30am & 3pm. Weekday services: 8am, 5.30pm
& a 12.30 service on Weds, Fris and Saints' Days.
Admission: Donation.

CONISHEAD PRIORY & MANJUSHRI BUDDHIST TEMPLE

Ulverston, Cumbria LA12 9QQ

Tel: 01229 584029   **Fax:** 01229 580080   **e-mail:** info@manjushri.org
www.conisheadpriory.org
Owner: Manjushri Kadampa Meditation Centre   **Contact:** Mr D Coote
A Victorian gothic mansion. Special features include decorative ceilings, a vaulted
great hall with fine stained glass and a 177 feet long cloister corridor. This historic
treasure has been rescued from collapse and is still under careful restoration. 'A very
important Gothic revival country house...', English Heritage. There is also a unique
Buddhist Temple in the former Kitchen garden.
Location: OS Ref. SD300 750. 2m S of Ulverston on Bardsea Coast Rd A5087.
Open: Easter - Oct: Sat, Sun & BHs, 2 - 5pm. Closed 21 May - 6 Jun & 16 Jul - 15 Aug.
Opening times sometimes vary, please telephone to confirm and for weekday details.
Admission: Free. House Tours and audio visual: Adult £2.50, Child/Conc: £1.50.
▣ ▮ ⓖPartial. WC. ☞ ⓕBy arrangement. ⓟ ▪
⛊Guide dogs only in House. In grounds, on leads. ▣ ✳

©National Trust Photographic Library/Scott Mackie

✳ Open All Year Index see page 43

Sizergh Castle & Garden.

DALEMAIN 🏛

PENRITH, CUMBRIA CA11 9TH

www.dalemain.com

Tel: 017684 86450 **Fax:** 017684 86223 **e-mail:** admin@dalemain.com
Owner: Robert Hasell-McCosh Esq   **Contact:** Marta Bakinowska - Administrator
Dalemain is a fine mixture of mediaeval, Tudor and early Georgian architecture. The
imposing Georgian façade strikes the visitor immediately but in the cobbled
courtyard the atmosphere of the north country Tudor manor is secure. The present
owner's family have lived at Dalemain since 1679 and have collected china, furniture
and family portraits.
Delightful and fascinating 5 acre plantsman's gardens set against the picturesque
splendour of the Lakeland Fells and Parkland. Richly planted herbaceous borders.
Rose Walk with over 100 old-fashioned roses and ancient apple trees of named
varieties. Magnificent Abies Cephalonica and Tulip Tree. Tudor Knot Garden. Wild
Garden with profusion of flowering shrubs and wild flowers and in early summer
the breathtaking display of blue Himalayan Poppies.

Location: OS Ref. NY477 269. On A592 1m S of A66. 4m SW of Penrith. From London,
M1, M6/J40: 5 hrs. From Edinburgh, A73, M74,M6/J40: 2 1/2 hrs.
Open: 20 Mar - 30 Oct: Sun - Thur. House: 11am - 4pm. Gardens/restaurant/
tearoom/gift shop/plant sales/museums: 10.30am - 5pm. Groups (10+) please book.
Winter: Gardens, restaurant & tearoom open for homemade food: 31 Oct - mid Mar:
Mon - Thur, 10am - 4pm.
Admission: House & Garden: Adult £6, Accompanied Child Free. Gardens only: Adult
£4, Accompanied Child Free. Visitors in wheelchairs Free. All prices include VAT.

ⓘNo photography in house. Moorings available on Ullswater. ▣ ▮ ☞
ⓖVisitors may drive into the Courtyard and alight near the gift shop. Electric scooter.
WCs. ☞ ⓕⓛLicensed. Groups must book for lunches/high teas.
ⓕ1hr tours. German and French translations. Garden tour for groups extra. ⓟ50 yds.
⛊Guide dogs in house only. No dogs in garden, allowed in grounds. ⓔTel for details.

©The Wordsworth Trust

DOVE COTTAGE
& THE WORDSWORTH MUSEUM
GRASMERE, CUMBRIA LA22 9SH
www.wordsworth.org.uk

Tel: 01539 435544   **Fax:** 01539 435748

e-mail: enquiries@wordsworth.org.uk

Owner: The Wordsworth Trust   **Contact:** Bookings Officer

Situated in the heart of the English Lake District, Dove Cottage is the beautifully preserved Grasmere home of England's finest poet William Wordsworth. Visitors are offered fascinating guided tours of his world-famous home. The award-winning Museum displays priceless Wordsworth manuscripts and memorabilia. Onsite tearooms and book and gift shop.

Location: OS Ref. NY342 070. Immediately S of Grasmere village on A591. Main car/coach park next to Dove Cottage Tea Rooms and Restaurant.

Open: All year: daily, 9.30am - 5.30pm (last admission 5pm). Closed 9 Jan - 7 Feb.

Admission: Adult £5.95, Child £3, OAP £5.30, Family Tickets available. Pre-arranged groups (10-60): Adult £4.75. Reciprocal discount ticket with Rydal Mount and Wordsworth House. (2004 prices.)

[i]No photography. 🏛 &Partial. WC. ▣ 🅃 Obligatory. PLimited. ■
🐕Guide dogs only. ✻ ▽ Tel for details.

FELL FOOT PARK 🐾
Newby Bridge, Cumbria LA12 8NN

Tel: 01539 531273   **Fax:** 01539 539926   **e-mail:** fellfootpark@nationaltrust.org.uk

Owner: The National Trust   **Contact:** Park Manager

Come and explore this lakeshore Victorian park on the edge of Windermere. A great place for the family, with boat hire, tearoom, play area, family activity sheets and wildlife room showing birds and bats who live around the park. Fantastic views of the Lakeland fells. Wonderful colour in spring.

Location: OS Ref. SD381 869. S end of Lake Windermere on E shore, entrance from A592. Near Aquarium of the Lakes and Haverthwaite Steam Railway.

Open: Daily, 9am - dusk.

Admission: Car park: 2hrs £2.50, 4hrs £4.50, all day £6. Coaches by arrangement.
🏛 &Partial. ▣ PCharge. 🐕On leads. ✻ ▽ Tel for details.

FURNESS ABBEY ♯
Barrow-in-Furness, Cumbria LH13 0TJ

Tel: 01229 823420

Owner: English Heritage   **Contact:** Visitor Operations Staff

Hidden in a peaceful green valley are the beautiful red sandstone remains of the wealthy abbey founded in 1123 by Stephen, later King of England. This abbey first belonged to the Order of Savigny and later to the Cistercians. There is a museum and exhibition.

Location: OS Ref. SD218 717. 1¹/₂ m NE of Barrow-in-Furness.

Open: 24 Mar - 30 Sept: daily, 10am - 6pm. 1 Oct - 31 Mar: Thur - Mon, 10am - 4pm. Closed 1 - 2pm in winter. Closed 24 - 26 Dec & 1 Jan. Times subject to change April 2005.

Admission: Adult £3.30, Child £1.70, Conc. £2.50. 15% discount for groups (11+).
[i]WC. 🏛 &Grounds. 🎧 Inclusive. P ■ 🐕In grounds, on leads. ✻
▽ Tel for details.

HARDKNOTT ROMAN FORT ♯
Ravenglass, Cumbria

Tel: 0161 242 1400

Owner: English Heritage   **Contact:** The North West Regional Office

This fort, built between AD120 and 138, controlled the road from Ravenglass to Ambleside.

Location: OS Ref. NY219 015. At the head of Eskdale. 9m NE of Ravenglass, at W end of Hardknott Pass.

Open: Any reasonable time. Access may be hazardous in winter.

Admission: Free.
P 🐕On leads. ✻

HERON CORN MILL & MUSEUM OF PAPERMAKING
Beetham Trust, Waterhouse Mills, Beetham, Milnthorpe LA7 7AR

Tel: 015395 65027   **Fax:** 015395 65033   **e-mail:** info@heronmill.org

Owner: Heron Corn Mill Beetham Trust   **Contact:** Mr Neil Stobbs

A fascinating visitor attraction. An 18th century corn mill and museum of papermaking offers hand-made paper demonstrations and art workshops for visitors.

Location: OS Ref. SD497 800. At Beetham. 1m S of Milnthorpe on the A6.

Open: Easter - 30 Sept: Tue - Sun & BHs, 11am - 5pm.

Admission: Adult £2, Child £1, OAP £1.50. Schools and groups welcome.

©National Trust Photographic Library/Geoffrey Frosh

HILL TOP 🐾
NEAR SAWREY, AMBLESIDE, CUMBRIA LA22 0LF
www.nationaltrust.org.uk

Tel: 01539 436269   **Fax:** 01539 436811   **e-mail:** hilltop@nationaltrust.org.uk

Owner: The National Trust   **Contact:** Ticket Office/Visitor Services Manager

Beatrix Potter wrote many of her famous children's stories in this little 17th century house, which contains her furniture and china. She bought Hill Top Farm 100 years ago and this will be celebrated throughout 2005. There is a traditional cottage garden attached. A selection of the original illustrations may be seen at the Beatrix Potter Gallery in Hawkshead. Shop specialises in Beatrix Potter items.

Location: OS Ref. SD370 955. 2m S of Hawkshead, in hamlet of Near Sawrey, behind the Tower Bank Arms.

Open: 19 Mar - 30 Oct: Sat - Wed & Good Fri, 10.30am - 4.30pm. Garden & Shop: Sat - Wed, 10.30am - 5pm, Thur & Fri, 10am - 5pm. Last admission 4pm. Admission by timed ticket. Group booking essential.

Admission: Adult £5, Child £2, Family £12. No reduction for groups. Discount for Beatrix Potter Gallery ticket holders (not groups). Garden: Free on Thur & Fri.
[i]No photography in house. 🏛 &Partial. PNone for coaches.
🐕Assistance dogs only. ▽ Tel for details.

HOLEHIRD GARDENS
Patterdale Road, Windermere, Cumbria LA23 1NP

Tel: 01539 446008

Owner: Lakeland Horticultural Society   **Contact:** The Hon Secretary

Over 10 acres of hillside gardens overlooking Windermere, including a walled garden and national collections of Astilbe, Hydrangea and Polystichum ferns. Organised and maintained entirely by volunteers.

Location: OS Ref. NY410 008. On A592, ³/₄ m N of junction with A591. ¹/₂ m N of Windermere. 1m from Townend.

Open: All year: dawn to dusk.

Admission: Free. Donation appreciated (at least £2 suggested).

Special Events Index see page 24

HOLKER HALL & GARDENS 🏛

CARK-IN-CARTMEL, GRANGE-OVER-SANDS, CUMBRIA LA11 7PL

www.holker-hall.co.uk

Tel: 01539 558328 **Fax:** 01539 558378 **e-mail:** publicopening@holker.co.uk

Owner: Lord Cavendish of Furness   **Contact:** Elizabeth Ward

Holker Hall, home of Lord and Lady Cavendish, shows the confidence, spaciousness and prosperity of Victorian style on its grandest scale. The New Wing was designed by architects Paley and Austin and built by the 7th Duke of Devonshire during 1871-4. Despite this grand scale, Holker is very much a family home with visitors able to wander freely throughout the New Wing. Varying in period and style, Louis XV pieces happily mix with the Victorian, including an early copy of the famous triple portrait of Charles I by Van Dyck. The award-winning gardens include formal and woodland areas covering 25 acres. Designated 'amongst the best in the world in terms of design and content' by the *Good Gardens Guide*. This inspiring garden includes a lime stone cascade, fountain, the Sunken Garden, the Elliptical and Summer Gardens and many rare plants and shrubs. Newly created Labyrinth designed by Lady Cavendish and international designer Jim Buchanen. Winner 2004 'Cumbria in Bloom Award for Creative & Adventurous Horticultural Development'.

Location: OS Ref. SD359 773. Close to Morecambe Bay, 5m W of Grange-over-Sands by B5277. From Kendal, A6, A590, B5277, B5278: 16m. Motorway: M6/J36.

Open: Hall & Gardens: 28 Mar - 31 Oct: daily except Sat, 10am - 5.30pm. Hall closes at 4.45pm. Food Hall/Courtyard Café/Gift Shop: open daily from 1 Mar, 10.30am - 5.30pm.

Admission: House & Garden: Adult £8.75, Child £5, Family £25.75. Groups (20-100): Adult £5, Child £3.50, OAP £4.50. Under 6yrs Free.

ℹ️ No photography in house. 📷 Holker Food Hall – produce from the estate. 🖼
🍽 ♿ Visitors alight at entrance. WCs. 🍷 Licensed. 🏨 🅕 By arrangement.
🅿 150 yds from Hall. ◼ 🐕 In grounds, on leads.

HUTTON-IN-THE-FOREST 🏛

PENRITH, CUMBRIA CA11 9TH

www.hutton-in-the-forest.co.uk

Tel: 017684 84449 **Fax:** 017684 84571 **e-mail:** info@hutton-in-the-forest.co.uk

Owner: Lord Inglewood   **Contact:** Edward Thompson

The home of Lord Inglewood's family since 1605. Built around a medieval pele tower with 17th, 18th and 19th century additions. Fine collections of furniture, paintings, ceramics and tapestries. Outstanding grounds with terraces, topiary, walled garden, dovecote and woodland walk through magnificent specimen trees.

Location: OS Ref. NY460 358. 6m NW of Penrith & 2 ½ m from M6/J41 on B5305.

Open: 25 Mar - 3 Apr & 1 May - 2 Oct: Thur, Fri, Suns & BHs., 12.30 - 4pm (last entry). Tearoom: As house: 11am - 4.30pm. Gardens & Grounds: Easter - Oct, daily except Sats, 11am - 5pm.

Admission: House, Gardens & Grounds: Adult £5, Child £2.50, Family £13.50. Gardens & Grounds: Adult £3, Child Free. (2004 prices.)

ℹ️ Picnic area. 📷 Gift stall. 🍽 By arrangement. ♿ Partial. ◼
🅕 Obligatory (except Jul/Aug & BHs). 🅿 ◼ 🐕 On leads. 📱 Tel for details.

Map 7

Owner:
Richard Gillow
Reynolds Esq

▶ **CONTACT**

Mrs C S Reynolds
Leighton Hall
Carnforth
Lancashire LA5 9ST

Tel: 01524 734474
Fax: 01524 720357

e-mail: info@
leightonhall.co.uk

▶ **LOCATION**

OS Ref. SD494 744

9m N of Lancaster,
10m S of Kendal,
3m N of Carnforth.
1^1/$_2$ m W of A6.
3m from M6/A6/J35,
signed from J35A.

Rail: Carnforth
Station 3m.

Bus: The Carnforth
Connect (line 1) bus
from Carnforth Railway
Station stops at the
gates of Leighton Hall
(info 01524 734311).

Air: Manchester
Airport 65m.

Taxi: Carnforth Radio
Taxis, 01524 732763.

CONFERENCE/FUNCTION

ROOM	SIZE	MAX CAPACITY
Music Room	24' x 21'6"	80
Dining Rm		30
Other		80

LEIGHTON HALL 🏛

www.leightonhall.co.uk

Leighton Hall is one of the most beautifully sited houses in the British Isles, situated in a bowl of parkland, with the whole panorama of the Lakeland Fells rising behind. The Hall's neo-gothic façade was superimposed on an 18th century house, which, in turn, had been built on the ruins of the original medieval house. The present owner is descended from Adam d'Avranches who built the first house in 1246.

The whole house is, today, lived in by the Reynolds family whose emphasis is put on making visitors feel welcome in a family home.

Mr Reynolds is also descended from the founder of Gillow and Company of Lancaster. Connoisseurs of furniture will be particularly interested in the many 18th century Gillow pieces, some of which are unique. Fine pictures, clocks, silver and *objéts d'art* are also on display.

Leighton Hall is home to a varied collection of Birds of Prey. These birds are flown daily during opening hours, weather permitting.

GARDENS
The main garden has a continuous herbaceous border with rose covered walls, while the Walled Garden contains flowering shrubs, a herb garden, and an ornamental vegetable garden with a caterpillar maze. Beyond is the Woodland Walk where wild flowers abound from early spring.

🛍 ❋ ℹ No photography in house. Gifts & unusual plants for sale.

▼ Product launches, conferences, seminars, filming, garden parties. Outdoor events include: overland driving, archery and clay pigeon shooting. Wedding receptions, buffets, lunches and dinners.

♿ Partial. WC. Visitors may alight at the entrance to the Hall. Ground floor only.

🅿 🍴 Booking essential for group catering, menus on request.

🚶 Obligatory. By prior arrangement owner may meet groups. The 45 minute tour includes information on the property, its gardens and history. House and flying display tour time: 2 hrs.

🅿 Ample for cars and coaches.

🏫 School programme: all year round. Choice of Countryside Classroom, Victorian Leighton or Local History. Sandford Award for Heritage Education winner in 1983 and 1989.

🐕 In Park, on leads.

❄ For booked groups & functions.

🔔 An unusual, but spectacular venue, Leighton Hall is a fairytale choice.

🎭 Visit website for details.

▶ **OPENING TIMES**
Summer

May - September
Tue - Fri (also
BH Sun & Mon)
2 - 5pm.

August only:
Tue - Fri and Sun
(also BH Mon)
12.30 - 5pm.

NB. Booked groups (25+)
at any time, all year by
arrangement.

Winter

1 October - 30 April
Open to booked
groups (25+).

▶ **ADMISSION**
Summer

House, Garden & Birds
Adult £5.50
Child (5-12yrs)....... £4.00
Student/OAP £5.00
Family (2+3) £17.00
Groups (25+)
Adult £4.50
Child (5-12yrs)....... £3.50
Family (2+3) £17.00

Child under 5yrs, Free

Grounds only
(after 4.30pm)
Per person £1.50

Winter

As above but groups by
appointment only.

Pre-booked Candlelit
Tours Nov - Jan.

Note: The owners reserve
the right to close or restrict
access to the house and
grounds for special events,
or at any other time without
prior notice.

ASTLEY HALL MUSEUM & ART GALLERY

ASTLEY PARK, CHORLEY PR7 1NP

www.chorley.gov.uk/astleyhall

Tel: 01257 515555 **Fax:** 01257 515556 **e-mail:** louisemccall@chorley.gov.uk
Owner: Chorley Borough Council   **Contact:** Louise McCall - Curator
Timber-framed Tudor house, with spectacular 17th century additions. Interiors include sumptuous plaster ceilings, fine 17th century oak furniture and tapestries, plus displays of fine and decorative art. Set in parkland.
Location: OS Ref. SD574 183. Off Hallgate, Astley Village, between A581 and B5252. Close to M61/J8 and M6/J28.
Open: Apr - Oct: Sat, Sun & BH Mons, 12 noon - 5pm. Weekday & Nov - Apr: by appointment only.
Admission: Free.
ℹ️No photography. 🅾️ 🆃 ♿Partial. Braille guide. ● 🅵By arrangement.
🔊 ■ 🅿️ ♿Guide dogs only. ▲ ✳️

BLACKBURN CATHEDRAL

Cathedral Close, Blackburn, Lancashire BB1 5AA

Tel: 01254 51491 **Fax:** 01254 689666   **Contact:** Mrs Alison Feeney
On an historic Saxon site in town centre. The 1826 Parish Church dedicated as the Cathedral in 1977 with new extensions to give a spacious and light interior.
Location: OS Ref. SD684 280. 9m E of M6/J31, via A59 and A677. City centre.
Open: Daily, 9am - 5pm. Sun services: at 8am, 9am, 10.30am and 4pm. Catering: Tues - Fri, 10am - 2.30pm or Sat by arrangement.
Admission: Free. Donations invited.

LOCAL FOOD

Lancashire Hotpot

This nourishing casserole uses scrag or best end of neck of lamb or mutton. It was a way of providing a nourishing meal from the very cheapest and most readily available ingredients. Today restaurants may try to smarten it up with the addition of kidneys, black pudding or borlotti beans, but the traditional recipe of layered lamb, onions and potatoes is hard to beat.

BROWSHOLME HALL 🏛

Clitheroe, Lancashire BB7 3DE

Tel: 01254 827160 **Fax:** 01254 827161 **e-mail:** rrp@browsholme.co.uk
www.browsholme.co.uk
Owner/Contact: Robert Parker
Ancestral home of the Parker Family, built in 1507 with a major collection of oak furniture and portraits, arms and armour, stained glass and many unusual antiquities from the Civil War to a fragment of a Zeppelin.
Location: OS Ref. SD683 452. 5m NW of Clitheroe off B6243.
Open: 22 May with Garden and Craft Fair. 28 - 31 May: daily; 28 June - 10 July: daily except Mons; 23 Aug - 4 Sept: daily, 2 - 4pm. Groups welcome by appointment.
Admission: Adult £4, Child £1.

GAWTHORPE HALL 🌿

Padiham, Nr Burnley, Lancashire BB12 8UA

Tel: 01282 771004 **Fax:** 01282 770178 **e-mail:** gawthorpe@nationaltrust.org.uk
Owner: The National Trust   **Contact:** Property Office
The house was built in 1600-05, and restored by Sir Charles Barry in the 1850s. Barry's designs have been re-created in the principal rooms. Gawthorpe was the home of the Shuttleworth family, and the Rachel Kay-Shuttleworth textile collections are on display in the house, private study by arrangement. Collection of portraits on loan from the National Portrait Gallery.
Location: OS Ref. SD806 340. M65/J8. On E outskirts of Padiham, ¾ m to house on N of A671. Signed to Clitheroe, then signed from 2nd set of traffic lights.
Open: Hall & Tearoom: 25 Mar - 2 Nov: daily except Mons & Fris, open Good Fri & BH Mons, 1 - 5pm. Last adm. 4.30pm. Garden: All year: daily, 10am - 6pm.
Admission: Hall: Adult £3, Accompanied Child Free (prices may change). Garden: Free. Groups must book.
♿Please ring in advance. ● ♿In grounds on leads. ✳️

HALL I'TH'WOOD

off Green Way, off Crompton Way, Bolton BL1 8UA

Tel: 01204 332370
Owner: Bolton Metropolitan Borough Council   **Contact:** Liz Shaw
Late medieval manor house with 17/18th century furniture, paintings and decorative art.
Location: OS Ref. SD724 116. 2m NNE of central Bolton. ¼ m N of A58 ring road between A666 and A676 crossroads.
Open: Apr - Oct: Wed - Sun, 11am - 5pm. Nov - Mar: Sat & Sun, 11am - 5pm.
Admission: Adult £2, Child/Conc. £1, Family £5.

Hoghton Tower.

Len Grant

HEATON HALL

HEATON PARK, PRESTWICH, MANCHESTER M25 2SW

www.manchestergalleries.org

Tel: 0161 2358888   **Fax** 0161 2358899

Owner: Manchester City Council

Heaton Hall is a magnificent James Wyatt house, built for Sir Thomas Egerton in 1772, and is one of Manchester's most impressive and important buildings. It is set in the middle of Heaton Park's rolling landscape, designed by William Eames and John Webb, much of which has recently been restored with the help of a Heritage Lottery Fund grant. The principal rooms of the Hall have been beautifully restored and are furnished in a style appropriate to the late 18th century,

with a collection of furniture, owned by English Heritage, that was designed by Wyatt for Heveningham Hall.

Location: OS Ref. SD833 044. NW Manchester, close to M60/J19. Main entrance off St Margaret's Road, off Bury Old Road - A665.

Open: Easter - end Sept. Telephone for details.

Admission: Free.

ⓘNo photography. ⊤ &Partial. WCs. ☻ ⓕBy arrangement. ℙAmple, but limited for coaches. ▦ ⊕In grounds, on leads. ⌂

▽ Corporate Hospitality see page 35

LOCAL FOOD

BLACK PUDDING

Black pudding is a traditional Lancashire delicacy, created in a time of hardship when nothing of an animal was wasted. The principal ingredient is fresh pigs' blood, to which is added cooked barley, onions, and pig fat. Then oatmeal, flour and rusk are used to thicken the mixture and finally herbs and spices are added as a final flavouring. The puddings are encased in cow's intestine and tied off in a ring, sphere or sausage shape. They can be eaten whole or the larger ones sliced and grilled. Traditionally black puddings are eaten as part of a full English breakfast.

HOGHTON TOWER 🏛

HOGHTON, PRESTON, LANCASHIRE PR5 0SH

www.hoghtontower.co.uk

Tel: 01254 852986   **Fax:** 01254 852109   **e-mail:** mail@hoghtontower.co.uk

Owner: Sir Bernard de Hoghton Bt   **Contact:** Office

Hoghton Tower, home of 14th Baronet, is one of the most dramatic looking houses in northern England. Three houses have occupied the hill site since 1100 with the present house re-built by Thomas Hoghton between 1560 - 1565. Rich and varied historical events including the Knighting of the Loin 'Sirloin' by James I in 1617.

Location: OS Ref. SD622 264. M65/J3. Midway between Preston & Blackburn on A675.

Open: Jul, Aug & Sept: Mon - Thur, 11am - 4pm. Suns, 1 - 5pm. BH Suns & Mons excluding Christmas & New Year. Group visits by appointment all year.

Admission: Gardens & House tours: Adult £5, Child/Conc. £4, Family £16. Gardens, Shop & Tearoom only: £2. Children under 5yrs Free. Private tours by arrangement (25+) £6, OAP £5.

◎ ⊤Conferences, wedding receptions. &Unsuitable. ☻ ⓕObligatory. ℙ ▦ ✳

LEIGHTON HALL 📖 *See page 428 for full page entry.*

MANCHESTER CATHEDRAL
Manchester M3 1SX
Tel: 0161 833 2220 **Fax:** 0161 839 6218 **www.**manchestercathedral.co.uk
In addition to regular worship and daily offices, there are frequent professional concerts, day schools, organ recitals, guided tours and brass-rubbing. The cathedral contains a wealth of beautiful carvings and has the widest medieval nave in Britain. Visitor Centre and restaurant.
Location: OS Ref. SJ838 988. Manchester.
Open: Daily. Visitor Centre: Mon - Sat, 10am - 4.30pm.
Admission: Donations welcome.
ℹ️ Visitor Centre. ✳️

MARTHOLME
Great Harwood, Blackburn, Lancashire BB6 7UJ
Owner: Mr & Mrs T H Codling **Contact:** Miss P M Codling
Part of medieval manor house with 17th century additions and Elizabethan gatehouse.
Location: OS Ref. SD753 338. 2m NE of Great Harwood off A680 to Whalley.
Open: Groups (8+) by written appointment only.
Admission: £4.50.

RUFFORD OLD HALL ✼
RUFFORD, Nr ORMSKIRK, LANCASHIRE L40 1SG
www.nationaltrust.org.uk

Tel: 01704 821254 **Fax:** 01704 823823 **e-mail:** ruffordhall@nationaltrust.org.uk
Owner: The National Trust **Contact:** The Property Manager
One of the finest 16th century buildings in Lancashire. The magnificent Great Hall contains an intricately carved movable screen and suits of armour, and is believed to have hosted Shakespeare. Collections of weapons, tapestries and oak furniture are found in the Carolean Wing and attractive gardens contain sculptures and topiary.
Location: OS Ref. SD463 160. 7m N of Ormskirk, in village of Rufford on E side of A59.
Open: House: 19 Mar - 30 Oct: Sat - Wed, 1 - 5pm. Garden: as house, 11am - 5.30pm. Shop & Tearoom: as house, 11am - 5pm. Open BHs & Good Fri.
Admission: House & Garden: Adult £4.70, Child £2.20, Family £11.50. Garden only: Adult £2.60, Child £1.20. Booked groups (15+): Adult £2.90, Child £1.10 (no groups on Suns & BH Mons).
ℹ️ No photography in house. 🅿️ ▼ 🅰️ Partial. ♥ Licensed. 🎫 By arrangement. 🎧 🅿️ Limited for coaches. ▦ ✗ In grounds, on leads. 🔔 ♻️ Tel for details.

🎭 **Special Events Index** see page 24

SAMLESBURY HALL
Preston New Road, Samlesbury, Preston PR5 0UP
Tel: 01254 812010 **Fax:** 01254 812174
Owner: Samlesbury Hall Trust **Contact:** Mrs S Jones - Director
Built in 1325, the hall is an attractive black and white timbered manor house set in extensive grounds. Weddings & events welcome. Antiques & crafts all year.
Location: OS Ref. SD623 305. N side of A677, 4m WNW of Blackburn.
Open: All year: daily except Sats: 11am - 4.30pm.
Admission: Adult £3, Child £1.25.

SMITHILLS HALL HISTORIC HOUSE
Smithills Dean Road, Bolton BL7 7NP
Tel: 01204 332377 **e-mail:** office@smithills.org
Owner: Bolton Metropolitan Borough Council **Contact:** Michelle Monks
14th century manor house with Tudor panelling. Stuart furniture. Stained glass.
Location: OS Ref. SD699 119. 2m NW of central Bolton, ½ m N of A58 ringroad.
Open: Apr - Sept: Tue - Sat, 11am - 5pm, Sun, 2 - 5pm. Last admission 4.15pm. Closed Mon except BH Mons.
Admission: Adult £3, Conc. £1.75, Family (2+3) £7.75.

TOWNELEY HALL ART GALLERY & MUSEUMS
Burnley BB11 3RQ
Tel: 01282 424213 **Fax:** 01282 436138 **www.**towneleyhall.org.uk
Owner: Burnley Borough Council **Contact:** Miss Susan Bourne
House dates from the 14th century with 17th and 19th century modifications. Collections include oak furniture, 18th and 19th century paintings. There is a Museum of Local Crafts and Industries and a Natural History Centre with an aquarium in the grounds.
Location: OS Ref. SD854 309. ½ m SE of Burnley on E side of Todmorden Road (A671).
Open: All year: Mon - Thur, 10am - 5pm. Sat & Sun, 12 noon - 5pm. Closed Fris. Closed Christmas - New Year.
Admission: Free. Guided tours: Tues, Weds & Thurs afternoons or as booked for groups.
🅿️ 🅰️ WC. 🎫 ✳️ ♻️ Tel for details.

TURTON TOWER
Chapeltown Road, Turton BL7 0HG
Tel: 01204 852203 **Fax:** 01204 853759 **e-mail:** turtontower@mus.lancscc.gov.uk
Owner: Lancashire County Council **Contact:** Judith Scanlon
Country house based on a medieval tower, extended in the 16th, 17th and 19th centuries.
Location: OS Ref. SD733 153. On B6391, 4m N of Bolton.
Open: Feb & Nov: Suns, 1 - 4pm. May - Sept: Mon - Thur, 11am - 5pm; Sat & Sun, 1 - 5pm. Apr: Sat - Wed, 1 - 5pm. Mar & Oct: Mon - Wed, 1 - 5pm. Sats & Suns 1 - 4pm.
Admission: Adult £3, Child Free, OAP £1.50. Season ticket available.

WARTON OLD RECTORY ♯
Warton, Carnforth, Lancashire
Tel: 0161 242 1400
Owner: English Heritage **Contact:** The North West Regional Office
A rare medieval stone house with remains of the hall, chambers and domestic offices.
Location: OS Ref. SD499 723. At Warton, 1m N of Carnforth on minor road off A6.
Open: Any reasonable time.
Admission: Free.
🐕 On leads. ✳️

Leighton Hall.

Formby Point.

www.hudsonsguide.co.uk

CROXTETH HALL & COUNTRY PARK

Liverpool, Merseyside L12 0HB

Tel: 0151 228 5311 **Fax:** 0151 228 2817

Owner: Liverpool City Council   **Contact:** Mrs Irene Vickers

Ancestral home of the Molyneux family. 500 acres country park. Special events and attractions most weekends.

Location: OS Ref. SJ408 943. 5m NE of Liverpool city centre.

Open: Parkland: daily throughout the year. Hall, Farm & Garden: Easter - Sept: daily, 10.30am - 5pm. Telephone for exact dates.

Admission: Parkland: Free. Hall, Farm & Garden: prices on application.

LIVERPOOL CATHEDRAL

Liverpool, Merseyside L1 7AZ

Tel: 0151 709 6271 **Fax:** 0151 702 7292

Owner: The Dean and Chapter   **Contact:** Lew Eccleshall

Sir Giles Gilbert Scott's greatest creation. Built last century from local sandstone with superb glass, stonework and major works of art, it is the largest cathedral in Britain.

Location: OS Ref. SJ354 893. Central Liverpool, ¹/₂ m S of Lime Street Station.

Open: 8am - 6pm. Sun services: 8am, 10.30am, 3pm, 4pm. Weekdays: 8am & 5.30pm, also 12.05pm on Fri. Sats: 8am & 3pm.

Admission: Donation. Lift to Tower and Embroidery Exhibition: £4.25 (concessions available).

LIVERPOOL METROPOLITAN
CATHEDRAL OF CHRIST THE KING

Liverpool, Merseyside L3 5TQ

Tel: 0151 709 9222 **Fax:** 0151 708 7274 **e-mail:** met.cathedral@boltblue.com

www.liverpoolmetrocathedral.org.uk

Owner: Roman Catholic Archdiocese of Liverpool   **Contact:** Rt Rev P Cookson

Modern circular cathedral with spectacular glass by John Piper and numerous modern works of art. Extensive earlier crypt by Lutyens. Grade II* listed.

Location: OS Ref. SJ356 903. Central Liverpool, ¹/₂ m E of Lime Street Station.

Open: 8am - 6pm (closes 5pm Suns in Winter). Sun services: 8.30am, 10am, 11am & 7pm. Weekday services: 8am, 12.15pm & 5.15pm. Sats, 9am & 6.30pm. Gift Shop & Restaurant: Mon - Sat, 10am - 5pm; Sun, 11am - 4pm.

Admission: Donation.

⬚ ♿ Except crypt. WCs. 🍴 📷 By arrangement. 🅿 Ample for cars. ⬛ 🐕 Guide dogs only. ✱

MEOLS HALL 🏛

Churchtown, Southport, Merseyside PR9 7LZ

Tel: 01704 228326 **Fax:** 01704 507185 **e-mail:** events@meolshall.com

www.meolshall.com

Owner: Robert Hesketh Esq   **Contact:** Pamela Whelan

17th century house with subsequent additions. Interesting collection of pictures and furniture. Tithe Barn available for wedding ceremonies and receptions all year.

Location: OS Ref. SD365 184. 3m NE of Southport town centre in Churchtown. SE of A565.

Open: 14 Aug - 14 Sept: daily, 2 - 5pm.

Admission: Adult £3, Child £1. Groups only (25+) £9 (inclusive of full afternoon tea).

🔝 Wedding ceremonies and receptions now available in the Tithe Barn.

♿ ♨ 🅿 🔊 ♨

PORT SUNLIGHT VILLAGE & HERITAGE CENTRE

95 Greendale Road, Port Sunlight CH62 4XE

Tel: 0151 6446466 **Fax:** 0151 6458973   **Contact:** The Centre

Port Sunlight is a picturesque 19th century garden village on the Wirral.

Location: OS Ref. SJ340 845. Follow signs from M53/J4 or 5 or follow signs on A41.

Open: All year, 10am - 4pm in summer; 11am - 4pm in winter.

Admission: Adult £1, Child 60p, Conc. 80p. Group rates on application.

SPEKE HALL GARDEN & ESTATE 🌿

The Walk, Liverpool L24 1XD

Tel: 0151 427 7231 **Fax:** 0151 427 9860 **Info Line:** 08457 585702

www.spekehall.org.uk **www.**nationaltrust.org.uk

Owner: The National Trust   **Contact:** The Property Manager

One of the most famous half-timbered houses in the country.

Location: OS Ref. SJ419 825. North bank of the Mersey, 6m SE of city centre. Follow signs for Liverpool John Lennon airport.

Open: House: 20 Mar - 31 Oct: Daily except Mons & Tues (open BH Mons), 1 - 5.30pm; 6 Nov - 5 Dec: Sats & Suns only, 1 - 4.30pm. Grounds: Daily, 11am - 5.30pm. Home Farm: dates as House, 11am - 5.30pm. Check for winter opening, additional opening Jul & Aug.

Admission: Adult £6, Child £3.50, Family £17. Grounds only: Adult £3, Child £1.50, Family £9.

©National Trust Photographic Library/Joe Cornish

Formby Point.

433

north east

Rugged and Roman – the North East region of Britain offers the visitor a wealth of history going back to the Roman occupation. But it does not just live in the past – 'The Angel of the North', the huge sculpture alongside the A1 at Gateshead, the wonderful architectural regeneration of Tyneside, and the stunning new Millennium Garden Project at Alnwick Castle are evidence of the area's enthusiasm for the modern alongside the ancient. As well as visiting the magnificent fortress castles at Alnwick, Bamburgh and Chillingham, time should be set aside to explore unusual properties such as Cragside, with its extraordinary collection of Victorian gadgets, and The Lady Waterford Murals at Ford, where in 1860 biblical murals were commissioned to decorate the walls of this beautiful building.

Farne Islands, Northumberland   ©National Trust Photographic Library/Joe Cornish.

English Heritage Events.

Bamburgh Castle, Northumberland.

Tynemouth Priory, Tyne & Wear.

Barnard Castle, Co. Durham

© English Heritage

co. durham

northumberland

tyne and wear

lindisfarne castle

fortress | pilgrimage | lutyens

© Mike Kipling

©National Trust Photographic Library/Andreas von Einsiedel

©National Trust Photographic Library/Andreas von Einsiedel

©National Trust Photographic Library/Andreas von Einsiedel

©National Trust Photographic Library/Andreas von Einsiedel

lindisfarne castle

n o r t h   e a s t

On a dramatic rockface sprouting from flat pasture and overlooking the sea at 'Holy Island' are the remnants of a dilapidated Tudor fort, since reinvented as a domestic house by Lutyens in the early 20th century.

Lindisfarne Castle stands boldly against the skyline of the island, whose fame grew out of the foundation of a monastic community by the Irish Evangelist St Aidan, as directed by King Oswald of Northumbria in 635AD. One of the most important centres of Christianity in Anglo-Saxon England, Lindisfarne became a place of pilgrimage after Benedictine Monks from Durham Cathedral had rebuilt the Priory in 1082 in the memory of St Cuthbert.

This once-key strategic border point, standing on Beblowe Crag, was first fortified in 1542, following the Dissolution of the Monasteries because of the need to suppress the devastating activities of the Scots on the English borders. The fort was restored by Elizabeth I, but it never encountered siege; and it was deemed militarily redundant after 1603 when England and Scotland became united. By 1715 the garrison had been reduced to seven men and the Volunteer Coast Artillery Detachment withdrew in 1893.

The Elizabethan fortress is the basis of the Castle, built from 1902 by Edwin Lutyens for his friend and founder of 'Country Life', Edward Hudson, and is the first such castle transformation Lutyens attempted. Edward Hudson had discovered the dilapidated remains in 1901. What followed was the reconstruction of the fort in the form of holiday house – a typically austere Lutyens creation with whitewashed walls and red herringbone brick floors.

Now the visitor can see the four living rooms and nine bedrooms created by the architect and the decorative themes he and Hudson loved so much, from the Flemish 17th century furniture to sea-faring memorabilia: Lutyens' ancestors were Dutch sailors. In the Castle are a 17th century Dutch brass chandelier and a wonderful rococo 17th century cabinet painted with scenes of Dutch life. A series of photographs of Lutyens' children were commissioned, portraying them as though they were in Vermeer paintings.

Lutyens excelled at the romantic revival of this fort; the architecture was sympathetic to its situation. The impressive entrance hall is reminiscent of the Norman nave at Durham Cathedral and in the Dining Room he installed neo-Gothic windows as a reminder of the Castle's past.

Outside, the landscape is pitted with remnants of 19th century lime kilns, but lying below and a short distance from the Castle is a Walled Garden, originally planted by Gertrude Jekyll with roses, fruit trees and sunflowers. The National Trust is recreating her beautiful 'summer' scheme at Lindisfarne, their first 20th century house, acquired in 1944.

▸ For further details about Lindisfarne Castle, see page 450.

© www.mikekipling.com

Map 8

THE BOWES MUSEUM

www.bowesmuseum.org.uk

Owner:
The Bowes Museum Ltd

▶ **CONTACT**

Barnard Castle
Co. Durham
DL12 8NP

Tel: 01833 690606
Fax: 01833 637163

e-mail: info@
bowesmuseum.org.uk

▶ **LOCATION**
OS Ref. NZ055 164

¹/₄ m E of Market Place
in Barnard Castle,
just off A66.

John and Joséphine Bowes had a passion for collecting beautiful works of art which led to the foundation of The Bowes Museum in 1892.

Although the amazing 19th century architecture replicates a French château, the building was purposefully designed as a museum. Its spacious galleries, flooded with natural light, house one of the best collections of European fine and decorative art to be found in this country.

The outstanding collection contains over 30,000 items of art, ceramics, furniture and textiles. Included within the collection are works by Canaletto, El Greco and Goya. However, the most loved piece is the Silver Swan automaton which plays everyday to the delight of visitors.

The wonderful museum story is retold as you wander through over 20 fascinating galleries with an audio guide and variety of interactive elements to inform and entertain.

The world class art at The Bowes is complemented by a series of international exhibitions. Highlights for 2005 include 'Toulouse-Lautrec and the Art of the French Poster', 'Boucher: The Art of Landscapes', Raphael's 'Madonna of the Pinks' and 'Sudan: Ancient Treasures'. Regional and national exhibitions are also represented with the exciting programme.

The Bowes is situated in the picturesque town of Barnard Castle. Set in large grounds of beautiful parkland and garden, you can enjoy a quiet stroll or explore the unusual tree trail.

Open all year, The Bowes Museum also offers the acclaimed Café Bowes, Museum Shop, and Coffee Bar, making this world class visitor attraction a great day out for all.

▶ **OPENING TIMES**

All year
Daily
11am - 5pm.

Closed 25/26 December &
1 January.

▶ **ADMISSION**

Adult £6.00
Child (under 16yrs) .... Free
Conc. £5.00
Disabled carers .... Free

Groups (20+)
Adult £5.00
Conc. £4.00

🛍️ Palatial rooms and 23 acres of parkland. Individual tailored packages for wedding or corporate function.

♿ Access to most of the Museum including gift shop, café and WCs. Wheelchair faciity is available. Signposted disabled parking and entrance.

☕ Licensed.

🧍 By arrangement.

🎧

🅿️ Ample.

🐾 In grounds.

🎭 Tel for details.

RABY CASTLE

www.rabycastle.com

Map 8

Owner:
The Lord Barnard

▶ CONTACT

Clare Simpson/
Catherine Turnbull
Raby Castle
Staindrop
Darlington
Co. Durham DL2 3AH

Tel: 01833 660202
Fax: 01833 660169

e-mail: admin@
rabycastle.com

▶ LOCATION

OS Ref. NZ129 218

On A688, 1m N of
Staindrop. 8m NE of
Barnard Castle, 12m
WNW of Darlington.

Rail: Darlington
Station, 12m.

Air: Durham Tees
Valley Airport,
20m.

The magnificent Raby Castle, in the beautiful North Pennines, has been home to Lord Barnard's family since 1626 when it was purchased by his ancestor, Sir Henry Vane the Elder, the eminent statesman and politician. The Castle was built mainly in the 14th century by the Nevill family on the site of an earlier manor house. The Nevills continued to live at Raby until 1569 when, after the failure of the Rising of the North, the Castle and its land were forfeited to the Crown.

The impressive Entrance Hall (below) was created into its present dramatic form by John Carr for the 2nd Earl of Darlington, to celebrate the coming of age of his heir in 1787. The roof was raised to enable carriages to pass through the Hall and the result is a stunning interior in the Gothic Revival style. Raby's treasures include an important collection of Meissen porcelain, fine furniture and artworks, including paintings by Munnings, De Hooch, Reynolds, Van Dyck, Batoni, Teniers, Amigoni, Vernet and De Vos.

There is a 200-acre Deer Park with two lakes and a beautiful walled garden with formal lawns, ancient yew hedges and an ornamental pond. The 18th century stable block contains a horse-drawn carriage collection including the State Coach last used by the family for the Coronation of Edward VII in 1902.

Part of the Stables has been converted into a gift shop and tearooms, where the former stalls have been incorporated to create an atmospheric setting. A Woodland Adventure Playground is close to the picnic area.

Heritage House Group Ltd

ℹ️ Film locations, product launches, corporate events, fairs & concerts. Raby Estates venison & game sold in tearooms. Soft fruit when in season. Lectures on Castle, its contents, gardens & history. No photography or video filming is permitted inside. Colour illustrated guidebook and slides are on sale.

🛍️ 🌼 🍷 ♿ Partial. WC.

☕ Licensed.

🏃 By arrangement for group 20+ or min charge £240, weekday am. Tour time: 1¹/₂ hrs. Discounted guidebooks £2.

🅿️ By arrangement (20+), weekday am. Primary & junior £3; Secondary £3.50.

🐕 Guide dogs welcome. On leads in park only.

🎭 Tel for details or see website.

▶ OPENING TIMES

May & September
Weds & Suns only.

June, July & August:
Daily except Sats.

BHs (incl. Easter):
Sat to following Wed.

Castle
1- 5pm.

Park & Gardens
11am - 5.30pm.

▶ ADMISSION

Castle, Park & Gardens
Adult £9.00
Child (5-15yrs) £4.00
OAP/Student £8.00
Family (2+3) £25.00
Groups (12+)
Adult £8.00
Child (5-15yrs). £3.00
OAP/Student £7.00
*Please book in advance for group visits.

Guided Tour (incl. reception, tea/coffee, must book)
20+ £12.00
or min charge £240.00

Park & Gardens
Adult £4.00
Child (5-15yrs) £2.50
OAP/Student £3.50
Groups (12+)
Adult £3.50
Child (5-15yrs). £2.50
OAP/Student £3.00

Season ticket
Park & Gardens
Adult £15.00
Child (5-15yrs) £7.50
OAP/Student £10.00

Castle, Park & Gardens
Adult £35.00
Child (5-15yrs) £20.00
OAP/Student £30.00

AUCKLAND CASTLE 🏛

BISHOP AUCKLAND, CO. DURHAM DL14 7NR

www.auckland-castle.co.uk

Tel: 01388 601627 **Fax:** 01388 609323 **e-mail:** auckland.castle@zetnet.co.uk

Owner: Church Commissioners **Contact:** The Manager

Principal country residence of the Bishops of Durham since Norman times and now the official residence of the present day Bishops. The Chapel, reputedly one of the largest private chapel in Europe, was originally the 12th century banquet hall. Chapel and State Rooms including the Throne Room, Long Dining Room and King Charles Dining Room are open to the public. Access to the adjacent Bishop's Park with its 18th century Deer House.

Location: OS Ref. NZ214 303. Bishop Auckland, N end of town centre.

Open: Easter Mon - 30 Sept: Suns & Mons (plus Weds in August) , 2 - 5pm. Last admission 4.30pm. The managment reserves the right to close the castle to visitors.

Admission: Adult £4, Child/Conc. £3. Child (up to 12yrs) Free. Special openings for groups (25+).

ℹ️Exhibitions. No indoor photography. 📷 📺Wedding receptions, functions. ♿ Wheelchair access to chapel, ground floor. WC. Stairwalker available for upstairs staterooms by prior arrangement. 🎫 🅿 ♨ 🐕Guide dogs only.

AUCKLAND CASTLE DEER HOUSE ⚏

Bishop Auckland, Durham

Tel: 0191 2691200

Owner: English Heritage **Contact:** The Regional Office

A charming building erected in 1760 in the Park of the Bishops of Durham so that the deer could shelter and find food.

Location: OS Ref. NZ216 305. In Bishop Auckland Park, just N of town centre on A689. About 500 yds N of the castle.

Open: Park opening times – see Auckland Castle.

Admission: Free.

🐕On leads.

BARNARD CASTLE ⚏

Barnard Castle, Castle House, Durham DL12 9AT

Tel: 01833 638212

Owner: English Heritage **Contact:** Visitor Operations Team

The substantial remains of this large castle stand on a rugged escarpment overlooking the River Tees. Parts of the 14th century Great Hall and the cylindrical 12th century tower, built by the Baliol family can still be seen. Sensory garden.

Location: OS92, NZ049 165. In Barnard Castle.

Open: 24 Mar - 30 Sept: daily, 10am - 6pm. 1 - 31 Oct: daily, 10am - 5pm. 1 Nov - 31 Mar: Thur - Mon, 10am - 4pm. Closed 24 - 26 Dec & 1 Jan. Closed 1 - 2pm. Times subject to change April 2005.

Admission: Adult £3.30, Child £1.70, Conc. £2.50. 15% discount for groups (11+).

ℹ️WCs in town. 📷 ♿Grounds. 🏠Inclusive. 🐕In grounds, on leads. ❄ 📺Tel for details.

BINCHESTER ROMAN FORT

Bishop Auckland, Co. Durham

Tel: 01388 663089 / 0191 3834212 (outside opening hours)

Owner: Durham County Council **Contact:** Deborah Anderson

Once the largest Roman fort in Co Durham, the heart of the site has been excavated.

Location: OS92 Ref. NZ210 312. 1¹/₂ m N of Bishop Auckland, signposted from A690 Durham - Crook and from A688 Spennymoor - Bishop Auckland roads.

Open: Easter BH, 1 May - 30 Sept: daily, 11am - 5pm.

Admission: Adult £2, Child/Conc. £1.

THE BOWES MUSEUM

See page 440 for full page entry.

CROOK HALL & GARDENS

Sidegate, Durham DH1 5SZ

Tel: 0191 3848028

Owner: Keith & Maggie Bell **Contact:** Mrs Maggie Bell

Medieval manor house set in rural landscape on the edge of Durham city.

Location: OS Ref. NZ274 432. ¹/₂ m N of city centre.

Open: Easter weekend, BHs, Suns in May & Sept; Jun, Jul & Aug: daily except Sats, 1 - 5pm.

Admission: Adult £4, Conc. £3.50, Family £12.

DERWENTCOTE STEEL FURNACE ⚏

Newcastle, Durham

Tel: 0191 2691200

Owner: English Heritage **Contact:** Regional Office

Built in the 18th century it is the earliest and most complete authentic steel making furnace to have survived.

Location: OS Ref. NZ131 566. 10m SW of Newcastle N of the A694 between Rowland's Gill and Hamsterley.

Open: 24 Mar - 30 Sept: Suns, 1 - 5pm. Times subject to change April 2005.

Admission: Free.

🅿 🐕On leads in restricted areas.

DURHAM CASTLE

Palace Green, Durham DH1 3RW

Tel: 0191 3343800 **Fax:** 0191 3343801 **Contact:** Mrs Julie Marshall

Durham Castle, founded in the 1070s, with the Cathedral is a World Heritage Site.

Location: OS Ref. NZ274 424. City centre, adjacent to cathedral.

Open: Mar - Sept: 10am - 12 noon & 2 - 4.30pm. Oct - Mar: 2 - 4pm.

Admission: Adult £3.50, Child £2.50, OAP £3, Family £8. Guide book £3.

DURHAM CATHEDRAL
Durham DH1 3EH

Tel: 0191 3864266   **Fax:** 0191 3864267   **e-mail:** enquiries@durhamcathedral.co.uk
Contact: Miss A Heywood
A World Heritage Site. Norman architecture. Burial place of St Cuthbert and the Venerable Bede.
Location: OS Ref. NZ274 422. Durham city centre.
Open: Summer: 30 May - 4 Sept: 9.30am - 8pm. Open only for worship and private prayer: All year: Mon - Sat, 7.30am - 9.30am and Suns, 7.45am - 12.30pm. The Cathedral is closed to visitors during evening recitals and concerts. Visitors welcome Mon - Sat, 9.30 - 5pm, Suns 12.30 - 3.30pm.
Admission: Cathedral: Request a donation of min. £4. Tower: Adult £2.50, Child (under 16) £1.50, Family £7. Monk's Dormitory: Adult £1, Child 30p, Family £2.10. AV: Adult £1.10, Child 30p, Family £2.

EGGLESTONE ABBEY ⌗
Durham

Tel: 0191 2691200

Owner: English Heritage   **Contact:** The Regional Office
Picturesque remains of a 12th century abbey, located in a bend of the River Tees. Substantial parts of the church and abbey buildings remain.
Location: OS Ref. NZ062 151. 1¹/₂ m SE of Barnard Castle on minor road off B6277.
Open: Daily, 10am - 6pm.
Admission: Free.
♿ 🅿 ⬛ On leads.

ESCOMB CHURCH
Escomb, Bishop Auckland DL14 7ST

Tel: 01388 458358

Owner: Church of England   **Contact:** Mrs E Kitching (01388 662265)
Saxon church dating from the 7th century built of stone from Binchester Roman Fort.
Location: OS Ref. NZ189 302. 3m W of Bishop Auckland.
Open: Summer: 9am - 8pm. Winter: 9am - 4pm. Key available from 22 Saxon Green, Escomb.
Admission: Free.

FINCHALE PRIORY ⌗
Finchale Priory, Brasside, Newton Hall DH1 5SH

Tel: 0191 3863828/ 2691200

Owner: English Heritage   **Contact:** Visitor Operations Team
These beautiful 13th century priory remains are located beside the curving River Wear.
Location: OS Ref. NZ297 471. 4¹/2 m NE of Durham.
Open: 24 Mar - 30 Sept: Sat, Sun & BHs, 10am - 6pm. Times subject to change April 2005.
Admission: Adult £2.30, Child £1.20, Conc. £1.70. 15% discount for groups (11+).
ⓘ WC. 📷 ▣ (Not managed by EH.) 🅿 On S side of river. ⬛ On leads.

PIERCEBRIDGE ROMAN FORT
Piercebridge, Co. Durham

Tel: 01325 460532

Owner: Darlington Borough Council   **Contact:** Heritage Manager
Visible Roman remains include the east gate and defences, courtyard building and Roman road. Also remains of a bridge over the Tees.
Location: OS Ref. NZ211 157. Through narrow stile and short walk down lane opposite car park off A67 NE of the village. Bridge via signposted footpath from George Hotel car park.
Open: At all times.
Admission: Free.

RABY CASTLE 🏛
See page 441 for full page entry.

ROKEBY PARK 🏛
Nr Barnard Castle, Co Durham DL12 9RZ

Tel: 01833 637334

Owner: Trustees of Mortham Estate   **Contact:** Mrs P I Yeats (Curator)
Rokeby, a fine example of a 18th century Palladian-style country house.
Location: OS Ref. NZ082 142. Between A66 & Barnard Castle.
Open: May BH Mon then each Mon & Tue from Spring BH until the first Tue in Sept: 2 - 5pm (last admission 4.30pm). Groups (25+) on other days by appointment.
Admission: Please telephone for details.

THE WEARDALE MUSEUM & HIGH HOUSE CHAPEL
Ireshopeburn, Co. Durham DL13 1EY

Tel: 01388 517433   **e-mail:** dtheatherington@argonet.co.uk
Contact: D T Heatherington
Small folk museum and historic chapel. Includes 1870 Weardale cottage room, John Wesley room and local history displays.
Location: OS Ref. NZ872 385. Adjacent to 18th century Methodist Chapel.
Open: Easter & May - Sept: Wed - Sun & BH, 2 - 5pm. Aug: daily, 2 - 5pm.
Admission: Adult £1.50, Child 50p.

© English Heritage

Finchale Priory.

North East - England

Map 10

Owner:
His Grace the Duke of
Northumberland

▶ **CONTACT**

Alnwick Castle
Estate Office
Alnwick
Northumberland
NE66 1NQ

Tel: 01665 510777
Info: 01665 511100
Group bookings:
01665 511367
Fax: 01665 510876
e-mail: enquiries@
alnwickcastle.com

▶ **LOCATION**

OS Ref. NU187 135

In Alnwick 1½ m
W of A1.
From London 6hrs,
Edinburgh 2hrs,
Chester 4hrs,
Newcastle 40mins
North Sea ferry
terminal 30mins.

Bus: From bus station
in Alnwick.

Rail: Alnmouth
Station 5m.
Kings Cross, London
3½hrs.

Air: Newcastle 40mins.

CONFERENCE/FUNCTION

ROOM	SIZE	MAX CAPACITY
The Guest Hall	100' x 30'	300

ALNWICK CASTLE 🏛

www.alnwickcastle.com   www.alnwickgarden.com

Set in magnificent 'Capability' Brown landscape, Alnwick Castle is the home of the Duke of Northumberland. Owned by his family, the Percies, since 1309, the Castle was a major stronghold during the Scottish wars.

Restorations by the First and Fourth Dukes have transformed this massive fortress into a comfortable family home. The Italian Renaissance-style State Rooms are filled with fine furniture, porcelain and paintings by Canaletto, Van Dyck and Titian.

Within the grounds are the recently refurbished museums of the Northumberland Fusiliers,

Northumberland Archaeology and the Percy Tenantry Volunteers 1798 - 1814. Quizzes and a location for the *Harry Potter* film make it a magical place for the whole family.

Events include: birds of prey demonstrations, live music, open-air theatre and Wellington's Redcoat camp.

The Castle's splendid Guest Hall is available for entertaining, concerts, wedding receptions and dinner dances. (Not open to the public.)

For details of events visit the website or telephone 01665 510777.

ℹ️ Conference facilities. Fashion shows, fairs, filming, parkland for hire. No photography inside the castle. No unaccompanied children.

🍽 Wedding receptions.

♿ Unsuitable.

☕ Coffee, light lunches and teas.

🅿️ 200 cars and 6 coaches.

📖 Guidebook and worksheet, special rates for children and teachers.

🐕 Guide dogs only.

❄️ Garden only.

🛡 Tel for details.

▶ **OPENING TIMES**

23 March - 28 October
Daily, 11am - 5pm.
Last admission to State
Rooms 4.15pm.

▶ **ADMISSION**

Castle

Adult £7.95
Child (6-15yrs)........ £2.95
Child (under 5yrs).... Free
Conc. £7.50

Pre-booked Groups
(14+, tel 01665 511350)
Adult £6.95
School £1.50

Discounts available with combined Castle and The Alnwick Garden ticket.

HHA members free access to Castle only.

444

Jarrold Colour Publications

Map 10

BAMBURGH CASTLE 🏛

www.bamburghcastle.com

Owner:
Trustees Lord Armstrong
dec'd.

▶ CONTACT

The Administrator
Bamburgh Castle
Bamburgh
Northumberland
NE69 7DF

Tel: 01668 214515

Fax: 01668 214060

e-mail: bamburghcastle
@aol.com

▶ LOCATION

OS Ref. NU184 351

42m N of
Newcastle-upon-Tyne.
20m S of Berwick upon
Tweed. 6m E of Belford
by B1342 from
A1 at Belford.

Bus: Bus service
200 yards.

Rail: Berwick-upon-
Tweed 20m.

Taxi: J Swanston
01289 306124.

Air: Newcastle-upon-
Tyne 45m.

Bamburgh Castle is the home of the Armstrong family. The earliest reference to Bamburgh shows the craggy citadel to have been a royal centre by AD 547. Recent archaeological excavation has revealed that the site has been occupied since prehistoric times.

The Norman Keep has been the stronghold for nearly nine centuries, but the remainder has twice been extensively restored, initially by Lord Crewe in the 1750s and subsequently by the 2nd Lord Armstrong at the beginning of the 20th century. This Castle was the first to succumb to artillery fire – that of Edward IV.

The public rooms contain many exhibits, including the loan collections of armour from HM Tower of London, the John George Joicey Museum, Newcastle-upon-Tyne and other private sources, which complement the castle's armour. Porcelain, china, jade, furniture from many periods, oils, water-colours and a host of interesting items are all contained within one of the most important buildings of Britain's national heritage.

VIEWS

The views from the ramparts are unsurpassed and take in Holy Island, the Farne Islands, one of Northumberland's finest beaches and, landwards, the Cheviot Hills.

▶ OPENING TIMES

12 March - 31 October
Daily, 11am - 5pm.
Last entry 4.30pm.

Tours by arrangement
at any time.

▶ ADMISSION

Summer
Adult £5.50
Child (6 - 15yrs) £2.50
OAP £4.50
Groups *
Adult £4.00
Child (6 - 15yrs) £2.00
OAP £3.00

* Min payment £50

Winter
Group rates only quoted.

ℹ️ Filming. No photography in house.

📷

♿ Limited access. WC.

☕ Tearooms for light refreshments. Groups can book.

🚶 By arrangement at any time, min charge out of hours £150.

🅿️ 100 cars, coaches park on tarmac drive at entrance.

🏫 Welcome. Guide provided if requested, educational pack.

🐕 Guide dogs only.

🔔

❄️

445

Map 10

Owner:
Sir Humphry
Wakefield Bt

▶ **CONTACT**

Administrator
Chillingham Castle
Northumberland
NE66 5NJ

Tel: 01668 215359
Fax: 01668 215463

e-mail: enquiries@
chillingham-castle.com

▶ **LOCATION**
OS Ref. NU062 258

45m N of Newcastle
between A697 & A1.
2m S of B6348
at Chatton.
6m SE of Wooler.

Rail: Alnmouth
or Berwick.

CONFERENCE/FUNCTION

ROOM	MAX CAPACITY
King James I Room	
Great Hall	100
Minstrels' Hall	60
2 x Drawing Room	
Museum	
Tea Room	35
Lower Gallery	
Upper Gallery	

CHILLINGHAM CASTLE 🏛

www.chillingham-castle.com

One of England's top 100 houses, rated 4-star in Simon Jenkins' *England's Thousand Best Houses*.

This remarkable castle, the home of Sir Humphry Wakefield Bt, with its alarming dungeons has, now and since the 1200s, been continuously owned by the family of the Earls Grey and their relations. You will see active restoration of complex masonry, metalwork and ornamental plaster as the great halls and state rooms are gradually brought back to life with antique furniture, tapestries, arms and armour as of old and even a torture chamber.

At first a 12th century stronghold, Chillingham became a fully fortified castle in the 14th century. Wrapped in the nation's history it occupied a strategic position as a fortress during Northumberland's bloody border feuds, often besieged and at many times enjoying the patronage

of royal visitors. In Tudor days there were additions but the underlying medieval character has always been retained. The 18th and 19th centuries saw decorative refinements and extravagances including the lake, garden and grounds laid out by Sir Jeffrey Wyatville, fresh from his triumphs at Windsor Castle. These contrast the ancient Wild Cattle in the park beyond (a separate tour).

GARDENS

With romantic grounds, the castle commands breathtaking views of the surrounding countryside. As you walk to the lake you will see, according to the season, drifts of snowdrops, daffodils or bluebells and an astonishing display of rhododendrons. This emphasises the restrained formality of the Elizabethan topiary garden, with its intricately clipped hedges of box and yew. Lawns, the formal gardens and woodland walks are all fully open to the public.

▶ **OPENING TIMES**
Summer
Easter
1 May - 30 September
Daily except some Sats,
Castle, 1 - 5pm,
Grounds & Tearoom,
12 noon - 5pm

Winter
October - April: Groups
any time by appointment.
All function activities
available.

▶ **ADMISSION**
Summer

Adult	£6.00
Child (under 16yrs)	£3.00
Child (under 5yrs)	£1.00
OAP	£5.50

Groups (10+)
Per person	£5.30
Tour	£25.00

⬜ 🌱

🍽 Corporate entertainment, lunches, drinks, dinners, wedding ceremonies and receptions.

♿ Partial.

☕ Booked meals for up to 100 people.

🚶 By arrangement.

🅿 Avoid Lilburn route, coach parties welcome by prior arrangement. Limited for coaches.

📖

🚫

🏨 Apartments.

🔔 Civil Wedding Licence.

❄

ALNWICK CASTLE 🏛 *See page 444 for full page entry.*

AYDON CASTLE ⌗
Corbridge, Northumberland NE45 5PJ
Tel: 01434 632450
Owner: English Heritage   **Contact:** Visitor Operations Team
One of the finest fortified manor houses in England, dating from the late 13th century. Its survival, intact, can be attributed to its conversion to a farmhouse in the 17th century.
Location: OS Ref. NZ002 663. 2m NE of Corbridge, on minor road off B6321 or A68.
Open: 24 Mar - 30 Sept: daily, 10am - 6pm. Times subject to change April 2005.
Admission: Adult £3.30, Child £1.70, Conc. £2.50. 15% discount for groups (11+).
ℹ WC. ⬛ ♿ Ground floor & grounds. 🅿 Limited. ⬛ 🐕 In grounds, on leads. ♨ Tel for details.

BAMBURGH CASTLE 🏛 *See page 445 for full page entry.*

© English Heritage Photo Library

BELSAY HALL, CASTLE & GARDENS ⌗
BELSAY, Nr PONTELAND, NORTHUMBERLAND NE20 0DX
www.english-heritage.org.uk/visits

Tel: 01661 881636 **Fax:** 01661 881043

Owner: English Heritage   **Contact:** Visitor Operations Team

Belsay is one of the most remarkable estates in Northumberland's border country. The buildings, set amidst 30 acres of magnificent landscaped gardens, have been occupied by the same family for nearly 600 years. The gardens, created largely in the 19th century, are a fascinating mix of the formal and the informal with terraced gardens, a rhododendron garden, magnolia garden, mature woodland and even a winter garden. The buildings comprise a 14th century castle, a manor house and Belsay Hall, an internationally famous mansion designed by Sir Charles Monck in the 19th century in the style of classical buildings he had encountered during a tour of Greece.

Location: OS87, NZ088 785. In Belsay 14m (22.4 km) NW of Newcastle on SW of A696. 7m NW of Ponteland. Nearest airport and station is Newcastle.

Open: 24 Mar - 30 Sept: daily, 10am - 6pm. 1 - 31 Oct: daily, 10am - 4pm. 1 Nov - 31 Mar: Thur - Mon, 10am - 4pm. Closed 24 - 26 Dec and 1 Jan. Times subject to change April 2005.

Admission: Adult £5.30, Child £2.70, Conc. £4, Family £13.30. 15% discount for groups (11+).

⬛ 🍴 ♿ Partial. WC. 🎫 During summer & weekends Apr - Oct. 🅿 ⬛ 🐕 In grounds, on leads. ❄ ♨ Tel for details.

BERWICK BARRACKS ⌗
The Parade, Berwick-upon-Tweed, Northumberland TD15 1DF
Tel: 01289 304493
Owner: English Heritage   **Contact:** Visitor Operations Team
Among the earliest purpose built barracks, these have changed very little since 1717. They house an exhibition 'By Beat of Drum', which recreates scenes such as the barrack room from the life of the British infantryman, the Museum of the King's Own Scottish Borderers and the Borough Museum with fine art, local history exhibition and other collections.
Location: OS Ref. NT994 535. On the Parade, off Church Street, Berwick town centre.
Open: 24 Mar - 30 Sept: daily, 10am - 6pm. 1 - 31 Oct: daily, 10am - 4pm. 1 Nov - 31 Mar: Thur - Mon, 10am - 4pm. Closed 24 - 26 Dec and 1 Jan. Times subject to change April 2005.
Admission: Adult £3.30, Child £1.70, Conc. £2.50. 15% discount for groups (11+).
⬛ 🅿 In town. ⬛ 🐕 In grounds, on leads. ❄ ♨ Tel for details.

BERWICK RAMPARTS ⌗
Berwick-upon-Tweed, Northumberland
Tel: 0191 269 1200
Owner: English Heritage   **Contact:** The Regional Office
A remarkably complete system of town fortifications consisting of gateways, ramparts and projecting bastions built in the 16th century.
Location: OS Ref. NT994 535. Surrounding Berwick town centre on N bank of River Tweed.
Open: Any reasonable time.
Admission: Free.
❄

BRINKBURN PRIORY

Long Framlington, Morpeth, Northumberland NE65 8AF

Tel: 01665 570628

Owner: English Heritage   **Contact:** Visitor Operations Staff

This late 12th century church is a fine example of early gothic architecture, almost perfectly preserved, and is set in a lovely spot beside the River Coquet.

Location: OS Ref. NZ116 984. 4¹/₂ m SE of Rothbury off B6344 5m W of A1.

Open: 24 Mar - 30 Sept: daily, 10am - 6pm. Times subject to change April 2005.

Admission: Adult £2.30, Child £1.20, Conc. £1.70. 15% discount for groups (11+).

🅿 ⬛ 🔲 On leads. 🔳 Tel for details.

CAPHEATON HALL

Newcastle-upon-Tyne NE19 2AB

Tel/Fax: 01830 530253

Owner/Contact: J Browne-Swinburne

Built for Sir John Swinburne in 1668 by Robert Trollope, an architect of great and original talent.

Location: OS Ref. NZ038 805. 17m NW of Newcastle off A696.

Open: By written appointment only.

🔳

CHERRYBURN – THOMAS BEWICK BIRTHPLACE 🌿

Station Bank, Mickley, Stocksfield, Northumberland NE43 7DD

Tel: 01661 843276   www.nationaltrust.org.uk

Owner: The National Trust   **Contact:** The Administrator

Birthplace of Northumbria's greatest artist, wood engraver and naturalist, Thomas Bewick, b1753. The Museum explores his famous works. Farmyard animals, picnic area, garden.

Location: OS Ref. NZ075 627. 11m W of Newcastle on A695 (400yds signed from Mickley Square). 1¹/₂ m W of Prudhoe.

Open: 18 Mar - 31 Oct: daily except Weds, 11am - 5pm. Last admission 4.30pm.

Admission: Adult £3.50, Child £1.75. Child under 5yrs Free. Tel for group rate.

🅿 🔲 Some steps. WC. 🍽 Morning coffee for booked groups. 🔳 Tel for details.

© English Heritage Photo Library.

CHESTERS ROMAN FORT & MUSEUM

CHOLLERFORD, Nr HEXHAM, NORTHUMBERLAND NE46 4EP

Tel: 01434 681379

Owner: English Heritage   **Contact:** Visitor Operations Team

The best preserved example of a Roman cavalry fort in Britain, including remains of the bath house on the banks of the River North Tyne. The museum houses a fascinating collection of Roman sculpture and inscriptions.

Location: OS87, NY913 701. 1¹/₂ m from Chollerford on B6318.

Open: 24 Mar - 30 Sept: daily, 9.30am - 6pm. 1 Oct - 31 Mar: daily, 10am - 4pm. Closed 24 - 26 Dec and 1 Jan. Times subject to change April 2005.

Admission: Adult £3.60, Child £1.80, Conc. £2.70. 15% discount for groups (11+).

🅿 🔲 Grounds. WC. 🍽 Summer only. 🅿 ⬛ 🔲 In grounds, on leads. 🔳 🔳 Tel for details.

CHILLINGHAM CASTLE 🏠   *See page 446 for full page entry.*

CHIPCHASE CASTLE 🏠

Wark, Hexham, Northumberland NE48 3NT

Tel: 01434 230203   Fax: 01434 230740

Owner/Contact: Mrs P J Torday

The castle overlooks the River North Tyne and is set in formal and informal gardens. One walled garden is used as a nursery specialising in unusual perennial plants.

Location: OS Ref. NY882 758. 10m NW of Hexham via A6079 to Chollerton. 2m SE of Wark.

Open: Castle: 1 - 28 Jun: daily, 2 - 5pm. Tours by arrangement at other times. Castle Gardens & Nursery: Easter - 31 Jul, Thur - Sun & BH Mons, 10am - 5pm.

Admission: Castle £5, Garden £3, concessions available. Nursery Free.

🔲 Unsuitable. 🎧 Obligatory. 🔳

CORBRIDGE ROMAN SITE

Corbridge, Northumberland NE45 5NT

Tel: 01434 632349

Owner: English Heritage   **Contact:** Visitor Operations Team

A fascinating series of excavated remains, including foundations of granaries with a grain ventilation system. From artefacts found, which can be seen in the site museum, we know a large settlement developed around this supply depot.

Location: OS Ref. NY983 649. ¹/₂ m NW of Corbridge on minor road, signposted for Corbridge Roman Site.

Open: 24 Mar - 30 Sept: daily, 10am - 6pm. 1 - 31 Oct: daily, 10am - 4pm. 1 Nov - 31 Mar: Sat & Sun, 10am - 4pm. Closed 1 - 2pm during winter & 24 - 26 Dec and 1 Jan. Times subject to change April 2005.

Admission: Adult £3.60, Child £1.80, Conc. £2.70. 15% discount for groups (11+).

🅿 🔲 Partial. 🎧 Inclusive. 🅿 Limited for coaches. ⬛ 🔲 In grounds, on leads. 🔳 🔳 Tel for details.

CRAGSIDE 🌿

Rothbury, Morpeth, Northumberland NE65 7PX

Tel: 01669 620150   **Fax:** 01669 620066   www.nationaltrust.org.uk

Owner: The National Trust   **Contact:** Property Manager

Revolutionary home of Lord Armstrong, Victorian inventor and landscape genius, Cragside sits on a rocky crag high above the Debdon Burn. Crammed with ingenious gadgets, it was the first house in the world lit electrically. Armstrong constructed 5 lakes, one of Europe's largest rock gardens and planted over 7 million trees and shrubs. Today, this magnificent estate can be explored on foot and by car and provides one of the last shelters for the endangered red squirrel. Children will love the tall trees, tumbling streams, adventure play area and labyrinth.

Location: OS Ref. NU073 022. ¹/₂ m NE of Rothbury on B6341.

Open: House: 22 Mar - 25 Sept: daily except Mons (open BH Mons), 1 - 5.30pm, last admission 1hr prior to closing time. Estate & Gardens: 22 Mar - 30 Oct, 10.30am - 7pm; 2 Nov - 18 Dec: 11am - 4pm.

Admission: House, Estate & Gardens: Adult £8.50, Child (5-17yrs) £4, Family (2+3) £20. Groups (15+) £7. Estate & Gardens: Adult £5.70, Child (5-17yrs) £2.60, Family (2+3) £14. Groups (15+) £4.70.

🅿 🔲 Partial. 🍽 🎟 🅿 ⬛ 🔲 🔲 In grounds, on leads. 🔳 Tel for details.

DUNSTANBURGH CASTLE # 🌿

c/o Grieves Garage, Embleton, Northumberland NE66 3TT

Tel: 01665 576231

Owner: The National Trust   **Guardian:** English Heritage
                              Contact: Visitor Operations Team

An easy, but bracing, coastal walk leads to the eerie skeleton of this wonderful 14th century castle sited on a basalt crag, rearing up more than 100 feet from the waves crashing on the rocks below. The surviving ruins include the large gatehouse, which later became the keep, and curtain walls.

Location: OS75, NU258 220. 8m NE of Alnwick.

Open: 24 Mar - 30 Sept: daily, 10am - 6pm. 1 - 31 Oct, daily, 10am - 4pm. 1 Nov - 31 Mar: Thur - Mon, 10am - 4pm. Closed 24 - 26 Dec and 1 Jan. Times subject to change April 2005.

Admission: Adult £2.60, Child £1.30, Conc. £2. 15% discount for groups (11+).

🅿 None. ⬛ 🔲 In grounds, on leads. 🔳

EDLINGHAM CASTLE

Edlingham, Alnwick, Northumberland

Tel: 0191 269 1200

Owner: English Heritage   **Contact:** The Regional Office

Set beside a splendid railway viaduct this complex ruin has defensive features spanning the 13th and 15th centuries.

Location: OS Ref. NU115 092. At E end of Edlingham village, on minor road off B6341 6m SW of Alnwick.

Open: Any reasonable time.

Admission: Free.

🔲 In grounds, on leads. 🔳

ETAL CASTLE ⚏

Cornhill-on-Tweed, Northumberland

Tel: 01890 820332

Owner: English Heritage   **Contact:** Visitor Operations Team

A 14th century castle located in the picturesque village of Etal. Award-winning exhibition about the castle, Border warfare and the Battle of Flodden.

Location: OS75, NT925 394. In Etal village, 10m SW of Berwick.

Open: 24 Mar - 30 Sept: daily, 10am - 6pm. Times subject to change April 2005.

Admission: Adult £3.30, Child £1.70, Conc. £2.50, Family £8.30. 15% discount for groups (11+).

ℹ WC in village. ▣ ♿ Partial. WC. ⏾ Inclusive. 🅿 Limited. ▦
🐕 In grounds, on leads. ☗ Tel for details.

HERTERTON HOUSE GARDENS

Hartington, Cambo, Morpeth, Northumberland   NE61 4BN

Tel: 01670 774278

Owner/Contact: C J "Frank" Lawley

One acre of formal garden in stone walls around a 16th century farmhouse, including a small topiary garden, physic garden, flower garden, fancy garden and gazebo.

Location: OS Ref. NZ022 881. 2m N of Cambo, just off B6342, Signposted (brown).

Open: 1 Apr - 30 Sept: Mons, Weds, Fri - Sun, 1.30 - 5.30pm.

Admission: Adult £2.80, Child (5-15yrs) £1. Groups by arrangement.

ℹ ♿ Unsuitable. 🉐 By arrangement. 🅿 Limited for coaches.
▦ Guided tours for adult students only. ✖

HOUSESTEADS ROMAN FORT ⚏ ✾

NR HAYDON BRIDGE, NORTHUMBERLAND   NE47 6NN

Tel: 01434 344363

Owner: The National Trust   **Guardian:** English Heritage

     Contact: Visitor Operations Team

Perched high on a ridge overlooking open moorland, this is the best known part of the Wall. The fort covers five acres and there are remains of many buildings, such as granaries, barrack blocks and gateways. A small exhibition displays altars, inscriptions and models.

Location: OS Ref. NY790 687. 2m NE of Bardon Mill.

Open: 24 Mar - 30 Sept: daily, 10am - 6pm. 1 Oct - 31 Mar: daily, 10am - 4pm. Closed 24 - 26 Dec and 1 Jan. Times subject to change April 2005.

Admission: Adult £3.60, Child £1.80, Conc. £2.70, Family £9. 15% discount for groups (11+).

▣ 🅿 Charge. ▦ 🐕 In grounds, on leads. ✖

LOCAL FOOD

Northumberland Twists

These are made from a yeast-dough and are cut into strips, twisted slightly and then brushed with sherry and sprinkled with a little sugar before baking.

HOWICK HALL GARDENS

Howick, Alnwick, Northumberland   NE66 3LB

Tel: 01665 577285   **e-mail:** estateoffice@howickuk.com

www.howickgarden.org.uk

Owner: Howick Trustees Ltd   **Contact:** Mrs D Spark

Romantically landscaped grounds surrounding the house in a little valley, with rare rhododendrons and flowering shrubs and trees.

Location: OS Ref. NU249 175. 6m NE of Alnwick. 1m E of B1339.

Open: Easter - Oct: daily 12 noon - 6pm.

Admission: Adult £3.50, Child (under 16yrs) Free, OAP £2.50. Season tickets available.

♿ Grounds partial. WC. 🅿 New car park. 🐕 Guide dogs only.

KIRKLEY HALL GARDENS

Ponteland, Northumberland   NE20 0AQ

Tel: 01670 841200   **Fax:** 01661 860047   **Contact:** Reception

Over 9 acres of beautiful gardens incorporating a Victorian walled garden, woodland walks, sunken garden and wildlife areas and ponds.

Location: OS Ref. NZ150 772. 10m from the centre of Newcastle upon Tyne. 2½ m N of Ponteland on byroad to Morpeth.

Open: All year: daily, 10am - 4pm.

Admission: Free.

THE LADY WATERFORD HALL & MURALS

Ford, Berwick-upon-Tweed   TD15 2QA

Tel: 01890 820503   **Fax:** 01890 820384

Owner: Ford & Etal Estates   **Contact:** Dorien Irving

Commissioned in 1860 the walls of this beautiful building are decorated with beautiful murals depicting Bible stories.

Location: OS Ref. NT945 374. On the B6354, 9m from Berwick-upon-Tweed, midway between Newcastle-upon-Tyne and Edinburgh, close to the A697.

Open: Mar - Oct: daily, 10.30am - 12.30pm & 1.30 - 5.30pm. By arrangement with the caretaker during winter months. Note: the Hall may be closed on occasion for private functions. Please telephone prior to travelling.

Admission: Adult £1.75, Child 75p, Child (under 12yrs) Free, Conc. £1.25. Groups by arrangement.

LINDISFARNE CASTLE ✾

Holy Island, Berwick-upon-Tweed, Northumberland   TD15 2SH

Tel: 01289 389244   **www**.nationaltrust.org.uk

Owner: The National Trust   **Contact:** Property Manager

Built in 1550 to protect Holy Island harbour from attack, the castle was restored and converted into a private house for Edward Hudson by Sir Edwin Lutyens in 1903.

Location: OS Ref. NU136 417. On Holy Island, ¾ m E of village, 6m E of A1 across causeway. Usable at low tide.

Open: 12 - 20 Feb & 12 Mar - 30 Oct: daily except Mon (but open BHs incl. Scottish BHs), 10.30am - 3pm or 12 noon - 4.30pm, depending on tides. Visitors are advised to check tide times before visiting.

Admission: Adult £5, Child £2.50, Family £12.50. Garden only: Adult £1, Child Free. Out of hours group tours (10+) by arrangement £6pp.

▣ NT Shop (in Main St). ▦ 🐕 In grounds, on leads.

Hadrian's Wall.

© English Heritage Photo Library

LINDISFARNE PRIORY ⌗

HOLY ISLAND, BERWICK-UPON-TWEED TD15 2RX

Tel: 01289 389200

Owner: English Heritage   **Contact:** Visitor Operations Team

The site of one of the most important early centres of Christianity in Anglo-Saxon England. St Cuthbert converted pagan Northumbria, and miracles occurring at his shrine established this 11th century priory as a major pilgrimage centre. The evocative ruins, with the decorated 'rainbow' arch curving dramatically across the nave of the church, are still the destination of pilgrims today. The story of Lindisfarne is told in an exhibition which gives an impression of life for the monks, including a reconstruction of a monk's cell.

Location: OS Ref. NU126 418. On Holy Island, check tide times.

Open: 24 Mar - 30 Sept: daily, 10am - 6pm. 1 - 31 Oct: daily, 10am - 4pm. 1 Nov - 31 Mar: Sat - Mon, 10am - 2pm. Closed 24 - 26 Dec and 1 Jan. Times subject to change April 2005.

Admission: Adult £3.60, Child £1.80, Conc. £2.70. 15% discount for groups (11+).
⬛ ♿Partial. Disabled parking. 🅿Charge. ⬛ 🐕Restricted. ✳ 📞Tel for details.

NORHAM CASTLE ⌗

Norham, Northumberland

Tel: 01289 382329

Owner: English Heritage   **Contact:** Visitor Operations Team

Set on a promontory in a curve of the River Tweed, this was one of the strongest of the Border castles, built c1160.

Location: OS75, NT907 476. 6m SW of Berwick.

Open: 24 Mar - 30 Sept: Sats & Suns, 10am - 6pm. Times subject to change April 2005.

Admission: Adult £2.60, Child £1.30, Conc. £2. 15% discount for groups (11+).
⬛ ♿Partial. ⬛Inclusive. ⬛ 🐕On leads. 📞Tel for details.

PRESTON TOWER 🏠

Chathill, Northumberland NE67 5DH

Tel: 01665 589227

Owner/Contact: Major T Baker Cresswell

The Tower was built by Sir Robert Harbottle in 1392 and is one of the few survivors of 78 pele towers listed in 1415. The tunnel vaulted rooms remain unaltered and provide a realistic picture of the grim way of life under the constant threat of "Border Reivers". Two rooms are furnished in contemporary style and there are displays of historic and local information. Visitors are welcome to walk in the grounds which contain a number of interesting trees and shrubs. A woodland walk to the natural spring from which water is now pumped up to the Tower for the house and cottages.

Location: OS Ref. NU185 253. Follow Historic Property signs on A1 7m N of Alnwick.

Open: All year: daily, 10am - 6pm.

Admission: Adult £1.50, Child 50p, Conc. £1. Groups £1.
♿Grounds. 🐕 ✳

PRUDHOE CASTLE ⌗

Prudhoe, Northumberland NE42 6NA

Tel: 01661 833459

Owner: English Heritage   **Contact:** Visitor Operations Team

Set on a wooded hillside overlooking the River Tyne are the extensive remains of this 12th century castle including a gatehouse, curtain wall and keep. Small exhibition and video presentation.

Location: OS88 Ref. NZ092 634. In Prudhoe, on minor road N from A695.

Open: 24 Mar - 30 Sept: daily, 10am - 6pm. Times subject to change April 2005.

Admission: Adult £3.30, Child £1.70, Conc. £2.50. 15% discount for groups (11+).
ℹWC. ⬛ ♿Partial. ⬛ 🅿Limited. ⬛ 🐕In grounds, on leads. 📞Tel for details.

SEATON DELAVAL HALL 🏠

SEATON SLUICE, WHITLEY BAY, NORTHUMBERLAND NE26 4QR

Tel: 0191 237 1493 / 0191 237 0786   **e-mail:** lordhastings@onetel.net.uk

Owner: Lord Hastings   **Contact:** Mrs Mills

The home of Lord and Lady Hastings, half a mile from Seaton Sluice, is the last and most sensational mansion designed by Sir John Vanbrugh, builder of Blenheim Palace and Castle Howard. It was erected 1718 - 1728 and comprises a high turreted block flanked by arcaded wings which form a vast forecourt. The centre block was gutted by fire in 1822, but was partially restored in 1862 and again in 1959 - 1962 and 1999 - 2000. The remarkable staircases are a visual delight, and the two surviving rooms are filled with family pictures and photographs and royal seals spanning three centuries as well as various archives. This building is used frequently for concerts and charitable functions. The East Wing contains immense stables in ashlar stone of breathtaking proportions. Nearby are the Coach House with farm and passenger vehicles, fully documented, and the restored ice house with explanatory sketch and description. There are beautiful gardens with herbaceous borders, rose garden, rhododendrons, azaleas, laburnum walk, statues, and a spectacular parterre by internationally famous Jim Russell, also a unique Norman Church.

Location: OS Ref. NZ322 766. $^1/_2$m from Seaton Sluice on A190, 3m from Whitley Bay.

Open: May & Aug BH Mons; Jun - 30 Sept: Weds & Suns, 2 - 6pm.

Admission: Adult £4, Child £1, OAP £3.50, Student £2. Groups (20+): Adult £3, Child/Student £1.

⬛ ♿Partial. WC. 🐕 🅿Free. ⬛ 🐕In grounds, on leads.

WALLINGTON ✤

CAMBO, MORPETH, NORTHUMBERLAND NE61 4AR

www.nationaltrust.org.uk

Tel: 01670 773600   **Fax** 01670 774420   **e-mail:** wallington@nationaltrust.org.uk

Owner: The National Trust   **Contact:** The Estate Office

Dating from 1688, the much-loved home of the Trevelyan family contains magnificent rococo plasterwork, fine ceramics and a collection of doll's houses. The Pre-Raphaelite Central Hall depicts floral wall paintings and a series of scenes of Northumbrian history by William Bell Scott.

There are extensive walks through a variety of lawns, shrubberies, lakes and woodland to the exuberant walled garden, which remain open throughout the year.

Location: OS Ref. NZ030 843. Near Cambo, 6m NW of Belsay (A696).

Open: House & Restaurant: 23 Mar - 30 Oct: daily except Tue, 1 - 5.30pm (closes 4.30pm from 5 Sep). Last admissions 1 hr (House)/30 min (Restaurant) prior to closing times. Walled garden: 1 Apr - 30 Sept: daily, 10am - 7pm. Oct: daily, 10am - 6pm. 1 Nov - 31 Mar: daily, 10am - 4pm. Shop: 5 Jan - 13 Feb: Wed - Sun, 10.30am - 4.30pm; 2 Mar - 4 Sep: daily (closed Tue during 2 Mar - 30 May), 10.30am - 5.30pm; 5 Sep - 30 Oct: daily except Tue, 10.30am - 4.30pm; 2 Nov -20 Dec: Wed - Sun, 10.30am - 4.30pm. Restaurant as shop. Farm shop: 1 Apr - 24 Dec: daily, 10.30am - 5pm; 28 Dec - 31 Mar (outside turnstile): 10.30am - 4pm. Grounds: daily in daylight hours.

Admission: House, garden & grounds: Adult £7.30, Child £3.65, Family £18.25, Groups £6.50. Garden & grounds only: Adult £5.20, Child £2.60, Family £13, Groups £4.60.

🗓 ⛲ 🍴 ♿Partial. ☝ 🎲 By arrangement. 🅿 ◼ ♨In grounds on leads. ▲ ✳ ♔ Tel for details.

WARKWORTH CASTLE ⌗

WARKWORTH, MORPETH, NORTHUMBERLAND NE66 0UJ

Tel: 01665 711423

Owner: English Heritage   **Contact:** Visitor Operations Team

The great towering keep of this 15th century castle, once the home of the mighty Percy family, dominates the town and River Coquet. Warkworth is one of the most outstanding examples of an aristocratic fortified residence. Upstream by boat from the castle lies Warkworth Hermitage, cutting into the rock of the river cliff (separate charge applies).

Location: OS Ref. NU247 057. 7m S of Alnwick on A1068.

Open: 24 Mar - 30 Sept: daily, 10am - 6pm. 1 - 31 Oct: daily, 10am - 4pm. 1 Nov - 31 Mar: Sat - Mon, 10am - 4pm (closed 1 - 2pm). Closed 24 - 26 Dec and 1 Jan. Times subject to change April 2005.

Admission: Adult £3.30, Child £1.70, Conc. £2.50, Family £8.30. 15% discount for groups (11+).

ⅈWC. 🗓 ♿Grounds. ♫Inclusive. 🅿 ◼ ♨ On leads. ✳ ♔ Tel for details.

WARKWORTH HERMITAGE ⌗

Warkworth, Northumberland

Tel: 01665 711423

Owner: English Heritage   **Contact:** Visitor Operations Team

Upstream by boat from the castle this curious hermitage cuts into the rock of the river cliff.

Location: OS Ref. NU247 057. 7 ½ m SE of Alnwick on A1068.

Open: 24 Mar - 30 Sept: Weds, Suns & BHs, 11am - 5pm. Times subject to change April 2005.

Admission: Adult £2.30, Child £1.20, Conc. £1.70.

🗓 ♿Grounds. ♫Inclusive. 🅿 ◼ ♨ On leads. ✳ ♔ Tel for details.

Belsay Pillar Hall.

Herterton House Gardens
© Andrew Lawson.

ARBEIA ROMAN FORT
Baring Street, South Shields, Tyne & Wear NE33 2BB
Tel: 0191 456 1369   **Fax:** 0191 427 6862
Owner: South Tyneside Metropolitan Borough Council   **Contact:** The Curator
Managed by: Tyne & Wear Museums
More than 1,500 years on, the remains at Arbeia represent the most extensively excavated example of a military supply base anywhere in the Roman Empire. Museum includes weapons, jewellery and tombstones.
Location: OS Ref. NZ365 679. Near town centre and Metro Station.
Open: Easter - Sept: Mon - Sat: 10am - 5.30pm, Suns, 1 - 5pm. Open BH Mons. Oct - Easter: Mon - Sat, 10am - 4pm. Closed 25/26 Dec, 1 Jan & Good Friday.
Admission: Free, except for Time Quest Gallery: Adult £1.50, Child/Conc. 80p.

BEDE'S WORLD MUSEUM
Church Bank, Jarrow, Tyne & Wear NE32 3DY
Tel: 0191 489 2106   **Fax:** 0191 428 2361
Managed by: Jarrow 700AD Ltd   **Contact:** Visitor Services
A museum telling the story of the Venerable Bede and Anglo-Saxon Northumbria.
Location: OS Ref. NZ339 652. Just off A19, S end of Tyne Tunnel. 300yds N of St Paul's.
Open: Apr - Oct: Mon - Sat, 10am - 5.30pm, Suns, 12 noon - 5.30pm. Nov - Mar: Mon - Sat, 10am - 4.30pm, Suns, 12 noon - 4.30pm. Also open BH Mons but closed Good Fri.
Admission: Adult £4.50, Conc. £3, Family £10. Groups by arrangement.

BESSIE SURTEES HOUSE ⌗
41 - 44 Sandhill, Newcastle, Tyne & Wear
Tel: 0191 269 1200
Owner: English Heritage   **Contact:** Reception
Two 16th and 17th century merchants' houses stand on the quayside near the Tyne Bridge. One is a rare example of Jacobean domestic architecture. 3 rooms open.
Location: OS Ref. NZ252 639. 41 - 44 Sandhill, Newcastle. Riverside. City centre.
Open: Weekdays only: 10am - 4pm. Closed BHs, 24 - 26 Dec and 1 Jan. Times subject to change April 2005.
Admission: Free.

GIBSIDE ⚘
Nr Rowlands Gill, Burnopfield, Newcastle-upon-Tyne NE16 6BG
Tel: 01207 541820   **e-mail:** gibside@nationaltrust.org.uk   **www**.nationaltrust.org.uk
Owner: The National Trust   **Contact:** The Property Manager
Gibside is one of the finest 18th century designed landscapes in the north of England. The Chapel was built to James Paine's design soon after 1760. Outstanding example of Georgian architecture approached along a terrace with an oak avenue. Walk along the River Derwent through woodland.
Location: OS Ref. NZ172 583. 6m SW of Gateshead, 20m NW of Durham. Entrance on B6314 between Burnopfield and Rowlands Gill.
Open: 7 Mar - 23 Oct: daily, 10am - 6pm. 24 Oct - 5 Mar: daily, 10am - 4pm.
Admission: Adult £3.50, Child £2, Family (2+4) £10, Family (1+3) £7. Booked groups £3.
Partial. By arrangement. Limited for coaches. On leads, in grounds. Tel for details.

NEWCASTLE CASTLE KEEP
Castle Keep, Castle Garth, Newcastle-upon-Tyne NE1 1RQ
Tel: 0191 232 7938
Owner: Newcastle City Council   **Contact:** Paul MacDonald
The Keep originally dominated the castle bailey. The 'new' castle was founded in 1080.
Location: OS Ref. NZ251 638. City centre between St Nicholas church and the High Level bridge.
Open: All year: daily, 9.30am - 5.30pm (4.30pm winter).
Admission: Adult £1.50, Child/Conc. 50p.

ST PAUL'S MONASTERY ⌗
Jarrow, Tyne & Wear
Tel: 0191 489 7052
Owner: English Heritage   **Contact:** The Regional Office – 0191 269 1200
The home of the Venerable Bede in the 7th and 8th centuries, partly surviving as the chancel of the parish church. It has become one of the best understood Anglo-Saxon monastic sites.
Location: OS Ref. NZ339 652. In Jarrow, on minor road N of A185. 300yds S of Bede's World.
Open: Any reasonable time.
Admission: Free.

SOUTER LIGHTHOUSE ⚘
Coast Road, Whitburn, Sunderland, Tyne & Wear SR6 7NH
Tel: 0191 529 3161   **Fax:** 0191 529 0902   **e-mail:** souter@nationaltrust.org.uk
www.nationaltrust.org.uk
Owner: The National Trust   **Contact:** The Property Manager
Dramatic red and white lighthouse tower on rugged coast. Built in 1871, the first to be powered by alternating electric current.
Location: OS Ref. NZ408 641. 2¹/₂m S of South Shields on A183. 5m N of Sunderland.
Open: 14 - 29 Feb & 19 Mar - 6 Nov: daily except Fri (open Good Fri), 11am - 5pm. Last admission 4.30pm.
Admission: Adult £3.80, Child £2.30, Family £10. Booked Groups (10+): Adult £3.30, Child £2. NT members Free: membership available from shop.
Partial. WCs. By arrangement. In grounds, on leads.

TYNEMOUTH PRIORY & CASTLE ⌗
North Pier, Tynemouth, Tyne & Wear NE30 4BZ
Tel: 0191 257 1090
Owner: English Heritage   **Contact:** Visitor Operations Team
The castle walls and gatehouse enclose the substantial remains of a Benedictine priory founded c1090 on a Saxon monastic site. Their strategic importance has made the castle and priory the target for attack for many centuries. In World War I, coastal batteries in the castle defended the mouth of the Tyne.
Location: OS Ref. NZ374 695. In Tynemouth.
Open: 24 Mar - 30 Sept: daily, 10am - 6pm. 1 - 31 Oct: daily, 10am - 4pm. 1 Nov - 31 Mar: Thur - Mon, 10am - 4pm (closed 1 - 2pm). Closed 24 - 26 Dec & 1 Jan. Times subject to change April 2005.
Admission: Adult £3.30, Child £1.70, Conc. £2.50, Family £5.80. 15% discount for groups (11+).
Grounds. By arrangement. In grounds, on leads. Tel for details.

WASHINGTON OLD HALL ⚘
The Avenue, Washington Village, District 4, Washington, Tyne & Wear NE38 7LE
Tel: 0191 416 6879   **Fax:** 0191 419 2065   **www**.nationaltrust.org.uk
Owner: The National Trust   **Contact:** The Property Manager
Jacobean manor house incorporating portions of 12th century house of the Washington family. Small Jacobean knot garden.
Location: OS Ref. NZ312 566. In Washington on E side of The Avenue. 5m W of Sunderland (2m from A1), S of Tyne Tunnel, follow signs for Washington District 4 and then village.
Open: 25 Mar - 30 Oct: Sun - Wed, 11am - 5pm. Last admission 4.30pm. Open Good Fri.
Admission: Adult £3.80, Child £2.30, Family £10. Booked groups (15+): Adult £3.30, Child £2. Membership available from reception.
Conferences. Ground floor and grounds. By arrangement. Limited. In grounds, on leads.

Tynemouth Priory.

Corporate Hospitality see page 35

Looking to Arran

Scotland

Scotland is loosely divided into the Highlands and the Lowlands, the latter made up of the Central plain and the Southern Uplands. The southernmost counties nearest the border with England are also known as The Borders. The cattle and sheep reared on Lowland pastures produce meat of the highest quality which is sought after worldwide. The Highlands, in their turn, provide wonderfully romantic scenery; mountains and moorlands, lochs and glens. This is the home of red deer, wild cats and golden eagles. Walk along the beaches on the west coast, some of which rank among the finest in the world, with just seals and seagulls for company, a perfect destination from which to escape the stress of urban living. First time visitors to Scotland can only scratch the surface of its cultural and social history. Edinburgh Castle is, of course, Scotland's most famous castle but there are so many others which merit a visit: fairytale Dunrobin on the east coast, Dunvegan on the Isle of Skye, Cawdor, home of the Thanes of Cawdor from the 14th century – the list is endless. Equally interesting, though perhaps less dramatic, is The Castle of Mey, the only home actually owned by the late Queen Elizabeth, The Queen Mother, and restored by her from a ruin. No visit to Scotland would be complete without a trip to a distillery. The soft water of the Highlands produces the finest malt whisky in the world.

Melrose Abbey.

Cawdor Castle, Highlands & Skye.

Urquhart Castle.

Melrose Abbey.

stirling castle

royal stronghold | unicorn tapestries | symbolism

stirling castle

s c o t l a n d

At magnificent Stirling Castle, looming above two of the most famous Scottish battlefields, Stirling Bridge and Bannockburn, a most remarkable project is taking shape.

At this Scottish stronghold, where Mary Queen of Scots was crowned in its Chapel Royal in 1543, the Royal Apartments of the Palace are being decorated and furnished as they might have looked in the 16th century during the reign of King James V.

An integral part of this process involves recreating 'The Hunt of the Unicorn', a series of seven tapestries dating from 1495-1505 and which are currently part of the medieval collection of the Metropolitan Museum of Art in New York. These scenes, telling the story of the Passion of Christ and culminating in the Crucifixion, used well-known contemporary religious symbolism: the Unicorn, with all its powerful mystery, depicted Christ. These tapestries were first recorded in France in the 17th century in documentation in the inventory of a wealthy French duke and were rediscovered in a barn in the 19th century, although their earlier origins are hazy.

Historic Scotland decided that this story, told in one of the world's finest medieval tapestries, should be recreated, based on the inventories of King James V which included a reference to a set of six pieces depicting the 'historie of the unicorne'.

Tapestries were an important decorative and practical feature of medieval castles and royal residences. They were indicators of social status by virtue of their beauty, craftsmanship and length of time they took to produce; and they kept out the damp, while being readily transferable elsewhere. Medieval tapestries were made from wool, silk and sometimes gold thread. Inventories at Stirling also show that there were more than 100 tapestries in the Royal Collection by 1539, many collected by James V and his father, from France and Flanders.

This traditional craft, supported by the US-based Quinque Foundation, is brought to life in the Castle by the West Dean Tapestry Studio of West Sussex who are now currently busy on the third tapestry of the series: 'The Unicorn is Killed and Brought to the Castle'; and visitors can watch it being recreated in the Castle's Nether Bailey. Two sections are complete: the first, 'The Unicorn in Captivity', took two years to weave and portrays the captured, but 'indestructible' unicorn tied to a pomegranate tree; and the second, a piece based on 'The Start of the Hunt', was completed in 2004. The whole project aims to bring to life the colourful history of the castle, following on from the success of the restoration of the Great Hall in 1999.

▸ For further details about Stirling Castle see page 498.

MERTOUN GARDENS 📷
St Boswells, Melrose, Roxburghshire TD6 0EA
Tel: 01835 823236 **Fax:** 01835 822474
Owner: His Grace the Duke of Sutherland **Contact:** Angela Dodds/Susan Murdoch
26 acres of beautiful grounds. Walled garden and well-preserved circular dovecote.
Location: OS Ref. NT617 318. Entrance off B6404 2m NE of St Boswells.
Open: Apr - Sept: weekends & Public Holiday Mons only, 2 - 6pm. Last admission
5.30pm.
Admission: Adult £2, Child 50p, OAP £1.50. Groups by arrangement: 10% reduction.
📷 By arrangement. 🅿 ✕

MONTEVIOT HOUSE GARDENS
JEDBURGH, ROXBURGHSHIRE TD8 6UQ

Tel: 01835 830380 (mornings only) / 01835 830704 **Fax:** 01835 830288
Owner: The Marquess of Lothian   **Contact:** The Administrator
The river garden planted with herbaceous shrub borders, has a beautiful view of
the River Teviot. A semi-enclosed rose garden with a collection of hybrid teas,
floribunda and shrub roses. The pinetum is full of unusual trees and nearby a
water garden of islands is linked by bridges.
Location: OS Ref. NT648 247. 3m N of Jedburgh. S side of B6400 (to Nisbet).
1m E of A68.
Open: House: 4 - 17 Jul: 12 noon - 4.15pm. Garden: Apr - Oct: daily, 12 noon -
5pm. Coach parties by prior arrangement.
Admission: House or Garden only: Adult £2.50. House & Garden: Adult £4.50.
Under 16yrs Free.
📷 ♿Partial. Parking & WCs. 📷By arrangement. 🅿

Floors Castle.

OLD GALA HOUSE
Scott Crescent, Galashiels TD1 3JS
Tel: 01750 20096 **Fax:** 01750 23282
Owner: Scottish Borders Council
Dating from 1583, the former house of the Lairds of Gala. Particularly memorable is
the painted ceiling dated 1635.
Location: OS Ref. NT492 357. S of town centre, signed from A7.
Open: Apr/May & Sept: Tue - Sat, 10am - 4pm. Jun - Aug: Mon - Sat, 10am - 4pm,
Suns, 1 - 4pm. Oct: Tue - Fri, 1 - 4pm, Sat, 10am - 4pm.
Admission: Free.

LOCAL FOOD

Haggis

*Although there any many references to haggis-like dishes
throughout Great Britain from as far back as the Middle
Ages, it is only in Scotland that the haggis has survived to
the present day. A mixture of oatmeal, liver, heart and
beef suet, it is encased in a sheep's stomach and then
steamed or boiled. Traditionally served with a single malt
whisky, haggis has become synonymous with Burns
Night, when it is often piped into dinner and then
addressed by the reciting of Burns' poem "To a Haggis".
When the line 'an cut you up wi' ready slight', is reached,
the haggis is cut open with a sharp knife. It is customary
for the guests to applaud the speaker then stand and
toast the haggis with a glass of whisky.*

📷 Accommodation Index see page 31

PAXTON HOUSE, GALLERY & COUNTRY PARK

BERWICK-UPON-TWEED TD15 1SZ

www.paxtonhouse.com

Tel: 01289 386291 **Fax:** 01289 386660 **e-mail:** info@paxtonhouse.com

Owner: The Paxton Trust   **Contact:** The Director

Award-winning country house and country park built from 1758-62 to the design of John Adam for Patrick Home, Laird of Wedderburn. The house boasts the pre-eminent collection of Chippendale furniture in Scotland and a fine collection of Regency furniture by William Trotter of Edinburgh. The largest picture gallery in a Scottish country house, with over 70 paintings from the National Galleries of Scotland. Enjoy the 80 acres of grounds and gardens, riverside and woodland walks, red squirrel and bird hides plus the salmon net fishing museum. Shops, stables tearoom and an ever-changing exhibition programme.

Location: OS Ref. NT931 520. 3m off the A1 Berwick-upon-Tweed bypass on B6461.

Open: Easter - 31 Oct: House: 11am - 5pm. Last house tour 4.15pm. Grounds: 10am - sunset. Open to groups/schools all year by appointment.

Admission: Adult £6, Child £3. Groups (pre-arranged, 12+). Adult £5, Child £2.50. Grounds only: Adult £3, Child £1.50.

ⁱNo photography. Conferences, weddings. Partial. Licensed. Obligatory. In grounds, on leads. Tel for details.

SMAILHOLM TOWER

Smailholm, Kelso

Tel: 01573 460365

Owner: In the care of Historic Scotland   **Contact:** The Steward

Set on a high rocky knoll this well preserved 16th century tower houses an exhibition of tapestries and costume dolls depicting characters from Sir Walter Scott's Minstrelsy of the Scottish Borders.

Location: OS Ref. NT638 347. Nr Smailholm Village, 6m W of Kelso on B6937.

Open: 1 Apr - 30 Sept: daily, 9.30am - 6.30pm. Oct: Sat - Wed, 9.30am - 4.30pm. Nov - Mar: Sats & Suns only, 9.30am - 4.30pm. Last tickets ½ hr before closing.

Admission: Adult £2.50, Child £1, Conc. £1.90.

€

Mellerstain House.

STRANRAER CASTLE

Stranraer, Galloway

Tel: 01776 705088 **Fax:** 01776 705835

Owner: Dumfries & Galloway Council **Contact:** John Pickin

Also referred to as the Castle of St John. A much altered 16th century L-plan tower house, now a museum.

Location: OS Ref. NX061 608. In Stranraer, towards centre, ¼ m short of the harbour.

Open: Easter - mid Sept: Mon - Sat, 10am - 1pm & 2 - 5pm.

Admission: Free.

SWEETHEART ABBEY

New Abbey Village

Tel: 01387 850397

Owner: In the care of Historic Scotland **Contact:** The Steward

Cistercian abbey founded in 1273 by Devorgilla, in memory of her husband John Balliol. A principal feature is the well-preserved precinct wall enclosing 30 acres.

Location: OS Ref. NX965 663. In New Abbey Village, on A710 8m S of Dumfries.

Open: 1 Apr - 30 Sept: daily, 9.30am - 6.30pm. Last ticket 6pm. 1 Oct - 31 Mar: Sat - Wed, 9.30am - 4.30pm. Last ticket 4pm.

Admission: Adult £2, Child 80p, Conc. £1.50.

THREAVE CASTLE

Castle Douglas

Tel: 07711 223101

Owner: The National Trust for Scotland **Contact:** Historic Scotland

Built by Archibald the Grim in the late 14th century, early stronghold of the Black Douglases. Around its base is an artillery fortification built before 1455 when the castle was besieged by James II. Ring the bell and the custodian will come to ferry you over. Long walk to property. Owned by The National Trust for Scotland but under the guardianship of Historic Scotland.

Location: OS Ref. NX739 623. 2m W of Castle Douglas on the A75.

Open: 1 Apr - 30 Sept: daily, 9.30am - 6.30pm. Last ticket 6pm.

Admission: Adult £3, Child £1.20, Conc. £2.25. Charges include ferry trip.

€

THREAVE GARDEN & ESTATE

Castle Douglas DG7 1RX

Tel: 01556 502575 **Fax:** 01556 502683

Owner: The National Trust for Scotland

The garden has a wide range of features and a good collection of plants. There are peat and woodland garden plants and a colourful rock garden. A garden for all seasons.

Location: OS Ref. NX752 605. Off A75, 1m SW of Castle Douglas.

Open: Estate & garden, All year:, daily, 9.30am - sunset. Walled garden & glasshouses: All year: daily 9.30am - 5pm. Visitor Centre, Countryside Centre & exhibition: 1 Feb - 31 Mar & 1 Nov - 23 Dec: daily, 10am - 4pm; 1 Apr - 31 Oct: daily 9.30am - 5.30pm. House: 1 Mar - 31 Oct: Wed - Fri & Sun, 11am - 4 pm (guided tours only, admission by timed ticket). **(2004 opening times.)**

Admission: House & garden: Adult £9, Conc. £6.50, Family £23. Groups: Adult £7, Child/School £1. Garden only: Adult £5, Conc. £3.75, Family £13.50. Groups: Adult £4, Child/School £1. **(2004 prices.)**

WHITHORN PRIORY

Whithorn

Tel: 01988 500508

Owner: In the care of Historic Scotland **Contact:** The Project Manager

The site of the first Christian church in Scotland. Founded as 'Candida Casa' by St Ninian in the early 5th century it later became the cathedral church of Galloway.

Location: OS Ref. NX445 403. At Whithorn on the A746. 18m S of Newton Stewart.

Open: 21 Mar - 31 Oct: daily, 10.30am - 5pm.

Admission: Adult £2.70, Child/Conc. £1.50. Joint ticket gives entry to Priory, Priory Museum and 'The Story of Whithorn'.

Special Events Index see page 24

Blairquhan from the book 'Historic Family Homes & Gardens from the Air'.

Edinburgh City, Coast & Countryside

DALMENY HOUSE

www.dalmeny.co.uk

Dalmeny House rejoices in one of the most beautiful and unspoilt settings in Great Britain, yet it is only seven miles from Scotland's capital, Edinburgh, fifteen minutes from Edinburgh airport and less than an hour's drive from Glasgow. It is an eminently suitable venue for group visits, business functions, meetings and special events, including product launches. Outdoor activities, such as off-road driving, can be arranged.

Dalmeny House, the family home of the Earls of Rosebery for over 300 years, boasts superb collections of porcelain and tapestries, fine paintings by Gainsborough, Raeburn, Reynolds and Lawrence, together with the exquisite Mentmore Rothschild collection of 18th century French furniture. There is also the Napoleonic collection, assembled by the 5th Earl of Rosebery, Prime Minister, historian and owner of three Derby winners.

The Hall, Library and Dining Room will lend a memorable sense of occasion to corporate receptions, luncheons and dinners. A wide range of entertainment can also be provided, from a clarsach player to a floodlit pipe band Beating the Retreat.

Map 10

Owner:
The Earl of Rosebery

▶ CONTACT

The Administrator
Dalmeny House
South Queensferry
Edinburgh
EH30 9TQ

Tel: 0131 331 1888
Fax: 0131 331 1788

e-mail: events@
dalmeny.co.uk

▶ LOCATION

OS Ref. NT167 779

From Edinburgh A90,
B924, 7m N, A90 ½ m.

On south shore
of Firth of Forth.

Bus: From St Andrew
Square to Chapel Gate
1m from House.

Rail: Dalmeny
station 3m.

Taxi: Queensferry Fare
Radio Cabs
0131 331 1041.

▶ OPENING TIMES

Summer
July and August
Sun - Tue, 2 - 5.30pm.
Last admission 4.30pm.

Winter
Open at other times by
appointment only.

▶ ADMISSION

Summer
Adult	£5.00
Child (10-16yrs)	£3.00
OAP	£4.00
Student	£4.00
Groups (20+)	£4.00

i Fashion shows, product launches, archery, clay pigeon shooting, shows, filming, background photography, small meetings and special events. Lectures on House, contents and family history. Helicopter landing area. House is centre of a 4½ m shore walk from Forth Rail Bridge to small foot passenger ferry at Cramond (ferry 9am - 1pm, 2 - 7pm in summer, 2 - 4pm winter, closed Fri). No fires, picnics or photography.

Y Conferences and functions, buffets, lunches, dinners.

& Partially suitable. Visitors may alight at entrance. WC.

▱ Teas, groups can book in advance.

Ẋ Obligatory. Special interest tours can be arranged outside normal opening hours.

P 60 cars, 3 coaches. Parking for functions in front of house.

Map 10

HOPETOUN HOUSE 🏛
Edinburgh

www.hopetounhouse.com

Hopetoun House is a unique gem of Europe's architectural heritage and undoubtedly 'Scotland's Finest Stately Home'. Situated on the shores of the Firth of Forth, it is one of the most splendid examples of the work of Scottish architects Sir William Bruce and William Adam. The interior of the house, with opulent gilding and classical motifs, reflects the aristocratic grandeur of the early 18th century, whilst its magnificent parkland has fine views across the Forth to the hills of Fife. The house is approached from the Royal Drive, used only by members of the Royal Family, notably King George IV in 1822 and Her Majesty Queen Elizabeth II in 1988.

Hopetoun is really two houses in one, the oldest part of the house was designed by Sir William Bruce and built between 1699 and 1707. It shows some of the finest examples in Scotland of carving, wainscotting and ceiling painting. In 1721 William Adam started enlarging the house by adding the magnificent façade, colonnades and grand State apartments which were the focus for social life and entertainment in the 18th century.

The house is set in 100 acres of rolling parkland including fine woodland walks, the red deer park, the spring garden with a profusion of wild flowers, and numerous picturesque picnic spots.

Hopetoun has been home of the Earls of Hopetoun, later created Marquesses of Linlithgow, since it was built in 1699 and in 1974 a charitable trust was created to preserve the house with its historic contents and surrounding landscape for the benefit of the public for all time.

Owner:
Hopetoun House
Preservation Trust

▶ CONTACT
Mhairi MacDougall
Hopetoun House
South Queensferry
Edinburgh
West Lothian
EH30 9SL

Tel: 0131 331 2451
Fax: 0131 319 1885

e-mail: marketing@
hopetounhouse.com

▶ LOCATION
OS Ref. NT089 790

2½ m W of Forth Road
Bridge.

12m W of Edinburgh
(25 mins. drive).

34m E of Glasgow
(50 mins. drive).

▶ OPENING TIMES
Summer
Easter Sun - 30 September:
Daily, 10am - 5.30pm.
Last admission 4.30pm.

Winter
By appointment only
for Groups (20+).

▶ ADMISSION
House & Grounds
Adult	£7.00
Child (5-16yrs)*	£4.00
Conc/Student	£6.00
Family (2+2)	£20.00
Additional Child	£2.50
Groups	£6.00

Grounds only
Adult	£3.50
Child (5-16yrs)*	£2.00
Conc/Student	£3.00
Family (2+2)	£9.00
Groups	£3.00

School Visits
Child	£5.25
Teachers	Free

*Under 5yrs Free.

Winter group rates on request.

Admission to Tearoom Free.

CONFERENCE/FUNCTION
ROOM	SIZE	MAX CAPACITY
Ballroom	92' x 35'	300
Tapestry Rm	37' x 24'	100
Red Drawing Rm	44' x 24'	100
State Dining Rm	39' x 23'	20
Stables	92' x 22'	200

📷 ℹ Private functions, special events, antiques fairs, concerts, Scottish gala evenings, conferences, wedding ceremonies and receptions, grand piano, helicopter landing. No smoking or flash photography in house.

🍽 Receptions, gala dinners.

♿ Licensed.

🍴 Licensed. Groups (up to 250) can book in advance, menus on request tel: 0131 331 4305.

🚶 By arrangement.

🅿 Close to the house for cars and coaches. Book if possible, allow 1-2hrs for visit (min).

▪ Special tours of house and/or grounds for different age/interest groups.

🐕 No dogs in house, on leads in grounds.

❄

John Freeman/ The Royal Collection © 2005 HM Queen Elizabeth II

Map 10

PALACE OF HOLYROODHOUSE
& THE QUEEN'S GALLERY
www.royal.gov.uk

Owner:
Official Residence of
Her Majesty The Queen

▶ **CONTACT**
Ticket Sales &
Information Office
Buckingham Palace
London SW1A 1AA

Tel: 0131 556 5100
Groups (15+):
020 7766 7321

Fax: 020 7930 9625

e-mail: holyrood@
royalcollection.org.uk

▶ **LOCATION**
OS Ref. NT269 739

Central Edinburgh,
end of Royal Mile.

The Palace of Holyroodhouse, the official residence in Scotland of Her Majesty The Queen, stands at the end of Edinburgh's Royal Mile against the spectacular backdrop of Arthur's Seat. This fine baroque palace is closely associated with Scotland's rich history. Today the Royal Apartments are used by The Queen for State ceremonies and official entertaining. They are finely decorated with magnificent works of art from the Royal Collection.

The Palace is perhaps best known as the home of Mary, Queen of Scots and was the setting for many dramatic episodes in her short and turbulent reign. Mary, Queen of Scots' chambers are housed in the Palace's west corner tower and are approached up a small winding staircase. These intimate apartments were home to Mary following her return from France in 1561.

The Queen's Gallery, Edinburgh

Opened in November 2002 as part of Her Majesty The Queen's Golden Jubilee celebrations. The Gallery provides purpose-built facilities and state-of-the-art environmental controls, which enable exhibitions of the most delicate works from the Royal Collection to be shown.

Holbein to Hockney: Drawings from the Royal Collection (19 November 2004 - 8 March 2005)

The Royal Library at Windsor Castle holds one of the world's greatest collections of works on paper. The 75 examples selected for the exhibition represent each important group of material in the Royal Collection. Among the artists represented are Dürer, Leonardo Da Vinci, Michelangelo, Raphael, Poussin, Canaletto and Merian.

Watercolours and Drawings from the Collection of Queen Elizabeth The Queen Mother (18 March - 25 September 2005)

The first exhibition devoted to the collection formed by Queen Elizabeth The Queen Mother includes many works that have never been shown before. It reflects the range of Queen Elizabeth's interests and her enthusiastic patronage and support of contemporary artists from the 1930s onwards.

▶ **OPENING TIMES**
Palace of Holyroodhouse
April - October:
Daily (closed 25 March, 17 - 29 May, 27 Jun - 10 Jul), 9.30am - 6pm.
Last admission 5pm.

November - February:
Daily (closed 25/26 December), 9.30am - 4.30pm, last admission 3.30pm.

Closed during Royal visits. Opening times are subject to change at short notice. Please check before planning a visit.

Private tours of the Palace and The Queen's Gallery are available for pre-booked groups (15+). Tel: 020 7766 7322.

The Queen's Gallery
Open daily (closed 7 - 18 Mar, 25 Mar, 28 Sept - 13 Oct, 25/26 December). Opening times as Palace.

Each exhibition is priced separately. Entry by timed ticket.

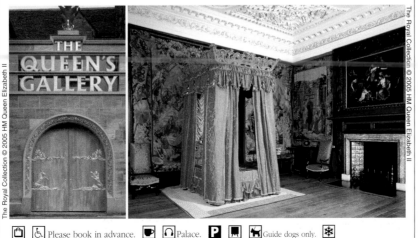

The Royal Collection © 2005 HM Queen Elizabeth II

The Royal Collection © 2005 HM Queen Elizabeth II

▶ **ADMISSION**
(Price incl. Audio tour)

For admission prices please call the Ticket Sales & Information Office on 0131 556 5100.
Groups (15+) discounts available.

Information correct at time of going to print.

⬜ ♿ Please book in advance. ☕ 🎧 Palace. 🅿 ▦ 🐕 Guide dogs only. ❄

Edinburgh City, Coast & Countryside

AMISFIELD MAINS
Nr Haddington, East Lothian EH41 3SA
Tel: 01875 870201 **Fax:** 01875 870620
Owner: Wemyss and March Estates Management Co Ltd **Contact:** M Andrews
Georgian farmhouse with gothic barn and cottage.
Location: OS Ref. NT526 755. Between Haddington and East Linton on A199.
Open: Exterior only: By appointment, Wemyss and March Estates Office, Longniddry, East Lothian EH32 0PY.
Admission: Please contact for details.

ARNISTON HOUSE 🏠
GOREBRIDGE, MIDLOTHIAN EH23 4RY
www.arniston-house.co.uk
Tel/Fax: 01875 830515 **e-mail:** henrietta.d.bekker2@btinternet.com
Owner: Mrs A Dundas-Bekker **Contact:** Miss H Dundas-Bekker
Magnificent William Adam mansion started in 1726. Fine plasterwork, Scottish portraiture, period furniture and other fascinating contents. Beautiful country setting beloved by Sir Walter Scott.
Location: OS Ref. NT326 595. Off B6372, 1m from A7, Temple direction.
Open: Apr, May & Jun: Tue & Wed; 1 Jul - 11 Sept: Sun - Fri, guided tours at 2pm & 3.30pm. Pre-arranged groups (10-50) accepted throughout the rest of the year.
Admission: Adult £5, Child £2, Conc. £4.
ℹ️No inside photography. ♿WC. 🎭Obligatory. 🅿️ In grounds, on leads. ❄️

BEANSTON
Nr Haddington, East Lothian EH41 3SB
Tel: 01875 870201 **Fax:** 01875 870620
Owner: Wemyss and March Estates Management Co Ltd **Contact:** M Andrews
Georgian farmhouse with Georgian orangery.
Location: OS Ref. NT546 763. Between Haddington and East Linton on A199.
Open: Exterior only: By appointment, Wemyss and March Estates Office, Longniddry, East Lothian EH32 0PY.
Admission: Please contact for details.

BLACKNESS CASTLE 🏰
Blackness
Tel: 01506 834807
Owner: In the care of Historic Scotland **Contact:** The Steward
One of Scotland's most important strongholds. Built in the 14th century and massively strengthened in the 16th century as an artillery fortress, it has been a Royal castle and a prison armaments depot and film location for *Hamlet*. It was restored by the Office of Works in the 1920s. It stands on a promontory in the Firth of Forth.
Location: OS Ref. NT055 803. 4m NE of Linlithgow on the Firth of Forth, off the A904.
Open: 1 Apr - 30 Sept: daily, 9.30am - 6.30pm, last ticket 6pm. 1 Oct - 31 Mar: daily, 9.30am - 4.30pm, last ticket 4pm. Closed Thur & Fri in winter.
Admission: Adult £3, Child £1.20, Conc. £2.25.
❄️ €

CRAIGMILLAR CASTLE 🏰
Edinburgh
Tel: 0131 661 4445
Owner: In the care of Historic Scotland **Contact:** The Steward
Mary Queen of Scots fled to Craigmillar after the murder of Rizzio. This handsome structure with courtyard and gardens covers an area of one and a quarter acres. Built around an L-plan tower house of the early 15th century including a range of private rooms linked to the hall of the old tower.
Location: OS Ref. NT285 710. 2½ m SE of Edinburgh off the A68.
Open: 1 Apr - 30 Sept: daily, 9.30am - 6.30pm, last ticket 6pm. 1 Oct - 31 Mar: daily, 9.30am - 4.30pm, last ticket 4pm. Closed Thur & Fri in winter.
Admission: Adult £3, Child £1.20, Conc. £2.25.
❄️ €

CRICHTON CASTLE 🏰
Pathhead
Tel: 01875 320017
Owner: In the care of Historic Scotland **Contact:** The Steward
A large and sophisticated castle with a spectacular façade of faceted stonework in an Italian style added by the Earl of Bothwell between 1581 and 1591 following a visit to Italy. Mary Queen of Scots attended a wedding here.
Location: OS Ref. NT380 612. 2½ m SSW of Pathhead off the A68.
Open: 1 Apr - 30 Sept: daily, 9.30am - 6.30pm, last ticket 6pm.
Admission: Adult £2.50, Child £1, Conc. £1.90.
€

DALMENY HOUSE
See page 477 for full page entry.

©Historic Scotland Photographic Library.

DIRLETON CASTLE & GARDEN 🏰
DIRLETON, EAST LOTHIAN EH39 5ER
Tel: 01620 850330
Owner: In the care of Historic Scotland **Contact:** The Steward
The oldest part of this romantic castle dates from the 13th century, when it was built by the De Vaux family. The renowned gardens, first laid out in the 16th century, now include a magnificent Arts and Crafts herbaceous border (the longest in the world) and a re-created Victorian Garden. In the picturesque village of Dirleton.
Location: OS Ref. NT516 839. In Dirleton, 2m W of North Berwick on the A198.
Open: Apr - Sept: daily, 9.30am - 6.30pm. Oct - Mar: daily, 9.30am - 4.30pm. Last ticket 30 mins before closing.
Admission: Adult £3.30, Child £1.30, Conc. £2.50. 10% discount for groups (10+).
📷 ♿Partially. 🅿️ Free if booked. 🐕Guide dogs only. ❄️ €

❄️ Open All Year Index see page 43

DUNGLASS COLLEGIATE CHURCH

Cockburnspath

Tel: 0131 668 8800

Owner: In the care of Historic Scotland

Founded in 1450 for a college of canons by Sir Alexander Hume. A handsome cross-shaped building with vaulted nave, choir and transepts.

Location: OS67 NT766 718. 1m NW of Cockburnspath. SW of A1.

Open: All year.

Admission: Free.

©Historic Scotland Photographic Library

EDINBURGH CASTLE

CASTLEHILL, EDINBURGH EH1 2NG

Tel: 0131 225 9846 **Fax:** 0131 220 4733

Owner: Historic Scotland   **Contact:** Barbara Smith

Scotland's most famous castle, dominating the capital's skyline and giving stunning views of the city and countryside. Home to the Scottish crown jewels, the Stone of Destiny and Mons Meg. Other highlights include St Margaret's Chapel, the Great Hall and the Scottish National War Memorial.

Location: OS Ref. NT252 736. At the top of the Royal Mile in Edinburgh.

Open: Apr - Sept: daily, 9.30am - 6pm. Oct - Mar: daily, 9.30am - 5pm. Last ticket 45 mins before closing.

Admission: Adult £9.80, Child £3.50, Conc. £7.50. Pre-booked school visits available free, except May - Aug.

Private evening hire. Partial. WCs. Courtesy vehicle. Licensed. In 6 languages. Ample (except Jun-Oct). Guide dogs.

THE GEORGIAN HOUSE

7 Charlotte Square, Edinburgh EH2 4DR

Tel: 0131 226 3318

Owner: The National Trust for Scotland

A splendid example of the neo-classical 'palace front'. Three floors are delightfully furnished as they would have been around 1796. There is an array of china and silver, pictures and furniture, gadgets and utensils.

Location: OS Ref. NT247 738. In Charlotte Square, 2 mins from west end of Princes Street. 10 mins from Tourist Information Centre.

Open: House & Shop: 1 - 31 Mar and 1 Nov - 24 Dec: daily 11am - 3pm; 1 Apr - 31 Oct: daily, 10am - 5pm. **(2004 opening times.)**

Admission: Adult £5, Conc. £3.75, Family £13.50. Groups: Adult £4, Child/School £1. **(2004 prices.)**

GLADSTONE'S LAND

477b Lawnmarket, Royal Mile, Edinburgh EH1 2NT

Tel: 0131 226 5856 **Fax:** 0131 226 4851

Owner: The National Trust for Scotland

Gladstone's Land was the home of a prosperous Edinburgh merchant in the 17th century. It is decorated and furnished with great authenticity to give visitors an impression of life in Edinburgh's Old Town some 300 years ago.

Location: OS Ref. NT255 736. In Edinburgh's Royal Mile, near the castle.

Open: 1 Apr - 31 Oct: Mon - Sat, 10am - 5pm, Sun, 2 - 5pm. **(2004 opening times.)**

Admission: Adult £3.50, Conc. £2.60, Family £9.50. Groups: Adult £2.80, Child/School £1. **(2004 prices.)**

GOSFORD HOUSE

LONGNIDDRY, EAST LOTHIAN EH32 0PX

Tel: 01875 870201   **Owner/Contact:** The Earl of Wemyss

Though the core of the house is Robert Adam, the family home is in the South Wing built by William Young in 1890. This contains the celebrated Marble Hall and a fine collection of paintings and works of art. The house is set in extensive policies with an 18th century Pleasure Garden and Ponds. Greylag geese and swans abound.

Location: OS Ref. NT453 786. Off A198 2m NE of Longniddry.

Open: 12 June - 7 Aug: Fri - Sun, 2 - 5pm.

Admission: Adult £6, Child £1.

In grounds, on leads.

GREYWALLS

MUIRFIELD, GULLANE, EAST LOTHIAN EH31 2EG

www.greywalls.co.uk

Tel: 01620 842144 **Fax:** 01620 842241 **e-mail:** hotel@greywalls.co.uk

Owner: Giles Weaver   **Contact:** Mrs Sue Prime

Stunning Edwardian Country House Hotel only 30 minutes from the centre of Edinburgh. Close to wonderful golf courses and beaches. Designed by Sir Edwin Lutyens with secluded walled gardens attributed to Gertrude Jekyll. Greywalls offers the delights of an award-winning menu and an excellent wine list in this charming and relaxed environment (non residents welcome).

Location: OS Ref. NT490 835. Off A198, 5m W of North Berwick, 30 mins from Edinburgh.

Open: Apr - Oct.

BURRELL COLLECTION

Pollok Country Park, 2060 Pollokshaws Road, Glasgow G43 1AT

Tel: 0141 287 2550   **Fax:** 0141 287 2597

Owner: Glasgow Museums

An internationally renowned, outstanding collection of art.

Location: OS Ref. NS555 622. Glasgow 15 min drive.

Open: All year: Mon - Thur & Sats, 10am - 5pm, Fri & Sun, 11am - 5pm. Closed 25/26 Dec & 1/2 Jan. **(2004 opening times.)**

Admission: Free. Small charge may apply for temporary exhibitions. **(2004 prices.)**

COLZIUM HOUSE & WALLED GARDEN

Colzium-Lennox Estate, off Stirling Road, Kilsyth G65 0RZ

Tel/Fax: 01236 828156

Owner: North Lanarkshire Council   **Contact:** Charlie Whyte

A walled garden with an extensive collection of conifers, rare shrubs and trees. Kilsyth Heritage Museum, curling pond, picnic tables, woodland walks.

Location: OS Ref. NS722 786. Off A803 Banknock to Kirkintilloch Road. 1/2 m E of Kilsyth.

Open: House available for weddings, conferences, etc. Walled garden: Apr - Sept: daily, 12 noon - 7pm; Oct - Mar: Sats & Suns, 12 noon - 4pm.

Admission: Free.

COREHOUSE

Lanark ML11 9TQ

Tel: 0131 667 1514

Owner: The Trustees of the late Lt Col A J E Cranstoun MC   **Contact:** Estate Office

Designed by Sir Edward Blore and built in the 1820s, Corehouse is a pioneering example of the Tudor Architectural Revival in Scotland.

Location: OS Ref. NS882 416. On S bank of the Clyde above the village of Kirkfieldbank.

Open: 8 May - 1 Jun & 11 - 18 Sep: Sat - Wed. Guided tours: weekdays: 1 & 2pm, weekends: 1.30 & 2.30pm. Closed Thur & Fri.

Admission: Adult £5, Child (under 14yrs)/OAP £2.

Obligatory.

CRAIGNETHAN CASTLE

Lanark, Strathclyde

Tel: 01555 860364

Owner: Historic Scotland   **Contact:** The Steward

In a picturesque setting overlooking the River Nethan and defended by a wide and deep ditch with an unusual caponier, a stone vaulted artillery chamber, unique in Britain.

Location: OS Ref. NS815 463. 5 1/2 m WNW of Lanark off the A72. 1/2 m footpath to W.

Open: 1 Apr - 30 Sept: daily, 9.30am - 6.30pm. Oct: Sat - Wed; Nov - Mar: Sats & Suns only, 9.30am - 4.30pm.

Admission: Adult £2.50, Child £1, Conc. £1.90.

€

New Lanark World Heritage Site.

GLASGOW CATHEDRAL

Glasgow

Tel: 0141 552 6891

Owner: Historic Scotland   **Contact:** The Steward

The only Scottish mainland medieval cathedral to have survived the Reformation complete. Built over the tomb of St Kentigern. Notable features in this splendid building are the elaborately vaulted crypt, the stone screen of the early 15th century and the unfinished Blackadder Aisle.

Location: OS Ref. NS603 656. E end of city centre. In central Glasgow.

Admission: Free.

GREENBANK GARDEN

Clarkston, Glasgow G76 8RB

Tel: 0141 639 3281

Owner: The National Trust for Scotland

Several small gardens including a parterre layout illustrating different aspects of gardening.

Location: OS Ref. NS563 566. Flenders Road, off Mearns Road, Clarkston. Off M77 and A726, 6m S of Glasgow city centre.

Open: Garden: All year: daily, 9.30am - sunset. Shop & tearoom: 3 Jan - 31 Mar: Sat/Sun, 2 - 4pm; 1 Apr - 31 Oct: daily, 11am - 5pm. House: 1 Apr - 31 Oct: Sun, 2 - 4pm. **(2004 opening times.)**

Admission: Adult £3.50, Conc. £2.60, Family £9.50. Groups: Adult £2.80, Child/School £1. **(2004 prices.)**

HOLMWOOD HOUSE

61 Netherlee Road, Cathcart, Glasgow G1 1EJ

Tel: 0141 637 2129

Owner: The National Trust for Scotland

Villa described as Alexander 'Greek' Thomson's finest domestic design, built in 1857-8.

Location: OS Ref. NS580 593. Netherlee Road, off Clarkston road (off A77 and B767).

Open: 1 Apr - 31 Oct: daily, 12 noon - 5pm. Morning visits available for pre-booked groups. **(2004 opening times.)**

Admission: Adult £3.50, Conc. £2.60, Family £9.50. Groups: Adult £2.80, Child/School £1. **(2004 prices.)**

HUTCHESONS' HALL

158 Ingram Street, Glasgow G1 1EJ

Tel: 0141 552 8391   **Fax:** 0141 552 7031

Owner: The National Trust for Scotland

Described as one of Glasgow city centre's most elegant buildings, the Hall by David Hamilton, replaced the earlier 1641 hospice founded by George and Thomas Hutcheson.

Location: OS Ref NS594 652. Glasgow city centre, near SE corner of George Square.

Open: Gallery, shop & function hall: 20 Jan - 24 Dec: Mon - Sat, 10am - 5pm. Hall on view subject to functions in progress. **(2004 opening times.)**

Admission: Function hall & A/V programme: Adult £2, Conc. £1. **(2004 prices.)**

DAVID LIVINGSTONE CENTRE

165 Station Road, Blantyre, Glasgow G72 9BT

Tel: 01698 823140

Owner: The National Trust for Scotland

Scotland's most famous explorer and missionary was born here in 1813 and today the Centre commemorates his life and work. Livingstone's childhood home - consisting of just one room - remains much as it would have done in his day.

Location: OS Ref NS690 575. In Blantyre town centre, at N end of Station Road.

Open: 1 Apr - 24 Dec: Mon - Sat, 10am - 5pm, Sun 12.30 - 5pm. **(2004 opening times.)**

Admission: Adult £3.50, Conc. £2.60, Family £9.50. Groups: Adult £2.80, Child/School £1. **(2004 prices.)**

MOTHERWELL HERITAGE CENTRE

High Road, Motherwell ML1 3HU

Tel: 01698 251000

Owner: North Lanarkshire Council   **Contact:** The Manager

Multimedia exhibition and other displays of local history. STB 4-Star attraction.

Location: OS Ref. NS750 570. In High Road, 200 yds N of A723 (Hamilton Road).

Open: All year. Wed - Sat, 10am - 5pm. Suns, 12 noon - 5pm. (closed 25/26 Dec & 1/2 Jan). Closed Mons & Tues.

Admission: Free.

NEW LANARK WORLD HERITAGE SITE

NEW LANARK MILLS, LANARK, S. LANARKSHIRE ML11 9DB

www.newlanark.org

Tel: 01555 661345 **Fax:** 01555 665738 **e-mail:** visit@newlanark.org

Owner: New Lanark Conservation Trust **Contact:** Rachael Love

Surrounded by native woodlands and close to the famous Falls of Clyde, this cotton mill village was founded in 1785 and became famous as the site of Robert Owen's radical reforms. Now beautifully restored as both a living community and attraction, the fascinating history of the village is interpreted in an award-winning Visitor Centre. Accommodation is available in the New Lanark Mill Hotel and Waterhouses, a stunning conversion from an original 18th century mill. New Lanark is now a World Heritage Site.

Location: OS Ref. NS880 426. 1m S of Lanark.

Open: All year: daily, 10.30am - 5pm (11am - 5pm Sept - May). Closed 25 Dec & 1 Jan.

Admission: Visitor Centre: Adult £5.95, Child/Conc. £3.95. Groups: 1 free/10 booked. ⓘ Conference facilities. ◫ ⊤ ⓢ Partial. WC. Visitor Centre wheelchair friendly. ▣ 𝑓 By arrangement. 🅿 5 min walk. ▣ ▣ In grounds, on leads. ▣ ✱

NEWARK CASTLE ⛫

Port Glasgow, Strathclyde

Tel: 01475 741858

Owner: In the care of Historic Scotland **Contact:** The Steward

The oldest part of the castle is a tower built soon after 1478 with a detached gatehouse, by George Maxwell. The main part was added in 1597 - 99 in a most elegant style. Enlarged in the 16th century by his descendent, the wicked Patrick Maxwell who murdered two of his neighbours.

Location: OS Ref. NS329 744. In Port Glasgow on the A8.

Open: 1 Apr - 30 Sept: daily, 9.30am - 6.30pm. Last ticket 6pm.

Admission: Adult £2.50, Child £1, Conc. £1.90.

€

POLLOK HOUSE ♛

Pollok Country Park, Pollokshaws Road, Glasgow G43 1AT

Tel: 0141 616 6410

Owner: The National Trust for Scotland

Three earlier castles here were replaced by the present house (c1740). The house contains an internationally famed collection of paintings as well as porcelain and furnishings appropriate to an Edwardian house.

Location: OS Ref. NS550 616. In Pollok Country Park, off M77/J1, follow signs for Burrell Collection.

Open: House, shop & restaurant: All year: daily, 10am - 5pm. Closed 25/26 Dec & 1/2 Jan. **(2004 opening times.)**

Admission: 1 Apr - 31 Oct: Adult £5, Conc. £3.75, Family £13.50. Groups: Adult £4, Child/School £1. 1 Nov - 31 Mar, admission free. Gardens, Country Park & Burrell Collection open all year: daily. Admission free. **(2004 prices.)**

ST MARY'S EPISCOPAL CATHEDRAL

300 Great Western Road, Glasgow G4 9JB

Tel: 0141 339 6691 **Fax:** 0141 334 5669 **Contact:** Very Rev Griff Dines

Newly restored, fine Gothic Revival church by Sir George Gilbert Scott, with outstanding contemporary murals by Gwyneth Leech. Regular concerts and exhibitions.

Location: OS Ref. NS578 669. 1/4 m after the Dumbarton A82 exit from M8 motorway.

Open: All year. Tue - Fri, 5.30 - 7.30pm, Sat, 9.30 - 10am. Sun services: 8.30am, 10am, 12 noon & 6.30pm.

SUMMERLEE HERITAGE PARK

Heritage Way, Coatbridge, North Lanarkshire ML5 1QD

Tel: 01236 431261

Owner: North Lanarkshire Council **Contact:** The Manager

STB 4-star attraction. 22 acres of industrial heritage including Scotland's only remaining electric tramway; a re-created addit mine and mine workers' cottages.

Location: OS Ref. NS729 655. 600yds NW of Coatbridge town centre.

Open: All year. Summer, 10am - 5pm. Winter: 10am - 4pm (closed 25/26 Dec & 1/2 Jan).

Admission: Free. Tram ride: Adult 80p, Child 45p.

THE TENEMENT HOUSE ♛

145 Buccleuch Street, Glasgow G3 6QN

Tel: 0141 333 0183

Owner: The National Trust for Scotland

A typical Victorian tenement flat of 1892, and time capsule of the first half of the 20th century.

Location: OS Ref. NS583 662. Garnethill (three streets N of Sauchiehall Street, near Charing Cross), Glasgow.

Open: 1 Mar - 31 Oct: daily, 1 - 5pm; weekday morning visits available for pre-booked educational and other groups. **(2004 opening times.)**

Admission: Adult £3.50, Conc. £2.60, Family £9.50. Groups: Adult £2.80, Child/School £1. **(2004 prices.)**

THE TOWER OF HALLBAR

Braidwood Road, Braidwood, Lanarkshire

Tel: 0845 090 0194 **Fax:** 0845 090 0174 **e-mail:** enquiries@vivat.org.uk

www.vivat.org.uk

Owner: The Vivat Trust **Contact:** Miss Lisa Simm

A 16th century defensive tower and Bothy set in ancient orchards and meadowland. Converted into self-catering holiday accommodation by The Vivat Trust and furnished and decorated in keeping with its history. Hallbar sleeps up to seven people, including facilities for a disabled person and their carer.

Location: OS Ref. NS842 471. S side of B7056 between Crossford Bridge & Braidwood.

Open: All year: Sats, 2 - 3pm, or by appointment. Also four open days a year.

Admission: Free.

ⓢ Partial. 𝑓 By arrangement. 🅿 Limited. ▣ In grounds, on leads. ▣ 3 single, 1 twin & 1 double. ✱

WEAVER'S COTTAGE ♛

Shuttle Street, Kilbarchan, Renfrew PA10 2JG

Tel: 01505 705588

Owner: The National Trust for Scotland

Typical cottage of an 18th century handloom weaver contains looms, weaving equipment and domestic utensils.

Location: OS Ref. NS402 633. Off A740 (off M8) and A737, at The Cross, Kilbarchan, (nr Johnstone, Paisley) 12m SW of Glasgow.

Open: 1 Apr - 30 Sep: Fri - Tue, 1 - 5pm; morning visits available for pre-booked groups. **(2004 opening times.)**

Admission: Adult £3.50, Conc. £2.60, Family £9.50. Groups: Adult £2.80, Child/School £1. **(2004 prices.)**

LOCAL FOOD

Forfar Bridies

The local equivalent of the Cornish pasty, these oval, meat-filled pasties are a favourite Scottish convenience food and are said to take their name from Mrs Maggie Bridie, a travelling food seller. They were eaten by farm workers, the casing of pastry allowing the Bridie to be eaten out of work-soiled hands. The crust was simply thrown away.

Map 10

Owner: Blair
Charitable Trust

▶ **CONTACT**

Administration Office
Blair Castle
Blair Atholl
Pitlochry
Perthshire PH18 5TL

Tel: 01796 481207
Fax: 01796 481487
e-mail: office@
blair-castle.co.uk

▶ **LOCATION**

OS Ref. NN880 660

From Edinburgh 80m,
M90 to Perth, A9,
follow signs for Blair
Castle, 1¹/₂ hrs.
Trunk Road A9 2m.

Bus: Bus stop 1m
in Blair Atholl.

Train: 1m, Blair Atholl
Euston-Inverness line.

Taxi: Elizabeth Yule,
01796 472290.

BLAIR CASTLE

www.blair-castle.co.uk

Perthshire's 5 star historic home. Blair Castle has been the ancient home and fortress of the Earls and Dukes of Atholl for over 725 years. Its central location makes it easily accessible from all major Scottish centres in less than two hours.

The castle has known the splendour of Royal visitations, submitted to occupation by opposing forces on no less than four occasions, suffered siege and changed its architectural appearance to suit the taste of successive generations.

Today 30 rooms of infinite variety display beautiful furniture, fine collections of paintings, arms, armour, china, costumes, lace and embroidery, Jacobite relics and other unique treasures giving a

stirring picture of Scottish life from the 16th to 20th centuries.

The Duke of Atholl has the unique distinction of having the only remaining private army in Europe - The Atholl Highlanders.

GARDENS

Blair Castle is set in extensive grounds. Near the car and coach parks, there is a picnic area, a deer park and a unique two acre plantation of large trees known as 'Diana's Grove.' It has been said that *"it is unlikely that any other two acres in the world contain such a number of different conifers of such heights and of such small age."* A restored 18th century garden re-opened to visitors in 1996.

<table>
<tr><td colspan="3">**FUNCTION**</td></tr>
<tr><td>ROOM</td><td>SIZE</td><td>MAX CAPACITY</td></tr>
<tr><td>Ballroom</td><td>88' x 36'</td><td>400</td></tr>
<tr><td>Ballroom Dining</td><td>36' x 25'</td><td>200</td></tr>
<tr><td>Exhibition Hall</td><td>55' x 27'</td><td>90</td></tr>
</table>

Fashion shows, equestrian events, shows, rallies, filming, highland and charity balls, piping championships, grand piano, helicopter pad, cannon firing by Atholl Highlanders, resident piper, needlework displays. No smoking.

Buffets, dinners, wedding receptions and banquets.

May alight at entrance. WC & wheelchair facilities.

Non-smoking. Seats up to 125. Private group lunches for up to 35 can be arranged in the Garry Room.

Audio visual presentation.

In English, German and French at no extra cost. Tour time 1¹/₂ hrs (max). Illustrated guide books (English, German, French and Italian) £4.

200 cars, 20 coaches. Coach drivers/couriers free, plus free meal and shop voucher, information pack.

Nature walks, deer park, ranger service & pony trekking, children's play area.

Grounds only. ❄

Event programme available on application.

▶ OPENING TIMES

Summer
19 March - 28 October
Daily, 9.30am - 4.30pm
(last admission).

Winter
Open for groups by arrangement.

▶ ADMISSION

House & Grounds

Adult	£6.90
Child (5-16yrs)	£4.30
Senior	£5.90
Student (with ID)	£5.60
Family	£17.50
Disabled	£2.20

Groups* (12+)
(Please book)

Adult	£5.55
Child(5-16yrs)	£4.10
Primary School	£3.10
Senior	£5.10
Student (with ID)	£4.55
Disabled	£2.00

Grounds only
(with access to restaurant, gift shop & WC)

Adult	£2.20
Child (5-16yrs)	£1.10
Senior/Student	£2.20
Family	£5.15
Disabled	Free
Scooter Hire	£3.00

Groups* (12+)
(Please book)

Adult	£2.00
Child (5-16yrs)	£1.00
Primary School	£1.00
Senior/Student	£2.00
Disabled	Free

* Group rates only apply when all tickets bought by the Driver, Courier or Group Leader at one time.

Map 10

Owner: The Earl of Strathmore & Kinghorne

▶ **CONTACT**

Mr David Adams
Castle Administrator
Estates Office
Glamis
by Forfar
Angus   DD8 1RJ

Tel: 01307 840393
Fax: 01307 840733

e-mail: enquiries@ glamis-castle.co.uk

▶ **LOCATION**

OS Ref. NO386 480

From Edinburgh M90,
A94, 81m.
From Forfar A94, 6m.
From Glasgow 93m.
Motorway: M90.
Rail: Dundee
Station 12m.
Air: Dundee
Airport 12m.
Taxi: K Cabs
01575 573744.

GLAMIS CASTLE 🏛

www.glamis-castle.co.uk

Glamis Castle is the family home of the Earls of Strathmore and Kinghorne and has been a royal residence since 1372. It was the childhood home of Her Majesty Queen Elizabeth The Queen Mother, the birthplace of Her Royal Highness The Princess Margaret and the legendary setting of Shakespeare's play Macbeth. Although the castle is open to visitors it remains a family home lived in and loved by the Strathmore family.

The castle, a five-storey 'L' shaped tower block, was originally a royal hunting lodge. It was remodelled in the 17th century and is built of pink sandstone. It contains the Great Hall, with its

magnificent plasterwork ceiling dated 1621, a beautiful family Chapel constructed inside the Castle in 1688, an 18th century billiard room housing what is left of the extensive library once at Glamis, a 19th century dining room containing family portraits and the Royal Apartments which have been used by Her Majesty Queen Elizabeth The Queen Mother.

The castle stands in an extensive park, landscaped towards the end of the 18th century, and contains the beautiful Italian Garden and the Pinetum which reflect the peace and serenity of the castle and grounds.

▶ **OPENING TIMES**

Summer

19 March - 31 October
Daily, 10am - 6pm.

Last admission 4.30pm.

Groups welcome. Out of hours visits can also be arranged.

Winter

1 November - 22 December

Special winter opening programme scheduled. Telephone for details.

▶ **ADMISSION**

Summer
Castle & Grounds
Adult £7.00
Child (5-16yrs) £3.80
OAP/Student £5.70
Family £20.00
Groups (20+)
Adult £6.00
Child (5-16yrs) £3.30
OAP/Student £5.20

Grounds only ticket available.

ℹ Fashion shoots, archery, equestrian events, shows, rallies, filming, product launches, highland games, new shopping development, grand piano. No photography in the castle.

🛍 Shopping pavilion.   ❋

🍽 The State Rooms are available for grand dinners, lunches and wedding receptions.

♿ Disabled visitors may alight at entrance. Those in wheelchairs will be unable to tour the castle but may visit the two exhibitions. WC.

☕🍴 Morning coffees, light lunches, afternoon teas. Self-service, licensed restaurant.

🚶 All visits are guided, tour time 50 - 60 mins. Tours leave every 10 - 15 mins. Tours in French, German, Italian and Spanish by appointment at no additional cost. Three exhibitions.

🅿 500 cars and 20 coaches 200 yds from castle. Coach drivers and couriers admitted free. Beware narrow gates; they are wide enough to take buses (10ft wide).

▪ One teacher free for every 10 children. Nature trail, family exhibition rooms, dolls' house, play park. Glamis Heritage Education Centre in Glamis village. Education pack. Winner of Sandford Award in 1997. Children's Quest.

🐕 In grounds, on leads.   ❋ 🎭 Tel for details.   €

CONFERENCE/FUNCTION

ROOM	SIZE	MAX CAPACITY
Dining Rm	84 sq.m	90
Restaurant	140 sq.m	100
16th century Kitchens		40

Perthshire, Angus & Dundee and The Kingdom of Fife

Map 10

Owner: The Earl of Mansfield

▶ CONTACT

The Administrator
Scone Palace
Perth PH2 6BD

Tel: 01738 552300
Fax: 01738 552588

e-mail: visits@
scone-palace.co.uk

▶ LOCATION

OS Ref. NO114 266

From Edinburgh
Forth Bridge M90,
A93 1hr.

Bus: Regular buses
from Perth.

Rail: Perth Station 3m.

Motorway: M90 from
Edinburgh.

Taxi: 01738 636777.

SCONE PALACE & GROUNDS 🏛

www.scone-palace.co.uk

Scone Palace is the home of the Earl and Countess of Mansfield and is built on the site of an ancient abbey. 1500 years ago it was the capital of the Pictish kingdom and the centre of the ancient Celtic church. In the intervening years, it has been the seat of the parliaments and crowning place of kings, including Macbeth, Robert the Bruce and Charles II. The State Rooms house a superb collection of *objets d'art*, including items of Marie Antoinette, bought by the 2nd Earl of Mansfield. Notable works of art are also on display, including paintings by Sir David Wilkie, Sir Joshua Reynolds, and Johann Zoffany. The Library boasts one of Scotland's finest collections of porcelain, including Sèvres, Ludwigsburg and Meissen, whilst the unique 'Vernis Martin' *papier mâché* may be viewed in the Long Gallery.

Gardens

The grounds of the Palace house magnificent collections of shrubs, with woodland walks through the pinetum containing David Douglas' original fir and the unique Murray Star Maze. There are Highland cattle and peacocks to admire and an adventure play area for children. The 100 acres of mature Policy Parks, flanked by the River Tay, are available for a variety of events, including corporate and private entertaining.

🖼 ℹ️ Receptions, fashion shows, war games, archery, clay pigeon shooting, equestrian events, garden parties, shows, rallies, filming, shooting, fishing, floodlit tattoos, product launches, highland games, parkland, cricket pitch, helicopter landing, croquet, racecourse, polo field, firework displays, adventure playground. No photography in state rooms. Gift shop & food shop.

🍴 Grand dinners in state rooms, buffets, receptions, wedding receptions, cocktail parties.

♿ All state rooms on one level, wheelchair access to restaurants. Stairlift in gift shop.

🍴 ☕ Licensed. Teas, lunches & dinners, can be booked, menus upon request, special rates for groups.

🚶 By arrangement. Guides in rooms, tour time 45 mins. French and German guides available by appointment.

🐕 Welcome.

🅿️ 300 cars and 15 coaches, groups please book, couriers and coach drivers free meal and admittance.

🐾 In grounds on leads.

❄️ €

▶ OPENING TIMES

Summer

25 March - 31 October
Daily: 9.30am - 6pm.

Last admission 5pm.

Evening tours by appointment.

Winter

By appointment.

Grounds only: Fri, 11am - 4pm.

▶ ADMISSION

Summer

Palace & Grounds

Adult	£6.95
Child (under 16yrs)	£4.00
Senior/Student	£5.95
Family	£22.00

Groups (20+)

Adult	£5.80
Child (5-16yrs)	£3.80
Senior/Student	£5.10

Grounds only

Adult	£3.50
Child (5-16yrs)	£2.20
Senior/Student	£3.00

Under 5s Free
Private Tour £40 supplement.

Winter

On application.

🎭 SPECIAL EVENTS

APR - SEPT
Perth Races (01738 551597).

JUL
Game Fair.

FEB & NOV
Antiques Fair.

Please telephone for further information.

CONFERENCE/FUNCTION

ROOM	SIZE	MAX CAPACITY
Long Gallery	140' x 20'	200
Queen Victoria's Rm	20' x 20'	20
Drawing Rm	48' x 25'	80

ABERDOUR CASTLE

Aberdour, Fife

Tel: 01383 860519

Owner: In the care of Historic Scotland   **Contact:** The Steward

A 14th century castle built by the Douglas family. The gallery on the first floor gives an idea of how it was furnished at the time. The castle has a 14th century tower extended in the 16th and 17th centuries, a delightful walled garden and a circular dovecote.

Location: OS Ref. NT193 854. In Aberdour 5m E of the Forth Bridge on the A921.

Open: 1 Apr - 30 Sept: daily, 9.30am - 6.30pm, last ticket 6pm. 1 Oct - 31 Mar: daily, 9.30am - 4.30pm, last ticket 4pm. Closed Thur & Fris in winter.

Admission: Adult £3, Child £1.20, Conc. £2.25.

ANGUS FOLK MUSEUM

Kirkwynd, Glamis, Forfar, Angus DD8 1RT

Tel: 01307 840288   **Fax:** 01307 840233

Owner: The National Trust for Scotland   **Contact:** The Manager

Where will you find cruisie lamps, pirn winders, cloutie rugs, bannock spades and a thrawcrook? All these items, and more, are to be found in the Angus Folk Museum.

Location: OS Ref. NO385 467. Off A94, in Glamis, 5m SW of Forfar.

Open: 1 Apr - 30 Jun & 1 - 30 Sep: Fri - Tue, 12 noon - 5pm; 1 Jul - 31 Aug: daily, 12 noon - 5pm. **(2004 opening times.)**

Admission: Adult £3.50, Conc. £2.60, Family £9.50. Groups: Adult £2.80, Child/School £1. **(2004 prices.)**

ARBROATH ABBEY

Arbroath, Tayside

Tel: 01241 878756

Owner: In the care of Historic Scotland   **Contact:** The Steward

The substantial ruins of a Tironensian monastery, notably the gate house range and the abbot's house. Arbroath Abbey holds a very special place in Scottish history. Scotland's nobles swore their independence from England in the famous 'Declaration of Arbroath' in 1320. New visitor centre.

Location: OS Ref. NO644 414. In Arbroath town centre on the A92.

Open: 1 Apr - 30 Sept: daily 9.30am - 6.30pm, last ticket 6pm. 1 Oct - 31 Mar: daily, 9.30am - 4.30 pm, last ticket 4pm.

Admission: Adult £3.30, Child £1.30, Conc. £2.50.

BALCARRES

Colinsburgh, Fife KY9 1HL

Tel: 01333 340206

Owner: Balcarres Trust   **Contact:** The Earl of Crawford

16th century tower house with 19th century additions by Burn and Bryce. Woodland and terraced gardens.

Location: OS Ref. NO475 044. $^1/2$ m N of Colinsburgh.

Open: Woodland & Gardens: 1 - 19 Feb & 4 Apr - 18 Jun, 2 - 5pm. House not open except by written appointment and 11 - 27 Apr, excluding Sun.

Admission: Adult £5. Garden only: £3.

By arrangement.

BALGONIE CASTLE

Markinch, Fife KY7 6HQ

Tel: 01592 750119   **Fax:** 01592 753103

Owner/Contact: The Laird of Balgonie

14th century tower, additions to the building up to 1702. Still lived in by the family. 14th century chapel for weddings.

Location: OS Ref. NO313 006. $^1/2$ m S of A911 Glenrothes - Leven road at Milton of Balgonie on to B921.

Open: All year: daily, 10am - 5pm.

Admission: Adult £3, Child £1.50, OAP £2.

BALHOUSIE CASTLE (BLACK WATCH MUSEUM)

Hay Street, North Inch Park, Perth PH1 5HR

Tel: 0131 310 8530

Owner: MOD   **Contact:** Major Proctor

Regimental museum housed in the castle.

Location: OS Ref. NO115 244. $^1/2$ m N of town centre, E of A9 road to Dunkeld.

Open: May - Sept: Mon - Sat, 10am - 4.30pm. Oct - Apr: Mon - Fri, 10am - 3.30pm. Closed 23 Dec - 5 Jan & last Sat in Jun.

Admission: Free.

J M BARRIE'S BIRTHPLACE

9 Brechin Road, Kirriemuir, Angus DD8 4BX

Tel: 01575 572646

Owner: The National Trust for Scotland

The creator of the eternal magic of *Peter Pan*, J M Barrie, was born here in 1860.

Location: OS Ref. NO388 542. On A926/B957, in Kirriemuir, 6m NW of Forfar.

Open: 1 Apr - 30 Jun & 1 - 30 Sep: Fri - Tue, 1 - 5pm; 1 Jul - 31 Aug: daily, 1 - 5pm. **(2004 opening times.)**

Admission: Adult £5, Conc. £3.75, Family £13.50. Groups: Adult £4, Child/School £1. Includes admission to Camera Obscura. **(2004 prices.)**

BARRY WATER MILL

Barry, Carnoustie, Angus DD7 7RJ

Tel: 01241 856761

Owner: The National Trust for Scotland

19th century meal mill. Waymarked walks. Picnic area.

Location: OS Ref. NO533 349. N of village between A92 & A930, 2m W of Carnoustie.

Open: 1 Apr - 30 Sep: Fri - Tue, 12 noon - 5pm. **(2004 opening times.)**

Admission: Adult £3.50, Conc. £2.60, Family £9.50. Groups: Adult £2.80, Child/School £1. **(2004 prices.)**

BLAIR CASTLE

See page 486 for full page entry.

BOLFRACKS GARDEN

Aberfeldy, Perthshire PH15 2EX

Tel: 01887 820344   **Fax:** 01887 829522   **e-mail:** info@bolfracks.fsnet.co.uk
www.bolfracks.com

Owner/Contact: Mr R A Price

A garden of approximately 4 acres with splendid views over the River Tay to the hills beyond. A walled garden contains a wide collection of trees, shrubs and perennials. Also a burn garden with rhododendrons, azaleas, meconopsis, primulas etc. with peat wall arrangements. Lots of bulbs and good autumn colour.

Location: OS Ref. NN822 481. 2m W of Aberfeldy on A827 towards Kenmore.

Open: 1 Apr - 31 Oct: daily, 10am - 6pm.

Admission: Adult £3, Child (under 16 yrs) Free.

Not ideal. Self catering cottages with fishing.

BRANKLYN GARDEN

Dundee Road, Perth PH2 7BB

Tel: 01738 625535

Owner: The National Trust for Scotland

Small garden with an impressive collection of rare and unusual plants.

Location: OS Ref. NO125 225. On A85 at 116 Dundee Road, Perth.

Open: 1 - 30 Apr & 1 Jul - 30 Sep: Fri - Tue 10am - 5pm; 1 May - 30 Jun: daily, 10am - 5pm. **(2004 opening times.)**

Admission: Adult £3.50, Conc. £2.60, Family £9.50. Groups: Adult £2.80, Child/School £1. **(2004 prices.)**

BRECHIN CASTLE

Brechin, Angus DD9 6SG

Tel: 01356 624566   **e-mail:** fay@dalhousieestates.co.uk
www.dalhousieestates.co.uk

Owner: Dalhousie Estates   **Contact:** Fay Clark

Dating from 1711 the Castle contains many family pictures and artefacts. Beautiful gardens.

Location: OS Ref. NO593 602. Off A90 on A935.

Open: 9 Jul - 7 Aug: guided tours only.

Admission: Adult £5. Child under 12yrs Free.

No photography. Unsuitable. Obligatory.

CAMBO GARDENS

Cambo Estate, Kingsbarns, St Andrews, Fife KY16 8QD

Tel: 01333 450054   **Fax:** 01333 450987   **e-mail:** cambo@camboestate.com
www.camboestate.com

Owner: Mr & Mrs T P N Erskine   **Contact:** Catherine Erskine

Victorian walled garden with burn, willow, waterfall and rose-clad bridges. Naturalistic plantings of rare and interesting herbaceous perennials, spectacular bulbs, including acres of woodland walks leading to sea carpeted in snowdrops, roses, September borders, woodland garden with colchicum meadow. "All seasons plantsman's paradise."

Location: OS Ref. NO603 114. 3m N of Crail. 7m SE of St Andrews on A917.

Open: All year: daily, 10am - dusk.

Admission: Adult £3.50, Child Free.

Conferences. Mail order snowdrops in the green. Limited for coaches. In grounds, on leads. 2 doubles & self-catering apartments/cottages.

LOCHLEVEN CASTLE

Loch Leven, Kinross

Tel: 0388 040483

Owner: In the care of Historic Scotland   **Contact:** The Steward

Mary Queen of Scots endured nearly a year of imprisonment in this 14th century tower before her dramatic escape in May 1568. During the First War of Independence it was held by the English, stormed by Wallace and visited by Bruce.

Location: OS Ref. NO138 018. On island in Loch Leven reached by ferry from Kinross off the M90.

Open: 1 Apr - 30 Sept: daily, 9.30am - 6.30pm, last ticket 6pm.

Admission: Adult £3.50, Child £1.30, Conc. £2.50. Prices include ferry trip.

€

MEGGINCH CASTLE GARDENS

Errol, Perthshire PH2 7SW

Tel: 01821 642222   **Fax:** 01821 642708

Owner: Captain Drummond of Megginch and Lady Strange

15th century castle, 1,000 year old yews, flowered parterre, double walled kitchen garden, topiary, astrological garden, pagoda dovecote in courtyard. Part used as a location for the film *Rob Roy*.

Location: OS Ref. NO241 245. 8m E of Perth on A90.

Open: Apr - Oct: Weds. Aug: daily, 2.30 - 6pm.

Admission: Adult £4, Child £1.

Partial. By arrangement. Limited for coaches. In grounds, on leads.

MONZIE CASTLE

Crieff, Perthshire PH7 4HD

Tel: 01764 653110

Owner/Contact: Mrs C M M Crichton

Built in 1791. Destroyed by fire in 1908 and rebuilt and furnished by Sir Robert Lorimer.

Location: OS Ref. NN873 244. 2m NE of Crieff.

Open: 14 May - 12 Jun: daily, 2 - 5pm. By appointment at other times.

Admission: Adult £3, Child £1. Group rates available, contact property for details.

©Historic Scotland Photographic Library

ST ANDREWS CASTLE

THE SCORES, ST ANDREWS, KY16 9AR

Tel: 01334 477196

Owner: Historic Scotland   **Contact:** David Eaton

This was the castle of the Bishops of St Andrews and has a fascinating mine and counter-mine, rare examples of medieval siege techniques. There is also a bottle dungeon hollowed out of solid rock. Cardinal Beaton was murdered here and John Knox was sent to the galleys when the ensuing siege was lifted.

Location: OS Ref. NO513 169. In St Andrews on the A91.

Open: Apr - Sept: daily, 9.30am - 6.30pm. Oct - Mar: Daily, 9.30am - 4.30pm. Last ticket 30 mins before closing.

Admission: Adult £4, Child £1.60, Conc. £3. 10% discount for groups (10+). Free pre-booked school visits. Joint ticket with St Andrews Cathedral available.

Visitor centre. Private evening hire. Partial. WCs. By arrangement. On street. Free if booked. Guide dogs. €

NORTHFIELD

Colinsburgh, Fife KY9 1HQ

Tel: 01333 340214   **e-mail:** enquiries@andersonofnorthfield.net
www.andersonofnorthfield.net

Owner: Margaret Aynscough   **Contact:** Mrs M E Aynscough

"Andersons of Northfield", formerly of St Germains and Bourhouse. Display of family portraits from late 1600s to present day, including Dewar, Naesmyth, Murray, Findlay, Seton and other branches of the family tree. Holiday accommodation available all year.

Location: OS Ref. NO468 033. East Neuk of Fife. 10m from St Andrews, 2m from Elie, 31m from Forth Road Bridge.

Open: 29 Apr - 8 May: 10am - 4pm.

Admission: Free - Donation for charity.

Partial. Limited. In grounds, on leads. All year.

ST ANDREWS CATHEDRAL

St Andrews, Fife

Tel: 01334 472563

Owner: Historic Scotland   **Contact:** The Administrator

The remains still give a vivid impression of the scale of what was once the largest cathedral in Scotland along with the associated domestic ranges of the priory.

Location: OS Ref. NO514 167. In St Andrews.

Open: 1 Apr - 30 Sept: daily, 9.30am - 6.30pm, last ticket 6pm. 1 Oct - 31 Mar: daily, 9.30am - 4.30pm, last ticket 4pm.

Admission: Adult £3, Child £1.20, Conc. £2.25. Joint entry ticket with St Andrews Castle available.

€

SCONE PALACE & GROUNDS   *See page 488 for full page entry.*

STOBHALL

Stobhall, Cargill, Perthshire PH2 6DR

Tel: 01821 640332   **www.**stobhall.com

Owner: Viscount Strathallan   **Contact:** The Administrator

Original home of the Drummond chiefs from the 14th century. Romantic cluster of small-scale buildings around a courtyard in a magnificent situation overlooking the River Tay, surrounded by formal and woodland gardens. 17th century painted ceiling in Chapel depicts monarchs of Europe and North Africa on horse (or elephant) back.

Location: OS Ref. NO132 343. 8m N of Perth on A93.

Open: Garden and Chapel: 7 - 22 May & 30 July - 7 Aug: daily, 2 - 5:30pm. Tours of the Folly and Drawing Room 2:30 & 4:30pm. Library by prior appointment.

Admission: Adult £5, Child £2, Conc. £3. Large group visits must be booked.

Partial. Please see website or ring for details. Limited. Coaches please book.

STRATHTYRUM HOUSE & GARDENS

St Andrews, Fife

Tel: 01334 473600

Owner: The Strathtyrum Trust   **Contact:** Elizabeth Smith

Location: OS Ref: NO490 172. Entrance from the St Andrews/Guardbridge Road which is signposted when open.

Open: 2 - 6 & 9 - 11 May, 6 - 10 Jun, 4 - 8 Jul, 1 - 5 Aug and 5 - 9 Sept: 2 - 4.30pm.

Admission: Adult £5, Child £2.50.

Free. Guide dogs only.

TULLIBOLE CASTLE

Crook of Devon, Kinross KY13 0QN

Tel: 01577 840236   **e-mail:** visit@tulbol.demon.co.uk
www.tulbol.demon.co.uk/visit.htm

Owner: Lord & Lady Moncreiff   **Contact:** Lord Moncreiff

Recognised as a classic example of the Scottish tower house. Completed in 1608, the Moncreiff family have lived here since 1747. The Castle is in a parkland setting with ornamental fishponds (moat), a roofless lectarn doocot, with a short walk to a 9th century graveyard and a ruined church.

Location: OS Ref. NO540 888. Located on the B9097 1m E of Crook of Devon.

Open: Last week in Aug - 30 Sept: Tue - Sun, 1 - 4pm. Admission every 1/2 hr with guided tours only.

Admission: Adult £3.50, Child/Conc. £2.50. Free as part of "Doors Open Day" (last weekend of Sept).

Unsuitable. Obligatory. Ample but limited for coaches. Guide dogs only. Twin x 1.

West Highlands & Islands, Loch Lomond, Stirling and Trossachs

© Historic Scotland.

ARGYLL'S LODGING

Map 10

Owner: Historic Scotland

▶ **CONTACT**

Neil Young
Argyll's Lodging
Castle Wynd
Stirling FK8 1EJ

Tel: 01786 431319

Fax: 01786 448194

▶ **LOCATION**

OS Ref. NS793 938

At the top and on E side of Castle Wynd in Stirling. One way route from town centre from Albert Street.

Rail: Stirling.

Air: Edinburgh or Glasgow.

This attractive townhouse, sitting at the foot of Stirling Castle, is decorated as it would have been during the 9th Earl of Argyll's occupation around 1680. Before coming into Historic Scotland's care the building was a youth hostel, but restoration revealed hidden secrets from the Lodging's past. Perhaps the best of these was a section of 17th century *trompe l'oeil* panelling in the dining room, created by painter David McBeath.

Visitors to Argyll's Lodging might wonder at the highly decorated walls and rich materials and colours used but the restoration relied on a household inventory of 1680 found among the then Duchess's papers. But no matter how rich the decoration, it cannot match the colourful lives of Argyll Lodging's inhabitants.

The 9th Earl, Archibald Campbell, was sentenced to death for treason and imprisoned in Edinburgh Castle. However he escaped when his stepdaughter smuggled him out dressed as her page. Archibald escaped to Holland, but his stepdaughter was arrested and placed in public stocks – a major humiliation. He didn't cheat death a second time, however. Joining plots over the succession following Charles II's death, he was captured and beheaded in 1685.

An earlier inhabitant of Argyll's Lodging, Sir William Alexander, was tutor to James VI's son, Prince Henry and in 1621 he attempted to colonise Nova Scotia in Canada. Great wealth eluded him all his life, however, and he died a bankrupt in 1640, leading to the town council taking over the lodging and selling it to the Earl of Argyll in the 1660s.

▶ **OPENING TIMES**

April - September
Daily, 9.30am - 6pm.

October - March
Daily, 9.30am - 5pm.

▶ **ADMISSION**

Adult £3.30
Child* £1.30
Conc. £2.50

*up to 16 years

©Historic Scotland Photographic Library

FUNCTION

ROOM	SIZE	MAX CAPACITY
Laigh Hall	11 x 6m	60 for receptions
High Dining Room	11 x 6m	26 for dinner
Both rooms:	120 for receptions	

Interpretation scheme includes computer animations; joint ticket with Stirling Castle available.

Evening receptions/dinners.

Partial. No wheelchair access to upper floor.

Ample parking for coaches and cars on Stirling Castle Esplanade.

Free pre-booked school visits scheme.

Guide dogs only. ✳ €

CRATHES CASTLE & GARDEN

Banchory AB31 3QJ

Tel: 01330 844525 **Fax:** 01330 844797

Owner: The National Trust for Scotland

The building of the castle began in 1553 and took 40 years to complete. Just over 300 years later, Sir James and Lady Burnett began developing the walled garden.

Location: OS Ref. NO733 969: On A93, 3m E of Banchory and 15m W of Aberdeen.

Open: Castle & Visitor Centre: 1 Apr - 31 Oct: daily 10am - 5.30pm (4.30pm in Oct). Restaurant & shop: 18 Jan - 31 Mar & 1 Nov - 21 Dec: Wed - Sun, 10am - 4pm; 1 Apr - 31 Oct: daily, 10am - 5.30pm (4.30pm in Oct). Admission to the castle is by timed ticket (limited numbers: entry may be delayed). Garden & grounds: All year: daily, 9am - sunset. **(2004 opening times.)**

Admission: Castle & Garden: Adult £9, Conc. £6.50. Groups: Adult £7, Child/School £1, Family £23. Car parking £2. Castle/walled garden/grounds only: Adult £7, Conc. £5.25. **(2004 prices.)**

CRUICKSHANK BOTANIC GARDEN

St Machar Drive, Aberdeen AB24 3UU

Tel: 01224 272704 **Fax:** 01224 272703

Owner: University of Aberdeen   **Contact:** R B Rutherford

Extensive collection of shrubs, herbaceous and alpine plants and trees. Rock and water gardens.

Location: OS Ref. NJ938 084. In old Aberdeen. Entrance in the Chanonry.

Open: All year: Mon - Fri, 9am - 4.30pm. Also May - Sept: Sats & Suns, 2 - 5pm.

Admission: Free.

DALLAS DHU DISTILLERY

Forres

Tel: 01309 676548

Owner: In the care of Historic Scotland   **Contact:** The Steward

A completely preserved time capsule of the distiller's craft. Wander at will through this fine old Victorian distillery then enjoy a dram. Visitor centre, shop and audio-visual theatre.

Location: OS Ref. NJ035 566. 1m S of Forres off the A940.

Open: 1 Apr - 30 Sept: daily, 9.30am - 6.30pm, last ticket 6pm. 1 Oct - 31 Mar: daily, 9.30am - 4.30pm, last ticket 4pm. Closed Thurs and Fris in winter.

Admission: Adult £4, Child £1.60, Conc. £3.

ⓘ Visitor centre. ⬜ ✳ €

DELGATIE CASTLE

TURRIFF, ABERDEENSHIRE AB53 5TD

www.delgatiecastle.com

Tel/Fax: 01888 563479 **e-mail:** jjohnson@delgatie-castle.freeserve.co.uk

Owner: Delgatie Castle Trust   **Contact:** Mrs Joan Johnson

Dating from 1030 the Castle is steeped in Scottish history yet still has the atmosphere of a lived in home. It has some of the finest painted ceilings, Mary Queen of Scots' bed-chamber and armour, Victorian clothes, fine furniture and paintings are displayed. Widest turnpike stair of its kind in Scotland. Clan Hay Centre.

Location: OS Ref. NJ754 506. Off A947 Aberdeen to Banff Road.

Open: 2 Apr - 25 Oct: daily, 10am - 5pm. Winter: Fri - Sun, 10am - 4pm. Closed Christmas & New Year.

Admission: Adult £4, Conc. £3. Groups (10+): £3.

ⓘ No photography. ⬛ 🅖 Ground floor. WC. 🍴 Home-baking and lunches. Ⓕ By arrangement. 🅿 ⬛ 🚌 🏠 6 x houses for self catering. ✳

DRUM CASTLE & GARDEN

Drumoak, by Banchory AB31 3EY

Tel: 01330 811204

Owner: The National Trust for Scotland   **Contact:** The Property Manager

Owned for 653 years by one family, the Irvines. The combination over the years of a 13th century square tower, a very fine Jacobean mansion house and the additions of the Victorian lairds make Drum Castle unique among Scottish castles.

Location: OS Ref. NJ796 004. Off A93, 3m W of Peterculter and 10m W of Aberdeen.

Open: 1 Apr - 31 May: daily, 12.30 - 5.30pm; 1 Jun - 31 Aug: daily, 10am - 5.30pm. Grounds: All year: daily, 9.30am - sunset. **(2004 opening times.)**

Admission: Castle & Garden: Adult £7, Conc. £5.25, Family £19. Groups: Adult £5.60, Child/School £1. Garden & grounds only: Adult £2.50, Conc. £1.90, Family £7. Groups: Adult £2, Child/School £1. **(2004 prices.)**

DRUMMUIR CASTLE

Drummuir, by Keith, Banffshire AB55 5JE

Tel: 01542 810332 **Fax:** 01542 810302

Owner: The Gordon-Duff Family   **Contact:** Joy Hoffman

Castellated Victorian Gothic-style castle built in 1847 by Admiral Duff. 60ft high lantern tower with fine plasterwork. Family portraits, interesting artefacts and other paintings.

Location: OS Ref. NJ372 442. Midway between Keith (5m) and Dufftown, off the B9014.

Open: 20/21 & 27/28 Aug and 5 - 23 Sept: Tours 2pm - 5pm.

Admission: Adult £2, Child £1.50. Pre-arranged groups: Adult £2, Child £1.50.

🅶 Ⓕ Obligatory. 🅿 🐕 In grounds on leads.

DUFF HOUSE

Banff AB45 3SX

Tel: 01261 818181 **Fax:** 01261 818900   **Contact:** The Chamberlain

One of the most imposing and palatial houses in Scotland, with a strong classical façade and a grand staircase leading to the main entrance.

Location: OS Ref. NJ691 634. Banff. 47m NW of Aberdeen on A947.

Open: Contact property for details.

Admission: Adult £5, Conc. £4, Family £12. Groups (10+): £4. Free admission to shop, tearoom, grounds & woodland walks.

DUNNOTTAR CASTLE

Dunnottar Castle Lodge, Stonehaven, Kincardineshire AB39 2TL

Tel: 01569 762173 **e-mail:** info@dunechtestates.co.uk

www.dunechtestates.co.uk   **Contact:** P McKenzie

Spectacular ruined cliff top fortress, home to the Earls Marischals of Scotland. The Crown Jewels of Scotland were hidden at this site, then smuggled away during the dark days of Cromwell's occupation.

Location: OS Ref. NO881 839. Just off A92. 1¹/₂ m SE of Stonehaven.

Open: Easter weekend - 28 Oct: Mon - Sat, 9am - 6pm, Suns, 2 - 5pm. 29 Oct - Easter Sat: Fri - Mon, 9.30am - dusk. Closed Tue - Thur. Last admission: 30 mins before closing.

Admission: Adult £4, Child £1.

ELGIN CATHEDRAL

Elgin

Tel: 01343 547171

Owner: Historic Scotland   **Contact:** The Steward

When entire this was perhaps the most beautiful of Scottish cathedrals, known as the Lantern of the North. 13th century, much modified after almost being destroyed in 1390 by Alexander Stewart, the infamous 'Wolf of Badenoch'. The octagonal chapterhouse is the finest in Scotland. You can see the Bishop's home at Spynie Palace, 2m north of the town.

Location: OS Ref. NJ223 630. In Elgin on the A96.

Open: 1 Apr - 30 Sept: daily, 9.30am - 6.30pm, last ticket 6pm. 1 Oct - 31 Mar: daily, 9.30am - 4.30pm, last ticket 4pm. Closed Thurs & Fris in winter.

Admission: Adult £3, Child £1, Conc. £2.30. Joint entry ticket with Spynie Palace: Adult £3.30, Child £1.30, Conc. £2.50.

✳ €

FYVIE CASTLE

Turriff, Aberdeenshire AB53 8JS

Tel: 01651 891266 **Fax:** 01651 891107

Owner: The National Trust for Scotland   **Contact:** The Property Manager

The five towers of the castle bear witness to the five families who have owned it. Fyvie Castle has a fine wheel stair and a collection of arms and armour and paintings, including works by Batoni, Raeburn, Romney, Gainsborough, Opie and Hoppner.

Location: OS Ref. NJ763 393. Off A947, 8m SE of Turriff, and 25m N of Aberdeen.

Open: 1 Apr - 30 Jun & 1 - 30 Sep: Fri - Tue, 12 noon - 5pm. 1 Jul - 31 Aug: daily, 11am - 5pm. Grounds: All year: daily, 9.30am - sunset. **(2004 opening times.)**

Admission: Adult £7, Conc. £5.25, Family £19. Groups: Adult £5.60, Child/School £1. Car parking £2. **(2004 prices.)**

HADDO HOUSE ♛

Tarves, Ellon, Aberdeenshire AB41 0ER

Tel: 01651 851440   **Fax:** 01651 851888

Owner: The National Trust for Scotland

Designed by William Adam in 1731 for William, 2nd Earl of Aberdeen. Much of the interior is 'Adam Revival' carried out about 1880 for John, 7th Earl and 1st Marquess of Aberdeen and his Countess, Ishbel.

Location: OS Ref. NJ868 348. Off B999, 4m N of Pitmedden, 10m NW of Ellon.

Open: House & Garden: Jun: Fri - Mon; 1 Jul - 31 Aug: daily, 11am - 4.30pm. Guided tours only, departing at set times. All admissions (incl members) from Stables Shop. Shop & tearoom: Good Fri - Easter Mon: daily; 1 May - 30 Jun & 1 Sep - 31 Oct: Fri - Mon; 1 Jul - 31 Aug: daily, 11am - 5pm. Aberdeenshire Council Country Park: All year: daily, 9.30am - sunset. **(2004 opening times.)**

Admission: Adult £7, Conc. £5.25, Family £19. Groups: Adult £5.60, Child/School £1. **(2004 prices.)**

HUNTLY CASTLE ⌂

Huntly

Tel: 01466 793191

Owner: In the care of Historic Scotland   **Contact:** The Steward

Known also as Strathbogie Castle, this glorious ruin stands in a beautiful setting on the banks of the River Deveron. Famed for its fine heraldic sculpture and inscribed stone friezes.

Location: OS Ref. NJ532 407. In Huntly on the A96. N side of the town.

Open: 1 Apr - 30 Sept: daily, 9.30am - 6.30pm, last ticket 6pm. 1 Oct - 31 Mar: daily, 9.30am - 4.30pm, last ticket 4pm. Closed Thurs & Fris in winter.

Admission: Adult £3.30, Child £1.30, Conc. £2.50.

✳ €

KILDRUMMY CASTLE ⌂

Alford, Aberdeenshire

Tel: 01975 571331

Owner: In the care of Historic Scotland   **Contact:** The Steward

Though ruined, the best example in Scotland of a 13th century castle with a curtain wall, four round towers, hall and chapel of that date. The seat of the Earls of Mar, it was dismantled after the first Jacobite rising in 1715.

Location: OS Ref. NJ455 164. 10m W of Alford on the A97. 16m SSW of Huntley.

Open: 1 Apr - 30 Sept: daily, 9.30am - 6.30pm, last ticket 6pm.

Admission: Adult £2.50, Child £1, Conc. £1.90.

€

KILDRUMMY CASTLE GARDEN

Kildrummy, Aberdeenshire

Tel: 01975 571203 / 571277   **Contact:** Alastair J Laing

Ancient quarry, shrub and alpine gardens renowned for their interest and variety. Water gardens below ruined castle.

Location: OS Ref. NJ455 164. On A97 off A944 10m SW of Alford. 16m SSW of Huntly.

Open: Apr - Oct: daily, 10am - 5pm.

Admission: Adult £3, Child Free.

LEITH HALL & GARDEN ♛

Huntly, Aberdeenshire AB54 4NQ

Tel: 01464 831216   **Fax:** 01464 831594

Owner: The National Trust for Scotland   **Contact:** The Property Manager

This mansion house is built around a courtyard and was the home of the Leith family for almost 300 years. With an enviable family record of military service over the centuries, the house contains a unique collection of military memorabilia displayed in an exhibition 'For Crown and Country'.

Location: OS Ref. NJ541 298. B9002, 1m W of Kennethmont, 7m S of Huntley.

Open: House & tearoom, Good Fri - Easter Mon: daily; 1 May - 30 Sep: Fri - Tue, 12 noon - 5pm. Garden & grounds: All year: daily 9.30am - sunset. **(2004 opening times.)**

Admission: Adult £7, Conc. £5.25, Family £19. Groups: Adult £5.60, Child/School £1. Garden and grounds only: Adult £2.50, Conc. £1.90, Family £7. Groups: Adult £2, Child/School £1. **(2004 prices.)**

LICKLEYHEAD CASTLE

Auchleven, Insch, Aberdeenshire AB52 6PN

Tel: 01464 821359

Owner: The Leslie family   **Contact:** Zoë Lemon

A beautifully restored Laird's Castle, Lickleyhead was built by the Leslies c1450 and extensively renovated in 1629 by John Forbes of Leslie, whose initials are carved above the entrance. It is an almost unspoilt example of the transformation from 'Chateau-fort' to 'Chateau-maison' and boasts many interesting architectural features.

Location: OS Ref. NJ628 237. Auchleven is 2m S of Insch on B992. Twin pillars of castle entrance on left at foot of village.

Open: 8 - 14 May: daily; 21 May - 17 Sept: Sats, 12 noon - 3pm.

Admission: Free.

♿Unsuitable. 🅿Limited. No coaches. 🐕In grounds, on leads.

PITMEDDEN GARDEN ♛

Ellon, Aberdeenshire AB41 0PD

Tel: 01651 842352   **Fax:** 01651 843188

Owner: The National Trust for Scotland   **Contact:** The Property Manager

The centrepiece of this property is the Great Garden which was originally laid out in 1675 by Sir Alexander Seton, 1st Baronet of Pitmedden.

Location: OS Ref. NJ885 280. On A920 1m W of Pitmedden village & 14m N of Aberdeen.

Open: 1 May - 30 Sep: daily, 10am - 5.30pm. Grounds: All year. **(2004 opening times.)**

Admission: Adult £5, Conc. £3.75, Family £13.50. **(2004 prices.)**

PLUSCARDEN ABBEY

Nr Elgin, Moray IV30 8UA

Tel: 01343 890257   **Fax:** 01343 890258

e-mail: monks@pluscardenabbey.org   **Contact:** Father Giles

Valliscaulian, founded 1230.

Location: OS Ref. NJ142 576. On minor road 6m SW of Elgin. Follow B9010 for first mile.

Open: All year: 4.45am - 8.30pm. Shop: 8.30am - 5pm.

Admission: Free.

PROVOST SKENE'S HOUSE

Guestrow, off Broad Street, Aberdeen AB10 1AS

Tel: 01224 641086   **Fax:** 01224 632133

Owner: Aberdeen City Council   **Contact:** Christine Rew

Built in the 16th century, Provost Skene's House is one of Aberdeen's few remaining examples of early burgh architecture. Splendid room settings include a suite of Georgian rooms, an Edwardian nursery, magnificent 17th century plaster ceilings and wood panelling.

Location: OS Ref. NJ943 064. Aberdeen city centre, off Broad Street.

Open: Contact property for details.

Admission: Free.

ST MACHAR'S CATHEDRAL TRANSEPTS ⌂

Old Aberdeen

Tel: 0131 668 8800

Owner: In the care of Historic Scotland

The nave and towers of the Cathedral remain in use as a church, and the ruined transepts are in care. In the south transept is the fine altar tomb of Bishop Dunbar (1514 - 32).

Location: OS Ref. NJ939 088. In old Aberdeen. ½ m N of King's College.

Admission: Free.

✳

SPYNIE PALACE ⌂

Elgin

Tel: 01343 546358

Owner: In the care of Historic Scotland   **Contact:** The Steward

Spynie Palace was the residence of the Bishops of Moray from the 14th century to 1686. The site is dominated by the massive tower built by Bishop David Stewart (1461-77) and affords spectacular views across Spynie Loch.

Location: OS Ref. NJ231 659. 2m N of Elgin off the A941.

Open: 1 Apr - 30 Sept: daily, 9.30am - 6.30pm. 1 Oct - 31 Mar: Sats & Suns, 9.30am - 4.30pm. Last ticket 30 mins before closing.

Admission: Adult £2.20, Child 75p, Conc. £1.60. Joint entry ticket with Elgin Cathedral: Adult £2.50, Child £1, Conc. £1.90.

✳ €

TOLQUHON CASTLE ⌂

Aberdeenshire

Tel: 01651 851286

Owner: In the care of Historic Scotland   **Contact:** The Steward

Tolquhon was built for the Forbes family. The early 15th century tower was enlarged between 1584 and 1589 with a large mansion around the courtyard. Noted for its highly ornamented gatehouse and pleasance.

Location: OS Ref. NJ874 286. 15m N of Aberdeen on the A920. 6m N of Ellon.

Open: 1 Apr - 30 Sept: daily, 9.30am - 6.30pm. 1 Oct - 31 Mar: Sats & Suns, 9.30am - 4.30pm. Last ticket 30 mins before closing.

Admission: Adult £2.50, Child £1, Conc. £1.90.

✳ €

DAVID WELCH WINTER GARDENS – DUTHIE PARK

Polmuir Road, Aberdeen, Grampian Highlands AB11 7TH

Tel: 01224 585310   **Fax:** 01224 210532   **e-mail:** wintergardens@aberdeen.nct.uk

www.aberdeencity.gov.uk

Owner: Aberdeen City Council   **Contact:** Alan Findlay

One of Europe's largest indoor gardens with many rare and exotic plants on show from all around the world.

Location: OS Ref. NJ97 044. Just N of River Dee, 1m S of city centre.

Open: All year: daily from 9.30pm.

Admission: Free.

✳

Map 12

Owner: The Dowager
Countess Cawdor

▶ **CONTACT**

The Secretary
Cawdor Castle
Nairn
Scotland IV12 5RD

Tel: 01667 404401

Fax: 01667 404674

e-mail: info@
cawdorcastle.com

▶ **LOCATION**

OS Ref. NH850 500

From Edinburgh
A9, 3¹/₂ hrs,
Inverness 20 mins,
Nairn 10 mins.
Main road: A9, 14m.

Rail: Nairn
Station 5m.

Bus: Inverness to Nairn
bus route 200 yds.

Taxi: Cawdor Taxis
01667 404315.

Air: Inverness
Airport 5m.

CONFERENCE/FUNCTION

ROOM	MAX CAPACITY
Cawdor Hall	40

CAWDOR CASTLE 🏛

www.cawdorcastle.com

This splendid romantic castle dating from the late 14th century was built as a private fortress by the Thanes of Cawdor, and remains the home of the Cawdor family to this day. The ancient medieval tower was built around the legendary holly tree.

Although the house has evolved over 600 years, later additions mainly of the 17th century were all built in the Scottish vernacular style with slated roofs over walls and crow-stepped gables of mellow local stone. This style gives Cawdor a strong sense of unity, and the massive, severe exterior belies an intimate interior that gives the place a surprisingly personal, friendly atmosphere.

Good furniture, fine portraits and pictures, interesting objects and outstanding tapestries are

arranged to please the family rather than to echo fashion or impress. Memories of Shakespeare's *Macbeth* give Cawdor an elusive, evocative quality that delights visitors.

GARDENS

The flower garden also has a family feel to it, where plants are chosen out of affection rather than affectation. This is a lovely spot between spring and late summer. The walled garden has been restored with a holly maze, paradise garden, knot garden and thistle garden. The wild garden beside its stream leads into beautiful trails through a spectacular mature mixed woodland, through which paths are helpfully marked and colour-coded. New are the Tibetan garden and traditional Scottish vegetable garden at Auchindoune.

ℹ 9 hole golf course, putting green, golf clubs for hire, Conferences, whisky tasting, musical entertainments, specialised garden visits. No photography, video taping or tripods inside.

🛍 Gift, book and wool shops.

🍷 Lunches, sherry or champagne receptions.

♿ Visitors may alight at the entrance. WC. Only ground floor accessible.

🍴 Licensed buttery, May-Oct, groups should book.

🅿 250 cars and 25 coaches. Two weeks' notice for group catering, coach drivers/couriers free.

▧ £3.00 per child. Room notes, quiz and answer sheet can be provided.

🐕 Guide dogs only.

▶ **OPENING TIMES**

Summer
1 May - 9 October
Daily: 10am - 5.30pm.

Last admission 5pm.

Winter

October - April
Groups by appointment, admission prices on application.

▶ **ADMISSION**

Summer
House & Garden
Adult £6.80
Child (5-15yrs) £4.00
OAP/Student £5.80
Family (2+5).......... £19.50

Groups (20+)
Adult £5.90
Child (5-15yrs) £3.50
OAP/Student £5.80

Garden only
Per person £3.50

🎭 **SPECIAL EVENTS**

JUN 4/5
Special Gardens Weekend: Guided tours of gardens.

DUNVEGAN CASTLE

www.dunvegancastle.com

Map 11

Owner: John Macleod of Macleod

▶ **CONTACT**

The Administrator
Dunvegan Castle
Isle of Skye
Scotland IV55 8WF

Tel: 01470 521206
Fax: 01470 521205
Seal Tel: 01470 521500

e-mail: info@
dunvegancastle.com

▶ **LOCATION**

OS Ref. NG250 480

1m N of village. NW corner of Skye.

From Inverness A82 to Invermoriston, A887 to Kyle of Lochalsh 82m. From Fort William A82 to Invergarry, A87 to Kyle of Lochalsh 76m.

Kyle of Lochalsh to Dunvegan 45m via Skye Bridge (toll).

Ferry: To the Isle of Skye, 'roll-on, roll-off', 30 minute crossing.

Rail: Inverness to Kyle of Lochalsh 3 - 4 trains per day - 45m.

Bus: Portree 25m, Kyle of Lochalsh 45m.

Dunvegan is unique. It is the only Great House in the Western Isles of Scotland to have retained its family and its roof. It is the oldest home in the whole of Scotland continuously inhabited by the same family – the Chiefs of the Clan Macleod. A Castle placed on a rock by the sea - the curtain wall is dated before 1200 AD – its superb location recalls the Norse Empire of the Vikings, the ancestors of the Chiefs.

Dunvegan's continuing importance as a custodian of the Clan spirit is epitomised by the famous Fairy Flag, whose origins are shrouded in mystery but whose ability to protect both Chief and Clan is unquestioned. To enter Dunvegan is to arrive at a place whose history combines with legend to make a living reality.

GARDENS

The gardens and grounds extend over some ten acres of woodland walks, peaceful formal lawns and a water garden dominated by two spectacular natural waterfalls. The temperate climate aids in producing a fine show of rhododendrons and azaleas, the chief glory of the garden in spring. One is always aware of the proximity of the sea and many garden walks finish at the Castle Jetty, from where traditional boats make regular trips to view the delightful Seal Colony.

ℹ️ Gift and craft shop. Boat trips to seal colony. Pedigree Highland cattle. No photography in castle.

♿ Visitors may alight at entrance. WC.

🍴 Licensed restaurant, (cap. 70) special rates for groups, menus upon request. Tel: 01470 521310. Open late peak season for evening meals.

🚶 By appointment in English or Gaelic at no extra charge. If requested owner may meet groups, tour time 45mins.

🅿️ 120 cars and 10 coaches. Do not attempt to take passengers to Castle Jetty (long walk). If possible please book. Seal boat trip dependent upon weather.

🏫 Welcome by arrangement. Guide available on request.

🐕 In grounds only, on lead.

🛏️ 4 self-catering units, 3 of which sleep 6 and 1 of which sleeps 7.

❄️

▶ **OPENING TIMES**

Summer
22 March - 31 October
Daily: 10am - 5.30pm.
Last admission 5pm.

Winter
1 November - mid March
Daily: 11am - 4pm.
Last admission 3.30pm.

Closed Christmas Day, Boxing Day, New Year's Day and 2 January.

▶ **ADMISSION**

Summer
Castle & Gardens
Adult £6.80
Child (5 -15yrs) £3.80
OAP/Student £5.80

Groups (10+) £5.80

Gardens only
Adult £4.50
Child (5 -15yrs) £2.50

Seal Boats
Adult £5.50
Child (5 -12yrs) £3.50

Child (under 5yrs)........ £1.50

Winter
Adult £5.00
Child* (5 -15yrs) £2.50
Conc. £3.50

Groups (10+) £3.50

BALLINDALLOCH CASTLE 🏰

Grantown-on-Spey, Banffshire AB37 9AX

Tel: 01807 500206 **Fax:** 01807 500210 **e-mail:** enquiries@ballindallochcastle.co.uk
www.ballindallochcastle.co.uk

Owner: Mr & Mrs Russell   **Contact:** Mrs Clare Russell

Ballindalloch is a much loved family home and one of the few castles lived in continuously by its original owners, the Macpherson-Grants, since 1546. Filled with family memorabilia and a magnificent collection of 17th century Spanish paintings. The Estate is home to the oldest herd of Aberdeen Angus cattle and the Castle grounds have beautiful rock and rose gardens and river walks to savour.

Location: OS Ref. NJ178 366. 14m NE of Grantown-on-Spey on A95, 22m S of Elgin on A95.

Open: Good Fri - 30 Sept: 10.30am - 5.30pm, closed Sats. Coaches all year by appt.

Admission: Castle & Grounds: Adult £6, Child (6-16yrs) £2.50, Conc. £5, Family (2+3) £12, Season ticket £12. Grounds only: Adult £2, Child (6-16yrs) £1, Season ticket £5. Groups: (20+) Adult £4, Child £2.

🖼 ♿ Ground floor & grounds. WC. ☕ 🅿 🎧 Audio-visual.
🐕 In grounds, on leads in dog walking area.

CASTLE LEOD

Strathpeffer IV14 9AA

Tel/Fax: 01997 421264 **e-mail:** cromartie@castle-leod.freeserve.co.uk

Owner/Contact: The Earl of Cromartie

15th century tower house of rose-pink stone complete with turrets. Lived in by the Mackenzie family, chiefs of the clan, for 500 years and still very much a home where the family ensure a personal welcome. Magnificent setting below Ben Wyvis and amongst some of the finest trees in Scotland.

Location: OS Ref. NH485 593. 1km E of Strathpeffer on the A834 Strathpeffer to Dingwall road.

Open: 14 - 17 Apr, 12 - 15 May, 9 - 12 Jun, 30 Jun - 3 Jul, 14 - 18 Sept & 13 - 16 Oct: 2 - 5.30pm (last admission 4.45pm).

Admission: Adult £5, Child £2, OAP/Student £4.

ℹ️ No coaches. 🚻 ♿ Grounds only. WC. 🎫 By arrangement, all year.
🅿 No coach parking. 🐕 Guide dogs only. 🛏 Tel for details.

The Queen Elizabeth Castle of Mey Trust

CASTLE OF MEY

THURSO, CAITHNESS KW14 8XH

www.castleofmey.org.uk

Tel: 01847 851473 **Fax:** 01847 851475

Owner: The Queen Elizabeth Castle of Mey Trust   **Contact:** James Murray

The home of The Queen Mother in Caithness and the only property in Britain that she owned. She bought the Castle in 1952, saved it from becoming a ruin and developed the gardens. It became her ideal holiday home because of the beautiful surroundings and the privacy she was always given.

Location: OS Ref. ND290 739. On A836 between Thurso and John O'Groats, just outside the village of Mey. 12m Thurso station, 18m Wick airport.

Open: 2 May - 28 Jul & 10 Aug - 29 Sept: daily (closed Fris), 10.30am - 4pm.

Admission: Adult £7, Child (16yrs and under) Free, Conc. £6. Booked groups (20+): £6. Gardens & grounds only: Adult £3.

ℹ️ No photography in the Castle. 🖼 🎫 ♿ Partial. 🎫 By arrangement. 🅿
🐕 In grounds, on leads.

CASTLE OF OLD WICK ⚓

Wick

Tel: 01667 460232

Owner/Contact: Historic Scotland

Essential work to safeguard the future of Scotland's best-preserved Norse castle has been completed and it has now reopened to the public. Visitors can now enjoy visiting this dramatically located castle once again. One of the oldest keeps in Scotland, the castle is a simple square keep of at least three storeys. In addition to the tower the site contains the low-lying ruins of other buildings. These have never been excavated and are largely covered by turf in order to protect them from damage.

Location: OS Ref. ND368 487. 1m S of Wick on Shore Road, E of A9.

Open: All year.

Admission: Free.

✳️

CAWDOR CASTLE 🏰

See page 502 for full page entry.

CULLODEN 🏰

Culloden Moor, Inverness IV1 2ED

Tel: 01463 790607 **Fax:** 01463 794294

Owner: The National Trust for Scotland

Culloden, the bleak moor which in 1746 saw the hopes of the young Prince Charles Edward Stuart crushed, and the end of the Jacobite Rising, the 'Forty-Five'.

Location: OS Ref. NH745 450. On B9006, 5m E of Inverness.

Open: Site: All year: daily. Visitor Centre, restaurant & shop, 1 - 28 Feb & 1 Nov - 31 Dec: daily, 11am - 4pm (closed 25/26 Dec); 1 - 31 Mar: daily, 10am - 4pm; 1 Apr - 30 Jun & 1 Sep - 31 Oct: daily, 9am - 6pm; 1 Jul - 31 Aug: daily, 9am - 7pm. **(2004 opening times.)**

Admission: Visitor Centre & Old Leanach Cottage: Adult £5, Conc. £3.75, Family £13.50. Groups: Adult £4, Child/School £1. **(2004 prices.)**

THE DOUNE OF ROTHIEMURCHUS 🏰

By Aviemore PH22 1QH

Tel: 01479 812345 **e-mail:** info@rothie.co.uk **www.**rothiemurchus.net

Owner: J P Grant of Rothiemurchus   **Contact:** Rothiemurchus Visitor Centre

The family home of the Grants of Rothiemurchus was nearly lost as a ruin and has been under an ambitious repair programme since 1975. This exciting project may be visited on selected Mondays throughout the season. Book with the Visitor Centre for a longer 2hr 'Highland Lady' tour which explores the haunts of Elizabeth Grant of Rothiemurchus, born 1797, author of *Memoirs of a Highland Lady*, who vividly described the Doune and its surroundings from the memories of her childhood.

Location: OS Ref. NH900 100. 2m S of Aviemore on E bank of Spey river.

Open: House: selected Mons. Grounds: May - Aug: Mon, 10am - 12.30pm & 2 - 4.30pm, also 1st Mon in the month during winter.

Admission: House only £1. Tour (booking essential, 4+) £10pp.

ℹ️ Visitor Centre. 🖼 🎫 Obligatory. 🅿 Limited. 🐕 In grounds, on leads.

Cawdor Castle.

DUNROBIN CASTLE 🏛
GOLSPIE, SUTHERLAND KW10 6SF
www.highlandescape.com

Tel: 01408 633177 **Fax:** 01408 634081 **e-mail:** info@dunrobincastle.net

Owner: The Sutherland Trust **Contact:** Keith Jones, Curator

Dates from the 13th century with additions in the 17th, 18th and 19th centuries. Wonderful furniture, paintings, library, ceremonial robes and memorabilia. Victorian museum in grounds with a fascinating collection including Pictish stones. Set in fine woodlands overlooking the sea. Magnificent formal gardens, one of few remaining French/Scottish formal parterres. Falconry display.

Location: OS Ref. NC850 010. 50m N of Inverness on A9. 1m NE of Golspie.

Open: 25 Mar - 15 Oct: Mon - Sat, 10.30am - 4.30pm, Suns, 12 noon - 4.30pm. 1 Jun - 30 Sept: Mon - Sat, 10.30am - 5.30pm, Suns, 12 noon - 5.30pm (Jul & Aug: Suns, opens at 10.30am.)

Admission: Adult £6.60, Child £4.70, Conc. £6, Family (2+2) £18. Booked groups: Adult £5.50, Child/Conc. £4.70.

🖻 🇹 ⑤Unsuitable for wheelchairs. 🖷 🍴 🇫By arrangement. 🅿 ✖

FORT GEORGE 🏰
ARDERSIER BY INVERNESS IV1 2TD

Owner: In the care of Historic Scotland **Contact:** Brian Ford

Tel/Fax: 01667 460232

Built following the Battle of Culloden to subdue the Highlands, Fort George never saw a shot fired in anger. One of the most outstanding artillery fortifications in Europe with reconstructed barrack room displays. The Queen's Own Highlanders' Museum.

Location: OS Ref. NH762 567. 11m NE of Inverness off the A96 by Ardersier.

Open: Apr - Sept: daily, 9.30am - 6.30pm. Oct - Mar: daily, 9.30am - 4.30pm. Last ticket sold 45 mins before closing.

Admission: Adult £6, Child £2.40, Conc. £4.50. 10% discount for groups (10+).

ⓘPicnic tables. 🖻 🇹Private evening hire. ⑤Wheelchairs available. WCs. 🖷In summer. 🅿 🅿 Free if pre-booked. 🐕In grounds, on leads. ✖ €

DUNVEGAN CASTLE 🏛   *See page 503 for full page entry.*

EILEAN DONAN CASTLE
Dornie, Kyle of Lochalsh, Wester Ross IV40 8DX

Tel: 01599 555202 **Fax:** 01599 555262 **e-mail:** info@donan.f9.co.uk

www.eileandonancastle.com **Contact:** Rod Stenson – Castle Keeper

Location: OS Ref. NG880 260. On A87 8m E of Skye Bridge.

Open: Mar & Nov: 10am - 3.30pm. Apr - Oct: 10am - 5.30pm.

Admission: Adult £4.90, Conc. £3.60.

GLENFINNAN MONUMENT ⚜
Inverness-shire PH37 4LT

Tel/Fax: 01397 722250

Owner: The National Trust for Scotland

The monument, situated on the scenic road to the Isles, is set amid superb Highland scenery at the head of Loch Shiel. It was erected in 1815 in tribute to the clansmen who fought and died in the Jacobite cause.

Location: OS Ref. NM906 805. On A830, 18m W of Fort William, Lochaber.

Open: Site: All year: daily. Visitor Centre, shop & snack-bar: 1 Apr - 30 Jun & 1 Sep - 31 Oct: daily, 10am - 5pm; 1 Jul - 31 Aug: daily, 9.30am - 5.30pm. **(2004 opening times.)**

Admission: Adult £2, Conc. £1 (honesty box). **(2004 prices.)**

HUGH MILLER'S COTTAGE ⚜
Cromarty IV11 8XA

Tel: 01381 600245

Owner: The National Trust for Scotland

Furnished thatched cottage of c1698, birthplace of eminent geologist and writer Hugh Miller. Exhibition and video.

Location: OS Ref. NH790 680. Via Kessock Bridge & A832, in Cromarty, 22m NE of Inverness.

Open: Good Fri - 30 Sep: daily; 1 - 31 Oct: Sun - Wed, 12 noon - 5pm. **(2004 opening times.)**

Admission: Adult £2.50, Conc. £1.90, Family £7. Groups: Adult £2, Child/School £1. **(2004 prices.)**

INVEREWE GARDEN ⚜
Poolewe, Ross & Cromarty IV22 2LQ

Tel: 01445 781200 **Fax:** 01445 781497

Owner: The National Trust for Scotland

In a spectacular lochside setting among pinewoods, Osgood Mackenzie's Victorian dreams have produced a glorious 50 acre mecca for garden lovers.

Location: OS Ref. NG860 820. On A832, by Poolewe, 6m NE of Gairloch, Highland.

Open: Garden: 1 Apr - 31 Oct: daily, 9.30am - 9pm; 1 Nov - 31 Mar: daily, 9.30am - 4pm (or sunset if earlier). Visitor Centre & shop, 1 Apr - 31 Oct: daily, 9.30am - 5pm (4pm in Oct). Restaurant, same dates, but opens at 10am. **(2004 opening times.)**

Admission: Adult £7, Conc. £5.25, Family £19. Groups: Adult £5.60 (pre-booked £5.25 in 2003), Child/School £1. **(2004 prices.)**

LOCAL FOOD

Scottish Shortbread

A sweet biscuit sold usually either as 'petticoat tails' or in sticks, Scottish shortbread is a teatime treat.

Highlands & Skye

©Historic Scotland Photographic Library

URQUHART CASTLE
DRUMNADROCHIT, LOCH NESS

Tel: 01456 450551

Owner: In the care of Historic Scotland   **Contact:** Euan Fraser

The remains of one of the largest castles in Scotland dominate a rocky promontory on Loch Ness. Most of the existing buildings date from the 16th century. New visitor centre with original artefacts, audio-visual presentation, shop and café.

Location: OS Ref. NH531 286. On Loch Ness, 1¹/₂m S of Drumnadrochit on A82.

Open: 1 Apr - 30 Sept: daily, 9.30am - 6.30pm, last ticket 5.45pm. 1 Oct - 31 Mar: daily, 9.30am - 4.30pm, last ticket 3.45pm.

Admission: Adult £6, Child £2.40, Conc. £4.50.

🄯 ♿Partial. WCs. 🖳 🅿 ⌂ 🔲Free if pre-booked. 🐕Guide dogs only. ❋ €

© Skyscan

Dunvegan Castle from the book 'Historic Family Homes & Gardens from the Air'.

BALFOUR CASTLE

Shapinsay, Orkney Islands KW17 2DY

Tel: 01856 711282 **Fax:** 01856 711283

Owner/Contact: Mrs Lidderdale

Built in 1848.

Location: OS Ref. HY475 164 on Shapinsay Island, 3¹/₂ m NNE of Kirkwall.

Open: May: Weds & Suns; Jun - Sept: Suns only, 2.15 - 5.30pm.

Admission: Adult £17, Child £8.50, including boat fare, guided tour, gardens & afternoon tea. Bookings essential.

BISHOP'S & EARL'S PALACES

Kirkwall, Orkney

Tel: 01856 875461

Owner: In the care of Historic Scotland   **Contact:** The Steward

The Bishop's Palace is a 12th century hall-house with a round tower built by Bishop Reid in 1541-48. The adjacent Earl's Palace built in 1607 has been described as the most mature and accomplished piece of Renaissance architecture left in Scotland.

Location: Bishop's Palace: OS Ref. HY447 108. Earl's Palace: OS Ref. HY448 108. In Kirkwall on A960.

Open: 1 Apr - 30 Sept: daily, 9.30am - 6.30pm, last ticket 6pm.

Admission: Adult £2.50, Child £1, Conc. £1.90. Joint entry ticket available for all the Orkney monuments: Adult £11, Child £3.50, Conc. £8.

€

BLACK HOUSE

Arnol, Isle of Lewis

Tel: 01851 710395

Owner: In the care of Historic Scotland   **Contact:** The Steward

A traditional Lewis thatched house, fully furnished, complete with attached barn, byre and stockyard. A peat fire burns in the open hearth. New visitor centre open and restored 1920s croft house.

Location: OS Ref. NB320 500. In Arnol village, 11m NW of Stornoway on A858.

Open: 1 Apr - 30 Sept: Mon - Sat, 9.30am - 6.30pm, last ticket 6pm. 1 Oct - 31 Mar: Mon - Thur & Sat, 9.30am - 4.30pm, last ticket 4pm.

Admission: Adult £4, Child £1.60, Conc. £3.

✳ €

BROCH OF GURNESS

Aikerness, Orkney

Tel: 01831 579478

Owner: In the care of Historic Scotland   **Contact:** The Steward

Protected by three lines of ditch and rampart, the base of the broch is surrounded by Iron Age buildings.

Location: OS Ref. HY383 268. At Aikerness, about 14m NW of Kirkwall on A966.

Open: 1 Apr - 30 Sept: daily, 9.30am - 6.30pm, last ticket 6pm.

Admission: Adult £3.30, Child £1.30, Conc. £2.50. Joint entry ticket available for all Orkney monuments: Adult £11, Child £3.50, Conc. £8.

€

CARRICK HOUSE

Carrick, Eday, Orkney KW17 2AB

Tel: 01857 622260

Owner: Mr & Mrs Joy   **Contact:** Mrs Rosemary Joy

17th century house of 3 storeys, built by John Stewart, Lord Kinclaven Earl of Carrick younger brother of Patrick, 2nd Earl of Orkney in 1633.

Location: OS Ref. NT227 773. N of island of Eday on minor roads W of B9063 just W of the shore of Calf Sound. Regular ferry service.

Open: Jun - Sept: occasional Suns by appointment only.

Admission: Adult £2.50, Child £1.

🎞 Obligatory.

JARLSHOF PREHISTORIC & NORSE SETTLEMENT

Shetland

Tel: 01950 460112

Owner: In the care of Historic Scotland   **Contact:** The Steward

Over 3 acres of remains spanning 3,000 years from the Stone Age. Oval-shaped Bronze Age houses, Iron Age broch and wheel houses. Viking Long Houses, medieval farmstead and 16th century laird's house.

Location: OS Ref. HY401 096. At Sumburgh Head, 22m S of Lerwick on the A970.

Open: 1 Apr - 30 Sept: daily, 9.30am - 6.30pm. Last adm. ¹/₂ hr before closing.

Admission: Adult £3.30, Child £1.30, Conc. £2.50.

€

MAESHOWE

Orkney

Tel: 01856 761606

Owner: In the care of Historic Scotland   **Contact:** The Steward

This world-famous tomb was built in Neolithic times, before 2700 BC. The large mound covers a stone-built passage and a burial chamber with cells in the walls. Runic inscriptions tell of how it was plundered of its treasures by Vikings.

Location: OS Ref. NY318 128. 9m W of Kirkwall on the A965.

Open: 1 Apr - 30 Sept: daily, 9.30am - 6.30pm. 1 Oct - 31 Mar: daily, 9.30am - 4.30pm except Suns am.

Admission: Adult £4, Child £1.60, Conc. £3. Joint entry ticket for all Orkney monuments available. Timed ticketing in place - please telephone for details. Admission, shop and refreshments at nearby Tormiston Mill.

✳ €

RING OF BRODGAR STONE CIRCLE & HENGE

Stromness, Orkney

Tel: 0131 668 8800

Owner/Contact: In the care of Historic Scotland

A magnificent circle of upright stones with an enclosing ditch spanned by causeways. Of late Neolithic date.

Location: OS Ref. HY294 134. 5m NE of Stromness.

Open: Any reasonable time.

Admission: Free.

✳

©Historic Scotland Photographic Library

SKARA BRAE & SKAILL HOUSE

SANDWICK, ORKNEY

Tel: 01856 841815

Owner: Historic Scotland/Major M R S Macrae   **Contact:** Ann Marwick

Skara Brae is one of the best preserved groups of Stone Age houses in Western Europe. Built before the Pyramids, the houses contain stone furniture, hearths and drains. Visitor centre and replica house with joint admission with Skaill House – 17th century home of the Laird who excavated Skara Brae.

Location: OS6 HY231 188. 19m NW of Kirkwall on the B9056.

Open: Apr - Sept: daily, 9.30am - 6.30pm. Oct - Mar: Mon - Sat, 9.30am - 4.30pm, Suns, 2 - 4.30pm.

Admission: Apr - Sept: Adult £6, Child £2.40, Conc. £4.50. Oct - Mar: Adult £4, Child £1.20, Conc. £3. 10% discount for groups (10+). Joint ticket with other Orkney sites available.

ℹ Visitor centre. 📷 ♿ Partial. WCs. 🍽 Licensed. 🅿
🎦 Free school visits when booked. 🐕 Guide dogs only. ✳ €

TANKERNESS HOUSE

Broad Street, Kirkwall, Orkney

Tel: 01856 873191 **Fax:** 01856 871560

Owner: Orkney Islands Council   **Contact:** Janette Park

A fine vernacular 16th century town house contains The Orkney Museum.

Location: OS Ref. HY446 109. In Kirkwall opposite W end of cathedral.

Open: Oct - Apr: Mon - Sat, 10.30am - 12.30pm & 1.30 - 5pm. May - Sept: Mon - Sat, 10.30am - 5pm, Suns, 2 - 5pm. Gardens always open.

Admission: Free.

Stackpole, South Wales. ©National Trust Photographic Library/Martin Trelawny

wales

wales

The traditional border between Wales and England is Offa's Dyke. The ditch and rampart earthwork was built by King Offa between 757 and 796AD, although whether as a defensive structure or merely to mark an agreed boundary between the Kingdom of Mercia and Wales, is not known. North Wales is a holiday area attracting lovers of coast and countryside alike. To the west lies Snowdon (Eryri as it is known in Welsh), the highest peak in England and Wales, a popular destination for climbers and walkers. The Snowdonia National Park offers mountain walks, forest trails and miles of golden sandy beaches. Clough Williams-Ellis' enchanting village of Portmeirion sits on its own private peninsula; with all the cottages available to rent, it is truly a unique place to stay. To the east, in contrast, is a gentler landscape of moorlands, valleys and the hills of the Welsh Borders. Further south, the Gower Peninsula – the first place in Britain to be designated as an Area of Outstanding Natural Beauty – is a haven for wildlife. South Wales, the heart of Wales' industrial past, has shed its coal pits and slag heaps and is now home to high-tech industries competing with the best in the world.

Stackpole – Beach and cliffs, South Wales
©National Trust Photographic Library/Martin Trelawny Farne Islands

Powis Castle Orangery Terrace, North Wales

Colby Woodland Garden, South Wales

Penbryn, South Wales

©National Trust Photographic Library/Joe Cornish

north wales

south wales

Porth Dinllaen , South Wales.

gwydir castle

spectres | atmospheric | gilded leatherwork

gwydir castle

n o r t h   w a l e s

The recovery of magical and mysterious Gwydir Castle is a restoration story like no other. Its current owners bought the wisteria-clad, semi-derelict property after discovering its crumbling frame in Snowdonia ten years ago.

Gwydir was disintegrating. One side of the house was collapsing and the chimney stacks were waving in the wind. Sizeable parts were perilously roofless and vulnerable to the elements. Its most recent inhabitants had been rats, bats, swallows and squatters. Now it is dazzlingly restored, testament to years of dedication and toil.

This, one of the most haunted houses in Wales, is a most exceptionally atmospheric place. The first castle was built at Gwydir in the 14th century by Howell Coetmore, who fought under the Black Prince at the Battle of Poitiers in 1356. It was rebuilt after the Wars of the Roses by Meredith, founder of the Wynn dynasty and a leading supporter of King Henry VII.

In the 1570s Gwydir was the home of Katherine of Berain, the 'Mother of Wales' and cousin to Queen Elizabeth I; and it has associations with both the Babington Plot and the Gunpowder Plot of 1605. There are also historical links with Lord Leicester, Inigo Jones and Bishop Morgan, translator of the Welsh Bible.

Grade I listed, much of what the visitor to Gwydir sees now, after a decade of repairing, restoration, limewashing and remarkable historical breakthroughs, dates from Meredith's house with 16th century additions. Now that the structure is secure, the owners have sought to recreate an Elizabethan interior using appropriate fabrics and furniture.

By far the most momentous recovery can be seen in the Dining Room. The 1640s panelling, 12-foot high baroque doorcase and fireplace, together with a frieze of gilded leatherwork which disappeared after the sale of Gwydir and its contents in 1921, was rediscovered still in unpacked boxes in the Metropolitan Museum of Art, New York. Stripped from its walls, a year prior to a devastating fire, it was bought by William Randolph Hearst, the legendary newspaper tycoon. It was returned to Wales in 1996 and reinstalled like a jigsaw, using a sepia photograph from 1908 for reference.

Outside in the famous gardens, where oranges and lemons were once grown and where peacocks still strut, are relics of different eras: see the Old Dutch Garden, with its yew topiary and octagonal fountain, or the Royal gardens, where oak trees were planted in the 19th century to commemorate the visit of the Duke and Duchess of York, later King George V and Queen Mary. You might not be alone: other 'visitors' to this gripping place include the spectre of a murdered servant girl, a prowling dog and the vision of a torch-lit procession on the Great Terrace.

The story of the restoration of Gwydir Castle is the subject of Judy Corbett's recently published book "Castles in the Air".

▶ For further details about Gwydir Castle, see page 518.

ABERCONWY HOUSE ❧
Castle Street, Conwy LL32 8AY

Tel: 01492 592246   **Fax:** 01492 585153

Owner: The National Trust

Dating from the 14th century, this is the only medieval merchant's house in Conwy to have survived the turbulent history of this walled town for nearly six centuries. Furnished rooms and an audio-visual presentation show daily life from different periods in its history.

Location: OS Ref. SH781 777. At junction of Castle Street and High Street.

Open: 18 Mar - 30 Oct: daily except Tues, 11am - 5pm. Last adm. 30 mins before close. Shop: 1 Mar - 31 Dec: daily (closed 25/26 Dec), 10am - 5pm (5.30pm 1 Apr - 30 Oct).

Admission: Adult £2.60, Child £1.30, Family (2+2) £6.50. Pre-booked groups (15+) Adult £2.10, Child £1. National Trust members Free.

ℹ️No indoor photography. 🅾️All year. 🎫By arrangement. 🏠
🅿️In town car parks only. ♿ 🦮 Guide dogs only.

BEAUMARIS CASTLE ✚
BEAUMARIS, ANGLESEY LL58 8AP

www.cadw.wales.gov.uk

Tel: 01248 810361

Owner: In the care of Cadw   **Contact:** The Custodian

The most technically perfect medieval castle in Britain, standing midway between Caernarfon and Conwy, commanding the old ferry crossing to Anglesey. A World Heritage Listed Site.

Location: OS Ref. SH608 762. 5m NE of Menai Bridge (A5) by A545. 7m from Bangor.

Open: 1 Apr - 31 May & Oct: daily, 9.30am - 5pm. 1 Jun - 30 Sept: daily, 9.30am - 6pm. 1 Nov - 31 Mar: Mon - Sat, 9.30am - 4pm, Suns 11am - 4pm.

Admission: Adult £3, Child (under 16 yrs)/Conc. £2.50, Child under 5yrs free, Family (2+3) £8.50. (Prices subject to review Mar 2005).

🅾️ ♿ 🎫 🅿️ 🦮 Guide dogs only. ❄️

BODELWYDDAN CASTLE
Bodelwyddan, Denbighshire LL18 5YA

Tel: 01745 584060 **Fax:** 01745 584563 **e-mail:** enquiries@bodelwyddan-castle.co.uk
www.bodelwyddan-castle.co.uk

Owner: Bodelwyddan Castle Trust   **Contact:** Kevin Mason

Set within 200 acres of historical parkland, Bodelwyddan Castle is the Welsh home of the National Portrait Gallery, displaying works from its 19th century collection. Complementary collection of sculpture and furniture in a period setting. Victorian games gallery. Temporary exhibitions and events.

Location: OS Ref. SH999 749. Follow signs off A55 expressway. 2m W of St Asaph, opposite Marble Church.

Open: Easter - end Oct: daily except Fri: 10.30am - 5pm. Winter: Sats & Suns, 10.30am - 4pm.

Admission: Adult £4.50, Child (5-16yrs) £2 (under 5yrs free), Conc. £4, Family (2+2) £12. Discounts for schools, groups & disabled. Season ticket available.

🅾️ 🍴 ♿ Partial. WCs. ♿ 🎫 By arrangement. 🏠 Free. 🅿️ ♿ 🦮 Guide dogs only. ❄️ 🔺
📺 Tel for details.

BODNANT GARDEN ❧
Tal-y-Cafn, Colwyn Bay LL28 5RE

Tel: 01492 650460 **Fax:** 01492 650448 **e-mail:** office@bodnantgarden.co.uk
www.bodnantgarden.co.uk

Owner: The National Trust

Bodnant Garden is one of the finest gardens in the country not only for its magnificent collections of rhododendrons, camellias and magnolias but also for its idyllic setting above the River Conwy with extensive views of the Snowdonia range. Visit in early Spring and be rewarded by the sight of masses of golden daffodils and other spring bulbs, as well as the beautiful blooms of the magnolias, camellias and flowering cherries. The spectacular rhododendrons and azaleas will delight from mid-April until late May, whilst the famous original Laburnum Arch is an overwhelming mass of yellow bloom from mid-May to mid-June. The herbaceous borders, roses, hydrangeas, clematis and water lilies flower from the middle of June until September. This 32-ha garden has many interesting features including the Lily Terrace, pergola, Canal Terrace, Pin Mill and the Dell Garden.

Location: OS Ref. SH801 723. 8 miles S of Llandudno and Colwyn Bay, off A470. Signposted from A55, exit at Junction 19.

Open: 12 Mar - 30 Oct: daily, 10am - 5pm (Tearoom from 11am).

Admission: Adult £5.50, Child £2.75. Groups (20+) £5. RHS members free.

🅾️ 🍴 ♿ Partial. WCs. 🅿️ 🦮 Guide dogs only.

BODRHYDDAN 🏠
Rhuddlan, Clwyd LL18 5SB

Tel: 01745 590414 **Fax:** 01745 590155 **e-mail:** bodrhyddan@hotmail.com
www.bodrhyddan.co.uk

Owner/Contact: Colonel The Lord Langford OBE DL

The home of Lord Langford and his family, Bodrhyddan is basically a 17th century house with 19th century additions by the famous architect, William Eden Nesfield, although traces of an earlier building exist. The house has been in the hands of the same family since it was built over 500 years ago. There are notable pieces of armour, pictures, period furniture, a 3,000 year old mummy, a formal parterre, a woodland garden and attractive picnic areas. Bodrhyddan is a Grade I listing, making it one of few in Wales to remain in private hands.

Location: OS Ref. SJ045 788. On the A5151 midway between Dyserth and Rhuddlan, 4m SE of Rhyl.

Open: Jun - Sept inclusive: Tues & Thurs, 2 - 5.30pm.

Admission: House & Gardens: Adult £4, Child £2. Gardens only: Adult £2, Child £1.

♿ Partial. ♿ 🎫 Obligatory. 🅿️

BRYN BRAS CASTLE
LLANRUG, CAERNARFON, GWYNEDD LL55 4RE

www.brynbrascastle.co.uk

Tel/Fax: 01286 870210 **e-mail:** holidays@brynbrascastle.co.uk

Owner: Mr & Mrs N E Gray-Parry   **Contact:** Marita Gray-Parry

Built in the Neo-Romanesque style in c1830, on an earlier structure, and probably designed by Thomas Hopper, it stands in the Snowdonian Range. The tranquil garden includes a hill-walk with fine views of Mt Snowdon, Anglesey and the sea. Bryn Bras, a much loved home, offers a delightful selection of apartments for holidays for twos within the Grade II* listed castle. Many local restaurants, inns.

Location: OS Ref. SH543 625. $^1/_2$ m off A4086 at Llanrug, $4^1/_2$ m E of Caernarfon.

Open: Only by appointment.

Admission: By arrangement. No young children please.

🛏️ 🏠 Self-catering Apartments for twos within castle. ❄️

CADW: Welsh Historic Monuments. Crown copyright

CADW: Welsh Historic Monuments. Crown copyright

CAERNARFON CASTLE ✠

CASTLE DITCH, CAERNARFON LL55 2AY

www.cadw.wales.gov.uk

Tel: 01286 677617

Owner: In the care of Cadw　　　　　　**Contact:** The Custodian

The most famous, and perhaps the most impressive castle in Wales. Taking nearly 50 years to build, it proved the costliest of Edward I's castles. A World Heritage Listed Site.

Location: OS Ref. SH477 626. In Caernarfon, just W of town centre.

Open: 1 Apr - 31 May & Oct: daily, 9.30am - 5pm. 1 Jun - 30 Sept: daily, 9.30am - 6pm. 1 Nov - 31 Mar: Mon - Sat, 9.30am - 4pm, Suns 11am - 4pm.

Admission: Adult £4.50, Child (under 16 yrs)/Conc. £3.50, Child under 5yrs free, Family (2+3) £12.50. (Prices subject to review Mar 2005.)

🔲 🅿 ⛟ Guide dogs only. ✳

NT Photographic Library / Matthew Antrobus

CHIRK CASTLE ✤

CHIRK LL14 5AF

Tel: 01691 777701　**Fax:** 01691 774706　**e-mail:** chirkcastle@nationaltrust.org.uk

Owner: The National Trust

700 year old Chirk Castle, a magnificent marcher fortress, commands fine views over the surrounding countryside. Rectangular with a massive drum tower at each corner, the castle has beautiful formal gardens with clipped yews, roses and a variety of flowering shrubs. Voted best National Trust garden in 1999. The dramatic dungeon is a reminder of the castle's turbulent history, whilst later occupants have left elegant state rooms, furniture, tapestries and portraits. The castle was sold for five thousand pounds to Sir Thomas Myddelton in 1595, and his descendants continue to live in part of the castle today.

Location: OS Ref. SJ275 388. 8m S of Wrexham off A483, 2m from Chirk village.

Open: Castle & Shop: 18 Mar - 30 Oct, Wed - Sun & BH Mons, 12 noon - 5pm (4pm in Oct), last admission 1/2 hr before closing. Garden: as Castle, 11am - 6pm (5pm in Oct), last admission 1hr before closing. Tearoom: as Castle, 11am - 5pm (4pm in Oct).

Admission: Adult £6.40, Child £3.20, Family £15.80. Pre-booked groups (15+): Adult £5, Child £2.50. Garden only: Adults £4, Child £2, Family £10. Pre-booked groups: Adult £3.20, Child £1.60.

ℹ No indoor photography. 🔲 🅲 🔽 ▣ Licensed. 🅵 By arrangement. 🅿 🔲 ⛟ Guide dogs only. 🔺 ▽ Tel for details.

COCHWILLAN OLD HALL

Talybont, Bangor, Gwynedd LL57 3AZ

Tel: 01248 355853

Owner: R C H Douglas Pennant　　　　**Contact:** Miss M D Monteith

A fine example of medieval architecture with the present house dating from about 1450. It was probably built by William Gryffydd who fought for Henry VII at Bosworth. Once owned in the 17th century by John Williams who became Archbishop of York. The house was restored from a barn in 1971.

Location: OS Ref. SH606 695. 3¹/₂ m SE of Bangor. 1m SE of Talybont off A55.

Open: By appointment.

Admission: Please telephone for details.

✳

Cadw: Welsh Historic Monuments. Crown Copyright

CONWY CASTLE ✠

CONWY LL32 8AY

www.cadw.wales.gov.uk

Tel: 01492 592358

Owner: In the care of Cadw　　　　　**Contact:** The Custodian

Taken together the castle and town walls are the most impressive of the fortresses built by Edward I, and remain the finest and most impressive in Britain. A World Heritage Listed Site.

Location: OS Ref. SH783 774. Conwy by A55 or B5106.

Open: 1 Apr - 31 May & Oct: daily, 9.30am - 5pm. 1 Jun - 30 Sept: daily, 9.30am - 6pm. 1 Nov - 31 Mar: Mon - Sat, 9.30am - 4pm, Suns 11am - 4pm.

Admission: Adult £3.75, Child (under 16yrs)/Conc. £3.25, Child under 5yrs free, Family (2+3) £10.75. Joint ticket for entry to Conwy Castle and Plas Mawr: Adult £6.50, Conc. £5.50, Family (2+3) £18.50. (Prices subject to review Mar 2005.)

🔲 🅵 By arrangement. 🅿 ⛟ Guide dogs only. ✳

CRICCIETH CASTLE ✠

Castle Street, Criccieth, Gwynedd LL52 0DP

Tel: 01766 522227　**www**.cadw.wales.gov.uk

Owner: In the care of Cadw　　　　　**Contact:** The Custodian

Overlooking Cardigan Bay, Criccieth Castle is the most striking of the fortresses built by the native Welsh Princes. Its inner defences are dominated by a powerful twin-towered gatehouse.

Location: OS Ref. SH500 378. A497 to Criccieth from Porthmadog or Pwllheli.

Open: 1 Apr - 31 May & Oct : daily, 10am - 5pm. 1 June - 30 Sept: daily, 10am - 6pm. (Nov - Mar open daily. Site staffed Fri + Sat 9.30am - 4pm, Sun 11am - 4pm.)

Admission: Adult £2.75, Child (under 16yrs)/Conc. £2.25, Child under 5yrs free, Family (2+3) £7.75. (Prices subject to review Mar 2005.)

🔲 🅿 ⛟ Guide dogs only. ✳

DENBIGH CASTLE ♣

Denbigh, Clwyd

Tel: 01745 813385   www.cadw.wales.gov.uk

Owner: In the care of Cadw   **Contact:** The Custodian

Crowning the summit of a prominent outcrop dominating the Vale of Clwyd, the principal feature of this spectacular site is the great gatehouse dating back to the 11th century. Some of the walls can still be walked by visitors.

Location: OS Ref. SJ052 658. Denbigh via A525, A543 or B5382.

Open: 1 Apr - 30 Sept: Mon - Fri, 10am - 5.30pm, Sats & Suns, 9.30am - 5.30pm. (Open and unstaffed at all other times with no admission charge.)

Admission: Castle: Adult £2.50, Child (under 16yrs)/Conc. £2, Child under 5 yrs free, Family (2+3) £7. (Prices subject to review Mar 2005.)

⬚ 🅿 ♿ Guide dogs only. ❋

DOLBELYDR

Trefnant, Denbighshire LL16 5AG

Tel: 01628 825925   www.landmarktrust.org.uk

Owner/Contact: The Landmark Trust

A 16th century, Grade II* listed building, a fine example of a 16th century gentry house and has good claim to be the birthplace of the modern Welsh language. It was at Dolbelydr that Henry Salesbury wrote his *Grammatica Britannica*. Dolbelydr is cared for by The Landmark Trust, a building preservation charity who let it for holidays. Full details of Dolbelydr and 178 other historic and architecturally important buildings are featured in the Landmark Trust Handbook (£9.50 refundable against a booking).

Location: OS Ref. SJ031 709.

Open: Available for holidays for max 6 people throughout the year. Open Days on 8 days throughout the year. Contact the Landmark Trust for details.

Admission: Free on Open Days.

🖼 ❋

DOLWYDDELAN CASTLE ♣

Blaenau Ffestiniog, Gwynedd

Tel: 01690 750366   www.cadw.wales.gov.uk

Owner: In the care of Cadw   **Contact:** The Custodian

Standing proudly on a ridge, this stern building remains remarkably intact and visitors cannot fail to be impressed with the great solitary square tower, built by Llewelyn the Great in the early 13th century.

Location: OS Ref. SH722 522. A470(T) Blaenau Ffestiniog to Betws-y-Coed, 1m W of Dolwyddelan.

Open: All Year: Mon - Sat, 9.30am - 6.30pm (4pm, 1 Oct - 31 Mar). Suns 11am - 4pm.

Admission: Adult £2, Child (under 16yrs)/Conc. £1.50, Child under 5 yrs free, Family (2+3) £5.50. (Subject to review Mar 2005).

🅿 ♿ Guide dogs only. ❋

ERDDIG ✿

Nr Wrexham LL13 0YT

Tel: 01978 355314   **Fax:** 01978 313333   **Info Line:** 01978 315151

Owner: The National Trust

One of the most fascinating houses in Britain, not least because of the unusually close relationship that existed between the family of the house and their servants. The beautiful and evocative range of outbuildings includes kitchen, laundry, bakehouse, stables, sawmill, smithy and joiner's shop, while the stunning state rooms display most of their original 18th & 19th century furniture and furnishings, including some exquisite Chinese wallpaper. The large walled garden has been restored to its 18th century formal design with Victorian parterre and yew walk, and also contains the National Ivy Collection. There is an extensive park with woodland walks.

Location: OS Ref. SJ326 482. 2m S of Wrexham.

Open: House: 19 Mar - 28 Sept & Oct: Sat - Wed, 12 noon - 5pm (Oct closes 4pm). Garden: 19 Mar - 29 Jun & 3 - 28 Sept: Sat - Wed, 11am - 6pm; 2 Jul - 31 Aug: Sat - Wed, 10am - 6pm; Oct: Sat - Wed, 11am - 5pm; 5 Nov - 18 Dec: Sats & Suns, 11am - 4pm.

Admission: All-inclusive ticket: Adult £7.40, Child £3.70, Family (2+3) £18.40. Pre-booked group (15+) £6, Child £3. Garden: Adult £3.80, Child £1.90, Family £9.60. Groups, Adult £3, Child £1.50. NT members Free.

⬚ ⓕ ♿ Partial. WCs. 🍴 Licensed. 📷 AV presentation. 🅿 🔲 ♿ Guide dogs only.

FFERM

Pontblyddyn, Mold, Flintshire

Tel/Fax: 01352 770217

Owner/Contact: Dr M Jones-Mortimer

17th century farmhouse. Viewing is limited to 7 persons at any one time. Prior booking is recommended. No toilets or refreshments.

Location: OS Ref. SJ279 603. Access from A541 in Pontblyddyn, 3½ m SE of Mold.

Open: 2nd Wed in every month, 2 - 5pm. Pre-booking is recommended.

Admission: £4.

🔲 ❋

GWYDIR CASTLE

LLANRWST, GWYNEDD LL26 0PN

www.gwydircastle.co.uk

Tel/Fax: 01492 641687   **e-mail:** info@gwydircastle.co.uk

Owner/Contact: Mr & Mrs Welford

Gwydir Castle is situated in the beautiful Conwy Valley and is set within a Grade 1 listed, 10 acre garden. Built by the illustrious Wynn family c1500, Gwydir is a fine example of a Tudor courtyard house, incorporating re-used medieval material from the dissolved Abbey of Maenan. Further additions date from c1600 and c1826. The important 1640s panelled Dining Room has now been reinstated, following its repatriation from the New York Metropolitan Museum.

Location: OS Ref. SH795 610. ½ m W of Llanrwst on B5106.

Open: 1 Mar - 31 Oct: daily, 10am - 4.30pm. Limited openings at other times. Occasional weddings on Sats.

Admission: Adult £3.50, Child £1.50. Group discount 10%.

ⓣ ♿ Partial. 🍴 By arrangement. ⓕ By arrangement. 🅿 🔲 🛏 2 doubles. 🔲

GYRN CASTLE

Llanasa, Holywell, Flintshire CH8 9BG

Tel/Fax: 01745 853500

Owner/Contact: Sir Geoffrey Bates BT

Dating, in part, from 1700, castellated 1820. Large picture gallery, panelled entrance hall. Pleasant woodland walks and fantastic views to the River Mersey and the Lake District.

Location: OS Ref. SJ111 815. 26m W of Chester, off A55, 4½ m SE of Prestatyn.

Open: All year by appointment.

Admission: £4. Discount for groups.

♿ Grounds. 🍴 By arrangement. ⓕ Obligatory. 🅿 Limited for coaches. 🐕 On leads. ❋

🎭 Special Events Index see page 24

CADW: Welsh Historic Monuments. Crown copyright

HARLECH CASTLE ✠

HARLECH LL46 2YH

www.cadw.wales.gov.uk

Tel: 01766 780552

Owner: In the care of Cadw   **Contact:** The Custodian

Set on a towering rock above Tremadog Bay, this seemingly impregnable fortress is the most dramatically sited of all the castles of Edward I. A World Heritage Listed Site.

Location: OS Ref. SH581 312. Harlech, Gwynedd on A496 coast road.

Open: 1 Apr - 31 May & Oct: daily, 9.30am - 5pm. 1 Jun - 30 Sept: daily, 9.30am - 6pm. 1 Nov - 31 Mar: Mon - Sat, 9.30am - 4pm, Suns 11am - 4pm.

Admission: Adult £3, Child (under 16yrs)/Conc. £2.50, Child under 5 yrs free, Family (2+3) £8.50. (Prices subject to review Mar 2005.)

🔲 🅿 🔲 Guide dogs only. ✽

HARTSHEATH

Pontblyddyn, Mold, Flintshire

Tel/Fax: 01352 770217

Owner/Contact: Dr M Jones-Mortimer

18th and 19th century house set in parkland. Viewing is limited to 7 persons at any one time. Prior booking is recommended. No toilets or refreshments.

Location: OS Ref. SJ287 602. Access from A5104, 3½ m SE of Mold between Pontblyddyn and Penyffordd.

Open: 1st, 3rd & 5th Wed in every month, 2 - 5pm.

Admission: £4.

🔲 ✽

ISCOYD PARK

Nr Whitchurch, Shropshire SY13 3AT

Owner/Contact: Mr P C Godsal

18th century Grade II* listed redbrick house in park.

Location: OS Ref. SJ504 421. 2m W of Whitchurch on A525.

Open: By written appointment only.

🔲 ✽

PENRHYN CASTLE 🦌

Bangor LL57 4HN

Tel: 01248 353084   **Infoline:** 01248 371337   **Fax:** 01248 371281

Owner: The National Trust

This dramatic neo-Norman fantasy castle sits between Snowdonia and the Menai Strait. Built by Thomas Hopper between 1820 and 1845 for the wealthy Pennant family, who made their fortune from Jamaican sugar and Welsh slate. The castle is crammed with fascinating things such as a 1-ton slate bed made for Queen Victoria.

Location: OS Ref. SH602 720. 1m E of Bangor, at Llandygai (J11, A55).

Open: Castle: 23 Mar - 30 Jun & 1 Sept - 2 Oct, daily (except Tues), 12 noon - 5pm; July - Aug, daily (except Tues), 11am - 5pm; Grounds, Shop & Tearoom: 23 Mar - 30 Jun & Sept - Oct: 11am - 5pm; Jul - Aug: daily except Tues, 10am - 5pm. Stableblock, Museums & Galleries as Grounds, Shop & Tearoom.

Admission: Adult £7, Child £3.50, Family (2+2) £17.50. Pre-booked groups (15+) £5.50. Garden & Stableblock Exhibitions only: Adult £5, Child £2.50. Audio tour: £1 (including NT members). NT members Free.

🔲 ▣ Licensed. 🔲 🔲 🔲 Guide dogs only. ▣

PLAS BRONDANW GARDENS 🏛

Plas Brondanw, Llanfrothen, Gwynedd LL48 6SW

Tel: 01743 239236

Owner: Trustees of the Second Portmeirion Foundation.

Italianate gardens with topiary.

Location: OS Ref. SH618 423. 3m N of Penrhyndeudraeth off A4085, on Croesor Road.

Open: All year: daily, 9am - 5pm. Coaches accepted, please book.

Admission: Adult £3, Subsequent adult £2pp, Child Free if accompanied by an adult.

Cadw: Welsh Historic Monuments. Crown Copyright

PLAS MAWR ✠

HIGH STREET, CONWY LL32 8EF

www.cadw.wales.gov.uk

Tel: 01492 580167

Owner: In the care of Cadw   **Contact:** The Custodian

The best preserved Elizabethan town house in Britain, the house reflects the status of its builder Robert Wynn. A fascinating and unique place allowing visitors to sample the lives of the Tudor gentry and their servants, Plas Mawr is famous for the quality and quantity of its decorative plasterwork.

Location: OS Ref. SH781 776. Conwy by A55 or B5106 or A547.

Open: 1 Apr - 31 May, Sept & Oct: Tues - Suns & BH Mons, 9.30am - 5pm (4pm in Oct). 1 Jun - 31 Aug: Tues - Suns & BH Mons, 9.30am - 6pm.

Admission: Adult £4.50, Child (under 16yrs)/Conc. £3.50, Child under 5yrs free, Family (2+3) £12.50. Joint ticket for entry to Conwy Castle and Plas Mawr: Adult £6.50, Conc. £5.50, Family (2+3) £18.50. (Prices subject to review Mar 2005.)

🔲 🅿 Limited. 🔲 🔲 Guide dogs only.

©The Landmark Trust

Dolbelydr.

North Wales

National Trust Photographic Library / Nick Meers

PLAS NEWYDD ✻
LLANFAIRPWLL, ANGLESEY LL61 6DQ

Tel: 01248 714795 **Infoline:** 01248 715272 **Fax:** 01248 713673

Owner: The National Trust

Set amidst breathtaking beautiful scenery and with spectacular views of Snowdonia. Fine spring garden and Australasian arboretum with an understorey of shrubs and wildflowers. Summer terrace, and, later, massed hydrangeas and Autumn colour. A woodland walk gives access to a marine walk on the Menai Strait. Rhododendron garden open April - early June only. Elegant 18th century house by James Wyatt, famous for its association with Rex Whistler whose largest painting is here. Military museum contains relics of 1st Marquess of Anglesey and Battle of Waterloo. A historic cruise, a boat trip on the Menai Strait operates from the property weather and tides permitting (additional charge). 5 seater buggy to rhododendron garden and woodland walk.

Location: OS Ref. SH521 696. 2m S of Llanfairpwll and A5.

Open: 19 Mar - 2 Nov: Sat - Wed & Good Fri. House: 12 noon - 5pm. Garden: 11am - 5.30pm. Last admission 4.30pm. Shop & Tearoom: daily except Thurs & Fri, 10.30am - 5.30pm (11am - 4pm from 5 Nov - 18 Dec). Walks as garden.

Admission: House & Garden: Adult £5, Child £2.50 (under 5yrs free), Family (2+3) £12. Groups (15+) £4.50. Garden only: Adult £3, Child £1.50. NT members Free.

🛈 No indoor photography. 🅿 Partial. WCs. Minibus from car park to house. 🍽 Licensed. 🎫 By arrangement. 🅿 ♿ Guide dogs only. 🛏 Tel for details.

NTPL/Andrew Butler

POWIS CASTLE & GARDEN ✻
Nr WELSHPOOL SY21 8RF

Tel: 01938 551929 **Infoline:** 01938 551944 **Fax:** 01938 554336

e-mail: powiscastle@nationaltrust.org.uk

Owner: The National Trust   **Contact:** Visitor Services Manager

The world-famous garden, overhung with enormous clipped yew trees, shelters rare and tender plants in colourful herbaceous borders. Laid out under the influence of Italian and French styles, the garden retains its original lead statues and, an orangery on the terraces. Perched on a rock above the garden terraces, the medieval castle contains one of the finest collections of paintings and furniture in Wales.

Location: OS Ref. SJ216 064. 1m W of Welshpool, car access on A483.

Open: Castle & Museum: 21 Mar - 30 Oct: Thur - Mon, 1 - 5pm (4pm 7 - 28 Apr & 5 Sept - 30 Oct). Coach House: 21 Mar - 30 Oct: Thur - Mon, 11am - 5pm (4pm, 7 - 28 Apr & 5 Sept - 30 Oct). Garden: 21 Mar - 30 Oct: Thur - Mon, 11am - 6pm (5.30pm, 7 - 28 Apr & 5 Sept - 30 Oct). Shop & Restaurant: 21 Mar - 30 Oct: Thur - Mon, 11am - 5.30pm (5pm, 7 - 28 Apr & 5 Sept - 30 Oct). Last entry 45 mins before closing.

Admission: Castle & Garden: Adult £8.80, Child £4.40, Family (2+3) £22. Groups (15+ booked): £7.80. Garden only: Adult £6.20, Child £3.10, Family (2+3) £15.20. Groups (15+ booked): £5.20. No groups rates on Suns or BHs. NT members & under 5s Free.

🛈 No indoor photography. 🅿 ♿ Partial. 🍽 Licensed. 🎫 By arrangement. 🅿 Limited for coaches. ♿ Guide dogs only.

PLAS YN RHIW ✻
Rhiw, Pwllheli LL53 8AB

Tel/Fax: 01758 780219

Owner: The National Trust

A small manor house, with garden and woodlands, overlooking the west shore of Porth Neigwl (Hell's Mouth Bay) on the Llyn Peninsula. The house is part medieval, with Tudor and Georgian additions, and the ornamental gardens have flowering trees and shrubs, divided by box hedges and grass paths, rising behind to the snowdrop wood.

Location: OS Ref. SH237 282. 16m SW of Pwllheli, 3m S of the B4413 to Aberdaron. No access for coaches.

Open: 18 Mar - 30 May: Thur - Mon; 1 Jun - 30 Sept: daily except Tues 12 noon - 5pm.; 1 - 23 Oct: Sats & Suns; 24 - 30 Oct: daily, 12 noon - 4pm (last entry 4.30pm).

Admission: Adult £3.40, Child £1.70, Family (2+3) £8.50. Groups: £2.80, Child £1.40. Gardens only: Adult £2.20, Child £1.10, Family (2+3) £5.50. Groups £1.70.

🅿 🎫 ♿ Partial. WCs. 🎫 By arrangement. 🅿 Limited. ♿ Guide dogs only.

PORTMEIRION
Portmeirion, Gwynedd LL48 6ET

Tel: 01766 770000 **Fax:** 01766 771331 **e-mail:** info@portmeirion-village.com

Owner: The Portmeirion Foundation   **Contact:** Mr R Llywelyn

Built by Clough Williams-Ellis as an 'unashamedly romantic' village resort.

Location: OS Ref. SH590 371. Off A487 at Minffordd between Penrhyndeudraeth and Porthmadog.

Open: All year: daily, 9.30am - 5.30pm. Closed 25 Dec.

Admission: Adult £6, Child £3, OAP £5, Family (2+2) £14.40.

RHUDDLAN CASTLE ✤
Castle Gate, Castle Street, Rhuddlan LL18 5AD

Tel: 01745 590777   www.cadw.wales.gov.uk

Owner: In the care of Cadw   **Contact:** The Custodian

Guarding the ancient ford of the River Clwyd, Rhuddlan was the strongest of Edward I's castles in North-East Wales. Linked to the sea by an astonishing deep water channel nearly 3 miles long, it still proclaims the innovative genius of its architect.

Location: OS Ref. SJ025 779. SW end of Rhuddlan via A525 or A547.

Open: 1 Apr - 30 Sept: daily, 10am - 5pm. Closed at all other times.

Admission: Adult £2.75, Child (under 16yrs)/Conc. £2.25, Child under 5 yrs free, Family (2+3) £7.75. (Prices subject to review Mar 2005.)

🅿 🅿 ♿ Guide dogs only.

RUG CHAPEL & LLANGAR CHURCH ✤
c/o Coronation Cottage, Rug, Corwen LL21 9BT

Tel: 01490 412025   www.cadw.wales.gov.uk

Owner: In the care of Cadw   **Contact:** The Custodian

Prettily set in a wooded landscape, Rug Chapel's exterior gives little hint of the wonders within. Nearby the attractive medieval Llangar Church still retains its charming early Georgian furnishings.

Location: Rug Chapel: OS Ref. SJ065 439. Off A494, 1m N of Corwen. Llangar Church: OS Ref. SJ064 423. Off B4401, 1m S of Corwen (obtain key at Rug).

Open: **Rug** – 1 Apr - 30 Sept: Wed - Sun (but open BH Mons & Tues), 10am - 5pm.

Llangar – 1 Apr - 30 Sept: Wed - Sun (but open BH Mons & Tues). Access is arranged daily at 2pm through Custodian at Rug Chapel; please telephone 01490 412025 for details.

Admission: Adult £2.50, Child (under 16yrs)/Conc. £2, Child under 5 yrs free, Family (2+3) £7. (Prices subject to review Mar 2005.)

🅿 ♿ Guide dogs only.

RUTHIN CASTLE

CASTLE STREET, RUTHIN, DENBIGHSHIRE LL15 2NU

www.ruthincastle.co.uk

Tel: 01824 702664 **Fax:** 01824 705978 **e-mail:** reservations@ruthincastle.co.uk

Owner: Ruthin Castle Limited

Set in 38 acres of gardens, amid the ruins and dungeons of the original Castle built in 1282, the Castle is now run as an hotel and, as such, open to visitors. It is a leading wedding venue with wonderful photographic opportunities and famed for its Mediaeval Banquets. Many of the 65 bedrooms are exceptionally large, with four-poster beds.

Location: OS Ref. SJ127 575. Just off Ruthin town square.

Open: All year: daily.

Admission: Free.

🔄 Partial. ▣Licensed. 🍴Licensed. 🅿Ample. 🐕Guide dogs only. 🏨Double x 63, Single x 2, En-suite x 65. ▲ ✳ €

TỶ MAWR WYBRNANT 🌿

Penmachno, Betws-y-Coed, Conwy LL25 0HJ

Tel: 01690 760213

Owner: The National Trust

Situated in the beautiful and secluded Wybrnant Valley, Tỷ Mawr was the birthplace of Bishop William Morgan, first translator of the entire Bible into Welsh. The house has been restored to its probable 16th-17th century appearance and houses a display of Welsh Bibles. A footpath leads from the house through woodland and the surrounding fields, which are traditionally managed.

Location: OS Ref. SH770 524. From A5 3m S of Betws-y-Coed, take B4406 to Penmachno. House is 2¹/₂ m NW of Penmachno by forest road.

Open: 20 Mar - 30 Sept: Tues - Sun, 12 noon - 5pm (4pm in Oct).

Admission: Adult £2.60, Child £1.30, Family £6.30. Booked groups (15+): Adult £2.10, Child £1. NT members Free.

🔄 Ground floor. 🅿 🐕 Guide dogs only.

VALLE CRUCIS ABBEY ✠

Llangollen, Clwyd

Tel: 01978 860326 **www**.cadw.wales.gov.uk

Owner: In the care of Cadw   **Contact:** The Custodian

Set in a beautiful valley location, Valle Crucis Abbey is the best preserved medieval monastery in North Wales, enhanced by the only surviving monastic fish pond in Wales.

Location: OS Ref. SJ205 442. B5103 from A5, 2m NW of Llangollen, or A542 from Ruthin.

Open: 1 Apr - 30 Sept: daily, 10am - 5pm. Unstaffed with no admission charge at all other times, generally between 10am - 4pm.

Admission: Adult £2, Child (under 16yrs)/Conc. £1.50, Child under 5 yrs free, Family (2+3) £5.50. (Prices subject to review Mar 2005.)

▣ 🅿 🐕 Guide dogs only. ✳

WERN ISAF

Penmaen Park, Llanfairfechan LL33 0RN

Tel: 01248 680437

Owner/Contact: Mrs P J Phillips

This Arts and Crafts house was built in 1900 by the architect H L North as his family home and it contains much of the original furniture and William Morris fabrics. It is situated in a woodland garden and is at its best in the Spring. It has extensive views over the Menai Straits and Conwy Bay. One of the most exceptional houses of its date and style in Wales.

Location: OS Ref. SH685 75. Off A55 midway between Bangor and Conwy.

Open: 16 - 31 Mar: daily except Mons, 1 - 4pm. 14 - 25 Sept: daily, 1 - 4pm. Closed 19 Sept.

Admission: £1

ST ASAPH CATHEDRAL

St Asaph, Denbighshire LL17 0RL

Tel: 01745 583429   **Contact:** Chapter Office

Britain's smallest ancient cathedral founded in 560AD by Kentigern, a religious community enclosed in a 'llan', hence Llanelwy.

Location: OS Ref. SJ039 743. In St Asaph, S of A55.

Open: Summer: 9am - 6pm. Winter: 9am - dusk. Sun services: 8am, 11am, 3.30pm. Morning Prayer: 9am.

TOWER

Nercwys, Mold, Flintshire CH7 4EW

Tel: 01352 700220 **e-mail:** enquiries@towerwales.co.uk **www**.towerwales.co.uk

Owner/Contact: Charles Wynne-Eyton

This Grade I listed building is steeped in Welsh history and bears witness to the continuous warfare of the time. A fascinating place to visit or for overnight stays.

Location: OS Ref. SJ240 620. 1m S of Mold.

Open: 2 - 16 & 20 - 30 May & 26 - 29 Aug: 2 - 4.30pm. Groups welcome at other times by appointment.

Admission: Adult £3, Child £2.

🏨

TREWERN HALL

Trewern, Welshpool, Powys SY21 8DT

Tel: 01938 570243

Owner: Chapman Family   **Contact:** M Chapman

Trewern Hall is a Grade II* listed building standing in the Severn Valley. It has been described as 'one of the most handsome timber-framed houses surviving in the area'. The porch contains a beam inscribed RF1610, though it seems likely that parts of the house are earlier. The property has been in the ownership of the Chapman family since 1918.

Location: OS Ref. SJ269 113. Off A458 Welshpool - Shrewsbury Road, 4m from Welshpool.

Opening: Last week in Apr, 1 - 31 May: Mon - Fri, 2 - 5pm.

Admission: Adult £2, Child/Conc. £1.

🔄 Unsuitable. 🅿Limited. None for coaches. 🐕

Powis Castle.

ABERCAMLAIS
Brecon, Powys LD3 8EY

Tel: 01874 636206   **Fax:** 01874 636964   **e-mail:** info@abercamlais.co.uk
www.abercamlais.co.uk

Owner/Contact: Mrs S Ballance
Splendid Grade II* mansion dating from middle ages, altered extensively in early 18th century with 19th century additions, in extensive grounds beside the river Usk. Still in same family ownership and occupation since medieval times. Exceptional octagonal pigeon house, formerly a privy.

Location: OS Ref. SN965 290. 5m W of Brecon on A40.

Open: Apr - Oct: by appointment.

Admission: Adult £5, Child Free.

ℹ️No photography in house. 🅰️ 🎥Obligatory. 🅿️ ❌

ABERDULAIS FALLS 🌿
Aberdulais, Vale of Neath SA10 8EU

Tel: 01639 636674   **Fax:** 01639 645069

Owner: The National Trust   **Contact:** The Property Warden
For over 300 years this famous waterfall has provided the energy to drive the wheels of industry, from the first manufacture of copper in 1584 to present day remains of the tinplate works. It has also been visited by famous artists such as J M W Turner in 1796. The site today houses a unique hydro-electrical scheme which has been developed to harness the waters of the Dulais river.

Location: OS Ref. SS772 995. On A4109, 3m NE of Neath. 4m from M4/J43, then A465.

Open: 4 Mar - 3 Apr: Fri - Sun, 11am - 4pm. 4 Apr - 30 Oct: Mon - Fri, 10am - 5pm; Sats & Suns & BH Mons, 11am - 6pm. 4 Nov - 18 Dec: Fri - Sun, 11am - 4pm; 19 - 21 Dec: 11am - 4pm.

Admission: Adult £3.20, Child £1.60, Family £8. Groups (15+): Adult £2.40, Child £1.20. Children must be accompanied by an adult.

🖥️ 🍴Light refreshments (summer only). 🅿️Limited. ❌

BLAENAVON IRONWORKS ✤
Nr Brecon Beacons National Park, Blaenavon, Gwent

Tel: 01495 792615   **Winter Bookings:** 01633 648081   **www.**cadw.wales.gov.uk

Owner: In the care of Cadw   **Contact:** The Custodian
The famous ironworks at Blaenavon were a milestone in the history of the Industrial Revolution. Visitors can view much of the ongoing conservation work as well as 'Stack Square' - a rare survival of housing built for pioneer ironworkers. Part of a World Heritage Site.

Location: OS Ref. SO248 092. Via A4043 follow signs to Big Pit Mining Museum and Blaenavon Ironworks. Abergavenny 8m. Pontypool 8m. From car park, cross road, then path to entrance gate.

Open: 5 Apr - 31 Oct: Mon - Fri, 9:30am - 4:30pm. Sats, 10am - 5pm. Suns, 10am - 4.30pm. For other times, telephone Torfaen County Borough Council, 01633 648081.

Admission: Adult £2, Child (under 16 yrs)/Conc. £1.50, Child under 5yrs free, Family (2+3) £5.50. (Prices subject to review March 2005.)

🖥️ 🅰️Partial. 🎥By arrangement. 🅿️ ❌Guide dogs only.

CAE HIR GARDENS
Cae Hir, Cribyn, Lampeter, Cardiganshire SA48 7NG

Tel: 01570 470839

Owner/Contact: Mr W Akkermans
This transformed 19th century smallholding offers a succession of pleasant surprises and shows a quite different approach to gardening.

Location: OS Ref. SN521 520. NW on A482 from Lampeter, after 5m turn S on B4337. Cae Hir is 2m on left.

Open: Daily, excluding Mons (open BH Mons), 1 - 6pm.

Admission: Adult £2.50, Child 50p, OAP £2. Groups: (20+) £2.

ABERGLASNEY GARDENS
LLANGATHEN, CARMARTHENSHIRE SA32 8QH

www.aberglasney.org

Tel/Fax: 01558 668998   **e-mail:** info@aberglasney.org.uk

Owner: Aberglasney Restoration Trust   **Contact:** Booking Department
Aberglasney is one of the most remarkable restoration projects of recent years. When acquired in 1995 the Mansion and grounds were so derelict they were considered by most to be beyond restoration. It was not until the undergrowth was cleared and extensive archaeological surveys undertaken, that the importance of this historical garden was realised. The parapet walkway, dating from 1600, is the only example that survives in the United Kingdom. The nine acre garden is already planted with many rare and unusual plants, giving interest throughout the year. Aberglasney is destined to become one of the most fascinating gardens in the country.

Location: OS Ref. SN581 221. 4m W of Llandeilo. Follow signs from A40.

Open: All year: daily (except Christmas Day). Apr - Sept: 10am - 6pm, last entry 5pm. Oct - Mar: 10.30am - 4pm.

Admission: Adult £6, Child £3, OAP £5. Booked groups (10+): Adult £5.50, Child £3, OAP £4.50.

🖥️ 🍴 🅰️Licensed. 🍴Licensed. 🎥Daily: 11.30am & 2.30pm. 🅿️Limited for coaches. ❌ ❌Guide dogs only. 🔲 ❌

CAERLEON ROMAN BATHS & AMPHITHEATRE ✚
High Street, Caerleon NP6 1AE

Tel: 01633 422518   **www**.cadw.wales.gov.uk

Owner: In the care of Cadw

Caerleon is the most varied and fascinating Roman site in Britain – incorporating fortress and baths, well-preserved amphitheatre and a row of barrack blocks, the only examples currently visible in Europe.

Location: OS Ref. ST340 905. 4m ENE of Newport by B4596 to Caerleon, M4/J25 (westbound), M4/J26 (eastbound).

Open: 1 Apr - 31 Oct: daily, 9.30am - 5pm. 1 Nov - 31 March: Mon - Sat, 9.30am - 5pm, Suns 12 noon - 5pm.

Admission: Adult £2.50, Child (under 16 yrs)/Conc. £2, Child under 5yrs free, Family (2+3) £7. (Prices subject to review March 2005.)

▣ ▣ ▣ Guide dogs only. ✳

CAERPHILLY CASTLE ✚
CAERPHILLY CF8 1JL
www.cadw.wales.gov.uk

Tel: 029 2088 3143

Owner: In the care of Cadw   **Contact:** The Custodian

Often threatened, never taken, this vastly impressive castle is much the biggest in Wales. 'Red Gilbert' de Clare, Anglo-Norman Lord of Glamorgan, flooded a valley to create the 30 acre lake, setting his fortress on 3 artificial islands. Famous for its leaning tower, its fortifications are scarcely rivalled in Europe.

Location: OS Ref. ST156 871. Centre of Caerphilly, A468 from Newport, A470, A469 from Cardiff.

Open: 1 Apr - 31 May & Oct: daily, 9.30am - 5pm. 1 Jun - 30 Sept: daily, 9.30am - 6pm. 1 Nov - 31 Mar: Mon - Sat, 9.30am - 4pm, Suns 11am - 4pm.

Admission: Adult £3, Child (under 16 yrs)/Conc. £2.50, Child under 5yrs free, Family (2+3) £8.50. (Prices subject to review March 2005.)

▣ ▣ ▣ Limited. ▣ Guide dogs only. ▲ ✳

CALDICOT CASTLE & COUNTRY PARK
Church Road, Caldicot, Monmouthshire NP26 4HU

Tel: 01291 420241   **Fax:** 01291 435094

e-mail: caldicotcastle@monmouthshire.gov.uk   **www.**caldicotcastle.co.uk

Owner: Monmouthshire County Council   **Contact:** Castle Development Officer

Caldicot's magnificent castle is set in fifty acres of beautiful parkland. Founded by the Normans, developed in royal hands in the Middle Ages and restored as a Victorian home. Discover the Castle's past with an audio tour. Visitors can relax in tranquil gardens, explore medieval towers, discover children's activities and play giant chess.

Location: OS Ref. ST487 887. From M4 take J23a and B4245 to Caldicot. From M48 take J2 and follow A48 & B4245. Castle signposted on B4245.

Open: Mar - Oct: Daily, 11am - 5pm. Please telephone for winter opening times.

Admission: Adult £3, Child/Conc £1.50. Groups (10 - 100): Adult £2, Child/Conc £1. (2004 prices.)

▣ ▼ ▣ Partial. WCs. ▣ ▣ By arrangement. ▣ ▣
▣ Free for formal educational visits. ▣ In Castle, on leads. ▲ ▣ Tel for details.

CARDIFF CASTLE
Castle Street, Cardiff CF10 3RB

Tel: 029 2087 8100   **Fax:** 029 2023 1417

Owner: City and County of Cardiff   **Contact:** Booking Office

2000 years of history, including Roman Walls, Norman Keep and Victorian interiors.

Location: OS Ref. ST181 765. Cardiff city centre, signposted from M4.

Open: 1 Mar - 30 Oct: daily, 9.30am - 6pm, last entry 5pm. Nov - Feb: daily, 9.30am - 5pm, last entry 4pm. Closed 25/26 Dec & 1 Jan.

Admission: Adult £6, Child/OAP £3.70.

CARMARTHEN CASTLE
Carmarthen, South Wales

Tel: 0126 7224923   **e-mail:** clgriffiths@carmarthenshire.gov.uk

Owner/Contact: The Conservation Department, Carmarthenshire County Council

The fortress, originally founded by Henry I in 1109, witnessed several fierce battles, notably in the 15th century when the Welsh hero Owain Glyndwr burnt the town and took the castle from the English.

Location: OS Ref. SN413 200. In the town centre.

Open: Throughout the year.

Admission: Free (guided tours while archaeologists continue to work at the site).

CARREG CENNEN CASTLE ✚
Tir-y-Castell Farm, Llandeilo

Tel: 01558 822291   **www**.cadw.wales.gov.uk

Owner: In the care of Cadw   **Contact:** The Custodian

Spectacularly crowning a remote crag 300 feet above the River Cennen, the castle is unmatched as a wildly romantic fortress sought out by artists and visitors alike. The climb from Rare Breeds Farm is rewarded by breathtaking views and the chance to explore intriguing caves beneath.

Location: OS Ref. SN668 190. Minor roads from A483(T) to Trapp village. 5m SE of A40 at Llandeilo.

Open: All Year: daily, 9.30am - 6.30pm (dusk, 1 Nov - 31 Mar).

Admission: Adult £3, Child (under 16 yrs)/Conc. £2.50, Child under 5yrs free, Family (2+3) £8.50. (Prices subject to review March 2005.)

▣ ▣ ▣ ▣ ▣ Guide dogs only. ✳

CASTELL COCH ✚
TONGWYNLAIS, CARDIFF CF4 7JS
www.cadw.wales.gov.uk

Tel: 029 2081 0101

Owner: In the care of Cadw   **Contact:** The Custodian

A fairytale castle in the woods, Castell Coch embodies a glorious Victorian dream of the Middle Ages. Designed by William Burges as a country retreat for the 3rd Lord Bute, every room and furnishing is brilliantly eccentric, including paintings of Aesop's fables on the drawing room walls.

Location: OS Ref. ST131 826. M4/J32, A470 then signposted. 5m NW of Cardiff city centre.

Open: Apr - May & Oct: daily, 9.30am - 5pm. 1 June - 30 Sept: daily, 9.30am - 6pm. Nov - Mar: Mon - Sat, 9.30am - 4pm, Suns 11am - 4pm.

Admission: Adult £3, Child (under 16 yrs)/Conc. £2.50, Child under 5yrs free, Family (2+3) £8.50. (Prices subject to review March 2005.)

▣ ▣ Partial. ▣ ▣ ▣ ▣ Guide dogs only. ▲ ✳

CADW: Welsh Historic Monuments. Crown Copyright

CADW: Welsh Historic Monuments. Crown Copyright

CHEPSTOW CASTLE ✠

Chepstow, Gwent

Tel: 01291 624065   www.cadw.wales.gov.uk

Owner: In the care of Cadw   **Contact:** The Custodian

This mighty fortress has guarded the route from England to South Wales for more than nine centuries. So powerful was this castle that it continued in use until 1690, being finally adapted for cannon and musket after an epic Civil War siege. This huge, complex, grandiosely sited castle deserves a lengthy visit.

Location: OS Ref. ST533 941. Chepstow via A466, B4235 or A48. 1½ m N of M48/J22.

Open: 1 Apr - 31 May & Oct: daily, 9.30am - 5pm. 1 Jun - 30 Sept: daily, 9.30am - 6pm. 1 Nov - 31 Mar: Mon - Sat, 9.30am - 4pm, Suns 11am - 4pm.

Admission: Adult £3, Child (under 16 yrs)/Conc. £2.50, Child under 5yrs free, Family (2+3) £8.50. (Prices subject to review March 2005.)

◻ ♿Partial. 🅿 🐕Guide dogs only. ✳

CILGERRAN CASTLE ✠ ❦

Cardigan, Dyfed

Tel: 01239 615007   www.cadw.wales.gov.uk

Owner: In the care of Cadw   **Contact:** The Custodian

Perched high up on a rugged spur above the River Teifi, Cilgerran Castle is one of the most spectacularly sited fortresses in Wales. It dates from the 11th - 13th centuries.

Location: OS Ref. SN195 431. Main roads to Cilgerran from A478 and A484. 3½ m SSE of Cardigan.

Open: All Year: daily, 9.30am - 6.30pm (dusk, 1 Nov - 31 Mar).

Admission: Adult £2.50, Child (under 16 yrs)/Conc. £2, Child under 5yrs free, Child under 5yrs free, Family (2+3) £7. (Prices subject to review March 2005.)

◻ 🅿 🐕Guide dogs only. ✳

CLYNE GARDENS

Mill Lane, Blackpill, Swansea SA3 5BD

Tel: 01792 401737

Owner: City and County of Swansea   **Contact:** Steve Hopkins

50 acre spring garden, large rhododendron collection, 4 national collections, extensive bog garden, native woodland.

Location: OS Ref. SS614 906. S side of Mill Lane, 500yds W of A4067 Mumbles Road, 3m SW of Swansea.

Open: All year.

Admission: Free.

COLBY WOODLAND GARDEN ❦

Amroth, Narbeth, Pembrokeshire SA67 8PP

Tel: 01834 811885   **Fax:** 01834 831766

Owner: The National Trust   **Contact:** The Centre Manager

An attractive woodland garden. Walks through secluded valleys along open woodland pathways.

Location: OS Ref. SN155 080. ½ m inland from Amroth beside Carmarthen Bay. Signs from A477.

Open: 18 Mar - 30 Oct: daily. Woodland Garden: 10am - 5pm; Walled Garden: 11am - 5pm; Shop/Gallery: 10am - 5pm; Tearoom: 10am - 4.30pm. Evenings visits by arrangement.

Admission: Adult £3.60, Child £1.80, Family £9. Groups: Adult £3, Child £1.50.

ℹ Gallery events. ◻ ▣

CORNWALL HOUSE

58 Monnow St, Monmouth NP25 3EN

Tel/Fax: 01600 712031

Owner/Contact: Ms Jane Harvey

Town house, dating back to at least the 17th century. Red brick garden façade in Queen Anne style, dating from 1752. Street façade remodelled in Georgian style (date unknown). Many original features, including fine staircase. Delightful town garden with original walled kitchen garden.

Location: OS Ref. SO506 127. Half way down main shopping street in Monmouth.

Open: 25 - 31 Mar, 1 - 3, 9/10, 16/17, 30 Apr, 1/2 May, 27 - 29 Aug, 10/11 & 17/18 Sept: 2 - 5pm.

Admission: Adult £4, Conc. £2.

♿ Grounds only. 𝑓 Obligatory. 🅿 Public car park nearby. 🐕Guide dogs only. €

CRESSELLY

Kilgetty, Pembrokeshire SA68 0SP

Fax: 01646 687045   **e-mail:** hha@cresselly.org.uk   www.cresselly.org.uk

Owner/Contact: H D R Harrison-Allen Esq MFH

Home of the Allen family for 250 years. The house is of 1770 with matching wings of 1869 and contains good plasterwork and fittings of both periods. The Allens are of particular interest for their close association with the Wedgwood family of Etruria and a long tradition of foxhunting. Grade II listed holiday cottages nearby on river.

Location: OS Ref. SN065 065. W of the A4075.

Open: Mon - Fri only. 2 - 6, 9 - 13, 16 - 20, 23 - 27 May & 6 - 10, 13 - 15 June: 10am - 1pm. Guided tours only, on the hour. Coaches and at other times by arrangement.

Admission: Adult £4, no children under 12.

♿ Ground floor only. 𝑓 Obligatory. 🅿 Coaches by arrangement. ▣ Holiday cottages.

CYFARTHFA CASTLE MUSEUM

Brecon Road, Merthyr Tydfil, Mid Glamorgan CF47 8RE

Tel/Fax: 01685 723112   **e-mail:** cyfarthacastle@fsmail.net

Owner: Merthyr Tydfil County Borough Council   **Contact:** Scott Reid

Castle originates from 1824/1825, now a museum and school.

Location: OS Ref. SO041 074. NE side of A470 to Brecon, ½ m NW of town centre.

Open: 1 Apr - 30 Sept: Mon - Sun, 10am - 5.30pm. Winter: Tue - Fri, 10am - 4pm, Sats & Suns, 12 noon - 4pm. Closed between Christmas and New Year.

Admission: Free.

DINEFWR ❦

Llandeilo SA19 6RT

Tel: 01558 825912   **Fax:** 01558 822036   **e-mail:** gdroff@nationaltrust.org.uk

Owner: The National Trust   **Contact:** The House Manager

Historic site with particular connections to the medieval Princes of Wales.

Location: OS Ref. SN625 225. On outskirts of Llandeilo.

Open: House & Park: 18 Mar - 30 Oct: daily except Tue & Wed, 11am - 5pm. Park open daily during school holidays.

Admission: House & Park: Adult £3.80, Child £1.90, Family £9. Groups (15+): £3. Park only: Adult £2.60, Child £1.30, Family £6. Groups: £2.10.

♿ ▣ 𝑓By arrangement. 🅿Limited for coaches. ▣ 🐕In grounds on leads. ✳

Llanerchaeron.

©National Trust Photographic Library/Andrew Butler

DYFFRYN GARDENS AND ARBORETUM 🏛
ST NICHOLAS, Nr CARDIFF CF5 6SU
www.dyffryngardens.org.uk

Tel: 029 2059 3328   **Fax:** 029 2059 1966

Owner: Vale of Glamorgan Council   **Contact:** Ms G Donovan

Dyffryn Gardens is a beautiful Grade I registered Edwardian garden, set in the heart of the Vale of Glamorgan countryside. The 55-acre gardens are the result of a unique collaboration between the eminent landscape architect, Thomas Mawson, and the passionate plant collector, Reginald Cory. The garden includes great lawns, herbaceous borders, many individual themed garden 'rooms' and a well established Arboretum including 14 champion trees. The gardens are being restored with grant assistance from the Heritage Lottery Fund, with completion of phase one expected in 2005. The gardens remain open throughout the restoration and there is an extensive annual events programme.

Location: OS Ref. ST095 723. 3m NW of Barry, J33/M4. 1¹/₂ m S of St Nicholas on A48.

Open: Easter - Sept: daily, 10am - 6pm. Oct: daily, 10am - 5pm.

Admission: Adult £3.50, Child/Conc. £2.50. Discount available for groups (15+).
🏠 🔳 ♿ 🍴 🎁 🅿 🍽 📷 ⛰ ✳ 🐕 Tel for details.

Skyscan

FONMON CASTLE 🏛
RHOOSE, BARRY, SOUTH GLAMORGAN CF62 3ZN

Tel: 01446 710206   **Fax:** 01446 711687   **e-mail:** sophie@fonmoncastle.fsnet.co.uk

Owner: Sir Brooke Boothby Bt   **Contact:** Sophie Katzi

Occupied as a home since the 13th century, this medieval castle has the most stunning Georgian interiors and is surrounded by extensive gardens. Available for weddings, concerts, corporate entertainment and multi-activity days.

Location: OS Ref. ST047 681. 15m W of Cardiff, 1m W of Cardiff airport.

Open: 1 Apr - 30 Sept: Tues & Weds, 2 - 5pm (last tour 4pm). Other times by appointment. Groups: by appointment.

Admission: Adult £5, Child Free.
ℹ️ Conferences. 🍴 By arrangement (up to 120). ♿ WC. 🅿
🐕 Guide dogs only. ⛰ ✳

Alex Ramsay

THE JUDGE'S LODGING
BROAD STREET, PRESTEIGNE, POWYS LD8 2AD
www.judgeslodging.org.uk

Tel: 01544 260650   **Fax:** 01544 260652   **e-mail:** info@judgeslodging.org.uk

Owner: Powys County Council   **Contact:** Gabrielle Rivers

Explore the fascinating world of the Victorian judges, their servants and felonious guests at this award-winning, totally hands-on historic house. From the stunning restored judge's apartments to the gas lit servants' quarters below. Follow an 'eavesdropping' audio tour featuring actor Robert Hardy. Damp cells, vast courtroom and local history rooms included.

Location: OS Ref. SO314 644. In town centre, off A44 and A4113. Easy reach from Herefordshire and mid-Wales.

Open: 1 Mar - 31 Oct: daily, 10am - 6pm. 1 Nov - 22 Dec: Wed - Sun, 10am - 4pm. Bookings by arrangement accepted all year.

Admission: Adult £4.50, Child £3.50, Conc. £3.95. Groups (10-80): Adult £3.95, Child/Conc. £3.50, Family £13.50.
🏠 🍴 ♿ Partial (access via lift). 🎁 By arrangement. 🎧 🅿 In town. 🛏
🐕 Guide dogs only. ✳

KIDWELLY CASTLE ♣
Kidwelly, West Glamorgan SA17 5BG

Tel: 01554 890104   **www**.cadw.wales.gov.uk

Owner: In the care of Cadw   **Contact:** The Custodian

A chronicle in stone of medieval fortress technology this strong and splendid castle developed during more than three centuries of Anglo-Welsh warfare. The half-moon shape stems from the original 12th century stockaded fortress, defended by the River Gwendraeth on one side and a deep crescent-shaped ditch on the other.

Location: OS Ref. SN409 070. Kidwelly via A484. Kidwelly Rail Station 1m.

Open: 1 Apr - 31 May & Oct: daily, 9.30am - 5pm. 1 Jun - 30 Sept: daily, 9.30am - 6pm. 1 Nov - 31 Mar: Mon - Sat, 9.30am - 4pm, Suns 11am - 4pm.

Admission: Adult £2.50, Child (under 16 yrs)/Conc. £2, Child under 5yrs free, Family (2+3) £7. (Prices subject to review March 2005.)

▢ ▢ ⓕ By arrangement. ▢ ℙ ☒ Guide dogs only. ✳

KYMIN ⚘
Kymin, Monmouth NP5 3SE

Tel/Fax: 01600 719241   **www**.nationaltrust.org.uk

Owner: The National Trust   **Contact:** The Custodian

Once visited by Nelson and set in 4ha (9acres) of woods and pleasure grounds, this property encompasses a small two-storey circular Georgian banqueting house and naval temple.

Location: OS Ref. SO528 125. 1m E of Monmouth between A466 and A4136.

Open: Round House: 25 Mar - 24 Oct: Sat - Mon, 11am - 4pm. Temple/Grounds: All year.

Admission: House: Adult £2, Child £1, Family £5. Groups (15+): £1.60. Grounds: Free.

☒ Partial. ℙ Limited, no coaches. ☒ Guide dogs only. ✳

LAMPHEY BISHOP'S PALACE ♣
Lamphey, Dyfed

Tel: 01646 672224   **www**.cadw.wales.gov.uk

Owner: In the care of Cadw   **Contact:** The Custodian

Lamphey marks the place of the spectacular Bishop's Palace but it reached its height of greatness under Bishop Henry de Gower who raised the new Great Hall. Today the ruins of this comfortable retreat reflect the power enjoyed by the medieval bishops.

Location: OS Ref. SN018 009. A4139 from Pembroke or Tenby. N of village (A4139).

Open: 1 Apr - 31 Mar: daily, 10am - 5pm. Closed at all other times.

Admission: Adult £2.50, Child (under 16 yrs)/Conc. £2, Child under 5yrs free, Family (2+3) £7. (Prices subject to review March 2005.)

▢ ▢ ℙ ☒ Guide dogs only. ✳

LAUGHARNE CASTLE ♣
King Street, Laugharne SA33 4SA

Tel: 01994 427906   **www**.cadw.wales.gov.uk

Owner: In the care of Cadw   **Contact:** The Custodian

Picturesque Laugharne Castle stands on a low ridge overlooking the wide Taf estuary, one of a string of fortresses controlling the ancient route along the South Wales coast.

Location: OS Ref. SN303 107. 4m S of A48 at St Clears via A4066.

Open: 1 Apr - 30 Sept: daily, 10am - 5pm. Closed at all other times.

Admission: Adult £2.75, Child (under 16 yrs)/Conc. £2.25, Child under 5yrs free, Family (2+3) £7.75. (Prices subject to review March 2005.)

▢ ℙ ☒ Guide dogs only.

LLANCAIACH FAWR MANOR
Nelson, Treharris CF46 6ER

Tel: 01443 412248   **Fax:** 01443 412688

Owner: Caerphilly County Borough Council   **Contact:** The Administrator

Tudor fortified manor dating from 1530 with Stuart additions. Costumed guides.

Location: OS Ref. ST114 967. S side of B4254, 1m N of A472 at Nelson, in the county borough of Caerphilly.

Open: All year: weekdays, 10am - 5pm. weekends, 10am - 6pm. Last admission 1½ hours before closing. Nov - Feb: closed Mons. Closed Christmas week.

Admission: Adult £4.95, Child/Conc. £3.25, Family £13.

LLANERCHAERON ⚘
Aberaeron, Ceredigion SA48 8DG

Tel: 01545 570200   **Infoline:** 01558 825147   **Fax:** 01545 571759

Owner: The National Trust   **Contact:** The Property Manager

A small 18th century Welsh gentry estate which survived virtually unaltered into the 20th century. The house was designed and built by John Nash in 1794-96. Llanerchaeron was a self sufficient estate – evident in the dairy, laundry, brewery and salting house of the service courtyard as well as the home farm buildings from the stables to the threshing barn. Llanerchaeron today is a working organic farm and the two restored walled gardens also produce home grown fruit and herbs. There are extensive walks around the estate and pleasure grounds.

Location: OS Ref. SN480 602. 2½m E of Aberaeron off A482.

Open: 18 Mar - 30 Oct: Wed - Sun & BH Mons. House: 11.30am - 4.30pm. Last entry to house 4pm. Home Farm & Garden: 11am - 5pm. Parkland: All year, daylight hours.

Admission: Adult £5.20, Child £2.60, Family £12.60. Groups (15+): Adult £4.20, Child £2.10. Home Farm & Garden only: Adult £4.20, Child £2.10. Discounted entry when walking, cycling or arriving at the property by public transport. Bike or foot: Adult £4.20, Child £2.10. NT members Free.

⚲ ⬛ ☒ ℙ ☒ ✳

LLANVIHANGEL COURT 🏛
Nr Abergavenny, Monmouthshire NP7 8DH

Tel: 01873 890217   **Fax:** 01873 890380   **www**.llanvihangel-court.co.uk

Owner/Contact: Julia Johnson

A Grade I Tudor Manor. The home in the 17th century of the Arnolds who built the imposing terraces and stone steps leading up to the house. The interior has a fine hall, unusual yew staircase and many 17th century moulded plaster ceilings. Delightful grounds. Includes 17th century features, notably Grade I stables.

Location: OS Ref. SO433 139. 4m N of Abergavenny on A465.

Open: 29 April - 3 May, 27 - 31 May & 15 - 29 Aug: 2.30 - 5.30pm. Last tour 5pm.

Admission: Adult £4, Child/Conc. £2.50.

ⓘ No inside photography. ☒ Partial. ⓕ ℙ Limited. ☒ ▲

MUSEUM OF WELSH LIFE
St Fagans, Cardiff CF5 6XB

Tel: 029 2057 3500   **Fax:** 029 2057 3490

St Fagans Castle, a 16th century building built within the walls of a 13th century castle.

Location: OS Ref. ST118 772. 4m W of city centre, 1½ m N of A48, 2m S of M4/J33. Entrance drive is off A4232 (southbound only).

Open: All year: daily, 10am - 5pm. Closed 24 - 26 Dec & 1 Jan.

Admission: Free.

Judge's Lodging.

Education Index see page 48

THE NATIONAL BOTANIC GARDEN OF WALES

CARMARTHENSHIRE SA32 8HG

www.gardenofwales.org.uk

Tel: 01558 667148   **Fax:** 01558 668933   **e-mail:** info@gardenofwales.org.uk

Owner: The National Botanic Garden of Wales   **Contact:** Helen Edwards

Four years after opening, the first national botanic garden of the new Millennium is blossoming into one of the most beautiful and stimulating gardens in the UK. Created within a 568 acre Regency parkland it is home to a unique and large collection of plants. The centrepiece is the awe inspiring largest single span glasshouse in the world, which houses Mediterranean plants from across the globe. The recently restored double walled garden is a major new feature displaying the family tree of plants. Visitors can also enjoy a large variety of themed outdoor gardens including the award winning Japanese and Apothecaries' Gardens, exhibitions, multi-media theatre, water features, adventure playground, mini-farm, restaurant, shop and plant sales. Further information is available at www.gardenofwales.org.uk

Location: OS159 Ref. SN518 175. $^{1}/_{4}$m from the A48 midway between Crosshands and Carmarthen. Clearly signposted from A48 and Carmarthen. Train & Bus in Carmarthen (7m).

Open: British Summer Time: 10am - 6pm. British Winter Time: 10am - 4.30pm. Closed Christmas Day.

Admission: Adult £7, Child £2, OAP/Students £5, Family (2+4) £16. Groups (10+): Adult £6, Child £1.50, OAP/Student £4.

⬚ ⬚ ⬚ ⬚ Free disability scooter hire, booking advisable. ⬚ Licensed. ⬚ Licensed. ⬚ By arrangement. ⬚ ⬚ ⬚ Guide dogs only. ⬚ ⬚

OXWICH CASTLE ✤

c/o Oxwich Castle Farm, Oxwich SA3 1NG

Tel: 01792 390359   **www**.cadw.wales.gov.uk

Owner: In the care of Cadw   **Contact:** The Custodian

Beautifully sited in the lovely Gower peninsula, Oxwich Castle is a striking testament to the pride and ambitions of the Mansel dynasty of Welsh gentry.

Location: OS159 Ref. SS497 864. A4118, 11m SW of Swansea, in Oxwich village.

Open: 1 Apr - 30 Sept: daily, 10am - 5pm. Closed at all other times.

Admission: Adult £2, Child (under 16 yrs)/Conc. £1.50, Child under 5yrs free, Family (2+3) £5.50. (Prices subject to review March 2005.)

⬚ ⬚ ⬚ Guide dogs only.

LOCAL FOOD

Bara Brith

This is literally translated as 'speckled bread'. Once a week, the stove was lit for baking day and, as the heat began to die down, a handful of currants was added to the last of the bread dough and this speckled bread became a treat. The flavour of this spiced, honey-glazed fruit bread is delicious when spread with salted Welsh butter, and it is no wonder that Bara Brith is still produced all over Wales.

PEMBROKE CASTLE

PEMBROKE SA71 4LA

www.pembrokecastle.co.uk

Tel: 01646 681510   **Fax:** 01646 622260   **e-mail:** pembroke.castle@talk21.com

Owner: Trustees of Pembroke Castle   **Contact:** Mrs A Williams

Pembroke Castle is situated within minutes of beaches and the breathtaking scenery of the Pembrokeshire Coastal National Park. This early Norman fortress, birthplace of the first Tudor King, houses many fascinating displays and exhibitions. Enjoy a picnic in the beautifully kept grounds, or on the roof of St. Anne's Bastion and take in the views along the estuary. Events every weekend in July and August.

Location: OS Ref. SM983 016. W end of the main street in Pembroke.

Open: All year. 1 Apr - Sept: daily, 9.30am - 6pm. Mar & Oct: daily, 10am - 5pm. Nov - Feb: daily, 10am - 4pm. Closed 24 - 26 Dec & 1 Jan. Brass rubbing centre open Summer months and all year by arrangement.

Admission: Adult £3, Child/Conc. £2. Groups (20+): Adult £2.60, OAP/Student £1.70.

⬚ ⬚ ⬚ Easter - Oct. ⬚ End of May - Sept by arrangement. ⬚ ⬚ In grounds on leads. ⬚ ⬚ Tel for details.

PICTON CASTLE

HAVERFORDWEST, PEMBROKESHIRE SA62 4AS

www.pictoncastle.co.uk

Tel/Fax: 01437 751326 **e-mail:** pct@pictoncastle.freeserve.co.uk

Owner: The Picton Castle Trust **Contact:** Mr D Pryse Lloyd

Built in the 13th century by Sir John Wogan, his direct descendants still use the Castle as their family home. The medieval castle was modernised in the 1750s, above the undercroft and extended around 1790 with fine Georgian interiors. The 40 acres of woodland and walled gardens are part of The Royal Horticultural Society access scheme for beautiful gardens. There is a unique collection of rhododendrons and azaleas, mature trees, unusual shrubs, wild flowers, fern walk, fernery, maze, restored dewpond, a herb collection labelled with medicinal remedies and a children's nature trail. The Picton Gallery is used for nationally acclaimed exhibitions. Events include spring and autumn plant sales.

Location: OS Ref. SN011 135. 4m E of Haverfordwest, just off A40.

Open: 1 Apr - 30 Sept: daily except Mon (open BH Mons), 10.30am - 5pm. Entrance to Castle by guided tours only, between 12 noon - 4pm. Oct: Gardens only, daily, 10.30am - dusk.

Admission: Castle, Garden & Gallery: Adult £5.95, Child £2.50, OAP £5.75. Garden & Gallery: Adult £4.95, Child £2.50, OAP £4.75. Groups (20+): reduced prices by prior arrangement.

No indoor photography. Licensed. Obligatory. In grounds, on leads. Tel for details.

RAGLAN CASTLE ✚

Raglan NP5 2BT

Tel: 01291 690228 **www.**cadw.wales.gov.uk

Owner: In the care of Cadw **Contact:** The Custodian

Undoubtedly the finest late medieval fortress-palace in Britain, it was begun in the 1430s by Sir William ap Thomas who built the mighty 'Yellow Tower'. His son William Lord Herbert added a palatial mansion defended by a gatehouse and many towered walls. The high quality is still obvious today.

Location: OS Ref. SO415 084. Raglan, NE of Raglan village off A40 (eastbound) and signposted.

Open: 1 Apr - 31 May & Oct: daily, 9.30am - 5pm. 1 Jun - 30 Sept: daily, 9.30am - 6pm. 1 Nov - 31 Mar: Mon - Sat, 9.30am - 4pm, Suns 11am - 4pm.

Admission: Adult £2.75, Child (under 16 yrs)/Conc. £2.25, Child under 5yrs free, Family (2+3) £7.75. (Prices subject to review March 2005.)

Guide dogs only.

ST DAVIDS BISHOP'S PALACE ✚

St Davids, SA62 6PE

Tel: 01437 720517 **www.**cadw.wales.gov.uk

Owner: In the care of Cadw **Contact:** The Custodian

The city of St Davids boasts not only one of Britain's finest cathedrals but also the most impressive medieval palace in Wales. Built in the elaborate 'decorated' style of gothic architecture, the palace is lavishly encrusted with fine carving.

Location: OS Ref. SM750 254. A487 to St Davids, minor road past the Cathedral.

Open: 1 Apr - 31 May & Oct: daily, 9.30am - 5pm. 1 Jun - 30 Sept: daily, 9.30am - 6pm. 1 Nov - 31 Mar: Mon - Sat, 9.30am - 4pm, Suns 11am - 4pm.

Admission: Adult £2.50, Child (under 16 yrs)/Conc. £2, Child under 5yrs free, Family (2+3) £7. (Prices subject to review March 2005.)

Partial. Guide dogs only.

ST DAVIDS CATHEDRAL

St Davids, Pembs SA62 6QW

Tel: 01437 720691 **Fax:** 01437 721885 **Contact:** Mr R G Tarr

Over eight centuries old. Many unique and 'odd' features.

Location: OS Ref. SM751 254. 5-10mins walk from car/coach parks: signs for pedestrians.

Open: Daily: 7.30am - 6.30pm. Suns: 12.30 - 5.30pm, may be closed for services in progress. Sun services: 8am, 9.30am, 11.15am & 6pm. Weekday services: 8am & 6pm. Weds extra service: 10am.

Admission: Donations. Guided tours (Adult £3, Child £1.20) must be booked.

STRATA FLORIDA ABBEY ✚

Ystrad Meurig, Pontrhydfendigaid SY25 6BT

Tel: 01974 831261 **www.**cadw.wales.gov.uk

Owner: In the care of Cadw **Contact:** The Custodian

Remotely set in the green, kite-haunted Teifi Valley with the lonely Cambrian mountains as a backdrop, the ruined abbey has a wonderful doorway with Celtic spiral motifs and preserves a wealth of beautiful medieval tiles.

Location: OS Ref. SN746 658. Minor road from Pontrhydfendigaid 14m SE of Aberystwyth by the B4340.

Open: 1 Apr - 30 Sept: Wed - Sun, 10am – 5pm. The monument will be open and unstaffed on Mondays and Tuesdays (except BH Mons). Open at all other times generally between 10am - 4pm, but unstaffed and with no admission charge.

Admission: Adult £2.25, Child (under 16 yrs)/Conc. £1.75, Child under 5yrs free, Family (2+3) £6.25. (Prices subject to review March 2005.)

Guide dogs only.

TINTERN ABBEY ✚

Tintern NP6 6SE

Tel: 01291 689251 **www.**cadw.wales.gov.uk

Owner: In the care of Cadw **Contact:** The Custodian

Tintern is the best preserved abbey in Wales and ranks among Britain's most beautiful historic sites. Elaborately decorated in 'gothic' architecture style this church stands almost complete to roof level. Turner sketched and painted here, while Wordsworth drew inspiration from the surroundings.

Location: OS Ref. SO533 000. Tintern via A466, from M4/J23. Chepstow 6m.

Open: 1 Apr - 31 May & Oct: daily, 9.30am - 6pm. 1 Jun - 30 Sept: daily, 9.30am - 6pm. 1 Nov - 31 Mar: Mon - Sat, 9.30am - 4pm, Suns 11am - 4pm.

Admission: Adult £3, Child (under 16 yrs)/Conc. £2.50, Child under 5yrs free, Family (2+3) £8.50. (Prices subject to review March 2005.)

Guide dogs only.

TREBERFYDD

Bwlch, Powys LD3 7PX

Tel: 01874 730205 **e-mail:** david.raikes@btinternet.com

www: treberfydd.net

Owner: David Raikes **Contact:** David Garnons-Williams

Treberfydd is a Victorian country house, built in the Gothic style in 1847 - 50. The house was designed by J L Pearson, and the garden and grounds by W A Nesfield.

Location: From A40 in Bwlch take road to Llangors, after 1/4 m turn left, follow lane for 2m until white gates and Treberfydd sign.

Open: 1 - 29 Aug. Guided tours of the House: 2 & 4pm, telephone or e-mail to secure a place on a tour. Grounds: 2 - 6pm.

Admission: Adult £2.50 (inc. tour), Child (under 12yrs) Free. Grounds: £2.50.

Partial. Obligatory. Limited. None for coaches. On leads, in grounds.

TREBINSHWN

Nr Brecon, Powys LD3 7PX

Tel: 01874 730653 **Fax:** 01874 730843

Owner/Contact: R Watson

16th century mid-sized manor house. Extensively rebuilt 1780. Fine courtyard and walled garden.

Location: OS Ref. SO136 242. 1 1/2m NW of Bwlch.

Open: Easter - 31 Aug: Mon - Tue, 10am - 4.30pm.

Admission: Free.

TREDEGAR HOUSE & PARK 🏛
NEWPORT, SOUTH WALES NP1 9YW

Tel: 01633 815880 **Fax:** 01633 815895 **e-mail:** tredegar.house@newport.gov.uk

Owner: Newport City Council   **Contact:** The Manager

South Wales' finest country house, ancestral home of the Morgan family. Parts of a medieval house remain, but Tredegar owes its reputation to lavish rebuilding in the 17th century. Visitors have a lively and entertaining tour through 30 rooms, including glittering State Rooms and 'below stairs'. Set in 90 acres of parkland with formal gardens. Winner of Best Public Park and Garden in Great Britain 1997. Craft workshops.

Location: OS Ref. ST290 852. M4/J28 signposted. From London 2¹/₂hrs, from Cardiff 20 mins. 2m SW of Newport town centre.

Open: Easter - Sept: Wed - Sun & BHs, 11.30am - 4pm. Evening tours & groups by appointment. Oct - Mar: Groups only by appointment.

Admission: Adult £5.40, Child Free (when accompanied by paying adult), Conc. £3.95. Special discounts for Newport residents. (2004 prices.)

ⓘConferences. No photography in house. 🖻 🔟 🔼Partial. WC. 🖝 🅵Obligatory. 🄿 🔳 ♿In grounds, on leads. ⬛ ⬛ Tel for details.

TREOWEN 🏛
Wonastow, Nr Monmouth NP25 4DL

Tel/Fax: 01600 712031   **e-mail:** john.wheelock@virgin.net   **www**.treowen.co.uk

Owner: R A & J P Wheelock   **Contact:** John Wheelock

Early 17th century mansion built to double pile plan with magnificent well-stair to four storeys.

Location: OS Ref. SO461 111. 3m WSW of Monmouth.

Open: May, Jun Aug & Sept: Fri, 10am - 4pm. Also 7/8, 14/15 & 21/22 May; 17/18 & 24/25 Sept: 2 - 5pm. HHA Friends Free on Fri only.

Admission: £5 (£3 if appointment made). Groups by appointment only.

🔟 🔳Entire house let, self-catering. Sleeps 24+. ⬛

TRETOWER COURT & CASTLE ✪
Tretower, Crickhowell NP8 2RF

Tel: 01874 730279   **www**.cadw.wales.gov.uk

Owner: In the care of Cadw   **Contact:** The Custodian

A fine fortress and an outstanding medieval manor house, Tretower Court and Castle range around a galleried courtyard, now further enhanced by a beautiful recreated medieval garden.

Location: OS Ref. SO187 212. Signposted in Tretower Village, off A479, 3m NW of Crickhowell.

Open: 22 - 31 Mar & Oct: daily, 10am - 4pm (5pm, 1 Apr - 30 Sept). Closed at all other times.

Admission: Adult £2.50, Child (under 16 yrs)/Conc. £2, Child under 5yrs free, Family (2+3) £7. (Prices subject to review March 2005.)

🖻 🖻 🄿 ♿Guide dogs only.

TUDOR MERCHANT'S HOUSE ⚜
QUAY HILL, TENBY SA70 7BX

Tel/Fax: 01834 842279

Owner: The National Trust   **Contact:** The Custodian

A late 15th century town house, characteristic of the building tradition of south west Wales.

Location: OS Ref. SN135 004. Tenby. W of alley from NE corner of town centre square.

Open: 18 Mar - 30 Oct: daily, 10am - 5pm (closed Sats).

Admission: Adult £2.20, Child £1.10, Family £5.50. Groups: Adult £1.80, Child 90p.

ⓘNo indoor photography. 🄿No parking. 🔳 ♿Guide dogs only.

TYTHEGSTON COURT
Tythegston, Bridgend CF32 0NE

e-mail: cknight@tythegston.com   **www**.tythegston.com

Owner/Contact: C Knight

Location: OS Ref. SS857 789. 2m E of Porthcawl on Glamorgan coast.

Open: By written appointment (no telephone calls please).

Admission: Adult £10, Child £2.50, Conc. £5.

🔟 🔼Partial. 🅵Obligatory. 🄿Limited. No coaches. ♿Guide dogs only.

USK CASTLE
Usk, Monmouthshire NP5 1SD

Tel: 01291 672563   **e-mail:** info@uskcastle.co.uk   **www**.uskcastle.com

Owner/Contact: J H L Humphreys

Romantic, ruined castle overlooking the picturesque town of Usk. Inner and outer baileys, towers and earthwork defences. Surrounded by enchanting gardens (open under NGS) incorporating The Castle House, the former medieval gatehouse.

Location: OS Ref. SO376 011. Up narrow lane off Monmouth road in Usk, opposite fire station.

Open: Castle ruins: daily, 11am - 5pm. Groups by appointment. Gardens: private visits welcome & groups by arrangement. House: Jun & BHs: 2 - 5pm (closed 25/26 Jun), small groups & guided tours only.

Admission: Castle ruins: Adult £2, Child Free. Gardens: Adult £2. House: Adult £5, Child £2.

🔟 🔼Partial. 🅵By arrangement. 🔳 🄿No coaches. ♿In grounds, on leads. ✴

WEOBLEY CASTLE ✪
Weobley Castle Farm, Llanrhidian SA3 1HB

Tel: 01792 390012   **www**.cadw.wales.gov.uk

Owner: In the care of Cadw   **Contact:** The Custodian

Perched above the wild northern coast of the beautiful Gower peninsula, Weobley Castle was the home of the Knightly de Bere family. Its rooms include a fine hall and private chamber as well as numerous 'garderobes' or toilets and an early Tudor porch block.

Location: OS Ref. SN477 928. B4271 or B4295 to Llanrhidian Village, then minor road for 1¹/₂ m.

Open: 1 Apr - 31 Oct: daily, 9.30am - 6pm (5pm, Nov - Mar).

Admission: Adult £2, Child (under 16 yrs)/Conc. £1.50, Child under 5yrs free, Family (2+3) £5.50. (Prices subject to review March 2005.)

🖻 🄿 ♿Guide dogs only. ✴

WHITE CASTLE ✪
Llantillio Crossenny, Gwent

Tel: 01600 780380   **www**.cadw.wales.gov.uk

Owner: In the care of Cadw   **Contact:** The Custodian

With its high walls and round towers reflected in the still waters of its moat, White Castle is the ideal medieval fortress. It was rebuilt in the mid-13th century by the future King Edward I to counter a threat from Prince Llywelyn the Last.

Location: OS Ref. SO380 167. By minor road 2m NW from B4233 at A7 Llantilio Crossenny. 8m ENE of Abergavenny.

Open: 1 Apr - 30 Sept: Wed - Sun, 10am - 5pm. The monument will be open and unstaffed on Mondays and Tuesdays (except BH Mons). Open at all other times generally between 10am - 4pm, but unstaffed and with no admission charge.

Admission: Adult £2, Child (under 16 yrs)/Conc. £1.50, Child under 5yrs free, Family (2+3) £5.50. (Prices subject to review March 2005.)

🖻 🄿 ♿Guide dogs only. ✴

LOCAL FOOD

Welsh Cakes

Welsh cakes are traditionally cooked on a griddle. Looking like a cross between a currant scone and a pancake, they are normally eaten cold served with butter and jam but they are much tastier hot from the pan. Slightly different from all other girdle (or griddle) cakes and scones because they are a little firmer. They were originally served to cold, tired and hungry travellers, on their arrival at an inn, while waiting for supper.

White Park Bay , Northern Ireland. ©National Trust Photographic Library/Joe Cornish

northern ireland

Northern Ireland's industrial past centres on its world-famous linen production and on the shipyards of Belfast. The ill-fated 'Titanic' was built here. Today, visitors to the province come largely to enjoy the stunning countryside and what it has to offer.

Fishing (both river and sea) and golf are two of the most popular attractions. The waters of Lough Erne and Lough Neagh – the biggest lake in the British Isles – encourage visiting sailors and the Mourne Mountains are a magnet for walkers and hikers.

There are many heritage properties both in private ownership and owned by the National Trust for Ireland that have fascinating histories. Mount Stewart was once the home of Lord Castlereagh and played host to many prominent political figures. Its magnificent gardens have been nominated as a World Heritage Site. The climate in Northern Ireland has encouraged many outstanding gardens to be created. Visit the oldest maze in Ireland in the 18th century walled garden at Seaforde Gardens.

Mount Stewart, Northern Ireland

Images courtesy of: © NTPL/Joe Cornish

Crom Estate, Northern Ireland

White Park Bay, Northern Ireland ©National Trust Photographic Library/Joe Cornish

Crom Estate, Northern Ireland

NT Photographic Library:/Joe Cornish

Castle Coole, Northern Ireland

©National Trust

northern
ireland

The Argory - West Front ©National Trust Photographic Library/Chris Hill

Mount Stewart - South Front Façade
©National Trust Photographic Library/Mike Williams

Castle Coole - South East Front ©National Trust Photographic Library/Chris Hill

Florence Court - East Front
©National Trust Photographic Library/Chris Hill

northern ireland

green ¦ linen ¦ curiosities

The Argory - Drawing Room
©National Trust Photographic Library/Chris Hill

The Argory -
Captain Shelton's
Bedroom
©National Trust Photographic
Library/Chris Hill

Florence Court
Staircase
©National Trust Photographic Library/Chris Hill

The Argory - Sundial Garden
©National Trust Photographic Library/Mike Williams

Mount Stewart - Main Hall
©National Trust Photographic Library/Chris Hill

Castle Coole - State Bedroom
©National Trust Photographic Library/Chris Hill

Castle Coole - Saloon
©National Trust Photographic Library
Chris Hill

Florence Court - Countess's Bedroom
©National Trust Photographic Library/Chris Hill

Mount Stewart - Italian Garden
©National Trust Photographic Library/Mike Williams

northern ireland

Northern Ireland is home to architectural and natural beauties, to curiosities and marvels, to oddities and spectacles. From 17th century plantation houses to world-renowned gardens there is abundance of National Trust properties of interest for visitors.

Castle Coole was built in the 18th century by James Wyatt overlooking stunning landscaped parkland on the edge of Enniskillen in Co Fermanagh. This neo-classical mansion was designed to inspire and excite and is temple-like in its appearance. There is a splendid Regency interior, with an elaborate state bedroom created for George IV in 1821. Sumptuous interiors are also a feature of Florence Court. This striking mansion, enclosed by rolling parkland and handsome gardens, has stirring views of the Cuilcagh Mountains. Following the reacquisition of many of the belongings of the once-owners, the Earls of Eniskillen, the visitor is greeted with an opulent rococo interior with luxuriant plasterwork adorning ceilings and wall panels. However the house still exerts a sense of lived-in homeliness. Among items returned were original paintings and notable Irish furniture, marking Florence Court as one of the most important houses in Ulster.

The Argory is a 19th century hill-top house, brimming with Victorian and Edwardian furniture and decoration, arranged as it was in 1900. This contrasts with the domestic unpretentious ambience of Springhill, a 17th century plantation house, and home to ten generations of the Conyngham family. Springhill has an exceptional library and gunroom and an excellent Irish costume collection.

For those seeking unusual architectural curiosities, Castle Ward is the most curious of them all. This peculiar abode, completed by 1772, has a two-fold fascination: one façade is classical; the other is gothic. This eccentricity was due to a difference in taste of Lord and Lady Ward, producing a hybrid house of contrasting styles. Also on the tranquil shores of Strangford Lough is Mount Stewart, home of the Londonderry family. This striking property once welcomed frequent prominent political visitors and famous guests. Visitors can see a full set of chairs once used at the Congress of Vienna. But it is the gardens, planted in the 1920s, which are world-renowned, with their rare and colourful flowers, and trees such as eucalyptus and mimosa. A vista across Strangford Lough can be enjoyed from the Temple of the Winds, a banqueting hall dating back to 1785. Rowallane is another magnificent garden with rare shrubs, planted among natural whinstone outcrops and dry-walled fields.

Another curiosity in Northern Ireland is the Carrick-a-Rede Rope Bridge. Traditionally set up for salmon fishing, this bridge crosses a 24 metres deep and 18 metres wide chasm to the tiny island of Carrick.

As of Spring 2005, visitors will also be able to enjoy the spectacular views from Divis and Black Mountain. The latter provide the backdrop to the Belfast skyline and up until their recent acquisition by the National Trust were inaccessible to the general public. For the local community and visitors alike, this marks a very exciting era and opens up the opportunity to explore and appreciate the local wildlife and countryside.

Northern Ireland has a natural beauty that provides a glorious backdrop to so many visitor attractions.

The Argory - Staircase
©National Trust Photographic Library/Chris Hill

ANTRIM CASTLE GARDENS
Randalstown Road, Antrim BT41 4LH

Tel: 028 9442 8000 **Fax:** 028 9446 0360 **e-mail:** clotworthyarts@antrim.gov.uk

Owner: Antrim Borough Council **Contact:** Philip Magennis

Situated adjacent to Antrim Town, the Sixmilewater River and Lough Neagh's shore, these recently restored, 17th century Anglo-Dutch water gardens are maintained in a manner authentic to the period. The gardens comprise of ornamental canals, round pond, ancient motte and a parterre garden planted with 17th century plants - many with culinary or medicinal uses. An interpretative display introducing the history of the gardens and the process of their restoration, along with a scale model of former Antrim Castle is located in the reception of Clotworthy Arts Centre.

Location: Outside Antrim town centre off A26 on A6.

Open: All year: Mon - Fri, 9.30am - 9.30pm (dusk if earlier). Sats, 10am - 5pm. Jul & Aug: also open Suns, 2 - 5pm.

Admission: Free. Charge for guided group tours (by arrangement only).

ARDRESS HOUSE & FARMYARD
64 Ardress Road, Portadown, Co Armagh BT62 1SQ

Tel/Fax: 028 3885 1236 **e-mail:** ardress@nationaltrust.org.uk **www**.ntni.org.uk

Owner: The National Trust **Contact:** The Custodian

A 17th century farmhouse with elegant 18th century additions by owner-architect George Ensor. Includes a display of antique farming implements in the farmyard.

Location: On B28, 5m from Moy, 5m from Portadown, 3m from M1/J13.

Open: 17 Mar: 2 - 6pm. 19 Mar - 25 Sept: Sats, Suns & BH/PHs, 2 - 6pm.

Admission: House tour: Adult £3.30, Child £1.70, Family £8.30. Groups £3 (outside normal hours £5).

Ground floor. WC. Obligatory. P On leads.

THE ARGORY
Moy, Dungannon, Co Tyrone BT71 6NA

Tel: 028 8778 4753 **Fax:** 028 8778 9598

e-mail: argory@nationaltrust.org.uk **www**.ntni.org.uk

Owner: The National Trust **Contact:** The Property Manager

The Argory is a handsome 19th century Victorian house furnished as it was in 1900, providing an excellent illustration of Victorian/Edwardian interior taste and interests.

Location: On Derrycaw road, 4m from Moy, 3m from M1/J13 or J14 (coaches J13).

Open: House: 17 Mar; 19 Mar - May: Sats, Suns & BH/PH (incl. 25 Mar - 1 Apr); Jun - Aug: daily; Sept: Sats & Suns, 1 - 6pm. 1 - 9 Oct: Sats & Suns, 1 - 5pm. Grounds: Oct - Apr: daily, 10am - 4pm; May - Sept: daily, 10am - 7pm (2 - 7pm on Event Days). Tearoom: as House, open at 2pm. Shop: as House.

Admission: House tour: Adult £4.50, Child £2.40, Family £11.40. Groups: £4.10 (outside normal hours £5). Grounds only: Car £2.50.

Ground floor. WC. Obligatory. P On leads.

BALLYWALTER PARK
Nr Newtownards, Co Down BT22 2PP

Tel: 028 4275 8264 **Fax:** 028 4275 8818

e-mail: enquiries@dunleath-estates.co.uk **www**.ballywalterpark.com

Owner: Lord Dunleath **Contact:** The Secretary, The Estate Office

Victorian mansion, situated in 40 acres of landscaped grounds, built in the mid-19th century by Charles Lanyon, with Edwardian additions by W J Fennell. Currently undergoing major restoration works. Self-catered (4 star) listed gatelodge overlooking beach available for holiday lets (sleeps four).

Location: 1km S of Ballywalter village.

Open: By appointment, please telephone the Estate Office.

Admission: House or Gardens: Adult £5. House and gardens: Adult £8. Groups (max 50): Adult £5.

No photography indoors. Pick-your-own, Jun - Aug. By prior arrangement. Obligatory. P Self-catering. Tel for details. €

BARONS COURT
Newtownstewart, Omagh, Co Tyrone BT78 4EZ

Tel: 028 8166 1683 **Fax:** 028 8166 2059 **Contact:** The Agent

The home of the Duke and Duchess of Abercorn, Barons Court was built between 1779 and 1782, and subsequently extensively remodelled by John Soane (1791), William and Richard Morrison (1819-1841), Sir Albert Richardson (1947-49) and David Hicks (1975-76).

Location: 5km SW of Newtownstewart.

Open: By appointment only.

Admission: Adult £5. Groups max. 50.

Partial. WCs. By arrangement. P €

CASTLE COOLE
Enniskillen, Co Fermanagh BT74 6JY

Tel: 028 6632 2690 **Fax:** 028 6632 5665 **e-mail:** castlecoole@nationaltrust.org.uk **www**.ntni.org.uk

Owner: The National Trust **Contact:** The Property Manager

One of the finest neo-classical houses in Ireland, built by James Wyatt in the late 18th century, and sited in a rolling landscape park right on the edge of Enniskillen.

Location: On A4, 1m from Enniskillen on A4, Belfast - Enniskillen road.

Open: House: 12 Mar - May: Sats, Suns & BH/PHs (incl. 25 Mar - 1 Apr), 12 noon - 6pm. Jun: daily except Thur, 1 - 6pm (from 12 noon Sats & Suns). Jul - Aug: daily; Sept: Sats & Suns, 12 noon - 6pm. 1 - 9 Oct: Sats & Suns, 1 - 5pm. Grounds: Daily, 10am - 4pm (8pm Apr - Sept). Last tour 1 hr before closing.

Admission: House Tour & Grounds: Adult £4.20, Child £2.10, Family £10.50. Groups: £3.50 (outside normal hours £4.50).

Partial. WC. P In grounds, on leads.

Mount Stewart.

NT Photographic Library.

CASTLE WARD & STRANGFORD LOUGH WILDLIFE CENTRE ✤
Strangford, Downpatrick, Co Down BT30 7LS

Tel: 028 4488 1204 **Fax:** 028 4488 1729 **e-mail:** castleward@nationaltrust.org.uk **www.ntni.org.uk**

Owner: The National Trust **Contact:** The Property Manager

Castle Ward is a beautiful 750 acre walled estate in a stunning location overlooking Strangford Lough. The mid-Georgian mansion is one of the architectural curios of its time, built inside and out in two distinct architectural styles.

Location: On A25, 7m from Downpatrick and $1^{1}/2$ m from Strangford.

Open: House & Wildlife Centre: 12 Mar - Apr: Sats, Suns & BH/PHs (incl. 25 Mar - 1 Apr); May: daily except Tues; Jun - Aug: daily; Sept - Oct: Sats & Suns, 1 - 6pm. Last tour 1 hr before closing. Grounds: Daily, 10am - 4pm (8pm May - Sept).

Admission: Grounds, Wildlife Centre & House Tour: Adult £5.30, Child £2.40, Family £13. Groups: £4.20 (outside normal hours £5.50). Grounds & Wildlife Centre only: Adult £3.70, Child £1.70, Family £9.10, Groups: £2.70.

🖼 🍽 ⛷ Ground floor & grounds. 🖪 🇮 Obligatory. 🅿 🚻 In grounds, on leads. 🏕 Caravan park, holiday cottages, basecamp. 🛏 ❄

CROM ESTATE ✤
Newtownbutler, Co Fermanagh BT92 8AP

Tel/Fax: 028 6773 8118 (Visitor Centre) 028 6773 8174 (Estate)

e-mail: crom@nationaltrust.org.uk **www.ntni.org.uk**

Owner: The National Trust **Contact:** The Visitor Facilities Manager

Crom is one of Ireland's most important nature conservation areas. It is set in 770 hectares of romantic and tranquil islands, woodland and ruins on the shores of Upper Lough Erne.

Location: 3m from A34, well signposted from Newtownbutler. Jetty at Visitor Centre.

Open: Grounds: 12 Mar - Jun: daily, 10am - 6pm; Jul & Aug: daily, 10am - 8pm; Sept: daily, 10am - 6pm; Oct: Sats & Suns, 12 noon - 6pm. All Suns: 12 noon - 6pm. Visitor Centre: 12 Mar - 24 Apr: Sats, Suns & BH/PHs (incl. 25 Mar - 1 Apr), 10am - 6pm; May - Sept: daily, 10am - 6pm; 1 - 9 Oct: Sats & Suns, 1 - 5pm.

Admission: Grounds & Visitor Centre: Car/Boat £4.70. Minibus £13, Coach £16.70, Motorbike £2.

🍽 🖪 🅿 🏕 7 x 4-star holiday cottages & play-area. 🛏

DERRYMORE HOUSE ✤
Bessbrook, Newry, Co Armagh BT35 7EF

Tel: 028 3083 8361 **www.ntni.org.uk**

Owner: The National Trust

An elegant late 18th century thatched cottage, built by Isaac Corry, who represented Newry in the Irish House of Commons. Park laid out in the style of 'Capability' Brown.

Location: On A25, 2m from Newry on road to Camlough.

Open: House: 5 May - 27 Aug: Thur - Sat (also BH Mons in Jul & Aug), 2 - 5.30pm. Grounds: Daily, 10am - 4pm (7pm May - Sept).

Admission: House tour: Adult £3, Child £1.50, Family £7.50. Groups: £2.20 (outside normal hours £4).

🅿 🚻 On leads.

FLORENCE COURT ✤
Enniskillen, Co Fermanagh BT92 1DB

Tel: 028 6634 8249 **Fax:** 028 6634 8873 **e-mail:** florencecourt@nationaltrust.org.uk **www.ntni.org.uk**

Owner: The National Trust **Contact:** The Property Manager

Florence Court is a fine mid-18th century house and estate set against the stunning backdrop of the Cuilcagh Mountains. House tour includes service quarters popular with all ages. Beautiful walled garden and lots of walks in grounds.

Location: 8m SW of Enniskillen via A4 and then A32 to Swanlinbar.

Open: House: 12 Mar - May: Sats, Suns & BH/PHs (incl. 25 Mar - 1 Apr); Jun: daily except Tues; Jul & Aug: daily; Sept: Sats & Suns: 12 noon - 6pm (from 1pm Mon - Fri in Jun); 1 - 9 Oct: Sats & Suns, 1 - 5pm. Last tour 1hr before closing. Grounds: Daily, 10am - 4pm (8pm Apr - Sept).

Admission: House tour: Adult £4, Child £2, Family £10. Groups: £3.50 (outside normal hours £4.50). Grounds only: Car £3, Minibus £15, Coach £20, Motorbike £1.50.

🖼 🍽 ⛷ Ground floor. WC. 🖪 🇮 Obligatory. 🅿 🚻 In grounds, on leads. 🏕 Holiday cottage. 🛏

GRAY'S PRINTING PRESS ✤
49 Main Street, Strabane, Co Tyrone BT82 8AU

Tel: 028 7188 0055 **www.ntni.org.uk**

Owner: The National Trust **Contact:** The Administrator

Historic printworks, featuring 18th century printing press and 19th century hand-printing machines. Tour includes audio-visual presentation.

Location: In the centre of Strabane.

Open: Apr - May: Sats; Jun - Sept: Tue - Sat, 2 - 5pm (from 11am Jul/Aug).

Admission: Press Tour: Adult £2.70, Child £1.60, Family £7. Group £2.20 (outside normal hours £3.50).

🇮 🔁

HEZLETT HOUSE & FARMYARD ✤
107 Sea Road, Castlerock, Coleraine, Co Londonderry BT51 4TW

Tel/Fax: 028 7084 8567 **e-mail:** downhillcastle@nationaltrust.org.uk **www.ntni.org.uk**

Owner: The National Trust **Contact:** The Custodian

Charming 17th century thatched house with 19th century furnishings. One of only a few pre-18th century Irish buildings still surviving.

Location: 5m W of Coleraine on Coleraine - Downhill coast road, A2.

Open: Jun - Aug. Please contact property directly for opening times - tel: 028 7084 8728.

Admission: Adult £3.70, Child £2.20, Family £9.60. Groups £3.10 (outside normal hours £4.50).

⛷ Ground floor. 🇮 Obligatory. 🅿 🚻 In grounds, on leads.

KILLYLEAGH CASTLE
Killyleagh, Downpatrick, Co Down BT30 9QA

Tel/Fax: 028 4482 8261 **e-mail:** gatehouses@killyleagh.plus.com **www.killyleaghcastle.com**

Owner/Contact: Mrs G Rowan-Hamilton

Oldest occupied castle in Ireland. Self-catering towers available to sleep 4-15. Swimming pool and tennis court available. Access to garden.

Location: At the end of the High Street.

Open: By arrangement. Groups (30-50): by appointment.

Admission: Adult £3.50, Child £2. Groups: Adult £2.50, Child £1.50.

ℹ No photography in house. 🍽 Wedding receptions. ⛷ Unsuitable. 🇮 Obligatory. 🅿 🚻 🛏 ❄

MOUNT STEWART ✤
NEWTOWNARDS, Co DOWN BT22 2AD

www.ntni.org.uk

Tel: 028 4278 8387 **Fax:** 028 4278 8569 **e-mail:** mountstewart@nationaltrust.org.uk

Owner: The National Trust **Contact:** The Property Manager

Home of the Londonderry family since the early 18th century, Mount Stewart was Lord Castlereagh's house and played host to many prominent political figures. The magnificent gardens planted in the 1920s have made Mount Stewart famous and earned it a World Heritage Site nomination. They feature a series of formal outdoor 'rooms', vibrant parterres, and formal and informal vistas, some with Strangford Lough views. Many rare and unusual plants thrive in the mild climate of the Ards, including eucalyptus, beschorneria, mimosa, and cordyline. The garden is also home to national collections of phormium and libertia. The house includes the famous painting 'Hambletonian', as well as the full set of chairs used at Congress of Vienna. The Temple of the Winds, a 1785 banqueting hall, is in the grounds. Café-bistro restaurant, gift shop and exhibition areas.

Location: On A20, 5m from Newtownards on the Portaferry road.

Open: House: 12 Mar - Apr: Sats, Suns & BH/PHs (inc. 25 Mar - 1 Apr); May - Sept: daily (closed Tues May/Jun & Sept); Oct: Sats & Suns, 12 noon - 6pm (from 1pm Mon - Fri May/Jun). Lakeside Gardens: All year: daily, 10am - sunset. Formal Gardens: Mar: Sats, Suns & BH/PHs, 10am - 4pm; Apr - Oct: daily, 10am - 6pm (8pm May - Sept). Temple of the Winds: Apr - Oct: Suns & BHs only, 2 - 5pm.

Admission: House Tour, Gardens & Temple: Adult £5.45, Child £2.70, Family £13.60. Group: £4.80 (outside normal hours £6). Gardens only: Adult £4.40, Child £2.30, Family £11.10. Group: £4.10 (outside normal hours £6).

🖼 🍽 ⛷ 🖪 🇮 Obligatory. 🅿 🚻 In grounds, on leads. 🛏 ❄ Lakeside area. 🍽 Tel for details. €

🎭 Special Events Index see page 24

Ireland

MUSSENDEN TEMPLE ❦
Castlerock, Co. Londonderry

Tel/Fax: 028 7084 8728　**e-mail:** downhillcastle@nationaltrust.org.uk
www.ntni.org.uk
Owner: The National Trust
Set on a stunning and wild headland with fabulous views over Ireland's north coast is the landscaped estate of Downhill.
Location: 1m W of Castlerock.
Open: Temple: 12 Mar - May: Sats, Suns & BH/PHs (incl. 25 Mar - 1 Apr); Jun - Aug: daily; Sept: Sats & Suns: 11am - 6pm (7.30pm Jul & Aug); Oct: Sats & Suns, 11am - 5pm. Grounds: All year, dawn - dusk.
Admission: Car park charge at Lion's Gate during Temple opening: Car £3.70, Minibus £7.40, Motorbike £2.30.
T P 🖼 On leads. ▲

ROWALLANE GARDEN ❦
Saintfield, Ballynahinch, Co Down　BT24 7LH

Tel: 028 9751 0131　**Fax:** 028 9751 1242

e-mail: rowallane@nationaltrust.org.uk　**www.ntni.org.uk**
Owner: The National Trust　　**Contact:** Head Gardener
Rowallane is a natural landscape of some 21 hectares, planted with an outstanding collection of trees, shrubs and other plants from many parts of the world, creating a beautiful display of form and colour throughout the year.
Location: On A7, 1m from Saintfield on road to Downpatrick.
Open: Oct - Mar: daily, 10am - 4pm (closed 25/26 Dec & 1 Jan). Apr - Sept: daily, 10am - 8pm.
Admission: Adult £3.70, Child £1.70, Family £9.10. Groups £2.80 (outside normal hours £3.50).
♿ Grounds. WC. ▣ Apr - Aug. 🖼 In grounds, on leads. ✳

SEAFORDE GARDENS 🏛
Seaforde, Co Down　BT30 8PG

Tel: 028 44811 225　**Fax:** 028 44811 370　**e-mail:** plants@seafordegardens.com
www.seafordegardens.com
Owner/Contact: Patrick Forde
18th century walled garden and adjoining pleasure grounds, containing many rare and beautiful trees and shrubs; many of them tender. There are huge rhododendrons and the National Collection of Eucryphias. The oldest maze in Ireland is in the centre of the walled garden, which can be viewed from the Mogul Tower. The tropical butterfly house contains hundreds of beautiful highly coloured butterflies; also a collection of parrots, insects and reptiles. The nursery garden contains many interesting plants for sale.
Location: 20m S of Belfast on the main road to Newcastle.
Open: Easter - end Sept: Mon - Sat, 10am - 5pm; Suns, 1 - 6pm. Gardens only: Oct - Mar: Mon - Fri, 10am - 5pm.
Admission: Butterfly House or Gardens: Adult £3, Child £2. Groups (10+): Adult £2.40, Child £1.50. Butterfly House & Gardens: Adult £5.50, Child £3. Groups: Adult £4.50, Child £2.70, Family (2+2) £15. RHS members Free access: Apr - Jun.
▣ 🎁 T ♿ 🍴 🎫 By arrangement. P ◨ 🖼 ✳ €

SPRINGHILL HOUSE & COSTUME COLLECTION ❦
20 Springhill Road, Moneymore, Co Londonderry　BT45 7NQ

Tel/Fax: 028 8674 8210　springhill@nationaltrust.org.uk　**www.ntni.org.uk**
Owner: The National Trust　　**Contact:** The Property Manager
A charming and atmospheric 17th century 'plantation' house, said by many to be one of the prettiest houses in Ulster. It was home to ten generations of the Conyngham family, originally from Ayr. 50 minutes drive from Belfast or Londonderry, 35 minutes from Coleraine.
Location: 1m from Moneymore on B18 to Coagh, 5m from Cookstown.
Open: 12 Mar - Jun: Sats, Suns & BH/PHs (incl. 25 Mar - 1 Apr); Jul & Aug: daily; Sept: Sats & Suns: 12 noon - 6pm; 1 - 9 Oct: Sats & Suns, 12 noon - 5pm.
Admission: House & Costume Collection Tour: Adult £4.10, Child £2.20, Family £10.40. Group £3.70 (outside normal hours £5).
▣ T ♿ Partial. WC. ▣ 🎫 P 🖼 In grounds, on leads. ▲

WELLBROOK BEETLING MILL ❦
20 Wellbrook Road, Corkhill, Co. Tyrone　BT80 9RY

Tel: 028 8674 8210/8675 1735　**e-mail:** wellbrook@nationaltrust.org.uk
www.ntni.org.uk
Owner: The National Trust　　**Contact:** The Custodian
Wellbrook is an 18th century water-powered beetling mill with the only working beetling engines on show in Northern Ireland. New exhibition on the history of linen and its importance to Ireland.
Location: 4m from Cookstown, following signs from A505 Cookstown - Omagh road.
Open: 12 Mar - Jun: Sats, Suns & BH/PHs (incl. 25 Mar - 1 Apr); Jul & Aug: daily; Sept: Sats & Suns: 1 - 6pm; 1 - 9 Oct: Sats & Suns, 1 - 5pm.
Admission: Mill Tour: Adult £3, Child £1.70, Family £7.70. Group: £2.50 (outside normal hours £3.50).
▣ P

WESTPORT HOUSE & GARDENS
THE DEMESNE, WESTPORT, Co MAYO

www.westporthouse.ie

Tel: 00353 (0)98 27766　**Fax:** 00353 (0)98 25206　**e-mail:** info@westporthouse.ie
Owner: Jeremy Altamont　　**Contact:** Karen Browne
Designed by the famous architects Richard Cassels and James Wyatt, Westport House is a fine example of an early 18th century Georgian mansion. It was built, and is still privately owned by, the Browne family who are direct descendants of the 16th century Pirate Queen, Grace O'Malley.

Westport House is situated in a magnificent parkland setting with a lake, terraces and gardens overlooking Clew Bay. There are several architecturally stunning rooms on show complete with original contents – artworks include landscapes by James Arthur O'Connor, Chalon, Barrett, Gibson and Carver, and portraits by such names as Reynolds, Beechy, Oppie, Brooks and Lavery; WaxWork Figures by Gems Display Figures, which are a tribute to the literary, arts and music achievements of the west of Ireland.
Location: W of Ireland.
Open: 1 Mar - 31 Oct: daily, 11.30am - 5pm. Tours accepted all year round by appointment.
Admission: Adult €11.50, Child €7.50, OAP €7.50. Group: €7.50. Discounts: Two for the price of one.
T Marquee - wedding receptions. P 🖼 In grounds, on leads.

LOCAL FOOD

Irish Soda Bread

Around 1850 it became common to make bread using baking soda, rather than yeast, in parts of rural Ireland. The practice of using baking soda started out of necessity. Yeast won't make dough rise unless the baker uses "strong" flour, which was scarce in parts of Ireland. So the leavening agents were buttermilk and baking soda (bicarbonate of soda). One of the disadvantages of this sort of bread is that it doesn't last very long, so daily bread baking was a necessity. Before baking, a cross is cut on the top with a knife, supposedly to ward off the devil.

Admission prices for properties in Northern Ireland are given in £ Sterling.

Admission prices for properties in the Republic of Ireland are given in Euros.

Opening Arrangements at Properties grant-aided by English Heritage

ENGLISH HERITAGE

ENGLISH HERITAGE

23 Savile Row, London W1S 2ET

I am very pleased to introduce this year's list of opening arrangements at properties grant-aided by English Heritage. Over half the properties are open free, but we give details of admission charges where appropriate. There is also a brief description of each property, information on parking and access for people with disabilities.

The extent of public access varies from one property to another. The size of the building or garden, their nature and function are all taken into account. Some buildings, such as town halls, museums or railway stations, are of course open regularly. For other properties, especially those which are family homes or work places, access may need to be arranged in a way that also recognises the vulnerability of the building or the needs of those who live or work in it. Usually this will mean opening by appointment or on an agreed number of days each year. This is made clear by each entry.

Some properties are open by written appointment only. In most cases you should still be able to make initial contact by telephone, but you will be asked to confirm your visit in writing. This is to confirm the seriousness of your interest just as you would for example when making a hotel booking. It also provides a form of identification, enabling owners to feel more confident about inviting strangers into their house.

It has always been a condition of grant-aid from English Heritage that the public should have a right to see the buildings to whose repair they have contributed. We therefore welcome feedback from visitors on the quality of their visit to grant-aided properties. In particular, please let us know if you are unable to gain access to any of the buildings on the list on the days or at the times specified, or if you have difficulty in making an appointment to visit and do not receive a satisfactory explanation from the owner. Please contact English Heritage Customer Services at Po Box 569, Swindon SN2 2YP (telephone: 0870 3331181; e-mail: customers@english-heritage.org.uk).

Information about public access is also included on our website (www.english-heritage.org.uk). The website is updated regularly to include new properties, any subsequent changes that have been notified to us or any corrections. We suggest that you consult our website for up-to-date information before visiting. If long journeys or special requirements are involved, we strongly recommend that you telephone the properties in advance, even if no appointment is required.

Finally, may I use this introduction to thank all those owners with whom we work. Their support for the access arrangements has been hugely encouraging. That the public can enjoy a visit to a grant-aided property is not only good in itself, it demonstrates that the historic environment is in a very real sense a common wealth, part of the richness and diversity that makes the English landscape — both urban and rural — so special. It also illustrates how crucially important the private owner is in maintaining that quality and distinctiveness.

I very much hope you enjoy the sites and properties you find in this list — from the famous to the many lesser-known treasures. They are all worth a visit — I hope we have helped you to find, and enjoy, them.

Neil Cossons.

BERKSHIRE

Welford Park

Welford, Newbury, Berkshire RG20 8HU
Red brick country house c1652 and remodelled in 1702, when a third storey was added and the front façade was decorated with Ionic columns. Other alterations were made in the Victorian period.
Grant Recipient: Mr J H L Puxley
Access Contact: Mr J H L Puxley
Tel: 01488 608691 **Fax:** 01488 608853
Open: 16 - 21 May, 30 May, 4 - 28 June (except 18 June & Suns) and 29 August: 11am - 5pm. Interior of house (4 principal rooms) by arrangement only.
P Spaces: 40. 80 more spaces within 1/4 mile walk.
Yes. No WC for the disabled. Guide Dogs: Yes
£ **House: Adult:** £5 **Child:** £3.50 **Other:** £3.50
Free entry to garden & grounds, except on occasional charity days.

BUCKINGHAMSHIRE

Claydon House

Middle Claydon, nr. Buckingham, Bucks MK18 2EY
18th century house with fine rococo decoration. A series of great rooms have wood carvings in Chinese and gothic styles, and tall windows overlook parkland and a lake. In continuous occupation by the Verney family for over 380 years, the house has mementoes of their relation Florence Nightingale who was a regular visitor.
www.nationaltrust.org.uk
Grant Recipient: The National Trust
Access Contact: The Custodian
Tel: 01296 730349 **Fax:** 01296 738511
E-mail: claydon@nationaltrust.org.uk
Open: House: 26 Mar - 30 Oct, daily except Thurs & Fri 1 - 5pm. Open BH Mons but closed Good Friday. Grounds: as house 1 - 5pm.
P Additional parking in parkland. Spaces: 30
Wheelchair access to ground floor with assistance and all of garden. WC for the disabled. Guide Dogs: Yes
£ **Adult:** £5, £1.10 (garden only) **Child:** £2.50
Family: £12.50, £4.20 (groups 15+ Sats & Mons - Weds)

Cliveden Mansion & Clock Tower

Cliveden, Taplow, Maidenhead, Bucks SL6 0JA
Built by Charles Barry in 1851, once lived in by Lady Astor now let as an hotel. Series of gardens, each with its own character, featuring roses, topiary, water gardens, a formal parterre, informal vistas, woodland and riverside walks.
www.nationaltrust.org.uk
Grant Recipient: The National Trust
Access Contact: Property Manager
Tel: 01628 605069 **Fax:** 01628 669461
E-mail: cliveden@nationaltrust.org.uk
Open: House (main ground floor rooms) and Octagon Temple: 2 Apr - 30 Oct, Thurs & Sun 3 - 5.30pm. Estate & garden: 16 Mar - 23 Dec daily 11am - 6pm (closes at 4pm from 1 Nov).
P Woodlands car park: open all year, daily 11am - 5.30pm (closes at 4pm Nov - Mar). Spaces: 300. Overflow car park with 1000 spaces available.
Wheelchair access to house. WC for the disabled. Guide Dogs: Yes
£ **House: Adult:** £1, **Child:** 50p.
Grounds: Adult: £7, **Child:** £3, **Family:** £17.50 (family), £7.50 (family: woodlands car park)
Woodlands Car Park: **Adult:** £3.50, **Child:** £1.50

Hall Barn Gothic Temple

Beaconsfield, Buckinghamshire HP9 2SG
Garden building in existence by 1740 but possibly c1725 and by Colen Campbell. Gothick Revival style hexagonal-shaped garden building. Situated in landscaped garden, laid out in 1680s.
Grant Recipient: 5th Baron Burnham's Will Trust
Access Contact: J A C Read
Open: By written application to Mrs Farncombe, Hall Barn, Windsor End, Beaconsfield, Buckinghamshire HP9 2SG.
P Parking available. No. £No.

Hughenden Manor Disraeli Monument

High Wycombe, Bucks HP14 4LA
The home of Prime Minster Benjamin Disraeli from 1848-1881. Hughenden has a red brick 'gothic' exterior. Much of his furniture, books and paintings remain. The garden has been recreated in the spirit of his wife, Mary Anne, with colourful designs. Park and woodland walks.
www.nationaltrust.org.uk
Grant Recipient: The National Trust
Access Contact: Property Manager
Tel: 01494 755573 **Fax:** 01494 474284
E-mail: hughenden@nationaltrust.org.uk
Open: House: 5 - 27 Mar, Sat & Sun 1 - 5pm; 30 Mar - 30 Oct, Wed - Sun (open Good Friday & BH Mons), 1 - 5pm. Gardens: as house 12 noon - 5pm. Park & woodlands all year. Note: long and steep walk to house entrance if arriving by public transport.
P Spaces: 100
Wheelchair access to ground floor of house, terrace, stable yard restaurant and shop. WC for the disabled. Guide Dogs: Yes
£ **House: Adult:** £5 **Child:** £2.50 **Family:** £12.50. **Garden: Adult:** £1.80 **Child:** 90p. Parks & woods free.

Stowe House

Buckingham, Bucks MK18 5EH
Mansion built 1680 and greatly altered and enlarged in the 18th century, surrounded by important 18th century gardens. House and gardens variously worked on by Vanbrugh, Gibbs, Kent and Leoni. Many of the greatest alterations carried out for Viscount Cobham, one of Marlborough's Generals, between 1715 and 1749. Gardens cover 325 acres and contain 6 lakes and 32 garden temples. Kent designed the Elysian Fields in the 1730s, one of the first experiments in 'natural' landscaping, and 'Capability' Brown worked here for 10 years as head gardener and was married in the church in the grounds in 1744. The House is now occupied by the Preservation Trust's tenant, Stowe School. The Gardens are owned by the National Trust.
www.stowe.co.uk
Grant Recipient: The Stowe House Preservation Trust
Access Contact: Lucy Beckett / Bill Kemp
Tel: 01280 818280 / 818282
Fax: 01280 818186
E-mail: sses@stowe.co.uk
Open: 19 - 20 Feb, 12 - 13 Mar, Sat & Sun for guided tour only at 2pm. 25 Mar - 17 Apr, Wed - Sun 12pm - 5pm (last adm. 4pm) with guided tour at 2pm (& Easter Mon). 30 May - 3 June, Wed - Sun for guided tour only at 2pm (and BH Mon). 3 July - 25 Aug, Wed - Sun (& BH Mon) 12pm - 5pm (last adm. 4pm) with guided tour at 2pm. 31 Aug - 16 Oct, Wed - Sun for guided tour only at 2pm. 19 - 20 Nov, 17 - 18 Dec, Sat & Sun for guided tour only at 2pm. Group visits by arrangement throughout the year. Information line tel: 01280 81866.
P Spaces: 30
Yes. WC for the disabled. Guide Dogs: Yes
£ **Adult:** £2 **Child:** £1 Guided tours (excluding group bookings): **Adult:** £3 **Child:** £1.50

Stowe Landscape Gardens

Buckingham, Bucks MK18 5EH
Extensive and complex pleasure grounds and park around a country mansion. Begun late 17th century but substantially developed in the 18th and 19th centuries by, among others, Charles Bridgeman, Sir John Vanbrugh, James Gibbs, William Kent and Lancelot 'Capability' Brown (Brown was originally head gardener here before leaving to set up his landscape practice). The park and gardens contain over 30 buildings, many of great architectural importance. Stowe was supremely influential on the English landscape garden during the 18th century.
www.nationaltrust.org.uk
Grant Recipient: The National Trust
Access Contact: Property Manager
Tel: 01280 822850 **Fax:** 01280 822437
E-mail: stowegarden@nationaltrust.org.uk
Open: 1 Jan - 28 Feb & 5 Nov - 31 Dec: Sat & Sun 10am - 4pm (last adm 3pm); 1 Mar - 30 Oct: daily, except Mon & Tues, 10am - 5.30pm (last adm 4pm). Open BH Mons and closed 28 May & 25 Dec.
P Spaces: 100
Partial. Self-drive battery cars available. WC for the disabled. Guide Dogs: Yes
£ **Adult:** £5.80 **Child:** £2.90 **Family:** £14.50

West Wycombe Park (West Portico)

West Wycombe, Bucks HP14 3AJ
House built early 18th century, extensively remodelled between 1750 and 1780 by Sir Francis Dashwood (creator of the Hell-Fire Club). Porticoes were added to the east and west fronts by Nicholas Revett (his work is relatively rare), and on the south, linking the wings, John Donovell added a two storey colonnade. Although the latter is based on Renaissance prototypes, it too is a rare feature. Frescoes were painted on the ceiling of the west Portico by one of the Borgnis.
www.nationaltrust.org.uk
Grant Recipient: The National Trust
Access Contact: Property Manager
Tel: 01494 513569
Open: Grounds only: 1 Apr - 31 May, daily 2 - 6pm except Fri & Sat (open Bank Hols). House & Grounds: 1 June - 31 Aug, daily 2 - 6pm except Fri & Sat. Weekdays: entry by guided tour every 20 minutes (approx). Last adm 5.15pm.
P Parking on site. Spaces: 30.
Wheelchair access to ground floor only. No WC for the disabled. Guide Dogs: Yes
£ **House & Grounds: Adult:** £5.40 **Child:** £2.70 **Grounds: Adult:** £2.80 **Child:** £1.40 **Family:** £13.50

Widmere Farm Chapel

Widmere, nr. Marlow, Bucks SL7 3DF
Chapel attached to farmhouse, early 13th century with traces of 14th century windows and later alterations, grade II*. 11th or 12th century crypt and medieval roof.
Grant Recipient: Mr G J White
Access Contact: Mr G J White
Tel: 01628 484204
Open: Access by arrangement.
P Parking on site. Spaces: 6 No £No

CAMBRIDGESHIRE

The Almonry

High Street, Ely, Cambs CB7 4JU
The Almonry (now a restaurant) is part of a long range of buildings which back onto the High Street on the north side of the Cathedral. Originally built by Alan of Walsingham soon after he became Sacrist in 1322, but mainly rebuilt in the 19th century.
www.cathedral.ely.anglican.org
Grant Recipient: The Dean & Chapter of Ely
Access Contact: The Events Manager
Tel: 01353 667735 **Fax:** 01353 665658
E-mail: j.leebetter@cathedral.ely.anglican.org
Open: Mon - Sat 10am - 5pm, Sun 11am - 5pm
P Town centre car parks. Parking for disabled in Cathedral car park by arrangement.
Wheelchair access to ground floor only. WC for the disabled. Guide Dogs: Yes
£No

Anglesey Abbey Gardens

Quy Road, Lode, Cambridge CB5 9EJ
98 acres of formal and landscape gardens surrounding a 17th century house on the site of a 12th century priory. Contains over 100 pieces of sculpture and a working 18th century water mill.
www.nationaltrust.org.uk
Grant Recipient: The National Trust
Access Contact: Property Manager
Tel: 01223 810080 **Fax:** 01223 810088
E-mail: angleseyabbey@nationaltrust.org.uk
Open: Garden: 2 - 20 Mar, 9 Nov - 18 Dec and 28 Dec - 19 Mar 2006, Wed - Sun 10.30am - 4.30pm; 23 Mar & 3 July & 7 Sept - 6 Nov, Wed - Sun 10.30am - 5.30pm; 6 July - 4 Sept, daily 10.30am - 5.30pm; Closed Good Fri & open BH Mons. House and mill are also open to the public. Please contact the National Trust for details.
P Spaces: 10
Grounds largely accessible for wheelchairs; level entrance to shop and restaurant; access to ground floor of House and lower floor of Mill only. WC for the disabled. Guide Dogs: Yes
£ **Adult:** £4.30 (garden only), £3.60 (winter) **Child:** £2.15 (garden only), £1.80 (winter)

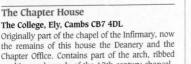

The Black Hostelry

The College, Ely, Cambs CB7 4DL
Built c1291-2 of Carr stone rubble with Barnack, or similar, stone dressings, upper storey is timber-framed and plastered on the south and east sides with stone on the west side. Has early 13th century undercroft with ribbed vaults, 13-14th century King Post roof, and 15th century red brick chimney and doorway. Constructed to accommodate visiting monks from other Benedictine monasteries.
www.cathedral.ely.anglican.org
Grant Recipient: The Dean & Chapter of Ely
Access Contact: The Events Manager
Tel: 01353 667735 **Fax:** 01353 665658
E-mail: j.leebetter@cathedral.ely.anglican.org
Open: By written arrangement with the Events Manager, The Chapter House, The College, Ely, Cambs CB7 4DL.
P Town centre car parks. Parking for disabled in Cathedral car park by arrangement.
♿ Wheelchair access to rear entrance hall only. WC for the disabled in Cathedral. Guide Dogs: Yes
£ No

Buckden Towers

High Street, Buckden, Cambs PE19 5TA
Former ecclesiastical palace set in 15 acres of gardens and parkland. Buildings include the Great Tower and the Inner Gatehouse (both constructed in the late 15th century) and the Victorian mansion. The grounds include an Elizabethan knot garden. Famous occupants include St Hugh of Lincoln (12th century) and Katherine of Aragon (1533-4).
www.claretcentre.fsnet.co.uk
Grant Recipient: The Claretian Missionaries
Access Contact: Mrs Margaret Caulfield
Tel: 01480 810344 **Fax:** 01480 811918
E-mail: claret_centre@claret.org.uk
Open: Guided tours by prior arrangement. Grounds open throughout the year. New visitor centre expected to open autumn 2005.
P Spaces: 50
♿ Yes. WC for the disabled. Guide Dogs: Yes
£ No

The Chapter House

The College, Ely, Cambs CB7 4DL
Originally part of the chapel of the Infirmary, now the remains of this house the Deanery and the Chapter Office. Contains part of the arch, ribbed vaulting and arcade of the 12th century chancel.
www.cathedral.ely.anglican.org
Grant Recipient: The Dean & Chapter of Ely
Access Contact: The Events Manager
Tel: 01353 667735 **Fax:** 01353 665658
E-mail: j.leebetterr@cathedral.ely.anglican.org
Open: By written arrangement with the Events Manager, The Chapter House, The College, Ely, Cambs CB7 4DL.
P Town centre car parks. Parking for disabled in Cathedral car park by arrangement.
♿ Wheelchair access to ground floor only. WC for the disabled in Cathedral. Guide Dogs: Yes
£ No

Elton Hall

Elton, nr. Peterborough, Cambs PE8 6SH
Grade I historic building and country house. Late 15th century gatehouse and chapel built by Sapcote family. Main entrance façade built by Sir Thomas Proby in the 17th century and remodelled by Henry Ashton for 3rd Earl of Carysfort in the 19th century. South Garden façade built between 1789 and 1812 in Gothic style.
Grant Recipient & Access Contact:
Sir William Proby Bt
Tel: 01832 280468 **Fax:** 01832 280584
E-mail: whp@eltonhall.com
Open: 30 May; Weds in June; Weds, Thurs and Suns in July & Aug, plus Aug BH Mon 2 - 5pm. Private groups by arrangement on weekdays Apr - Oct.
P Parking 300m from the Hall. Spaces: 500
♿ Full access to garden. Access to house is difficult. Please telephone 01832 280468. WC for the disabled. Guide Dogs: Yes
£ Adult: £6 (house), £3 (garden)
Child: Free if accompanied

Madingley Post Mill

Mill Farm, Madingley Road, Coton, Cambs CB3 7PH
Historic post mill with machinery intact.
Grant Recipient & Access Contact:
Mr Matthew Mortlock
Tel: 01954 211047 **Fax:** 01954 210752
E-mail: mattcb37ph@aol.com
Open: Weekdays & Sats 11am - 4pm by telephone arrangement.
P At American Cemetery (next door). Spaces: 5
♿ Wheelchair access around base of Windmill only. No WC for the disabled. Guide Dogs: Yes
£ No

The Manor

Hemingford Grey, Huntingdon, Cambs PE28 9BN
Built c1130 and one of the oldest continuously inhabited houses in Britain. Made famous as Green Knowe by the author Lucy Boston. Her patchwork collection is also shown. Four acre garden with topiary, old roses and herbaceous borders.
www.greenknowe.co.uk
Grant Recipient: Mrs Diana Boston
Access Contact: Mrs Diana Boston
Tel: 01480 463134 **Fax:** 01480 465026
E-mail: diana_boston@hotmail.com
Open: House: all year (except May) to individuals or groups by arrangement. May: guided tours at 11am & 2pm (booking advisable). Garden: all year, daily 11am - 5pm (4pm in winter).
P For disabled only adjacent to property. Spaces: 2
♿ Wheelchair access to garden and dining room only. WC for the disabled. Guide Dogs: Yes
£ Adult: £5, £2 (garden only) Child: £1.50, Free (garden only) Other: £4, £2 (garden only)

Minster Precincts

Peterborough Cathedral, Peterborough, Cambs PE1 1XS
The Minster Precincts incorporate many remains from the medieval monastery of which the Cathedral church was a part. These include the richly decorated 13th century arcades of the former infirmary, the originally 13th century Little Prior's Gate and the 15th century Table Hall.
www.peterborough-cathedral.org.uk
Grant Recipient: The Dean & Chapter of Peterborough Cathedral
Access Contact: The Chapter of Peterborough Cathedral
Tel: 01733 343342 **Fax:** 01733 552465
E-mail: a.watson@peterborough-cathedral.org.uk
Open: All year, exterior only.
P City centre car parks (nearest 5 minute walk).
♿ Wheelchair access and WC in Cathedral restaurant and Tourist Information Centre. Guide Dogs: Yes
£ No

The Old Palace

Sue Ryder Care, Palace Green, Ely, Cambs CB7 4EW
Grade I listed building formerly a bishops palace opposite cathedral, with an Elizabethan promenading gallery, bishops chapel and monks' room. 2 acre garden contains the oldest plane tree in Europe. Used as a neurological centre for the physically disabled.
Grant Recipient: The Sue Ryder Care
Access Contact: Mrs Mavis Garner
Tel: 01353 667686 **Fax:** 01353 669425
E-mail: mavis.garner@suerydercareely.org.uk
Open: By arrangement for access to the Long Gallery and Chapel. Gardens: open during the Open Gardens Scheme May - June. Other events held throughout the year, contact Mrs Garner for details.
P Nearest car park: St Mary's Street & Barton Road.
♿ Wheelchair access to garden and Long Gallery. WC for the disabled. Guide Dogs: Yes
£ Charge on garden open days: adult £3, child 50p

Prior Crauden's Chapel

The College, Ely, Cambs CB7 4DL
Private chapel built by Prior Crauden in 1524-5 of Barnack stone ashlar with clunch carved interior, over a 13th century vaulted undercroft. Has windows in the "Decorated" style, octagonal entrance and tower with spiral staircase, richly carved interior and a 14th century mosaic tile floor.
www.cathedral.ely.anglican.org
Grant Recipient: The Dean & Chapter of Ely Cathedral
Access Contact: The Events Manager
Tel: 01353 667735 **Fax:** 01353 665658
E-mail: j.leebetter@cathedral.ely.anglican.org
Open: By written arrangement with the Events Manager, The Chapter House, The College, Ely, Cambs CB7 4DL.
P Town centre car parks. Parking for disabled in Cathedral car park by arrangement.
♿ Wheelchair access to the undercroft only. WC for disabled in Cathedral. Guide Dogs: Yes
£ No

Queen's Hall

The Gallery, Ely, Cambs CB7 4DL
Built by Prior Crauden c1330 of Carr stone rubble with Barnack, or similar, stone dressings and much brick patching. Has original undercroft with ribbed vaulting, 14th century pointed arched windows with curvilinear tracery and corbels carved in the shape of crouching figures. Reputedly constructed for entertaining Queen Philippa, wife of Edward III.
Grant Recipient: The Dean & Chapter of Ely Cathedral
Access Contact: The Assistant Bursar
Tel: 01353 660700 **Fax:** 01353 662187
E-mail: nigelc@kings-ely.cambs.sch.uk
Open: By written arrangement with the Assistant Bursar, the King's School, Ely, Cambs CB7 4DN.
P Town centre car parks. Parking for disabled in Cathedral car park by arrangement. Spaces: 5
♿ Wheelchair access to ground floor only. WC for the disabled in Cathedral. Guide Dogs: Yes
£ No

Sir John Jacob's Almshouse Chapel

Church Street, Gamlingay, Cambs SG19 3JH
Built 1745 of Flemish bond red brick with plain tiled roof, in keeping with adjoining terrace of 10 almshouses constructed 80 years before. Now used as parish council offices.
Grant Recipient: The Trustees of Sir John Jacob's Almshouses
Access Contact: Mrs K Rayner and Mr G Barham
Tel: 01767 650310 **Fax:** 01767 650310
E-mail: gamlingaypc@lineone.net
Open: The office is generally open on Mon, Wed & Fri, 9.15am - 3pm.
P On-street parking.
♿ WC for the disabled. Guide Dogs: Yes   £ No

Thorpe Hall Hospice

Sue Ryder Care, Longthorpe, Peterborough, Cambs PE3 6LW
Built in the 1650s by Peter Mills for Oliver St John, Oliver Cromwell's Lord Chief Justice. Ground floor retains many original features.
Grant Recipient: Sue Ryder Care
Access Contact: Mr Bruce Wringe
Tel: 01733 330060 **Fax:** 01733 269078
E-mail: thorpe@sueryderthorpe.fsnet.co.uk
Open: Access to the Hall by arrangement. Gardens: open all year.
P Spaces: 150 ♿ Yes. WC for the disabled. Guide Dogs: Yes
£ Donations welcome

The Verger's House & The Old Sacristy

High Street, Ely, Cambs CB7 4JU
The Old Sacristy is part of a long range of buildings which back onto the High Street on the north side. Originally built by Alan of Walsingham soon after he became sacrist in 1322, but mainly rebuilt in the 19th century.
www.cathedral.ely.anglican.org
Grant Recipient: The Dean & Chapter of Ely
Access Contact: The Events Manager
Tel: 01353 667735 **Fax:** 01353 665658
E-mail: j.leebetterr@cathedral.ely.anglican.org
Open: By written arrangement with the Events Manager, The Chapter House, The College, Ely, Cambs CB7 4DL.

P Town centre car parks. Parking for disabled in Cathedral car park by arrangement.

Wheelchair access to ground floor only. WC for the disabled in Cathedral. Guide Dogs: Yes

£ No

Wimpole Estate

Arrington, Royston, Cambs SG8 0BW

18th century house set in extensive wooded park. Interior features work by Gibbs, Flitcroft and Soane. The park was landscaped by Bridgeman, Brown and Repton featuring a grand folly, Chinese bridge and lake. Walled garden restored to a working vegetable garden - best seen from June to Aug.

www.nationaltrust.org.uk

Grant Recipient: The National Trust

Access Contact: Property Manager

Tel: 01223 206000 **Fax:** 01223 207838

E-mail: wimpolehall@nationaltrust.org.uk

Open: Hall: 19 Mar - 31 July & 3 Sept - 30 Oct, daily except Thurs & Fri 1pm - 5pm. Aug, daily except Fri 1pm - 5pm. 6 - 27 Nov, Sun 1 - 4pm. BH Mons 11am - 5pm & Good Fri 1 - 5pm. Garden: 1 - 16 Mar, 31 Oct - 21 Dec & 7 Jan - 28 Feb 2006, daily except Thurs & Fri 11am - 4pm; 19 Mar - 31 July & 3 Sept - 30 Oct, daily except Thurs & Fri 10.30am - 5pm; Aug, daily except Fri 10.30am - 5pm; 27 Dec - 3 Jan 2006, daily 11am - 4pm.

P Spaces: 500

Wheelchair access to garden (gravel paths) and restaurant. Disabled visitors may be set down near Hall. Telephone in advance for details. WC for the disabled. Guide Dogs: Yes

£ **Adult:** £6.60, £2.70 (garden only)

Child: £3.40 **Joint Ticket with Wimpole Home Farm:** Adult £10.20, Child £5.50, Family £25.

CHESHIRE

Bache House Farm

Chester Road, Hurleston, Nantwich, Cheshire CW5 6BO

A timber-framed house with slate roof dating from 17th century with an 18th century extension. The house is a four square house with two gables at the rear. The interior shows timbers in the house walls and an oak staircase.

Grant Recipient: P R Posnett

Access Contact: R J Posnett

Tel: 01829 260251

Open: By arrangement at all reasonable times.

P Spaces: 10 No £ No

Belmont Hall

Great Budworth, Northwich, Cheshire CW9 6HN

Country house, built 1755, initial design by James Gibbs, with fine plasterwork interiors. Set in parkland. Now a private day school with family apartments in the East Wing. Also accessible is surrounding farmland, woods and medieval moat.

Grant Recipient: The Trustees of Belmont Hall

Access Contact: Mr R C Leigh

Tel: 01606 891235 **Fax:** 01606 892349

E-mail: asmleigh@hotmail.com

Open: Guided tours during the school holidays and on weekends by prior arrangement with the Estate Manager, Belmont Hall, Great Budworth, Northwich, Cheshire CW9 6HN (tel:01606 891235). Please note: the property and adjacent area are also open by way of a Countryside Stewardship Educational Access Agreement for schools as well as adult parties.

P Unlimited free parking on site. Guide Dogs: Yes

£ **Adult:** £5

Bramall Hall

Bramhall Park, Stockport, Cheshire SK7 3NX

Black and white timber-framed manor house dating back to the 14th century, with subsequently several renovations (many during the Victorian period). Contains 14th century wallpaintings, an Elizabethan plaster ceiling and Victorian kitchen and servants quarters.

www.stockport.gov.uk/tourism/bramall

Grant Recipient: Stockport Metropolitan Borough Council

Access Contact: Ms Caroline Egan

Tel: 0161 485 3708 **Fax:** 0161 486 6959

E-mail: bramall.hall@stockport.gov.uk

Open: Good Fri - end Sept: Mon - Sun 1 - 5pm. Bank Hols 11am - 5pm. Oct - 1 Jan: Tues - Sun 1 - 4pm. Bank Hols 11am - 4pm. 2 Jan - Easter: weekends only 1 - 4pm.

P Pay parking. Spaces: 60

Wheelchair access to ground floor only. WC for the disabled. Guide Dogs: Yes

£ **Adult:** £3.95 **Child:** £2.50 **Conc:** £2.50

Capesthorne Hall

Macclesfield, Cheshire SK11 9JY

Jacobean style hall with a collection of fine art, sculpture, furniture, tapestry and antiques from Europe, America and the Far East. The Hall dates from 1719 when it was originally designed by the Smith's of Warwick. Altered in 1837 by Blore and rebuilt by Salvin in 1861 following a disastrous fire.

www.capesthorne.com

Grant Recipient: Mr William Arthur Bromley-Davenport

Access Contact: Mrs Gwyneth Jones

Tel: 01625 861221 **Fax:** 01625 861619

E-mail: info@capesthorpe.com

Open: Apr - Oct: Sun, Wed and Bank Hols. Gardens and Chapel 12 noon - 5.00pm, Hall from 1.30 - 4pm (Last adm 3.30pm). Parties on other days by arrangement.

P Spaces: 2000

Wheelchair access to ground floor and butler's pantry. WC for the disabled. Guide Dogs: Yes

£ **Adult:** £6 (Suns & BHs), £4 (garden & chapel) **Child:** £3 (5-18 yrs), £2 (garden & chapel only) **Senior:** £5, £3 (garden & chapel), £15 (family). Wed only: £10 (Car: 4 people) £25 (minibus) £50 (coach)

Dixon's Almshouses

1-6 The Pit, Little Heath Lane, Christleton, Chester, Cheshire CH3 7AN

Originally six almshouses, built in 1868 by J. Oldrid Scott in Tudor style in memory of James Dixon of Littleton. A good, early example of Victorian timber framing. Order of Malta Homes carried out a major refurbishment in 1998 which won a council award for design.

Grant Recipient: Order of Malta Homes Trust

Access Contact: Mrs Beth Harding

Tel: 01522 813120

E-mail: b.harding@osjct.co.uk

Open: Property can be viewed from the outside with access to the interior by arrangement with the Reverend Peter Lee (tel: 01244 335663).

P On-street parking. No £ No

Highfields

Audlem, nr. Crewe, Cheshire CW3 0DT

Small half-timbered manor house dating back to c1600.

Grant Recipient: Mr J B Baker

Access Contact: Mrs Susan Baker

Tel: 01630 655479

Open: Guided tour of hall, drawing room, dining room, parlour, bedrooms and gardens by prior written arrangement.

P Spaces: 20

Wheelchair access to ground floor only, WC for the disabled with assistance (down 2 steps). Guide Dogs: Yes

£ **Adult:** £4 **Child:** £2

Lightshaw Hall Farm

Lightshaw Lane, Golborne, Warrington, Cheshire WA3 3UJ

16th century timber-framed farmhouse largely rebuilt in the 18th and 19th centuries. Historical evidence suggests there was an estate and probably a house on the site by the end of the 13th century if not before. The west range is supposed to represent the solar apartments of an early post-medieval house. External walls were replaced by bricks in the 18th and 19th centuries. Timber trusses and main roof timbers survive.

Grant Recipient & Access Contact: Mrs J Hewitt

Tel: 01942 717429

Open: All year by telephone arrangement.

P Spaces: 20

Wheelchair access to ground floor only. Video and photographs for those unable to climb stairs. No WC for the disabled. Guide Dogs: Yes £ No

Lyme Park

Disley, Stockport, Cheshire SK12 2NX

Home to the Legh family for 600 years, Lyme Park comprises a 1400 acre medieval deer park, a 17 acre Victorian garden and a Tudor hall which was transformed into an Italianate palace in the 18th century. Location for 'Pemberley' in the BBC TV's production of *Pride and Prejudice*.

www.nationaltrust.org.uk

Grant Recipient: Stockport Metropolitan Borough Council

Access Contact: Mr Philip Burt

Tel: 01663 762023 **Fax:** 01663 765035

E-mail: lymepark@nationaltrust.org.uk

Open: Hall: 21 Mar - 30 Oct, daily except Wed and Thurs 1 - 5pm. Garden: 21 Mar - 30 Oct, Fri - Tues 11am - 5pm, Wed & Thurs 1 - 5pm; Nov - 15 Dec, weekends 12 - 3pm. Park: Apr - Oct, daily 8am - 8.30pm; Nov - Mar, daily 8am - 6pm.

P Spaces: 1500. Park entry: £4 per car.

Wheelchair access to garden, first floor of house, parts of park, shop and restaurant. WC for the disabled. Guide Dogs: Yes

£ **Adult:** £6.20 **Child:** £3.10 NT members free

Rode Hall

Church Lane, Scholar Green, Cheshire ST7 3QP

Country house built early - mid 18th century, with later alterations. Set in a parkland designed by Repton. Home to the Wilbraham family since 1669.

www.rodehall.co.uk

Grant Recipient & Access Contact: Sir Richard Baker Wilbraham Bt

Tel: 01270 873237 **Fax:** 01270 882962

E-mail: rodehall@scholargreen.fsnet.co.uk

Open: Hall & Gardens: 1 Apr - 30 Sept, Wed & Bank Hols (closed Good Fri) 2 - 5pm; Gardens: Tues & Thurs 2 - 5pm. Snowdrop Walks: 8 - 27 Feb 12pm - 4pm.

P Parking for disabled available adjacent to entrance by arrangement. Spaces: 200

Wheelchair access with assistance to ground floor. WC for the disabled. Guide Dogs: Yes

£ **Adult:** £5 (house & garden), £3 (garden) **Child:** (over 12s): £3.50 (house & garden), £2 (garden) **Senior:** £3.50 (house & garden), £2 (garden)

St Chad's Church Tower

Wybunbury, Nantwich, Cheshire CW5 7LS

Grade II* listed 15th or 16th century church tower, rest of Church demolished in 1977. 96ft high and containing six restored bells, spiral staircase, charity boards, monuments and affords panoramic views over the South Cheshire plain. Bells are rung every Thurs evening.

www.wybunburytower.org.uk

Grant Recipient: Wybunbury Tower Preservation Society

Access Contact: Mrs D Lockhart

Tel: 01270 841481 **Fax:** 01270 842659

Open: Sat 11 June 'Fig Pie Wakes' (local race and festival) 1 - 5pm. Heritage Open Days 11am - 4pm. Other times by arrangement with Mrs D Lockhart (tel:01270 841481) or Mr John Colbert (tel:01270 841158).

P Spaces: 20

Wheelchair access to ground floor only. No WC for the disabled. Guide Dogs: Yes

£ **Adult:** £2 **Child:** £1

CLEVELAND

Marske Hall

Marske by the Sea, Redcar and Cleveland TS11 6AA

Country house built by Sir William Pennyman in 1625. 2 storeys with 3-storey projecting towers in a 9-bay range forming a symmetrical front approx. 115ft long. Altered in the late 19th and 20th centuries. Varied uses during 20th century include as quarters for the Royal Flying Corps in WWI, Army quarters in WWII, school 1948-58 and since 1963 a Cheshire Foundation nursing home.

Grant Recipient: Teesside Cheshire Homes

Access Contact: Mrs Sue O'Brien

Tel: 01642 482672 **Fax:** 01642 759973

E-mail: marske@ney.leonard-cheshire.org.uk

Open: Hall by arrangement only. Grounds open to public at all fund raising events such as the Summer Fete.

P Spaces: 20 •

& Yes. WC for the disabled. Guide Dogs: Yes **£** No

CO DURHAM

Barnard Castle Market Cross

Barnard Castle, Co. Durham, DL12 8EL

Two-storey building dating from 1747 with a colonnaded ground floor and enclosed upper storey. Two slate roofs crowned by a bell tower and gilded weather vane with two bullet holes from 1804. Formerly used as Town Hall, butter market, lock-up, Court room and fire station.

Grant Recipient: Teesdale District Council

Access Contact: Mr James Usher

Tel: 01833 696209 **Fax:** 01833 637269

E-mail: j.usher@teesdale.gov.uk

Open: Colonnaded area (ground floor) is open to the public at all times. The first floor is only accessible through organised tours with keys available from Teesdale House, Galgate, Barnard Castle, Co. Durham DL12 8EL (tel: 01833 696209) by special arrangement.

P On-street parking. **&** No **£** No

Croxdale Hall

Durham, County Durham DH6 5JP

18th century re-casing of an earlier Tudor building, containing comfortably furnished mid-Georgian rooms with Rococo ceilings. There is also a private chapel in the north elevation, walled gardens, a quarter-of-a-mile long terrace, an orangery and lakes which date from the mid-18th century.

Grant Recipient: Captain G M Salvin

Access Contact: Mr W H T Salvin

Tel: 01833 690100 **Fax:** 01833 637004

E-mail: whtsalvin@aol.com

Open: By arrangement on Tues & Weds from the first Tues in May to the second Wed in July, 10am - 1pm.

P Spaces: 20 **&** Partial. WC for the disabled. Guide Dogs: No

£ £7.50 (Free under 16yrs)

Durham Castle

Palace Green, Durham, Co. Durham DH1 3RW

Dating from 1072, the Castle was the seat of the Prince Bishops until 1832. Together with the Cathedral, the Castle is a World Heritage site. It now houses University College, the Foundation College of Durham University, and is a conference, banqueting and holiday centre in vacations.

www.durhamcastle.com

Grant Recipient: University of Durham

Access Contact: The Master

Tel: 0191 33 44104 **Fax:** 0191 33 43801

E-mail: M.E.Tucker@dur.ac.uk

Open: Easter - end of Sept: guided tours daily from 10am - 4pm; 1 Oct - Easter Mon: Wed, Sat & Sun (afternoons only). Tours may not take place when the Castle is being used for functions.

P Parking in city car parks.

& Wheelchair access to courtyard only. WC for the disabled inaccessible to wheelchairs. Guide Dogs: Yes

£ Adult: £5 **Child:** £2.50 (3-14yrs) **Senior:** £2.50

Group (10+): £3 **Child:** £2 (3-14yrs) **Family:** £10

Former Stockton & Darlington Railway Booking Office

48 Bridge Road, Stockton-on-Tees, Co. Durham TS18 3AX

Original booking office of the Stockton and Darlington Railway. Cottage of plain brick with slate roof facing railway line. A bronze tablet on the gable ends "Martin 1825 the Stockton and Darlington Company booked first passenger, thus marking an epoch in the history of mankind". The first rail of the Railway was laid outside the building. Now used as an administration office and accommodation for single homeless men.

Grant Recipient: Stockton Church's Mission to the Single Homeless

Access Contact: Ms Margaret McCarthy

Tel: 01642 800322 **Fax:** 01642 800322

Open: Mon - Fri, 9am - 3pm.

P Opposite side of road. Spaces: 50

& Wheelchair access to exterior of site. No WC for the disabled. Guide Dogs: Yes

£ No

Hamsteels Hall

Hamsteels Lane, Quebec, Co. Durham DH7 9RS

Early 18th century farmhouse with 19th century alterations. Panelled window shutters; ground-floor room with full early 18th century panelling; similar panelling and cupboards in first-floor room. Good quality dogleg stair with turned balusters.

Grant Recipient: Mr G F Whitfield

Access Contact: Mrs June Whitfield

Tel/Fax: 01207 520 388

E-mail: june@hamsteelshall.co.uk

Open: By arrangement.

P Spaces: 8

& Wheelchair access to Dining Room and Front Parlour only. No WC for the disabled. Guide Dogs: No

£ No

Low Butterby Farmhouse

Croxdale & Hett, Co. Durham DH6 5JN

Stone built farmhouse constructed on medieval site incorporating elements of 17th, 18th and 19th century phases of development.

Grant Recipient: The Trustees of Captain GM Salvin's 1983 Settlement

Access Contact: Mr W H T Salvin

Tel: 01833 690100 **Fax:** 01833 637004

E-mail: whtsalvin@aol.com

Open: By written or telephone arrangement with Mr W H T Salvin, The Estate Office, Egglestone Abbey, Barnard Castle, Co. Durham DL12 9TN.

P Spaces: 2

& Limited wheelchair access with assistance (some changes in floor level). No WC for the disabled. Guide Dogs: No.

£ No

Raby Castle

PO Box 50, Staindrop, Darlington, Co Durham DL2 3AY

Medieval castle, built in the 14th century. Once the seat of the Nevills, it has been home to Lord Barnard's family since 1626. Contains a collection of art, fine furniture and highly decorated interiors. Also has a deer park, gardens, carriage collection and woodland adventure playground.

www.rabycastle.com

Grant Recipient: Lord Barnard TD

Access Contact: Miss Catherine Turnbull

Tel: 01833 660888/660202 **Fax:** 01833 660169

E-mail: admin@rabycastle.com

Open: Easter & BH weekends, Sat - Wed; May & Sept, Wed & Sun only; June, July & Aug, daily except Sat. Castle open 1 - 5pm. Garden and park 11am - 5.30pm. Educational visits and private guided tours including tea/coffee reception (groups 20+) available weekday mornings from Easter to the end of Sept by arrangement.

P Spaces: 500

& Limited wheelchair access to lower floor with assistance (3 steps to entrance and some internal steps to be negotiated). 3 wheelchairs available. WC for the disabled. Guide Dogs: Yes

£ Adult: £9 (castle, park & gardens), £4 (park & gardens) **Child:** Age 5-15 £4 (castle, park & gardens), £2.50 (park & gardens) **Other:** £8 (castle, park & gardens), £3.50 (park & gardens), £25 (family), £15, £7.50 & £10 (season ticket park & gardens). Group rates available.

Rectory Farm Barn

Hall Walks, Easington, Peterlee, Co. Durham SR8 3BS

Barn, possibly 13th century with extensive alterations. May originally have been an oratory connected with Seaton Holme. Limestone rubble construction; first floor contains medieval windows. Purchased by Groundwork in 1997 and recently renovated. Listed Grade II*.

Grant Recipient: Groundwork East Durham

Access Contact: Mr Peter Richards

Tel: 0191 5273333 **Fax:** 0191 5273665

E-mail: peter.richards@groundwork.org.uk

Open: Access to the exterior at all reasonable times.

P Available.

& Yes. WC for the disabled. Guide Dogs: Yes

£ No

CORNWALL

Caerhays Castle & Garden

Gorran, St Austell, Cornwall PL26 6LY

Built by John Nash in 1808. Set in 60 acres of informal woodland gardens created by J C Williams, who sponsored plant hunting expeditions to China at the turn of the 19th century.

www.caerhays.co.uk

Grant Recipient: The Trustees of Charles Williams (Caerhays Estate)

Access Contact: Mrs M Kemp

Tel: 01872 501144/501312 **Fax:** 01872 501870

E-mail: estateoffice@caerhays.co.uk

Open: House: 14 Mar - 31 May (incl Bank Hols), Mon - Fri 1 - 4pm. Conducted tours every 45 minutes. Gardens: 14 Feb - 31 May, daily 10am to 5.30pm (last entry 4.30pm).

P Spaces: 500

& Limited wheelchair access to gardens (area around castle). Access to ground floor of castle with assistance, please telephone 01872 501144 or 01872 501312 in advance to check. WC for the disabled. Guide Dogs: Yes

£ Adult: £9.50 (garden & house), £5.50 (house tour only), £5.50 (gardens) **Child:** £3.50 (garden & house), £2.50 (house tour only), £2.50 (gardens). Under 5s free **Other:** £5 (groups 15+, house tour), £6.50 (groups, garden tour), £4 (groups, garden without tour)

Cotehele

St Dominick, Saltash, Cornwall PL12 6TA

Cotehele, situated on the west bank of the River Tamar, was built mainly between 1485-1627. Home of the Edgcumbe family for centuries. Its granite and slatestone walls contain intimate chambers adorned with tapestries, original furniture and armour.

www.nationaltrust.org.uk

Grant Recipient: The National Trust

Access Contact: Mr Lewis Eynon

Tel: 01579 351346 **Fax:** 01579 351222

E-mail: cotehele@nationaltrust.org.uk

Open: House & restaurant: 19 Mar - 30 Sept daily except Fri (but open Good Fri), 11am - 5pm; 1 - 31 Oct 11am - 4.30pm. Mill: 19 Mar - 30 June daily except Fri (but open Good Fri), 1pm - 5.30pm. 1 July - 31 Aug open daily. 1 Sept - 30 Sept daily except Fri, 1pm - 5.30pm. 1 - 31 Oct daily except Fri, 1pm - 4.30pm. Garden: daily all year round 10.30am - dusk. Light refreshments available 12 Feb - 19 Mar 11am - 4pm and on Fridays from 19 Mar - 31 Oct 11am - 5pm (4.30pm Oct).

P Spaces: 100. Parking space available for pre-booked coaches.

& Wheelchair access to house (hall, kitchen and Edgcumbe Room only), garden, area around house, restaurant and shop. Ramps available. Woodland walks: some paths accessible. WC for the disabled. Guide Dogs: Yes

£ Adult: £7.40 (house, garden & mill). £4.40 (garden & mill) **Child:** £3.70 (house, garden & mill), £2.20 (garden & mill) **Other:** £18.50 (family: house, garden & mill), £11 (family: garden & mill), £6.40 (pre-booked groups)

Cullacott Farmhouse

Werrington, Launceston, Cornwall PL15 8NH

Grade I listed medieval hall house, built in the 1480s as a long house, and extended 1579. Contains wall paintings of fictive tapestry, Tudor arms, St James of Compostella and remains of representation of St George and the Dragon. Extensively restored 1995-7 but still retains many original features. Now used as holiday accommodation.

www.cullacottholidays.co.uk

Grant Recipient: Mr & Mrs J Cole

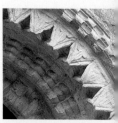

Access Contact: J Cole
Tel: 01566 772631
E-mail: marycole@cullacottholidays.co.uk
Open: By arrangement.
P Spaces: 20
♿ Wheelchair access to Great Hall, through passage and WC for the disabled. Guide Dogs: Yes
£ Adult: £2 Child: Free

Godolphin House

Godolphin Cross, Helston, Cornwall, TR13 9RE
Tudor-Stuart mansion of granite round a courtyard. For many generations seat of the Godolphin family who were courtiers from the 16th to the 18th century, the 1st Earl (who was born here) rose to be Queen Anne's Lord Treasurer. Has late Elizabethan stables with wagon collection and a large medieval and other gardens.
www.godolphinhouse.com
Grant Recipient: Mrs L M P Schofield
Access Contact: Mrs Joanne Schofield
Tel/Fax: 01736 763194
E-mail: godo@euphony.net
Open: Easter Mon - end Sept. Call for dates and times. Groups all year by arrangement.
P Spaces: 100. Parking for 3 coaches.
♿ Wheelchair access to all of the house except one room, but no access to the stables and gardens may be difficult. WC for the disabled. Guide Dogs: Yes
£ Adult: £6 (house & gardens) Child: £1.50 (5-15 yrs) Gardens: £2

Mount Edgcumbe House & Country Park

Cremyll, Torpoint, Cornwall PL10 1HZ
Grade II former home of the Earls of Mount Edgcumbe in Grade I registered landscape park of 850 acres. Includes 52 listed buildings and 16 acres of formal gardens. 16th - 18th centuries. Spectacular setting above River Tamar and Plymouth Sound. Landscape noted by Horace Walpole and Alexander Pope in 18th century. Used as starting point for D-Day landings by American troops in 1944.
www.mountedgcumbe.gov.uk
Grant Recipient: Mount Edgcumbe Country Park Joint Committee
Access Contact: The Manager
Tel: 01752 822236 Fax: 01752 822199
Open: Country Park (with listed structures): all year from dawn to dusk. Mount Edgcumbe House and Earls Garden: 27 Mar - 29 Sept, Thurs - Sun and BH Mons 11am - 4.30pm.
P Spaces: 120
♿ Wheelchair access to flat areas of garden and most of house. WC for the disabled. Guide Dogs: Yes
£ Adult: £4.50 (house only) Child: £2.25
Other: £3.50 (concessions & groups)

Porth-en-Alls Lodge

Prussia Cove, St Hilary, Cornwall TR20 9BA
Originally a chauffeur's lodge, built c1910-1914 and designed by Philip Tilden. It is built into the cliff and sits in close proximity to the main house. The Chauffeur's lodge is one of a number of historic houses on the Porth-en-Alls Estate.
Grant Recipient: Trustees of Porth-en-Alls Estate
Access Contact: Mr P Tunstall-Behrens
Tel/Fax: 01736 762 014
E-mail: penapc@dial.pipex.com
Open: Available as self-catering holiday lets throughout the year. Members of the public may view the property by arrangement, but only if it is unoccupied at the time.
P Public car park approx. 1/2 mile from the Lodge, off the A394 (near Rosudgeon village). Spaces: 50
♿ Wheelchair access to the lodge is difficult. No WC for the disabled. Guide Dogs: Yes
£ No

Tregrehan

Par, Restormel, Cornwall, PL24 2SLJ
Mid 19th century gardens and pleasure grounds designed by W A Nesfield together with significant 19th and 20th century plant collections. Concentrating on genera from warm temperate regions. An important green gene bank of known source plants. 1846 glasshouse range in walled garden. Set in 18th and 19th century parkland.
Grant Recipient: Mr T C Hudson
Access Contact: Mr T C Hudson
Tel/Fax: 01726 814389
Open: Mid Mar - mid June: Wed - Sun and Bank Hols (closed Easter Sun) 10.30am - 5pm; mid June - end Aug, Weds only 2 - 5pm.
P Spaces: 50
♿ Wheelchair access to 10 acres of garden. WC for the disabled. Guide Dogs: Yes
£ Adult: £4

Tresco Abbey Gardens

Tresco Estate, Isles of Scilly, Cornwall TR24 0QQ
25 acre garden with plants mainly from the Mediterranean region. Plant groups include protea, aloe from South Africa, succulents from Canary Isles and palms from Mexico. All grown outside all year round. Unique, frost-free climate.
www.tresco.co.uk
Grant Recipient: Tresco Estate
Access Contact: Mr Michael Nelhams
Tel: 01720 424105 Fax: 01720 422868
E-mail: mikenelhams@tresco.co.uk
Open: Daily 10am - 4pm.
P No
♿ Wheelchair access to all garden areas but some gravel slopes which may be difficult. WC for the disabled. Guide Dogs: Yes
£ Adult: £8.50 Child: Free (under 14)
Other: £12.50 (weekly ticket)

Trevelver Farmhouse

St Minver, Wadebridge, Cornwall PL27 6RJ
Remains of manor house now farmhouse. Dining room with 17th century painted panelling, a painted frieze and an over-mantle painted picture.
Grant Recipient & Access Contact: Mr Wills
Tel: 01208 863415 Fax: 01208 869024
Open: By arrangement at any reasonable time. Access to dining room only.
P Spaces: 4 ♿ No £ No

CUMBRIA

13-26 Lowther Village

Penrith, Cumbria CA10 2HG
Dwelling houses in a model village built 1766-73 by Robert Adam as estate houses for Sir James Lowther, part of a model village which was never completed.
Grant Recipient & Access Contact:
Lowther & District Housing Association Ltd
Tel: 01931 712577 Fax: 01931 712679
E-mail: jacky@lowtherdha.fsnet.co.uk
Open: Access to exterior at all times.
P Available. ♿ No £ No

Brantwood

Coniston, Cumbria LA21 8AD
Brantwood, situated on Coniston Water, was the former home of Victorian writer and artist, John Ruskin, from 1872 to 1900. Displays a collection of paintings by Ruskin and his circle, his furniture, books and personal items. Video, bookshop, craft gallery and restaurant on site. Gardens include the Harbour Walk and Professor's Garden where Ruskin experimented with native flowers and fruit.
www.brantwood.org.uk
Grant Recipient: Brantwood Education Trust Ltd
Access Contact: Mr Howard Hull
Tel: 015394 41396 Fax: 015394 41263
E-mail: enquiries@brantwood.org.uk
Open: All year: mid Mar - mid Nov, daily 11am - 5.30pm; mid Nov - mid Mar, Wed - Sun 11am - 4.30pm (closed Christmas Day and Boxing Day).
P Spaces: 50
♿ Wheelchair access to house, toilets and restaurant only. WC for the disabled. Guide Dogs: Yes
£ Adult: £5.50 Child: £1 Other: £4 (student)

Coop House

Netherby, nr. Carlisle, Cumbria CA6 5PX
Stands on the bank of the River Esk where 'coops' or traps were set to catch salmon. This summerhouse was built c1765 by Dr Robert Graham as an ornament in the landscape around Netherby Hall and as a place to enjoy the river. By 1980 it was completely derelict.
www.landmarktrust.co.uk
Grant Recipient: The Landmark Trust
Access Contact: Mr Toby Hawkins
Tel: 01628 825920 Fax: 01628 825417
E-mail: thawkins@landmarktrust.org.uk
Open: The Landmark Trust is an independent charity, which rescues small buildings of historic or architectural importance from decay or unsympathetic improvement. Landmark's aim is to promote the enjoyment of these historic buildings by making them available to stay in for holidays. Coop House can be rented by anyone, at all times of the year, for periods ranging from a weekend to three weeks. Bookings can be made by telephoning the Booking Office on 01628 825925. As the building is in full-time use for holiday accommodation, it is not normally open to the public. However the public can view the building by prior arrangement by telephoning the access contact (Toby Hawkins on 01628 825920) to make an appointment. Potential visitors will be asked to write to confirm the details.
P No ♿ No. Guide Dogs: Yes £ No

Crown & Nisi Prius Court

The Courts, English Street, Carlisle, Cumbria CA3 8NA
Former Crown Court in Carlisle situated at southern entrance to the city. One of a pair of sandstone towers built in the early 19th century as replicas of the medieval bastion. The towers were built to house the civil and criminal courts, used until the 1980s.
Grant Recipient: Cumbria Crown Court
Access Contact: Mr Mike Telfer
Tel: 01228 606116
Open: Guided Tours July and Aug Mon - Fri 1pm & 2.30pm (excl Aug BH Mon).
P Town centre car parks.
♿ Wheelchair access to Grand Jury Room, Court No.2 and Public Area Crown Court Room. WC for the disabled. Guide Dogs: Yes
£ Adult: £3 Child: £2 (age 5-15) Other: £2.50

Dean Tait's Lane Arch

Carlisle, Cumbria CA3 8TZ
16th century stone arch across the Dean Tait Lane pedestrian footpath and adjoining the Prior Slee Gatehouse.
Grant Recipient: The Chapter of Carlisle Cathedral
Access Contact: Mr T I S Burns
Tel: 01228 548151 Fax: 01228 547049
E-mail: office@carlislecathedral.org.uk
Open: Exterior visible at all times – the arch spans a public footpath.
P No ♿ Yes. No WC for the disabled. Guide Dogs: Yes £ No

Dixon's Chimney

Shaddongate, Carlisle, Cumbria CA2 5TZ
270ft chimney, formerly part of Shaddongate Mill. Built in 1836 by Peter Dixon. At its original height of 306ft the chimney was the tallest cotton mill chimney to have been constructed. Structural problems meant that the decorative stone capping had to be removed in the 1950s.
Grant Recipient: Carlisle City Council
Access Contact: Mr Peter Messenger
Tel: 01228 871195 Fax: 01228 817199
E-mail: PeterMe@carlisle-city.gov.uk
Open: Chimney can be viewed from Shaddongate and Junction Street.
P No ♿ No £ No

Kirkby Hall Wallpaintings

Kirkby-in-Furness, Cumbria LA17 7UX
Chapel in west wing, accessible only from trap door in dairy passage. Wallpaintings in red ochre and black consisting of panels with stylised trees, animals and birds with texts above of the Lord's Prayer, Creed, Ten Commandments and Galations 5, 16-21 from the Great Bible of 1541.

Grant Recipient: Holker Estates Company Ltd
Access Contact: Mr D P R Knight
Tel: 015395 58313 **Fax:** 015395 58966
E-mail: estateoffice@holker.co.uk
Open: By written arrangement with the Holker Estate Office, Cark-in-Cartmel, Grange-over-Sands, Cumbria LA11 7PH (tel:015395 58313).
P Spaces: 3 No No

Levens Hall
Kendal, Cumbria LA8 0PD
Elizabethan house built around a 13th century pele tower, containing fine furniture, panelling, plasterwork and an art collection. The gardens, which include much topiary, were laid out in the late 17th century by Monsieur Beaumont for Colonel James Grahme and are of national importance.
www.levenshall.co.uk
Grant Recipient: Mr C H Bagot
Access Contact: Mr PE Milner
Tel: 01539 560321 **Fax:** 01539 560669
E-mail: email@levenshall.fsnet.co.uk
Open: House: 12 Apr - 13 Oct, Sun - Thurs 12 noon - 5pm (Last adm 4.30). Garden: as house 10am - 5pm. Admission prices are under review at time of publication, please check with Mr Milner at the Estate Office for current information.
P Spaces: 80
House unsuitable for wheelchair users due to stairs and narrow doorways but all other facilities (topiary garden, plant centre, gift shop, and tea room) are accessible. A DVD tour of the House is available in the Buttery during opening hours. A mobility buggy is available for hire. WC for the disabled. Guide Dogs: Yes
£ **Adult:** £7.50 (house & garden), £5.80 (garden)
Child: £3.70 (house & garden), £2.60 (garden)

Muncaster Castle
Ravenglass, Cumbria CA18 1RQ
Large house incorporating medieval fortified tower, remodelled by Anthony Salvin for the 4th Lord Muncaster in 1862-66. Ancestral home of the Pennington family for 800 years containing a panelled Hall and octagonal library. Headquarters of the World Owl Trust. Woodland garden, Lakeland setting. World-famous rhododendrons, camelias and magnolias with a terrace walk along the edge of the Esk valley.
www.muncastercastle.co.uk
Grant Recipient: Mrs P R Gordon-Duff-Pennington
Access Contact: Mrs Iona Frost-Pennington
Tel: 01229 717614 **Fax:** 01229 717010
E-mail: info@muncaster.co.uk
Open: Castle: 13 Feb - 6 Nov, daily (except closed Sat) 12 noon - 5pm (or dusk if earlier). Gardens, Owl Centre and Maze open throughout the year 10.30am - 6.30pm (or dusk if earlier). Refreshments available.
P Spaces: 150
Wheelchair access to ground floor of Castle only but other attractions and facilities accessible. The hilly nature of the site can create access difficulties so please ask for further information on arrival. WC for the disabled. Guide Dogs: Yes
£ **Adult:** £9 (Castle, Gardens, Owls & Maze), £6 (Gardens, Owls & Maze)
Child: £6 (Castle, Gardens, Owls & Maze), £4 (Gardens, Owls & Maze). Under 5s free
Other: £25 (family: Castle, Gardens, Owls & Maze), £18 (family: Gardens, Owls & Maze)

Orthwaite Hall Barn
Uldale, Wigton, Cumbria CA7 1HL
Grade II* listed agricultural barn. Former house adjoining later Hall, probably late 16th or early 17th century, now used for storage and housing animals.
Grant Recipient: Mrs S Hope
Access Contact: Mr Jonathan Hope
Tel: 016973 71344
Open: By telephone arrangement.
P Spaces: 3 No wheelchair access. Guide Dogs: Yes
£ No

Prior Slee Gatehouse
Carlisle Cathedral, Carlisle, Cumbria CA3 8TZ
Dated 1528, the Gatehouse would have replaced an earlier one. It has a large chamber over the gate, with two Tudor fireplaces. Graffiti carved in the stonework is believed to include merchants' marks. One of two integral lodges survives on the north-east side of the building. Now used as residential accommodation.
Grant Recipient: The Chapter of Carlisle Cathedral
Access Contact: Mr T I S Burns
Tel: 01228 548151 **Fax:** 01228 547049
E-mail: office@carlislecathedral.org.uk
Open: By arrangement with Mr T I S Burns, The Chapter of Carlisle Cathedral, 7 The Abbey, Carlisle, Cumbria CA3 8TZ.
P Parking in nearby City centre car parks. 2 disabled parking spaces in Cathedral grounds.
WC for the disabled is nearby (approx. 200 yards). Guide Dogs: Yes £ No

Prior's Tower
The Abbey, Carlisle, Cumbria CA3 8TZ
This Grade I listed three storey pele tower type building was constructed c1500. It formed part of the Prior's Lodgings and until relatively recently was part of the Deanery. Of special interest is the magnificent ceiling of 45 hand-painted panels dating from c1510 and associated with Prior Senhouse.
Grant Recipient: The Chapter of Carlisle Cathedral
Access Contact: Mr T I S Burns
Tel: 01228 548151 **Fax:** 01228 547049
E-mail: office@carlislecathedral.org.uk
Open: By arrangement with Mr T I S Burns, The Chapter of Carlisle Cathedral, 7 The Abbey, Carlisle, Cumbria CA3 8TZ.
P Nearby City centre car parks. 2 disabled parking spaces in Cathedral grounds.
WC for the disabled is nearby (approx. 100 yards). Guide Dogs: Yes
£ No

Sizergh Castle
nr. Kendal, Cumbria LA8 8AE
Sizergh Castle has been the home of the Strickland family for over 760 years. Its core is the 14th century pele tower, later extended and containing some fine Elizabethan carved wooden chimney-pieces and inlaid chamber. The Castle is surrounded by gardens, including a rock garden.
www.nationaltrust.org.uk
Grant Recipient: The National Trust
Access Contact: Property Manager
Tel: 015395 60070 **Fax:** 015395 61621
E-mail: sizergh@nationaltrust.org.uk
Open: Castle: 23 Mar - 30 Oct, daily except Fri & Sat 1.30 - 5.30pm. Garden: 23 Mar - 30 Oct, daily except Fri & Sat 12.30 - 5.30pm. Closed Good Fri.
P Spaces: 250. Parking for disabled visitors available near the house.
Wheelchair access to Castle Lower Hall and garden gravel paths only. WC for the disabled. Guide Dogs: Yes
£ **Adult:** £5.80, £3.50 (garden only)
Child: £2.90, £1.70 (garden only)
Other: £14.50 (family), £4.80pp (pre-booked parties, min. 15 persons, not BHs)

Smardale Gill Viaduct
Kirkby Stephen, Cumbria
Rail overbridge, built 1860-1 by Sir Thomas Bouch for the South Lancashire and Durham Union Railway. 550ft long with 14 arches spanning Scandal Beck at Smardale Gill, a National Nature Reserve. A well-preserved example of a large road bridge on this line.
Grant Recipient: The Trustees of the Northern Viaduct Trust
Access Contact: Mr Michael Sewell
Tel: 01768 371456
Open: All year, access by footpaths only from Newbiggin-on-Lune or Smardale. Path along former railway.
P Parking at Smardale. Spaces: 8
Wheelchair access from Smardale only. No WC for the disabled. Guide Dogs: Yes
£ No

St Anne's Hospital
Boroughgate, Appleby, Cumbria
17th century almshouses. There are 13 dwellings and a chapel set round a cobbled courtyard. Founded by Lady Anne Clifford in 1653.
Grant Recipient: The Trustees of St Anne's Hospital
Access Contact: Lord Hothfield
Tel: 017683 51487 **Fax:** 017683 53259
E-mail: lulieant@aol.com
Open: All year, daily 9am - 5pm.
P On-street parking. Spaces: 50
Guide Dogs: Yes £ No

Wray Castle
Low Wray, Ambleside, Cumbria
A large Gothic mock castle and arboretum. Built in the 1840s over looking the western shore of Lake Windermere.
www.nationaltrust.org.uk
Grant Recipient: The National Trust
Access Contact: Property Manager
Tel: 015394 36269 **Fax:** 015394 36811
Open: Castle (entrance hall only): June, July and Aug by prior arrangement, contact property manager (tel: 015394 36269). Garden and grounds all year. Telephone the property manager for further details.
P Spaces: 20 No No

DERBYSHIRE

Assembly Rooms
The Crescent, Buxton, Derbyshire SK17 6BH
The Crescent was designed by John Carr of York and built by the Fifth Duke of Devonshire between 1780-89. It provided hotels, lodgings and a suite of elaborately decorated Assembly Rooms. The front elevation of three storeys is dominated by Doric pilasters over a continuous rusticated ground floor arcade.
Grant Recipient: Derbyshire County Council
Access Contact: Mr Allan Morrison
Tel: 01629 580000 **Fax:** 01629 585143
E-mail: allan.morrison@derbyshire.gov.uk
Open: Exterior accessible from public highway. No interior access until refurbishment works completed, other than special agreement.
P On-street parking available. No No

Barlborough Hall
Barlborough, Chesterfield, Derbyshire S43 4TL
Built by Sir Francis Rhodes in the 1580s, the Hall is square in plan and stands on a high basement with a small internal courtyard to provide light. Contains Great Chamber, now a chapel, bearing a date of 1584 on the overmantel whilst the porch is dated 1583. Now a private school.
Grant Recipient: The Governors of Barlborough Hall School
Access Contact: Mr C F A Bogie
Tel: 01246 435138 **Fax:** 01246 435090
Open: By arrangement only 29 Mar - 11 Apr, 31 May - 5 June, 4 July - 3 Sept and most weekends throughout the year. External visits (without guide) any evening after 6pm or weekend.
P Spaces: 50 No. Guide Dogs: Yes
£ No

Bennerley Viaduct
Erewash Valley, Ilkeston, Derbyshire
Disused railway viaduct over the Erewash vally, c1878-9, and approximately 500 yards long with 15 piers. It is one of two remaining wrought iron lattice-girder bridges in the British Isles.
Grant Recipient: Railway Paths Ltd
Access Contact: Mr Simon Ballantine
Tel/Fax: 01548 550 331
E-mail: simonb@sustrans.org.uk
Open: There is access to the viaduct by a public footpath running underneath it, but the deck itself is inaccessible.
P No No No

Buxton Opera House
Water Street, Buxton, Derbyshire SK17 6XN
The Buxton Opera House was designed by Frank Matcham and opened in 1903. Its Baroque guilded plasterwork and painted ceiling panels by De Jong were restored in Spring 2001 following extensive research into the original colour scheme.
www.buxton-opera.co.uk
Grant Recipient: High Peak Borough Council

Access Contact: Mr Graham Dentith
Tel: 01298 72050 Fax: 01298 27563
E-mail: genmanager@buxtonopera.co.uk
Open: The theatre is open all year round for performances (mostly evenings), exact schedule varies. Theatre tours are offered most Sat mornings. Box Office and Foyer open Mon - Sat 10am - 6pm (or 8pm) and some Suns.
P Limited on-street parking.
Wheelchair access to stalls only. WC for the disabled. Guide Dogs: Yes
£ Adult: £2 Child: Free

Calke Abbey

Ticknall, Derbyshire DE73 1LE
Baroque mansion, built 1701-3 for Sir John Harpur and set in a landscaped park. Little restored, Calke is preserved by a programme of conservation as a graphic illustration of the English house in decline. It contains the natural history collection of the Harpur Crewe family, an 18th century state bed and interiors that are essentially unchanged since the 1880s.
www.nationaltrust.org.uk
Grant Recipient: The National Trust
Access Contact: Property Manager
Tel: 01332 863822 Fax: 01332 865272
E-mail: calkeabbey@nationaltrust.org.uk
Open: House, garden and Church: 26 Mar - 30 Oct: daily except Thurs and Fri. House: 1 - 5.30pm (ticket office opens at 11am). Garden and Church: 11am - 5.30pm. Park: most days until 9pm or dusk if earlier. Timed ticket system is in operation. All visitors (including NT members) require a ticket from the ticket office.
P Spaces: 75
Wheelchair access to ground floor of house, stables, shop and restaurant. Garden and park partly accessible. WC for the disabled. Guide Dogs: Yes
£ Adult: £6.30   Child: £3.10 Other: £15.70 (family), £3.80 (garden only)

Catton Hall

Catton, Walton-on-Trent, Derbyshire DE12 8LN
Country house built c1741 by Smith of Warwick for Christopher Horton. Property owned by the same family since 1405. Contains an interesting collection of 17th and 18th century pictures, including Royal and Family portraits; also Byron and Napoleon memorabilia. Gardens, which run down to the River Trent, include a family chapel.
www.catton-hall.com
Grant Recipient: Mr R Neilson
Access Contact: Mrs C Neilson
Tel: 01283 716311 Fax: 01283 712876
E-mail: kneilson@catton-hall.com
Open: 4 Apr - 10 Oct, tours of the house, chapel and gardens every Mon at 2pm. Group tours (15 or more) at any time by arrangement.
P Unlimited parking.
Wheelchair access by separate entrance to all rooms. No WC for the disabled. Guide Dogs: Yes
£ Adult: £4 Conc: £3

Cromford Mill

Mill Lane, Cromford, nr. Matlock, Derbyshire DE4 3RQ
Grade I listed mill complex established by Sir Richard Arkwright in 1771. The world's first successful water powered cotton spinning mill situated in the Derwent Valley Mills World Heritage Site. Currently being conserved by the Arkwright Society, an educational charity. The Mill is home to four shops and a restaurant.
www.arkwrightsociety.org.uk
Grant Recipient: The Arkwright Society
Access Contact: Mr Jon Charlton
Tel: 01629 823256 Fax: 01629 824297
E-mail: info@arkwright.net
Open: Daily 9am - 5pm, closed on Christmas Day. Free entry to main site, charges for guided tours.
P Spaces: 100
Wheelchair access to shops, lavatories and restaurant. WC for the disabled. Guide Dogs: Yes
£ Adult: £2 Child: £1.50 Other: £1.50

Hardwick Hall

Doe Lea, Chesterfield, Derbyshire S44 5QJ
A late 16th century 'prodigy house' designed by Robert Smythson for Bess of Hardwick. Contains an outstanding collection of 16th century furniture, tapestries and needlework. Walled courtyards enclose gardens, orchards and herb garden.
www.nationaltrust.org.uk
Grant Recipient: The National Trust
Access Contact: Property Manager
Tel: 01246 850430 Fax: 01246 854200
E-mail: hardwickhall@nationaltrust.org.uk
Open: 23 Mar - 30 Oct: daily except Mon, Tues & Fri (but open BH Mons & Good Fri), 12 noon - 4.30pm. Garden: Wed - Sun, 11am - 5.30pm. Parkland: daily, 8am - 6pm (close 5.30pm in winter).
P Spaces: 200
WC for the disabled. Guide Dogs: Yes
£ Adult: £7.20   Child: £3.60   Other: £18(family), £3.90 (garden only), £9.70 (joint ticket with Hardwick Old Hall, EH property)

Kedleston Hall

Derby, Derbyshire DE22 5JH
A classical Palladian mansion built 1759-65 for the Curzon family and little altered since. Robert Adam interior with state rooms retaining their collection of paintings and original furniture. The Eastern museum houses a range of objects collected by Lord Curzon when Viceroy of India (1899-1905). Set in 800 acres of parkland and 18th century pleasure ground, garden and woodland walks.
www.nationaltrust.org.uk
Grant Recipient: The National Trust
Access Contact: Property Manager
Tel: 01332 842191 Fax: 01332 841972
E-mail: kedlestonhall@nationaltrust.org.uk
Open: House: 19 Mar - 31 Oct: daily except Thurs & Fri 12 noon - 4.30pm. Garden: daily 10am - 6pm. Park: All year (occasional day restrictions may apply in Dec and Jan 2006); 19 Mar - 31 Oct 10am - 6pm; 1 Nov - Mar 2005 10am - 4pm.
P Winter admission for park only, parking charge of £2.70. Spaces: 60
Wheelchair access to ground floor of house via stairclimber, garden, restaurant and shop. WC for the disabled. Guide Dogs: Yes
£ Adult: £6.30   Child: £3   Family: £15.50 . Park & garden only: £2.80

Masson Mills

(Sir Richard Arkwright's), Derby Road, Matlock Bath, Derbyshire DE4 3PY
Sir Richard Arkwright's 1783 showpiece Masson Mills are the finest surviving example of one of Arkwright's cotton mills. The "Masson Mill pattern" of design was an important influence in nascent British and American mill development. Museum with historic working textile machinery. Part of the Derwent Valley Mills World Heritage Site.
www.massonmills.co.uk
Grant Recipient: Mara Securities Ltd
Access Contact: Museum Reception
Tel: 01629 581001 Fax: 01629 581001
Open: All year except Christmas Day & Easter Day: Mon - Fri 10am - 4pm, Sat 11am - 5pm & Sun 11am - 4pm.
P Spaces: 200
Wheelchair access to most areas. WC for the disabled. Guide Dogs: No
£ Adult: £2.50 Child: £1.50 (schools £1 per child) Other: £2

St Ann's Hotel

The Crescent, Buxton, Derbyshire SK17 6BH
The Crescent was designed by John Carr of York and built by the Fifth Duke of Devonshire between 1780-89. It provided hotels, lodgings and a suite of elaborately decorated Assembly Rooms. The front elevation of three storeys is dominated by Doric pilasters over a continuous rusticated ground floor arcade.
Grant Recipient: High Peak Borough Council
Access Contact: Mr Richard Tuffrey
Tel: 01457 851653 Fax: 01457 860290
E-mail: richard.tuffrey@highpeak.gov.uk
Open: Exterior accessible from public highway. No interior access until refurbishment works completed.
P On-street parking available.   No £ No

Sudbury Hall

Sudbury, Ashbourne, Derbyshire DE6 5HT
17th century house with rich interior decoration including wood carvings by Laguerre. The Great Staircase (c1676) with white-painted balustrade with luxuriantly carved foliage by Edward Pierce, is one of the finest staircases of its date in an English house. 19th century service wing houses the National Trust Museum of Childhood.
www.nationaltrust.org.uk
Grant Recipient: The National Trust
Access Contact: Property Manager
Tel: 01283 585305 Fax: 01283 585139
E-mail: sudburyhall@nationaltrust.org.uk
Open: Hall: 6 Mar - 30 Oct: Wed - Sun (but open BH Mons & Good Fri) 1 - 5pm. Museum: 6 Mar - 30 Oct: as Hall 1 - 5pm; 3 - 11 Dec: Sat & Sun only 11am - 4pm. Grounds: as House to 30 Oct 11am - 6pm.
P Car park is a short distance from the Hall; six-seater volunteer driven buggy available. Spaces: 100
Wheelchair access to lake, tea room and shop. Ground floor access to museum. Access to Hall difficult – please contact the Property Manager in advance. WC for the disabled. Guide Dogs: Yes
£ Adult: £5 (house), £5.50 (museum), £8 (house & museum) Child: £2 (house), £3.50 (museum), £4.50 (house & museum) Family: £11.50 (house), £12.50 (museum), £20 (house & museum)

Tissington Hall

Tissington, Ashbourne, Derbyshire DE6 1RA
Grade II* listed Jacobean manor house altered in the 18th century and extended in the 20th. Contains fine furniture, pictures and interesting early 17th century panelling. Home of the FitzHerbert family for over 500 years.
www.tissington-hall.com
Grant Recipient/Access Contact:
Sir Richard FitzHerbert Bt
Tel: 01335 352200 Fax: 01335 352201
E-mail: tisshall@dircon.co.uk
Open: 28 Mar - 1 Apr, 30 May - 3 June and 29 Aug inclusive. 19 July - 30 Aug Tues - Fri.
P Spaces: 100
Wheelchair access to gardens and various rooms. Guide Dogs: by arrangement. WC for the disabled. Guide Dogs: Yes
£ Adult: £5.50 (house & garden), £2 (garden) Child: (10-16yrs): £2.50 (house & garden), £1 (garden) Other: £4.50 (house & garden), £2 (garden)

DEVON

21 The Mint

Exeter, Devon EX4 3BL
The refectory range of St Nicholas Priory, converted into a substantial town house in the Elizabethan period and later into tenements. Features include medieval arch-braced roof, traces of the Norman priory and later Elizabethan panelling. Recently restored, now dwellings and meeting room.
Grant Recipient: Exeter Historic Buildings Trust
Access Contact: Katharine Chant
Tel: 01392 436000 / 496653
Fax: 01392 496653
E-mail: the-chants@tiscali.co.uk
Open: Every Mon throughout the year 2 - 4pm (except Bank Hols). Also Easter Sat (26 Mar), May Day Bank Holiday (2 May), Spring Bank Holiday (28 - 30 May), first Sat in July (2 July) and first Sat in Aug for Exeter Living History Weekend 11am - 4pm. Heritage Open Days 11am - 4pm. Pre-booked groups at any time throughout the year.
P No
Wheelchair access to ground floor and courtyard garden only. No WC for the disabled. Guide Dogs: Yes
£ No, but meeting room available for hire

Anderton House/Rigg Side

Goodleigh, North Devon, Devon
Anderton House also known as Rigg Side. 1970-1 to the designs of Peter Aldington and

John Craig for Mr and Mrs Anderton. The inspiration for its profile is taken from the longhouses of Devon. Timber frame, forming a two-row grid of double posts and beams with a tent roof, set half proud of concrete block walls and glazed clerestory and stained tiled gabled roof. Timber linings and ceilings internally, with tiled floors. Its sliding doors give views of the Devon countryside.

www.www.landmarktrust.org.uk
Grant Recipient: The Landmark Trust
Access Contact: Mr Toby Hawkins
Tel: 01628 825920 **Fax:** 01628 825417
E-mail: thawkins@landmarktrust.org.uk
Open: The Landmark Trust is an independent charity, which rescues small buildings of historic or architectural importance from decay or unsympathetic improvement. Landmark's aim is to promote the enjoyment of these historic buildings by making them available to stay in for holidays. Anderton House can be rented by anyone, at all times of the year, for periods ranging from a weekend to three weeks. Bookings can be made by telephoning the Booking Office on 01628 825925. As the building is in full-time use for holiday accommodation, it is not normally open to the public. However the public can view the building by prior arrangement by telephoning the access contact (Toby Hawkins on 01628 825920) to make an appointment. Potential visitors will be asked to write to confirm the details of their visit.
Ⓟ No
Ⓖ Wheelchair access to kitchen, bedrooms and dining room. No WC for the disabled. Guide Dogs: Yes
£ No.

Ayshford Chapel

Ayshford, Burlescombe, Devon
Grade I listed private medieval chapel with a simple medieval screen. Distinctive stained glass of 1848 and 17th century monuments to the Ashford family.
www.friendsoffriendlesschurches.org.uk
Grant Recipient: Friends of Friendless Churches
Access Contact: Mr & Mrs Kelland
Tel: 01884 820271
Open: At any reasonable time. Keyholder lives nearby.
Ⓟ On-street parking. Spaces: 2
Ⓖ Wheelchair access possible with assistance: access to church through field and up one step. No WC for the disabled. Guide Dogs: Yes
£ No

Broomham Farm

King's Nympton, Devon EX37 9TS
Late medieval Grade II* listed Devon long-house of stone and cob construction with thatched roof. Contains a smoking room. Currently undergoing renovation.
Grant Recipient: Mr Clements
Access Contact: Miss J Clements
Tel: 01769 572322
Open: By telephone arrangement.
Ⓟ Spaces: 3 Ⓖ No £ No

Coldharbour Mill

Uffculme, Devon EX15 3EE
Woollen mill built by Thomas Fox between 1797-1799. Grade II* listed building. Now a working textile mill museum with demonstrations of textile machinery. Exhibition gallery, picnic area, café, waterside walks and shop.
www.coldharbourmill.org.uk
Grant Recipient: The Coldharbour Mill Trust
Access Contact: Mr Ashley Smart
Tel: 01884 840960 **Fax:** 01884 840858
E-mail: info@coldharbourmill.org.uk
Open: Mar - Oct: daily 10.30am - 5.30pm. Nov - Feb: Sundays only 10.30am - 5.30pm.
Ⓟ Spaces: 100
Ⓖ Wheelchair access to the mill via lift. Café not accessible and some areas of the steam complex. WC for the disabled. Guide Dogs: Yes
£ Adult: £5.75 Child: £2.75 Family: £16.00 (provisional prices, please check)

Colleton Manor Chapel

Chulmleigh, Devon EX18 7JS
Small chapel over gatehouse, possibly one mentioned in licence of 1381. Stone walls, slate roof, west wall recently rebuilt in stone and cob. Plain interior with Edwardian matchboard panelling and exposed timbers. Still used as a chapel.
Grant Recipient & Access Contact:
Mr and Mrs Phillips
Tel: 01769 580240
Open: By telephone arrangement with Mr & Mrs Phillips at Colleton Manor
Ⓟ Spaces: 3 Ⓖ No
£ Voluntary donation requested towards chapel maintenance

Cookworthy Museum of Rural Life in South Devon

The Old Grammar School, 108 Fore Street, Kingsbridge, Devon TQ7 1AW
17th century schoolroom with 19th century annex in Tudor style. Original entrance arch. Now a local museum with Victorian kitchen, Edwardian pharmacy and walled garden.
www.devonmuseums.net
Grant Recipient: William Cookworthy Museum Society
Access Contact: Miss Margaret Lorenz
Tel: 01548 853235
E-mail: wcookworthy@talk21.com
Open: 31 Mar - 31 Oct: Mon - Sat 10.30am - 5pm (Oct 10am - 4pm). Booked groups all year (contact Mr Clifford Peach at the Cookworthy Museum). Local History Resource Centre open all year.
Ⓟ Public car park on Fore Street, 100 metres from Museum. Spaces: 100
Ⓖ Wheelchair access with assistance to Victorian kitchen, photographic display, Farm Gallery, walled garden and shop and Local Heritage Resource Centre. WC for the disabled. Guide Dogs: Yes
£ Adult: £2 Child: 90p Seniors: £1.50 Family: £5

Dartington Hall

Dartington, Totnes, Devon TQ9 6EL
Medieval mansion and courtyard built 1388-1399 by John Holland, Earl of Huntingdon and later Duke of Exeter, half brother to Richard II. Set in a landscaped garden and surrounded by a 1200 acre estate. The Champernowne family owned Dartington for 400 years before selling the estate to Leonard and Dorothy Elmhirst who founded the Dartington Hall Trust.
www.dartington.u-net.com
Grant Recipient: The Dartington Hall Trust
Access Contact: Mrs K Hockings
Tel: 01803 847002 **Fax:** 01803 847007
E-mail: trust@dartingtonhall.org.uk
Open: All year for courses, events and activities. The Hall, courtyard and gardens are accessible for external viewing all year. Access to the interior by arrangement. Coach parties by arrangement only.
Ⓟ Spaces: 250
Ⓖ Wheelchair access to Great Hall, courtyard and top garden paths. WC for the disabled. Guide Dogs: Yes
£ Some activities have an entry fee

Exeter Custom House

The Quay, Exeter, Devon EX1 1NN
Located on the historic quayside, the Custom House was constructed in 1680-1 and is the earliest purpose-built customs house in Britain. Contains many original fittings and 3 exceptionally ornamental plaster ceilings by John Abbot of Frithelstock (amongst the finest such work of this date in the south west).
www.exeter.gov.uk/visiting/attractions
Grant Recipient: Exeter City Council
Access Contact: Tourism Promotions Officer
Tel: 01392 265203 **Fax:** 01392 265695
E-mail: guidedtours@exeter.gov.uk
Open: Tours: May - Sept, Thurs & Sat at 2pm (lasts 30 minutes).
Ⓟ Cathedral & Quay car park (75 metres). Spaces:

400. 5 disabled public spaces in front of Custom House.
Ⓖ Wheelchair access to ground floor stair area only. WC for the disabled in car park. Guide Dogs: Yes
£ No

Finch Foundry

Sticklepath, Okehampton, Devon EX20 2NW
19th century water-powered forge, which produced agricultural and mining hand tools. Still in working order with regular demonstrations. The foundry has three water-wheels driving the huge tilt hammer and grindstone.
www.nationaltrust.org.uk
Grant Recipient: The National Trust
Access Contact: Mr Roger Boney
Tel/Fax: 01837 840046
E-mail: rboney@nationaltrust.org.uk
Open: 21 Mar - 31 Oct: daily except Tues, 11am - 5.30pm (Last adm 5pm). Tea room/shop as Foundry.
Ⓟ Access to car park is narrow and unsuitable for coaches and wide vehicles. Spaces: 50
Ⓖ Wheelchair access to museum and workshop is difficult, Foundry can be viewed through shop window. No WC for the disabled. Guide Dogs: Yes
£ Adult: £3.50 Child: £1.70 (5-16 yrs, Under 5yrs Free.)

Higher Thornham

Romansleigh, South Molton, Devon EX36 4JS
16th century through passage house, remodelled in the 17th century. Built of stone and cob, with a thatched roof. Beamed ceilings on ground floor and one moulded door frame. Recently renovated using traditional materials.
Grant Recipient & Access Contact:
Mr S W Chudley
Open: By written arrangement 1 May - end of Sept: Mon or Fri 2 - 4.30pm. Dogs not allowed and children must be accompanied by an adult. No Photography. Guide dog access to ground floor only.
Ⓟ Spaces: 2
Ⓖ No. Guide Dogs: Yes
£ Adult: £4 Child: £1.50

Kilworthy Farm Cow Houses & Granary

Tavistock Hamlets, Devon PL9 0JN
Kilworthy Farm was part of the Duke of Bedford's Devon estates. The farm buildings dated 1851 consist of three parallel ranges of cowhouses situated over an undercroft of granite construction. A two storey granary adjoins the cowhouses to the east and a stableyard of single storey buildings lies separately to the west. An unusually large and complete example of a planned farmyard covering all functions of the farm for dairy and arable. The cowhouses with underground dung pit are of exceptional interest.
Grant Recipient: Mesdames Coren, Dennis & Edworthy
Access Contact: Mrs Sandra Vallance
Tel: 01822 614477 **Fax:** 01822 614477
Open: 25 July - 20 Aug, daily except Sun and excluding Thurs in Aug; Easter Sat & Easter Mon; both May & the Aug BH weekends. At other times by arrangement with Mr & Mrs A Vallance 10am - 5pm. Guided tour to start at 11am & 2pm, or by special arrangement.
Ⓟ Please ensure access for farm traffic is not obstructed. Spaces: 4
Ⓖ Wheelchair access to the ground floor of the granary and the lengthwise walkways of the cowhouses. The undercroft is cobbled and the central passages are passable but rough. Guide dogs are welcome but as a working farm care is requested. No WC for the disabled.
£ Adult: £3 (includes info leaflet & guided tour) Child: £1 (under 10)

Lawrence Castle Haldon Belvedere

Higher Ashton, nr. Dunchideock, Exeter, Devon EX6 7QY
Grade II* listed building built in 1788 as the centrepiece to a 11,600 acre estate. Stands 244 metres above sea level overlooking the cathedral city of Exeter, the Exe estuary and the surrounding countryside. Contains a spiral staircase and miniature ballroom.
www.haldonbelvedere.co.uk

Opening arrangements at properties grant-aided by English Heritage

Grant Recipient:
Devon Historic Buildings Trust
Access Contact: Mr Ian Turner
Tel: 01392 833668 **Fax:** 01392 833668
E-mail: turner@haldonbelvedere.co.uk
Open: 6 Mar - 30 Oct: Sundays & Bank Hols 2 - 5pm. At other times by prior arrangement. Grounds open all year. Further public access under review at time of publication, please check the English Heritage website or with the access contact for current information.
P Spaces: 15. Parking for disabled adjacent to building.
Wheelchair access to ground floor only. No WC for the disabled. Guide Dogs: Yes
£ Adult: £2 **Child:** Free
Wheelchair bound visitors: Free

Lynton Town Hall

Lee Road, Lynton, Devon EX35 6HT
Grade II* listed Town Hall. Cornerstone laid 1898, opened by the donor Sir George Newnes, 15 Aug 1900. Neo-Tudor design with Art Nouveau details: a very striking building. Now functions as Town Hall and community facility.
Grant Recipient: Lynton & Lynmouth Town Council
Access Contact: Mr Dwyer
Tel: 01598 752384 **Fax:** 01598 752677
E-mail: ltc@northdevon.gov.uk
Open: Mon - Fri 9.30am - 11.00am. Other times by arrangement.
P No
Wheelchair access to ground floor only. No WC for the disabled. Guide Dogs: Yes
£ No

Old Quay Head

The Quay, Ilfracombe, Devon EX34 9EQ
Grade II* listed quay originally constructed early in the 16th century by William Bourchier, Lord Fitzwarren. The Quay was paved with stone in the 18th century and extended further in the 19th. This extension is marked by a commemorative stone plaque at its southern end. The Quay separates the inner harbour basin from the outer harbour.
Grant Recipient: North Devon District Council
Access Contact: Lieutenant Commander R Lawson
Tel: 01271 862108
Open: All year.
P Charges apply from Mar - Oct. Places for disabled available. Spaces: 144
WC for the disabled immediately adjacent to the Old Quay Head. Guide Dogs: Yes
£ No

Saltram House

Plympton, Plymouth, Devon PL7 1UH
A remarkable survival of a George II mansion, complete with its original contents and set in a landscaped park. Robert Adam worked here on two occasions to create the state rooms and produced what are claimed to be the finest such rooms in Devon. These show his development as a designer, from using the conventional Rococo, to the low-relief kind of Neo-Classical detail that became his hallmark and with which he broke new ground in interior design.
www.nationaltrust.org.uk
Grant Recipient: The National Trust
Access Contact: Carol Murrin
Tel: 01752 333500 **Fax:** 01752 336474
E-mail: saltram@nationaltrust.org.uk
Open: House: 23 Mar - 30 Sept daily except Fri (but open Good Fri), 12 noon - 4.30pm. 1 Oct - 30 Oct daily except Fri, 11.30am - 3.30pm. Garden: 23 Mar - 31 Oct daily except Fri (but open Good Fri), 11am - 5pm. 1 Nov - 22 Dec daily except Fri, 11am - 4pm.
P 500 metres from house, 30 marked spaces on tarmac, remainder on grass. Spaces: 250
Wheelchair access to first floor via lift (66cm wide by 86.5cm deep), restaurant, tea room, ticket offices over cobbles. Wheelchairs available at house. WC for the disabled. Guide Dogs: Yes
£ Adult: £7 (house & garden), £3.50 (garden only) **Child:** £3.50 (house & garden), £1.80 (garden only). Under 5s Free
Other: £17.50 (family). £6 (Groups 15+)

Smeaton's Tower

The Hoe, Plymouth, Devon PL1 2NZ
Re-sited upper part of the former Eddystone Lighthouse. Built 1759 by John Smeaton, erected here on new base in 1882. Circular tapered tower of painted granite with octagonal lantern. When this lighthouse was first constructed it was considered to be an important technical achievement.
Grant Recipient: Plymouth City Museum & Art Gallery
Access Contact: Mr Andrew Gater
Tel: 01752 304386 **Fax:** 01752 256361
E-mail: andrew.gater@plymouth.gov.uk
Open: Easter - end Oct, daily 10am - 4pm; beginning Nov - Easter, Tues - Sat 10am - 3pm.
P On-street parking. Spaces: 40 No
£ Adult: £2.25 Child: £1.25

South Molton Town Hall and Pannier Market

South Molton, Devon EX36 3AB
Guild Hall, dating from 1743 and Grade I listed. Incorporates Court Room, Old Assembly Room and Mayor's Parlour with Museum on ground floor. Adjacent to Pannier Market and New Assembly Room.
Grant Recipient: South Molton Town Council
Access Contact: Mr Malcolm Gingell
Tel: 01769 572501 **Fax:** 01769 574008
E-mail: smtc@northdevon.gov.uk
Open: Museum open Mar - Oct, Mon - Thurs & Sat. All other rooms used for meetings, functions etc as and when required. Constable Room rented by Devon County Council.
P In Pannier Market except Thurs & Sats.
All areas except Court Room, Mayor's Parlour & Old Assembly Room. WC for the disabled. Guide Dogs: Yes
£ No

Ugbrooke Park

Chudleigh, Devon TQ13 0AD
House and chapel built c1200 and redesigned by Robert Adam in the 1760s for the 4th Lord Clifford. Chapel and library wing in Adam's characteristic castle style. Set in 'Capability' Brown landscaped park with lakes and 18th century Orangery. Home of the Lords Clifford of Chudleigh for 400 years.
www.ugbrooke.co.uk
Grant Recipient: Clifford Estate Company Ltd
Access Contact: Lord Clifford
Tel: 01626 852179 **Fax:** 01626 853322
E-mail: cliffordestate@btconnect.com
Open: 10 July - 8 Sept: Tue, Wed, Thur, Sun and Aug BH Mon 1 - 5.30pm. Group tours and private functions by prior arrangement.
P Spaces: 200
Yes. WC for the disabled. Guide Dogs: Yes
£ Adult: £5.50 (house & garden), £3 (garden) **Child:** £3 (house & garden), £2 (garden) **Senior:** £5 (house & garden)

DORSET

Blandford Forum Town Hall & Corn Exchange

Market Place, Blandford Forum, Dorset DT1 7PY
The Town Hall built by the Bastard Brothers and completed in 1734, has a Portland stone facade. On the ground floor is a loggia with 3 semi-circular arches enclosed by iron gates. The former magistrates room and the mid 20th century Council Chamber sit at 1st floor level. Attached to the rear of the building is the Corn Exchange, built in 1858, with interesting elliptical roof-trusses.
www.blandford-tc.co.uk
Grant Recipient: Blandford Forum Town Council
Access Contact: The Town Clerk
Tel: 01258 454500 **Fax:** 01258 454432
E-mail: admin@blandford-tc.co.uk
Open: Open to the public throughout the year for markets, civic functions and other events. At other times by prior telephone arrangement with The Town Clerk, Mon - Fri 9.30am - 12.30pm.
P On-street meter parking, except on market days on Thurs and Sats. Other parking in the town. Spaces: 20

Wheelchair access to ground floor only. WC for the disabled. Guide Dogs: Yes
£ No

The Chantry

128 South Street, Bridport, Dorset DT6 3PA
14th or 15th century two-storey stone rubble house, originally situated on a promontory of the River Brit. At one time known as the "Prior's House", more probably the house of a chantry priest. Interesting internal details including fragments of 17th century domestic wall paintings.
www.vivat.org.uk
Grant Recipient: The Vivat Trust Ltd
Access Contact: Mrs F Lloyd
Tel: 0845 090 2212 **Fax:** 0845 090 0174
E-mail: enquiries@vivat.org.uk
Open: Heritage Open Days in Sept 10am - 5pm. At other times by prior arrangement with The Vivat Trust (tel:0845 090 2212, fax:0845 090 0174, email:enquiries@vivat.co.uk).
P Spaces: 1. Additional on-street parking.
Wheelchair access with difficulty through back entrance to kitchen and sitting room on ground floor. No WC for the disabled. Guide Dogs: Yes
£ No

Highcliffe Castle

Rothesay Drive, Highcliffe-on-Sea, Christchurch, Dorset BH23 4LE
Cliff-top mansion built in the 1830s by Charles Stuart. Constructed in the romantic, picturesque style, much of its stonework is medieval coming from France. Exterior has been restored, interior houses changing exhibitions and the 16th century stained glass Jesse window. Gift shop and tea rooms on site with 14 acre cliff-top park.
www.highcliffecastle.co.uk
Grant Recipient: Christchurch Borough Council
Access Contact: Mr David Hopkins
Tel: 01425 278807 **Fax:** 01425 280423
E-mail: d.hopkins@christchurch.gov.uk
Open: 1 Feb - 31 Oct: daily 11 am - 5pm. Also some evenings for special events. Tea Rooms open all year 10am - late afternoon; grounds all year from 7am.
P Charged parking in Council car park Apr - Sept (free Oct - Mar) with additional parking in Highcliffe Village (1 mile from Castle). Spaces: 120
Currently no wheelchair access to the building but there are toilet facilities for the disabled at the site. Guide Dogs: Yes
£ Adult: £2 **Child:** Free **Other:** HHA/Season Ticket holders free

EAST RIDING OF YORKSHIRE

Church of Our Lady & St Everilda

Everingham, East Riding of Yorkshire YO42 4JA
Roman Catholic parish church for Everingham, built between 1836 and 1839 to the designs of Agostino Giorgiola. Interior has columned walls and a barrelled ceiling with a semi-dome above the high altar. Also of note are the altar, font and statues and the 1839 organ by William Allen.
Grant Recipient: The Herries Charitable Trust
Access Contact: Mr N J M Turton
Tel/Fax: 01759 304105
E-mail: nturton@btconnect.com
Open: Key available during reasonable hours by telephoning 01430 861443 or 01759 302226.
P Spaces: 12
No. Guide Dogs: Yes
£ No

Constable Mausoleum

Halsham, nr. Kingston-upon-Hull, East Riding of Yorkshire
The Constable Mausoleum was commissioned by Edward Constable in 1792, built by Atkinson and York and completed in 1802 at a cost of £3,300. It comprises a central domed rotunda of stone, internally lined with black marble and surrounded by heraldic shields. The external raised and railed podium is part of a vaulted ceiling to the crypt below, in which various generation of the Constable family are interned.
Grant Recipient & Access Contact: Mr John Chichester-Constable

Tel: 01964 562316   Fax: 01964 563283
E-mail: info@burtonconstable.co.uk
Open: By written arrangement with Mr John Chichester-Constable, South Wing - Estate Office, Burton Constable Hall, nr Kingston-upon-Hull, East Riding of Yorkshire HU11 4LN.
P On street parking. Spaces: 1
No. WC for the disabled at Halsham Arms approximately 300 metres.   £ No

Maister House

160 High Street, Kingston-upon-Hull, East Riding of Yorkshire HU1 1NL
Rebuilt in 1743 during Hull's heyday as an affluent trading centre, this house is a typical but rare survivor of a contemporary merchant's residence. The restrained exterior belies the spectacular plasterwork staircase inside. The house is now let as offices.
www.nationaltrust.org.uk
Grant Recipient: The National Trust
Access Contact: Property Manager
Tel: 01482 324114   Fax: 01482 227003
Open: Daily except Sat & Sun (closed Good Fri and all Bank Hols) 10am - 4pm. Access is to entrance hall and staircase only. Unsuitable for groups. No WC.
P No   No. Guide Dogs: Yes   £ Donations welcome

Old Lighthouse

Flamborough, nr. Bridlington, East Riding of Yorkshire
Grade II* light tower, built in 1674. 24 metres high, designed for a coal and brushwood fire to have been burnt on top although it is uncertain whether it was ever lit. The octagonal tower has four floors, several windows and a fireplace so it was possibly built to be lived in.
Grant Recipient: East Riding of Yorkshire Council
Access Contact: Mr N Hall MBE
Tel: 01262 850583
Open: 28 May, Sat from 2 July to 10 Sept 2 - 4pm. Access at other times by arrangement with Mr Hall, Prospect House, Carter Lane, Flamborough YO15 1LW. Tel: 01262 850583. Opening times may change, please check with Mr Hall before visiting.
P Public parking at Flamborough headland, 1/4 mile
No   £ Donations requested.

Stamford Bridge Viaduct

Stamford Bridge, East Riding of Yorkshire
Built 1847 for the York & North Midland Railway Company, East Riding lines. Mainly red brick with 10 unadorned round brick arches. The railway line was closed in the mid 1960s and is now repaired as part of a circular pedestrian walkway around the village.
Grant Recipient: East Riding of Yorkshire Council
Access Contact: Mr Darren Stevens
Tel: 01482 391678   Fax: 01482 391660
E-mail: darren.stevens@eastriding.gov.uk
Open: The site is permanently open as a footpath.
P Informal parking for approximately 20 cars near sports hall.
No. Guide Dogs: Yes   £ No

ESSEX

The Great Dunmow Maltings

Mill Lane, Great Dunmow, Essex CM6 1BD
Grade II* maltings complex (listed as Boyes Croft Maltings, White Street), early 16th century and later, timber-framed and plastered, part weatherboarding and brick. The building exhibits the entire floor malting process whilst the Great Dunmow Museum Society occupies the ground floor with displays of local history. The first floor is available for community use.
Grant Recipient: Great Dunmow Maltings Preservation Trust
Access Contact: Mr David A Westcott
Tel/Fax: 01371 873958
E-mail: david.westcott2@btinternet.com
Open: Open all year: Sat, Sun and Bank Hols 11am - 4pm. In addition, from Easter - end Oct: Tues 11am - 4pm. Groups at any reasonable time by arrangement. Closed over Christmas/New Year

holiday week.
P Public car park nearby (pay and display, free on Sun & BHs). Spaces: 100
Yes. WC for the disabled. Guide Dogs: Yes
£ Adult: £1   Child: 50p   Senior: 50p

Harwich Redoubt Fort

behind 29 Main Road, Harwich, Essex CO12 3LT
180ft diameter circular fort commanding the harbour entrance built in 1808 to defend the port against a Napoleonic invasion. Surrounded by a dry moat, there are 11 guns on the battlements. 18 casements which originally sheltered 300 troops in siege conditions now house a series of small museums.
www.harwich-society.com
Grant Recipient: The Harwich Society
Access Contact: Mr A Rutter
Tel/Fax: 01255 503429
E-mail: info@harwich-society.com
Open: 1 May - 31 Aug: daily 10am - 4pm. Rest of year: Sundays only 10am - 4pm.
P No
No. No WC. Guide Dogs: Yes
£ Adult: £1   Child: Accompanied children free

Hylands House

Hylands Park, London Road, Widford, Chelmsford, Essex CM2 8WQ
Grade II* listed building, surrounded by 600 acres of landscaped parkland, partly designed by Humphry Repton. Built c1730, the original house was a red brick Queen Anne style mansion, subsequent owners set about enlarging the property, which produced a neo-classical style house. Internal inspection of the house reveals its Georgian and Victorian features.
www.chelmsfordbc.gov.uk/hylands
Grant Recipient: Chelmsford Borough Council
Access Contact: Mrs Linda Palmer
Tel: 01245 496800   Fax: 01245 496804
E-mail: linda.palmer@chelmsford.gov.uk
Open: Suns & Bank Hols (except Christmas Day) all year & Mons between Apr - end Sept 11am - 6pm. Mons between Oct - end Mar 11am - 4pm. Tea Room: Suns throughout the year & Mons between Apr - end Sept 11am - 4.30pm; Mons between Oct - end Mar 11am - 4.30pm. Group visits by arrangement with Mrs Ceri Lowen, Assistant Hylands House Manager, Leisure Services, Chelmsford Borough Council, Civic Centre, Duke Street, Chelmsford, Essex CM1 1JE (tel:01245 496800). Events programme.
P Spaces: 84. 4 parking spaces for disabled, coaches by arrangement. Please note that during construction work this will be reduced – with alternative parking nearby.
Yes. WC for the disabled. Guide Dogs: Yes
£ Adult: £3.30   Child: Free (under 16)   Other: £2.30

John Webb's Windmill

Fishmarket Street, Thaxted, Essex CM6 2PG
Brick tower mill built in 1804 consisting of five floors. Has been fully restored as a working mill. On two floors there is a museum of rural and domestic bygones. There is also a small picture gallery of early photographs of the mill and the surrounding countryside.
Grant Recipient: Thaxted Parish Council
Access Contact: Mr L A Farren
Tel/Fax: 01371 830285
Open: May - Sept, Sat - Sun & Bank Hols, 2pm - 6pm. Groups during weekdays by special arrangement. For further information please contact Mr L A Farren, Borough Hill, Bolford Street, Thaxted, Essex CM6 2PY (tel: 01371 830285).
P Public parking in Thaxted. Spaces: 80
Wheelchair access to ground floor only. WC for the disabled in public car park in Margaret Street. Guide Dogs: Yes
£ Adult: £1   Child: Free

Old Friends Meeting House

High Street, Stebbing, Essex CM6 3SG
The Stebbing Meeting House is the earliest Quaker meeting House in Essex. Built c1674 it is a particularly fine and complete example of an early Quaker meeting house and its historical importance is recognised by its Grade II* listing.

Grant Recipient: The Trustees of the Old Friends Meeting House
Access Contact: Mr R T Guyer
Tel: 01371 856155
E-mail: clareguyer@aol.com
Open: By prior telephone or written arrangement with Mr R T Guyer, Fermoy Cottage,The Downs, Stebbing, Essex CM6 3RD (tel: 01371 856155).
P Spaces: 10
Wheelchair access to ground floor. WC for the disabled. Guide Dogs: Yes
£ No

Valentines Mansion

Emerson Road, Ilford, Essex IG1 4XA
Valentines Mansion is a late 17th century house, largely Georgian in appearance with Regency additions. Of particular interest is the unusual curved early 19th century porte cochere. The exterior was extensively repaired and restored in 2000.
Grant Recipient: London Borough of Redbridge
Access Contact: Mr Nigel Burch
Tel: 020 8708 3619   Fax: 020 8708 3178
E-mail: nigel.burch@redbridge.gov.uk
Open: 10 May for annual May Fair and for London Open House weekend in Sept. At other times by prior arrangement with Nigel Burch, Chief Leisure Officer, London Borough of Redbridge, Lynton House, 255/259 High Road, Ilford, Essex IG1 1NY (tel:020 8708 3619).
P No
Wheelchair access to ground floor only. No WC for the disabled. Guide Dogs: Yes
£ No

GLOUCESTERSHIRE

Acton Court

Latteridge Road, Iron Acton, South Gloucestershire BS37 9TJ
Seat of the Poyntzes, an influential courtier family who occupied the house until 1680 when it was converted into a farm house. A Tudor range, constructed in 1535 to accommodate King Henry VIII and Queen Anne Boleyn survives along with part of the North range. The rooms are unfurnished but contain important traces of original decoration.
www.actoncourt.com
Grant Recipient: Rosehill Corporation
Access Contact: Ms Lisa Kopper
Tel: 01454 228224   Fax: 01454 227256
E-mail: actonct@dircon.co.uk or info@actoncourt.com
Open: Guided tours and events 14 June - 21 Aug. Closed Mon except Aug Bank Holiday. Pre-booking essential. Ring information line for details 01454 228224.
P Spaces: 40
Wheelchair access to ground floor only. WC for the disabled. Guide Dogs: Yes
£ Adult: £5   Child: £3.50   Other: £3.50 (senior citizens & disabled), £100 (exclusive group tours maximum 25). Special events priced separately

Chastleton House

Chastleton, Moreton-in-Marsh, Gloucestershire GL56 0SU
Jacobean house filled with a mixture of rare and everyday objects, furniture and textiles collected since 1612. Continually occupied for 400 years by the same family. Emphasis here lies on conservation rather than restoration.
www.nationaltrust.org.uk
Grant Recipient: The National Trust
Access Contact: The Custodian
Tel/Fax: 01608 674355
E-mail: chastleton@nationaltrust.org.uk
Open: 23 Mar - 1 Oct: Wed - Sat, 1 - 5pm (Last adm 4pm); 5 Oct - 29 Oct: Wed - Sat 1 - 4pm (Last adm 3pm). Visitor numbers limited, pre-booking advised (tel: 01494 755585). Groups by written arrangement with the Custodian.
P Spaces: 50
Wheelchair access to ground floor with assistance and parts of garden only. WC for the disabled. Guide Dogs: Yes
£ Adult: £6   Child: £3   Other: £15 (family), Private View £7.50 (£2.50 NT members)

Chavenage

Tetbury, Gloucestershire GL8 8XP

Elizabethan Manor House (c1576), contains tapestry rooms, furniture and relics from the Cromwellian Period. Has been the home of only two families since the time of Elizabeth I. Used as a location for television and film productions.
www.chavenage.com

Grant Recipient: Trustees of the Chavenage Settlement

Access Contact: Miss Caroline Lowsley-Williams

Tel: 01666 502329   Fax: 01453 836778

E-mail: info@chavenage.com

Open: May – Sept: Thurs, Sun and Bank Hols 2 – 5pm; plus Easter Sun & Mon. Groups at other times by arrangement.

Ⓟ Spaces: 40

♿ Wheelchair access to ground floor only. Parking for disabled near front door. WC for the disabled. Guide Dogs: Yes

£ Adult: £5   Child: £2.50

Dyrham Park

Dyrham, nr. Chippenham, Gloucestershire SN14 8ER

17th century house set within an ancient deer park, woodlands and formal garden. The house was furnished in the Dutch style and still has many original contents including paintings, ceramics, furniture and 17th century tapestries. The Victorian domestic rooms include the kitchen, larder, bakehouse, dairy and tenants' hall.

Website Address: www.nationaltrust.org.uk

Grant Recipient: The National Trust

Access Contact: Visitor Services Manager

Tel: 01179 372501   Fax: 01179 371353

E-mail: dyrhampark@nationaltrust.org.uk

Open: House: 18 Mar – 30 Oct, daily except Wed & Thurs 12 noon – 4.45pm (Last adm to house 4.15pm). Garden: as for house 11am – 5pm or dusk if earlier. Park: all year (closed 25 Dec) 11am – 5pm or dusk if earlier. BH Mons & Good Fri 11am – 5pm.

Ⓟ Spaces: 250. Free shuttle bus from car park to house.

♿ Wheelchair access to all but four upstairs rooms. A photograph album of these rooms is available. WC for the disabled. Guide Dogs: Yes

£ Adult: £8.80, £3.40 (grounds only), £2.25 (park only when house & garden closed)
Child: £4.35, £1.70 (grounds only), £1.10 (park only when house & garden closed)
Family: £21.75 (house & grounds), £7.75 (grounds only)

East Banqueting House

Calf Lane, Chipping Campden, Gloucestershire

The East Banqueting House stands opposite the West Banqueting House across a broad terrace that ran in front of Sir Baptist Hick's mansion, which was deliberately destroyed by the Royalists in 1645 only 30 years after it had been built. It is elaborately decorated with spiral chimney stacks, finials and ebullient strapwork parapets. Steep staircases.

www.landmarktrust.co.uk

Grant Recipient: The Landmark Trust

Access Contact: Mr Toby Hawkins

Tel: 01628 825920   Fax: 01628 825417

E-mail: thawkins@landmarktrust.org.uk

Open: The Landmark Trust is an independent charity, which rescues small buildings of historic or architectural importance from decay or unsympathetic improvement. Landmark's aim is to promote the enjoyment of these historic buildings by making them available to stay in for holidays. East Banqueting House can be rented by anyone, at all times of the year, for periods ranging from a weekend to three weeks. Bookings can be made by telephoning the Booking Office on 01628 825925. The public can also view the building on eight Open Days throughout the year (dates to be set) or by prior arrangement; telephone the access contact Toby Hawkins on 01628 825920 to make an appointment. Potential visitors will be asked to write to confirm the details of their visit.

Ⓟ In town only.   ♿ No. Guide dogs: Yes.   £ No

Ebley Mill

Westward Road, Stroud, Gloucestershire GL5 4UB

19th century riverside textile mill, now restored and converted into offices occupied by Stroud District Council. Has Gothic-style clock tower and block designed by George Bodley.

www.stroud.gov.uk

Grant Recipient: Stroud District Council

Access Contact: Mr D Marshall

Tel: 01453 754646   Fax: 01453 754942

E-mail: information@stroud.gov.uk

Open: Mon – Thurs 8.45am – 5pm; Fri 8.45am – 4.30pm. Closed Bank Hols. Tours by arrangement.

Ⓟ Spaces: 30

♿ Yes. WC for the disabled. Guide Dogs: Yes

£ No

Elmore Court Entrance Gates

Elmore, Gloucestershire GL2 3NT

Early 18th century carriage and pedestrian gateway, with 19th century flanking walls. By William Edney, blacksmith of Bristol for Sir John Guise at Rendcomb. Gateway was removed from Rendcomb and re-erected here in early 19th century.

Grant Recipient/Access Contact:
Trustees of the Elmore Court Estate

Tel: 01452 720293

Open: Visible at all times from public highway.

Ⓟ Off-road parking on forecourt in front of Gates. Spaces: 5

♿ Yes. No WC for the disabled. Guide Dogs: Yes

£ No

Frampton Manor Barn

(The Wool Barn, Manor Farm), The Green, Frampton-on-Severn, Gloucestershire GL2 7EP

Grade I listed timber framed barn built c1560. Re-used worked stones in ashlar plinth wall were found during repair works.

www.framptoncourtestate.uk.com

Grant Recipient & Access Contact:
Mr P R H Clifford

Tel: 01452 740698   Fax: 01452 740698

E-mail: clifford.fce@farming.co.uk

Open: During normal office hours (8.30am – 4.30pm Mon – Fri). Other times by arrangement (tel:01452 740698).

Ⓟ Spaces: 30

♿ Yes. WC for the disabled. Guide Dogs: Yes

£ Adult: £1 Child/Conc: Free (special rates for schools)

The Malt House

High Street, Chipping Campden, Gloucestershire GL55 6AH

18th century malt house converted to a dwelling in 1905. Now part of a hotel and used as a conference room.

Grant Recipient: Seymour House Hotel Ltd

Access Contact: The Director

Tel: 01386 840429   Fax: 01386 840369

E-mail: enquiry@seymourhousehotel.com

Open: Open to the public at all times except when in use for functions.

Ⓟ Spaces: 30 ♿ Guide Dogs: Yes £ No

Newark Park

Ozleworth, Wotton-under-Edge, Glos GL12 7PZ

Tudor hunting lodge built c1550 for one of Henry VIII's courtiers, Sir Nicholas Poyntz (who married into the equally wealthy Berkeley family), reputedly with stone from the destroyed Kingswood Abbey. Enlarged in early 17th century and then remodelled into a castellated country house by James Wyatt in the late 18th century. Retains many original features and is located on the edge of a 40ft cliff with outstanding views of the surrounding countryside.

www.nationaltrust.org.uk

Grant Recipient: The National Trust

Access Contact: Property Manager

Tel/Fax: 01985 842644

E-mail: newarkpark@nationaltrust.org.uk

Open: 6 Apr – 26 May Wed and Thurs 11am – 5pm; 1 June – 30 Oct Wed, Thurs, Sat & Sun 11am – 5pm. Garden only: 4 – 19 Feb Sat & Sun 11am – 5pm. Open BH Mons, Good Fri, and Easter Sat &

Sun 11am – 5pm.

Ⓟ Spaces: 10   ♿ No. Guide Dogs: Yes

£ Adult: £4.70 Child: £2.30 Family: £12

Regan House

23 Lansdowne Terrace, Cheltenham, Gloucestershire

Regency house, now flats. Richly detailed stone façade with portico. Mews arch between No. 22 and Regan House.

Grant Recipient: Abel Developments/Forward Construction

Access Contact: Mr Mark Davis ARICS

Tel: 01242 260266

Open: Access to the exterior only at all times.

Ⓟ Spaces: 2   ♿ No. Guide Dogs: Yes £ No.

St Mary Magdalene Chapel

Hillfield Gardens, London Road, Gloucestershire

Chancel of former church serving the inmates of St Mary Magdalene Hospital, originally a leper hospital, then later almshouses. Medieval graffiti visible on exterior, perhaps mementos of visiting pilgrims. Interior contains south and west doorways rebuilt after the church was demolished in 1861 and tomb of 13th century lady, removed from St Kyneburgh's Chapel near the South Gate in 1550.

Grant Recipient: Gloucester Historic Buildings Trust Ltd

Access Contact: Mr Richard Sermon

Tel: 01452 396340   Fax: 01452 396622

E-mail: culture@gloucester.gov.uk

Open: Repair work due to be completed early 2005. For further information please contact Mr Richard Sermon, Gloucester City Council, Herbert Warehouse, The Docks, Gloucestershire GL1 2EQ (tel:01452 396340). When open, access will be by prior arrangement and as part of the Heritage Open Days weekend. Exterior accessible at all times in public park.

Ⓟ No

♿ Wheelchair access to exterior and to interior with assistance (entrance steps to be negotiated). No WC for the disabled. Guide Dogs: Yes

£ No

Stancombe Park Temple

Dursley, Gloucestershire GL11 6AU

One in a series of buildings built in the folly gardens at Stancombe Park, in the form of a Greek temple.

www.thetemple.info

Grant Recipient: Mr N D Barlow

Access Contact: Mrs G T Barlow

Tel: 01453 542815

E-mail: nicb@nicbarlow.com

Open: All year by telephone arrangement.

Ⓟ Spaces: 50

♿ No. Guide Dogs: Yes

£ Adult: £3 (charity donation for visits to garden)
Other: No charge is made for anyone specifically wishing to see the temple only

Stanley Mill

Kings Stanley, Stonehouse, Gloucestershire GL10 3HQ

Built 1813, with large addition c1825, of Flemish bond red brick with ashlar dressings and Welsh slate roof. Early example of fireproof construction (which survived a major fire in 1884).

Grant Recipient: Stanley Mills Ltd

Access Contact: Mr Mark Griffiths

Tel: 01453 821800

Open: By written arrangement as the Mill is used by various manufacturing companies.

Ⓟ By written arrangement.   ♿ No   £ No

West Banqueting House

Chipping Campden, Gloucestershire

The West Banqueting House stands opposite the East Banqueting House across a broad terrace. It is elaborately decorated with spiral chimney stacks, finials and strapwork parapets.

www.landmarktrust.org.uk

Grant Recipient: The Landmark Trust

Access Contact: Mr Toby Hawkins

Tel: 01628 825920   Fax: 01628 825417

E-mail: thawkins@landmarktrust.org.uk

Open: The Landmark Trust is an independent

charity, which rescues small buildings of historic or architectural importance from decay or unsympathetic improvement. Landmark's aim is to promote the enjoyment of these historic buildings by making them available to stay in for holidays. West Banqueting House can be rented by anyone, at all times of the year, for periods ranging from a weekend to three weeks. Bookings can be made by telephoning the Booking Office on 01628 825925. The public can also view the building on eight Open Days throughout the year (dates to be set) or by prior arrangement; telephone the access contact Toby Hawkins on 01628 825920 to make an appointment. Potential visitors will be asked to write to confirm the details of their visit.

Ⓟ In town only. Ⓖ No. Guide dogs: Yes. Ⓔ No

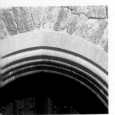

Wick Court

Overton Lane, Arlingham,
Gloucestershire GL2 7JJ
Medieval, 16th and 17th century Grade II* listed manor house with a range of farm buildings enclosed by a moat. The house is now a Farms for City Children centre.
www.farmsforcitychildren.co.uk
Grant Recipient: Farms for City Children
Access Contact: Ms Heather Tarplee
Tel: 01452 741023 **Fax:** 01452 741366
E-mail: wickcourt@yahoo.co.uk
Open: 5 - 23 Jan; 29 May - 6 June; 23 July - 2 Sept. At other times by arrangement with Heather Tarplee, Farm School Manager (tel:01452 741023).
Ⓟ Spaces: 20
Ⓖ Wheelchair access to ground floor of manor house only. WC for the disabled. Guide Dogs Yes
Ⓔ Adult: £2.50 (guided tour).

Woodchester Park Mansion

Nympsfield, Stonehouse,
Gloucestershire GL10 3TS
Grade I listed Victorian mansion, abandoned incomplete in 1870. One of the most remarkable houses of its period and uniquely exhibiting its construction process. Set in a large landscaped park (possibly by 'Capability' Brown). The building is also a site of special scientific interest housing 2 nationally important populations of endangered bats.
www.woodchestermansion.org.uk
Grant Recipient: Woodchester Mansion Trust
Access Contact: The Office Manager
Tel: 01453 861541 **Fax:** 01453 861337
Open: Easter - Oct: every Sun, 1st weekend in month (Sat & Sun) & BH weekends (Sat/Sun/Mon) 11am - 4pm. Groups/private visits welcome by arrangement.
Ⓟ Spaces: 60. Parking is 1 mile from Mansion, access via woodland walk. Minibus service available.
Ⓖ No. No WC for the disabled. Guide Dogs Yes
Ⓔ Adult: £5 Child: Free with parents
English Heritage & National Trust members: £4

GREATER MANCHESTER

1830 Warehouse

The Museum of Science & Industry in
Manchester, Liverpool Road, Castlefield,
Manchester, Greater Manchester M3 4FP
Former railway warehouse, c1830, originally part of the Liverpool Road Railway Station (the oldest surviving passenger railway station in the world) which was the terminus of the Liverpool and Manchester Railway built by George Stephenson and his son Robert. Now part of The Museum of Science and Industry in Manchester.
www.msim.org.uk
Grant Recipient: The Museum of Science & Industry in Manchester
Access Contact: Miss Val Smith
Tel: 0161 832 2244 **Fax:** 0161 833 1471
E-mail: marketing@msim.org.uk
Open: Daily (except 24/25/26 Dec) 10am - 5pm.
Ⓟ Spaces: 50
Ⓖ Yes. WC for the disabled. Guide Dogs: Yes
Ⓔ No. Free entry to all to main museum building. Charge for special exhibitions.

Albion Warehouse

Penny Meadow, Ashton-under-Lyne,
Greater Manchester OL6 6HG
School, now warehouse. Built 1861-2 by Paull and Ayliffe in Italianate style.
Grant Recipient: G A Armstrong Ltd
Access Contact: Mr David Armstrong
Tel/Fax: 0161 339 5353
E-mail: enquiries@gaarmstrong.co.uk
Open: Mon - Sat 9am - 5pm. Closed Suns, Bank Hols, Christmas Day & New Year's Day.
Ⓟ Spaces: 10
Ⓖ No. Guide Dogs: Yes Ⓔ No

Dam House

Astley Hall Drive, Astley, Tyldesley,
Greater Manchester M29 7TX
17th century house with extensive additions in the 19th century. Formerly a hospital, now a community facility. Retains many original and Regency features.
www.damhouse.org
Grant Recipient: Morts Astley Heritage Trust
Access Contact: Mrs Helen Bolton
Tel/Fax: 01942 876417
Open: Daily 9am - 5pm.
Ⓟ Parking at rear. Spaces: 50
Ⓖ Yes. WC for the disabled. Guide Dogs: Yes Ⓔ No

Hall i' th' Wood Museum

Green Way, Bolton,
Greater Manchester BL1 8UA
Grade I listed manor house, early 16th century, where Samuel Crompton invented and built his spinning mule in 1779. Part of the Hall is timber-framed and shows the development of a house in the 16th and 17th centuries. Now a museum.
www.boltonmuseums.org.uk
Grant Recipient: Bolton Metropolitan Borough Council
Access Contact: Miss Elizabeth Shaw
Tel: 01204 332370 **Fax:** 01204 332215
E-mail: hallithwood@bolton.gov.uk
Open: 8 Jan - 22 Mar Sat & Sun, 11am - 5pm; 23 Mar - 30 Oct Wed - Sun, 11am - 5pm (Last adm 4.15pm); 31 Oct - end Mar 2006 Sat & Sun, 11am - 5pm (Last adm 4.15pm).
Ⓟ Spaces: 8 Ⓖ No Ⓔ Adult: £2 Child/Senior: £1

Heaton Park Temple

Prestwich, Greater Manchester M25 2SW
Grade II* listed ornamental temple. Probably late 18th century, by James Wyatt. Situated on a hill in Heaton Park near Heaton Hall. The form is a simple, small rotunda of Tuscan columns with domed roof and lantern. It is said that Sir Thomas Egerton may have used the structure as an observatory.
www.manchester.gov.uk/leisure/parks/heaton.htm
Grant Recipient: Manchester City Council
Access Contact: Mr Edward Flanagan
Tel: 0161 773 1085 **Fax:** 0161 798 0107
E-mail: e.flanagan@notes.manchester.gov
Open: The temple can be viewed externally 365 days a year. Access to the interior by prior arrangement or when local artist is in residence (usually during summer months). Internal access also available in the winter through the park warden's team: please phone for details (tel: 0161 773 1085 x207).
Ⓟ Spaces: 500
Ⓖ External viewing only possible: pathway to the temple on a steep incline. WC for the disabled. Guide Dogs: Yes
Ⓔ No

Manchester Law Library

14 Kennedy Street, Manchester M2 4BY
Built in Venetian Gothic style in 1885 to a design by Manchester architect, Thomas Hartas. Has stained glass windows by Evans of Birmingham.
www.manchester-law-library.co.uk
Grant Recipient: The Manchester Incorporated Law Library Society
Access Contact: Mrs Jane Riley
Tel: 0161 236 6312 **Fax:** 0161 236 6119
E-mail: librarian@manchester-law-library.co.uk
Open: By telephone or written arrangement.
Ⓟ No Ⓖ No. Guide Dogs: Yes Ⓔ No

Old Grammar School

Boarshaw Road, Middleton,
Greater Manchester M24 6BR
Endowed by Elizabeth I in 1572, completed in 1584 with house added 1830s. Restored in 1998. Grade II* listed building with fine original oak beams and items of historical and local interest. An important early example of a building type for which there was little architectural precedent.
Grant Recipient: The Old Grammar School Trust
Access Contact: Revd Canon N J Feist
Tel/Fax: 0161 643 2693
E-mail: nickjfeist@ntlworld.com
Open: All year except Christmas/New Year period: Tues, Wed & Thurs 2 - 4pm. Parties by arrangement on 0161 643 7442 or 0161 643 2693. Regular programme of events and use by community groups.
Ⓟ Spaces: 9
Ⓖ Yes. WC for the disabled. Guide Dogs: Yes
Ⓔ £1 donation per person requested.

Ordsall Hall

Ordsall Lane, Salford,
Greater Manchester M5 3AN
Ordsall Hall is a Grade I listed early 16th century timber-framed house, extended in brick and incorporating the remains of the original 14th century house. Once an important manor house and home to the wealthy and influential Radclyffe family.
www.ordsallhall.org.uk
Grant Recipient: Salford City Council
Access Contact: The Director of Development Services
Tel: 0161 793 3770 **Fax:** 0161 793 3738
E-mail: malcolm.sykes@salford.gov.uk
Open: Mon - Fri 10am - 4pm; Sun 1 - 4pm. Closed on Sat, Christmas Day and New Year's Day. For further information contact the Director of Development Services at Salford City Council (tel:0161 793 3600) or Ordsall Hall (tel:0161 872 0251, fax:0161 872 4951).
Ⓟ Free parking in grounds. Spaces: 40
Ⓖ Wheelchair access to ground floor only. WC for the disabled. Guide Dogs: Yes
Ⓔ No

Portico Library

57 Mosley Street, Manchester,
Greater Manchester M2 3HY
19th century subscription library with Reading Room and Gallery, situated in Manchester city centre. 25,000 volumes, mainly 19th century. Particularly valuable for Victorian studies. Gallery shows mainly art exhibitions of new and established artists' work - local, national and international. Occasionally literary/local history exhibitions also shown.
www.theportico.org.uk
Grant Recipient: The Trustees of the Portico Library
Access Contact: Emma Marigliano
Tel: 0161 236 6785 **Fax:** 0161 236 6803
E-mail: librarian@theportico.org.uk
Open: Mon - Fri and 3rd Sun of each month: 9.30am - 4.30pm. Closed over Christmas period (usually 22 Dec - 2 Jan) & Bank Hols.
Ⓟ No Ⓖ No. Guide Dogs: Yes Ⓔ No

Staircase House

30a/31 Market Place, Stockport,
Greater Manchester SK1 3XE
Timber framed town house. Dating from 1460, enlarged in 16th and 17th centuries and altered in 18th, 19th and 20th centuries. Early panelled rooms and an important 17th century caged newel staircase from which the house takes its name. Damaged by fire, but restored by Stockport Council. Due to open Autumn 2005 with a new museum 'The Stockport Story'. Interpretation charts the history of the house and its evaluation to WWII.
Grant Recipient: Stockport Metropolitan Borough Council
Access Contact: Mrs Angela Stead
Tel: 0161 474 3279
E-mail: Angela.Stead@Stockport.Gov.UK
Open: From autumn 2005. Daily 1pm - 5pm.
Ⓟ Town centre car parks and street parking.
Ⓖ Yes. WC for the disabled. Guide Dogs: Yes
Ⓔ No

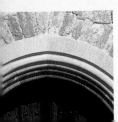

Victoria Baths

Hathersage Road, Manchester M13 0FE

Swimming pool complex built 1903 - 1906, with 2 pools, Turkish and Russian Bath suite, Aeratone and extensive stained glass and tilework.

www.victoriabaths.org.uk

Grant Recipient: The Manchester Victoria Baths Trust

Access Contact: Ms Gill Wright

Tel: 0161 224 2020 **Fax:** 0161 224 0707

E-mail: info@victoriabaths.org.uk

Open: Mar - Oct, the first Sun in each month 12 - 4pm, and additional opening days including Heritage Open Days in Sept, but please ring to confirm. At other times by prior arrangement with Ms Gill Wright of the Manchester Victoria Baths Trust, Studio 20, Imex Business Park, Hamilton Road, Longsight, Manchester M13 0PD (tel: 0161 224 2020).

P On-street parking during the week. Use of large adjacent car park at weekends.

♿ Wheelchair access to ground floor with assistance. Most of the building can be seen from the ground floor. No WC for the disabled. Guide Dogs: Yes

£ Adult: £2 (proposed - admission charges may be introduced in 2005, please ring to confirm.)

HAMPSHIRE

Avington Park

Winchester, Hampshire SO21 1DB

Palladian mansion dating back to the 11th century, enlarged in 1670 by the addition of two wings and a classical Portico surmounted by three statues. Visited by Charles II and George IV. Has highly decorated State rooms and a Georgian church in the grounds.

www.avingtonpark.co.uk

Grant Recipient & Access Contact:
Mrs Sarah Bullen

Tel: 01962 779260 **Fax:** 01962 779864

E-mail: enquiries@avingtonpark.co.uk

Open: May - Sept: Sun & Bank Hols (also every Mon in Aug) 2.30 - 5.30pm. Other times by arrangement.

P Spaces: 150

♿ Wheelchair access to ground floor only. Church with assistance (one step to interior). WC for the disabled. Guide Dogs: Yes

£ Adult: £4 Child: £2

Boathouse No. 6

Portsmouth Naval Base, Portsmouth PO1 3LJ

Large Victorian naval boathouse constructed 1845. Designed by Captain James Beatson of the Royal Engineers, it is one of the first examples of a brick building constructed around a metal frame. Its massive cast iron beams are inscribed with their load-bearing capacity.

Grant Recipient: Portsmouth Naval Base Property Trust

Access Contact: Mr Mark Meacher

Tel: 023 9282 0921 **Fax:** 023 9286 2437

Open: All year except Christmas Eve and Christmas Day, 10am - 5.30pm (Apr - Oct) and 10am - 5pm (Nov - Mar). Groups by arrangement.

P Spaces: 150. Additional parking 500 metres from the site.

♿ Yes. WC for the disabled. Guide Dogs: Yes

£ Adult: £9.70 Child: £8 Family: £33

Breamore Home Farm Tithe Barn

Breamore, nr. Fordingbridge, Hampshire SP6 2DD

Late 16th century tithe barn with dwarf walls supporting a timber-frame and external cladding under a tiled roof with massive timber aisle posts, double doors in the centre of each side and an area of threshing boards.

Grant Recipient: Breamore Ancient Buildings Conservation Trust

Access Contact: Mr Michael Hulse

Tel/Fax: 01725 512858

Open: Weekdays by arrangement. with Mr Michael Hulse of Breamore House.

P Spaces: 10

♿ Yes. No WC for the disabled. Guide Dogs: Yes

£ No

Calshot

Activities Main Hanger, Games Hanger & FFF Hanger, Calshot, Fawley, Hampshire SO45 1BR

Part of the most outstanding group of early aircraft structures of this type in Britain and the largest hanger built for use by fixed-wing aircraft during World War 1. Now an activities centre.

Grant Recipient: Hampshire County Council

Access Contact: Mr Peter Davies

Tel: 01962 841841 **Fax:** 01962 841326

E-mail: arccpd@pbrs.hants.gov.uk

Open: Daily except Christmas Day, Boxing Day & New Year's Day.

P Ample free on-site.

♿ Yes. WC for the disabled. Guide Dogs: Yes

£ No

Highclere Castle & Park

Highclere, Newbury, Hampshire RG20 9RN

Early Victorian mansion rebuilt by Sir Charles Barry in 1842, surrounded by 'Capability' Brown parkland with numerous listed follies including Heavens Gate, an 18th century eye-catching hill-top landscape feature and The Temple, c1760, altered by Barry in mid 19th century, a regular classical circular structure. Family home of the 8th Earl and Countess of Carnarvon.

www.highclerecastle.co.uk

Grant Recipient: Executors of the 7th Earl of Carnarvon & Lord Carnarvon

Access Contact: Mr Alec Tompson

Tel: 01223 351421 **Fax:** 01223 324554

E-mail: agent@hwdean.co.uk

Open: 1 June - 31 Aug, Mon - Fri, plus May BH Mons (2 and 30 May). Gates open 10am, Castle 11am - 4pm. Last adm 3pm.

P Unlimited parking.

♿ Wheelchair access to ground floor only. WC for the disabled. Guide Dogs: Yes

£ Adult: £7.50 Child: £4 Senior: £6

Houghton Lodge Gardens

Stockbridge, Hampshire SO20 6LQ

Landscaped pleasure grounds and a park laid out c1800 with views from higher ground over informal landscape (Grade II*) surrounding the 18th century Cottage Ornée (Grade II*). Chalk cob walls enclose ancient espaliers, greenhouses and herb garden. Formal topiary 'Peacock' Garden, snorting topiary dragon and wild flowers. A popular TV Film location.

www.houghtonlodge.co.uk

Grant Recipient & Access Contact:
Captain M W Busk

Tel: 01264 810502 **Fax:** 01264 810063

E-mail: info@houghtonlodge.co.uk

Open: 1 Mar - 30 Sept: Sat, Sun & Bank Hols 10am - 5pm; Mon, Tues, Thurs and Fri 2pm - 5pm.

P Parking available.

♿ Yes. WC for the disabled. Guide Dogs: Yes

£ Adult: £5 Child: Free Groups: £4.50

Manor Farmhouse

Hambledon, Hampshire PO7 4RW

12th century stone built house with later medieval wing. 17th and 18th century re-fronting of part and minor renovation.

Grant Recipient & Access Contact:
Mr Stuart Mason

Tel: 023 92632433

Open: By arrangement only.

P Spaces: 2 **♿** Yes. No WC for the disabled. Guide Dogs: Yes

£ No

St Michael's Abbey

Farnborough, Hampshire GU14 7NQ

Grade I listed church and Imperial Mausoleum crypt of Napoleon III and his family. Abbey Church also built for the Empress Eugenie so the monks could act as custodians of the tombs. Now a Benedictine priory, raised to Abbey status in 1903.

www.farnboroughabbey.org

Grant Recipient: Empress Eugenie Memorial Trust

Access Contact: Fr Magnus Wilson

Tel: 01252 546105 **Fax:** 01252 372822

E-mail: prior@farnboroughabbey.org

Open: Sat & Public Holidays at 3.30pm. Contact Fr Magnus Wilson, Bursar, or Fr D C Brogan, Prior, for further information.

P No **♿** No **£** No

Whitchurch Silk Mill

28 Winchester Street, Whitchurch, Hampshire RG28 7AL

Grade II* watermill built c1800 and has been in continuous use as a silk weaving mill since the 1820s. Now a working museum, the winding, warping and weaving machinery installed between 1890 and 1927 produces traditional silks for theatrical costume, historic houses, fashion and artworks.

www.whitchurchsilkmill.org.uk

Grant Recipient: Hampshire Buildings Preservation Trust

Access Contact: General Manager

Tel: 01256 892065 **Fax:** 01256 893882

E-mail: silkmill@btinternet.com

Open: Mill & shop: Tues - Sun 10.30am - 5pm (Last adm 4.15pm). Mill and shop closed Mondays (except Bank Hols) and between Christmas and New Year.

P Free parking next to Mill, 2 disabled spaces next to shop and in adjacent car park. Spaces: 20

♿ Wheelchair access to ground floor, shop and gardens. Stairlift to be installed to first floor for 2005. WC for the disabled. Guide Dogs: Yes

£ Adult: £3.50 Child: £1.75 Other: £3 Family: £8.75

HEREFORDSHIRE

Chandos Manor

Rushall, Ledbury, Herefordshire HR8 2PA

Farmhouse, probably late 16th century with 18th century extensions. Timber-frame, partly rendered.

Grant Recipient: Mr Richard White

Access Contact: Mr Richard White

Tel: 01531 660208

Open: Easter - Sept: Sundays by arrangement.

P Spaces: 12

♿ No. Guide Dogs: Yes

£ Donations to charity requested

Chapel Farm

Wigmore, nr. Leominster, Herefordshire HR6 9UQ

Timber-framed farmhouse c1400 of rectangular plan, originally a hall-house with first floor inserted in the 16th century. Contains an open roof with foliate carved windbraces, ornate post-heads and late Elizabethan wall painting. Associated with the Lollards around 1400.

Grant Recipient & Access Contact: Mr M Pollitt

Open: By written arrangement Mondays (except Bank Hols) May - Sept 2 - 4.30pm. Max 2 persons per visit. No children under 16 and no animals.

P Spaces: 1 **♿** No **£** No

Eastnor Castle

nr. Ledbury, Herefordshire HR8 1RL

Norman-style castellated mansion set in the western slopes of the Malvern Hills. Constructed 1812 - 1820 and designed by Sir Robert Smirke, the castle has 15 state and other rooms fully-furnished and open to visitors. The decoration includes tapestries, paintings, armour and a drawing room by Augus Pugin.

www.eastnorcastle.com

Grant Recipient: Mr J Hervey-Bathurst

Access Contact: Mr S Foster

Tel: 01531 633160 **Fax:** 01531 631776

E-mail: enquiries@eastnorcastle.com

Open: Easter - end Sept: Sun & BH Mons, plus every day in July & Aug except Sat, 11am - 5pm.

P Spaces: 150

♿ Wheelchair access to grounds and ground floor with assistance (always available). WC for the disabled. Guide Dogs: Yes

£ Adult: £7 Child: £4 Senior: £6

Hergest Court

Kington, Herefordshire HR5 3EG

House dates back to 1267 and was the ancestral home of the Clanvowe and Vaughan families. It is

an unusual example of a fortified manor in the Welsh Marches. It has literary associations with Sir John Clanvowe and Lewis Glyn Cothi.
Grant Recipient & Access Contact: Mr W L Banks
Tel: 01544 230160   **Fax:** 01544 232031
E-mail: gardens@hergest.co.uk
Open: By arrangement with the Hergest Estate Office, Kington, Herefordshire HR5 3EG. Bookings by phone or fax with five days' notice.
Ⓟ Spaces: 5
♿ Wheelchair access to ground floor only. No WC for the disabled. Guide Dogs: Yes
£ **Adult:** £4   **Child:** Free   **Groups:** £3.50

The Painted Room

Town Council Offices, Church Street, Ledbury, Herefordshire HR8 1DH
The wall paintings, discovered here in 1989, are a unique example of domestic wall painting dating from the Tudor period. They are clearly the work of a commoner, created to imitate the rich tapestries or hangings that would have been found in the homes of the gentry.
Grant Recipient: Ledbury Town Council
Access Contact: Mrs J McQuaid
Tel: 01531 632306   **Fax:** 01531 631193
E-mail: ledburytowncouncil@ledbury.org.uk
Open: Easter - end Sept: guided tours Mon - Fri 11.00am - 1pm & 2 - 4pm; Sun 2 - 5pm (from end of May - end Sept). Rest of year: Mon, Tues, Wed & Fri 10am - 2pm, if member of staff available. Tours may be arranged out of these hours at a cost of £1 per adult (min. 10 persons). Children's parties are free.
Ⓟ Town centre car parks nearby.
♿ Guides are aware of the location of the nearest WC for the disabled. Guide Dogs: Yes
£ No charge when open normally (£1 for adults on out of hours tours) but donations welcome

HERTFORDSHIRE

Berkhamsted Town Hall

196 High Street, Berkhamsted, Hertfordshire HP4 3AP
Berkhamsted Town Hall and Market House, built in 1859, also housed the Mechanics' Institute. It has a gothic façade and retains much of the original stonework. There are three rooms: the Great Hall, Clock Room, Sessions Hall. In the Great Hall many of the original features have been preserved, including the fireplace and barrel vaulted ceiling.
Grant Recipient: Berkhamsted Town Hall Trust
Access Contact: Ms Janet Few
Tel: 01442 862288
E-mail: janet_few@lineone.net
Open: Mon - Fri 10am - 1pm. At other times the Town Hall is let for functions. Additional opening by arrangement with the Town Hall Manager (tel:01442 862288).
Ⓟ Parking in nearby public car parks.
♿ Yes. WC for the disabled.   Guide Dogs: Yes
£ No

Bridgewater Monument

Aldbury, Hertfordshire HP4 1LT
The monument was erected in 1832 to commemorate the Duke of Bridgewater. It is the focal point of Ashridge Estate which runs across the borders of Hertfordshire and Buckinghamshire along the main ridge of the Chilterns.
www.nationaltrust.org.uk
Grant Recipient: The National Trust
Access Contact: Property Manager
Tel: 01442 851227   **Fax:** 01442 850000
E-mail: ashridge@nationaltrust.org.uk
Open: Monument: 19 Mar - 30 Oct, Sat, Sun and BH Mons 12 noon - 5pm; Mon - Fri by arrangement, weather permitting. Estate: open all year. Visitor Centre: 21 Mar - 9 Dec, daily Mon - Fri 1 - 5pm; Sat, Sun, BH Mons & Good Fri 12 noon - 5pm.
Ⓟ Spaces: 100
♿ Wheelchair access to monument area, monument drive and visitor centre. WC for the disabled. Guide Dogs: Yes
£ Adult: £1.30   Child: 60p

Cromer Windmill

Ardeley, Stevenage, Hertfordshire SG2 7QA
Grade II* postmill dated 1674, last surviving postmill in Hertfordshire. Restored to working order (but not actually working). Houses displays about Hertfordshire's lost windmills, television and video display on the history of Cromer Mill and audio sound effects of a working mill.
www.hertsmuseums.org.uk
Grant Recipient: Hertfordshire Building Preservation Trust
Access Contact: Ms Cristina Harrison
Tel: 01279 843301/07944 928552
Fax: 01279 843301
E-mail: cristinaharrison@btopenworld.com
Open: Sat before National Mill Day, ie. second Sun in May. Thereafter Sun & Bank Hols, and second and fourth Sat, until Heritage Open Days, 2.30 - 5pm. 30 minute video available for schools and other groups. Guided tours. Special parties by prior arrangement with Ms Cristina Harrison, The Forge Museum, High Street, Much Hadham, Hertfordshire SG10 6BS (tel:01279 843301 or 07944 928552). Refreshments available.
Ⓟ Spaces: 20
♿ Wheelchair access to ground floor only but video of upper floors showing all the time. No WC for the disabled. Guide Dogs: Yes
£ **Adult:** £1.50   **Child:** 25p

Ducklake House Wallpainting

Springhead, Ashwell, Baldock, Hertfordshire SG7 5LL
16th century wall painting, located on the ground floor, containing classical grotesques holding cartouches.
Grant Recipient & Access Contact: Mr P W H Saxton
Open: By written arrangement to view the wall painting only.
Ⓟ Spaces: 1   ♿ No   £ No

Folly Arch

Hawkshead Road, Little Heath, Potters Bar, Hertfordshire EN6 1NN
Grade II* listed gateway and folly, once the entrance to Gobions estate. Circa 1740 for Sir Jeremy Sambrooke, probably by James Gibbs. Red brick with large round-headed arch and thin square turrets.
Grant Recipient: Mr R J Nicholas
Access Contact: Mr and Mrs Nicholas
Tel: 01707 663553
E-mail: m-f-robnic@mac.com
Open: The Arch is on the boundary between public open space and a private garden and can be viewed from public ground at any time.
Ⓟ On street parking.
♿ Yes. No WC for the disabled.   Guide Dogs: Yes
£ **Adult:** £8.50 (£7.50 group)   **Child:** £8
Senior: £8 (£7 group)

Knebworth House

Knebworth, nr. Stevenage, Hertfordshire SG3 6PY
Originally a Tudor manor house, rebuilt in gothic style in 1843. Contains rooms in various styles, which include a Jacobean banqueting hall. Set in 250 acres of parkland with 25 acres of formal gardens. Home of the Lytton family since 1490.
www.knebworthhouse.com
Grant Recipient: Knebworth House Education & Preservation Trust
Access Contact: Mrs Christine Smith
Tel: 01438 812661   **Fax:** 01438 811908
E-mail: info@knebworthhouse.com
Open: Daily: 26 Mar - 10 Apr, 28 May - 5 June, 1 July - 31 Aug; Weekends and Bank Hols: 19 - 20 Mar, 16 Apr - 22 May, 11 - 26 June, 3 - 25 Sept. Gardens, Park & Playground: 11.00am - 5.30pm. House: 12.00pm - 5.00pm (Last adm 4.15pm).
Ⓟ 50-75 parking spaces on gravel, unlimited space on grass.
♿ Wheelchair access to ground floor of House only. Gravel paths around gardens and House but level route from car park to House entrance. WC for the disabled.   Guide Dogs: Yes
£ **Adult:** £8.50 (£7.50 group)   **Child:** £8
Senior: £8 (£7 group)

The Old Clockhouse

Cappell Lane, Stanstead Abbots, Hertfordshire SG12 8BU
Grammar school, now private residence, c1636 also used for Sun services in 17th century.
Grant Recipient & Access Contact: Mr Michael Hannon
Tel: 01920 871495
Open: Access to exterior at all times; Bell Tower can only be viewed from High Street.
Ⓟ Public car park in Stansted Abbots High Street.
♿ No   £ No

Redbournbury Mill

Redbournbury Lane, Redbourn Road, St Albans, Hertfordshire AL3 6RS
Grammar school, now private residence, c1636 also used for Sun services in 17th century.
www.redbournmill.co.uk
Grant Recipient: Mr J T James
Access Contact: Mrs A L James
Tel: 01582 792874   **Fax:** 01582 792874
E-mail: redbrymill@aol.com
Open: 21 Mar - 3 Oct: Sun 2.30 - 5pm, plus Easter, late May & Aug BHs. National Mills Weekend, Heritage Open Days & New Year's Day open all day. Special events all year. Private parties by arrangement. Refreshments available. Milling demonstrations. Organic flour and bread for sale.
Ⓟ Spaces: 30
♿ Wheelchair access to ground floor only. No WC for the disabled. Guide Dogs: No
£ **Adult:** £1.50   **Child:** 80p   **Other:** 80p

Torilla

11 Wilkins Green Lane, Nast Hyde, Hatfield, Hertfordshire AL10 9RT
'Torilla' (house at Nast Hyde) was built by F R S Yorke in 1935 in the international style and features a flat roof, 2 balconies and a large double height living room. Constructed of concrete with large steel framed windows. F R S Yorke was a key figure in the evolution of modern architecture in Britain.
Grant Recipient & Access Contact: Mr Alan Charlton
Tel: 01707 259582
Open: By arrangement (written or telephone) 11am - 5pm on Sun 15 May and Sun 14 Aug. At other times by written arrangement.
Ⓟ Spaces: 5
♿ Wheelchair access to ground floor only. No WC for the disabled. Guide Dogs: Yes
£ No

Woodhall Park

Watton-at-Stone, Hertfordshire SG14 3NF
Country house, now school. Designed and built by Thomas Leverton in 1785 in neo-Classical style. Normally associated with London houses, this is one of his few country houses. Highly decorated interiors which include the Print Room with walls covered in engraved paper, reproductions of paintings with frames, ribbons, chains, busts, candelabra and piers with vases.
Grant Recipient & Access Contact: The Trustees of R M Abel Smith 1991 Settlement
Tel: 01920 830286   **Fax:** 01920 830162
E-mail: woodhallest@dial.pipex.com
Open: At all reasonable times, preferably school holidays, by arrangement with the Trustees.
Ⓟ Parking limited to 10 spaces during school terms. Spaces: 30
♿ Wheelchair access to ground floor only. No WC for the disabled. Guide Dogs: Yes
£ No

KENT

The Archbishops' Palace

Mill Street, Maidstone, Kent ME15 6YE
14th century Palace built by the Archbishops of Canterbury. Much altered and extended over the centuries, the interior contains 16th century panelling and fine wood or stone fireplaces. Now used as Kent County Council's Register Office.
Grant Recipient: Maidstone Borough Council
Access Contact: Mrs Maggie Taylor
Tel: 01622 701920
E-mail: maidstone.register-office@kent.gov.uk

Opening arrangements at properties grant-aided by English Heritage

Open: Open throughout the year for weddings and at other times by prior arrangement with the Registrar.
P Public parking in town centre car parks (pay and display). Spaces: 100
No. Guide Dogs: Yes **£** No

Chiddingstone Castle

Chiddingstone, nr. Edenbridge, Kent TN8 7AD
Tudor mansion subsequently twice remodelled by the Streatfeilds whose seat it was. William Atkinson "Master of the picturesque" is responsible for the romantic design, c1805, of the building as it is today. Rescued from dereliction by Denys Bower in the 20th century, now managed by a charitable trust.
www.chiddingstone-castle.org.uk
Grant Recipient: Trustees of the Denys Eyre Bower Bequest
Access Contact: Miss M R Eldridge MBE
Tel: 01892 870347
Open: Apr and May: Easter & Spring Bank Hols only. June - Sept: Thurs, Sun & Bank Hols. Weekdays: 2pm - 5.30pm. Sun & Bank Hols: 11.30am - 5.30pm (last admittance 5pm). Groups (min. 20), including school groups, throughout the year by arrangement. No mobile phones.
P Disabled parking available at entrance. Spaces: 50
Wheelchair access to ground floor (includes everything except the Egyptian collection) and tea room. WC for the disabled. Guide Dogs: Yes
£ Adult: £5 Child: £3 (5-15, under 5 free but must be accompanied by an adult)

Church House

72 High Street, Edenbridge, Kent TN8 5AR
Late 14th century timber-framed farmhouse, Tudor additions include fireplace and 18th century brick frontage. Now houses the Eden Valley Museum which illustrates economic and social changes during the 14th to 20th centuries.
www.evmt.org.uk
Grant Recipient: Edenbridge Town Council
Access Contact: Mrs Jane Higgs
Tel: 01732 868102 **Fax:** 01732 867866
E-mail: curator@evmt.org.uk
Open: Oct - Mar: Tues and Wed 2 - 4.30pm; Thurs and Sat 10am - 4.30pm. Apr - Sept: Tues, Wed, Sun 2 - 4.30pm; Thurs and Sat 10am - 4.30 pm. Private/educational groups by prior arrangement.
P Free parking in town centre car park, 200 yards from House. Spaces: 150
Wheelchair access grnd floor only (visual computer link to upstairs). WC for the disabled. Guide Dogs: Yes
£ Adult: £2 Child: 75p Other: 75p (disabled)

Cobham Hall and Dairy

Cobham, Kent DA12 3BL
Gothic-style dairy in grounds of Cobham Hall, built by James Wyatt c1790.
Grant Recipient: Cobham Hall Heritage Trust
Access Contact: Mr N G Powell
Tel: 01474 823371 **Fax:** 01474 825904
E-mail: cobhamhall@aol.com
Open: Easter - July / Aug: Hall open Wed & Sun 2 - 5pm (last tour 4.30pm). Please telephone to confirm opening times. At other times (and coach parties) by arrangement. Self-guided tour of Gardens and Parkland (historical/conservation tour by arrangement).
P Spaces: 100
Wheelchair access to ground floor, manual assistance required for first floor access. WC for the disabled. Guide Dogs: Yes
£ Adult: £4.50 Conc: £3.50

Crabble Corn Mill

Lower Road, River, nr. Dover, Kent CT17 0UY
Georgian watermill with millpond, cottages and gardens. Guided and non-guided tours and demonstrations of milling techniques. Flour produced and sold on site. Cafeteria and art gallery. Available for group tours, functions and events.
Grant Recipient: Crabble Corn Mill Trust
Access Contact: Mr Anthony Skaveley
Tel/Fax: 01304 823292

E-mail: miller@ccmt.org.uk
Open: Feb - Apr: Sun 11am - 5pm. Apr - Sept: Daily 11am - 5pm. Open to group visits all year round by prior arrangement (contact Alan Davis, Tony Staveley, Anne Collins or Anthony Reid, tel: 01304 823292).
P In recreation ground opposite site. Spaces: 32
Wheelchair access to ground and first floor, art gallery, cafeteria and milling floor. No WC for the disabled. Guide Dogs: Yes
£ Mill Tour: Adult: £4 Child: £3 (age 5-15yrs) Seniors/Students: £3 Family: £9

Dover Town Hall

Biggin Street, Dover, Kent CT16 1DL
The Town Hall incorporates the remains of a medieval hospital, 14th century chapel tower, 19th century prison, town hall and assembly rooms. The Maison Dieu Hall of c1325 was originally part of a hospital founded by Hubert de Burgh in the early 13th century. The Town Hall designed by Victorian Gothic architect William Burges was built in 1881 on the site of the hospital.
www.dover.gov.uk/townhall/home.htm
Grant Recipient: Dover District Council
Access Contact: Mr Steve Davis
Tel: 01843 296111 (Admin)
E-mail: dover@leisureforce.co.uk
Open: Normally open during the week for functions and other bookings. Guided tours to be organised on two Sundays per month June - Sept and one Sun per month Oct - May. To ensure access please telephone in advance (tel: 01843 296111).
P Parking at the rear of the building.
Yes. WC for the disabled. Guide Dogs: Yes
£ No

Gad's Hill Place

Higham, Rochester, Kent ME3 7PA
Former home of Charles Dickens, who lived here from 1856 until his death in 1870 whilst writing The Mystery of Edwin Drood. Built c1780 with Dickensian additions, it is now an Independent School and stands in 11 acres of playing fields and gardens.
Grant Recipient: Gad's Hill School
Access Contact: Mrs Katherine Hersey-Meade
Tel: 01634 318825 **Fax:** 01474 822977
E-mail: info@gadshill.org or ghp@significantevents.co.uk
Open: Opening arrangements under review at time of publication, please check the English Heritage website or with the access contact for current information.
P Spaces: 70
Access for certain types of wheelchair only, please check with the Place for details. WC for the disabled. Guide Dogs: Yes
£ Adult: £4 Child: £2.50

Herne Windmill

Mill Lane, Herne Bay, Kent CT6 7DR
Kentish smock mill built 1789, worked by wind until 1952 and then by electricity until 1980. Bought by Kent County Council in 1985, which carried out some restoration. Now managed by Friends of Herne Mill on behalf of the County Council. Much of the original machinery is in place, some is run for demonstration and the sails used when the wind conditions permit.
www.kentwindmills.co.uk
Grant Recipient: Kent County Council
Access Contact: Mr Ken Cole
Tel: 01227 361326
Open: Easter - end Sept: Sun and Bank Hols, plus Thurs in Aug, 2 - 5pm. National Mills Weekend, Sat & Sun, 2 - 5pm. For further information contact Ken Cole, Secretary, Friends of Herne Mill (tel:01227 361326) or John Fishpool (Chairman) on (tel: 01227 366863).
P In Mill grounds. Free on-street parking (Windmill Road). Spaces: 6
Wheelchair and guide dog access to ground floor of Mill and meeting room. WC for the disabled. Guide Dogs: Yes
£ Adult: £1 Child: 25p (accompanied by adult)

Ightham Mote

Ivy Hatch, Sevenoaks, Kent TN15 0NT
Moated manor house covering 650 years of

history from medieval times to 1960s. Extended visitor route now includes the newly refurbished north-west quarter with Tudor Chapel, Billiards Room and Drawing Room, South West Quarter and apartments of Charles Henry Robinson, the American donor of Ightham Mote to the National Trust. Interpretation displays and special exhibition featuring conservation in action.
www.nationaltrust.org.uk
Grant Recipient: The National Trust
Access Contact: Property Manager
Tel: 01732 810378 **Fax:** 01732 811029
E-mail: ighthammote@nationaltrust.org.uk
Open: 18 Mar - 30 Oct, daily except Tues and Sat. House: 10.30am - 5.30pm; Garden 10.00am - 5.30pm. Estate open all year Dawn - Dusk.
P Spaces: 420
Wheelchair access to ground floor with help and part of the exterior only. WC for the disabled. Guide Dogs: Yes
£ Adult: £7 Child: £3.50 Other: £17.50 (family), £5.50 (groups), no reduction on Sun or BHs

Penshurst Place Park

Tonbridge, Kent TN11 8DG
Open parkland, formerly a medieval deer park, circa 80 hectares. Scattered mature trees, lake with a small island and Lime Avenue originally planted in 1730s.
www.penshurstplace.com
Grant Recipient: Lord De L'Isle
Access Contact: Mr Ian R Scott
Tel: 01892 870307 **Fax:** 01892 870866
E-mail: ianscott@penshurstplace.com
Open: Footpaths through parkland open 365 days a year.
P Parking available. Spaces: 50
No. Guide Dogs: Yes **£** No

Somerhill

Tonbridge, Kent TN11 0NJ
Grade I Jacobean mansion with Victorian addition set in 150 acres of parkland. Now used as a school, but original ceilings, panelling and stables have been retained.
Grant Recipient: Somerhill Charitable Trust Ltd
Access Contact: Diane M Huntingford
Tel: 01732 352124 **Fax:** 01732 363381
Open: By written or telephone arrangement with Diane Huntingford, Bursar, plus the Sunday of Heritage Open Days weekend.
P Spaces: 170
Wheelchair access to ground floor only. No WC for the disabled. Guide Dogs: Yes
£ No

LANCASHIRE

Gawthorpe Hall

Padiham, nr. Burnley, Lancashire BB12 8UA
An Elizabethan property in the heart of industrial Lancashire. Restored and refurbished in the mid 19th century by Sir Charles Barry. There are many notable paintings on display loaned to the National Trust by the National Portrait Gallery, and a collection of needlework, assembled by the last family member to live there, Rachel Kay-Shuttleworth.
www.nationaltrust.org.uk
Grant Recipient: The National Trust
Access Contact: Property Manager
Tel: 01282 771004 **Fax:** 01282 770178
E-mail: gawthorpehall@nationaltrust.org.uk
Open: Hall: 25 Mar - 2 Nov, daily except Mon and Fri (but open Good Fri and BH Mons) 1 - 5pm. Garden: all year 10am - 6pm.
P Spaces: 50
Wheelchair access to garden only. WC for the disabled. Guide Dogs: Yes
£ Adult: £3 Child: Free when accompanied by an adult Other: £1.50 (concessions), garden free

Grand Theatre

33 Church Street, Blackpool, Lancashire FY1 1HT
Grade II* 1200-seat theatre designed by Frank Matcham, 1894. Major restoration ongoing.
www.blackpoolgrand.co.uk
Grant Recipient: Blackpool Grand Theatre Trust Ltd
Access Contact: Mr David Fletcher

⊞ Opening arrangements at properties grant-aided by English Heritage

Tel: 01253 290111 Fax: 01253 751767
E-mail: info@blackpoolgrand.co.uk
Open: Daily. Tours take place on a semi-regular basis. Shows in the auditorium once or twice a day. Contact David Fletcher (tel: 01253 290111) for more information.
Ⓟ In West Street car park (2 min walk). Spaces: 200
♿ Wheelchair access to stalls and bar. WC for the disabled. Guide Dogs: Yes
£ Adult: £5 (guided tour) Child: £3.50
Charges made for performances, Free on open days

Hoghton Tower

Hoghton, Preston, Lancashire PR5 0SH
16th century fortified manor house, ancestral home of the de Hoghton family since William the Conqueror. Associated with many kings and queens (the Banqueting Hall is where James I knighted the Loin of Beef 'Sirloin') and William Shakespeare. Various staterooms open to the public, as well as a Tudor horse-drawn well, dungeons and underground passages.
www.hoghtontower.co.uk
Grant Recipient:
Hoghton Tower Preservation Trust
Access Contact: Mr John Graver
Tel: 01254 852986 Fax: 01254 852109
E-mail: mail@hoghtontower.co.uk
Open: July - Sept: Mon - Thurs, 11am - 4pm (Sun 1 - 5pm). Guided tours: Bank Holiday Suns/Mons (excluding Christmas and New Year); private tours throughout the year by prior arrangement.
Ⓟ Spaces: 250
♿ Wheelchair access to Gardens, Banqueting Hall and Kings Hall. WC for the disabled. Guide Dogs: Yes
£ Adult: £5 Conc: £4 Family: £16

India Mill Chimney

Bolton Road, Darwen, Blackburn, Lancashire BB3 1AE
Chimney, 1867, built as part of cotton spinning mill. Brick with ashlar base. Square section, 300 feet high, in the style of an Italian campanile. Rests on foundation stone said to have been the largest single block quarried since Cleopatra's Needle. Listed Grade II*.
Grant Recipient & Access Contact: Brookhouse Managed Properties Ltd
Open: Chimney visible from public highway (no interior access).
Ⓟ On-street parking.
♿ Yes. No WC for the disabled. Guide Dogs: Yes
£ No

Judges' Lodgings

Church Street, Lancaster, Lancashire LA1 1YS
The home of Thomas Covell, Keeper of the Castle at the time of the Lancashire witch trials in 1612. For two centuries a Judges' Lodgings, now a museum with Regency period rooms, Gillow furniture, portraits by Wright of Derby, Romney and Lawrence. Museum of Childhood with historic doll collection.
www.lancsmuseums.gov.uk
Grant Recipient: Lancashire County Council
Access Contact: Anthea Dennett
Tel: 01524 32808 Fax: 01524 846315
E-mail: anthea.dennet@mus.lancscc.gov.uk
Open: Good Fri - 30 June: Mon - Fri 1 - 4pm, Sat - Sun 12noon - 4pm. 1 July - 30 Sept: Mon - Fri 10am - 4pm, Sat - Sun 12noon - 4pm. Oct: Mon - Fri 1pm - 4pm, Sat - Sun 12noon - 4pm. Open Bank Holiday weekends.
Ⓟ Large car park nearby.
♿ Wheelchair access to ground floor only via side entrance. Please telephone in advance. No WC for the disabled. Guide Dogs: Yes
£ Adult: £2 Child: Free (accompanied by adult)
Conc: £1

Leighton Hall

Carnforth, Lancashire LA5 9ST
Country House, 1765, probably by Richard Gillow, with earlier remains. Gothic south-east front early 19th century, possibly by Thomas Harrison. Tower at west end of the façade 1870 by Paley and Austin. Ancestral home of the Gillow family with fine furniture, paintings and objets d'art.
www.leightonhall.co.uk

Grant Recipient: Mr Richard Reynolds
Access Contact: Mr & Mrs Richard Reynolds
Tel: 01524 734474 Fax: 01524 720357
E-mail: leightonhall@yahoo.co.uk
Open: May - Sept: 2 - 5pm, Tues - Fri (also Bank Holiday Suns & Mons). Aug only: 12.30pm - 5pm, Tues - Fri & Sun (also BH Mon). Groups of 25+ all year by arrangement. The owner reserves the right to close or restrict access to the Hall and grounds for special events (please see our web site for up to date information).
Ⓟ Spaces: 100
♿ Wheelchair access to ground floor, shop and tea rooms. WC for the disabled. Guide Dogs: Yes
£ Adult: £5.50 Child: £4 (age 5- 12)
Senior/Student: £5 Family: £17 Groups (25+): Adult £4.50, Child £3.50

Rufford Old Hall

Rufford, nr. Ormskirk, Lancashire L40 1SG
Fine 16th century building with intricately carved movable wooden screen and hammerbeam roof. Owned by the Hesketh family for 400 years, the house contains collections of 16th and 17th century oak furniture, arms, armour and tapestries.
www.nationaltrust.org.uk
Grant Recipient: The National Trust
Access Contact: Property Manager
Tel: 01704 821254 Fax: 01704 823823
E-mail: ruffordoldhall@nationaltrust.org.uk
Open: House:19 Mar - 30 Oct, daily except Thurs and Fri 1 - 5pm. Garden: as house 11am - 5.30pm. Shop & Restaurant: 11am - 5pm. Open BH Mons & Good Fri. Winter opening: please telephone for details.
Ⓟ Spaces: 130
♿ Wheelchair access to ground floor, restaurant, shop and garden. WC for the disabled. Guide Dogs: Yes
£ Adult: £4.70 Child: £2.20 Family: £11.50
Garden only: £2.90 Booked Groups: £2.90 (adult) £1.10 (child).

Samlesbury Hall

Preston New Road, Samlesbury, Preston, Lancashire PR5 0UP
Built in 1325, the hall is an attractive black and white timbered manor house set in extensive grounds. Independently owned and administered since 1925 by The Samlesbury Hall Trust whose primary aim is to maintain and preserve the property for the enjoyment and pleasure of the public. Currently open to the public as an antiques/craft centre.
www.samlesburyhall.co.uk
Grant Recipient: Samlesbury Hall Trust
Access Contact: Ms Sharon Jones
Tel: 01254 812010/01254 812229
Fax: 01254 812174
E-mail: samlesburyhall@btconnect.com
Open: Daily except Sat, 11am - 4.30pm. Open Bank Hols. For Christmas closing times please contact the Hall (tel:01254 812010 or 01254 812229).
Ⓟ Additional parking for 100 cars in overflow car park.
Spaces: 70
♿ Wheelchair access to ground floors of historical part of Hall. WC for the disabled. Guide Dogs: Yes
£ Adult: £3 Child: £1.25 (age 4-16)

Stonyhurst College

Stonyhurst, Clitheroe, Lancashire BB7 9PZ
16th century manor house, now home to a Catholic independent co-education boarding and day school. Contains dormitories, library, chapels, school-rooms and historical apartments.
www.stonyhurst.ac.uk
Grant Recipient: Stonyhurst College
Access Contact: Miss Frances Ahearne
Tel: 01254 826345 Fax: 01254 826732
E-mail: domestic-bursar@stonyhurst.ac.uk
Open: House: 18 July - 29 Aug daily (except Fri), plus Aug BH Mon, 1 - 5pm; Gardens: 1 July - 29 Aug daily (except Fri), plus Aug BH Mon, 1 - 5pm. Coach parties by arrangement.
Ⓟ Spaces: 200
♿ Limited wheelchair access but assistance is available by arrangement. WC for the disabled. Guide Dogs: Yes
£ Adult: £5.50 Conc: £4.50

Todmorden Unitarian Church

Honey Hole Road, Todmorden, Lancashire OL14 6LE
Grade I church with a large wooded burial ground and ornamental gardens designed by John Gibson, 1865-69. Victorian Gothic style with tall tower and spire. Detached smaller burial ground nearby and listed lodge in churchyard. Lavish interior with highly decorated fittings and furnishings. One of the most elaborate Non conformist churches of the High Gothic Revival.
www.hct.org.uk
Grant Recipient: Historic Chapels Trust
Access Contact: Mr Rob Goldthorpe
Tel: 01706 815648
E-mail: rob.goldthorpe@btinternet.com
Open: At all reasonable times by application to the keyholder, Mr Rob Goldthorpe, 14 Honey Hole Close, Todmorden, Lancashire OL14 6LH or by calling at the caretaker's house, Todmorden Lodge, at the entrance to the churchyard.
Ⓟ Spaces: 10
♿ Yes. WC for the disabled. Guide Dogs: Yes
£ No

LEICESTERSHIRE

7 King Street

Melton Mowbray, Leicestershire LE13 1XA
Dating from 1330, this is the oldest secular building in Melton Mowbray. The building has Medieval roof timbers, a 16th century timber-framed extension and has been modified and gentrified through the centuries. Listed Grade II*, the building was at risk for many years. Restoration by Melton Mowbray Borough Council was completed in 2004 and is the Council's Tourist Information Centre.
Grant Recipient: Melton Borough Council
Access Contact: Mr Richard Spooner MA IHBC
Tel: 01664 502387 Fax: 01664 410283
E-mail: rspooner@melton.gov.uk
Open: Mon - Sat (hours to be determined). Access to the upper floors by prior arrangement.
Ⓟ Public car park adjacent (Pay and Display)
♿ Ground floor rooms. WC for the disabled. Guide Dogs: Yes £ No

Rearsby Packhorse Bridge

Rearsby, Leicestershire LE7 4YE
Low narrow medieval bridge, perhaps 16th century, comprising 7 arches of random granite masonry and brick coping. On the upstream side there are 4 cutwaters, 3 of granite and 1 of brick. The bridge has recently been restored.
Grant Recipient: Leicestershire County Council
Access Contact: Mr P Steer
Tel: 0116 265 7151 Fax: 0116 265 7135
E-mail: psteer@leics.gov.uk
Open: In use as a public highway.
Ⓟ Street parking.
♿ Yes. No WC for the disabled. Guide Dogs: Yes
£ No

Stanford Hall

Lutterworth, Leicestershire LE17 6DH
William and Mary house, built by the Smiths of Warwick (begun 1697), for Sir Roger Cave, ancestor of present owner whose family home it is. Visitors see every room on the ground floor (except modern kitchen), the "flying staircase" and two bedrooms. Contents include collection of Royal Stuart paintings.
Grant Recipient: Lady Braye
Access Contact: Mr Robert Thomas
Tel: 01788 860250 Fax: 01788 860870
E-mail: enquiries@stanfordhall.co.uk
Open: 27 Mar - 25 Sept Sun & BH Mons 1.30pm - 5.30pm (Last adm 5pm). On BH Suns & Mons Grounds open at 12noon and earlier on Event Days. Open day or evening during the Season for pre-booked parties of 20+.
Ⓟ Spaces: 1500. Parking for disabled adjacent to the house.
♿ Wheelchair access to the Park, the Gardens, the Motorcycle Museum, the 1898 Flying Machine and the ground floor of the Hall if entrance steps can be negotiated. WC for the disabled. Guide Dogs: Yes
£ Adult: £5 (house and grounds), £3 (grounds), Child: £2 (house & grounds), £1 (grounds)
Groups (20+): £4.75 (adult), £1.80 (child)

Tomb of Andrew Lord Rollo

St Margaret's Church, Canning Place, Leicester
Grade II* listed tomb of 1765. Each face has a large rectangular plaque with ornate carved pilaster panels. The west front has a long inscription on the slate plaque recording the life and exploits of Andrew Lord Rollo, who died in 1765. The remaining three fronts each have a shallow carved relief of Lord Rollo's arms and military trophies.
Grant Recipient: The Abbey Parish PCC
Access Contact: Mr Jack Adams
Tel: 0116 2897432
Open: The churchyard is open at all times.
P Spaces: 3
⑁ Yes. No WC for the disabled. Guide Dogs: Yes
£ No

LINCOLNSHIRE

12 Minster Yard

Lincoln, Lincolnshire LN2 1PJ
House of early 14th, late 17th and 19th centuries.
Grant Recipient:
Dean & Chapter of Lincoln Cathedral
Access Contact: Mrs Carol Heidschuster
Tel: 01522 527637 **Fax:** 01522 575 688
E-mail: worksmanager@lincolncathedral.com
Open: By written arrangement with the Works Manager, Lincoln Cathedral, 28 Eastgate, Lincoln LN2 4AA.
P No ⑁ No. Guide Dogs: Yes £ No

13/13a Minster Yard

Lincoln, Lincolnshire LN2 1PW
Houses, mid-18th century, with late 18th and 19th century alterations.
Grant Recipient:
Dean & Chapter of Lincoln Cathedral
Access Contact: Mrs Carol Heidschuster
Tel: 01522 527637 **Fax:** 01522 575 688
E-mail: worksmanager@lincolncathedral.com
Open: By written arrangement with the Works Manager, Lincoln Cathedral, 28 Eastgate, Lincoln LN2 4AA.
P No ⑁ No. Guide Dogs: Yes £ No

17 Minster Yard

Lincoln, Lincolnshire LN2 1PX
13th and 14th century building with 15th century additions. Sacked in 1644 and restored 1671-94 and 1704-32 with internal alterations, c1813, by William Fowler. Further additions to the building were made in the late 19th century.
Grant Recipient: Dean & Chapter of Lincoln Cathedral
Access Contact: Mrs Rachel Harrison
Tel/Fax: 01522 787267
E-mail: education@lincolncathedral.com
Open: By written arrangement with the Works Manager, Lincoln Cathedral, 28 Eastgate, Lincoln LN2 4AA.
P No ⑁ No. Guide Dogs: Yes £ No

18/18a Minster Yard

Lincoln, Lincolnshire LN2 1PX
13th and 14th century building with 17th century additions. Remodelled and extended in 1827 and re-fronted 1873 by J L Pearson.
Grant Recipient:
Dean & Chapter of Lincoln Cathedral
Access Contact: Mrs Carol Heidschuster
Tel: 01522 527637 **Fax:** 01522 575 688
E-mail: worksmanager@lincolncathedral.com
Open: By written arrangement with the Works Manager, Lincoln Cathedral, 28 Eastgate, Lincoln LN2 4AA.
P No ⑁ No. Guide Dogs: Yes £ No

3/3a Vicars Court

Lincoln, Lincolnshire LN2 1PT
Former priests' vicars lodgings, now 2 houses. Begun late 13th century by Bishop Sutton and completed c1309. Altered 15th century, re-roofed and altered late 16th, 17th, 18th and 19th centuries.
Grant Recipient: Dean & Chapter of Lincoln Cathedral
Access Contact: Mrs Carol Heidschuster

Tel: 01522 527637 **Fax:** 01522 575688
E-mail: worksmanager@lincolncathedral.com
Open: By written arrangement with the Works Manager, Lincoln Cathedral, 28 Eastgate, Lincoln LN2 4AA.
P No ⑁ No. Guide Dogs: Yes £ No

Arabella Aufrere Temple

Brocklesby Park, Grimsby, Lincolnshire DN41 8PN
Garden Temple of ashlar and red brick with coupled doric columns on either side of a central arch leading to a rear chamber. Built c1787 and attributed to James Wyatt. Inscription above inner door: "Dedicated by veneration and affection to the memory of Arabella Aufrere."
Grant Recipient: The Earl of Yarborough
Access Contact: Mr H A Rayment
Tel: 01469 560214 **Fax:** 01469 561346
E-mail: office@brocklesby-estate.co.uk
Open: 1 Apr - 31 Aug: viewable from permissive paths through Mausoleum Woods at all reasonable times.
P Free parking in village or walks car park, 1/4 mile from site. Spaces: 10
⑁ No £ No

Brocklesby Mausoleum

Brocklesby Park, Grimsby, Lincolnshire DN41 8PN
Family Mausoleum designed by James Wyatt and built between 1787 and 1794 by Charles Anderson Pelham, who subsequently became Lord Yarborough, as a memorial to his wife Sophia who died at the age of 33. The classical design is based on the Temples of Vesta at Rome and Tivoli.
Grant Recipient: The Earl of Yarborough
Access Contact: Mr H A Rayment
Tel: 01469 560214 **Fax:** 01469 561346
E-mail: office@brocklesby-estate.co.uk
Open: Exterior: 1 Apr - 31 Aug: viewable from permissive paths through Mausoleum Woods at all reasonable times. Interior (excluding private crypt) by prior arrangement with the Estate Office. Admission charge for interior.
P Free parking in village or walks car park, 1/4 mile from site. Spaces: 10
⑁ No. Guide Dogs: Yes
£ Adult: £2 (charge for interior)

Burghley House

Stamford, Lincolnshire PE9 3JY
Large country house built by William Cecil, Lord High Treasurer of England, between 1555 and 1587, and still lived in by descendants of his family. Eighteen State Rooms, many decorated by Antonio Verrio in the 17th century, housing a collection of artworks including 17th century Italian paintings, Japanese ceramics, European porcelain and wood carvings by Grinling Gibbons and his followers. There are also four State Beds, English and continental furniture, and tapestries and textiles. 'Capability' Brown parkland.
www.burghley.co.uk
Grant Recipient: Burghley House Preservation Trust Ltd
Access Contact: Mr Philip Gompertz
Tel: 01780 752451 **Fax:** 01780 480125
E-mail: burghley@burghley.co.uk
Open: 25 Mar - 30 Oct: daily (except Fri and 3 Sept) 11am - 4.30pm. By guided tour only apart from Sun when there are guides in each room.
P Parking for disabled available close to visitors' entrance. Spaces: 500
⑁ Yes. Please telephone the Property Manager for information on wheelchair access. WC for the disabled. Guide Dogs: Yes
£ Adult: £8.20 Child: £3.70 Senior.Student: £7.20 Groups (20+): £7pp Schools (up to 15yrs): £3.80pp Family: £21

Fydell House gates, piers and railings

South Street, Boston, Lincolnshire PE21 6HU
Fronted by renewed, grant-aided, gates, gate piers and railings Fydell House was built in 1726 with minor 19th century alterations. Example of a small 18th century stately home. It contains links between Boston England and Boston Mass and houses the adult educational Pilgrim College Ltd.
Grant Recipient/Access Contact: Boston Preservation Trust Ltd

Open: Access to the exterior at all reasonable times. Open throughout the year (except Bank Hols) but in term time access to rooms is limited.
P Public car park nearby. ⑁ Yes. WC for the disabled. Guide Dogs: Yes £ No

Harding House

48-54 Steep Hill, Lincoln, Lincolnshire LN2
Grade II listed house of the 16th century, remodelled in the 18th and restored in the 20th. Built of coursed rubble and brick with a pantile roof. The building is divided up into several studios predominately used for a variety of craft uses.
Grant Recipient: Lincoln City Council
Access Contact: Mr Mark Wheater
Tel: 01522 873464 **Fax:** 01522 560049
E-mail: mark.wheater@lincoln.gov.uk
Open: During normal shop opening hours.
P No ⑁ No. WC for the disabled at Westgate car park, Castle Hill. Guide Dogs: Yes £ No

Harlaxton Manor

Harlaxton, Grantham, Lincolnshire NG32 1AG
Grade I listed county house 1832-1844. Elizabethan, Revival style. Now a university. The owner, Gregory Gregory, acted largely as his own architect, in collaboration with Anthony Salvin 1832-1838. The interior decoration, c1837-1854, incorporates important plasterwork probably by Bernasconi.
www.ueharlax.ac.uk
Grant Recipient: University of Evansville-Harlaxton College
Access Contact: Mr Ian Welsh
Tel: 01476 403000 **Fax:** 01476 403030
E-mail: iwelsh@ueharlax.ac.uk
Open: 5 June and 22 Aug 11am - 5pm open house. Guided tours (for approx. 20 plus) at other times by prior arrangement.
P Spaces: 150 ⑁ Yes. WC for the disabled. Guide Dogs: Yes
£ Adult: £5 Child: £2 Other: Guided tours (incl refreshments): £4.80 Conc: £4

Heggy's Cottage

Hall Road, Haconby, nr. Bourne, Lincolnshire PE10 0UY
Built c1500 of mud and stud construction, a good example of early conversion to two storeys. Restored to its original state in 1995.
Grant Recipient: J E Atkinson & Son
Access Contact: Mrs J F Atkinson
Tel: 01778 570790
Open: By written arrangement with Mrs J F Atkinson, Haconby Hall, nr. Bourne, Lincolnshire PE10 0UY.
P Spaces: 1 ⑁ No £ No

Jews' Court

(the Society for Lincolnshire History & Archaeology), 2/3 Steep Hill, Lincoln, Lincolnshire LN2 1LS
Grade I two storey stone building, c12th century, with cellar and attic. Traditionally the medieval synagogue. Now used by the Society for Lincolnshire History & Archaeology and for worship.
www.lincolnshirepast.org.uk
Grant Recipient: Jews' Court Trust
Access Contact: Ms Pearl Wheatley
Tel/Fax: 01522 521337
Open: Open daily except Sun, 10am - 4pm. Also closed over the Christmas period.
P Ample public parking within 300 yards.
⑁ Access for wheelchairs is not possible. Electric stair-lift is available for access to first floor. Several days notice is required as two trained staff members need to be in attendance. Guide Dogs: Yes £ No

Kyme Tower

Manor Farm, South Kyme, Lincoln, Lincolnshire LN4 4JN
23.5m high tower with one storey and a stair turret. Remainder of a fortified medieval manor house, built on the site of an Auginian priory, itself built on an Anglo-Saxon religious establishment. There are also visible earthworks of the former moat and fishponds.
Grant Recipient: The Crown Estate Commissioners

Access Contact: Mr W B Lamyman
Tel: 01526 860603
Open: By telephone arrangement with Mr W B Lamyman of Manor Farm (tel: 01526 860603). At least one week's notice required.
🅿Spaces: 3 ♿No £No

Lincoln Castle

Castle Hill, Lincoln, Lincolnshire LN1 3AA
Lincoln Castle was begun by William the Conqueror in 1068. For 900 years the castle has been used as a court and prison. Many original features still stand and the wall walks provide magnificent views of the cathedral, city and surrounding countryside.
www.lincolnshire.gov.uk/lincolncastle
Grant Recipient: Lincolnshire County Council
Access Contact: Mr Peter Allen
Tel: 01522 511068 Fax: 01522 512150
E-mail: allenp@lincolnshire.gov.uk
Open: Mon - Sat: 9.30am - 5.30pm. Sun 11am - 5.30pm. Winter closing at 4pm. Also closed 24 - 26 Dec, 31 Dec & 1 Jan.
🅿Paid parking available in the Castle / Cathedral area.
♿Wheelchair access to grounds, Magna Carta exhibition, audio visual presentation and café. WC for the disabled. Guide Dogs: Yes
£Adult: £3.70 Child: £2.15 (under 5s free) Conc: £2.15 Family: £9.60

Monksthorpe Chapel

Spilsby, East Lindsey, Lincolnshire
Resembling a brick barn, this remote chapel with outdoor bapistry was used by local Baptists as a secluded place of worship and is one of the two best surviving examples in England. It was substantially altered to its present appearance in the early 19th century.
Grant Recipient/Access Contact:
The National Trust
Tel: 01909 486411 Fax: 01909 486377
Open: 30 Mar - 29 Sept: Wed & Thurs 2 - 5pm. Stewarded some Saturdays: 9 Apr, 14 May, 11 June, 9 July, 13 Aug, & 10 Sept. Services: 23 Apr, 28 May, 11 June, 23 July, 27 Aug, 1 Oct and 10 Dec. At other times access by key collected from Gunby Hall, £10 returnable deposit required.
🅿No. ♿No. £No.

Shodfriars Hall

South Street, Boston, Lincolnshire
Guildhall, now shops and offices. Timber frames with jettied first and second floors. Dating from c1400, restored and extended by Sir George Gilbert Scott in 1873. Listed Grade II*.
Grant Recipient: Baddow Investments Ltd
Access Contact: Mr David Shaw
Open: During normal office hours and at other times by arrangement with Mr Shaw, Baddow Investments Ltd, Coach House, PO Box 76, Boston Road, Swineshead, Lincolnshire PE20 3NW
🅿No ♿No £No

St Peter

Sotby, Lincolnshire
Grade II* listed church dating from early 12th and 13th centuries.
Grant Recipient/Access Contact: Mr B F Cotton
Tel: 01507 533681
Open: Key available by prior arrangement with Sandra Meaking, Chapel Cottage, Moor Lane, Sotby, Lincolnshire. Tel (evenings): 01507 343662.
🅿Roadside parking.
♿Partial. Grass entry to building and small step. No WC for the disabled. Guide dogs: Yes
£No.

Tattershall Castle

Tattershall, Lincoln, Lincolnshire LN4 4LR
A vast fortified and moated red-brick tower, built c1440 for Ralph Cromwell, Treasurer of England. The building was rescued from becoming derelict by Lord Curzon 1911-14 and contains four great chambers with enormous Gothic fireplaces, tapestries and brick vaulting. Gatehouse with museum room.
www.nationaltrust.org.uk
Grant Recipient: The National Trust
Access Contact: The Custodian

Tel/Fax: 01526 342543
E-mail: tattershallcastle@nationaltrust.org.uk
Open: 5 Mar - 20 Mar and 5 Nov - 11 Dec: Sat & Sun 12 noon - 4pm; 26 Mar - 30 Oct: Sat - Wed 11am - 5.30pm (11am - 4pm in Oct). Ground floor of Castle may occasionally be closed for functions or events.
🅿Spaces: 40
♿Wheelchair access to ground floor via ramp. Photograph album of inaccessible parts of Castle. WC for the disabled. Guide Dogs: Yes
£Adult: £3.70 Child: £1.90 Family: £9.30

Uffington Manor Gatepiers

Main Street, Uffington, nr. Stamford, Lincolnshire PE9 4SN
Pair of Grade II* listed gate piers, possibly by John Lumley c1700, surmounted by urns with wrought iron entrance gates with a coat of arms over of later 19th century date.
Grant Recipient & Access Contact:
Mr David Pike
Tel: 01780 751944 Fax: 01780 489218
Open: Can be viewed from public roadway, otherwise by written arrangement.
🅿Spaces: 2 ♿No. Guide Dogs: Yes £No

Westgate House

Westgate, Louth, Lincolnshire LN11 9YQ
Grade II* Georgian town house in brick and stone, with 1775 neo-classical additions and proto-Regency remodelling c1799 on the Westgate façade. Interior contains fine plasterwork, mahogany doors, Carrara fireplaces and other fine details. Used as a school 1937-1980s but now in course of restoration as a residence by the present owners, after dereliction.
Grant Recipient: Professor P Byrne
Access Contact: Professor & Mrs P Byrne
Tel: 01507 354388
Open: Ground floor only. Guided visits between 11.30am - 4pm, by prior arrangement. Evening group visits for societies, etc, by prior arrangement.
🅿Public parking in town centre (5 mins walk).
♿No. Guide Dogs: Yes
£Adult: £3 Child: Free (when accompanied by an adult) Other: Evening Group visits (max 30): £5pp, including wine and canapés

LONDON

Benjamin Franklin's House

36 Craven Street, London WC2N 5NF
A 1730s terraced house with c1792 alterations. Part of the Craven family's 18th century development of their Brewhouse estate, laid out by Flitcroft. Listed Grade I for historical associations. The world's only remaining home of the diplomat, scientist, inventor, writer, and philosopher Benjamin Franklin. Due to open to the public in Jan 2006, in time for Franklin's 300th 'birthday'. The house will feature a 'museum as theatre' historical experience that reveals the role Franklin and the house played on the eve of the American Revolution and Age of Enlightenment. A student science centre featuring hands-on experimentation with Franklin's London science, and a scholarship centre for promoting Anglo-American research and understanding.
www.thersa.org/Franklin
Grant Recipient: Friends of Benjamin Franklin House
Access Contact: Dr Marcia Balisciano
Tel: 020 8808 8772 Fax: 020 8808 4118
E-mail: BenjaminFranklinHouse@Msn.com
Open: Limited viewing by prior arrangement until building work completed when the house will open to the public.
🅿No ♿No. Guide Dogs: Yes £No

Bruce Castle Museum

(Haringey Libraries Archives & Museum Service), Lordship Lane, London N17 8NU
Limited viewing by prior arrangement until building work completed when the house will open to the public.
www.haringey.gov.uk
Grant Recipient: London Borough of Haringey

Access Contact: Ms Deborah Hedgecock
Tel: 020 8808 8772 Fax: 020 8808 4118
E-mail: museum.services@haringey.gov.uk
Open: Museum: Wed - Sun 1 - 5pm plus Easter Mon, May Day, late May Bank Holiday and Aug Bank Holiday. Closed Good Fri, Christmas Day, Boxing Day and New Year's Day. Groups at other times by prior arrangement. Archive: Wed - Thurs 1 - 4.45pm, Fri 9.15am - 12noon and 1 - 4.45pm, Sat 1 - 4.45pm. Visitors to the archive are advised to book an appointment.
🅿Spaces: 15
♿Yes. WC for the disabled. Guide Dogs: Yes
£No

Brunswick Square Gardens

Brunswick Square, London WC1
A public park originally part of the grounds of the Foundling Hospital, founded by Sir Thomas Coram.
www.camden.gov.uk
Grant Recipient: London Borough of Camden
Access Contact: Mr Martin Stanton
Tel: 020 7974 1693 Fax: 020 7974 1543
E-mail: martin.stanton@camden.gov.uk
Open: During daylight hours throughout the year.
🅿On street parking.
♿Yes. No WC for the disabled. Guide Dogs: Yes
£No

Charlton House Gateway

Charlton Road, London SE7 8RE
Located on the front lawn of Charlton House, the arch (previously known as the Gateway) marks the original front boundary to the House. The House is a Grade I listed Jacobean mansion, built between 1607 and 1612 by Sir Adam Newton with later additions.
www.greenwich.gov.uk
Grant Recipient: London Borough of Greenwich
Access Contact: Mr Edward Schofield
Tel: 020 8856 3951 Fax: 020 8856 4162
E-mail: edward.schofield@greenwich.gov.uk
Open: At anytime, all year. (Charlton House: Mon - Fri 9am - 10pm, Sat 10am - 5pm. Closed on Sun)
🅿Spaces: 25
♿Yes. WC for the disabled. Guide Dogs: Yes £No

Clissold House

Stoke Newington Church Street, London N16
House built c1770 for Jonathan Hoare, a Quaker banker. Located in middle of Clissold park, a late 18th Century park, developed in 1880s into a public park.
Grant Recipient: London Borough of Hackney
Access Contact: Ms Carole Stewart
Tel: 020 8356 7476 Fax: 020 8356 7575
E-mail: carole.stewart@hackney.gov.uk
Open: Café is open all year, daily 9am - 7pm.
🅿 On street parking. ♿No £No

College of Arms

Queen Victoria Street, London EC4V 4BT
Built in 1670s/1680s to the design of Francis Sandford and Morris Emmett to house the Heralds' offices, on the site of their earlier building, Derby Place, which was destroyed in the Great Fire of 1666. The principal room is Earl Marshal's Court, which is two floors high with gallery, panelling and throne. New record room added 1842 and portico and terrace in 1867.
www.college-of-arms.gov.uk
Grant Recipient: College of Arms
Access Contact: The Bursar
Tel: 020 7248 2762 Fax: 020 7248 6448
E-mail: enquiries@college-of-arms.gov.uk
Open: Earl Marshal's Court only: all year (except Public Holidays and State and Special Occasions), Mon - Fri 10am - 4pm. Group tours of Record Room (max 20) and lecture in evenings after 6pm by prior arrangement with Officer-in -Waiting (tel. 020 7248 2762).
🅿No ♿No. Guide Dogs: Yes £No

Countess of Derby's Almshouses

Church Hill, Harefield, London UB9 6DU
16th century range, established in 1636 for poor women of good character in the Parish of Harefield, known as the Countess of Derby's

Almshouses. Four stacks of paired or tripled diagonal brick chimney stacks. Originally housed six residents in 'one up one down' 'apartments' each with their own front door and staircase, hence the windows at first floor level. Converted to accommodate four on the ground floor only in the 1950s and has undergone conversion again in 2003/4 into two self-contained flats. Listed Grade II*. There is a Grade I listed memorial by Maximilian Colt to Lady Alice, the Dowager Countess of Derby, who bequeathed the Almshouses in her Will dated 1636, in St Mary's Parish Church, Harefield (100 metres from the Almshouses).

www.harefieldcharities.co.uk

Grant Recipient: Harefield Parochial Charities

Access Contact: Mrs Joyce Willis/ Mr John Ross

Tel: 01895 822657 / 01895 823058

Fax: 01895 823644

E-mail: hpc@harefieldcharities.co.uk

Open: Access to exterior from main road, Church Hill, Harefield.

Ⓟ On-street parking. ♿No 💷No

Dissenters' Chapel

Kensal Green Cemetery, Harrow Road, London W10 4RA

Grade II* building within Grade II* cemetery. Cemetery dates from 1832 and is London's oldest. The Chapel was designed in Greek Revival style by John Griffith in 1834. It is now used by the Friends of Kensal Green Cemetery as a headquarters, exhibition space and art gallery and as a centre for their guided walks, lectures and special events.

www.hct.org.uk or www.kensalgreen.co.uk

Grant Recipient: Historic Chapels Trust

Access Contact: Mr Tom Bolton

Tel: 020 8671 0801

E-mail: teabolton@hotmail.com

Open: Cemetery: daily; Dissenters' Chapel: Sun afternoons and at other times by prior arrangement. Guided tours of chapels and cemetery for modest charge, also tours of the Catacombs 1st and 3rd Sun in every month.

Ⓟ In adjacent streets, parking for disabled in cemetery.

♿ Yes. WC for the disabled. Guide Dogs: Yes

💷 £5 (donation requested for guided tours only)

Dr Johnson's House

17 Gough Square, London EC4A 3DE

Fine 18th century town house in the heart of the City of London. Here Dr Johnson compiled his dictionary (published 1755). Original staircase and woodwork throughout and collection of prints, paintings and Johnson memorabilia.

www.drjohnsonshouse.org

Grant Recipient: Dr Johnson's House Trust

Access Contact: The Curator Dr Johnson's House Trust

Tel/Fax: 020 7353 3745

E-mail: curator@drjohnsonshouse.org

Open: Mon - Sat: May - Sept 11am - 5.30pm, Oct - Apr 11am - 5pm. Closed Sun & Bank Hols.

Ⓟ On-street metered. ♿No. WC for the disabled. Guide Dogs: Yes

💷 **Adult:** £4 **Child:** £1 **Conc:** £3

Dulwich College

College Road, Dulwich, London SE21 7LD

Dulwich College was founded in 1619; the main buildings date from 1866-70 by the younger Charles Barry and are listed Grade II*. Three blocks lined by arcades in ornate Northern Italian Renaissance style. Close to Dulwich Village.

www.dulwich.org.uk

Grant Recipient: Dulwich College

Access Contact: Ms Julia Field

Tel: 020 8693 3737 **Fax:** 020 8693 6319

E-mail: skinneraw@dulwich.org.uk

Open: Exterior visible from South Circular. Interior by prior arrangement with the Bursar.

Ⓟ 200 parking spaces in school holidays. Spaces: 50

♿ Wheelchair access with help (a few steps at entrance). WC for the disabled. Guide Dogs: Yes

💷 Tour and archives: £4, £6

Fulham Palace Stableyard Wall

Bishop's Avenue, London SW6

Home to the Bishops of London for over a thousand years to 1973. The two storey medieval west court is red brick with terracotta roof tiles. The mainly three storey Georgian east court is brown and yellow brick with parapets and slate roofs. Set in historic grounds near the river.

Grant Recipient: London Borough of Hammersmith & Fulham

Access Contact: Ms Stella Washington

Tel: 020 8753 4960

E-mail: stella.washington@lbhf.gov.uk

Open: The Palace grounds are open daily throughout the year during daylight hours, admission is free. Museum of Fulham Palace: Mar - Oct, Wed - Sun 2 - 5pm; Nov - Feb, Thurs - Sun 1 - 4pm. Tours of principal rooms and gardens every 2nd and 4th Sun. Restoration works due to begin Apr 2005 will affect access to the Museum and Palace: please check for current information. Open for London Open House subject to restoration programme.

Ⓟ On-street meter parking. Spaces: 50

♿ Prior notice required for wheelchair users wishing to visit ground floor to enable the ramp to be installed. Gardens accessible. WC for the disabled. Guide Dogs: Yes. 💷No

Garrick's Temple

Hampton Court Rd, Richmond-upon-Thames, London TW12 2EN

The actor-manager David Garrick built the Temple in 1756 to celebrate the genius of William Shakespeare. The Temple was restored between 1997-1999 and now houses an exhibition of Garrick's acting career and life at Hampton, while the grounds have been landscaped to echo their original 18th century layout.

www.hampton-online.co.uk

Grant Recipient: London Borough of Richmond-upon-Thames

Access Contact: Mark De Novellis/ Sara Bird

Tel: 020 8831 6000 **Fax:** 020 8744 0501

E-mail: m.denovellis@richmond.gov.uk

Open: Temple: Sun, Apr - Sept 2 - 5pm. Also pre-arranged visits for small groups throughout the year (tel:020 8831 6000). Lawn: all year 7.30am - dusk.

Ⓟ On Molesey Hurst, access via Ferry, running all day in summer.

♿ Wheelchair access to lawn gardens only. No WC for the disabled. Guide Dogs: Yes 💷 No

Gunnersbury Park Temple

Gunnersbury Park, Popes Lane, Acton, London W3 8LQ

Grade II* listed Temple. Built before 1760. Red brick with stone Doric portico. Situated in Gunnersbury Park, the estate of Princess Amelia in the 18th century. The 185 acre park became a public park in 1926.

Grant Recipient: London Borough of Hounslow

Access Contact: The Curator

Tel: 020 8992 1612 **Fax:** 020 8752 0686

E-mail: gp-museum@cip.org.uk

Open: Park open daily 8am - dusk. The interior will be open for London Open House and at other times by prior arrangement. The Temple is used for events throughout the year and is available for hire.

Ⓟ Spaces: 120.

♿ Wheelchair access to the exterior only. There are two toilets for disabled within the park, but not in close proximity to the Temple. Guide Dogs: Yes

💷 No

Hackney Empire

291 Mare Street, London E8 1EJ

Hackney Empire, designed and built by Frank Matcham in 1901, is one of the finest surviving variety theatres in Britain. Restoration and renovation completed 2004, providing modern facilities and access for all.

www.hackneyempire.co.uk

Grant Recipient: Hackney Empire Ltd

Access Contact: Mr S Thomsett

Tel: 020 8510 4500 **Fax:** 020 8510 4530

E-mail: info@hackneyempire.co.uk

Open: Performances throughout the year.

Ⓟ On-street parking. ♿Yes. WC for the disabled. Guide Dogs: Yes

💷 Charges are made for performances and some organised tours.

Highpoint

North Hill, Highgate, London N6 4BA

Two blocks of flats built in 1935 and 1938 by Lubetkin and Tecton. Constructed of reinforced concrete with decorative features.

Grant Recipient: Mantra Ltd

Access Contact: Mr Stephen Ellman

Tel: 020 7554 5800 **Fax:** 020 7554 5801

E-mail: smc@grossfine.com

Open: By arrangement with Mr Stephen Ellman of Gross Fine, 14/16 Stephenson Way, London NW1 2HD.

Ⓟ No ♿No. Guide Dogs: Yes 💷No

Himalaya Palace Cinema (formerly Liberty Cinema)

14 South Road, Southall, London UB1 1RT

Former cinema, later market hall. 1928. An early work by George Coles; the only known example of cinema built in the Chinese style. Street elevation faced with coloured glazed tiles with red pantiled pagoda roofs. Interior badly fire damaged. Repaired and returned to use as a three screen cinema showing Bollywood, Tamil, Telugu and Afganistan movies.

Grant Recipient: Himalaya Carpets Ltd

Access Contact: Mr S Pandher

Tel: 020 8574 6193 **Fax:** 020 8574 2317

E-mail: himalayacarpets@tiscali.co.uk

Open: Daily 10.30am-11.30pm. Non public areas by prior arrangement.

Ⓟ Council car park at rear of cinema.

♿ Yes. No WC for the disabled. No guide Dogs.

💷 **Adult:** £3.95 (before 2pm), £5.95 other times **Child/Senior:** £3.95 (all times)

The House Mill

Three Mill Lane, Bromley-by-Bow, London E3 3DU

Industrial water mill, originally built 1776 as part of a distillery. Contains four floors with remains of un-restored machinery, four water wheels and gearing. Originally had 12 pairs of millstones and has unique survival of Fairbairn-style "silent millstone machinery".

Grant Recipient: River Lea Tidal Mill Trust

Access Contact: Ms Patricia Wilkinson

Tel: 020 8539 6726 **Fax:** 020 8539 2317

E-mail: pwilkinson@whippx.demon.co.uk

Open: Sun of National Mills Week, Heritage Open Days & the first Sun of each month Apr - Dec: 11am - 4pm. Other Suns May - Oct: 2 - 4pm. Groups by arrangement with Ms Patricia Wilkinson, 1B Forest Drive East, Leytonstone, London E11 1JX. For further information tel. 020 8539 6726.

Ⓟ Nearby.

♿ Yes. WC for the disabled. Guide Dogs: Yes

💷 **Adult:** £3 **Child:** Free **Other:** £1.50

Kew Bridge Steam Museum

Kew Bridge Pumping Station, Green Dragon Lane, Brentford, London TW8 0EN

19th century Victorian waterworks with original steam pumping engines which are operated every weekend. "Water for Life" gallery exploring 2000 years of London's water.

www.kbsm.org

Grant Recipient & Access Contact: Kew Bridge Engines Trust & Water Supply Museum Ltd

Tel: 020 8568 4757 **Fax:** 020 8569 9978

E-mail: info@kbsm.org

Open: Daily 11am - 5pm. Closed Good Fri and 18 Dec 2004 - 3 Jan 2005. Subject to change. Contact the Museum for up-to-date information.

Ⓟ Spaces: 45 ♿ Wheelchair access to 80% of museum. Two wheelchairs available. WC for the disabled. Guide Dogs: Yes

💷 **Adult:** £4.60 **Child:** £2.50 **Other:** £3.70

Mappin Terrace Café

London Zoo, Regents Park, London NW1 4RY

The café was designed by John James Joass and built between 1914-20. It was funded by John Newton Mappin. It is a single story red-brick building with a pantiled roof. It is characterised by

paired Tuscan columns, french windows, bracketed eaves and pavilion towers at three angles.
Grant Recipient/Access Contact: Zoological Society of London
Tel: 020 7722 3333
Open: On view to visitors to London Zoo which is open daily except 25 Dec.
P Spaces: 300. Car park £7 and 250 yards away.
Yes. WC for the disabled. No guide Dogs.
£ **Adult:** £13 **Child:** £9.75 **Other:** £11

Orleans House Gallery
Riverside, Twickenham, London TW1 3DJ
Orleans House Gallery comprises the Octagon Room with its fine Baroque interior, and the surviving wing/orangery of the 18th century Orleans House, the rest having been demolished in 1926. Overlooking the Thames and residing in preserved natural woodland, the Gallery presents a programme of temporary exhibitions, organises educational projects/activities and is responsible for the Richmond Borough Art Collection.
www.richmond.gov.uk/orleanshouse
Grant Recipient: London Borough of Richmond-upon-Thames
Access Contact: Mr Mark De Novellis
Tel: 020 8831 6000 **Fax:** 020 8744 0501
E-mail: m.denovellis@richmond.gov.uk
Open: All year, Tues - Sat 1 - 5.30pm; Sun 2 - 5.30pm. Oct - Mar, closes 4.30pm. Grounds open every day from 9am until dusk. For Bank Holiday and Christmas opening hours please call in advance.
P Spaces: 60
Wheelchair access to ground floor only. WC for the disabled. Guide Dogs: Yes £ No

Pitzhanger Manor-House and Gallery
Walpole Park, Mattock Lane, London W5 5EQ
Pitzhanger Manor-House is set in Walpole Park, Ealing and was owned and rebuilt by architect and surveyor Sir John Soane (1753-1837). Much of the house has been restored to its early 19th century style and a Victorian wing houses a collection of Martinware Pottery (1877-1923). Pitzhanger Manor Gallery opened in 1996 in a 1940s extension and exhibitions of professional contemporary art in all media are shown in both the House and Gallery.
www.ealing.gov.uk/pmgallery&house
Grant Recipient: London Borough of Ealing
Access Contact: Pitzhanger Manor-House and Gallery
Tel: 020 8567 1227 **Fax:** 020 8567 0596
E-mail: pmgallery&house@ealing.gov.uk
Open: Tues - Fri 1pm - 5pm, Sat 11am - 5pm. Summer Sun openings (ring for details). Closed Bank Hols, Christmas and Easter.
P For orange badge holders. Parking meters – 2 spaces.
Access for certain types of wheelchair only with assistance (domestic lift and some steps), please phone in advance for further information. WC for the disabled. Guide Dogs: Yes £ No

Priory Church of the Order of St John
St John's Square, Clerkenwell, London EC1M
Remains of the Priory Church of the Knights Hospitallers' London headquarters, including choir and 12th century crypt. Museum in adjacent St John's Gate presents information on the Order of St John and conducts guided tours.
www.sja.org.uk/history
Grant Recipient: The Order of St John of Jerusalem
Access Contact: Ms Pamela Willis
Tel: 020 7324 4071 **Fax:** 020 7336 0587
E-mail: museum@nhq.sja.org.uk.
Open: Guided tours: Tues, Fri & Sat 11am and 2.30pm. Other days and times by arrangement with the Museum.
P Metered parking available in St John's Square.
Wheelchair access to Church with assistance, but not the crypt. WC for the disabled at St John's Gate. WC for the disabled at St John's Gate. Guide Dogs: Yes
£ Donations requested for guided tours

The Queen's Chapel of the Savoy
Savoy Hill, Strand, London WC2R 0DA
Originally part of a hospital founded in 1512 by Henry VII. Rebuilt by Robert Smirke after a fire in 1864, from which time the ceiling covered with heraldic emblems dates. Recently restored.
Grant Recipient: Duchy of Lancaster
Access Contact: Mr Phillip Chancellor
Tel: 020 7836 7221 **Fax:** 020 7379 8088
Open: All year except Aug and Sept: Tues - Fri 11.30am - 3.30pm; Sun for Morning Service only. Closed the week after Christmas Day & the week after Easter Day.
P Parking on meters in adjoining streets.
Wheelchair access to chapel via portable ramps. No WC for the disabled. Guide Dogs: Yes
£ No

Rainham Hall
The Broadway, Rainham, Havering, London RM13 9YN
Georgian house built in 1729 to a symmetrical plan and with fine wrought iron gates, carved porch and interior panelling plasterwork.
www.nationaltrust.org.uk
Grant Recipient: The National Trust
Access Contact: Property Manager
Tel: 01708 555 360
Open: Apr - end Oct: Wed & BH Mons 2 - 6pm. Sat by written arrangement with the tenant of the Hall.
P On-street pay-and-display parking nearby.
Wheelchair access to ground floor only. Guide dogs by arrangement. WC for the disabled. Guide Dogs: Yes
£ **Adult:** £2.20 **Child:** £1.10 **Other:** No group reductions

Richmond Weir & Lock
Riverside, Richmond-upon-Thames, London
The lock and weir are important examples in the history of hydraulic engineering. Constructed in 1894 to control river levels between Richmond and Teddington at half-tide level, the weir was engineered to ensure that the river remained navigable at all times. Operated and maintained by the Port of London Authority since its establishment in 1909, the machinery was designed and built by Ransomes & Rapier.
www.portoflondon.co.uk
Grant Recipient: Port of London Authority
Access Contact: Mr James Trimmer
Tel: 020 7743 7900 **Fax:** 020 7743 7998
E-mail: james.trimmer@pola.co.uk
Open: The lock and weir are open at all times for passage by river except for 3 weeks in Nov/Dec for major maintenance undertaken by the Port of London Authority. The footbridge over the lock is open 6.30am - 9.30pm British Summer Time and 6.30am - 7.30pm GMT.
P On-street parking. Please note this area is liable to flooding at high spring tides. Spaces: 50
No £ No

The Round Chapel (Clapton Park United Reformed Church)
1d Glenarm Road, London E5 0LY
Grade II* listed United Reformed Church, c1871. Horseshoe-shaped plan with roof and gallery supported by iron pillars. Detailed columns form a continuous iron arcade at roof level with latticework effects. Contemporary pulpit with double flight of stairs, organ and organ case.
Grant Recipient: Hackney Historic Buildings Trust
Access Contact: Dr Ann Robey
Tel: 020 8525 0706 **Fax:** 020 8986 0029
E-mail: roundchapel@pop3.poptel.org.uk
Open: Many public/community events take place in the Round Chapel which the public can attend, it is also available to hire for private events, otherwise access by arrangement.
P Spaces: 3
Wheelchair access to ground floor only. WC for the disabled. Guide Dogs: Yes
£ No

Royal Geographical Society (with the Institute of British Geographers)
Lowther Lodge, 1 Kensington Gore, London SW7 2AR
Built by Norman Shaw, c1874-5, as a private house with a 2-acre garden for the Lowthers, the Lodge was one of the earliest and most influential works in the Queen Anne style. Bought by the RGS in 1912 and extended by them in 1930 to provide a lecture theatre. 'Unlocking the Archives' project, supported by the Heritage Lottery Fund, is underway. It will provide improved access, education facilities & increased conservation storage facilities for the Society's extensive heritage collections.
www.rgs.org
Grant Recipient: Royal Geographical Society
Access Contact: Ms Denise Prior
Tel: 020 7591 3090 **Fax:** 020 7591 3091
E-mail: d.prior@rgs.org
Open: Weekdays (except Public and Bank Hols) 10am - 5pm. Closed between Christmas and New Year. Foyle Reading Room can be visited for private study and research, using maps, library, journals, documents and photographs. Education events: a programme for school and adult groups. School groups (11-15 years) by arrangement. For further details check www.rgs.org and www.unlockingthearchives.rgs.org
P On-street parking.
Partial access, contact House Manager for details. WC for the disabled. Guide Dogs: Yes
£ Entry to Foyle Reading Room free to education users and Society members, otherwise £10 per day. Exhibition free to all.

The Royal Institution of Great Britain
21 Albemarle Street, London W1S 4BS
Houses the Michael Faraday Museum and a 200 year old lecture theatre. Regular public lectures on scientific themes.
www.rigb.org
Grant Recipient: Royal Institution of Great Britain
Access Contact: Mr Alan Winter
Tel: 020 7409 2992 **Fax:** 020 7629 3569
E-mail: alanw@ri.ac.uk
Open: Mon - Fri 9am - 5pm. Faraday Lecture Theatre open for public lectures/events on various days of the week, usually starting at 7pm. Lecture lists published on RI website (www.rigb.org). RI closed on Bank Hols, weekends, and from 24 Dec - beginning Jan.
P No
Yes. WC for the disabled. Guide Dogs: Yes
£ **Adult:** £1 (museum), £8 (lecture) **Child:** 50p (museum), £5 (lecture) **Other:** Schools free

St Alban (now the Landmark Arts Centre)
Ferry Road, Teddington, London TW11 9NN
Grade II* former church, c1889, in French-Gothic style by architect William Niven. A number of intended architectural features were never in the end built, due to insufficient funds (hence the incomplete flying buttresses for example). Redundant as a church in 1977. Following renovation now used as an Arts Centre with a variety of arts events, classes and private events.
www.landmarkartscentre.org
Grant Recipient: London Diocesan Fund
Access Contact: Mr Graham Watson
Tel: 020 8614 8036 **Fax:** 020 8614 8080
E-mail: grahamgwatson@aol.com
Open: Normally open Mon - Fri 10am - 5pm (shorter hours at weekends when public events are held), visitors are advised to contact Lorna Henderson at the Landmark Arts Centre (tel:020 8977 7558, fax:020 8977 4830, email. landmarkinfo@aol.com) to check. Visits at other times by prior arrangement with Lorna Henderson, subject to staff availability.
P Spaces: 4. Additional on-street parking nearby.
Yes. WC for the disabled. Guide Dogs: Yes
£ Admission charges for some public events

St Ethelburga's Centre for Reconciliation and Peace
78 Bishopgate, London EC2N 4AG
Church of St Ethelburga the Virgin built in the late 14th and early 15th centuries. Devastated by a terrorist bomb in Apr 1993 and re-opened in Nov 2002, after restoration, for use as a Centre for Reconciliation and Peace.
www.stethelburgas.org
Grant Recipient: St Ethelburga's Centre for Reconciliation & Peace
Access Contact: Mr Simon Keyes
Tel: 020 7496 1610 **Fax:** 020 7638 1440
E-mail: enquiries@stethelburgas.org
Open: Wed 11am - 3pm and first Fri in every

month 12 noon - 2.30pm. Groups may visit at other times by arrangement. Details of services, public lectures and other events available from the website or by telephone.
Ⓟ No Ⓗ Yes. WC for the disabled. Guide Dogs: Yes
£ No

St Matthias Old Church

113 Poplar High Street, Poplar, London E14 0AE
Built by in 1650-54 by the East India Company, St Matthias Old Church is the oldest building in Docklands. Declared redundant in 1977, the building became derelict. In 1990 the building was restored and is now used as a community arts/cultural centre.
Grant Recipient: London Diocesan Fund
Access Contact: Mrs Kathleen Haley
Tel: 020 7987 0459 **Fax:** 020 7531 9973
Open: Mondays: 11am - 1pm.
Ⓟ Car park for limited number of cars. Ⓗ Yes. WC for the disabled. Guide Dogs: Yes £ No.

St Pancras Chambers

Euston Road, London NW1 2QR
Grade I listed Gothic-style building fronting St Pancras Station. Built as the Midland Grand Hotel between 1868 and 1876 to designs by Sir George Gilbert Scott. Key features are its impressive grande gothic façade and sweeping 'fairytale' staircase.
www.lcrproperties.co.uk
Grant Recipient: British Railways Board/London & Continental Stations & Property Ltd
Access Contact: Mrs Laura Walsham
Tel: 020 7843 4253 **Fax:** 020 7843 4255
E-mail: lwalsham@lcsp.co.uk
Open: The front entrance and former ground floor coffee lounge are generally open each weekday 11.30am - 3.30pm without charge (except during filming and events). Public tours take place Sat & Sun 11am and 1.30pm every weekend and last approx. 1 hour (max 25 on a first come first serve basis). These tours are conducted by experienced guides who have a unique understanding of the building and its history. Please note that tours involve climbing several flights of stairs and that there are no working lifts or other facilities for disabled visitors. For further information on guided tours please telephone 020 7843 4253. Access arrangements may change or be restricted depending on the progress of refurbishment proposals. Please check with the access contact before visiting.
Ⓟ No Ⓗ No
£ Adult: £7.50 (private tour), £5 (public tour)
Child: Free (must be accompanied by a paying adult)

St Paul's Steiner Project

1 St Paul's Road, London N1 2QH
Grade II* listed church, 1826-28 by Sir Charles Barry. Perpendicular in style. Converted to a 'cradle to grave' education and cultural centre, including a Steiner school, multi use community performance space, adult education and information centre.
Grant Recipient: St Paul's Steiner Project
Access Contact: Ms Jane Gerhard
Tel: 020 7226 4454 **Fax:** 102 7226 2062
E-mail: st.pauls.school@btinternet.com
Open: 4 Feb, 11 Mar, 20 May, 17 June 9am - 1pm. At other times by arrangement with 2 days notice.
Ⓟ Pay and display. Ⓗ Ground floor. WC for the disabled. Guide Dogs: Yes £ No

Walpole's House

St Mary's College, Strawberry Hill, Waldegrave Road, Twickenham, London TW1 4SX
Bought by Horace Walpole in 1749 and over the next half century converted into his own vision of a 'gothic' fantasy with 14 rooms open to the public containing chimneypieces based on Medieval tombs and a collection of 16th century painted glass roundels. Reputedly the first substantial building of the Gothic Revival.
Grant Recipient: St Mary's, Strawberry Hill
Access Contact: Head of Catering and Conference Services
Tel: 020 8240 4044 **Fax:** 020 8255 4255
E-mail: gallaghs@smuc.ac.uk

Open: 1 May - 25 Sept, Sun only 2 - 3.30pm. Guided group tours (minimum 10 people) by prior arrangement on any day except Sat.
Ⓟ Spaces: 60
Ⓗ Wheelchair access to ground floor and grounds with difficulty – doorways are small. WC for the disabled. Guide Dogs: Yes
£ Adult: £5.50 Other: £4.75.

Wapping Hydraulic Power Pumping Station

Wapping Wall, London E1W 3ST
The Wapping Hydraulic Power Station was built by the London Hydraulic Power Company in 1890. One of the five London Stations of its kind, it harnessed Thames water to provide power throughout the central London area. The showcase building of the LHPC, it was used as a model for power stations in Argentina, Australia, New York and Europe. Now houses an art gallery and restaurant.
Grant Recipient & Access Contact:
Women's Playhouse Trust
Tel: 020 7680 2080 **Fax:** 020 7680 2081
E-mail: info@wapping-wpt.com
Open: Mon - Fri: 12 noon - Midnight. Sat 10am - Midnight, Sun 10am - 6pm. Open all year with the exception of Christmas & New Year Bank Hols.
Ⓟ Spaces: 30 Ⓗ Yes. WC for the disabled. Guide Dogs: Yes £ No

Whitechapel Art Gallery

Whitechapel High Street, London E1 7QX
Grade II* listed Arts and Crafts building constructed in the late 1890s by C H Townsend. Occupied by the Whitechapel Art Gallery, which was founded in 1901 by the Revd Canon Barnett 'to bring great art to the people of the East End'.
www.whitechapel.org
Grant Recipient: Trustees of the Whitechapel Art Gallery
Access Contact: Mr Tom Wilcox
Tel: 020 7522 7865 **Fax:** 020 7377 1685
E-mail: TomWilcox@whitechapel.org
Open: All year: Tues - Sun 11am - 6pm, Thurs 11am - 9pm. Various exhibitions (5 - 6 per year).
Ⓟ Paid parking in Spreadeagle Yard to the left of the gallery off Whitechapel High Street.
Ⓗ Yes. WC for the disabled. Guide Dogs: Yes
£ No, but one exhibition per year will have entrance fee

MERSEYSIDE

Broughton Hall Conservatory

Convent of Mercy, Yew Tree Lane, West Derby, Liverpool, Merseyside L12 9HH
Victorian conservatory of rectangular shape with an entrance porch at one end and an access bay to main building, at the other. The cast iron structure is mounted on a stone plinth. The elevations are divided into a series of panels with decorated cast iron circular columns. From the capitols spring semi-circular arches. These form the bases of the frieze moulding which runs round the periphery of the building. The flooring is of quarry tiles.
Grant Recipient: The Institute of Our Lady of Mercy
Access Contact: The Sister Superior
Tel: 0151 228 9232 **Fax:** 0151 259 0677
Open: By written arrangement only, Mon - Sat 10am - 4pm. No access on Sun or Bank Hols.
Ⓟ Spaces: 4 Ⓗ Yes. WC for the disabled. Guide Dogs: Yes £ No

Liverpool Collegiate Apartments

Shaw Street, Liverpool, Merseyside L6 1NR
Grade II* former school built 1843 of red sandstone in Tudor Gothic style, gutted by fire and now converted into residential block.
Grant Recipient: Urban Splash Ltd
Access Contact: Mr Bill Maynard
Tel: 0161 839 2999 **Fax:** 0161 839 8999
E-mail: billmaynard@urbansplash.co.uk
Open: Exterior only, visible from Shaw Street.
Ⓟ No Ⓗ Yes. No WC for the disabled. Guide Dogs: No £ No

Meols Hall

Churchtown, Southport, Merseyside PR9 7LZ
17th century house with 18th and 19th century alterations. Substantially rebuilt in 1960-94 by the amateur architect Roger Hesketh, using materials from other houses demolished after the Second World War. For its mix of old and new Meols Hall has been acclaimed as one of the most convincing country houses created since the war.
www.meolshall.com
Grant Recipient & Access Contact:
Mr Robert Hesketh
Tel: 01704 228326 **Fax:** 01704 507185
E-mail: events@meolshall.com
Open: 30 Apr, 1 & 2 May (as part of the Meols Hall Garden & Leisure Show), 14 Aug - 14 Sept daily 2 - 5pm.
Ⓟ Spaces: 200
Ⓗ Yes. WC for the disabled. Guide Dogs: Yes
£ Adult: £3 Child: £1 Other: Concession for Garden Festival visitors only in May

Sefton Park

Liverpool, Merseyside L18 3JD
108 hectare public park, designed in 1867, the first to introduce French influence to the design of parks through the designer Edouard André who had worked on the design of major Parisian parks. Sefton Park is Grade II* registered and contains several listed statues and other features. The Grade II* listed Palm House, 1896 by Mackenzie and Moncur, is an octagonal iron frame structure which appears as 3 domed roofs, one above the other.
www.palmhouse.org.uk
Grant Recipient: Liverpool City Council
Access Contact: Ms Emma Reid
Tel: 0151 726 9304 **Fax:** 0151 726 2419
E-mail: info@palmhouse.org.uk
Open: Park open at all times. Palm House: Jan - 31 Mar: Mon - Sun 10.30am - 4pm, may be closed on Tues and Thurs for events; 1 Apr - 31 Dec: Mon - Sat 10.30am - 5pm, Sun 10.30am - 4pm, may be closed on Tues and Thurs and from 4pm for events. The Trust reserves the right to shut the Palm House on other occasions and will endeavour to give as much notice as possible on the website and information line (tel: 0151 726 2415).
Ⓟ On-street parking available on edge of park.
Ⓗ Yes. No WC for the disabled. Guide Dogs: Yes
£ No

Speke Hall

The Walk, Liverpool, Merseyside L24 1XD
One of the most important timber framed manor houses in the country, dating from 1530. The interior spans many periods: the Great Hall and priest holes evoke Tudor times, the Oak Parlour and smaller rooms, some with William Morris wallpapers, show the Victorian desire for privacy and comfort. There is some Jacobean plasterwork and intricately carved furniture. Restored garden and woodland walks.
www.nationaltrust.org.uk
Grant Recipient: The National Trust
Access Contact: Property Manager
Tel: 0151 427 7231 **Fax:** 0151 427 9860
E-mail: spekehall@nationaltrust.org.uk
Open: House: 19 Mar - 30 Oct, Wed - Sun (open Bank Hols); Nov and Dec, Sat & Sun only. Times: Mar - mid Oct 1 - 5.30pm; mid Oct - Dec 1 - 4.30pm. Woodland and garden: open daily throughout the year, closed 24 - 26 and 31 Dec, 1 Jan. Times: Mar - mid Oct 11am - 5.30pm; mid Oct - mid Mar 2004 11am - dusk.
Ⓟ Spaces: 400. 500 yards from property. Courtesy shuttle service available.
Ⓗ Wheelchair access to ground floor of house. WC for the disabled. Guide Dogs: Yes
£ Adult: £6.25, £3.25 (grounds only) Child: £3.50, £1.75 (grounds only) Other: £19 (family), £10 grounds only)

NORFOLK

Church of St Mary the Virgin

Houghton-on-the-Hill, Norfolk PE37 8DP
Ancient church at least 900 years old. Many original features remain including double splay

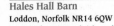

windows, keyhole chancel, Roman brick arch, 12th century North door and early wall paintings. All areas open.
www.saintmaryschurch.org.uk
Grant Recipient: Norfolk County Council
Access Contact: Mr & Mrs R Davey
Tel: 01760 440470
E-mail: steward@cathedral.org.uk
Open: All year at any reasonable time.
ⓅSpaces: 40. ♿Yes. No WC for the disabled. Guide Dogs: Yes £No

The Deanery

56 The Close, Norwich, Norfolk NR1 4EG
13th century with later additions, originally the Prior's lodgings. It remains the residence of the Dean of Norwich. The interior is closed to the public.
www.cathedral.org.uk
Grant Recipient: The Chapter of Norwich Cathedral
Access Contact: Mr Tim Cawkwell
Tel: 01603 218300   **Fax:** 01603 766032
E-mail: steward@cathedral.org.uk
Open: Exterior visible from The Close which is open to visitors during daylight hours throughout the year.
ⓅNo ♿Yes. No WC for the disabled. Guide Dogs: No £No

Felbrigg Hall

Felbrigg, Norwich, Norfolk NR11 8PR
17th century house containing its original 18th century furniture and paintings. The walled garden has been restored and features a working dovecote, small orchard and the national collection of Colchicum. The park is renowned for its fine and aged trees.
www.nationaltrust.org.uk
Grant Recipient: The National Trust
Access Contact: Property Manager
Tel: 01263 837444   **Fax:** 01263 837032
E-mail: felbrigg@nationaltrust.org.uk
Open: House: 19 Mar to 30 Oct: daily except Thurs and Fri, 1 - 5pm. Garden: 19 Mar to 30 Oct: daily except Thurs and Fri, 11am to 5pm (21 July - 2 Sept: daily 11am - 5pm) Estate walks: daily, dawn to dusk.
ⓅVisitors with disabilities may be set down at Visitor Reception by arrangement. Spaces: 200
♿Wheelchair access to ground floor, photograph album of first floor. Garden, shop & bookshop (ramp), tearoom & restaurant accessible. WC for the disabled. Guide Dogs: Yes
£Adult: £6.60   Child: £3.10   Family: £16.20
Gardens only: £2.60

Hales Hall Barn

Loddon, Norfolk NR14 6QW
Late 15th century brick and thatch barn 180ft long, built by James Hobart, Henry VII's Attorney General. Queen post roof, and crown post roof to living accommodation, and richly patterned brickwork. The Barn and similar sized gatehouse, ranged around defended courtyards, are all that remains of the house that once stood on this site. Large garden with topiary and yew hedges, and national collections of citrus, grapes and figs.
www.haleshall.com
Grant Recipient & Access Contact:
Mr & Mrs Terence Read
Tel: 01508 548507   **Fax:** 01508 548040
E-mail: judy@haleshall.com
Open: All year, Tues - Sat 10am - 5pm (or dusk if earlier); plus Easter - Oct, Sun afternoons and BH Mons 11am - 4pm. Closed 25 Dec - 5 Jan and Good Fri. Garden with yew and box topiary included in admission charge. Parties and guided tours by prior arrangement with Mr or Mrs Terence Read, Hales Hall, Loddon, Norfolk NR14 6QW (tel.01508 548507). Barn and garden may be used for wedding receptions, particularly Sat afternoon: telephone to ensure access.
ⓅSpaces: 40
♿Yes. WC for the disabled. Guide Dogs: Yes
£Adult: £2 (including guide)   Child: Free
Other: £1.50, £3 (guided tours by arrangement)

King's Lynn Custom House

Purfleet Quay, King's Lynn, Norfolk PE30 1HP
Built 1683 as a merchants' exchange, became

official Custom House in 1703. Building purchased by the Crown in 1717 for £800 and was used by HM Customs until 1989. The Borough Council of King's Lynn and West Norfolk obtained a lease of the building in 1995 and restored it.
Grant Recipient: King's Lynn & West Norfolk Council
Access Contact: Mrs Karen Cooke
Tel: 01553 763044   **Fax:** 01553 819441
E-mail: kings-lynn.tic@west-norfolk.gov.uk
Open: Daily 10.30am - 4pm. Opening times likely to be longer during summer months, check with the access contact for current information.
ⓅPublic car parks, plus many pay and display spaces within 10 minute walk.
♿Wheelchair access to ground floor only. No WC for the disabled. Guide Dogs: Yes £No

Old Buckenham Cornmill

Green Lane, Old Buckenham, Norfolk NR17
Mill with the largest diameter tower in England, which had five sets of stones when it was working. Once owned by the Colmans of Norwich and Prince Duleep Singh. Built by John Burlingham in 1818.
www.norfolkwindmills.co.uk
Grant Recipient: Norfolk Windmills Trust
Access Contact: Mrs A L Rix
Tel: 01603 222708   **Fax:** 01603 224413
E-mail: amanda.rix@norfolk.gov.uk
Open: Apr - Sept: second Sun of each month 2 - 5pm. Groups at other times by prior arrangement with Mrs A L Rix, Conservation Officer, Building Conservation Section, Dept of Planning & Transportation, Norfolk County Council, County Hall, Martineau Lane, Norwich, Norfolk NR1 2SG.
ⓅSpaces: 6 ♿No £Adult: 70p Child: 30p

Old Hall

Norwich Road, South Burlingham, Norfolk NR13 4EY
Small Elizabethan manor house with a painted stucco fireplace, painted stucco mermaids and scrollwork on the front porch, and a long gallery of hunting scenes in grisaille, c1600.
Grant Recipient & Access Contact:
Mr P Scupham
Tel: 01493 750804
E-mail: goodman@dircon.co.uk
Open: By prior telephone arrangement with Mr P Scupham or Ms M Steward. No access for guide dogs to the Long Gallery.
ⓅSpaces: 8. 12 extra parking spaces available in small attached meadow.
♿Wheelchair access to ground floor and garden, painted gallery inaccessible.   No WC for the disabled. Guide Dogs: Yes
£No

Oxburgh Hall

Oxborough, King's Lynn, Norfolk PE33 9PS
Moated manor house with Tudor gatehouse, was built in 1482 by the Bedingfeld family who still live there. The rooms show the development from medieval austerity to Victorian comfort, and include a display of embroidery by Mary, Queen of Scots and Bess of Hardwick. Gardens include a French Parterre and woodland walks, as well as a Catholic chapel.
www.nationaltrust.org.uk
Grant Recipient: The National Trust
Access Contact: Property Manager
Tel: 01366 328258   **Fax:** 01366 328066
E-mail: oxburghhall@nationaltrust.org.uk
Open: House: 19 Mar - 30 Oct: daily except Thurs and Fri, 1 - 5pm, Bank Hols 11am - 5pm (Last adm 4.30pm). Garden: 8 Jan - 13 Mar, 5 Nov - 18 Dec and 7 Jan - 26 Feb: Sat & Sun, 11am - 4pm; 19 Mar - 31 July and 3 Sept - 30 Oct: daily except Thurs and Fri, 11am - 5.30pm; Aug: daily 11am - 5.30pm; : daily except Thurs and Fri 11am - 5.30pm;
ⓅSpaces: 100
♿Wheelchair access to 4 ground floor rooms (shallow ramp), difficult stairs to upper floors. Garden largely accessible, restaurant and shop accessible. WC for the disabled. Guide Dogs: Yes
£Adult: £6 Child: £3 Other: £15.80 (family), £3 (garden & estate only)

Ruined Church of St Peter

Wiggenhall St Peter with Wigge, Norfolk
Former parish church, largely 15th century, now ruined. South aisle was demolished in 1840.
Grant Recipient: Wiggenhall St Peter PCC
Access Contact: Mrs Darby
Tel: 01553 617329
Open: At all times.
ⓅSpaces: 2 ♿No £No

Shotesham Park Dairy Farm Barn

Newton Flotman, Norfolk NR15 1XA
Built c1500 with later additions, part weather-boarded and part-rendered 5-bay timber framed barn with double queen post thatched roof.
Grant Recipient: Norfolk Historic Buildings Trust/ Mr Christopher Bailey
Access Contact: Mr John Nott
Tel: 01508 470113
Open: All year by arrangement with either Mr John Nott (tel:01508 470113) or Mr Christopher Bailey (tel:01508 499285).
ⓅThe Barn is in a busy farmyard but parking can usually be found (apart from at harvest time) for at least two cars by prior arrangement. Spaces: 2
♿Partial. Wheelchair access with assistance, rough surface outside Barn. WC for the disabled. Guide Dogs: Yes £No

St Andrew's Hall

St Andrew's Plain, Norwich, Norfolk NR3 1AU
Remains of medieval friary, including the nave (St Andrew's Hall), choir (Blackfriars Hall), crypt, cloisters, private chapel (Beckets) and chapter house. Hammerbeam roof in nave, medieval bosses in choir and a 13th century 7-light East Window. A civic hall in use since 1540.
www.norwich.gov.uk
Grant Recipient: Norwich City Council
Access Contact: Mr Russell Wilson
Tel: 01603 628477   **Fax:** 01603 762182
E-mail: TheHalls@norwich.gov.uk
Open: Mon - Sat 9am - 4pm. Subject to events.
ⓅParking in multi-storey car park in city centre. Blue Badge on site, Orange Badge if space is available.
♿Partial. Wheelchair access to ground floor only. WC for the disabled. Guide Dogs: Yes £No

St Benet's Level Mill

Ludham, Norfolk
Typical example of a Broadland drainage mill with tapering red brick tower, white boat shaped cap, sails and fantail. Built in 18th century and altered over the years, it became redundant in the 1940s. Ground and first floors accessible. Information boards on site.
Grant Recipient: Crown Estates Commissioners
Access Contact: Mr D L Ritchie
Tel: 01692 678232   **Fax:** 01692 678055
E-mail: Laurie@DLRitchie.fsnet.co.uk
Open: Open days: second Sun in May and first Sun in Aug. At other times by prior arrangement with Mr D L Ritchie at Hall Farm, Ludham, Great Yarmouth, Norfolk NR29 5NU (tel:01692 678232) or Mrs Jenny Scaff, Carter Jonas, 6-8 Hills Road, Cambridge CB2 1NH (tel:01223 346628).
ⓅNo ♿No. Guide dogs: Yes £No

St Clement, Colegate

Norwich, Norfolk NR3 1BQ
15th century church, now a pastoral care and counselling centre. Has a slender tower decorated with lozenges of flushwork (patterns made from flint and stone).
Grant Recipient: Norwich Historic Churches Trust
Access Contact: Reverend Jack Burton
Tel: 01603 622747
Open: Daily 10am - 4pm (sometimes longer). Occasionally closed when steward on leave.
ⓅIn city centre car parks. ♿Partial. Wheelchair access to Nave at street level. No WC for the disabled. Guide Dogs: Yes £No

St Lawrence

The Street, South Walsham, Norfolk NR13 6DQ
Medieval church destroyed by fire and rebuilt in 1832 as a parish church and used for worship until c1890. Formerly redundant but now

re-licensed for worship. Now houses St Lawrence Centre for Training and the Arts, open to the public and used for exhibitions, classes and concerts. Access to Sacristan's Garden.
www.st-lawrence.org.uk
Grant Recipient: South Walsham Parochial Church Council
Access Contact: Mrs Caroline Linsdell
Tel: 01603 270522
Open: Daily 9am - 6pm or dusk in winter.
P Spaces: 8
Yes. WC for the disabled. Guide Dogs: Yes £ No

St Martin at Oak
Norwich, Norfolk
15th century former church, now redundant.
Grant Recipient: Norwich Historic Churches Trust
Access Contact: Mrs J Jones
Tel: 07867 801995 **Fax:** 01603 722008
E-mail: hall.farm@btinternet.com
Open: By arrangement with the tenant. Please telephone 07867 801995 for details.
P In city centre car parks. No £ No

St Martin at Palace
Norwich, Norfolk NR3 1RW
Medieval former church, now housing the Norfolk Association for the Care and Resettlement of Offenders (NACRO). Has a fine 16th century tomb for Lady Elizabeth Calthorpe.
Grant Recipient: Norwich Historic Churches Trust
Access Contact: Mr Richard Hawthorn
Tel: 01603 763555
E-mail: Richard@norfolkacro.org
Open: By written arrangement.
P In city centre car parks.
No. WC for the disabled. Guide Dogs: Yes
£ No

St Mary's Abbey
West Dereham, Norfolk
The present six bay house is the remains of the service block of Sir Thomas Dereham's Renaissance style mansion, which he built after 1689 incorporating the surviving parts of a Premonstratensian Abbey founded in 1188 by Hubert Walter. Had become a ruin and was only recently restored, with the building re-roofed, re-fenestrated and a first floor and stair tower added. The house is now a private residence.
Grant Recipient: Mr G Shropshire
Access Contact: Mrs Ann King
Tel: 01353 727200 **Fax:** 01353 727325
Open: By arrangement with Mrs Ann King, G's Marketing Ltd, Barway, Ely, Cambridgeshire CB7 5TZ (tel: 01353 727200, Mon-Fri only). Up to one month's notice may be required.
P Spaces: 20 Yes. WC for the disabled available on request, although they are not specifically designed for such use. Guide Dogs: Yes £ No

St Mary
Fordham, Norfolk
Medieval aisleless church in rural landscape, now redundant. Listed Grade II*.
Grant Recipient: Fordham St Mary Preservation Trust
Access Contact: Mr Robert Bateson
Tel: 01366 388399 **Fax:** 01366 385859
bateson@rannerlow.co.uk
Open: Key may be available from farm opposite church or by prior arrangement with Robert Bateson (tel: 01366 388399).
P Available. Spaces: 12 No. Guide Dogs: Yes
£ No

St Peter & St Paul
Tunstall, Norfolk
Chancel and ruined nave and tower of medieval church.
Grant Recipient: Tunstall (Norfolk) Church Preservation Trust
Access Contact: The Secretary
Tel/Fax: 01493 700279
Open: Normally all year. If locked, it is due to severe weather. Key available at the Manor House in Tunstall.
P Spaces: 6 Yes. Wheelchair access across uneven path. No WC for the disabled. Guide Dogs: Yes £ No

Thurne Dyke Drainage Mill
Thurne Staithe, Thurne, Norfolk
Broadland drainage mill c1820 with classic 'hained' appearance and turbine pump. Originally 2 storey tapering circular whitewashed brick tower but raised to 3 storeys in mid 19th century, with timber weatherboarded boat shaped cap, sails and fan.
www.norfolkwindmills.co.uk
Grant Recipient: Norfolk Windmills Trust
Access Contact: Ms A Yardy
Tel: 01603 222705 **Fax:** 01603 224413
Open: Apr - Sept: second and fourth Sun of each month; National Mills weekend (second weekend in May) 2 - 6pm and at other times by arrangement.
P No. No £ No

Waxham Great Barn
Sea Palling, Norfolk NR1 2DH
Grade I listed barn, 1570s-80s, with later additions. Flint with ashlar dressings and thatched roof. Much of its fabric is reused material from dissolved monasteries.
Grant Recipient: Norfolk County Council
Access Contact: Ms Caroline Davison
Tel: 01603 222706 **Fax:** 01603 224413
E-mail: caroline.davison.pt@norfolk.gov.uk
Open: Provisional: 19 Mar - 30 Oct, daily 10.30am - 4.30pm. Visitors should ring nearer the time to confirm opening times.
P Free. Spaces: 100 Wheelchair access with assistance (gravel path from car park to Barn). WC for the disabled. Guide Dogs: Yes
£ Adult: £2.50 Child: Free

NORTH YORKSHIRE

Aiskew Water Cornmill
Bedale, North Yorkshire DL8 1AW
Grade II* watermill, late 18th and early 19th century. Sold in 1918 in a major dispersal of estate properties. Roof and main structure restored. Restoration of interior with original wooden machinery is planned.
www.farmattraction.co.uk
Grant Recipient: David Clark
Access Contact: Jared and Duncan Clark
Tel: 01677 422125 **Fax:** 01677 425205
E-mail: oakwood.ent@btinternet.com
Open: Access to the exterior at all reasonable times.
P Spaces: 40
Wheelchair access. No WC for the disabled.
Guide Dogs: Yes
£ No

Beningbrough Hall
**Shipton-by-Beningbrough,
Yorkshire YO30 1DD**
Country house, c1716, contains an impressive Baroque interior. A very high standard of craftsmanship is displayed throughout, most of the original work surviving with extremely fine woodcarving and other ornate decoration, and an unusual central corridor running the full length of the house. Over 100 pictures on loan from the National Portrait Gallery are on display. There is a fully equipped Victorian laundry and walled garden.
www.nationaltrust.org.uk
Grant Recipient: The National Trust
Access Contact: Property Manager
Tel: 01904 470666 **Fax:** 01904 470002
E-mail: beningbrough@nationaltrust.org.uk
Open: House: 27 Mar - 30 June, daily except Thurs and Fri 12 noon - 5pm; 1 July - 31 Aug daily except Thurs 12 noon - 5pm; 1 Sept - 31 Oct daily except Thurs and Fri 12 noon - 5pm. Grounds and shop: as house 11am - 5.30pm. Restaurant: as house 11am - 5pm.
P Spaces: 250 Partial. Wheelchair access (ramped) to ground floor only. WC for the disabled. Guide Dogs: Yes
£ Adult: £6.50 (house), £5.30 (garden & exhibition)
Child: £3.20 (house), £2.70 (garden & exhibition)
Other: £14.50 (family, house), £13 (family, garden & exhibition). Discount for cyclists

Castle Howard
York, North Yorkshire YO60 7DA
Large stately home dating from the beginning of the 18th century and designed by Sir John Vanbrugh. Situated in 10,000 acres of landscaped grounds, which includes numerous monuments.
www.castlehoward.co.uk
Grant Recipient: The Hon Simon Howard
Access Contact: Mr D N Peake
Tel: 01653 648444 **Fax:** 01653 648529
E-mail: estatemanager@castlehoward.co.uk
Open: 1 Mar - 6 Nov: daily 11am - 4.00pm (Grounds only from 10am); Nov - mid-Mar: grounds open most days but please telephone for confirmation in Nov, Dec and Jan.
P Spaces: 300 Wheelchair access to all but chapel and first floor of exhibition wing. WC for the disabled. Guide Dogs: Yes
£ Adult: £9.50 Child: £6.50 Other: £8.50 (prices are provisional)

Cawood Castle
nr. Selby, North Yorkshire
This decorated gatehouse, and wing to one side, is all that remains of the castle, once a stronghold of the Archbishops of York. Visitors have included Thomas Wolsey, Henry III, Edward I, and Henry VIII. In the 18th century it was used as a courtroom eventually ending up in domestic use. Extremely steep spiral staircase.
www.landmarktrust.co.uk
Grant Recipient: The Landmark Trust
Access Contact: Mr Toby Hawkins
Tel: 01628 825920 **Fax:** 01628 825417
E-mail: thawkins@landmarktrust.org.uk
Open: The Landmark Trust is an independent charity, which rescues small buildings of historic or architectural importance from decay or unsympathetic improvement. Landmark's aim is to promote the enjoyment of these historic buildings by making them available to stay in for holidays. Cawood Castle can be rented by anyone, at all times of the year, for periods ranging from a weekend to three weeks. Bookings can be made by telephoning the Booking Office on 01628 825925. As the building is in full-time use for holiday accommodation, it is not normally open to the public. However the public can view the building by prior arrangement by telephoning the access contact (Toby Hawkins on 01628 825920) to make an appointment. Potential visitors will be asked to write to confirm the details of their visit.
P Spaces: 1 No. Guide dogs: Yes. £ No

Duncombe Park
Helmsley, York, North Yorkshire YO62 5EB
Recently restored family home of Lord and Lady Feversham. Originally built in 1713 and then rebuilt after a fire in 1879 largely to the original design. Early 18th century gardens.
www.duncombepark.com
Grant Recipient: Lord Feversham
Access Contact: Duncombe Park Estate Office
Tel: 01439 770213 **Fax:** 01439 771114
E-mail: liz@duncombepark.com
Open: Easter Sun 27 Mar and Easter Mon 28 Mar 10am - 5pm. 1 May - 30 Oct, Sun - Thurs: House & Garden 12 noon - 5.30pm (tours hourly 12.30pm - 3.30pm lasting 11/4 hours, Last adm to gardens and parkland 4.30pm). Parkland Centre Tea room, shop & parkland walks 11am - 5.30pm (last orders in tearoom 5.15pm). Special Events throughout the year. Duncombe Park reserve the right to alter opening arrangements without prior notice - please telephone to check.
P Spaces: 200 Wheelchair access to ground & first floor only. WC for the disabled. Guide Dogs: Yes
£ Adult: £6.50 (house & gardens), £3.50 (gardens & parkland), £2 (parkland)
Child: £3 (10-16, house & garden), £2 (10-16, gardens & parkland), £1 (10-16, parkland)
Other: £5 (concessions, house & garden), £13.50 (family, house & garden), £4.75 (groups, house & garden), £25.00 (family season ticket)

Fountains Hall
**Studley Royal, Ripon,
North Yorkshire HG4 3DY**
Elizabethan mansion, built between 1589 and 1604 for Stephen Proctor. Three rooms; the Stone Hall, the Arkell Room, and the Reading Room, all unfurnished, are open to the public. The

conservation of a fourth room, the Great Chamber, has recently been completed. This upper room features an ornate chimney piece depicting the Biblical story of the Judgement of Solomon. The mansion is situated within a World Heritage Site which also includes the ruins of a 12th century Cistercian Abbey, monastic water mill and Georgian water garden.
www.fountainsabbey.org.uk
Grant Recipient: The National Trust
Access Contact: Property Manager
Tel: 01765 608888 **Fax:** 01765 601002
E-mail: fountainsenquiries@nationaltrust.org.uk
Open: As part of the Fountain's Abbey and Studley Royal Estate. Jan - Feb, 10am - 4pm; Mar - Oct, 10am - 6pm; Nov - Dec, 10am - 4pm. Estate closed 24, 25 Dec & Fri in Jan, Nov & Dec.
Ⓟ Spaces: 500 ♿ Yes. WC for the disabled. Guide Dogs: Yes
£ **Adult:** £5.50 **Child:** £3 **Family:** £15

Giggleswick School Chapel

Giggleswick, Settle, North Yorkshire BD24 0DE
Built 1897-1901 by T G Jackson for Walter Morrison as a gift to the school to commemorate the Diamond Jubilee of Queen Victoria. Constructed of Gothic banded rockfaced millstone grit sandstone and limestone, with lead hipped roof to nave and copper covered terracotta dome to chancel. Contains Italian sgraffito work throughout.
www.giggleswick.org.uk
Grant Recipient: The Governors of Giggleswick School
Access Contact: The Bursar and Clerk to the Governors
Tel: 01729 893000/893012 **Fax:** 01729 893150
E-mail: bursar@giggleswick.org.uk
Open: Mon - Fri 9 am - 5pm, closed Bank Hols. Other times by arrangement. Visitors must report to reception to obtain the key to the Chapel.
Ⓟ Spaces: 25 ♿ Wheelchair access to ground floor only. WC for the disabled in main school premises. Guide Dogs: Yes
£ No

Hackfall

Grewelthorpe, North Yorkshire
Developed as a wild gothic woodland landscape in the 18th century, remains of a number of man-made features can still be seen. The woodland is known to have existed since at least 1600 and the ground flora is characteristic of ancient woodland. Beech, oak, ash and wild cherry can also be seen together with spindle, an unusual tree found in chalk and limestone. The site is very steep and paths can sometimes be narrow and difficult to negotiate.
www.woodland-trust.org.uk
Grant Recipient: The Woodland Trust
Access Contact: Ms Dilys Machin
Tel: 01476 581146 **Fax:** 01476 590808
E-mail: dilysmachin@woodland-trust.org.uk
Open: The site is open to the public at all times. For further information contact Dilys Machin (tel:01476 581146).
Ⓟ Parking on opposite side of road. Spaces: 6
♿ No £ No

Hovingham Hall

Hovingham, York, North Yorkshire YO62 4LU
Palladian house built c1760 by Thomas Worsley to his own design. Unique entry through huge riding school. Extensive gardens in a parkland setting. The private cricket ground in front of the house is reported to be the oldest in England.
www.hovingham.co.uk
Grant Recipient: Mr William Worsley
Access Contact: Mrs Kathryn Lamprey
Tel: 01653 628771 **Fax:** 01653 628668
E-mail: office @hovingham.co.uk
Open: 6 June - 9 July: Mon - Sat 12.30pm - 4.30pm (closed Sun). Tours hourly 12.30pm - 3.30pm.
Ⓟ Spaces: 80 ♿ Wheelchair access to ground floor. WC for the disabled in adjacent village hall. WC for the disabled. Guide Dogs: Yes
£ **Adult:** £5.50 **Child:** £3 **Conc:** £5
Gardens: £3.50

Jervaulx Abbey

Ripon, North Yorkshire HG4 4PH
Ruins of Cistercian Abbey moved to this site in 1156, built of sandstone ashlar in Early English style. Remains of nave, transepts and choir, with a cloister on the south side of the nave, flanked by a chapter house to the east and a kitchen and dorter to the south.
Grant Recipient & Access Contact:
Mr Ian Burdon
Tel: 01677 460391/01677 460226
E-mail: ba123@btopenworld.com
Open: At any reasonable time throughout the year.
Ⓟ Spaces: 55 ♿ Wheelchair access to church, infirmary, frater & cloisters. Uneven terrain and steps on other parts of site. WC for the disabled. Guide Dogs: Yes
£ **Adult:** £2 (honesty box) **Child:** £1.50 (honesty box)

Kiplin Hall

Scorton, Richmond, North Yorkshire DL10 6AT
Grade I listed Jacobean house with 19th century additions. Built in 1620 by George Calvert, 1st Lord Baltimore, founder of the State of Maryland, USA, the Hall contains fine paintings and furniture collected by four families over four centuries. Recent major restoration work has brought the Hall back to life as a comfortable Victorian family home.
www.kiplinhall.co.uk
Grant Recipient: Kiplin Hall Trust
Access Contact: Ms Dawn Webster
Tel: 01748 818178 **Fax:** 01748 818178
E-mail: info@kiplinhall.co.uk
Open: Easter weekend, daily, 2 - 5pm. May and Sept: Sun and Tues, 2 - 5pm; June - Aug: Sun - Wed, 2 - 5pm; BH Mons, 2 - 5pm. Special events, contact the Hall for further details.
Ⓟ Free parking a short walk along drive to Hall, overflow into coach area. Disabled parking adjacent to Hall, 12 spaces.
♿ Wheelchair access to ground floor and tea room only. No WC for the disabled. Guide Dogs: Yes
£ **Adult:** £4.00 **Child:** £2 **Other:** £3

Markenfield Hall

Ripon, North Yorkshire HG4 3AD
Fortified moated manor house, built 1310-1323 for John de Markenfield (Chancellor of the Exchequer to Edward II), with further additions and alterations in the 16th, 18th and 19th centuries. Restored 1981-4 and 2001-3.
www.markenfield.com
Grant Recipient: Lady Deirdre Curteis
Access Contact: The Administrator
Tel: 01765 692303 **Fax:** 01765 607195
Open: 1 - 14 May and 19 June - 1 July 2 - 5pm. Groups with guided tour by appointment all year.
Ⓟ Spaces: 25
♿ Wheelchair access to ground floor only. No WC for the disabled. Guide Dogs: Yes £ **Adult:** £3 **Child:** £2 **Other:** £2 (senior citizens), £60 (minimum charge groups out of opening times)

Ormesby Hall

Church Lane, Ormesby, Middlesbrough, North Yorkshire TS7 9AS
A mid-18th century Palladian mansion, notable for its fine plasterwork and carved wood decoration. The Victorian laundry and kitchen with scullery and game larder are interesting. 18th century stable block, attributed to Carr of York, is leased to the Cleveland Mounted Police. Large model railway and garden with holly walk.
www.nationaltrust.org.uk
Grant Recipient: The National Trust
Access Contact: Property Manager
Tel: 01642 324188 **Fax:** 01642 300937
E-mail: ormesbyhall@nationaltrust.org.uk
Open: Hall: 30 Mar - 2 Nov, daily except Mon, Fri & Sat (but open Good Fri & BH Mons) 1.30 - 5pm (Last adm 4.30pm). Shop & tea room: as Hall 12.30 - 5pm.
Ⓟ 100 metres from House. Spaces: 100
♿ Wheelchair access to ground floor of Hall (shallow step at entrance), shop, tea room and garden. No WC for the disabled. Guide Dogs: Yes
£ **Adult:** £4.10, £2.90 (garden, railway & exhibition only) **Child:** £2, £1.30 (garden, railway & exhibition only) **Family:** £10.50

Ribblehead Viaduct

Ribblehead, North Yorkshire
Railway viaduct, 1870-74, rockfaced stone and brick. 104 feet high at highest point. Largest and most impressive of the viaducts of the Settle - Carlisle line of the Midland Railway.
Grant Recipient: British Rail
Access Contact: Mr Simon Brooks
Tel: 0161 228 8584 **Fax:** 0161 228 8790
E-mail: david.wiggins@networkrail.co.uk
Open: Viewing from ground level only. Strictly no access from Network Rail property.
Ⓟ On-street parking in Cave. ♿ No £ No

St Margaret's Church

(National Centre for Early Music), Walmgate, York, North Yorkshire YO1 9TL
14th century church with highly decorated 12th century Romanesque doorway (removed from chapel of the ruined hospital of St Nicholas, probably during 1684-5 rebuilding of church (orange-red brick tower of same date) occasioned by Civil War damage). Now houses the National Centre for Early Music and used for concerts, music educational activities, conferences, recordings and events.
www.ncem.co.uk
Grant Recipient: York Early Music Foundation
Access Contact: Mrs G Baldwin
Tel: 01904 632220 **Fax:** 01904 612631
E-mail: info@ncem.co.uk
Open: All year, Mon - Fri 10am - 4pm. Also by prior arrangement. Access is necessarily restricted when events are taking place.
Ⓟ 2 disabled parking places. Spaces: 9
♿ Yes. WC for the disabled. Guide Dogs: Yes
£ No

St Paulinus

Brough Park, Richmond, North Yorkshire DL10 7PJ
Catholic neo-Gothic chapel designed by Bonomi with priest's accommodation and school room in undercroft.
Grant Recipient & Access Contact:
Mr Greville Worthington
Tel: 01748 812127
E-mail: grev@saintpaulinus.co.uk
Open: By prior arrangement.
Ⓟ Spaces: 2
♿ Downstairs accessible to wheelchair users.. Guide Dogs: Yes
£ No

St Saviour's Church

(Archaeological Resource Centre), St Saviourgate, York, North Yorkshire YO1 8NN
Church on site by late 11th century, present building dates from the 15th and extensively remodelled in 1845. Now houses the Archaeological Resource Centre, which contains an archaeological collection excavated by the York Archaeological Trust and promotes access to archaeological material through hands-on displays.
www.yorkarchaeology.co.uk
Grant Recipient: York Archaeological Trust
Access Contact: Miss Christine McDonnell
Tel: 01904 654324 / 619264 **Fax:** 01904 663024
E-mail: cmcdonnell@yorkarchaeology.co.uk
Open: School terms: Mon - Sat 10am - 3.30pm (Last adm 3.30pm). School holidays: Mon - Sat 11am - 3pm. Groups by prior arrangement during school term. 24-hour information line (01904 643211); advance bookings (01904 543403). Visitors who simply want to view the building may look round free of charge, otherwise admission charged for entrance to Archaeological Resource Centre. Sensory garden on architectural theme.
Ⓟ Disabled on-street parking at entrance; public car parks nearby.
♿ Full wheelchair access for exhibition areas, but no access to offices on mezzanine floor. WC for the disabled. Guide Dogs: Yes
£ **Adult:** £4.50 (ARC) **Child:** £4 **Family:** £15 Carers/enablers free when helping disabled person

The Mount School Lindley Murray Summerhouse

**Dalton Terrace, York,
North Yorkshire YO24 4DD**

Grade II* listed summerhouse built c1774, formerly situated in the grounds of Holgate House, York. Octagonal timber structure on raised stepped circular base with lead ogee roof and decorated with Doric columns. Restored in 1997.
Grant Recipient: The Mount School
Access Contact: Ms Anne Bolton
Tel: 01904 667506 **Fax:** 01904 667524
E-mail: abolton@mount.n-yorks.sch.uk
Open: By arrangement Mon - Fri all year (except Bank Hols) 9am - 4.30pm.
Ⓟ Spaces: 3
♿ Yes. WC for the disabled. Guide Dogs: Yes
£ Donations welcome.

Scampston Hall

Scampston, Malton, North Yorkshire, YO17 8NG

Late 17th century country house, extensively remodelled in 1801 by Thomas Leverton. Contains Regency interiors and an art collection. Set in a parkland designed by 'Capability' Brown with 10 acres of lakes and a Palladian bridge.
www.scampston.co.uk
Grant Recipient & Access Contact:
Sir Charles Legard Bt
Tel: 01944 758224 **Fax:** 01944 758700
E-mail: legard@scampton.co.uk
Open: 23 June - 24 July (closed Mon) 1.30 - 5pm.
Ⓟ Spaces: 50
♿ Wheelchair access to ground floor only. WC for the disabled. Guide Dogs: Yes
£ Adult: £5 (house, garden & park)

Thompson Mausoleum

Little Ouseburn Churchyard, Little Ouseburn, North Yorkshire YO26 9TS

18th century Mausoleum in magnesian limestone. It is a rotunda encircled by 13 Tuscan columns, above which a frieze and cornice support a plain drum and ribbed domed roof. Listed Grade II*. Built for the use of the Thompson family of Kirby Hall.
Grant Recipient: Little Ouseburn Mausoleum Ltd
Access Contact: Mr H Hibbs
Tel: 01423 330414
E-mail: helier@clara.net
Open: Always available to view from the outside, interior visible through a replica of the original wrought iron gate. Access to interior by arrangement and upon completion of repairs (scheduled to complete 2004). Contact Mr Hibbs, Friends of Ouseburn Mausoleum Ltd, Hilltop Cottage, Little Ouseburn, North Yorks YO26 9TD (tel:01423 330414) for current information.
Ⓟ Spaces: 4
♿ Wheelchair access with assistance (gravel path & grass). No WC for the disabled. Guide Dogs: Yes
£ No

NORTHAMPTONSHIRE

Boughton Park

Boughton, Northamptonshire NN16 9UP

Extensive remains of formal gardens of late 17th and early 18th century around a country house rebuilt at the same time, set in a park developed from a late medieval deer park. Beyond the park are avenues and rides, also part of the landscape of the late 17th and early 18th centuries. The grant aided Lily pool is approximately 100 metres south of the House.
www.boughtonhouse.org.uk
Grant Recipient: Boughton Estates Ltd
Access Contact: Mr C B Sparrow MRICS
Tel: 01536 482308
E-mail: csparrow@boughtonestate.co.uk
Open: 1 May - 1 Sept daily (except Fri in May - July) 1 - 5pm.
Ⓟ Spaces: 100
♿ Partial. No WC for the disabled. Guide Dogs: Yes
£ Adult: £1.50 (grounds), £6 (house & grounds)
Child/Conc: £1 (grounds), £5 (house & grounds)

Harrowden Hall Garden Statues

Wellingborough, Northamptonshire NN9 5AD

Early 18th century Harrowden Hall retains its surprisingly unaltered contemporary garden containing a number of garden features, including statues by the Dutch sculptor Van Nost, of which one has recently been repaired.
Grant Recipient: Wellingborough Golf Club
Access Contact: Mr Roy Tomlin
Tel: 01933 677234 **Fax:** 01933 67937
E-mail: secretary@wellingboroughgolfclub.com
Open: By written arrangement with Mr B R Baumgart, PBF Housing Association, 2 Devonia Road, London N1 8JJ, access will be arranged through the manager of the Residential Home.
Ⓟ Spaces: 100
♿ Yes. WC for the disabled. Guide Dogs: Yes £ No

Laxton Hall

Corby, Northamptonshire NN17 3AU

Stone built 18th century manor house, enlarged and modified in 19th century and set in 60 acres of parkland. Stable block by Repton. Formerly a boys' school, now a residential home for elderly Poles.
Grant Recipient: Polish Benevolent Housing Association Ltd
Access Contact: Mr B R Baumgart
Tel: 020 7359 8863 **Fax:** 020 7226 7677
E-mail: pbf.pmk@ukonlinke.co.uk
Open: By prior written arrangement with Mr BR Baumgart, PBF Housing Association, 2 Devonia Road, London N1 8JJ, access will be arranged through the manager of the Residential Home.
Ⓟ Spaces: 10
♿ Wheelchair access to ground floor only. WC for the disabled. Guide Dogs: Yes £ No

The Manor House

Hardwick, Wellingborough, Northamptonshire NN9 5AL

Manor house dating back to the 12th century. The exterior of the building has been restored including a fine example of a Collyweston roof. Now part of a modern working farm.
Grant Recipient & Access Contact:
Mr Siddons
Tel: 01933 678785 **Fax:** 01933 678166
E-mail: siddons@siddons.fsbusiness.co.uk
Open: By prior arrangement with Mr Siddons (please allow at least 48 hours' notice).
Ⓟ Spaces: 4 ♿ No £ No

NORTHUMBERLAND

27/28 Market Place

Hexham, Northumberland NE46 3PB

Grade II* listed 4 storey house built 1749. Ground floor is a shop and the upper floors have been converted into flats. Imposing rear elevation to Back Row.
Grant Recipient: Two Castles Housing Association
Access Contact: Ms Julie Cuthbert
Tel: 0191 261 4774 **Fax:** 0191 2619629
E-mail: julie.cuthbert@twocastles.org.uk
Open: Exterior only.
Ⓟ No ♿ No £ No

Belford Hall

Belford, Northumberland NE70 7EY

Country house, 1754-56 by James Paine, wings and rear entrance added 1818 by John Dobson. The property stood derelict for 40 years until it was restored by the North East Civic Trust and the Monument Trust between 1984-87.
Grant Recipient: North East Civic Trust
Access Contact: Ms Sheila Fairbairn
Tel: 01668 213794
Open: Interior: any day 9am - 5pm, subject to prior arrangement with Ms Fairbairn (tel:01668 213794) or Mr Corpe (tel: 01668 213097), but excluding Christmas and Easter. Exterior: any day 9am - 5pm (3pm in winter months), but excluding Christmas and Easter. No public toilets.
Ⓟ Spaces: 8 ♿ Wheelchair access to ground floor with assistance (three steps to main entrance). No WC for the disabled. Guide Dogs: Yes £ No

Cragside

Rothbury, Morpeth, Northumberland NE65 7PX

High Victorian mansion by Norman Shaw, with original furniture and fittings including William Morris' stained glass and earliest wallpapers. Built for the inventor-industrialist and armaments manufacturer, Lord Armstrong, who installed the world's first hydro-electric lighting. The mansion is set in a 1,000-acre wooded estate, with rock garden, formal garden, man-made lakes and hydro-electric machinery.
www.nationaltrust.org.uk
Grant Recipient: The National Trust
Access Contact: Mr John O'Brien
Tel: 01669 620333 x101 **Fax:** 01669 620066
E-mail: cragside@nationaltrust.org.uk
Open: House: Tues - Sun (& BH Mons) 22 Mar - 25 Sept 1 - 5.30pm (Last adm 4.30pm); Estate and formal gardens: Tues - Sun (& BH Mons) 22 Mar - 30 Oct 10.30am - 7pm (Last adm 5pm). Wed - Sun 2 Nov - 18 Dec 11am - 4pm (Last adm 3pm).
Ⓟ Spaces: 400
♿ Wheelchair access to ground floor of house and one landing area on first floor. WC for the disabled. Guide Dogs: Yes
£ Adult: £8.50 (house & garden), £5.70 (estate only)
Child: £4 (house & garden), £2.60 (estate only)
Other: £20 (family, house & garden), £14 (family, estate), £7 (booked groups 15 +, house & garden), £4.70 (booked groups 15 +, estate)

High Staward Farm

Langley-on-Tyne, Hexham, Northumberland NE47 5NS

Georgian farmhouse standing inside a walled garden surrounded by the farm steading. Has a ging gang, threshing machine, pig stys with stone troughs and a blacksmiths shop. Most of the house and buildings are of dressed stone and the house has flagged floors, ceiling hooks, cheeseboard and rail, large pantry and servants staircase. Still a working hill farm.
Grant Recipient & Access Contact:
Mr R J Coulson
Tel: 01434 683619
Open: By prior arrangement.
Ⓟ Spaces: 2
♿ No. Guide Dogs: Yes £ No

Lady's Well

Holystone, Harbbottle, Northumberland

The Lady's Holy Well is considered to be of Roman origin and is located on a halting place along the Roman road. The main feature of the well today is a rectangular stone tank which is fed by a natural spring.
Grant Recipient: The National Trust
Access Contact: Mr John O'Brien
Tel: 01669 620333 ext. 101
Fax: 01669 620066
Open: Open at all times.
Ⓟ No ♿ No. Guide Dogs: Yes £ No

Lambley Viaduct

Lambley, Tynedale, Northumberland

17 arch stone viaduct, 100ft high and 1650ft long, spanning the South Tyne river. Originally carried single track, now used as a footpath.
www.npht.com
Grant Recipient: British Rail Property Board/North Pennines Heritage Trust
Access Contact: Mr David Flush
Tel: 01434 382045 **Fax:** 01434 382294
E-mail: np.ht@virgin.net
Open: At all times as part of the South Tyne Trail between Featherstone Park and Alston.
Ⓟ Spaces: 30
♿ Yes. No WC for the disabled. Guide Dogs: Yes
£ No

Lindisfarne Castle

Holy Island, Berwick-upon-Tweed, Northumberland TD15 2SH

Built in 1550 to protect Holy Island harbour from attack, the castle was converted into a private house for Edward Hudson by Sir Edwin Luytens in 1903. Small walled garden was designed by Gertrude Jekyll. 19th century lime kilns in field by the castle.

www.nationaltrust.org.uk
Grant Recipient: The National Trust
Access Contact: Property Manager
Tel: 01289 389244 **Fax:** 01289 389349
Open: Castle: 12 Feb - 20 Feb daily except Mon; 12 Mar - 30 Oct daily except Mon (open Scottish & English BH Mons). Open for 4½ hours either 10.30am - 3pm or 12 noon - 4.30pm, depending on the tide. Garden: All year, 10am - dusk.
P Local authority car park 1 mile from site.
No. Guide Dogs: Yes
£ **Adult:** £5   **Child:** £2.50   **Other:** £12.50 (family), NT members free, £6 (groups 10+ out-of-hours by arrangement.)

Little Harle Tower

Kirkwhelpington, Newcastle-upon-Tyne, Northumberland NE19 2PD
Medieval tower with 17th century range and a Victorian wing which contains a recently restored 1740s drawing room. It has been one family's home since 1830 though part is now let.
Grant Recipient: Mr J P P Anderson
Access Contact: Mr Simon Rowarth
Tel/Fax: 01434 609000
E-mail: simon.rowarth@youngscs.com
Open: By arrangement (at least two weeks' notice required) with Mr Simon Rowarth of Youngs, 3 Wentworth Place, Hexham, Northumberland NE46 1XB.
P Spaces: 6
Wheelchair access to ground floor only. No WC for the disabled. Guide Dogs: Yes £ Donations to the church requested.

Mitford Hall Camellia House

Morpeth, Northumberland NE61 3PZ
East wing and conservatory of country house built c1820 by John Dobson, detached from main house by demolition of north-east wing in the 20th century. The conservatory houses a superb specimen of a red flowering camellia dating to c1826.
Grant Recipient: Shepherd Offshore plc
Access Contact: Mr B Shepherd
Tel: 01670 512637 **Fax:** 0191 2639872
Open: By written arrangement during the summer.
P Spaces: 3
Wheelchair access by prior arrangement. Ordinary toilet on site may be accessible for some disabled persons, please contact Hall for further information. Guide Dogs: Yes
£ No

Netherwitton Hall

Morpeth, Northumberland NE61 4NW
Grade I listed mansion house built c1685 by Robert Trollope for Sir Nicholas Thornton. Access to main ground floor rooms and external elevations. Built as a family home and remains the current family home.
Grant Recipient & Access Contact:
Mr J H T Trevelyan
Tel: 01670 772 249 **Fax:** 01670 772 510
Open: By arrangement at least 24 hours in advance on 2 May - 30 May & 6 - 14 June, Mon - Fri 11am - 2pm by compulsory tour. Groups at other times by arrangement.
P Spaces: 20
Use of ramps up external steps. No WC for the disabled. Guide Dogs: Yes
£ **Adult:** £3   **Child:** £1

Pottergate Tower

Pottergate, Alnwick, Northumberland
Built as part of the town's defences, Pottergate Tower was one of the many gates providing access into Alnwick. Rebuilt in 1768 to a design by Mr Henry Bell with a crown spire (removed in 1812). Above the archway is a St Michael and Dragon (the symbol of the Town), a blank roundel (formerly with a clock) and a memorial tablet: 'This tower was rebuilt at the expense of the Borough of Alnwick and the new foundation laid Apr 28 AD. 1768.' The Tower is approximately 50 feet in height and has a spiral stone staircase leading on an inner room. Listed Grade II*.
Grant Recipient: The Freemen of Alnwick
Access Contact: Mr Dennis Nixon
Tel/Fax: 01665 603517

Open: To the exterior at all times; to the interior by prior arrangement.
P No
Guide dogs and wheelchair access to the exterior only. Guide dogs: No.
£ No

Seaton Delaval Hall

Seaton Sluice, Whitley Bay, Northumberland NE26 4QR
Country house, 1718-29 by Sir John Vanbrugh for Admiral George Delaval. Listed Grade I. The house comprises a centre block between two arcaded pedimented wings. In 1822 the centre block was gutted by fire and was partially restored in 1862-63, and again in 1959-62 and 1999-2000. Extensive gardens with statues and also a Norman church.
Grant Recipient: The Lord Hastings
Access Contact: Mrs Mills
Tel/Fax: 0191 2371493
Email: lordhastings@onetel.com
Open: May and Aug BH Mons; 1 June - 30 Sept: Wed & Sun, 2 - 6pm.
P Spaces: 50
Wheelchair access to Stables, Tea Room, Coach House, Ice House, Norman Church and gardens. WC for the disabled. Guide dogs: Yes
£ **Adult:** £4 **Child:** £1 **Senior:** £3.50 **Student:** £1, **Groups** (20+): **Adult** £2.50

St Cuthbert's Chapel

Farne Islands, Northumberland
St Cuthbert's Chapel was completed in 1370. By the early 19th century it was in a ruinous condition. Restored in 1840 by Archdeacon Thorp it includes some fine 17th century woodwork from Durham Cathedral and a memorial to Grace Darling. Remains of an original window.
www.nationaltrust.org.uk
Grant Recipient: The National Trust
Access Contact: Mr John Walton
Tel/Fax: 01665 720651
E-mail: john.walton@nationaltrust.org.uk
Open: 25 Mar - 30 Apr & 1 Aug - 30 Sept: daily 10.30am - 6pm. 1 May - 31 July (breeding season) daily Staple Island 10.30am - 1.30pm, Inner Farne 1.30 - 5pm.
P Public parking in Seahouses (nearest mainland village).
Inner Farne is accessible for wheelchairs (telephone the Property Manager in advance). Staple Island is not accessible. WC for the disabled on Inner Farne. Guide dogs are allowed on boat but not on islands.
£ **Adult:** £5 (breeding season), £4 (outside breeding season) **Child:** £2.50 (breeding season), £2 (outside breeding season) **Other:** £2.50 (booked school parties, breeding season, per island), £2 (outside breeding season, per island). Admission fees do not include boatmen's charges

St Michael's Pant

Alnwick, Northumberland
St Michael's Pant (drinking fountain) was built in 1765 by Matthew Mills, designed by Mr Bell. St Michael and Dragon (the symbol of the Town) on top of an octagonal drum, gargoyle for the water spout with large square trough which measures approximately ten square metres. Listed Grade II*.
Grant Recipient: The Freemen of Alnwick
Access Contact: Mr D Nixon
Tel/Fax: 01665 603517
Open: To the exterior at all times.
P No.
Yes. No WC for the disabled. Guide Dogs: Yes
£ No

Swinburne Castle

Hexham, Northumberland NE48 4DQ
Kitchen range 1600-1650, incorporating earlier fabric and with later alterations, stands at right angles to the footprint of the now demolished (1966) mid 18th century house which stood on the site of the medieval castle. East (laundry) wing 1770, restored in 2000. Orangery, early 19th century.
Grant Recipient: Trustees of R W Murphy
Access Contact: Major R P Murphy
Tel: 01434 681610

Open: 1, 4 - 8, 11- 15, 18 - 22, 25 - 29 Apr; 2 - 6, 30 May; 29 Aug.
P Spaces: 6
Wheelchair access to East Wing ground floor only. No WC for the disabled. Guide Dogs: No
£ No

The Tower

Elsdon, Northumberland NE19 1AA
14th century Tower House, residence of the Rector until 1961 and originally used as a refuge from the Border Reivers. Fine example of a medieval tower house and listed Grade I.
Grant Recipient & Access Contact:
Dr J F Wollaston
Fax: 01830 520904
Open: By previously arranged guided visit, weekends only, 1 Apr - 30 Oct.
P Spaces: 30
No. Guide Dogs: Yes
£ **Adult:** £5

Vindolanda Roman Fort

Bardon Mill, Hexham, Northumberland, NE47 7NJ
Roman Fort and civilian settlement in central sector of Hadrian's Wall with active excavation and education programmes. The site is owned and administered by the Vindolanda Charitable Trust and has an on-site museum, with full visitor services, reconstructed Roman buildings and gardens.
www.vindolanda.com
Grant Recipient: Vindolanda Trust
Access Contact: Mrs Patricia Birley
Tel: 01434 344277 **Fax:** 01434 344060
E-mail: info@vindolanda.com
Open: 14 Feb - 14 Nov. Feb - Mar & Oct - Nov: daily 10am - 5pm. Apr - Sept: daily 10am - 6pm.Winter 2005 to be decided.
P Coach parking available on-site. Spaces: 60
Wheelchair access to parts of the archaeological site and all of the museums, gardens and open air museum. WC for the disabled. Guide Dogs: Yes
£ **Adult:** £4.50 (10% reduction for EH members) **Child:** £2.90 (10% reduction for EH members) **Other:** £3.80 (10% reduction for EH members)

Wallington Hall & Clock Tower

Cambo, Morpeth, Northumberland NE61 4AR
Dating from 1688, the house was home to many generations of the Blackett and Trevelyan family. Contains Rococo plasterwork, fine ceramics, paintings and a doll's house collection. Pre-Raphaelite central hall with scenes from Northumbrian history. Hall, Clock Tower and stable buildings set among lawns, lakes and woodland with walled garden.
www.nationaltrust.org.uk
Grant Recipient: The National Trust
Access Contact: Property Manager
Tel: 01670 773600 **Fax:** 01670 774420
E-mail: wallington@nationaltrust.org.uk
Open: House: daily except Tues; 23 Mar - 4 Sept 1pm - 5.30pm; 5 Sept - 30 Oct 1pm - 4.30pm. Walled garden: daily; 1 Apr - 30 Sept 10am - 7pm; 1 Oct - 31 Oct 10am - 6pm; 1 Nov - 31 Mar 10am - 4pm. Grounds: daily in daylight hours.
P Spaces: 500
Lift to first floor for visitors with mobility problems. WC for the disabled. Guide Dogs: Yes
£ **Adult:** £7.30 (house & gardens), £5.20 (gardens only) **Child:** £3.65 (house & gardens), £2.60 (gardens only) **Other:** £18.25 (family, house & gardens), £13.00 (family, gardens only), £6.50 (groups 15+ house & gardens), £4.60 (groups 15+ gardens only)

NOTTINGHAMSHIRE

Kiln Warehouse

Mather Road, Newark, Nottinghamshire NG24 1FB
Grade II* former warehouse. Early example of the use of massed concrete construction. Interior completely destroyed by fire in the early 1990s, the exterior walls have been restored and warehouse converted into offices.
Grant Recipient: British Waterways Midlands & South West

Access Contact: Mrs Karen Tivey
Tel: 0115 950 7577 Fax: 0115 950 7688
E-mail: karen@fhp.co.uk
Open: The exterior walls for which the property is notable can be viewed without arrangement. Access to the internal courtyard is by prior arrangement with Karen Tivey of Fisher Hargreaves Proctor, Chartered Surveyors, 10 Oxford Street, Nottingham NG1 5BG (tel: 0115 950 7577).
P Parking is available on adjacent land.
Yes. WC for the disabled. Guide Dogs: Yes £No

Upton Hall
(the British Horological Institute)
Upton, Newark, Nottinghamshire NG23 5TE
Grade II* listed house in Greek revival style, 1832, incorporating the earlier 17th century house. Large addition and interior remodelled in 1895. During the Second World War the house was a school for partially-sighted children. Now houses the British Horological Institute watch and clock museum featuring clocks from the 17th - 20th centuries.
www.bhi.co.uk/tour/start.htm
Grant Recipient & Access Contact:
British Horological Institute
Tel: 01636 813795 Fax: 01636 812258
E-mail: clocks@bhi.co.uk
Open: Museum Open Days: Sun, 27 Mar and Sun, 30 Oct 11am - 5pm. Groups and guided tours (min 10 people) by appointment.
P Coach parking available. Spaces: 50
Wheelchair access to ground floor only. No WC for the disabled. Guide Dogs: Yes
£ Adult: £3.50 Child: £2 (under 10s free)
Other: £3 (seniors), £10 (family)

OXFORDSHIRE

Aston Martin Heritage Trust
Drayton St Leonard, Wallingford, Oxfordshire OX10 7BG
15th century tithe barn, 6 bays. Constructed of elm with hipped roof. Listed Grade II*.
Grant Recipient: Aston Martin Owners Club
Access Contact: Mr Robert Ellis
Tel: 01865 400414 Fax: 01865 400200
E-mail: secretary@amheritrust.org
Open: Wed afternoons, 2 - 4pm. At other times by arrangement.
P Spaces: 30
Wheelchair access to ground floor only. WC for the disabled. Guide Dogs: Yes £No

Blenheim Palace & Park
Woodstock, Oxfordshire OX20 1PX
Ancestral home of the Dukes of Marlborough and birthplace of Winston Churchill. Built between 1705-22 for John Churchill, the 1st Duke, in recognition of his victory at the Battle of Blenheim in 1704. Designed by Sir John Vanbrugh, the house contains in its many state rooms a collection of paintings, furniture, bronzes and the Marlborough Victories tapestries. A five-room Churchill Exhibition includes his birth room. 'Capability' Brown park and gardens.
www.blenheimpalace.com
Grant Recipient: Duke of Marlborough
Access Contact: Mr K Timms
Tel: 01993 810531 Fax: 01993 813527
E-mail: kevantimms@blenheimpalace.com
Open: Palace: 12 Feb - 11 Dec, daily 10.30am - 5.30pm (Last adm 4.45pm), Nov & Dec closed Mon & Tues. Park: daily (except Christmas Day) 9am - 6pm (Last adm 4.45pm).
P Spaces: 10,000
Yes. WC for the disabled. Guide Dogs: Yes
£ Adult: £11.50 off peak, £13.00 peak
Child: £6 off peak, £7.50 peak
Senior: £9 off peak, £10.50 peak

Clattercote Priory Farm
Claydon, Banbury, Oxfordshire OX17 1QB
Founded c1150, the Priory is now a family house - part farmhouse, part tenanted. A rare example of a Gilbertine Priory with cellars and 'chapel', probably medieval.
Grant Recipient/Access Contact: Mr Adrian Taylor
Tel/Fax: 01295 690476

E-mail: clattercote1@aol.com
Open: By prior written arrangement.
P Spaces: 4
No. Guide Dogs: Yes
£ Adult: £5 (to cancer charity)

Cornbury Park
Charlbury, Oxford, Oxfordshire OX7 3EH
400 acre deer park adjacent to Wychwood forest containing newly restored/replanted beech avenues, ancient English oak trees and several ancient monuments.
www.cornburypark.co.uk
Grant Recipient: The Lord Rotherwick
Access Contact: Helen Spearman/ Richard Watkins/Lindsey Sculter
Tel: 01608 811276 Fax: 01608 811252
E-mail: estate@cpark.co.uk
Open: 1 Mar - 31 Oct: Tues and Thurs 10am - 4pm. Please note that a permit is required for access to the Park; permit must be applied for in advance. Organised educational access walks for groups by arrangement.
P Spaces: 20 No £No

Culham Manor Dovecote
The Green, Culham, Oxfordshire OX14 4LZ
Dovecote constructed from brick and stone, with a datestone above the door of 1685. Reputed to be the second largest dovecote in England, formed of two large cells each with an entry lantern for dove access. In total, it has over 3,000 nesting boxes.
Grant Recipient & Access Contact:
Mr James Wilson MacDonald
Tel: 01235 527009 Fax: 01865 744520
E-mail: wil.mac@virgin.net
Open: By prior arrangement (telephone: evenings, fax/e-mail: anytime).
P Spaces 20 No. Guide dogs: Yes. £No

Farnborough Hall
Farnborough, Banbury, Oxfordshire OX17 1DU
Mid-18th century honey-coloured stone built home of the Holbech family for over 300 years, contains impressive plasterwork. Set in grounds with 18th century temples, a Terrace Walk and an obelisk.
www.nationaltrust.org.uk
Grant Recipient: The National Trust
Access Contact: Mr & Mrs G Holbech
Tel: 01295 690002
E-mail: farnboroughhall@nationaltrust.org.uk
Open: House and garden: 2 Apr - 28 Sept, Wed and Sat 2pm - 5.30pm. 1 and 2 May, Sun and Mon 2pm - 5.30pm. Terrace walk: same days as house.
P Spaces: 10
Wheelchair access to ground floor of house and garden. Terrace Walk may be difficult as it is very steep. No WC for the disabled. Guide Dogs: Yes
£ Adult: £4, £2 (Terrace Walk only) Child: £2
Family: £11

Freeman Mausoleum
St Mary's Churchyard, Fawley, Henley-on-Thames, Oxon RG9 6HZ
Built in 1752 for the Freeman family who owned the Fawley Estate. Design by John Freeman based on the mausoleum of Cecilia Metella on the Appian Way in Rome, which he visited while on his Grand Tour. It contains 30 coffin slots with 12 being filled by the Freemans before they sold the Estate in 1850.
Grant Recipient: St Mary's Parochial Church Council
Access Contact: Mr R A Sykes
Tel/Fax: 01491 573778
Open: Mausoleum permanently open. For further information please contact Mr R A Sykes (tel: 01491 573778).
P On-street parking adjacent to church. Spaces: 10
Yes. No WC for the disabled. Guide Dogs: Yes £No

Martyrs' Memorial
St Giles, Oxford, Oxfordshire OX1
Erected in 1841-3 and designed by Sir George Gilbert Scott, in commemoration of Protestant martyrs, Archbishop Cranmer, Bishops Ridley and Latimer who were burnt to death in 1555 and

1556. The memorial is hexagonal in plan and takes the form of a steeple of three stages reaching a height of 21 metres.
Grant Recipient: Oxford City Council
Access Contact: Mr Nick Worlledge
Tel: 01865 252147 Fax: 01865 252144
E-mail: nworlledge@oxford.gov.uk
Open: Accessible at all times.
P No.
Wheelchair access to the Gothic Temple with assistance. No WC for the disabled. Guide Dogs: Yes £No

The Old Rectory Dovecote
Mill Street, Kidlington, Oxford, Oxfordshire OX5 2EE
Large round medieval dovecote.
Grant Recipient & Access Contact:
Ms Felicity Duncan
Tel: 01865 513816
Open: Daily, 10am - 5.30pm.
P No No. Guide Dogs: Yes £No

Shotover Park
Wheatley, Oxfordshire OX33 1QS
Early 18th century garden follies. The Gothic Temple (designer unknown) lies east of the house at the end of a long canal vista. Has a battlemented gable with a central pinnacle and a rose-window, below which is an open loggia of three pointed arches. The other Temple west of the house, designed by William Kent, is of a domed octagonal construction.
Grant Recipient & Access Contact:
Sir John Miller
Tel: 01865 872450 or 874095
Open: Access to Temples at all reasonable times (lie close to public rights of way). Parking for a few cars at the Gothic Temple, otherwise other arrangements can be made in advance with Sir John Miller on 01865 872450 or Mrs Price on 01865 874095.
P Spaces: 50
Wheelchair access to the Gothic Temple with assistance. WC for the disabled. Guide Dogs: Yes £No

Swalcliffe Tithe Barn
Shipston Road, Swalcliffe, Banbury, Oxon OX15 5DR
15th century barn built for the Rectorial Manor of Swalcliffe by New College, who owned the Manor. Constructed between 1400 and 1409, much of the medieval timber half-cruck roof remains intact. It is now a museum.
www.oxfordshire-collections.org.uk
Grant Recipient: Oxfordshire Historic Building Trust Ltd
Access Contact: Mr Martyn Brown
Tel: 01993 814114 Fax: 01993 813239
E-mail: martyn.brown@oxfordshire.gov.uk
Open:Easter - end of Sept: Sun and Bank Hols, 2 - 5pm. At other times by prior arrangement (contact Jeff Demmar tel: 01295 788278).
P Spaces: 10 Yes. WC for the disabled. Guide Dogs: Yes £No

SHROPSHIRE

2/3 Milk Street
Shrewsbury, Shropshire SY1 1SZ
Timber-framed two and a half storey building dating from the 15th century with later alterations and additions. Medieval shop front to rear. Still a shop.
Grant Recipient: Mr M J Cockle
Access Contact: Mr H Carter
Tel: 01743 236789 Fax: 01743 242140
E-mail: htc@pooks.co.uk
Open: Ground floor open 6 days a week all year. Mon - Sat 9.30am - 5.30pm. Upper floor flats can be visited only by prior arrangement with Mr H Carter, Pooks, 26 Claremont Hill, Shrewsbury, Shropshire SY1 1RE (tel: 01743 236789).
P No Wheelchair access to ground floor only. No WC for the disabled. Guide Dogs: Yes £No

Attingham Park

Atcham, Shrewsbury, Shropshire SY4 4TP
Built 1785 by George Steuart for the 1st Lord Berwick, with a picture gallery by John Nash. Contains Regency interiors, Italian neo-classical furniture and Grand Tour paintings. Park landscaped by Repton in 1797.
www.nationaltrust.org.uk
Grant Recipient: The National Trust
Access Contact: The Property Manager
Tel: 01743 708162/708123   **Fax:** 01743 708175
E-mail: attingham@nationaltrust.org.uk
Open: House: 4 Mar - 30 Oct, daily except Wed & Thurs 12 - 5pm (Last adm 4.30pm). Guided tours 12 noon - 1pm only. Park: all year except Christmas Day, Mar - end Oct 10am - 8pm, Nov - Feb 10am - 5pm.
Ⓟ Spaces: 150
♿ Wheelchair access: to lower ground and ground floors only (house), drives and paths (grounds), and shop. WC for the disabled. Guide Dogs: Yes
💷 **Adult:** £5.80, £3.00 (park & grounds)
Child: £2.90, £1.50 (park & grounds)
Family: £14   **Booked Groups (15+):** £4.90

Benthall Hall

Broseley, Shropshire TF12 5RX
16th century stone house situated on a plateau above the gorge of the River Severn, with mullioned and transomed windows, carved oak staircase, decorated plaster ceilings and oak panelling. Also has a restored plantsman's garden, old kitchen garden and a Restoration church.
www.nationaltrust.org.uk
Grant Recipient: The National Trust
Access Contact: The Custodian
Tel: 01952 882159
E-mail: benthall@nationaltrust.org.uk
Open: 27 Mar - 24 Sept. House: Mar - June: Tues and Wed 2pm - 5.30pm and July - Sept: Tues, Wed and Sun 2pm - 5.30pm. Garden: Mar - June: Tues and Wed 1.30pm - 5.30pm and July - Sept: Tues, Wed and Sun 1.30 - 5.30. Open Bank Holiday Suns and Mons. Groups by prior arrangement with the custodian.
Ⓟ Spaces: 50
♿ Wheelchair access to ground floor of Hall and part of garden only. No WC for the disabled. Guide Dogs: Yes
💷 **Adult:** £4.20
Child: £2.10
Other: £2.60 and £1.30 (garden only)

Blodwell Summerhouse

Blodwell Hall, Llanyblodwell, Oswestry, Shropshire SY10 8LT
Square red brick summerhouse with ashlar dressings and slate roof, built 1718, at end of terrace in a restored formal garden.
Grant Recipient: Trustees of the Bradford Estate
Access Contact: Mr R J Taylor
Tel: 07977 239955
Open: By prior arrangement.
Ⓟ Spaces: 2
♿ Yes No WC for the disabled. Guide Dogs: Yes
💷 No

Broseley Pipeworks

King Street, Broseley, Shropshire TF8 7AW
19th century clay pipe factory comprising a three storey factory range, bottle kiln, workers cottage and school room. Contents include pipe-making machinery and collection of smoking pipes. Main rooms contain the original equipment installed in the 1880s and used until the site was abandoned at the end of the 1950s.
www.ironbridge.org.uk
Grant Recipient: Ironbridge Gorge Museum Trust
Access Contact: Mr Glen Lawes
Tel: 01952 435 900   **Fax:** 1952 435 999
E-mail: information@ironbridge.org.uk
Open: Apr to end of Oct 1 - 5pm.
Ⓟ Spaces: 10. Overflow at adjacent site for 20.
♿ Wheelchair access to ground floor and yard. WC for the disabled. Guide Dogs: Yes
💷 **Adult:** £3.10 **Child:** £1.70 **Senior:** £2.30

Dudmaston

Quatt, Bridgnorth, Shropshire WV15 6QN
Queen Anne mansion of red brick with stone dressings, situated in parkland overlooking the Severn. Contains furniture, Dutch flower paintings, contemporary paintings and sculpture. Gardens, wooded valley and estate walks starting from Hampton Loade.
www.nationaltrust.org.uk
Grant Recipient: The National Trust
Access Contact: The Administrator
Tel: 01746 780866   **Fax:** 01746 780744
E-mail: dudmaston@nationaltrust.org.uk
Open: 27 Mar - 28 Sept: House: Tues, Wed and Sun 2 - 5.30pm; Garden: Mon, Tues, Wed and Sun 12 noon - 6pm; Shop: open same days as house 1 - 5.30pm; Tea Room: open same days as garden 11.30am - 5.30pm.
Ⓟ Spaces: 150
♿ Wheelchair access to main and inner halls, Library, oak room, No 1 and Derby galleries, old kitchen, garden and grounds (some estate walks), shop and tea room. WC for the disabled. Guide Dogs: Yes
💷 **Adult:** £4.75   **Child:** £2.40 **Family:** £11, £3.50 (garden only), **Booked Groups (15+)** £3.75

Hospital of the Holy and Undivided Trinity

Hospital Lane, Clun, Shropshire SY7 8LE
Founded in 1607 by Henry Howard, Earl of Northampton and built in 1618 with alterations of 1857. Dwellings and other rooms arranged around a square courtyard. A well preserved example of a courtyard-plan almshouses.
Grant Recipient: The Trustees of Trinity Hospital
Access Contact: Mrs J S Woodroffe
Tel: 01588 672303
Open: Gardens and chapel open each day apart from Christmas Day. The Dining Hall and quadrangle: 25, 26 and 27 June 2 - 6pm. At other time by prior arrangement.
Ⓟ Spaces: 70
♿ Yes. No WC for the disabled. Guide Dogs: Yes
💷 No

Jackfield Tile Museum & Factory

Jackfield, Telford, Shropshire TF8
Home to the Craven Dunnill factory, where decorative tiles were mass-produced from 1874 until just after the Second World War. Surviving example of a purpose-built Victorian tile factory and continues to manufacture products today.
www.ironbridge.org.uk
Grant Recipient: Ironbridge Gorge Museum Trust
Access Contact: Mr Glen Lawes
Tel: 01952 435 900 **Fax:** 01952 435 999
E-mail: information@ironbridge.org.uk
Open: Daily 10am - 5pm. Closed 24 and 25 Dec and 1 Jan 2006.
Ⓟ Free car park.
♿ Yes. WC for the disabled. Guide Dogs: Yes
💷 **Adult:** £4.50 **Child:** £2.70 **Other:** £4.15

John Rose Building

High Street, Coalport, Telford, Shropshire TF8 7HT
A range of china painting workshops, centre part dating from late 18th century, outer wings rebuilt early 20th century. Restored and converted to a Youth Hostel, with café, Coalport China Museum, craft workshops and shop. Main entrance is paved with mosaic celebrating the amalgamation of Coalport, Swansea and Nantgarw brands. Coalbrookdale cast iron windows of large dimension line both major elevations.
www.ironbridge.org.uk
Grant Recipient: Ironbridge Gorge Museum Trust
Access Contact: Mr Glen Lawes
Tel: 01952 435 900 **Fax:** 01952 435 999
E-mail: information@ironbridge.org.uk
Open: Open all year except Jan. Café: 10am - 5pm daily. Workshops: 11am - 5pm Mon - Fri.
Ⓟ Museum car park. Spaces: 65
♿ Youth Hostel: wheelchair access to ground and first floor (stair lift) with WC for the disabled & shower facilities. China Museum: majority accessible, visiting guide available on arrival. WC for the disabled. Guide Dogs: Yes 💷 No

Langley Gatehouse

Acton Burnell, Shrewsbury SY5 7PE
This gatehouse has two quite different faces: one is of plain dressed stone; the other, which once looked inwards to long demolished Langley Hall, is timber-framed. It was probably used for the Steward or important guests. It was rescued from a point of near collapse and shows repair work of an exemplary quality.
www.landmarktrust.co.uk
Grant Recipient: The Landmark Trust
Access Contact: Mr Toby Hawkins
Tel: 01628 825920 **Fax:** 01628 825417
E-mail: thawkins@landmarktrust.org.uk
Open: The Landmark Trust is an independent charity, which rescues small buildings of historic or architectural importance from decay or unsympathetic improvement. Landmark's aim is to promote the enjoyment of these historic buildings by making them available to stay in for holidays. Langley Gatehouse can be rented by anyone, at all times of the year, for periods ranging from a weekend to three weeks. Bookings can be made by telephoning the Booking Office on 01628 825925. As the building is in full-time use for holiday accommodation, it is not normally open to the public. However the public can view the building by prior arrangement by telephoning the access contact (Toby Hawkins on 01628 825920) to make an appointment. Potential visitors will be asked to write to confirm the details of their visit.
Ⓟ Spaces: 2 ♿ No. Guide Dogs: Yes 💷 No

Loton Hall

Alberbury, Shropshire SY5 9AJ
Country house, c1670, but extensively altered and enlarged in the early 18th and 19th centuries. Set in parkland which includes the ruins of the early 13th century Alberbury Castle. Home of the Leighton family since the 14th century.
Grant Recipient: Sir Michael Leighton
Access Contact: Mr Mark Williams
Tel: 01691 655334 **Fax:** 01691 657798
Open: House: 10 Jan - 14 Apr, Mon & Thurs by guided tour only at 10am or 12 noon. Garden and castle can also be viewed at the same times.
Ⓟ Spaces: 30
♿ No. Guide Dogs: Yes
💷 **Adult:** £5 **Child:** Free **Senior:** £3

The Lyth

Ellesmere, Shropshire SY12 0HR
Grade II* listed small country house, c1820, with minor later additions. Cast-iron verandah with trellised supports, one of the earliest and largest examples in the country. Birthplace of E & D Jebb, founders of Save the Children.
Grant Recipient & Access Contact: Mr L R Jebb
Tel: 01691 622339 **Fax:** 01691 624134
Open: To the exterior on the following Sundays: 10 Apr, 22 May, 18 Sept, 9 Oct, 2 - 6pm. At other times by arrangement with Mr Lionel Jebb.
Ⓟ Spaces: 40
♿ Yes. No WC for the disabled. Guide Dogs: Yes
💷 **Adult:** £2 **Child:** £1 (charity donation for visits to garden)

Newport Guildhall

High Street, Newport, Shropshire TF10 7TX
15th century timber framed Guildhall now used as town council offices and registered as a venue for Civil Weddings.
www.newportsaloptowncouncil.co.uk
Grant Recipient: Newport Town Council
Access Contact: Miss Dee Halliday
Tel: 01952 814338 **Fax:** 01952 825353
E-mail: townclerk@newportsaloptowncouncil.co.uk
Open: Mon - Fri 9am - 1pm (closed Bank Hols). 3 other Special Open Days in July & Aug planned, please contact Town Council for details.
Ⓟ Spaces: 5 ♿ Wheelchair access via chair lift to first floor. No WC for the disabled. Guide Dogs: Yes 💷 No

The Old Mansion

St Mary's Street, Shrewsbury, Shropshire SY1 1UQ
Early 17th century house with original staircase.

The building was renovated in 1997 and now provides 4 bedroom suites for the Prince Rupert Hotel.

Grant Recipient: Mr A Humphreys
Access Contact: Mr J H L Humphreys
Tel: 01291 672 563
Open: By prior arrangement with the Prince Rupert Hotel (tel: 01743 499955).
Ⓟ Public car park in town centre. Ⓐ No Ⓔ No

Old Market Hall

The Square, Shrewsbury, Shropshire SY1 1HJ
Old market hall and court house, dated 1596 and listed Grade I. Recently repaired and refurbished to accommodate a Film and Digital Media Centre, including auditorium and café/bar.
www.musichall.co.uk
Grant Recipient: Shrewsbury & Atcham Borough Council
Access Contact: Miss Lezley Picton
Tel: 01743 281287 **Fax:** 01743 281283
E-mail: lezley@musichall.co.uk
Open: Daily 10am - 11pm. Auditorium closed to public when film being screened. Current screening times: Mon - Sun evening films. Matinee films on most days.
Ⓟ No
Ⓐ Yes. WC for the disabled. Guide Dogs: Yes
Ⓔ No. Charges for performances only (Adult £4.50, Child £3)

Pradoe

West Felton, Oswestry, Shropshire SY11 4ER
Georgian country house set in park and garden designed by John Webb. Grade II* listed house contains furniture dating from 1803 - 1812 during initial occupation by the Kenyon family. Attached service ranges, walled kitchen garden and outbuildings including dairy, brewhouse and carpenter's shop, contain original early 19th century features, recently restored.
Grant Recipient & Access Contact:
Colonel John F Kenyon
Tel: 01691 610218 **Fax:** 01691 610913
Open: 1 June - end of Sept, Mon and Tues 10am - 12pm or 1- 3pm by arrangement.
Ⓟ Spaces: 50 Ⓐ Wheelchair access to gardens only. No WC for the disabled. Guide Dogs: Yes
Ⓔ Adult: £4, £3 (groups of not more than 30) Child: £2

Weston Park

**Weston-under-Lizard, Shifnal,
Shropshire TF11 8LE**
Stately home, built 1671, designed by Lady Wilbraham. Houses collection of paintings by Van Dyck, Gainsborough, Lely and Stubbs, and is surrounded by 1000 acres of 'Capability' Brown parkland and formal gardens. Formerly home to the Earls of Bradford, now held in trust for the nation by The Weston Park Foundation.
www.weston-park.com
Grant Recipient: Weston Park Foundation
Access Contact: Mr Colin Sweeney
Tel: 01952 852100 **Fax:** 01952 850430
E-mail: enquiries@weston-park.com
Open: 26 Mar - 4 Sept, weekends and Bank Hols only. Daily during Easter and Whitweek. Most days throughout July & Aug except for 30 July & 18 - 24 Aug. House: 1pm - 5pm (Last adm 4.30pm). Park & Gardens: 11am - 7pm (Last adm 5pm).
Ⓟ Spaces: 300 Ⓐ Wheelchair access to all areas except open parkland and some formal gardens. WC for the disabled. Guide Dogs: Yes
Ⓔ Adult: £3 (house), £3.50 (park)
Child: £2 (house), £2.50 (park)
Other: £2.50 (house), £3 (park) seniors; £11 (park), £16 (house & park) family

Yeaton Peverey Hall

**Yeaton Peverey, Shrewsbury,
Shropshire SY4 3AT**
Mock Jacobean country house, 1890-2 by Aston Webb. Previously a school, now reinstated as a family home. Principal rooms on the ground floor open to visitors.
Grant Recipient & Access Contact:
Mr Martin Ebelis
Tel: 01743 851185 **Fax:** 01743 851186
E-mail: mae@earlstone.co.uk
Open: 14/15 Mar, 18/9 Apr, 9/10 May, 6 June:

12 noon - 5pm. When family is in residence by arrangement with written confirmation or introduction through known contact.
Ⓟ Parking adjacent to the property for disabled. Spaces: 6
Ⓐ Yes. No WC for the disabled. Guide Dogs: Yes.
Ⓔ Adult: £5 Child: £2

SOMERSET

29 Queen Square railings

Bristol BS1 4ND
Fronted by repaired, grant-aided railings, 29 Queen Square is an early Georgian town house, 1709-11, listed Grade II*. Brick with limestone dressings. One of the few surviving original houses in Queen Square which was laid out in 1699 and has claim to be the largest square in England.
Grant Recipient: The Queen Square Partnership
Access Contact: Reception
Tel: 0117 975 0700
E-mail: southwest@english-heritage.org.uk
Open: Access to the exterior at all reasonable times.
Ⓟ Paid parking in Queen Square and The Grove (behind 29 Queen Square)
Ⓐ Yes. Guide Dogs: Yes Ⓔ No

Bath Assembly Rooms

Bennett Street, Bath, Somerset BA1 2QH
Built in 1771 by John Wood the Younger, now owned by the National Trust and administered by Bath and North East Somerset District Council. Each of the rooms has a complete set of original chandeliers. The Museum of Costume is located on the lower ground floor.
www.museumofcostume.co.uk
Grant Recipient: Bath City Council/National Trust
Access Contact: Ms Rosemary Harden
Tel: 01225 477752 **Fax:** 01225 444793
E-mail: rosemary_harden@bathnes.gov.uk
Open: Daily: Jan, Feb, Nov and Dec 11am - 5pm; Mar - Oct 11am - 6pm when not in use for pre-booked functions. Last adm is one hour before closing. Telephone in advance (01225 477789) to check availability. There are no pre-booked functions during the day during Aug. Closed Christmas Day and Boxing Day.
Ⓟ On street car parking (pay and display)
Ⓐ Yes. WC for the disabled. Guide Dogs: Yes
Ⓔ No, but charge for Museum of Costume

British Empire and Commonwealth Museum

**Clock Tower Yard, Temple Meads,
Bristol BS1 6QH**
Museum housed in world's earliest surviving railway terminus, which was completed in 1840 and was originally part of the Great Western Railway designed by IK Brunel. Over 220ft long with timber and iron roof spans of 72ft, this Grade I listed building has been nominated as a World Heritage Site. Contains the Passenger shed and the adjoining former Engine and Carriage shed.
www.empiremuseum.co.uk
Grant Recipient: Empire Museum Ltd
Access Contact: Mrs Barbara Ward
Tel: 0117 925 4980 **Fax:** 0117 925 4983
E-mail: barbara.ward@empiremuseum.co.uk
Open: Daily 10am - 5pm, except 25 and 26 December. Access to exterior is unrestricted.
Ⓟ Spaces: 15. Additional parking in Station car park.
Ⓐ Yes. WC for the disabled. Guide Dogs: Yes
Ⓔ Adult: £6.50 Child: £3.95 Other: £5.50 (subject to change)

Clevedon Pier

The Beach, Clevedon, Somerset BS21 7QU
Pier with attached toll house built c1860s to serve steamers bound for South Wales. Wrought and cast iron structure and shelters consisting of eight 100ft arched spans leading to a landing stage. The exceptionally slender spans are constructed from riveted broad-gauge railway track as designed by W H Barlow for the Great Western Railway. Scottish baronial style toll house contains shop and art gallery. Pier restored in 1999 after partial collapse 30 years earlier and is one of only two Grade I listed piers. This pier is of

outstanding importance for its delicate engineering and the relationship of pier to landward buildings, which creates an exceptionally picturesque ensemble.
www.clevedonpier.com
Grant Recipient: The Clevedon Pier and Heritage Trust
Access Contact: Mrs Mikhael Comerford
Tel: 01275 878846 **Fax:** 01275 790077
E-mail: clevedonpier@zoom.co.uk
Open: All year except Christmas Day: Mon - Wed 10am - 5pm, Thurs - Sun 9am - 5pm.
Ⓟ On seafront. Ⓐ No wheelchair access to art gallery. No WC for the disabled. Guide Dogs: Yes
Ⓔ Adult: £1 Child: 50p

Englishcombe Tithe Barn

**Rectory Farmhouse, Englishcombe, Bath,
Somerset BA2 9DU**
Early 14th century cruck framed tithe barn. Recently restored with new crucks, masonry and straw lining to the roof, and filigree windows unblocked. There are masons' and other markings on the walls.
Grant Recipient & Access Contact:
Mrs Jennie Walker
Tel: 01225 425073
E-mail: tithebarn@ntlworld.com
Open: Bank Holidays, 2 - 6pm; all other times by arrangement with Mrs Walker (tel:01225 425073). Closed 20 Dec 2004 - 8 Jan 2005 and month of Feb.
Ⓟ Spaces: 34
Ⓐ Yes. WC for the disabled. Guide Dogs: Yes Ⓔ No

Fairfield, Stogursey

nr. Bridgwater, Somerset TA5 1PU
Elizabethan manor house, medieval in origin and listed Grade II*. Undergoing repairs. Occupied by the same family for over 800 years. Woodland garden with views of the Quantocks.
Grant Recipient: Lady Gass
Access Contact: Mr D W Barke
Tel: 01722 327087 or 01278 732251
Fax: 01722 413229
Open: House: 27 Apr - 1 July: Wed, Thurs, Fri and Bank Hols by guided tour at 2.30pm and 3.30pm. Groups at other times by prior arrangement. Dates to be confirmed. Please contact the house or check the English Heritage website for current information. Garden: open for NGS and other charities on dates advertised in Spring. No inside photography. No dogs except Guide Dogs.
Ⓟ No parking for coaches. Spaces: 30
Ⓐ Yes. WC for the disabled. Guide Dogs: Yes
Ⓔ Adult: £4 Child: £1
Other: Admission charges in aid of Stogursey Church

Forde Abbey

Chard, Somerset TA20 4LU
Cistercian monastery founded in 1140 and dissolved in 1539 when the church was demolished. The monks' quarters were converted in 1640 into an Italian style "palazzo" by Sir Edmund Prideaux. Interior has plaster ceilings and Mortlake tapestries.
www.fordeabbey.co.uk
Grant Recipient: Trustees of the Roper Settlement
Access Contact: Mrs Clay
Tel: 01460 220231
E-mail: forde.abbey@virgin.net
Open: Gardens: daily 10am - 4.30pm. House: Apr - Oct; Tues - Fri, Sun & BHs 12 noon - 4pm.
Ⓟ Spaces: 500
Ⓐ Wheelchair access to ground floor and garden. WC for the disabled. Guide Dogs: Yes
Ⓔ Adult: £7.50 Child: Free Senior: £7 (provisional prices)

Gants Mill

Gants Mill Lane, Bruton, Somerset BA10 0DB
Working watermill with deeds dating back to owner John le Gaunt in 1290. Corn grinding demonstrations, demonstrations of hydropower plant and historical displays. Designer water garden with sculptures, ponds, streams, rose pergolas. Collections of iris, delphiniums, penstemons, day lilies and dahlias. Riverside walk.
www.gantsmill.co.uk
Grant Recipient: Mr Brian Shingler

Access Contact: Brian & Alison Shingler
Tel: 01749 812393
E-mail: shingler@gantsmill.co.uk
Open: 15 May - end Sept, Sun, Thurs & Bank Hols 2 - 5pm. Groups by arrangement. Refreshments available.
P Spaces: 40. Parking for disabled close to site.
Wheelchair access to gardens only. No WC for the disabled. Guide Dogs: Yes
£ **Adult:** £5   **Child:** £1   Group reductions available.

Great House Farm
Theale, Wedmore, Somerset BS28 4SJ
17th century farmhouse with Welsh slate roof, oak doors and some original diamond paned windows. Inside is a carved well staircase with two murals on the walls. There are four servants' rooms at the top, three of which are dark and occupied by Lesser Horseshoe bats.
Grant Recipient & Access Contact:
Mr A R Millard
Tel: 01934 713133
Open: Apr - Aug: Tues and Thurs 2 - 6pm by prior telephone arrangement.
P Spaces: 6
No. Guide Dogs: Yes
£ **Adult:** £2 **Child:** Free **Senior:** £1

Gurney Manor
Cannington, Somerset TA5 2MW
Late medieval house built around a courtyard. Used as a tenant farm before converted into flats in the 1940s, now restored to its original undivided state.
www.landmarktrust.co.uk
Grant Recipient: The Landmark Trust
Access Contact: Mr Toby Hawkins
Tel: 01628 825920   **Fax:** 01628 825417
E-mail: thawkins@landmarktrust.org.uk
Open: The Landmark Trust is an independent charity, which rescues small buildings of historic or architectural importance from decay or unsympathetic improvement. Landmark's aim is to promote the enjoyment of these historic buildings by making them available to stay in for holidays. Gurney Manor can be rented by anyone, at all times of the year, for periods ranging from a weekend to three weeks. Bookings can be made by telephoning the Booking Office on 01628 825925. As the building is in full-time use for holiday accommodation, it is not normally open to the public. However the public can view the building by prior arrangement by telephoning the access contact (Toby Hawkins on 01628 825920) to make an appointment. Potential visitors will be asked to write to confirm the details of their visit.
P Spaces: 3 No. Guide Dogs: Yes £ No

Hall Farm High Barn
Stogumber, Taunton, Somerset TA4 3TQ
17th century Grade II* listed building with seven bays of red local sandstone rubble with jointed cruck roof. South wall supported by four buttresses but there are none on the North wall. There are blocked windows on the South wall and two stub walls extend north. Lines of joist holes were provided for internal flooring and the two main entrances were to the north and south.
Grant Recipient & Access Contact:
C M & R Hayes
Tel: 01984 656321
Open: By prior arrangement with C M & R Hayes at Hall Farm.
P Spaces: 4
Yes. No WC for the disabled. Guide Dogs: Yes
£ No

Hestercombe
Cheddon Fitzpaine, Taunton, Somerset TA2 8LG
Formal gardens, featuring terraces, rills and an orangery, designed by Sir Edwin Lutyens and Gertrude Jekyll. The newly restored Landscape Garden was designed by Bampfylde in 1750 and comprises 40 acre pleasure grounds with classical temples and a Great Cascade.
www.hestercombegardens.com
Grant Recipient: Somerset County Council
Access Contact: Mr Philip White

Tel: 01823 413923   **Fax:** 01823 413747
E-mail: info@hestercombegardens.com
Open: Daily, excluding Christmas Day, 10am - 5pm (last admission).
P Spaces: 100
Limited wheelchair access to Gardens. Full access to toilets and tea room. WC for the disabled. Guide Dogs: Yes
£ **Adult:** £5.20 **Child:** £1.20 (age 5-15) **Senior:** £4.90 **Groups** (20+): £4.40

Lancin Farmhouse
Wambrook, Chard, Somerset TA20 3EG
14th century farmhouse with old oak beams, fireplaces with the original smoking thatch, flagstone floors and breadoven.
Grant Recipient: Mr S J Smith
Access Contact: Mrs R A Smith
Tel: 01460 62290
Open: 19 Apr, 10am - 2pm. 21 Apr; 3 and 26 May; 7 and 23 June; 7 and 19 July; 1 and 29 Sept, 9.30am - 2.30pm. At other times Tues, Wed or Thurs 10am - 5pm by prior arrangement.
P Spaces: 5 No £ **Adult:** £2.

Orchard Wyndham
Williton, Somerset TA4 4HH
Manor house, originally medieval but with many subsequent alterations and additions. Family home of the Wyndhams and their ancestors, the Orchards and Sydenhams, for 700 years.
Grant Recipient: The Wyndham Estate
Access Contact: Dr K S H Wyndham
Tel: 01984 632309   **Fax:** 01984 633526
E-mail: wyndhamest@btinternet.com
Open: 28 July - 29 Aug: (Thurs & Fri 2 - 5pm, BH Mon 11am - 5pm, by guided tour (groups of max. 8 persons, last tour 4pm). At other times by arrangement (at least 2 weeks notice requested).)
P Spaces: 25
Wheelchair access to ground floor and gardens only. No WC for the disabled. Guide Dogs: Yes
£ **Adult:** £6 **Child:** £2 (under 12)

Prior Park College Old Gymnasium
Ralph Allen Drive, Bath, Somerset BA2 5AH
Built for Ralph Allen in the mid-18th century as an early and successful demonstration of the quality of Bath stone. The Chapel and Old Gymnasium are part of the mid-19th century additions to adapt the property as a Catholic seminary for Bishop Baines. Now a boarding and day school.
www.priorpark.co.uk
Grant Recipient: Governors of Prior Park College
Access Contact: C J Freeman
Tel: 01225 837491   **Fax:** 01225 835753
E-mail: bursar@priorpark.co.uk
Open: Group tours during school holidays, otherwise by prior arrangement. Please telephone in advance. Further public access under review at time of publication, please check the English Heritage website, or with the access contact for current information.
P Spaces: 50
No wheelchair access to Old Gymnasium. WC for the disabled. Guide Dogs: Yes
£ Please telephone for prices.

Rowes Leadworks
('Wildscreen at Bristol' and Firehouse restaurant), Harbourside, Bristol BS1 5DB
A former leadworks built in the 19th century. One of a few surviving structures associated with the industrial character of this area with a goods station and nearby warehouses. Now transformed into a restaurant/bar, The Firehouse Rotisseries. Attached to this is a modern canopied, large open structure, the entrance to 'Wildscreen at Bristol' which features imagery and interactive exhibits of the natural world. It includes an IMAX cinema and living botanical house.
www.at-bristol.org.uk
Grant Recipient: Bristol City Council
Access Contact: Professor John Durant
Tel: 0117 9092000   **Fax:** 0117 9157200
E-mail: john.durant@at-bristol.org.uk
Open: All venues: daily 10am - 6pm. Possible late openings for August (please ring for confirmation). Public squares and spaces around the leadworks open all year round.

P Pay parking operated by Bristol City Council. Spaces: 500
Wheelchair access. WC for the disabled. Guide Dogs: Yes
£ Free to view building but charges for access to 'Wildscreen at Bristol' and the IMAX theatre.

Rowlands Mill
Rowlands, Ilminster, Somerset TA19 9LE
Grade II* stone and brick 3-storey millhouse and machinery, c1620, with a mill pond, mill race, overshooting wheel and waterfall. The millhouse is now a holiday let but the machinery has separate access and is in working condition.
Grant Recipient & Access Contact:
Mr P G H Speke
Tel/Fax: 01460 52623
Open: Millhouse Fri and machinery Mon - Fri 10am - 4pm by written arrangement (at least 1 week's notice required). Heritage Open Days machinery only unless a Fri, then whole building.
P Spaces: 7
Wheelchair access to ground floor only. No WC for the disabled. Guide Dogs: Yes
£ **Adult:** £3 **Child:** Free

Royal West of England Academy
Queen's Road, Clifton, Bristol BS8 1PX
Bristol's first Art Gallery, founded in 1844 and Grade II* listed. A fine interior housing five naturally lit art galleries, a new commercial gallery and a permanent fine art collection. Open to the public throughout the year.
www.rwa.org.uk
Grant Recipient: Royal West of England Academy
Access Contact: Miss Clare Wood
Tel: 0117 9735129   **Fax:** 0117 9237874
E-mail: info@rwa.org.uk
Open: Mon - Sat 10am - 5.30pm, Sun 2pm - 5pm. BHs 11am - 4pm. Closed 25 Dec - 1 Jan & Easter Day.
P 5 spaces for Disabled Badge Holders only.
Wheelchair access to New Gallery on ground floor and Main Galleries accessible by lift. Downstairs gallery not accessible. No WC for the disabled. Guide Dogs: Yes
£ **Adult:** £3 **Child:** Free (under 16) **Conc:** £2

St George's Bristol
Great George Street, Bristol, Somerset BS1 5RR
Grade II* listed Georgian former church, c1821-3, by Robert Smirke in Greek Revival style, now 550 seater concert hall. A Waterloo church, built as a chapel-of-ease to Cathedral of St Augine, and converted to a concert hall in 1987. The crypt now houses a café and art gallery.
www.stgeorgesbristol.co.uk
Grant Recipient: St George's Bristol
Access Contact: Ms Jo Webb
Tel: 0117 929 4929   **Fax:** 0117 927 6537
E-mail: j.webb@stgeorgesbristol.co.uk
Open: For seasonal concert programmes - mainly evenings, some lunchtimes and Sun afternoons, contact Box Office on 0117 9230359 for brochure. Free access to crypt and art gallery from 1 hour before concerts. Tours can be arranged if dates comply with events schedule.
P Disabled parking & evenings only. Pay & display around building and 2 NCPs within 5 mins walk. Spaces: 3
Wheelchair access via Charlotte Street. The auditorium stalls, crypt/café/gallery and Box Office are accessible but preferable if you ring in advance as entry is not straightforward. WC for the disabled. Guide Dogs: Yes
£ No, but tickets required for concerts

St Margaret's Almshouses
Taunton, Somerset
Converted 16th century almshouses built on site of 12th century leper hospital. Listed Grade II*. 16th century conversion/repair undertaken though services of Abbot Beve of Glastonbury Abbey. Remained as almshouses until 1938 when it became HQ of the Rural Community Council and Somerset Guild of Craftsmen. Building stood unused from the late 1980s and became derelict. Purchased, repaired and converted into social housing by the Somerset Building Preservation Trust in 1999. Occupied by

tenants of Falcon Rural Housing.
Grant Recipient: Somerset Buildings Preservation Trust
Access Contact: Mrs Erica Adams
Tel: 01823 669022 **Fax:** 01823 669022
E-mail: erica.adams1@tiscali.co.uk
Open: By arrangement only with Falcon Rural Housing (tel: 01823 667343).
🅿Limited parking.
♿Partial. Wheelchair access to ground floor. Guide dogs: Yes (by prior arrangement). No WC for the disabled. 💷No

Temple of Harmony
Halswell Park, Goathurst, Bridgwater, Somerset TA5 2DH
18th century folly, a copy of the Temple of Verilis, forms part of the 18th century Pleasure Gardens at Halswell House. Restored in 1994.
www.somersite.co.uk/temple.htm
Grant Recipient: Somerset Buildings Preservation Trust
Access Contact: Mr Richard Mathews
Tel/Fax: 01278 786012
E-mail: richard.p.mathews@totalise.co.uk
Open: 1 June - end Sept: Sat & Sun 2 - 5pm, plus Easter Weekend & May Day BH. Any other day by arrangement with Mrs J Hirst, Honorary Treasurer, The Halswell Park Trust, 27 Durliegh Road, Bridgwater, Somerset TA6 7HX (tel: 01278 429342).
🅿Spaces: 4 ♿No. Guide Dogs: Yes
💷Adult: £1 Child/Senior: 50p

SOUTH YORKSHIRE

Hickleton Hall
Hickleton, South Yorkshire DN5 7BB
Georgian Mansion, grade II* listed, built in the 1740s to a design by James Paine with later additions. The interior is noted for its plasterwork ceilings. Set in 15 acres of formal gardens laid out in the early 1900s, the Hall is now a residential care home.
Grant Recipient: Sue Ryder Care
Access Contact: Mrs A J Towriss
Tel: 01709 892070 **Fax:** 01709 890140
Open: By prior arrangement with Mrs Towriss at Sue Ryder Care, Mon - Fri 2 - 4pm.
🅿Available.
♿Wheelchair access to Hall only; no access to gardens. WC for the disabled. Guide Dogs: Yes
💷No

The Lyceum Theatre
Tudor Square, Sheffield, South Yorkshire S1 1DA
Grade II* listed theatre built 1897. The only surviving example of the work of WGR Sprague outside London. Its special features include a domed corner tower, a lavish Rococo auditorium (1097 seats) and a proscenium arch with a rare open-work valance in gilded plasterwork. A notable example of a theatre of the period, with a largely unaltered interior.
www.sheffieldtheatres.co.uk
Grant Recipient: The Lyceum Theatre Trust
Access Contact: The Box Office
Tel: 0114 249 6000 **Fax:** 0114 249 6003
Open: Performances throughout the year. 21 scheduled backstage tours per year. All tours commence at 10.30am. Group guided tours by prior arrangement. Contact the Box Office (tel: 0114 249 6000) or check the website for further information.
🅿National Car Park adjacent to the theatre. Spaces: 600
♿Wheelchair access all areas except 2 private entertaining rooms. WC for the disabled. Guide Dogs: Yes
💷Adult: £3 (backstage tour)
Other: Charge for performances

Moated Site & Chapel
Thorpe Lane, Thorpe-in-Balne, Doncaster, South Yorks DN6 0DY
Medieval chapel, moated site and fishponds. Built 12th century with 13th, 14th, 15th and 19th century alterations. Restored and re-roofed in

1994/5. In 1452 the chapel was the scene of the forcible abduction of Joan, wife of Charles Nowel, by Edward Lancaster of Skipton in Craven, which resulted in the passing of an Act of Parliament for the redress of grievance and the better protection of females.
Grant Recipient: Mr Attey
Access Contact: Mrs Attey
Tel/Fax: 01302 883160
Open: By prior arrangement with Mrs Attey at the Manor House, Thorpe Lane, Thorpe-in-Balne, nr. Doncaster, South Yorks DN6 0DY.
🅿Spaces: 10
♿Partial. Through the double doors at the front of the chapel facing Thorpe Lane – shallow wide step. Guide Dogs: Yes
💷No, but donations for charity welcomed. St Mary's Church, Kirk Bramwith, near Doncaster

STAFFORDSHIRE

Barlaston Hall
Barlaston, nr. Stoke-on-Trent, Staffordshire ST12 9AT
Mid-18th century Palladian villa attributed to Sir Robert Taylor, with public rooms containing some fine examples of 18th century plasterwork. Extensively restored during the 1990s.
Grant Recipient & Access Contact:
Mr James Hall
Fax: 01782 372391
E-mail: wadey54@aol
Open: 9 Mar - 14 Sept: Tues 2 - 5pm. No groups.
🅿Spaces: 6 ♿No 💷Adult: £2.50 Child: £1.50
Other: No charge for Historic Houses Association members

Biddulph Grange Garden
Biddulph, Stoke-on-Trent, Staffordshire ST8 7SD
Garden with series of connected compartments designed to display specimens from James Bateman's extensive and wide ranging plant collection. Visitors are taken on a miniature tour of the world featuring the Egyptian court, China, a Scottish glen, as well as a pinetum and rock areas.
www.nationaltrust.org.uk
Grant Recipient: The National Trust
Access Contact: Property Manager
Tel: 01782 517999 **Fax:** 01782 510624
E-mail: biddulphgrange@nationaltrust.org.uk
Open: 19 Mar - 30 Oct: Wed - Fri 12 noon - 6pm and Sat & Sun 11am - 6pm (High Season). 5 Nov - 18 Dec: Sat & Sun 11am - 3pm (Low Season).
🅿Spaces: 100 ♿Wheelchair access to Lime Avenue, Lake, Pinetum, Cheshire Cottage, Egypt and East Terrace. Steps and undulating terrain throughout the garden. WC for the disabled. Guide Dogs: Yes
💷Adult: £4.80 (High Season), £2 (Low Season) Child: £2.40 (High Season), £1 (Low Season)
Other: £12 (family, High Season), £5 (family, Low Season)

Cheddleton Flint Mill
Cheddleton, Leek, nr. Stoke-on-Trent, Staffordshire ST13 7HL
18th century complex for grinding flint comprising two working watermills. South Mill modified in 19th century and now contains displays relating to the pottery industry.
www.ex.ac.uk/~akoutram/cheddleton-mill
Grant Recipient:
Cheddleton Flint Mill Industrial Heritage Trust
Access Contact: Mr E E Royle, MBE
Tel: 01782 502907
Open: Apr - Sept (including Bank Hols), Sat - Sun 1pm - 5pm. Weekdays by arrangement (tel:01782 502907).
🅿Spaces: 18
♿Wheelchair access to ground floor only. Disabled toilet planned for 2005. Guide Dogs: No
💷No

Claymills Pumping Engines
Victorian Pumping Station, The Sewage Works, Meadow Lane, Stretton, Burton-on-Trent, Staffordshire DE13 0DA
Large Victorian steam-operated sewage pumping

station built in 1885. Four beam engines housed in two Italianate engine houses, two operational on steaming weekends. Boiler house with range of five Lancashire boilers, large Victorian steam-operated workshop with blacksmith's forge, steam hammer, and steam driven machinery. 1930s dynamo house with very early D.C. generating equipment, earliest dynamo 1889 (all operational). The site houses the largest number of steam engines in Britain still working in their original state (19).
www.claymills.org.uk
Grant Recipient: Severn Trent Water Ltd
Access Contact: Mr Roy Barratt
Tel: 01283 534960 **Fax:** 07092 275554
E-mail: roybarratt@yahoo.co.uk
Open: Thurs & Sats for static viewing. Steaming weekends 10am - 5pm: Easter 27 & 28 Mar, Early May BH 1 & 2 May, End of May BH 29 & 30 May, 28 & 29 Aug, Heritage Open Days (non steaming) 10 & 11 Sept, Burton Festival (combined with S/T) 18 & 19 Sept, 23 & 24 Oct, 1 & 2 Jan 2006. Admission charged for steaming weekends, donations requested on other open days. Refreshments available.
🅿For disabled adjacent to site. 6 coaches. Spaces: 100
♿Wheelchair access to ground floor only (boiler house, workshop, refreshments, engine house). WC for the disabled. Guide Dogs: Yes
💷Adult: £3 Child/Seniors: £2 Family: £7

Clifton Hall
Clifton Campville, Staffordshire B79 0BE
Small country house built in 1705, perhaps by Francis Smith of Warwick for Sir Charles Pye. Two monumental wings flanking a courtyard, the intention being to link them with a central main building which was never constructed. This strange history explains why the Hall unusually developed out of what would have been the servants' wing.
Grant Recipient & Access Contact:
Mr Richard Blunt
Tel/Fax: 01827 373681
Open: By prior arrangement only, any weekday 9am - 5pm all year.
🅿Spaces: 10
♿Yes No WC for the disabled. Guide Dogs: Yes
💷Adult: £4.50 Child/Conc: £2

Hamstall Ridware Manor
Hamstall Ridware, Staffordshire WS15 3RS
Small scheduled ancient monument known as 'The Porch', with stone balcony, now restored and two stone fireplaces. Restored oak doors and windows. Some carvings on the stone balcony. Interior is made up of two rooms.
Grant Recipient & Access Contact:
Mr and Mrs Shore
Tel: 0121 382 6540 office hrs only
Open: By arrangement with Mr and Mrs Shaw.
🅿No. ♿Wheelchair access to exterior only. Steps into building. No WC for the disabled. Guide Dogs: Yes
💷Lower Rock Houses only Adult: 50p Child: 25p

Kinver Edge (Hill Fort)
nr. Stourbridge, Staffordshire
A sandstone ridge covered in woodland and heath with Iron Age hill fort with views across surrounding countryside. Famous Holy Austin Rock Houses, inhabited until 1950s, have been restored and parts are open to visitors at selected times.
www.nationaltrust.org.uk
Grant Recipient: The National Trust
Access Contact: The Warden
Tel: 01384 872418
E-mail: kinveredge@nationaltrust.org.uk
Open: Kinver Edge is open at all times free of charge. Holy Austin Rock House grounds: daily, Apr - Sept 9am - 7pm, Oct - Mar 9am - 4pm. Upper Terrace: Wed, Sat & Sun, 2 Apr - 28 Sept 2 - 5pm, Oct - Mar 2 - 4pm. Lower Rock Houses: 2 Mar - 27 Nov, Sat & Sun 2 - 4pm. Other times for guided tours by arrangement with Custodian (tel:01384 872553). Booking line tel: 01384 872553.
🅿Spaces: 100 ♿Lower houses have access path for disabled. No WC for the disabled. Guide Dogs: Yes
💷Lower Rock Houses only Adult: 50p Child: 25p

Shugborough

Milford, Stafford, Staffordshire ST17 0XB

The present house was begun c1695. Between 1760 and 1770 it was enlarged and again partly remodelled by Samuel Wyatt at end of 18th century. The interior is particularly notable for its plaster work and other decorations. Ancestral home of the Earls of Lichfield. Houses the Staffordshire County Museum, Georgian working farm and Rare Livestock Breed project.
www.staffordshire.gov.uk
Grant Recipient: The National Trust
Access Contact: Property Manager
Tel: 01889 881388 **Fax:** 01889 881323
E-mail: shugborough.promotions@ staffordshire.gov.uk
Open: House, servants' quarters, farm and gardens: 18 Mar - 31 Oct, daily 11am - 5pm (Last adm 4.30pm). Opening times may vary, telephone to check. Tours for booked groups daily from 10.30am. Evening tours also available.
P Spaces: 60
Wheelchair access to ground floor of house and museum only. WC for the disabled. Guide Dogs: Yes
£ **Adult:** £8 (House & servants' quarters, farm & garden) **Child:** £5 (House & servants' quarters, farm & garden) **Other:** £20 (family- all sites), NT members: free to house only, £5 all inclusive ticket

Sinai House

Shobnall Road, Burton on Trent, Staffordshire DE14 2BB

Timber-framed E-shaped house, two-thirds derelict, on moated hill-top site, dating from the 13th century. House built variously during 15th, 16th and 17th centuries with later additions, including wall paintings and carpenters marks. 18th century bridge and plunge pool in the grounds.
Grant Recipient & Access Contact:
Ms C A Newton
Tel: 01283 544161/01889 561000
Fax: 01889 563258
E-mail: knewton@brookesvernons.co.uk
Open: By prior arrangement only.
P Spaces: 10.
Temporary ramps to internal steps can be arranged. No WC for the disabled. Guide Dogs: Yes
£ Donations requested

South Fortification Wall

The Close, Lichfield, Staffordshire WS13 7LD

External wall comprising remaining part of medieval building. Set in grounds adjacent to Cathedral Visitors' Centre and at the rear of Cathedral Coffee shop.
www.lichfield.cathedral.org
Grant Recipient & Access Contact: The Dean & Chapter of Lichfield Cathedral
Tel: 01543 306100 **Fax:** 01543 306109
E-mail: enquiries@lichfield-cathedral.org
Open: Grounds: daily 9am - 5pm.
P Public car parks nearby.
Yes. WC for the disabled. Guide Dogs: Yes
£ No

Speedwell Castle

Bargate Street, Brewood, Staffordshire ST19 9BB

Grade I listed. Mid 18th century, red brick designed in the manner of Strawberry Hill. Reputed to have been built by William Rock (d.1753) from the proceeds of betting on the racehorse Speedwell.
Grant Recipient: Penk Holdings Ltd
Access Contact: Mr A S Monckton
Tel: 01902 850214 **Fax:** 01902 850354
Open: The façade can be viewed from Bargate Street and Stafford Street (interior not open to the public).
P No No. Guide Dogs: Yes £ No

St Mary's (Lichfield Heritage Centre)

Market Square, Lichfield, Staffordshire WS13 6LG

Grade II* medieval guild church, rebuilt 1868-70 by James Fowler. Many original features are preserved and the building is a prominent landmark in the city. Now houses a Community Centre comprising a Heritage Centre, Social Centre for senior citizens, coffee and gift shops, as well as continuing to function as the parish church.
www.lichfieldheritage.org.uk
Grant Recipient: The Guild of St Mary's Centre
Access Contact: Mrs Bazeley
Tel: 01543 256611 **Fax:** 01543 414749
E-mail: info@lichfieldheritage.org.uk
Open: Lichfield Heritage Centre: open daily 10.30am - 5pm (Last adm 4pm).
P Pay-&-display nearby
Yes. WC for the disabled. Guide Dogs: Yes
£ **Adult:** £3.50 **Child:** £1 (age 5-14, under 5s free)
Other: £2.50 (concessions), £8 (family)

SUFFOLK

Abbey Farm Barn

Snape, Saxmundham, Suffolk IP17 1RQ

Grade II* listed Aisled barn. Circa 1300. Built by resident monks living in adjacent Priory (no remains standing above ground). Refurbished and still used by farmer for storage.
Grant Recipient & Access Contact:
Mr & Mrs Raynor
Tel: 01728 688088 **Fax:** 01728 688989
E-mail: thecartshed@onetel.net.uk
Open: By prior arrangement.
P Spaces: 1 No £ No

Christchurch Mansion

Christchurch Park, Soane Street, Ipswich, Suffolk IP4 2BD

16th century red brick mansion with some blue brick diapering, set in fine parkland in the centre of town. The Mansion and its collections trace the lives of the three wealthy families who made it their home. Paintings, English domestic furniture, kitchen and servants' area.
www.ipswich.gov.uk/tourism/guide/mansion.htm
Grant Recipient: Ipswich Borough Council
Access Contact: Mr Tim Heyburn
Tel: 01473 433550 **Fax:** 01473 433558
E-mail: tim.heyburn@ipswich.gov.uk
Open: Nov - Mar: Tues - Sat 10am - 4pm, Sun 2.30 - 4pm. Apr - Oct: Tues - Sat 10am - 4pm, Sun 2.30 - 4.30pm. For further information please contact Tim Heyburn, or the Mansion (Tel: 01473 433554, fax: 01473 433564).
P Public parking within 400m. Spaces: 1200. Parking for disabled adjacent to the Mansion.
Wheelchair access to most of ground floor and Wolsey Art Gallery. No WC for the disabled. Guide dogs: Yes.
£ No

Culford School Iron Bridge

Culford, Bury St Edmunds, Suffolk IP28 6TX

Constructed for the second Marquis Cornwallis in the late 1790s by Samuel Wyatt, brother of James, to a design patented by Wyatt. The bridge, in Culford Park, is one of the earliest surviving bridges with an unmodified cast-iron structure, being the earliest known example with hollow ribs.
Grant Recipient: Methodist Colleges and Schools
Access Contact: Michael Wooley
Tel: 01284 729318 **Fax:** 01284 729077
E-mail: bursar@culford.co.uk
Open: Access to the iron bridge and Culford Park is available at any time throughout the year.
P Spaces: 100
Disabled access may be difficult as over grass and rough track. Toilet facilities are only available when Culford School is open and ramps in place. No WC for the disabled. Guide Dogs: Yes
£ No

Elms Farm Wallpaintings

Old Station Road, Mendlesham, Suffolk IP14 5RS

Wealden hall house dating from 1480, wallpaintings consist of 16th century floral design

and Biblical texts in the upper hall and solar and 17th century armorial patterning in the parlour.
Grant Recipient & Access Contact:
Mrs Pamela Gilmour
Open: By prior written arrangement.
P Spaces: 10 No £ No

Flatford Mill

Willy Lott's House & Flatford Bridge Cottage, Flatford, East Bergholt, Colchester, Suffolk CO7 6OL

Flatford watermill, 1733 datestone, incorporating possibly earlier but altered former granary range to rear and further 19th century range adjoining granary. Later alterations. The mill was in the possession of the Constable family from the mid 18th century. Willy Lott's farmhouse, late 16th century - 17th century. Grade I listing of both buildings reflects their significance in the life and work of John Constable. Both buildings are leased by the National Trust to the Field Studies Council. Flatford Bridge Cottage 16th century thatched cottage, upstream from Flatford Mill houses an exhibition on John Constable.
www.nationaltrust.org.uk
Grant Recipient: The National Trust
Access Contact: Property Manager
Tel: 01206 298260 **Fax:** 01206 299193
E-mail: flatfordbridgecottage@nationaltrust.org.uk
Open: Flatford Mill and Willy Lott's House are owned by the National Trust and leased to the Field Studies Council which runs arts-based courses for all age groups (for information on courses tel: 01206 298283). There is no general public access to these buildings, but the Field Studies Council will arrange tours for groups. Flatford Bridge Cottage is open Mar and Apr daily except Mon and Tues 11am - 5.00pm; May to end Sept daily 10am - 5.30pm; Oct daily 11am - 4pm; Nov and Dec daily except Mon and Tues 11am - 3.30pm. Closed Christmas and New Year. 7 Jan 2006 - 26 Feb Sat & Sun 11am - 3.30pm. For further information contact the Property Manager on 01206 298260.
P Private pay car park 200 meters from Flatford Bridge Cottage. Parking near the Cottage is available for disabled visitors. Spaces: 2000
Wheelchair access to tea-garden and shop. Lavatory for disabled available in car park owned by Babergh DC, 23 metres from the Cottage. WC for the disabled. Guide Dogs: Yes
£ No

Horseman's House

Boundary Farm, Framsden, Suffolk IP14 6LH

Mid 17th century brick stable. Gable ended with brick pinnacles along upper edge with panels of diaper work in dark headers below round vents/owl holes. Original three bay, two storey structure housed horseman above his charges in unusually ornate accommodation for all.
Grant Recipient & Access Contact: Mr Bacon
Tel/Fax: 01728 860370
E-mail: info@boundaryfarm.co.uk
Open: By prior arrangement with Mr Bacon.
P Spaces: 4
Wheelchair access to ground floor stable and outside of building. WC for the disabled. Guide Dogs: Yes £ No

Ickworth House and Park

Horringer, Bury St Edmunds, Suffolk IP29 5QE

The Earl of Bristol created this eccentric house, with its central rotunda and curved corridors, in 1795 to display his collections. These include paintings by Titian, Gainsborough and Velasquez and a Georgian silver collection. The house is surrounded by an Italianate garden set in a 'Capability' Brown park with woodland walks, deer enclosure, vineyard, Georgian summerhouse and lake.
www.nationaltrust.org.uk
Grant Recipient: The National Trust
Access Contact: Property Manager
Tel: 01284 735270 **Fax:** 01284 735175
E-mail: ickworth@nationaltrust.org.uk
Open: House: 25 Mar - 30 Sept: daily except Wed and Thurs 1 - 5pm (Last adm 4.30pm). Closes 4.30pm in Oct. Garden: 1 Jan - 21 Mar: daily 10am - 4pm; 25 Mar - 30 Oct: daily 10am - 5pm (Last adm 4.30pm); 31 Oct - 23 Dec: daily except Sat & Sun 10am - 4pm. Park open daily 7am -

7pm but closed Christmas Day.

P Spaces: 2000

Wheelchair access to House: ramped access (restricted access in House for large powered vehicles/chairs); lift to first floor; stairlift to basement (shop and restaurant) suitable for wheelchair users able to transfer; wheelchair on each floor. Garden largely accessible, some changes of level, gravel drive and paths. WC for the disabled. Guide Dogs: Yes

£ Adult: £6.70, £3.10 (park & garden only)
Child: £3.00, 90p (park & garden only)

Somerleyton Hall & Gardens

Somerleyton, Lowestoft, Suffolk NR32 5QQ
Early Victorian stately home, built in Anglo-Italian style for Sir Morton Peto by John Thomas upon former Jacobean mansion. Contains fine furnishings, paintings, ornate carved stonework and wood carving, and state rooms. Set in twelve acres of historic gardens including a yew hedge maze.
www.somerleyton.co.uk
Grant Recipient: The Rt Hon Lord Somerleyton GCVO
Access Contact: Mr Edward Knowles
Tel: 01502 730224 **Fax:** 01502 732143
E-mail: enquiries@somerleyton.co.uk
Open: 4 Apr - 31 Oct: Thurs, Sun and Bank Hols, plus Tues and Wed in July and Aug, 11am - 5.30pm. Admission charges under review at time of publication, please check with the Hall for current information.
P Spaces: 200 Yes. WC for the disabled. Guide Dogs: Yes
£ Adult: £5.80 **Child:** £2.90 **Senior:** £5.50
Family: £16.40 (provisional prices)

St Bartholomew

Shipmeadow, Beccles, Suffolk NR34 8HL
Redundant medieval former parish church with 16th century tower, now converted into a house. 12th century nave and chancel in flint, later tower in brick and flint, with a variety of window styles.
Grant Recipient & Access Contact:
Mr Nick Caddick
Tel: 020 7404 0404 **Fax:** 020 7404 0505
E-mail: nick.caddick@talk21.com
Open: By prior arrangement with Mr Nick Caddick, 5 New Square, Lincolns Inn, London WC2A 3RJ (tel:020 7404 0404).
P Additional parking available on verge. Spaces: 4
Wheelchair access to porch & lower part of nave (subject to a low step at front door). No WC for the disabled. Guide Dogs: Yes
£ No

St John Lateran

Hengrave Hall, Hengrave, Bury St Edmunds, Suffolk IP28 6LZ
Grade 1 listed parish church dedicated to St John Lateran. Circular tower in coursed flint, possibly pre-Conquest. 13th century chancel with later additions. Noted for several of its monuments. Now known as the Church of Reconciliation, it reflects the present ecumenical vision of Hengrave Hall as a Christian retreat and conference centre and home of the Hengrave Community of Reconciliation.
www.hengravehallcentre.org.uk
Grant Recipient: Hengrave Hall Centre
Access Contact: Ms Madeleine Alberts
Tel: 01284 701561 **Fax:** 01284 702950
E-mail: administrator@hengravehallcentre.org.uk
Open: Church is open throughout the year, although the Hall is closed to visitors 24 - 27 Dec. Tours of the Hall by prior arrangement with the Administrator.
P Free 50 metres from Church, 25 metres from Hall. Overflow car park near Church. Spaces: 100
Wheelchair access to Church and ground floor of Hall only. WC for the disabled. Guide Dogs: Yes
£ Donations to Church welcome

St Lawrence

Dial Lane, Ipswich, Suffolk IP1 1DL
15th century aisleless church with a 97 foot west tower, enlarged in the 19th century and recently restored. Declared redundant in 1975. Owned by Ipswich Borough Council.
Grant Recipient: Ipswich Historic Churches Trust
Access Contact: Mr J S Hall

Tel: 01473 232300/406270
Fax: 01473 406385
E-mail: james-hall@birketts.co.uk
Open: By prior arrangement with Mr Hall (tel: 01473 406270), office hours and weekdays only. At least 24 hours' notice required. At other times and days subject to longer notice.
P In town centre car parks (10 min walk).
No **£** No

St Peter

College Street, Ipswich, Suffolk IP4 1DD
Large medieval church near the docks, owned by Ipswich Borough Council and redundant since the 1970s. Noted for a Tournai font and adjacent to Thomas Wolsey's gateway. Empty and unused.
Grant Recipient: Ipswich Historic Churches Trust
Access Contact: Mr J S Hall
Tel: 01473 232300/406270
Fax: 01473 406385
E-mail: james-hall@birketts.co.uk
Open: May - Nov, most Thurs 1.30 - 3.30pm (advisable to check in advance). Otherwise by prior arrangement with Mr Hall (tel: 01473 406270), office hours and weekdays only. 24 hours' notice required. At other times and days subject to longer notice.
P Car parks in town centre (1/2 mile).
Wheelchair access to all of church apart from the vestry and parts of the chancel. No WC for the disabled. Guide Dogs: Yes
£ No

Theatre Royal

Westgate Street, Bury St Edmunds, Suffolk IP33 1QR
A rare example of a late Georgian playhouse. Built 1819, later used as a warehouse, but restored and re-opened as a theatre in 1965. Constructed of white brick and stucco with a slate roof.
www.theatreroyal.org
Grant Recipient: The National Trust
Access Contact: The Administrator
Tel: 01284 755127 **Fax:** 01284 706035
E-mail: admin@theatreroyal.org
Open: Jan - end of May: Mon to Sat, 11am - 4pm subject to theatrical activity. Guided tours for groups available – pre-booking essential.
P Limited parking in Westgate Street.
Wheelchair access to front of house and wheelchair boxes only. WC for the disabled. Guide Dogs: Yes
£ No, but admission charge for performances & theatre tours

Woodbridge Lodge

Rendlesham, nr. Woodbridge, Suffolk IP12 2RA
Late 18th century small gothic folly. Originally a gatehouse to Rendlesham Hall, now part of a dwelling house.
Grant Recipient & Access Contact: Dr C P Cooper
Tel: 01394 460642
Open: Exterior only by arrangement.
P Spaces: 3 No **£** No

SURREY

Carew Manor Dovecote (Beddington Park)

Church Road, Beddington, Wallington, Surrey SM6 7NH
Early 18th century large octagonal brick dovecote with c1200 interior nesting boxes and original potence (circular ladder).
www.sutton.gov.uk
Grant Recipient: London Borough of Sutton
Access Contact: Ms Valary Murphy
Tel: 020 8770 4781 **Fax:** 020 8770 4777
E-mail: valary.murphy@sutton.gov.uk
Open: Open on the following Sundays: 24 Apr, 15 May, 3 July, 25 Sept, 2 - 5pm. Guided tours of Carew Manor at 2pm and 3.30pm. Groups at other times by prior arrangement with Valary Murphy, The Heritage Service, Central Library, St Nicholas Way, Sutton, Surrey SM1 1EA (tel: 020 8770 4781).
P Spaces: 30 No. Guide Dogs: Yes
£ Adult: £3.25 **Child:** £2 **Other:** Charges for guided tours of dovecote & Carew Manor, otherwise dovecote is free

Clandon Park

West Clandon, Guildford, Surrey GU4 7RQ
Palladian mansion, built c1730 by Venetian architect Giacomo Leoni with a two-storeyed Marble Hall, collection of 18th century furniture, porcelain, textiles, carpets, the Ivo Forde Meissen collection of Italian comedy figures and a series of Mortlake tapestries. Grounds contain grotto, sunken Dutch garden, Maori Meeting House and Museum of the Queen's Royal Surrey Regiment.
www.nationaltrust.org.uk
Grant Recipient: The National Trust
Access Contact: Property Manager
Tel: 01483 222482 **Fax:** 01483 223479
E-mail: clandonpark@nationaltrust.org.uk
Open: House: 13 Mar - 30 Oct, daily except Mon, Fri & Sat (but open Good Fri, Easter Sat & BH Mons) 11am - 5pm (Last adm 4.30pm). Museum: as for house 12 noon - 5pm. Garden: as for house 11am - 5pm.
P Spaces: 200
Wheelchair access to lower ground floor and five steps to ground floor. Lift for all floors planned for 2005. WC for the disabled. Guide Dogs: Yes
£ Adult: £6 **Child:** £3 **Family:** £15, £5 (group, Tues, Weds, Thurs & after 2pm Suns)

Great Fosters

Stroude Road, Egham, Surrey TW20 9UR
Grade II* registered garden. Laid out in 1918 by WH Romaine-Walker in partnership with GH Jenkins, incorporating earlier features. The site covers 50 acres and is associated with a late 16th century country house, converted to an hotel in 1927. The main formal garden is surrounded on three sides by a moat thought to be of medieval origin and is modelled on the pattern of a Persian carpet. Garden also includes a sunken rose garden and avenue of lime trees.
www.greatfosters.co.uk
Grant Recipient/Access Contact: Mr Richard Young
Tel: 01784 433822 **Fax:** 01784 472455
E-mail: enquiries@greatfosters.co.uk
Open: At any time throughout the year.
P Spaces: 200
Wheelchair access to ground floor of the house and most of the gardens. WC for the disabled. Guide Dogs: Yes **£** No

Great Hall

Virginia Park, Christchurch Rd, Virginia Water, Surrey GU25 4BH
By W H Crossland for Thomas Holloway and opened 1884. Built of red brick with Portland stone dressings and slate roofs in Franco-Flemish Gothic style. Formerly part of the Royal Holloway Sanatorium.
Grant Recipient:
Virginia Park Management Co Ltd
Access Contact: Ms Liz Adams
Tel: 01344 845276 **Fax:** 01344 842428
E-mail: virginia.park@btinternet.com
Open: Entrance Hall, Staircase and Great Hall of former Sanatorium open on the following Wed & Sun 10am - 4pm: Feb 16 & 27, Mar 23 & 27, Apr 13, 20 & 24, May 11, 18 & 22, June 15, 22 & 26, July 13, 20 & 24, Aug 10, 17 & 21, Sept 14, 21 & 25, Oct 12, 19 & 23, Nov 9, 23 & 27. At other times by telephone arrangement with the Estate Office.
P Public car park nearby at Virginia Water Station.
Wheelchair access with assistance (steps into building to be negotiated). Downstairs entrance Hall but not the Great Hall (no lift). WC for the disabled. Guide Dogs: Yes
£ Adult: £3

Painshill Park

Portsmouth Road, Cobham, Surrey KT11 1JE
Restored Grade I 18th century landscape garden of 150 acres, created by Charles Hamilton between 1738 and 1773. Contains a Gothic temple, Chinese bridge, ruined abbey, Turkish tent, grotto and 14 acre serpentine lake fed by a large waterwheel. Europa Nostra medal winner for 'Exemplary Restoration'.
www.painshill.co.uk
Grant Recipient: Painshill Park Trust Ltd
Access Contact: Miss Sarah AM Hallett
Tel: 01932 868113 **Fax:** 01932 868001

E-mail: info@painshill.co.uk

Open: Apr - Oct: Tues - Sun and Bank Hols 10.30am - 6pm (Last adm 4.30pm); Nov - Mar (except Christmas Day and Boxing Day): Wed, Sun and Bank Hols 11am - 4pm or dusk if earlier (Last adm 3pm). Guided tours for groups of 10 plus by prior arrangement.

P Spaces: 400. Parking for 8 coaches.

Wheelchair access to most of the site, apart from the Grotto and Alpine Valley. Wheelchairs and electric buggies available on request. Pre-book one week in advance. WC for the disabled. Guide Dogs: Yes

£ **Adult:** £7 **Child:** £3.50 (under 5's free) **Other:** £6 **Family (2+2):** £20

The Old Mill

Outwood Common, nr. Redhill, Surrey RH1 5PW

England's oldest working windmill, built in 1665.

www.outwoodwindmill.co.uk

Grant Recipient & Access Contact: Mrs Sheila Thomas

Tel/Fax: 01342 843458

E-mail: info@outwoodwindmill.co.uk

Open: Easter - Oct: Sun & BHs 2 - 6pm, plus parties by arrangement.

P Spaces: 12

Wheelchair access to ground floor of the mill only. WC for the disabled. Guide Dogs: Yes

£ **Adult:** £2 **Child:** £1

SUSSEX

De La Warr Pavilion

The Marina, Bexhill-on-Sea, East Sussex TN40 1DP

The "People's Palace" built in 1935 by architects Erich Mendholson and Serge Chermayeff was the first steel-framed building in this country. Its circular staircase and sweeping sea views make it unique.

www.dlwp.com

Grant Recipient: Rother District Council

Access Contact: Mr Alan Haydon

Tel: 01424 787900 **Fax:** 01424 787940

E-mail: info@dlwp.com

Open: Daily 10am - 5pm. Closed Christmas Day.

P Pay car park. Spaces: 100.

Yes. WC for the disabled. Guide Dogs: Yes

£ No

The Dovecote

Alciston, East Sussex BN8 6NS

14th century dovecote of flint facings with green sand stone dressings on a chalk rubble core with chalk blocks and nesting boxes internally.

www.firleplace.co.uk

Grant Recipient: Trustees of the Firle Estate Settlement

Access Contact: Mr Duncan Leslie

Tel: 01273 858567 **Fax:** 01273 858570

E-mail: duncan@firleplace.co.uk

Open: Access to the dovecote is by arrangement with the Estate Office.

P No The outside is accessible to wheelchair users. Guide dogs: Yes £ No

The Flushing Inn

4 Market Street, Rye, East Sussex TN31 7LA

15th century timber-framed building, now a restaurant, with large recently restored 16th century wallpainting.

www.theflushinginn.com

Grant Recipient & Access Contact: Mr Flynn

Tel: 01797 223292 **Fax:** 01797 229748

E-mail: j.e.flynn@talk21.com

Open: Restaurant: Wed - Sun for lunches and dinners, Mon lunch only & Tues closed. Closed first 2 weeks in Jan & June. Unless dining, visiting to view the Fresco is restricted to 10.30 - noon.

P Parking on-street but restricted to 1 hour, otherwise public parking elsewhere in Rye.

Wheelchair access to Fresco with assistance (entrance steps to be negotiated). No WC for the disabled. Guide Dogs: Yes

£ No

High Beeches Gardens Conservation Trust

High Beeches, Handcross, West Sussex RH17 6HQ

25 acre garden with woodland, open glades, natural wildflower meadows and water gardens. Many rare plants to be seen in all seasons. Tree trails. Tea Room/restaurant in restored Victorian farm.

www.highbeeches.com

Grant Recipient: The Trustees of High Beeches Conservation Trust

Access Contact: The Hon Mrs Boscawen

Tel: 01444 400589 **Fax:** 01444 401543

E-mail: gardens@highbeeches.com

Open: 18 Mar - 30 June and 1 Sept - 31 Oct: 1 - 5pm (Last adm 4.30pm), closed Weds. July and Aug: 1 - 5pm, closed Sat and Wed. All coaches and Guided Tours by prior arrangement. Tea room open all year except Weds.

P Disabled parking adjacent to tea room. Spaces: 100

Wheelchair access to tea room & tea garden only. WC for the disabled. Guide Dogs: Yes

£ **Adult:** £5 **Child:** Free **Other:** Concessions for groups

Lamb House

(Coromandel Lacquer Panels), 3 Chapel Hill, Lewes, East Sussex BN7 2BB

The incised lacquer panels in the study of Lamb House are a unique surviving example of imported late 17th century Chinese lacquer work that remains as decorative wall panelling. Recently restored.

Grant Recipient & Access Contact: Prof. Paul Benjamin

Tel: 01273 475657

E-mail: p.r.benjamin@sussex.ac.uk

Open: Weekends only by telephone or e-mail arrangement.

P On-street parking.

Steps to front door. Wheelchair access to ground floor only. No WC for the disabled. Guide Dogs: No £ No

Ouse Valley Viaduct

Balcombe, West Sussex

The most important surviving architectural feature of the original layout of the London – Brighton railway, the Grade II* Ouse Valley Viaduct has 37 circular arches, is 492 yards long and 92 feet high. Designed by John Rastrick with stonework accredited to David Mocatta, it is known for its pierced piers, ornate limestone parapets and pavilions. Built 1839-1841.

Grant Recipient: Railtrack plc (now Network Rail)

Access Contact: Network Rail

Open: Public access at all times on the footpath running underneath the viaduct. It is possible to view the viaduct from Borde Hill Lane without walking across the field.

P Limited on-street parking.

Wheelchair users can view viaduct from Borde Hill Lane. No WC for the disabled. Guide Dogs: Yes £ No

Parham House

Parham Park, nr. Pulborough, West Sussex RH20 4HS

Granted to the Palmer family in 1540 by Henry VIII, the foundation stone of this grey-stone Elizabethan house was laid in 1577. From the panelled Great Hall to the Long Gallery running the length of the roof-space, the house contains a collection of paintings, furniture and needlework.

www.parhaminsussex.co.uk

Grant Recipient: Parham Park Ltd

Access Contact: Ms Patricia Kennedy

Tel: 01903 742021 **Fax:** 01903 746557

E-mail: pat@parhaminsussex.co.uk

Open: 27 Mar - 29 Sept: Wed, Thurs, Sun and BH Mons & Tue & Fri during Aug (also Sats 9 July and 10 Sept). Gardens open at 12 noon, House at 2pm with last entry at 5pm.

P For disabled close to the house. Spaces: 300

Wheelchair access to ground floor only by prior arrangement, there is a reduced admission charge for wheelchair users and carers. Free loan of recorded tour tape. WC for the disabled. Guide Dogs: Yes

£ **Adult:** £6.50 **Child:** £2.50 (age 5-15) **Senior:** £5.50 **Family:** £15.50

Petworth House

Petworth, West Sussex GU28 0AE

Late 17th century mansion in 'Capability' Brown landscaped park. The house contains the Trust's largest collection of pictures including Turners and Van Dycks, as well as sculpture, furniture and Grinling Gibbons' carvings. Also there are the Servants' Quarters with interesting kitchens and other service rooms. Extra rooms open Mon, Tues and Wed afternoon by kind permission of Lord and Lady Egremont.

www.nationaltrust.org.uk

Grant Recipient: The National Trust

Access Contact: Property Manager

Tel: 01798 344970 **Fax:** 01798 342963

E-mail: petworth@nationaltrust.org.uk

Open: House and Servants' Quarters: 19 Mar - 30 Oct, daily except Thurs and Fri (but open Good Fri), 11am - 5pm (Last adm to house 4.30pm, Servants' Quarters 5pm). Extra rooms shown weekday afternoons (but not BH Mons) as follows: Mon: White and Gold Room and White Library; Tues and Wed: three bedrooms on first floor. Park: daily, all year, except 25 Dec and afternoons of open-air concerts in July.

P For house & park on A283, 800 yards away. Spaces: 150

Wheelchair access to ground floor of house, shop and tea room. WC for the disabled. Guide Dogs: Yes

£ **Adult:** £7.50 **Child:** £4 **Family:** £19 £6.50 (booked groups 15+)

Rotunda Temple

Brightling Park, Rother, East Sussex

Built c1812 as an eyecatcher by Sir Robert Smirke for John Fuller, wealthy philanthropist and eccentric. Small circular building with colonnade and dome: the centre-piece of Brightling Park.

Grant Recipient/Access Contact: Mr H C Grissell

Tel: 01424 838207 **Fax:** 01424 838467

E-mail: Henry@grissell.freeserve.co.uk

Open: By arrangement only. Otherwise Temple can be viewed from public footpaths and other permitted access routes through Park.

P Parking in surrounding roads.

No WC for the disabled. Guide Dogs: Yes £ No

The Royal Pavilion

Brighton, East Sussex BN1 1EE

Former seaside residence of George IV in Indian style with Chinese-inspired interiors. Originally a neo-classical villa by Henry Holland was built on the site in 1787, but this was subsequently replaced by the current John Nash building constructed between 1815-23.

www.royalpavilion.org.uk

Grant Recipient: Brighton & Hove City Council

Access Contact: Ms Cara Bowen

Tel: 01273 292810 **Fax:** 01273 292871

E-mail: cara.bowen@brighton-hove.gov.uk

Open: Apr - Sept, daily 9.30am - 5.45pm (Last adm 5pm); Oct - Mar, daily 10am - 5.15pm (Last adm 4.30pm); closed 25 and 26 Dec. Admission charges are valid until 31 Mar 2005, for rates after that date please check the English Heritage website or with the Royal Pavilion for current information.

P NCP car park on Church Street. Parking for disabled is available in the grounds of the Pavilion by arrangement.

Wheelchair access to ground floor only, reduced rate of admission is payable. WC for the disabled. Guide Dogs: Yes

£ **Adult:** £5.95 (see above), £2.30 (local residents, Oct - Feb only) **Child:** £3.50 under 16 (Oct - Feb, local residents free with paying adult) **Conc:** £4.20 **Family:** £15.40 (2 adults, 4 children), £9.45 (1 adult, 4 children) Prices valid until 31.3.05.

St Hugh's Charterhouse

Henfield Road, Partridge Green, Horsham, West Sussex RH13 8EB

Large monastery covering 10 acres. One large cloister of over 100 square yards comprising 34 four-room hermitages where the monks live. The fore part is a smaller cloister about 200ft square

which contains the cells of the Brothers and their work places. There is also a large church, library, refectory, Brothers' Chapel and other monastic buildings. The large quad encloses a cemetery. The spire is 203ft high and has a five-bell chime.
www.parkminster.org.uk
Grant Recipient: St Hugh's Charterhouse
Access Contact: Fr John Babeau
Tel/Fax: 01403 864231
Open: By arrangement, with due respect for the rules of the Charterhouse monastery. For further details please contact the monastery.
P Spaces: 20 No. Guide Dogs: Yes £ No

St Mary-in-the-Castle

**Pelham Crescent, Hastings,
East Sussex TN34 3AF**
Built in 1828, architect Joseph Kay, it forms an integral part of the design of Pelham Crescent. The Church has a horseshoe-shaped auditorium with gallery and is now used as an arts centre.
www.hastings.gov.uk
Grant Recipient: Friends of St Mary-in-the-Castle
Access Contact: Ms Penny Precious
Tel: 01424 781635/01424 781122
Fax: 01424 781133
E-mail: pprecious@hastings.gov.uk
Open: Guided tours Tues - Sat by arrangement. Arts activities run throughout the year. Contact the Bookings Office (Tel: 01424 781072 or 781625), the access contact or check the website for further information (www.hastings.gov.uk).
P Pay & Display parking opposite. Spaces: 400
Yes. WC for the disabled. Guide Dogs: Yes
£ Tours free but donations accepted. Events individually priced.

The Shell House

**Goodwood House, Chichester,
West Sussex PO18 0PX**
One-room Shell House dating from 1740s. Walls and ceiling decorated with hundreds of thousands of shells in classical design, with coffering, niches and cornucopia. Floor with inset horses teeth.
Grant Recipient: Goodwood Estate Company Ltd
Access Contact: Curator's Secretary
Tel: 01243 755048 **Fax:** 01243 755005
E-mail: curator@goodwood.co.uk
Open: By written arrangement, usually on set Connoisseurs' Days (13 & 26 Apr, 18 May, 20 Sept, 20 Oct) or on Sun mornings Apr - Sept. Two weeks' notice preferred. Bookings can be made with the Curator's Secretary (tel:01243 755048).
P 30 metres from house. Steps between car park & house. Spaces: 4
WC for the disabled available only when Goodwood House is open to the public. Guide Dogs: No
£ Adult: £3.50 (Connoisseurs' Day as part of House visit), £5 (other days) Child: £2 (under 12s, accompanied)

Shipley Windmill

Shipley, nr. Horsham, West Sussex RH13 8PL
Grade II* listed smock mill with five floors, built 1879 and restored in 1990 to full working order. Once owned by the Sussex writer and poet, Hilaire Belloc, who lived nearby. The milling process is demonstrated on open days for the benefit of visitors.
www.shipleywindmill.org.uk
Grant Recipient: Shipley Windmill Charitable Trust
Access Contact: Ms Penny Murray
Tel: 01243 777642 **Fax:** 01243 777848
E-mail: penny.murray@westsussex.gov.uk
Open: Easter - Oct: first, second and third Sun of each month, plus BH Mons. Also National Mills Day, Shipley Festival (May) and the Sun of the Heritage Open Days weekend.
P Spaces: 10
Wheelchair access to ground floor of mill and engine shed. No WC for the disabled. Guide dogs: No.
£ Adult: £2 Child: £1 Seniors: £1.50

Stanmer House

Stanmer, Brighton, East Sussex BN1 9PZ
Grade I listed country house. Built 1722-7, though incorporating part of an earlier house, with additions of the early 19th century and of 1860. Palladian style by the architect Nicholas

Dubois.
Grant Recipient: Brighton and Hove Council
Access Contact: Mr Michael Holland
Tel: 01273 724300 **Fax:** 01273 206681
Open: By arrangement from autumn 2005 to the principal rooms on the ground floor only.
P Public car park approx 500 metres.
WC for the disabled is adjacent to property.
£ No.

Tithe Barn

**Court Farm, East Street, Brighton,
West Sussex BN1 9PB**
Grade II* listed medieval tithe barn. Mainly of timber construction with thatched roof.
Grant Recipient: Brighton and Hove County Council
Access Contact: Mr Richard Butler
Tel: 01273 291440 **Fax:** 01273 291467
E-mail: richard.butler@brighton-hove.gov.uk
Open: By arrangement with Richard Butler, Brighton and Hove County Council (or Beth Turner at Cluttons 01622 756000) and Eric Huxham – tenant at Court Farm (07802 453842).
P On-street parking within Falmer village.
Barn within working farm so access can be muddy. Guide dogs are welcome but as a working farm care is requested. No WC for the disabled. Guide Dogs: Yes
£ No

TYNE & WEAR

Freemasons Hall

**Queen Street East, Sunderland,
Tyne & Wear SR1 2HT**
Grade I listed oldest purpose-built Masonic meeting place in the world, c1785. Contains an ornate Lodge Room which remains virtually unaltered with elaborate thrones from 1735. Also has a cellar is in its original condition and the last remaining example of a Donaldson organ which was specially constructed for the building in 1785.
Grant Recipient: Queen Street Masonic Temple Ltd
Access Contact: Mr Colin Meddes
Tel: 0191 522 0115
E-mail: colinmeddes@hotmail.com
Open: Guided tours all year by arrangement.
P Spaces: 80
Five external steps to main entrance: guides available to assist wheelchair users. Disabled access ramp due to be installed 2005. WC for the disabled. Guide Dogs: Yes £ No

High Level Bridge

Gateshead, Tyne & Wear
Grade I listed railway and road bridge of ashlar and cast iron, 1849, designed by Robert Stephenson. One of the finest pieces of architectural iron work in the world.
Grant Recipient: Network Rail
Access Contact: Mr Ian Kitching
Tel: 01904 650232 **Fax:** 01904 650304
E-mail: ian.kitching@networkrail.co.uk
Open: Best viewed from adjacent riverbanks or via access road/footpath under bridge. Also may be viewed from the footways which cross the lower deck of the bridge. Access to the lower deck is normally available at all times, but between Apr and Oct 2005 it will be closed to the public to enable major refurbishment to take place. No access to the upper deck of the bridge.
P On-street parking.
Footways across the lower deck of the bridge are accessible for wheelchairs. No WC for the disabled. Guide Dogs: Yes
£ No

Literary & Philosophical Society

**23 Westgate Road, Newcastle-upon-Tyne,
Tyne & Wear NE1 1SE**
Grade II* listed 1825 private library and society rooms designed by John Green in Greek revival style. Extended in late 19th century. Interior shows classical stucco ornament on friezes, wrought-iron balconies and spiral stair to library gallery. The library contains over 140,000 books, many of which are old and rare.
www.litandphil.org.uk
Grant Recipient: Literary & Philosophical Society
Access Contact: Ms Kay Easson
Tel: 0191 232 0192 **Fax:** 0191 261 4494
E-mail: library@litandphil.org.uk

Open: Mon, Wed, Thurs & Fri: 9.30am - 7pm. Tues 9.30am - 8pm. Sat 9.30am - 1pm. The Society is closed on public and Bank Hols. Visitors are welcome to view the building free of charge. However, annual subscription is charged for use of the private library.
P On-street parking on Westgate Road. Spaces: 10
Stairlift inside building allows wheelchair access, but no exterior ramp. No WC for the disabled. Guide Dogs: No
£ No

Theatre Royal

**Grey Street, Newcastle-upon-Tyne,
Tyne & Wear NE1 6BR**
Victorian theatre opened in 1837, rebuilt in 1899 by Frank Matcham in a richly-ornamented style. Classical façade with rare Hanoverian coat of arms. Traditional 4-tier 1,294 seat auditorium hosting annual programme of touring productions and international companies.
www.theatre-royal-newcastle.co.uk
Grant Recipient: Newcastle Theatre Royal Trust Ltd
Access Contact: Mr Peter Sarah
Tel: 0191 232 0997 **Fax:** 0191 261 1906
E-mail: peter.sarah@newcastle.gov.uk
Open: Regular tours available depending on production schedule, contact theatre on 0870 905 5060 or 0191 232 0997 for details.
P Public car parks in City centre.
Wheelchair access to foyer, café and stalls. WC for the disabled. Guide Dogs: Yes
£ Adult/Child: £3.50 (Tours, some free)

Washington Old Hall,

**The Avenue, Washington Village, District 4,
Washington, Tyne & Wear NE38 7LE**
17th century manor house, incorporating the 12th century remains of the home of George Washington's ancestors. Recreated 17th century interiors and displays of 'Washingtonabilia' celebrating the close connection with the USA. Permanent exhibition on the recent tenement period of the property. Jacobean knot-garden and Nuttery.
www.nationaltrust.org.uk
Grant Recipient: The National Trust
Access Contact: Property Manager
Tel: 0191 4166879 **Fax:** 0191 4192065
E-mail: washingtonoldhall@nationaltrust.org.uk
Open: 25 Mar - 30 Oct: Sun - Wed & Good Fri 11am - 5pm.
P Spaces: 10
Wheelchair access to ground floor of house and upper garden. WC for the disabled. Guide Dogs: Yes
£ Adult: £3.80 Child: £2.30
Other: £10 (family), £3.30 (£2 child, groups 10+)

WARWICKSHIRE

The Bath House

**Walton, Stratford-upon-Avon,
Warwickshire LE17 5RG**
Designed in 1748 by the architect Sanderson Miller. The upper room, where the bathers recovered, is decorated with dripping icicles and festoons of sea shells - the work of Mrs Delaney, better known for her flower pictures. Narrow steep staircases.
www.landmarktrust.co.uk
Grant Recipient: The Landmark Trust
Access Contact: Mr Toby Hawkins
Tel: 01628 825920 **Fax:** 01628 825417
E-mail: thawkins@landmarktrust.org.uk
Open: The Landmark Trust is an independent charity, which rescues small buildings of historic or architectural importance from decay or unsympathetic improvement. Landmark's aim is to promote the enjoyment of these historic buildings by making them available to stay in for holidays. The Bath House can be rented by anyone, at all times of the year, for periods ranging from a weekend to three weeks. Bookings can be made by telephoning the Booking Office on 01628 825925. As the building is in full-time use for holiday accommodation, it is not normally open to the public. However the public can view the building by prior arrangement by telephoning the access contact (Toby Hawkins on 01628 825920) to make an appointment. Potential visitors will be asked to write to confirm the details of their visit.
P Spaces: 1   No. Guide Dogs: Yes £ No

Charlecote Park

Wellesbourne, Warwick,
Warwickshire CV35 9ER
Owned by the Lucy family since 1247, Sir Thomas built the house in 1558. Now much altered, it is shown as it would have been a century ago. The balustraded formal garden gives onto a deer park landscaped by 'Capability' Brown.
www.nationaltrust.org.uk
Grant Recipient: The National Trust
Access Contact: Property Manager
Tel: 01789 470277 **Fax:** 01789 470544
E-mail: charlecote.park@nationaltrust.org.uk
Open: House: 5 Mar - 30 Sept, daily except Wed & Thurs 12 noon - 5pm; 1 Oct - 30 Oct, daily except Wed & Thurs 12 noon - 4.30pm. Park and gardens: 5 Mar - 30 Oct, daily except Wed & Thurs 10.30am - 6pm; 5 Nov - 18 Dec, Sat & Sun 11am - 4pm. Open Weds following BH Mons & Weds in July & Aug.
Ⓟ Spaces: 200. Overflow car park available.
♿ Wheelchair access to ground floor of house, restaurant & shop. WC for the disabled. Guide Dogs: Yes
£ **Adult:** £6.60 **Child:** £3.30 **Family:** £16 **Group:** £5.60

Lord Leycester Hospital

High Street, Warwick, Warwickshire CV34 4BH
14th century chantry chapel, Great Hall, galleried courtyard and Guildhall. Acquired by Robert Dudley, Earl of Leicester in 1571 as a home for his old soldiers. Still operating as a home for ex-servicemen.
Grant Recipient: Patron & Governors of Lord Leycester Hospital
Access Contact: Lieut. Colonel G F Lesinski
Tel/Fax: 01926 491422
E-mail: lordleycester@btinternet.com
Open: Tues - Sun 10am - 4pm (winter), 10am - 5pm (summer), plus BH Mons. Closed Good Fri and Christmas Day.
Ⓟ Spaces: 15
♿ Wheelchair access to ground floor only. WC for the disabled. Guide Dogs: Yes
£ **Adult:** £4.90, £2 (garden only)
Child: £3.90, free (garden only)
Other: £4.40, £2 (garden only)

Nicholas Chamberlaine's Almshouses' Pump House

All Saints Square, Bedworth, Nuneaton, Warwickshire CV12 8NR
Built 1840 of English bond brick with sandstone dressings and stone pyramid roof in Tudor Gothic style. Contains original cast-iron pump. Stands in front of the almshouses and originally provided water for the residents, illuminated at night.
Grant Recipient: Nicholas Chamberlaine's Hospital Charity
Access Contact: Mr David Dumbleton
Tel: 024 76227331 **Fax:** 024 76221293
E-mail: j.russell@rotherham-solicitors.co.uk
Open: Two sessions Sat & Sun of Heritage Open Days weekend and at other times by prior arrangement with Mr David Dumbleton, Clerk to the Governors, Nicholas Chamberlaine's Hospital Charity, Rotherhams and Co, 8/9 The Quadrant, Coventry, Warwickshire CV1 2EG. Exterior visible from All Saints Square at all times.
Ⓟ Public car parks nearby.
♿ Yes. WC for the disabled. Guide Dogs: Yes
£ No

Packwood House

Lapworth, Solihull, Warwickshire B94 6AT
Originally a 16th century house, Packwood has been much altered over the years and today is the vision of Graham Baron Ash who recreated a Jacobean house in the 1920s and 30s. Houses collection of 16th century textiles and furniture. Yew garden based on Sermon on the Mount.
www.nationaltrust.org.uk
Grant Recipient: The National Trust
Access Contact: Property Manager
Tel: 01564 783294 **Fax:** 01564 782706
E-mail: packwood@nationaltrust.org.uk
Open: House: 2 Mar - 6 Nov, daily except Mon and Tues (but open Bank Hols and Good Fri) 12 - 4.30pm. Gardens: as house 11am - 4.30pm in Mar, Apr, Oct and Nov, 11am - 5.30pm May - Sept. Park and woodland walks all year, daily. On

busy days admission to the house may be by timed ticket.
Ⓟ Spaces: 140
♿ Wheelchair access to ground floor. Garden largely accessible. WC for the disabled. Guide Dogs: Yes
£ **Adult:** £6 (house & garden), £3 (grounds)
Child: £3 (house & garden), £1.50 (grounds)
Other: £15 (family), discount for combined ticket to Packwood House and Baddesley Clinton

Polesworth Nunnery Gateway

22-24 High St, Polesworth, Tamworth, Warwickshire B78 1DU
Abbey gatehouse, late 14th century with later alterations. Upper floors now in residential use.
Grant Recipient: Polesworth PCC
Access Contact: Mr W E Thompson
Tel: 01827 706861
E-mail: polesworthabbey@aol.com
Open: Exterior at all reasonable times, ground floor interior by prior arrangement with Mr W E Thompson, 46 Kiln Way, Polesworth, nr Tamworth, Warwickshire B78 1JE.
Ⓟ In Abbey driveway for approx. 20 vehicles.
♿ Wheelchair access to ground floor only. No WC for the disabled. Guide Dogs: Yes
£ No

Ragley Hall

Alcester, Warwickshire B49 5NJ
Family home of the Marquess and Marchioness of Hertford. Built in 1680 to a design by Robert Hooke in the Palladian style, with portico added by Wyatt in 1780. Contents include baroque plasterwork by James Gibb, family portraits by Sir Joshua Reynolds and a mural by Graham Rust completed in 1983. Surrounding park designed by 'Capability' Brown.
www.ragleyhall.com
Grant Recipient: Marquess of Hertford & Earl of Yarmouth
Access Contact: Mr Alan Granger
Tel: 01789 762090 **Fax:** 01789 764791
E-mail: info@ragleyhall.com
Open: 19 Mar - 2 Oct, Thurs - Sun (plus BH Mons) 11am - 6pm (Last adm 4.30pm). Sat closing times may vary subject to events and functions. Park and gardens are open daily in school holidays. Group (20+) rates available: £5.00, adults & seniors, £3.00 child & school group.
Ⓟ Spaces: 4,000
♿ Yes. Wheelchair access via lift to first floor. WC for the disabled. Guide Dogs: Yes
£ **Adult:** £7.50 **Child:** £4.50 (age 5-16)
Other: £6.50 (seniors & Orange/Blue Badge), £25 (family). Season: £75 (family), £25 (single).

Stoneleigh Abbey

Kenilworth, Warwickshire CV8 2LF
16th century house built on site and incorporating remains of Cistercian Abbey founded in 1155. West wing designed by Francis Smith of Warwick between 1714-26 and northern wing reconstructed in 19th century by Charles S Smith of Warwick. South wing c1820. West wing contains a range of State Apartments. Also has restored Regency riding stables, 19th century conservatory and Humphrey Repton landscaped riverside gardens.
www.stoneleighabbey.org
Grant Recipient: Stoneleigh Abbey Preservation Trust (1996) Ltd
Access Contact: Estate Office
Tel: 01926 858535 **Fax:** 01926 850274
E-mail: enquiries@stoneleighabbey.org
Open: Good Fri - end of Oct: Tue, Wed, Thurs & Sun, plus BHs. Opening arrangements may change, please check with the Preservation Trust for current information.
Ⓟ Spaces: 400
♿ Yes. WC for the disabled. Guide Dogs: Yes
£ **Adult:** £6 **Child:** £2.50 **Senior:** £4
Grounds only: £2.50

WEST MIDLANDS

The Big House

44 Church Street, Oldbury, West Midlands B69 3AE
Grade II* 3-storey house dating from c1730. Originally with agricultural land and later the

house and offices of a solicitor in 1857 when the land was sold. Restored and reopened in 2002 as Civic offices.
Grant Recipient: Sandwell Metropolitan Borough Council
Access Contact: Civic Affairs Officer
Tel: 0121 569 3041 **Fax:** 0121 569 3050
E-mail: ann_oneill@sandwell.gov.uk
Open: By arrangement with the Mayor's office via the Civic Affairs officer (tel: 0121 569 3041). The Mayor will also hold "Open House" at various times throughout the year.
Ⓟ Market Street Public Car Park (30 spaces). Disabled parking (4 spaces) adjacent.
♿ Yes. WC for the disabled. Guide Dogs: Yes £ No

Red House Glassworks

Wordsley, Stourbridge, West Midlands DY8 4AZ
Built around 1790, the Cone was used for the manufacture of glass until 1936 and is now one of only four left in the Country. Reaching 100ft into the sky, the Cone enclosed a furnace where glass was made for 140 years. In its 200 year history, the site has remained virtually unaltered and therefore provides an interesting insight into the history and tradition of glassmaking. Glassmaking demonstrations and exhibitions tell the story of glassmaking in the area and the history of the glassworks.
www.redhousecone.co.uk
Grant Recipient: Dudley Metropolitan Borough Council
Access Contact: Ms Sarah Hall
Tel: 01384 812752 **Fax:** 01384 812751
E-mail: sarah.hall@dudley.gov.uk
Open: Jan - 31 Mar, daily 10am - 4pm. 1 Apr - 31 Oct, daily 10am - 5pm.
Ⓟ Spaces: 40
♿ Full wheelchair access to the Cone, glassmaking area and all display areas. Lift to upper floor and galleries. Some studios are inaccessible. WC for the disabled. Guide Dogs: Yes
£ **Adult:** £3 **Child:** Free. **Other:** £2.50

Soho House Museum

Soho Avenue, Handsworth, Birmingham, West Midlands B18 5LB
Soho House Museum is the former home of Matthew Boulton, Birmingham industrialist, entrepreneur and partner of James Watt. Designed by James and Samuel Wyatt, the house was once a meeting place of the Lunar Society and contains period rooms and displays on Boulton's manufacturing activities. The visitor centre houses a temporary exhibition gallery.
www.bmag.org.uk
Grant Recipient: Birmingham Museums & Art Gallery
Access Contact: Curator Manager
Tel: 0121 554 9122 **Fax:** 0121 554 5929
Open: 25 Mar (Good Fri) - 30 Oct, Tues - Sun 11.30am - 4pm, also open BH Mons.
Ⓟ Spaces: 23
♿ Yes. WC for the disabled. Guide Dogs: Yes £ No

St James

Great Packington, Meriden, nr. Coventry, West Midlands CV7 7HF
Red brick building with four domes topped by finials in neo-classical style. Built to celebrate the return to sanity of King George III. The organ was designed by Handel for his librettist, Charles Jennens, who was the cousin of the 4th Earl of Aylesford, who built the church.
Grant Recipient: St James Great Packington Trust
Access Contact: Packington Estate Office
Tel: 01676 522020 **Fax:** 01676 523399
E-mail: jameschurch@packingtonestate.co.uk
Open: Mon - Fri 9am - 5pm: key can be obtained from the Estate Office at Packington Hall, preferably by phoning in advance (see 01676 522020). At other times by prior arrangement with Lord Guernsey (tel:01676 522274).
Ⓟ Spaces: 10
♿ Wheelchair access with assistance (entrance steps and heavy door to be negotiated). No WC for the disabled. Guide Dogs: Yes
£ Donations towards restoration welcomed

Wightwick Manor

Wightwick Bank, Wolverhampton, West Midlands WV6 8EE
Built 1887, the house is a notable surviving example of the Arts and Crafts Movement. Contains original William Morris wallpapers and fabrics, Pre-Raphaelite paintings, Kempe glass

Opening arrangements at properties grant-aided by English Heritage

and de Morgan ware. Also has a 17 acre Victorian/Edwardian garden designed by Thomas Mawson.
www.nationaltrust.org.uk
Grant Recipient: The National Trust
Access Contact: Property Manager
Tel: 01902 761400 **Fax:** 01902 764663
E-mail: wightwickmanor@nationaltrust.org.uk
Open: By guided tour only 4 Mar - 24 Dec: Thurs and Sat (also Bank Holiday Sun and Mon to ground floor only) 12.30 - 5pm. Also family open days Weds in Aug 12.30 - 5pm. Admission by timed ticket issued from 11am at Visitor Reception. Other days by prior arrangement. Garden: Wed, Thurs, Sat and Bank Holiday Sun and Mon 11am - 6pm. First Thurs and Sat of each month: no guided tours, free flow only. Booking line open Thurs & Fri only (tel: 01902 760100).
Ⓟ For coach parking please telephone 01902 760100. Spaces: 50
♿ Wheelchair access to ground floor only. WC for the disabled. Guide Dogs: Yes
£ **Adult:** £6.30, £3.20 (garden only)
Child: £3.20, children free for garden only
Other: £3.20(students), £15.50 (family)

WEST YORKSHIRE

Bolling Hall Museum

Bowling Hall Road, Bradford, West Yorkshire BD4 7LP
Furnished house, mainly 17th and 18th centuries with some earlier parts. Large stained glass window with armorial glass, fine collection of 16th century oak furniture. Now a free public museum.
www.bradford.gov.uk
Grant Recipient: Bradford Metropolitan District Council
Access Contact: Miss Liz McIvor
Tel: 01274 723057 **Fax:** 01274 726220
E-mail: Liz.mcivor@bradford.gov.uk
Open: All year: Wed, Thurs and Fri 11am - 4pm; Sat 10am - 5pm; Sun 12 noon - 5pm. Closed on Mons (except Bank Hols) and Christmas Day, Boxing Day and Good Fri.
Ⓟ Free. 100 metres from Museum. Spaces: 75
♿ Wheelchair access to ground floor only. WC for the disabled. Guide Dogs: Yes
£ No

Bramham Park Lead Lads Temple

Wetherby, West Yorkshire LS23 6ND
Park folly, in the form of an open temple in the classical style, built in the 1750s by local craftsmen on the instructions of Harriet Benson (about a mile from the house in woodland called Black Fen, close to a public footpath). The 'Lead Lads' were classical lead figures that stood on the three small blocks at the apex and base of the front pediment, and were lost to vandals many years ago.
Grant Recipient: Trustees of the Bramham Settled Estate
Access Contact: The Estate Office
Tel: 01937 846000 **Fax:** 01937 846007
E-mail: enquiries@bramhampark.co.uk
Open: Close to a public footpath and accessible most of the year (closed 6 - 12 June & 15 Aug - 2 Sept).
Ⓟ Car park for visitors to Bramham Park (1 mile)
♿ WC for the disabled is not on site, but in visitors' car park (1 mile)
£ No charge for visitors via the footpath but charge made for visitors to the house and gardens

City Varieties Music Hall

Swan Street, Leeds, West Yorkshire LS1 6LW
Music hall built in 1865. Grade II* listed. Used as the location for BBC TV's "Good Old Days".
www.cityvarieties.co.uk
Grant Recipient: Leeds Grand Theatre & Opera House Ltd
Access Contact: Mr Peter Sandeman
Tel: 0113 3917777 **Fax:** 0113 2341800
E-mail: info@cityvarieties.co.uk
Open: Heritage Open Days: organised tours. Other times by arrangement.
Ⓟ No ♿ No. Guide Dogs: Yes
£ Charges for performances only.

Crossley Pavilion

The People's Park, King Cross Road, Halifax, West Yorkshire HX1 1EB
Grade II* listed building, designed by Sir Joseph Paxton and constructed in 1857. Contains seating and a statue of the park's benefactor, Sir Francis Crossley (1860), by Joseph Durham. Four gargoyle fountains supply pools flanking each side of the pavilion, set on formal terrace, balustrades and steps.
www.calderdale.gov.uk/tourism/parks/peoples.html
Grant Recipient: Calderdale Metropolitan Borough Council
Access Contact: People's Park Development Officer
Tel/Fax: 01422 323824
Open: The Park: daily 8am - dusk. The Pavilion: visits by prior arrangement with Calderdale Metropolitan Borough Council Leisure Services, 25 Bedford Street North, Halifax, West Yorkshire HX1 5BH. Public toilets open during park hours. Information Centre open by prior arrangement as above.
Ⓟ On-street in Park Road (up to 10 spaces). Limited spaces in adjacent college.
♿ There is one step into the pavilion, otherwise full wheelchair access. WC for the disabled. Guide Dogs: Yes £ No

Friends Meeting House

off Bolton Road, Addingham, nr. Ilkley, West Yorkshire LS29
Land for burial ground purchased in 1666, followed by construction of Meeting House in 1669. A simple single cell building with rubblestone walls, mullioned windows, stone-slated roof and stone-flagged floor. Contains loose benches and an oak minister's stand of an unusual panelled design with turned balusters.
www.hct.org.uk
Grant Recipient: Historic Chapels Trust
Access Contact: Barry Cody
Tel: 01756 710587
Open: At all reasonable times by application to keyholders Mr & Mrs Barry Cody, Riverview Cottage, Farfield, nr Addingham, West Yorks LS29 0RQ.
Ⓟ Spaces: 2 ♿ No. Guide Dogs: Yes £ No

Harewood House

Harewood, Leeds, West Yorkshire LS17 9LQ
Designed in neo-classical style by John Carr and completed in 1772. Contains Adam interiors, Chippendale furniture, an art collection and museum. Home of the Earl and Countess of Harewood.
www.harewood.org
Grant Recipient: The Trustees of Harewood House Trust Ltd
Access Contact: Mr Terence Suthers
Tel: 0113 218 1010 **Fax:** 0113 218 1002
E-mail: business@harewood.org
Open: Daily 4 Feb - 6 Nov: Grounds & Bird Garden open 10am - 4.30pm (Last adm 4pm); House and Terrace Gallery 11am - 4.30pm (Last adm 4pm). Grounds close at 6pm. Grounds and Bird Garden also open weekends between 6 Nov and 11 Dec. Guide dogs are not allowed in the Bird Garden but a free sound guide is available for the partially sighted visitor and a babysitter for the dog.
Ⓟ Unlimited overflow parking on grass. Spaces: 200
♿ Yes. WC for the disabled. Guide Dogs: Yes
£ **Adult:** £10(weekdays), £11 Suns & BHs
Child: £5.50
Other: £8.20 (senior), £30.50 (family), season tickets & concessions for disabled groups, 50% reduction for arrivals by public transport, students free Wed (provisional prices)

Huddersfield Station

St George's Square, Huddersfield, West Yorkshire HD1 1JF
Designed by J P Pritchett of York and built by local builder Joseph Kaye using local ashlar sandstone, the station is the oldest of the seven Grade I listed station buildings in use for railway passengers having opened on 3 Aug 1847. When the foundation stone was laid the year before a public holiday was declared and church bells were rung from dawn till dusk. The grandeur of the station is the result of it having been built at the joint expense of the Huddersfield & Manchester Rail & Canal Company and the Manchester & Leeds Railway Company.
Grant Recipient: Kirklees Metropolitan Council
Access Contact: Head of Design & Property Service
Open: Operational building open to the public every day except Christmas Day and Boxing Day. Please note that the building may also be closed on other days specified by Railtrack plc or other railway operators.
Ⓟ One hour stay maximum in station car park. Spaces: 20
♿ Full wheelchair access to main buildings. Access with assistance to inner platforms. No WC for the disabled. Guide Dogs: Yes
£ No

National Coal Mining Museum for England

Caphouse Colliery, New Road, Wakefield, West Yorkshire WF4 4RH
A colliery complex dating back to the 18th century with an underground tour into authentic coal workings. There are two major galleries of social history and technology and most of the historic buildings are open to the public. Facilities include a research library, restaurant, shop and education services.
www.ncm.org.uk
Grant Recipient: The National Coal Mining Museum for England Trust Ltd
Access Contact: Dr M Faull
Tel: 01924 848806 **Fax:** 01924 840694
E-mail: info@ncm.org.uk
Open: All year, daily 10am - 5pm except 24 - 26 Dec and 1 Jan.
Ⓟ Spaces: 120
♿ Wheelchair access to all galleries and historic buildings and underground (limited tour) but not the screens. WC for the disabled. Guide Dogs: Yes
£ No

Nostell Priory

Doncaster Road, Nostell, Wakefield, West Yorkshire WF4 1QE
Country house, c1736-1750, by James Paine for Sir Rowland Winn 4th baronet. Later Robert Adam was commissioned to complete the State Rooms. On display is a collection of Chippendale furniture, designed especially for the house, an art collection with works by Pieter Breughel the Younger and Angelica Kauffmann, an 18th century dolls' house, complete with its original fittings and Chippendale furniture and an unrestored 18th century Muniments Room. Other attractions include lakeside walks, historic park, family croquet, giant chess set and open day for cabinets.
www.nationaltrust.org.uk
Grant Recipient: The National Trust
Access Contact: Property Manager
Tel: 01924 863892 **Fax:** 01924 866846
E-mail: nostellpriory@nationaltrust.org.uk
Open: House: 27 Mar - 31 Oct, daily except Mon and Tues (open Good Fri and Bank Hols) 1 - 5.00pm; 6 Nov - 19 Dec, Sat & Sun only 12 noon - 4pm. Grounds, shop and tearoom: 6 - 21 Mar, weekends only 11am - 4.00pm; 27 Mar - 31 Oct, as house: grounds 11am - 6pm, shop and tearoom 11am - 5.30pm; 6 Nov - 19 Dec, as house 11am - 4.30pm.
Ⓟ Spaces: 120
♿ Wheelchair access to ground floor of house with lift to first floor, tea room, children's playground and shop. No WC for the disabled. Guide Dogs: Yes
£ **Adult:** £6, £3.50 (grounds only)
Child: £3, £2.50 (grounds only)
Other: £15 (family, no family ticket for grounds only)

The Roundhouse

Wellington Road, Leeds, West Yorkshire LS12 1DR
Grade II* railway roundhouse built in 1847 for the Leeds and Thirsk Railway by Thomas Granger. In full use by the North-Eastern Railway until 1904, now home to Leeds Commercial Van and Truck Hire.
Grant Recipient: Wellbridge Properties Ltd
Access Contact: Mr J D Miller
Tel: 0113 2435964 **Fax:** 0113 246 1142
E-mail: sales@leedscommercial.co.uk
Open: By written arrangement with the occupiers, Leeds Commercial, who manage the property as a working garage, or call in during office hours.
Ⓟ Free. Spaces: 100
♿ Yes. WC for the disabled. Guide Dogs: Yes
£ No

Temple Newsam House

Leeds Museums and Galleries, Leeds, West Yorkshire LS15 0AE
Tudor-Jacobean mansion set in 1200 acres. Birthplace of Henry Lord Darnley, husband of

Mary Queen of Scots, and later the home of the Ingram family, Viscounts Irwin. Over 30 rooms open to the public housing a fine and decorative arts museum with collections of furniture, metalwork and ceramics.
www.leeds.gov.uk/templenewsam
Grant Recipient: Leeds City Council
Access Contact: Mr Anthony Wells-Cole
Tel: 0113 264 7321 **Fax:** 0113 260 2285
E-mail: tnewsamho.leeds@virgin.net
Open: Jan - Dec daily except Mon (open BH Mons) 10.30am - 5.00pm (4pm in winter). Last adm 45 minutes before closing.
🅿Spaces: 200
♿Wheelchair access to all public areas except the first floor of the south wing. WC for the disabled. Guide Dogs: Yes
💷**Adult:** £3 (includes Audio Tour) **Child:** £2 (5-16); Free (under 5) **Family:** £8

Theatre Royal & Opera House
**Drury Lane, Wakefield,
West Yorkshire WF1 2TE**
A 500 seat Victorian Theatre designed by Frank Matcham. Notable for the quality of decoration in the auditorium, it provides a year-round programme of events.
www.wakefieldtheatres.co.uk
Grant Recipient: Wakefield Theatre Royal & Opera House
Access Contact: Mr Murray Edwards
Tel: 01924 215531 **Fax:** 01924 215525
E-mail: murray@wakefieldtheatres.co.uk
Open: Programme of events published in Feb, July and Nov. Guided tours once a month on Sat, groups on weekdays by prior arrangement, contact the Box Office Tel: 01924 211311 for further information.
🅿Spaces: 150
♿Wheelchair access to stalls area only. WC for the disabled. Guide Dogs: Yes
💷**Adult:** £3. Admission charge for performances.

WILTSHIRE

Avoncliffe Aqueduct
Kennet & Avon Canal, Westwood, Wiltshire
19th century limestone aqueduct carrying the Kennet and Avon Canal over the River Avon and the railway line. The canal towpath crosses alongside the canal providing a foot link to Bradford-on-Avon or Bath.
www.britishwaterways.co.uk
Grant Recipient: British Waterways
Access Contact: Mr Kent Daniels
Tel: 01452 318000
E-mail: kentdaniels@britishwaterways.co.uk
Open: At all times.
🅿Spaces: 12
♿ Top of aqueduct is accessible for wheelchairs from the small car park beside the canal.
 No WC for the disabled. Guide Dogs: Yes 💷No

Barton Grange Farm West Barn
Bradford-on-Avon, Wiltshire
Part of Barton Farm, once a grange of Shaftesbury Abbey (the richest nunnery in England), which includes the adjacent 14th century Tithe Barn. The West Barn was destroyed by fire in 1982 but has subsequently been rebuilt by the Preservation Trust and is now used as an 'Interpretation Centre'.
www.bradfordheritage.co.uk/PAGES/project.htm
Grant Recipient: Bradford-on-Avon Preservation Trust Limited
Access Contact: Mr Chris Penny
Tel: 01225 866551
E-mail: chrispenny@lineone.net
Open: May - Sept, weekends and Bank Hols 12 noon - 4pm. Also open at other times throughout the year, please check with Mr Penny for further details.
🅿Pay parking (15 spaces) near the site. Pay parking (200 spaces) at railway station.
♿Wheelchair access to main building but not galleries. Entrance pathways are loose gravel. WC for the disabled. Guide Dogs: Yes 💷No

The Cloisters
Iford Manor, Bradford-on-Avon, Wiltshire BA15 2BA
Small stone-built cloister in gardens of Manor, completed 1914 by Harold Peto and based on 13th century Italian style. Interesting early contents. Used for concerts and opera evenings during the summer.

www.ifordmanor.co.uk
Grant Recipient/Access Contact: Mrs Cartwright-Hignett
Tel: 01225 863146 **Fax:** 01225 862364
Open: Gardens only: Apr - Oct, Sundays & Easter Mon 2 - 5pm; May - Sept, daily (except Mon & Fri), 2 - 5pm. Children under 10 not encouraged at weekends. Coaches and groups by arrangement only outside normal opening hours.
🅿Spaces: 100
♿Wheelchair access by arrangement to Cloisters & part of the gardens. WC for the disabled. Guide Dogs: Yes
💷**Adult:** £4 **Child:** £3.50 (10-16, under 10 free) **Conc:** £3.50

Hemingsby
56 The Close, Salisbury, Wiltshire SP1 2EL
14th century canonical residence with spacious 18th century rooms and medieval Great Hall. Contains 15th century linenfold panelling. Large and interesting garden. Home of Canon William Fideon, a Greek scholar who escaped from Constantinople in 1453, and Canon Edward Powell, advocate of Catherine of Aragon and later hanged for denying the Act of Supremacy.
Grant Recipient: The Dean & Chapter of Salisbury Cathedral
Access Contact: Mr Peter Edds
Tel: 01722 555100 **Fax:** 01722 555109
Open: By prior arrangement only. Exterior can be viewed at all times.
🅿No ♿No. Guide Dogs: Yes
💷No, but donations for charity gratefully received

Lacock Abbey
Lacock, nr. Chippenham, Wiltshire SN15 2LG
Founded in 1232 and converted into a country house c1540, the fine medieval cloisters, sacristy, chapter house and monastic rooms of the Abbey have survived largely intact. The handsome 16th century stable courtyard has half timbered gables, a clockhouse, brewery and bakehouse. Victorian woodland garden. Former residents include William Fox Talbot 'the father of modern photography'.
www.nationaltrust.org.uk
Grant Recipient: The National Trust
Access Contact: Property Manager
Tel: 01249 730227 **Fax:** 01249 730501
Open: Abbey: 19 Mar - 30 Oct, daily 1 - 5.30pm (closed Tues and Good Fri). Museum, cloisters and garden: 26 Feb - 30 Oct, daily 11am - 5.30pm (closed Good Fri). Museum also open winter weekends, but closed 25 Dec - 2 Jan.
🅿Spaces: 300
♿Wheelchair access to Abbey is difficult as four sets of stairs. Garden, cloisters and museum are accessible (non-wheelchair stairlift in museum). Limited parking in Abbey courtyard by arrangement. WC for the disabled at Red Lion car park, High Street, and abbey courtyard, RADAR lock. Guide Dogs: Yes
💷**Adult:** £7.40 (Abbey, museum, cloisters & garden), £6.00 (Abbey & garden), £4.60 (garden, cloisters & museum)
Child: £3.70 (Abbey, museum, cloisters & garden), £3.00 (Abbey & garden), £2.30 (garden, cloisters & museum)
Other: £18.90 (family: Abbey, museum, cloisters & garden), £15.30 (family: Abbey & garden), £11.80 (family: garden, cloisters & museum). Group rates

Lady Margaret Hungerford Almshouses
Pound Pill, Corsham, Wiltshire SN13 9HT
Fine complex of Grade I listed 17th Almshouses, Schoolroom, Warden's House and Stables. Schoolroom with original 17th century furniture and Exhibition Room. Recently restored. Lady Margaret Hungerford founded the Almshouses for the care of six poor people and the schoolroom for educating poor children. Arms of the foundress are well displayed.
Grant Recipient: Trustees Of The Lady Margaret Hunderford Charity
Access Contact: Mr R L Tonge
Tel/Fax: 01225 742471
E-mail: rtonge@northwilts.gov.uk
Open: 3 Apr - 2 Oct Tues, Wed, Sat, and Sun 12.30pm - 3.30pm; Other dates: Sats 12.30pm - 3.30pm. Closed Dec and Jan. Groups welcome by appointment.
🅿In the town within 100 yards. Spaces: 100
♿Wheelchair access to ground floor only. WC for the disabled. Guide Dogs: Yes
💷**Adult:** £2 **Child:** 50p **Seniors/Conc:** £1.75

Larmer Tree Gardens
nr Tollard Royal, Salisbury, Wiltshire SP5 5PY
Created by General Pitt Rivers in 1880 as a pleasure grounds for 'public enlightenment and entertainment', the Larmer Tree Gardens are set high on the Cranbourne Chase providing exceptional views of the surrounding countryside. One of the most unusual gardens in England containing an extraordinary collection of colonial and oriental buildings, a Roman Temple and an Open Air Theatre.
www.larmertreegardens.co.uk
Grant Recipient & Access Contact: Trustees of MALF Pitt-Rivers No. 1 Discretionary Settlement
Tel: 01725 516228 **Fax:** 01725 516449
E-mail: larmer.tree@rushmore-estate.co.uk
Open: 1 Apr - 31 Oct, daily except Sat and Fri throughout July, 11am - 5.30pm. Please telephone for winter opening times.
🅿Spaces: 500
♿Wheelchair access to the sunken dell is difficult. WC for the disabled. Guide Dogs: Yes
💷**Adult:** £3.75 **Child:** £2.50 **Other:** £3

Lydiard Park
Lydiard Tregoze, Swindon, Wiltshire SN5 3PA
Ancestral home of the Bolingbrokes, the restored Palladian mansion contains family furnishings and portraits, plasterwork, rare 17th century painted window and room dedicated to 18th century society artist Lady Diana Spencer.
Grant Recipient: Swindon Borough Council
Access Contact: Mrs Sarah Finch-Crisp
Tel: 01793 770401 **Fax:** 01793 770968
Open: House: Mon - Sat 10am - 5pm. Nov - Feb early closing at 4pm. Grounds all day, closing at dusk.
🅿Spaces: 400
♿Yes. WC for the disabled. Guide Dogs: Yes
💷**Adult:** £2 **Child:** £1 **Other:** £1 (Swindon Card Holders)

Merchant's House
132 High Street, Marlborough, Wiltshire SN8 1HN
17th century town house built by the Bayly family, mercers between 1653 and c1700. Situated prominently in the High Street it contains a unique stripe-painted dining room c1665, painted balustrading to the oak staircase and a panelled chamber of the Commonwealth period.
www.themerchantshouse.co.uk
Grant Recipient: Merchant's House (Marlborough) Trust
Access Contact: Mr Michael Gray
Tel/Fax: 01672 511491
E-mail: manager@themerchantshouse.co.uk
Open: Easter - end Sept: Fri & Sat 11am - 4pm. Other times by arrangement with the Secretary at Merchant's House.
🅿Public parking in High St. Disabled visitors can park outside the building.
♿No. Guide Dogs: Yes 💷**Adult:** £3 **Child:** 50p

Old Bishop's Palace
**Salisbury Cathedral School,
1 The Close, Salisbury, Wilts SP1 2EQ**
13th century building, much altered over the centuries, with 13th century undercroft, Georgian drawing room and a chapel.
Grant Recipient: Salisbury Diocesan Board of Finance
Access Contact: Mr Neil Parsons
Tel: 01722 555302 **Fax:** 01722 410910
E-mail: bursar@salisburycathedralschool.com
Open: Guided tours on 10 days in July/Aug. Details can be obtained from the Visitors' Office at Salisbury Cathedral (tel: Jan Leniston on 01722 555124).
🅿No
♿No. WC for the disabled in the cloister (100 yards). Guide Dogs: No 💷**Adult:** £2.50

Salisbury Cathedral Education Centre (Wren Hall)
56c The Close, Salisbury, Wiltshire SP1 2EL
Originally north wing of adjacent Braybrook House, early 18th century. Former choristers' school (founded 13th century). Many of the original fixtures and fittings are still present. Items of particular interest are the teacher's and head teacher's desks, original wood panelling and various photographs and artefacts from the history of the schoolroom.
www.salisburycathedral.org.uk/education.php
Grant Recipient:
The Dean & Chapter of Salisbury Cathedral

Access Contact: Mr Peter Ebbs
Tel: 01722 555180
Open: By prior arrangement.
P As part of Close parking arrangements for members of the public.
No. WC for the disabled in the Close. Guide Dogs: Yes
£ Donation to work of Centre invited

Sarum College

19 The Close, Salisbury, Wiltshire SP1 2EE
Grade I listed house, c1677, attributed to Sir Christopher Wren. In the 1870s collegiate buildings were added, designed by William Butterfield. The college is an ecumenical education, training and conference centre.
www.sarum.ac.uk
Grant Recipient: Trustees of Salisbury & Wells Theological College/Sarum College
Access Contact: Mrs Linda Cooper
Tel: 01722 424800   **Fax:** 01722 338508
E-mail: admin@sarum.ac.uk
Open: Daily during term-time, please check with College for details of term-times.
P Spaces: 37
Wheelchair access to ground floor only. WC for the disabled. Guide Dogs: Yes
£ No

Wilton House

Wilton, Salisbury, Wiltshire SP2 0BJ
Ancestral home of the Earls of Pembroke for over 450 years, rebuilt by Inigo Jones and John Webb in the Palladian style with further alterations by James Wyatt c1801. Contains 17th century state rooms and an art collection including works by Van Dyck, Rubens, Joshua Reynolds and Brueghel. Surrounded by landscaped parkland.
www.wiltonhouse.com
Grant Recipient: Wilton House Charitable Trust
Access Contact: Mr Ray Stedman
Tel: 01722 746720   **Fax:** 01722 744447
E-mail: tourism@wiltonhouse.com
Open: 24 Mar - 30 Oct: 10.30am - 5.30pm (Last adm 4.30pm). House closed on Sat but grounds open. House and gardens open on Bank Hols.
P Spaces: 200
Yes. WC for the disabled. Guide Dogs: Yes
£ Adult: £9.75 Child: £5.50 Senior: £8. Group rates on application

WORCESTERSHIRE

Abberley Hall Clock Tower

Great Witley, Worcester, Worcestershire WR6 6DD
Victorian folly, built 1883-4, by J P St Aubyn in a fantastic mixture of 13th and 14th century Gothic styles. 161ft tall, it can be seen from six counties.
Grant Recipient: Abberley Hall Ltd
Access Contact: Mr J G W Walker
Tel: 01299 896275   **Fax:** 01299 896875
E-mail: johnwalker@abberleyhall.co.uk
Open: 22 and 23 July; other times by prior arrangement.
P Spaces: 20 No **£** Adult: £3 Child: £1.50

Abbey Gateway
(formerly Priory Gatehouse)

Abbey Road, Malvern, Worcestershire WR14 3ES
15th century gatehouse of the Benedictine Monastery in Malvern. Extended and restored,

notably during 16th and 19th centuries. Now houses the Malvern Museum, an independent voluntary-run local museum.
Grant Recipient: Malvern Museum Society Ltd
Access Contact: The Curator
Tel: 01684 567811
Open: 25 Mar - 31 Oct: daily 10.30am - 5pm. Closed Weds in term time. (Opening hours are always subject to the availability of volunteers).
P On-street parking. Paid parking within ¼ mile.
Wheelchair access restricted due to narrow winding staircase. Full access to sales area only. Audio tape (50p) and information folder are available as an alternative 'tour' of displays. No WC for the disabled. Guide Dogs: Yes
£ Adult: £1.50 Child: 50p (age 7 or over)

Hanbury Hall

Hanbury, Droitwich, Worcestershire WR9 7EA
Built in 1701, this William and Mary-style house contains painted ceilings and staircase. It has an orangery, ice house and Moorish gazebos. The re-created 18th century garden is surrounded by parkland and has a parterre, wilderness, fruit garden, open grove and bowling green pavilions.
www.nationaltrust.org.uk
Grant Recipient: The National Trust
Access Contact: Property Manager
Tel: 01527 821214   **Fax:** 01527 821251
E-mail: hanburyhall@nationaltrust.org.uk
Open: 5 - 20 Mar, Sat & Sun. 21 Mar - 31 Oct, Sat - Wed. House: 1 - 5pm. Garden: 11am - 5.30pm. Closed 11 -13 Mar for Homes & Gardens Exhibition.
P Spaces: 150. Car parking 200 metres from house. Buggy transfer available.
Wheelchair access to ground floor, gardens, tea room and shop. WC for the disabled. Guide Dogs: Yes
£ Adult: £5.70, £3.70 (garden only)
Child: £2.80, £1.90 (garden only)
Other: £13.50 (family), £4.80 (group)

Harvington Hall

Harvington, nr. Kidderminster, Worcestershire DY10 4LR
An Elizabethan moated manor house. Contains one of the best known series of priests' hides in the country and extensive traces of an ambitious scheme of wall paintings of late 16th or early 17th century.
www.harvingtonhall.org.uk
Grant Recipient: Roman Catholic Diocese of Birmingham
Access Contact: Mrs S Breeden
Tel: 01562 777846   **Fax:** 01562 777190
E-mail: thehall@harvington.fsbusiness.co.uk
Open: Mar - Oct: Sat & Sun 11.30am - 5pm; Apr - Sept: Wed - Sun 11.30am - 5pm. Groups and schools by arrangement at any time.
P Spaces: 100
Wheelchair access to ground floor, gardens, tea room and shop. Video of upper floors available. WC for the disabled. Guide Dogs: Yes
£ Adult: £4.50 Child: £3 Seniors: £3.80
Family: £12.50 Garden: £1

Hopton Court Conservatory

Cleobury Mortimer, Kidderminster, Worcestershire DY14 0EF
Grade II* listed conservatory, c1830, of cast iron with a rounded archway leading to a rear room roofed with curved glass. Two rooms either side, one housing the boiler beneath to supply heat by way of cast iron grilles running around the floor

of the interior.
www.hoptoncourt.co.uk
Grant Recipient: Mr C R D Woodward
Access Contact: Mr Christopher Woodward
Tel: 01299 270734   **Fax:** 01299 271132
E-mail: chris@hoptoncourt.fsnet.co.uk
Open: Weekends of 3/4 May and 7/8 May, 10am - 4.30pm. At other times by arrangement.
P Spaces: 150
Yes. WC for the disabled. Guide Dogs: Yes
£ Adult: £3.50

Lower Brockhampton

Bringsty, Worcestershire WR6 5UH
A late 14th century moated manor house with a detached half-timbered 15th century gatehouse. Also, the ruins of a 12th century chapel. Woodland walks.
www.nationaltrust.org.uk
Grant Recipient: The National Trust
Access Contact: Property Manager
Tel: 01885 488099   **Fax:** 01885 482151
E-mail: brockhampton@nationaltrust.org.uk
Open: House: 5 Mar - 27 Mar, Sat & Sun (open BH Mons & Good Fri) 12 noon - 4pm; 1 Apr - 30 Oct, Wed - Sun 12 noon - 5pm (until 4pm in Oct). Woodland walks open all year, daily during daylight hours.
P Spaces: 60. Parking for disabled near house. Car parking free at house, £2 charge for non NT members at estate car park.
Partial. WC for the disabled in estate car park. Guide Dogs: Yes
£ Adult: £3.60 Child: £1.80
Family: £8.50 Car Park: £2
Estate free to pedestrians

St Michael's Ruined Nave & West Tower

Abberley, Worcestershire
Ruins of tower, nave (both 12th century) and south aisle (c1260). Walls standing approximately 4ft high with many surviving features from Medieval church. 12th century chancel and south chapel, c1260, repaired in 1908 and still used for services.
Grant Recipient: Abberley Parochial Church Council
Access Contact: Mrs M A Nott
Tel: 01299 896392
Open: At all times.
P Also parking at Manor Arms Hotel. Spaces: 7
Yes. Full wheelchair access to ruins but help required to visit interior of church. No WC for the disabled. Guide Dogs: Yes
£ Donations welcome (place in Green Box)

Walker Hall

Market Square, Evesham, Worcestershire WR11 4RW
16th century timber-framed building adjoining Norman gateway, much altered. In the late 19th century the floor was removed and it became an open hall. In 1999 it was repaired and refitted to form offices (first floor) and a retail unit (ground floor).
Grant Recipient/Access Contact:
Messrs Saggers & Rhodes
Tel: 01386 446623   **Fax:** 01386 48215
E-mail: wds@ricsonline.org
Open: Access to interior by arrangement only.
P Parking in town centre car parks. Spaces: 500
Wheelchair and guide dog access to ground floor only. WC for the disabled. Guide Dogs: Yes
£ Charitable donation only

Key: **P** Parking information.   Disabled access.   **£** Admission prices.

Information carried in this Section is based on that supplied by English Heritage. Every effort has been made to ensure that the information given is accurate and while believed to be at the time of going to press, opening times, entrance charges and facilities available at properties may be changed at the discretion of the owners. If long journeys are involved, visitors are advised to telephone the property to ensure the opening times are as published. The publishers do not accept responsibility for any consequences that may arise from errors or omissions.

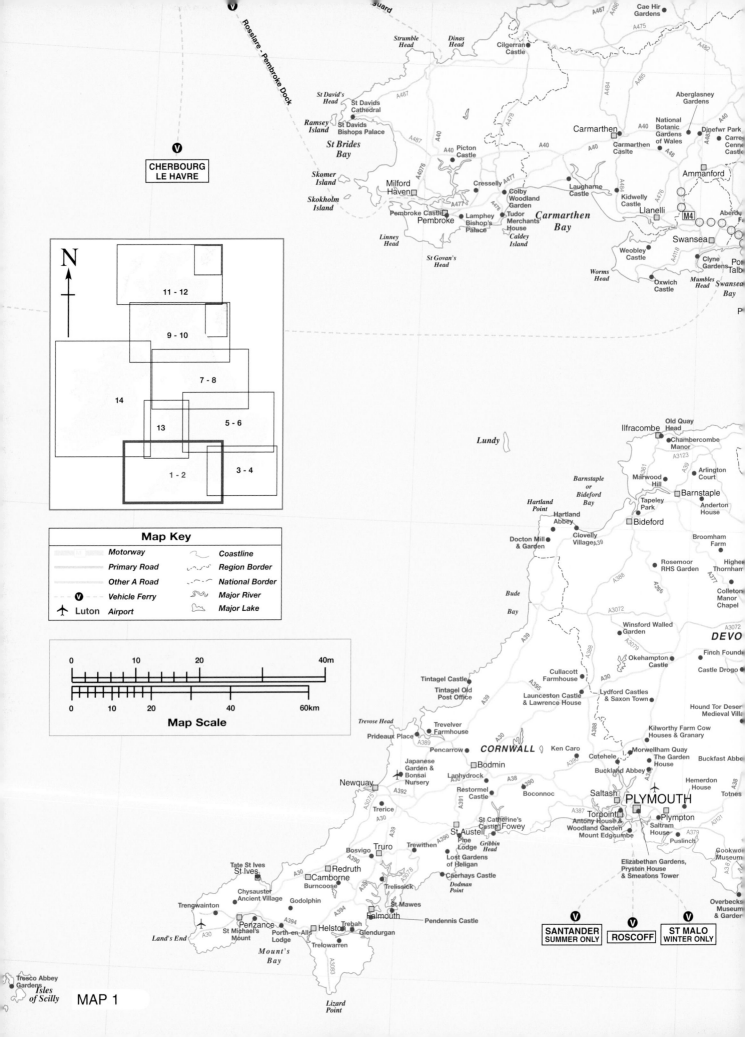

MAP 1

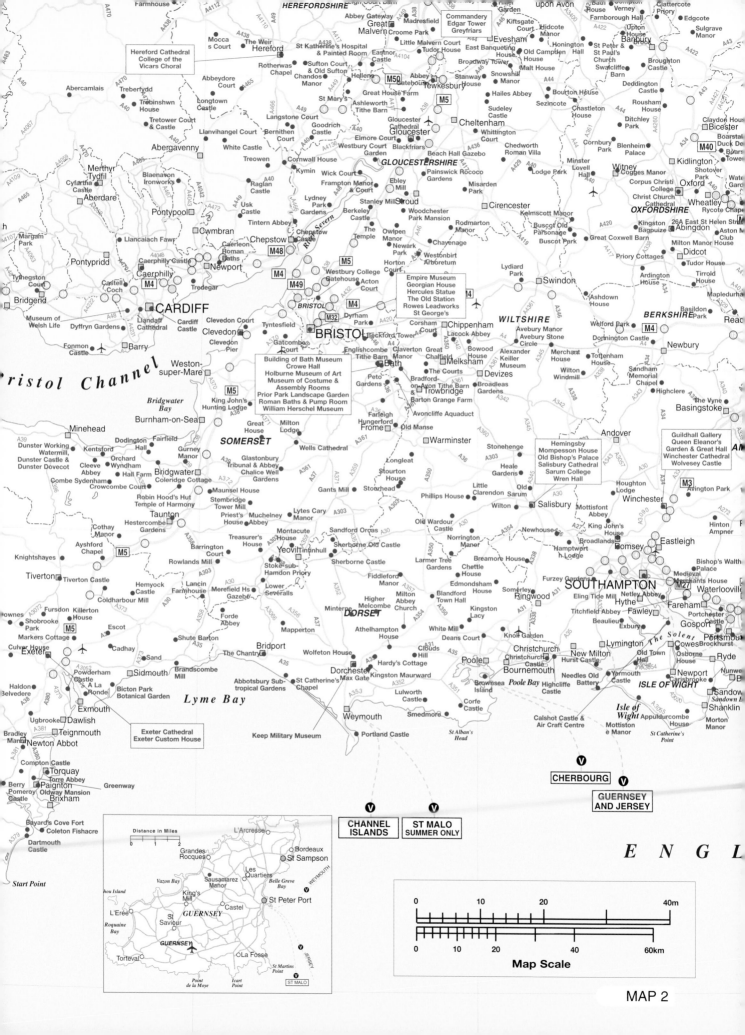

MAP 2

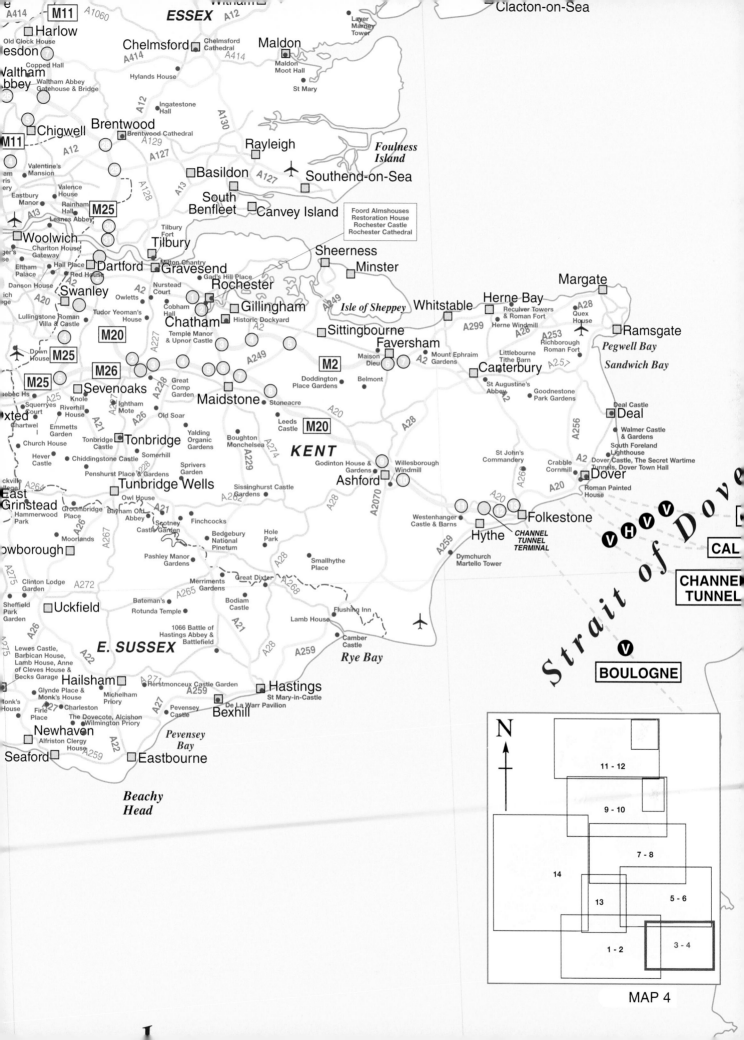

MAP 5

Counties / regions:
MERSEYSIDE, GREATER MANCHESTER, W. YORKSHIRE, S. YORKSHIRE, CHESHIRE, DERBYSHIRE, NOTTINGHAMSHIRE, STAFFORDSHIRE, SHROPSHIRE, LEICESTERSHIRE, WEST MIDLANDS, WORCESTERSHIRE, WARWICKSHIRE, HEREFORDSHIRE, NORTHAMPTONSHIRE, GLOUCESTERSHIRE, BUCKINGHAMSHIRE, OXFORDSHIRE

Cities:
LIVERPOOL, MANCHESTER, SHEFFIELD, STOKE-ON-TRENT, NOTTINGHAM, DERBY, LEICESTER, WOLVERHAMPTON, BIRMINGHAM, COVENTRY

Boxed lists:

Convent Conservatory
Croxteth Hall
Liverpool Cathedral
Liverpool Cathedral
Church of Christ the King
Liverpool Collegiate

Crossley Pavilion
Holdsworth Hse
Gazebo
Marlborough Hall

1830 Warehouse
Law Library
Heaton Hall
Cathedral
Victoria Baths
Ordsall Hall
Portico Library

Chester Roman

2/5 & 23/24 The Close
10 The Close
St Mary's
Samual Johnson

Newdigate House
Nottingham Castle

2/3 Milk Street
Coleham Pumping Station
Lord Hill Column
Old Mansion
Shrewsbury Castle
Shrewsbury Museum & Art Gallery

Soho House
Selly Manor
Botanical Gardens

The Commandery
Edgar Tower
The Greyfriars

Hereford Cathedral
College of Vicars
Choral

Blackfriars
Gloucester

Selected place names / sites:
Lytham Hall, Harris Museum, Blackburn, Accrington, Townley Hall, Halifax, W. Yorkshire, Oakwell, Batley, Castleford, Goole, M62, M18, M180, M181
Lytham St Anne's, Hoghton Tower, Oswaldtwistle, Rawtenstall, Todmorden, Brighouse, Shibden Hall, Bagshaw Museum, Dewsbury, Theatre Royal, Pontefract, Thorne, Epworth Old Rect
Leyland, Darwen, M65, Turton Tower, Rochdale, Huddersfield, Wakefield Cathedral, Nostell Priory, M62
Meols Hall, M61, M6, Chorley, Astley Hall, Smithills, Bolton, Bury, M66, Middleton, Oldham, Albion Warehouse, Hemsworth, M1, Moated Site, Brodsworth Hall, Doncaster
Formby, Ormskirk, Standish, Wigan, Kirklees Hall Farm, Lightshaw Hall Farm, GREATER MANCHESTER, Salford, Cannon Hall, Barnsley, Hickleton Hall, Cusworth Hall, Mansion House
Ince Blundell Hall, Skelmersdale, M58, Kirkby, St Helens, Dam House, Wentworth Castle, Cawthorne, Wortley Hall, Conisbrough Castle, Gainsborough Old Hall
Crosby, Bootle, Wallasey, Sefton Park, Widnes, Runcorn, Warrington, Altrincham, Sale, M60, Stockport, Cheadle, Wortley Hall, S. YORKSHIRE, Clifton Park, Rotherham, Worksop, Retford
Birkenhead, Port Sunlight, Speke Hall, Norton Priory, Dunham Massey, Bramall Hall, Lyme Park, Bishop's House, Lyceum Theatre, Roche Abbey, Hodsock Priory
Bebington, Ness, M53, Frodsham, Tabley House, Arley Hall, Belmont Hall, Tatton Park, Knutsford, Wilmslow, Bank Hall Mill, Peveril Castle, Eyam Hall, Renishaw Hall, Dronfield, Staveley, Clumber Park
Ellesmere Port, Flint, Northwich, Nether Alderley Mill, Hare Hill, Macclesfield, Buxton, Assembly Rooms, Opera House, Chatsworth, Chesterfield, Bolsover Castle
Chester, Dixon's Almshouses, Peover Hall, Capesthorne Hall, Gawsworth Hall, Pavilion Gardens, Haddon Hall, Caudwell's Mill, Hardwick Hall Old Hall, Rufford Abbey
CHESHIRE, Holmston Hall Barn, Congleton, Rode Hall, Little Moreton Hall, Dunwood Hall, DERBYSHIRE, Masson Mills, Clay Cross, M1, Mansfield, Sutton in Ashfield, NOTTINGHAMSHIRE, Carlton Hall
Beeston Castle, Sandbach, Biddulph Grange, Biddulph, Leek, Casterne Hall, Masson Mills, Matlock, Kirkby in Ashfield, Herb Garden, Winkburn Hall, Newark
Crewe, Woodhey, Bache House Farm, Kidsgrove, Ford Green Flint Mill, Cheddleton Flint Mill, Tissington Hall, Wingfield Manor, Cornfield Hall, Newstead Abbey, Papplewick, Newark Townha & Kiln Wareho
Nantwich, Dorfold Hall, St Chad's, Newcastle-under-Lyme, Whitmore Hall, STOKE-ON-TRENT, Ashbourne, Ripley, Hucknall, Upton Hall
Wrexham, Cholmondeley Castle, Combermere, Highfields, Belper, D H Lawrence Heritage, Eastwood
Erddig, Iscoyd Park, Dorothy Clive, Oakley Hall, STAFFORDSHIRE, Stone, Kedleston Hall, Bennerley Viaduct, Ilkeston, NOTTINGHAM
Valle Crucis Abbey, Chirk Castle, Hawkstone Hall, Wollerton Old Hall, Barlaston Hall, Sandon Hall, Sudbury Hall, Dale Abbey, Wollaton, DERBY, W Bridgford, Beeston
Oswestry, Blodwell Summerhouse, The Lyth, Hodnet Hall, Yeaton Peverey, Ancient High House, Stafford, Stafford Castle, Catton Hall, Sinai Park, Burton upon Trent, Melbourne Hall, Elvaston Castle, M1, Long Eaton, Thrumpton Hall
The Judge's Lodging, Adcote School, Moreton Corbet Castle, Newport Guildhall, Newport, Rugeley, Shugborough, Speedwell Castle, Claymills Pumping Station, Swadlincote, Staunton Harold, Loughborough, Melton Mowbray
Trewern Hall, Longner Hall, Haughmond Abbey, Loton Hall, M6, Cannock, Weston Park, Boscobel House, Lichfield, Ashby-de-la-Zouch, Coalville, Rearsby Packhorse Bridge
Powis Castle, Shrewsbury, Attingham Park, Wroxeter Roman City, Telford, M54, Brosely Pipeworks, Chillington Hall, Brownhills, Wall Roman Site, Tamworth, Clifton Hall, Donington le Heath, Bradgate Park, LEICESTERSHIRE, Quenby Hall
SHROPSHIRE, Cound Hall, Buildwas Abbey, Benthall Hall, Moseley Old Hall, Walsall, Aldridge, M42, Polesworth Nunnery, Kirkby Muxloe Castle, LEICESTER, Oakham Castle
Acton Burnell Castle, Wenlock Guildhall & Priory, Rose Building, Wightwick Manor, Sutton Coldfield, Middleton Hall, Bosworth Battlefield, M69, Wigston, Lyddingto Bede Hou
Langley Chapel & Gatehouse, Preen Manor Gardens, Morville Hall, Bridgnorth, Willenhall, W Bromwich, M6, Hinckley, Arbury Hall, M1, Market Harborough, Rockingham Castle
Shipton Hall, Dudley, Stourbridge, Halesowen, BIRMINGHAM, Bedworth, Chamberlain's Almshouses, Stanford Hall, Rushton Triangular Lodge, Kelmarsh Hall
Clun Castle, Stokesay Castle, Dudmaston, Detton Hall, Kinver Camp, Halesowen Abbey, Hagley Hall, Solihull, WEST MIDLANDS, St James Church, M42, Coventry Cathedral, COVENTRY, Rugby, Coton Manor, NORTHAMPTON, Wellingbo
Bromfield Priory Gatehouse, Ludlow Castle, Hopton Court Conservatory, Mawley Hall, Kidderminster, Harvington Hall, WORCESTERSHIRE, Hartlebury, Baddesley Clinton, Stoneleigh Abbey, Ryton Gardens, M45, Cottesbrooke, Lamport Hall
The Judge's Lodging, Croft Castle, Abbeley Hall Clock Tower, St Michael's Ruined Nave & West Tower, Witley Court, Stourport-on-Severn, Bromsgrove, M42, Redditch, Hanbury Hall, Packwood House, M40, Kenilworth Castle, Leamington Spa, Charlecote House, Compton Verney, Canons Ashby, Stoke Park Pavilions, M1
Hergest Court & Hergest Croft, Berrington Hall, Droitwich, Wichenford Dovecote, Hawford Dovecote, Coughton Court, Warwick, Warwick Castle, Lord Leycester Hospital, Farnborough Hall, Edgcote, Cowp & Newtw Museu
Cwmmau Farmhouse, Hampton Court, Lower Brockhampton, Leigh Court Barn, Worcester, Madresfield Court, Spetchley Park, Ragley Hall, Mary Arden's House, Hillers Garden, Charlecote House, Clattercote Priory Farm, Sulgrave Manor, Milton Keynes
HEREFORDSHIRE, Abbey Gateway, Great Malvern, Croome Park, Little Malvern Court, Bath House, Stratford upon Avon, Anne Hathaway's Cottage, Upton House, Banbury, Wakefield Lodge, Northampton, 78 Derngate, Northampton Cathed
Hereford, The Weir, Moccas Court, Old Sufton & Sufton Court, Painted Room, Eastnor Castle, Tudor House, Evesham, Hidcote Manor, Kiftsgate Court, Honington Hall, St Peter & St Paul's Church, Brook Cottage, Broughton Castle, Stowe House & Landscape Gardens
Rotherwas Chapel, Hellens, M50, Old Campden House, Bourton House, Sezincote, Chastleton House, Rousham Park, Buckingham Chantry Chapel, BUCKINGHAMSHIRE
Abbeydore Court, Chandos Manor, St Catherine's Hospital, Abbey Gatehouse, Tewkesbury, M5, Hailes Abbey, Snowshill Manor, Sudeley Castle, Deddington Castle, Swalcliffe Barn, Bicester, Claydon House
Longtown Castle, Tretower Court & Castle, Langstone Court, Goodrich Castle, Elmore Court Entrance Gates, Gloucester, Holst Birthplace Museum, Cheltenham, Whittington Court, Ditchley Park, Cornbury Park, Blenheim Palace, Kidlington, Aylesbury
Abergavenny, White Castle, Westbury Court Garden, Beach Hall Gazebo, Chedworth Roman Villa, Lodge Park, Minster Lovell, Witney, Christchurch Cath, Corpus Christi Col, Oxford, Waterperry Gardens, Thame
Big Pit, Blaenavon Ironworks, Pontypool, Treowen, GLOUCESTERSHIRE, Painswick Rococo Garden, Misarden Park, Court Farm Dovecote, Cogges Manor, Nether Winchenden House, M40, Wycombe
Raglan Castle, Frampton Manor & Frampton Court, Stanley Mill, Ebley Mill, Cirencester, Kelmscott Manor, Buscot Old Parsonage, Kingston Bagpuize House, Milton Manor House, Didcot, Tudor House, Stonor
Lydney Park, Woodchester Park Mansion, Stroud, Buscot Park, Great Coxwell Barn, The Garden House Cottages, Priory Farm Cottages, Widmere Farm Chapel
Llancaiach Fawr Manor, Chepstow Castle, Tintern Abbey, Berkeley Castle, Owlpen Manor, Rodmarton Manor, Chavenage, Westonbirt Arboretum, Abingdon, Aston Martin Heritage Trust, Freeman Mauso
Penhow Castle, M48, M5, Horton, Stinchcombe, The Newark Park, Temple, Weston-under-, Kingstone, The Garden House Cottages
A4046

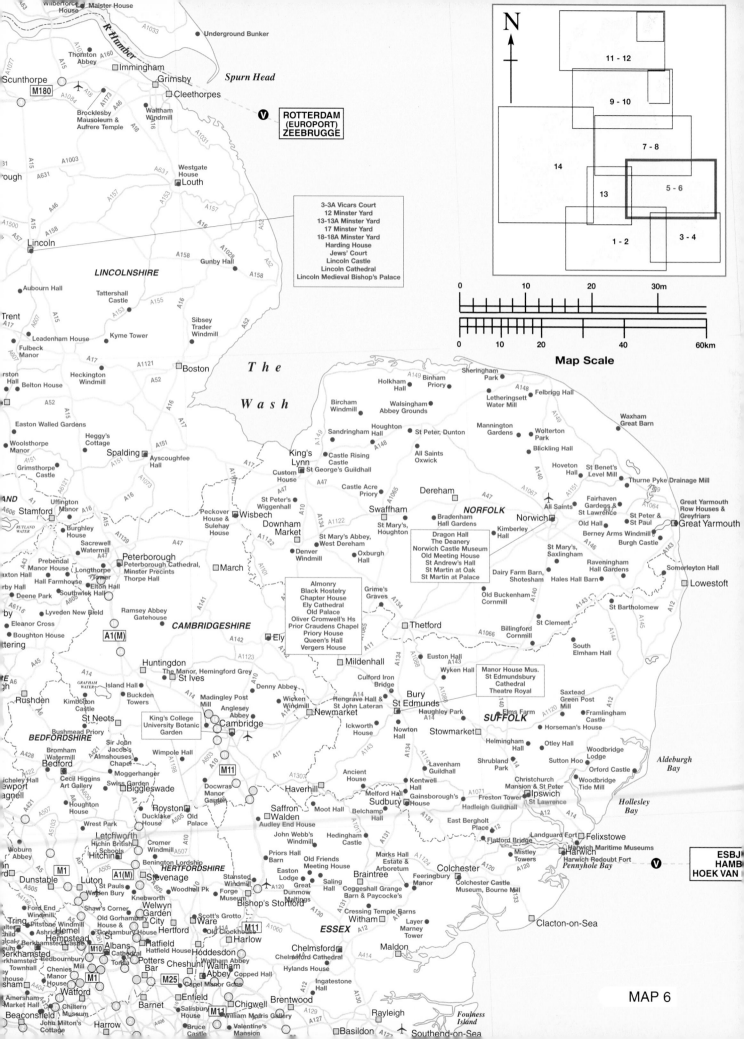

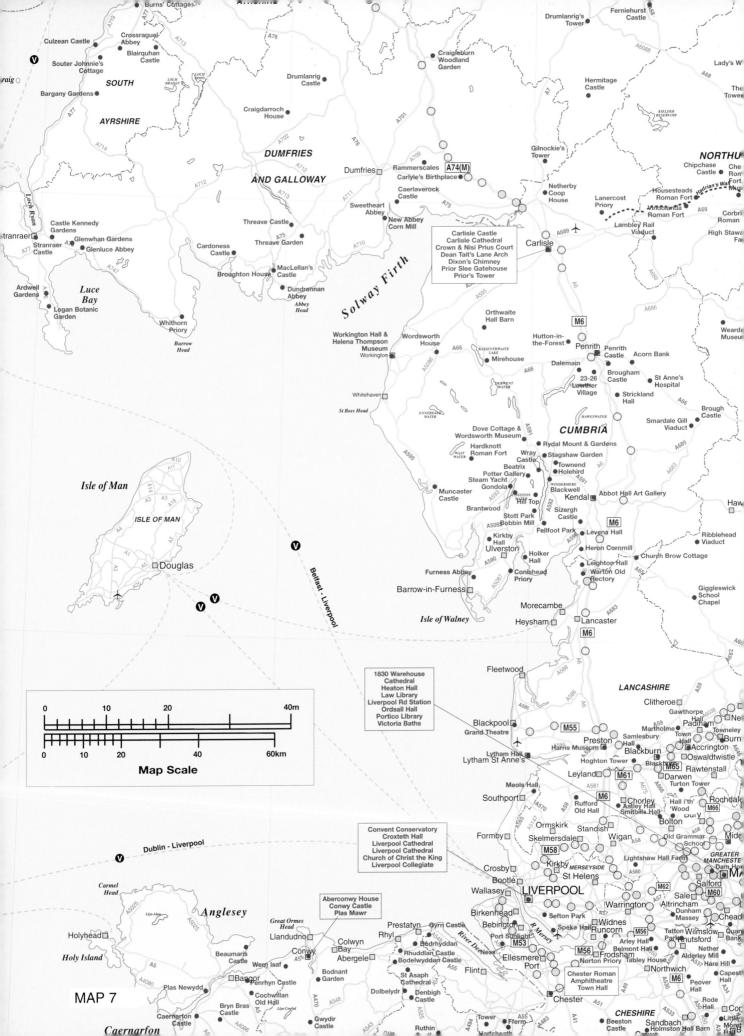

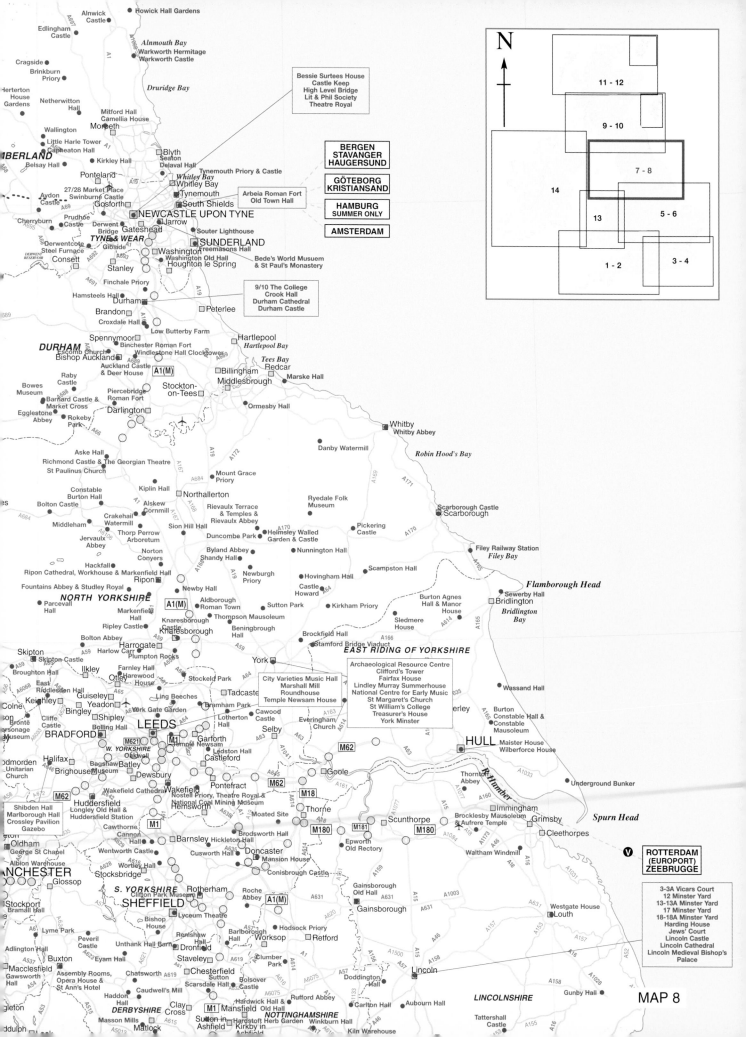

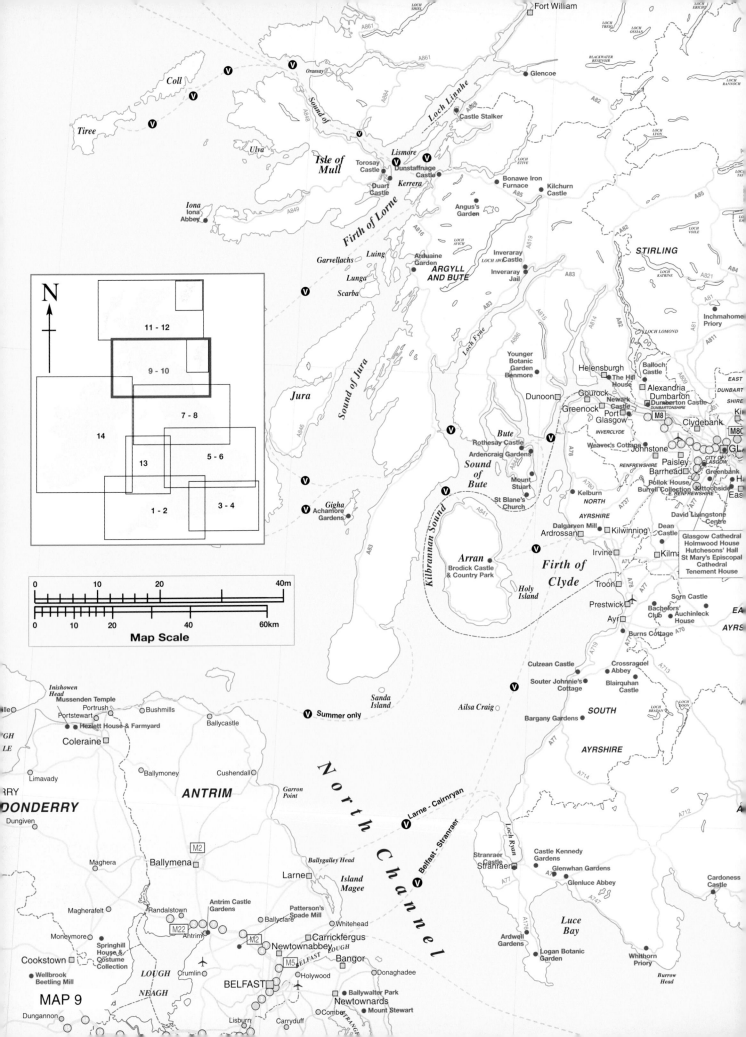

MAP 9

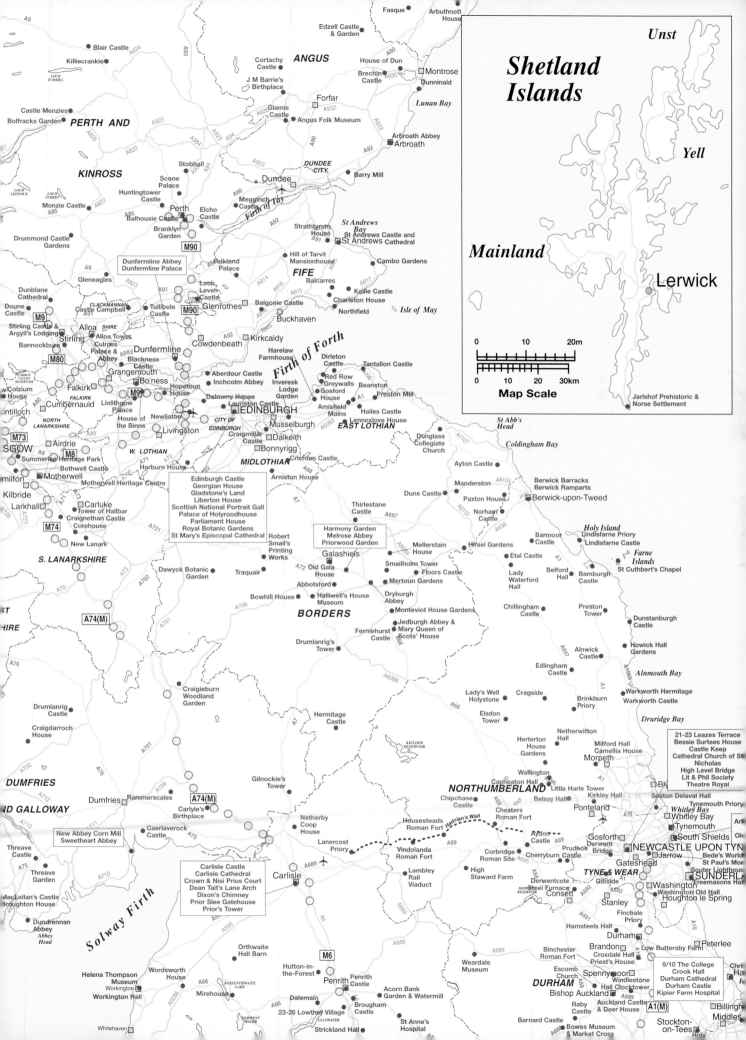

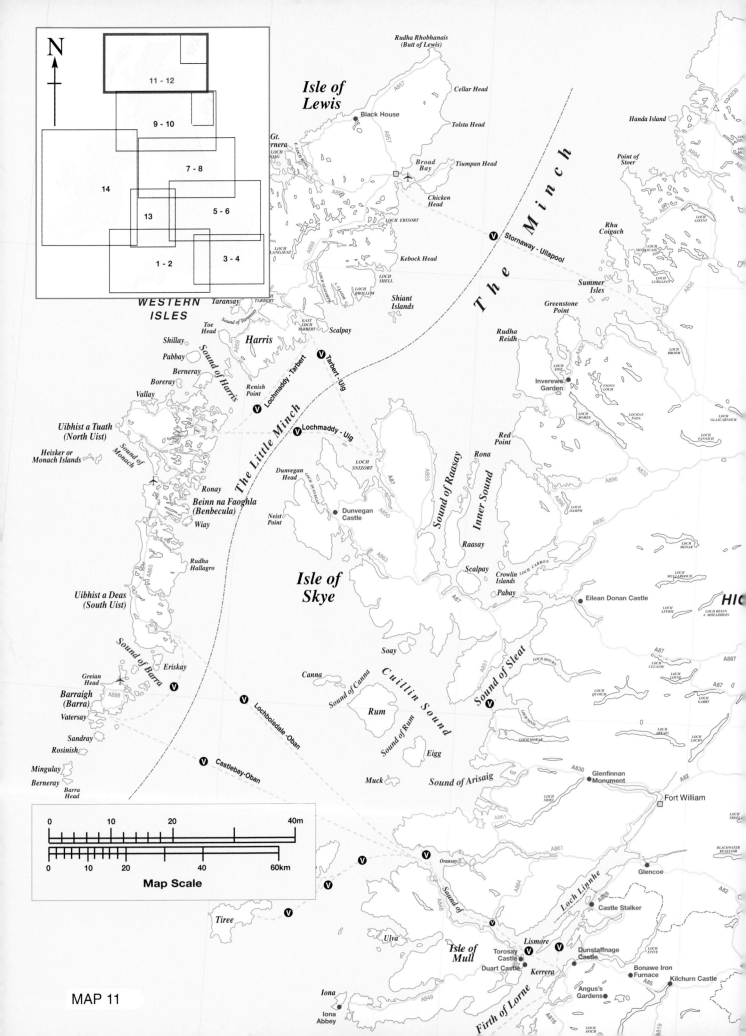

N

11 - 12

9 - 10

7 - 8

14

13

5 - 6

1 - 2

3 - 4

WESTERN ISLES

Isle of Lewis

Rudha Rhobhanais
(Butt of Lewis)

Cellar Head

A857

Black House

Tolsta Head

Handa Island

A894

LOCH
ST...

A859

Gt.
Bernera
LOCH
ROAG

Broad
Bay

Tiumpan Head

Point of
Stoer

A857

Chicken
Head

A859

LOCH ERISORT

Kebock Head

Stornaway - Ullapool Ⓥ

A835

LOCH
ASSYNT

Rhu
Coigach

LOCH
LURGAINN

LOCH
SIONASCAIG

Summer
Isles

T h e   M i n c h

LOCH
SHELL

Shiant
Islands

LOCH
BROLLUM

Shiant
Islands

Greenstone
Point

LOCH
BROOM

A832

Taransay

TARBERT

Sound of Taransay

EAST
LOCH
TARBERT

Scalpay

Rudha
Reidh

Toe
Head

Harris

A859

Lochmaddy - Tarbert Ⓥ

Tarbert - Uig Ⓥ

Inverewe
Garden

LOCH
EWE

FIONN
LOCH

A832

LOCH
FANNICH

Shillay

Pabbay

Berneray

Sound of Harris

Renish
Point

Ⓥ

Red
Point

LOCH
MAREE

LOCHAN
FADA

LOCH
GLASCARNOCH

A896

Boreray

Vallay

Lochmaddy - Uig Ⓥ

Dunvegan
Head

LOCH DUNVEGAN

LOCH
SNIZORT

Rona

Uibhist a Tuath
(North Uist)

Sound of Monach

The Little Minch

Neist
Point

Dunvegan
Castle

A850

A87

A855

Sound of Raasay

Inner Sound

LOCH
DAMPH

A890

A896

LOCH
MONAR

LOCH
MULLARDOCH

Heisker or
Monach Islands

Ronay

Beinn na Faoghla
(Benbecula)

Wiay

A863

Raasay

Scalpay

Crowlin
Islands

Pabay

LOCH CARRON

Eilean Donan Castle

HIG

LOCH
AFFRIC

LOCH BEINN
A' MHEADHOIN

A865

Rudha
Hallagro

A87

Uibhist a Deas
(South Uist)

**Isle of
Skye**

Soay

A851

Sound of Sleat

LOCH HOURN

LOCH
CLUANIE

A87

A887

LOCH
QUOICH

A87

LOCH
GARRY

Sound of Barra

Greian
Head

Eriskay

Ⓥ

Canna

Sound of Canna

Cuillin Sound

Rum

Sound of Rum

Eigg

LOCH
ARKAIG

LOCH
LOCHY

LOCH
MORAR

LOCH NEVIS

**Barraigh
(Barra)**

A888

Lochboisdale - Oban Ⓥ

Vatersay

Sandray

Rosinish

Castlebay-Oban Ⓥ

Muck

Sound of Arisaig

A830

Glenfinnan
Monument

LOCH
SHIEL

A861

Fort William

LOCH
TREIG

A82

Mingulay

Berneray

Barra
Head

Tiree Ⓥ

Ⓥ

Ⓥ

Oransay

Ⓥ

Sound of

A848

Ⓥ

Ulva

**Isle of
Mull**

Iona

Iona
Abbey

Torosay
Castle

Duart Castle

Lismore

Ⓥ

Kerrera

Ⓥ

Dunstaffnage
Castle

Angus's
Gardens

A884

Firth of Lorne

A816

Loch Linnhe

A828

Castle Stalker

Glencoe

A82

BLACKWATER
RESERVOIR

LOCH
ETIVE

Bonawe Iron
Furnace

Kilchurn Castle

A85

LOCH
AVICH

A819

LOCH
FYNE

Map Scale

0   10   20   40m

0   10   20   40   60km

Map Scale

MAP 11

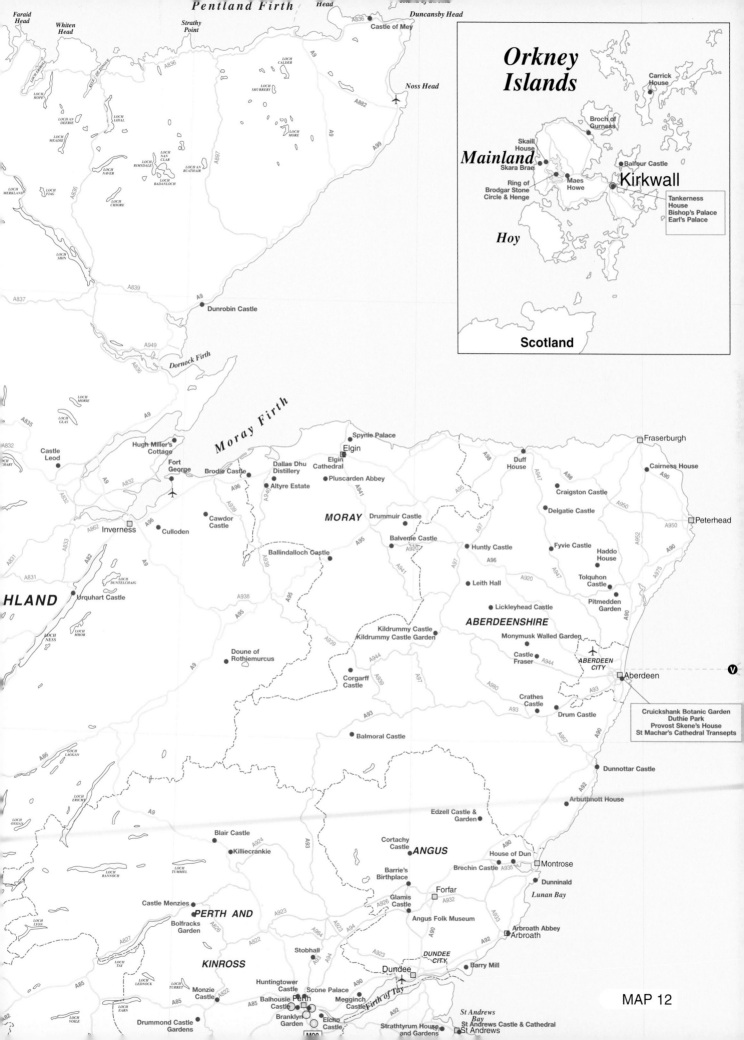

Pentland Firth

Faraid Head
Whiten Head
Strathy Point
Head
Duncansby Head
Castle of Mey
Noss Head

LOCH HOPE
LOCH ERIBOLL
LOCH MEADIE
LOCH LOYAL
LOCH NAVER
LOCH MERKLAND
LOCH FIAG
LOCH SHIN
LOCH AN DEERIE
LOCH RIMSDALE
LOCH BADANLOCH
LOCH NAN CLAR
LOCH CHIORE
LOCH AN RUATHAIR
LOCH CALDER
LOCH SHURRERY
LOCH MORE

A836
A9
A836
A838
A897
A839
A9
A837
A836
A882

Orkney Islands

Carrick House
Broch of Gurness
Skaill House
Skara Brae
Mainland
Balfour Castle
Ring of Brodgar Stone Circle & Henge
Maes Howe
Kirkwall

Tankerness House
Bishop's Palace
Earl's Palace

Hoy

Scotland

Dunrobin Castle

Dornoch Firth

A949
A836

Moray Firth

LOCH MORIE
LOCH GLASS
LOCH … HART
LOCH NESS
LOCH MHOR
LOCH DUNTELCHAIG

A835
A832
A833
A831
A82
A831
A9

Castle Leod
Hugh Miller's Cottage
Fort George
Brodie Castle
Dallas Dhu Distillery
Spynie Palace
Elgin
Elgin Cathedral
Duff House
Fraserburgh
Cairness House
Altyre Estate
Pluscarden Abbey
Craigston Castle
Inverness
Cawdor Castle
Culloden
MORAY
Drummuir Castle
Delgatie Castle
Peterhead
Ballindalloch Castle
Balvenie Castle
Huntly Castle
Fyvie Castle
Haddo House
HLAND
Urquhart Castle
Leith Hall
Tolquhon Castle
Pitmedden Garden
Lickleyhead Castle
ABERDEENSHIRE
Doune of Rothiemurcus
Kildrummy Castle
Kildrummy Castle Garden
Monymusk Walled Garden
Corgarff Castle
Castle Fraser
ABERDEEN CITY
Aberdeen
Crathes Castle
Drum Castle

A96
A862
A832
A96
A938
A939
A95
A95
A941
A940
A96
A95
A941
A920
A939
A944
A93
A97
A98
A947
A950
A952
A90
A975
A920
A947
A980
A93
A957
A90

Cruickshank Botanic Garden
Duthie Park
Provost Skene's House
St Machar's Cathedral Transepts

Balmoral Castle

Dunnottar Castle

Arbuthnott House

Edzell Castle & Garden

Blair Castle
Killiecrankie
Cortachy Castle
ANGUS
House of Dun
Barrie's Birthplace
Brechin Castle
Montrose
Dunninald
Lunan Bay
Castle Menzies
Glamis Castle
Forfar
Bolfracks Garden
Angus Folk Museum
Arbroath Abbey
Arbroath
Stobhall
KINROSS
Barry Mill
Monzie Castle
Huntingtower Castle
Scone Palace
DUNDEE CITY
Dundee
Balhousie Perth Castle
Megginch Castle
Branklyn Garden
Elcho Castle
Firth of Tay
St Andrews Bay
Drummond Castle Gardens
Strathtyrum House and Gardens
St Andrews Castle & Cathedral
St Andrews

LOCH LYON
LOCH LAGGAN
LOCH ERICHT
LOCH OSSIAN
LOCH RANNOCH
LOCH TUMMEL
LOCH TAY
LOCH LYON
LOCH LEDNOCK
LOCH TURRET
LOCH EARN
LOCH VOIL

A86
A889
A9
A924
A93
A827
A85
A822
A923
A94
A984
A923
A90
A92
A933

PERTH AND

MAP 12

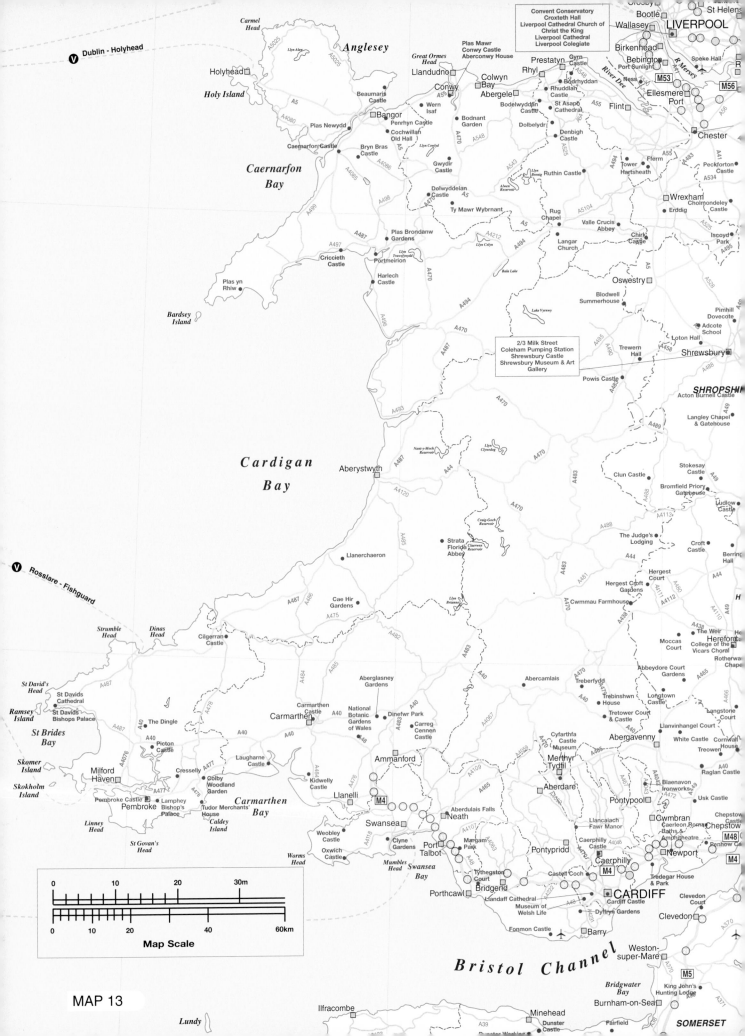

MAP 13

Map Scale
0 10 20 30m
0 10 20 40 60km

Map Scale

| 0 | 10 | 20 | 40 | 60m |
| 0 | 10 | 20 | 40 | 60 | 80 | 90km |

MAP 14

Tory Island
Horn Head
Fanad Head
Malin Head
Inishtrahull

North Channel

Islay
Rhinns Point
Laggan Bay
Gigha
Achamore Gardens

Mussenden Temple
Carndonagh
Portrush
Bushmills
Ballycastle
Hezlett House & Farmyard
Coleraine

DONEGAL
LONDONDERRY
LONDONDERRY
ANTRIM
Antrim Castle Gardens
Patterson's Spade Mill
Carrickfergus

Gray's Printing Press
Strabane
TYRONE
Barons Court
Springhill House & Costume Collection
BELFAST
Ballywalter Park

Wellbrook Beetling Mill
Mount Stewart

FERMANAGH
The Argory
Ardress
Rowallane Garden
Florence Court
Castle Coole
DOWN
Killyleagh Castle
Castle Ward
Crom Estate
MONAGHAN
ARMAGH
Seaforde Gardens
Derrymore House

MAYO
SLIGO
LEITRIM
CAVAN
LOUTH

ROSCOMMON
LONGFORD
Westport House & Gardens

GALWAY
WESTMEATH
MEATH
DUBLIN

Galway Bay
Aran Islands
OFFALY
KILDARE
DUBLIN
Dun Laoghaire

CLARE
LAOIS
WICKLOW

TIPPERARY
LIMERICK
CARLOW

KILKENNY
WEXFORD

KERRY
CORK
WATERFORD
WATERFORD

Dingle Bay
Bantry Bay

CORK

St Davids Cathedral & St Davids Bishops Palace

Dublin - Douglas (Summer Only)

CHERBOURG LE HAVRE

Rosslare - Fishguard
Rosslare - Pembroke Dock

ROSCOFF
ST MALO Summer Only
CHERBOURG Summer Only
LE HAVRE Summer Only

Cork - Swansea

LONDON DETAIL

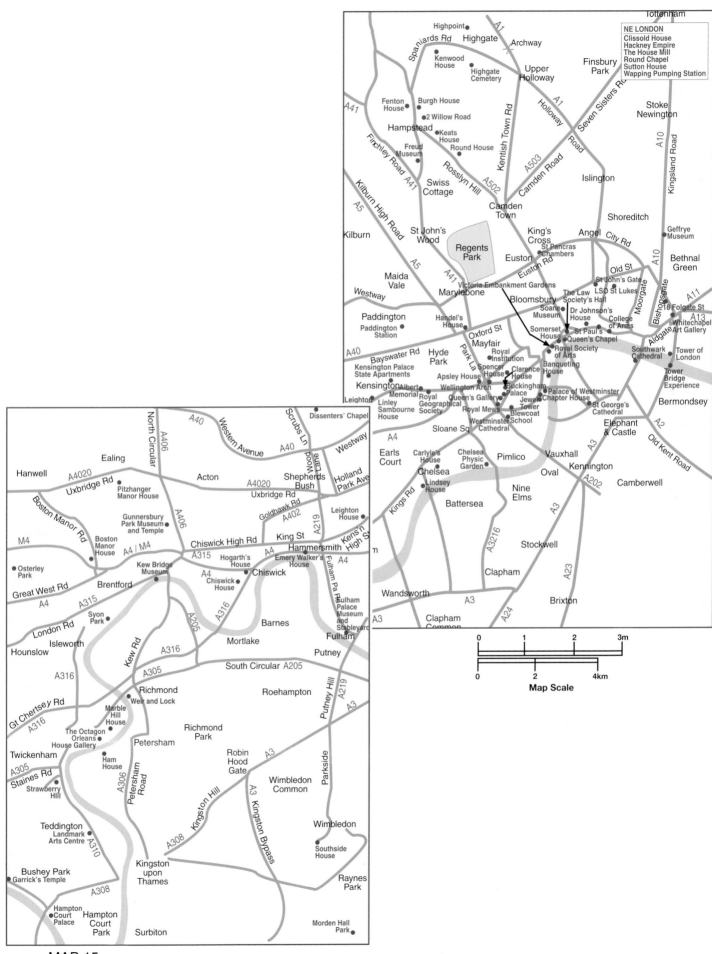

NE LONDON
Clissold House
Hackney Empire
The House Mill
Round Chapel
Sutton House
Wapping Pumping Station

Tottenham

Highpoint
Highgate
Archway
Spaniards Rd
Kenwood House
Highgate Cemetery
Upper Holloway
Finsbury Park
Stoke Newington
A1
A1
Holloway
Seven Sisters Rd
Kingsland Road
A10
Fenton House
Burgh House
2 Willow Road
Hampstead
Keats House
Round House
Freud Museum
Swiss Cottage
Kentish Town Rd
Camden Road
Islington
Shoreditch
Geffrye Museum
Bethnal Green
A41
A41
A5
Finchley Road
A41
Rosslyn Hill
A502
A503
Kilburn High Road
Kilburn
St John's Wood
Camden Town
King's Cross
Angel
City Rd
A10
A5
Regents Park
Euston
St Pancras Chambers
Old St
St John's Gate
Moorgate
Bishopsgate
A11
Maida Vale
Euston Rd
LSO St Lukes
A13
18 Folgate St
Whitechapel Art Gallery
Westway
Marylebone
Victoria Embankment Gardens
Bloomsbury
The Law Society's Hall
Dr Johnson's House
Aldgate
A41
Paddington
Handel's House
Soane Museum
College of Arms
Paddington Station
Oxford St
Mayfair
Somerset House
St Paul's
Queen's Chapel
Southwark Cathedral
Tower of London
A40
Bayswater Rd
Hyde Park
Royal Institution
Royal Society of Arts
Banqueting House
Tower Bridge Experience
Kensington Palace State Apartments
Spencer House
Clarence House
Palace of Westminster
Bermondsey
Kensington
Albert Memorial
Apsley House
Wellington Arch
Queen's Gallery
Buckingham Palace
Chapter House
St George's Cathedral
A2
Leighton
Linley Sambourne House
Royal Geographical Society
Royal Mews
Jewel Tower
Blewcoat School
Elephant & Castle
Old Kent Road
Dissenters' Chapel
Westminster Cathedral
Sloane Sq
Earls Court
Carlyle's House
Chelsea Physic Garden
Pimlico
Vauxhall
Kennington
A3
Chelsea
Oval
Camberwell
A202
Kings Rd
Lindsey House
Nine Elms
Battersea
A3216
Stockwell
A23
Clapham
Wandsworth
A3
Brixton
A24
Clapham Common

West London Inset

North Circular
A406
Western Avenue
A40
Scrubs Ln
Wood Lane
Westway
Ealing
Hanwell
A4020
Uxbridge Rd
Pitzhanger Manor House
Acton
A4020
Uxbridge Rd
Shepherds Bush
Holland Park Ave
Boston Manor Rd
A406
Gunnersbury Park Museum and Temple
Goldhawk Rd
A402
A219
Leighton House
Kens'n High St
M4
Boston Manor House
A4 / M4
Chiswick High Rd
King St
Hammersmith
Fulham Pa Rd
Osterley Park
Hogarth's House
Emery Walker's House
A4
Great West Rd
Kew Bridge Museum
A4
Chiswick House
Chiswick
A316
Fulham Palace Museum and Stableyard
A4
Brentford
A315
A316
Barnes
Fulham
London Rd
Syon Park
Mortlake
Putney
Hounslow
Isleworth
A316
South Circular A205
A316
A305
Richmond
Roehampton
Putney Hill
A219
Gt Chertsey Rd
Weir and Lock
Richmond Park
A3
A316
Marble Hill House
The Octagon
Orleans House Gallery
Petersham
Robin Hood Gate
A3
Parkside
Twickenham
Ham House
Petersham Road
Wimbledon Common
A305
Kingston Hill
Staines Rd
Strawberry Hill
Kingston Bypass
A3
Teddington Landmark Arts Centre
A306
A310
Kingston upon Thames
Wimbledon
A308
Bushey Park
Garrick's Temple
Southside House
A308
Hampton Court Palace
Hampton Court Park
Surbiton
Raynes Park
Morden Hall Park

Map Scale
0 1 2 3m
0 2 4km

MAP 15

EDINBURGH & YORK DETAIL

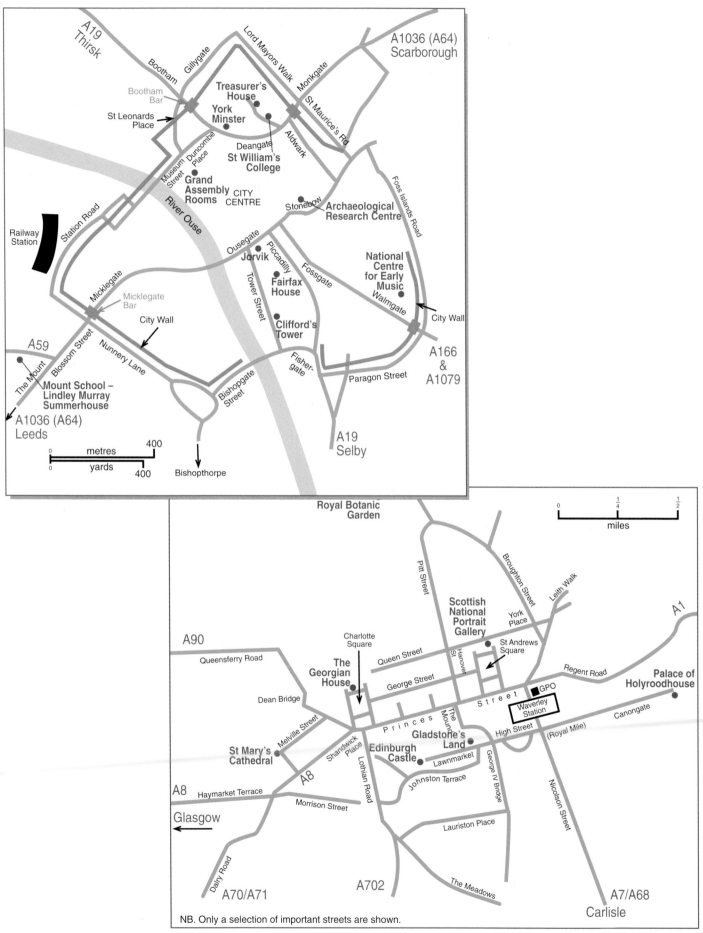

York map:

A19 Thirsk
A1036 (A64) Scarborough
Bootham
Gillygate
Lord Mayors Walk
Monkgate
Bootham Bar
St Maurice's Rd
Treasurer's House
York Minster
St Leonards Place
Aldwark
Deangate
St William's College
Museum Street
Duncombe Place
Grand Assembly Rooms
CITY CENTRE
River Ouse
Station Road
Stonebow
Archaeological Research Centre
Foss Islands Road
Railway Station
Ousegate
Piccadilly
Jorvik
Fairfax House
Fossgate
National Centre for Early Music
Micklegate
Micklegate Bar
City Wall
Tower Street
Walmgate
City Wall
Clifford's Tower
A59
Blossom Street
Nunnery Lane
Fisher-gate
A166 & A1079
The Mount
Mount School – Lindley Murray Summerhouse
Bishopgate Street
Paragon Street
A1036 (A64) Leeds
A19 Selby
Bishopthorpe

0 metres 400
0 yards 400

Edinburgh map:

Royal Botanic Garden
0 ¼ ½ miles
A90
Pitt Street
Broughton Street
Leith Walk
Scottish National Portrait Gallery
York Place
A1
Queensferry Road
Charlotte Square
Queen Street
Hanover St
St Andrews Square
Regent Road
The Georgian House
George Street
GPO
Palace of Holyroodhouse
Dean Bridge
Street
Waverley Station
Melville Street
Princes
The Mound
Canongate
St Mary's Cathedral
Shandwick Place
Gladstone's Land
High Street (Royal Mile)
A8
Lothian Road
Edinburgh Castle
Lawnmarket
George IV Bridge
A8 Haymarket Terrace
Johnston Terrace
Nicolson Street
Glasgow
Morrison Street
Lauriston Place
Dairy Road
A70/A71
A702
The Meadows
A7/A68
Carlisle

NB. Only a selection of important streets are shown.

MAP 16

C

M

T